Trail Map: How to Read This Report

- We have prepared this report with many audiences in mind, and believe it is possible to satisfy most investors seeking information on the subject of the rapidly growing, commercial Internet. We hope this report will be used as a reference for identifying risks, rewards, market opportunities, investment ideas, company competitive strategies, products, and how the Internet works. Since this report was published during the ski season, we offer some trail identifiers to help the reader navigate through the report.

Double Diamond — Already know the technology and companies but want to understand their strategies:

Read Chapters 1, 3, 10, 15, 16, and browse 11.

Intermediate — Browser-literate and knows own e-mail address:

Read Chapters 1, 2, 3, 5, 6, 7, 8, 9, 10, 11, 12, 14, 15, 16, 17, 18, and 19.

Expert — Already read all those "other" reports:

Read Chapters 1, 2, 3, 5, 6, 7, 9, 10, 14, 15, 16, 19, and browse 11.

Novice — Never heard of Motley Fool, cnet, or Yahoo:

Read Chapter 1, and read Chapters 2 through 19.

- Generally speaking, mastering Sections II, III, and IV can make the reader sound **smart at cocktail parties**; knowing Sections I and V can **impress your accountant**; and dropping a few URLs from Chapter 12 during dinner will **wow the kids**.

the Internet Report

the Internet Report

MORGAN STANLEY

Mary Meeker and Chris DePuy

HarperBusiness

A Division of HarperCollins*Publishers*

HarperCollins books may be purchased for educational, business, or sales promotional use. For information please write: Special Markets Department, HarperCollins Publishers, Inc., 10 East 53rd Street, New York, NY 10022.

FIRST EDITION

ISBN 0-88730-826-0

96 97 98 99 00 COM 10 9 8 7 6 5 4 3 2 1

Acknowledgments

The authors would like to thank the individuals who helped make this book possible. A report of this scope would not have been possible without a lot of hard work and a lot of support from many people.

First, without the tireless efforts and extensive contributions of Samantha McCuen, the report would simply not have been published. Samantha worked with Morgan Stanley for almost six years, most recently in the technology equity research group, before joining Sandler Capital in January as an investor focusing on PC software and new media companies.

In Morgan Stanley's equity research group, many analysts with expertise in various sectors contributed to the report. They include George Kelly (Data Networking); Chuck Phillips (Enterprise Software); Steve Milunovich (Server Hardware); Neil Danzger (Telecommunications Equipment); Mark Wolfenberger (Computer Services); Alan Rieper (Semiconductors); Doug Arthur (Publishing); Stephanie Comfort (Telecommunications Services); Rich Bilotti (Cable Television); David Hilder (Financial Services); Steve Roach (Economist); and Mike Sorell (Emerging Growth). Gillian Munson, Bob Austrian, Alison Manolovici, and Tony Scott offered invaluable sanity checks and feedback. Mayree Clark, Phil Friedman, and George Kelly were key advocates in committing the resources we needed for this project.

Morgan Stanley's Technology investment banking team has also been critical in helping us uncover emerging companies in all areas of technology, most recently related to the Internet. In our (admittedly partial, but unqualified) opinion, our technology banking team is second to none. We would like to single out Frank Quattrone, Bill Brady, Drew Guevara, Tim Walsh, Dave Weiden, Jim Liang, and Chris Pasko for their contributions to "The Internet Report."

While the aforementioned folks helped us get this report near the goal line, without Morgan Stanley's editorial and production group, the report never would have made it into the end zone. We would like to thank our two crack editors and technophiles, Fred Miller and Andy McCann, as well as our graphics and printing team, Claudette Bell, Alison Pitman, Ramona Boston, and Joe Darragh.

In addition to the contributions of these and other Morgan Stanley employees, many pioneers in the field, experts, advisers, and friends have generously shared invaluable insights that have made their way into this report, not just over the last year, but over the last decade. To you, we hope that our descriptions of your companies and concepts do justice to your visions and entrepreneurial efforts. May the next ten years in technology be as exciting as the last ten years have been. . . .

Mary Meeker, Chris DePuy
New York, February 1996

Table of Contents

Chapter 3 *(cont.)*

Chapter 4

Chapter 5

Chapter 6

Chapter 7

Chapter 8

Chapter 9

Chapter 10

TABLES

Chapter 11

Chapter 14

Chapter 15

Chapter 16

Chapter 17

Chapter 18

Chapter 19

Data Networking Equipment

Internet Security Equipment and Software

Internet Service Providers

PCs, Servers, and Semiconductors

Section I:
Introduction

Technology/New Media:
Chapter 1: The Internet Report

Introduction

- Our recommended portfolio of Internet-related stocks consists of **Cisco**, **Ascend**, **Cascade Communications**, **America Online**, and **Intuit**. We also like **Netscape**, but given the volatility in the stock, its lack of liquidity, and strong performance since its IPO, we believe investors should hold off in the near term until it becomes more seasoned. Many other companies should also benefit from growth in the Internet, but we have attempted to select for our portfolio those with especially high levels of reward/risk related to the Internet. Investors have already rewarded all Internet-related companies with extremely high valuations: The five stocks in our Internet portfolio rose, on an unweighted average, 257% in 1995 and at year-end traded at, on average, 7.3 times C1996E revenue and 59 times C1996E EPS. **Yes, we are excited about Internet investment opportunities and the performance of the stocks, and yes, we are nervous about the valuation levels.** In order to mitigate valuation/execution risk, investors must take a long-term, portfolio approach, and we recommend building positions over time. While in the short term, making money in Internet-related companies has been like shooting fish in a barrel, over the long run, selectivity and patience will be key as companies/technologies/stocks come and go.

- The companies we favor are leaders in three key areas of Internet development: **Internet Infrastructure**, **Internet Software and Services**, and **Internet Content and Aggregation**.

- **Infrastructure** The three data networking equipment companies that our networking analysts, George Kelly and Neil Danzger, are recommending are **Cisco, Ascend** and **Cascade**; all three look well positioned as early beneficiaries of the rapid Internet build, which has only just begun.

- **Software and Services** The companies we highlight — **Intuit** and **Netscape** — are in leadership positions in each of their respective operating spaces and should continue to support strong growth during the coming years.

- **Content and Aggregation** We believe **America Online** has a share in each of four critical areas: service, content organization and aggregation, and venture funding. We believe that the company is strategically well positioned (though not without risk to changes in its business model) to benefit from growth in online services and the Internet.

- In this lengthy report, we describe various aspects of this arena (including Internet, Intranet, and Online products) and propose frameworks for analyzing its emerging markets. Two things are certain: **Growth will be significant** (in fits and starts) and investors will vacillate between riding the growth wave and worrying about risk/reward and valuations; and **companies, strategies, and the very structure of the market will change rapidly**. When we first set out to write this report, we wanted it to answer all the questions about the Internet. The goal was impossible to achieve; by its very nature, the Internet is chaotic and can only be described clearly in hindsight. Consider this report our puck on the ice at the beginning of a very long game.

Summary and Investment Conclusion

In this report we attempt to describe what may be one of the hottest new markets to develop in years — the growth in PC-based communications and the Internet. We like the Internet investment theme for the following reasons:

- Due to technological advances in PC-based communications, a new medium — with the Internet, the World Wide Web, and TCP/IP at its core — is emerging rapidly. **The market for Internet-related products and services appears to be growing more rapidly than the early emerging markets for print publishing, telephony,**

film, radio, recorded music, television, and personal computers.

• In our opinion, we have entered what we call *"The Great Communications Backfill Opportunity."* By our estimates, there are something like 150 million PC users worldwide who in time will become more active Internet users (we estimate about 7%, or 10 million, were active users in 1995). In short, there's lots of upside.

By way of comparison, since 1980 and the sale of the first PC —an initial base of zero — the PC industry has created more than $250 billion in net shareholder value. Now we are embarking on an industry just beginning to tap the base of 150 million PC users. In the first 15 years of what might be called the enhanced-communications industry, or whatever it ends up being called, we feel that over time the shareholder value created from developments in the Internet (starting in 1994, for the sake of argument) could exceed that created in the first 15 years of the PC revolution.

• Based on our market growth estimates, we are still at the very early stages of a **powerful secular growth cycle** for Internet-related stuff. Remember how Microsoft's Windows cured for about seven years before it became a runaway hit in 1990 with the launch of Windows 3.0? Well, the Internet — TCP/IP in particular — has been curing for about 15 years, and the rollout of the graphical Web browser (Mosaic) in 1993 is having a significant impact on market growth analogous to the launch of Windows 3.0.

• There are two major market opportunities for Internet usage: **enterprise** and **consumer**. A recent survey by Dataquest showed that in 60% of 100 medium to large organizations in the U.S., all departments had some access to the Internet. Similarly, the rapid take-off of America Online shows that consumer adoption of online/Internet access, while still less than 8% of U.S. homes, is growing quickly. The enterprise market is dominated by access for information services (internal or external), while the consumer market will likely be dominated by online/Internet entertainment and information services.

• At a minimum, e-mail should become pervasive. So should Internet/Web access: **E-mail is the "killer application" of the Internet today**, and browsing through information services the "killer app" of tomorrow.

• Using the **Internet as an information distribution vehicle** offers companies the ability to reduce distribution costs, support costs, and cost of goods sold — and eventually to target focused customer bases. On the flip side, lower costs and easier distribution open markets for new competitors in publishing, marketing/advertising, commerce, and software development. Dislocations of traditional companies in these areas are likely in time as new business models based on free trials, subscribers, advertising, and transactions emerge.

Today, the amount of money being made from Web pages (mostly free, with limited advertising) is insignificant. But the authors of this report, over the course of the last several years (thanks to some T-1 lines plus some nice notebook PCs), have spent a lot of time gathering information (and being entertained) via online services and the Web. And our conclusion is that the value of these experiences has risen to the point where it's worth paying for.

• As the Internet continues to evolve, **market opportunities for equipment/infrastructure providers should be huge**. Opportunities for well-positioned software/services companies and content/aggregation companies will also be significant.

• **New companies will emerge and poorly positioned companies will die**.

• It's likely that **development of the Internet won't be as easy as it sometimes appears**. Bob Metcalfe, inventor of Ethernet and founder of 3Com, recently offered a list of provoking thoughts about what could crush the Internet, soon: *Money* — Investors will tire of investing in companies that lose money; *Digital Money* — Transaction costs will be too high; *Measurement* — Advertisers will only invest significant dollars when they have tangible user data; *Monopolies* — Telcos will be slow to reduce costs for high-speed Internet access, and the Internet will become constipated as more users try to send more stuff over the same infrastructure; *Security* — Major security breaches will occur that undermine user confidence; *Compatibility* — Fights for control for standards will tear the Web; *Capacity* — The Internet will become chronically overloaded, and the current flat-rate usage business models of vendors will not provide enough investment dollars to appropriately expand capacity; *Privacy* — Well-publicized privacy violations will occur; *Video* — Video delivery capabilities will be delayed; and *Pornography* — Porn' on the Web will become an even bigger political issue. (Like it or not, pornography has been one of the major, early-stage drivers of many new mass media; Playboy, it should be added, currently has the most popular Web site.)

Do we think that all these problems will appear? No. Will some? Yes. It's just tough to predict which and when, although the likeliest problems, we believe, will relate to security and capacity.

Put simply, change takes time and dislocations happen. In times of euphoria (when it's assumed the sky's the limit) it's also easy to forget developments on the "company" side. For instance, while Sun's Java may be great, if Microsoft NT erodes Sun's server share, Sun has issues; while Netscape's browser may seem ubiquitous, Microsoft's freeware, over time, may be an issue; while UUNET's revenue growth may be awesome, competitive pressures are sure to rise; while Compaq's Internet server business may be ramping, what happens if desktop PC prices collapse? While Microsoft's margins may be rising, what if the Internet causes a platform shift; and if the Internet ramps up really fast for consumers, what happens to America Online's business model?

Don't get us wrong, we are extremely excited about the long-term growth prospects of the Internet/Intranet/Online stuff, and many of the aforementioned companies. It's just that, no doubt, there will be bumps along the way. There always have been, always will be. Been there. Done that.

This report violates a lot of the rules they taught us in Wall Street Analyst school. It's long; it describes a lot of industry topics that aren't investment-relevant; it's short on investment ideas.

If all you care about is stock picking, **the number of pure-play investment vehicles related to the Internet is shockingly short** (and way too risky for your grandmother, anyway). From a short list, our even shorter list of favorite stocks follows. We like these stocks long-term but are scared about some of their short-term valuation risks. Many of the Internet-related stocks have traded up based on a simple phenomenon: Demand for the shares of semi-illiquid companies has exceeded supply. For a broader list of Internet-related companies, see Chapter 16.

We think it's a good idea for investors interested in an Internet-play to take a portfolio approach to these stocks, as in owning a basket to bring down the risk profile. For all the interest the Internet has received, there aren't a lot of ways for institutional investors (who require liquidity) to invest in the sector, and while these companies should have an estimated $6.5 billion in combined revenue in C1996, at year-end 1995 they carried a collective market capitalization of $36 billion (or $11.2 billion, if you exclude Cisco and Intuit).

For now, we are excluding the Internet Service Providers (ISPs), such as UUNET, PSINet, and Netcom from our list. While the top-line growth opportunities for these companies look significant, we believe that barriers to entry are relatively low (there are more than 3,000 ISPs, and the number is rapidly rising) and that pricing pressure will remain an issue. Clearly, following their unweighted average 73% 1995 rise, these stocks have shown caution to be a mistake — and given the enthusiasm for the Internet stocks generally, it may well remain a mistake for some time to come. But we prefer to wait and see.

The ISP companies have been early to market with superior service offerings, and while the telcos should in theory own this market, they have not proven adept at demonstrating this. Our cautious view is not that investors should not own these stocks, it's simply that we believe infrastructure providers like Cisco, Ascend, and Cascade — which sell products to UUNET, PSINet, and Netcom and have shares in excess of 75% in their markets — are a better, safer way (as a derivative) for investors to play the ISPs' dramatic growth.

No doubt, there will be a full pipeline of pure-play Internet companies that will go public in the next several years (manic market permitting). To put this trend in perspective for investors, consider the last big IPO boom, which was

Table 1.1
Recommended Internet Stock Portfolio

	Price (12/29/95)	1995 YTD Return	Mkt. Cap ($B)	Mkt. Cap/ C1996E Rev.	P/E C1996E
Cisco Systems	$75	112%	$21.3	5.7	25
Ascend Comm.	41	696	4.9	15.2	69
Cascade Comm.	85	176	2.6	7.4	66
America Online	38	168	3.8	2.5	61
Intuit	78	134	3.4	5.5	76
Mean		**257**			

related to the development of the PC industry, say 1980–94 (see our report, The Technology IPO Yearbook, Autumn, 1994, for details). In those 15 years, 581 tech companies went public and created more than $240B in net market capitalization. At the end of 1994, 45% of the companies traded at prices below their IPO price, and only 16 ten-bagger stocks had been created (or 3% of the companies that went public in the 15-year time period). In addition, only 17 of the top 100 PC software companies in 1981 (as defined in Jeff Tarter's *Soft-Letter* newsletter) were still on the list in 1995. For the losers, the reasons for poor performance were typically related to competitive pressures and low barriers to entry, overhyped expectations, technology obsolescence, and poor management execution.

"Caveat emptor" should be the mantra for the brave souls who tread in Internet investment waters. But the good news is that the next Microsofts, Ciscos, Oracles, and Compaqs are being created. When looking for investment ideas in new markets, we default to our favorite maxims from Don Valentine of Sequoia Capital, who is known as one of the toughest and smartest technology venture capitalists in Silicon Valley. Don follows several simple rules in choosing early-stage tech investments: (1) Find "monster" markets that can be really big, like the Internet; (2) find good technology and good technologists who can stay ahead of competitive threats; (3) find outstanding leaders/management teams that can drive the technologies and markets forward; and (4) buy companies, not products, and try to find companies that have achieved critical mass with their products — or can achieve it, and can create some form of "barriers to entry." Easier said than done, but an important checklist nonetheless.

How to Read This Report

If all you care about are stocks, your reading may be finished. However if you want to put on your geek hat, your consultant hat, or your start-up company hat, read on.... just don't read this cover-to-cover; jump around to the areas that you are interested in, as you would on the Net.

This introduction is intended to give the big picture and a couple of stock ideas. At the beginning of each chapter, we summarize the highlights in a few bullet points. In Chapter 3 we analyze the size of the markets. In Chapter 8 we describe, in detail, the Internet strategies for Netscape, Microsoft, America Online, Sun Microsystems, Adobe, and Macromedia. In Chapter 10 we analyze the positioning of companies in the subsegment Internet markets. In Chapter 11 we give brief descriptions of what lots of companies are doing about the Internet, and in Chapter 12 we present our favorite cool sites on the Web. The other chapters describe various areas and issues surrounding the Internet such as history, software environment, technical and administrative stuff, infrastructure, and company financials.

Background Thoughts — You Want Action? We Got Action. . .

No doubt, something's happening. PC sales are cruising along at healthy (though slowing) rates. Microsoft is marketing Windows 95 as if every breathing body were a potential customer. **Morgan Stanley chief economist Steve Roach posits that consumers are buying PCs instead of cars.** How can all of these wonderful things actually be happening — especially in the tough climate of the '90s?

It is tough out there — layoffs, stagnant real wages, and longer work days are only part of the malaise that is gripping the American worker/consumer. In part, because of these developments, households are operating in a much more income-constrained environment than ever before. That implies that when they find something new they like (i.e., computers) they must give up something in return (i.e., cars). The numbers certainly bear this out. When the current recovery commenced in 1Q91, our estimates suggest that cars and trucks accounted for 12% of total discretionary consumption; some 18 quarters later (3Q95), this ratio was essentially unchanged at 12%. Over this same period, the share of discretionary consumption going to electronics — computers, video and audio equipment, cable TV, and video cassette rentals — rose from 6% in 1Q91 to 10% in 3Q95. In the income-stretched 1990s, families have financed their entry into the Information Age by redefining the trade-offs that have long shaped discretionary spending choices.

But there's more to it than that. It's also a cultural thing. The local radio station is taking song requests via e-mail. Actress Sandra Bullock, an avid America Online user, worked to get the lead role in the summer film *The Net,* then hosted an online chat forum on America Online and 2,000 people (a chat record at the time) joined in to participate. MTV then decided to host Michael Jackson in a similar session, only to be followed by online distribution of speeches and Internet video updates from the U.S. tour of the Pope (yes, THE Pope)! The local coffee shop in Telluride, Colorado (The Steaming Bean), has a PC with an Internet connection for its customers.

Finally, tech stocks have (with fits and starts) experienced one of the most powerful rallies ever. What's going on? We call it "The Great Communications Backfill Opportunity." Over the last ten years, Bill Gates of Microsoft has been the most vocal repeater of the mantra "A PC on Every Desktop." Now we are getting to the point where PCs, while not on every desktop (or every lap), are supporting the kind of presence/momentum where even your mother thinks that Bill could be right. Over the last nine years, Intel has shipped over 300 million x86 chips for PCs: 35 million Pentiums, 125 million 486s, 72 million 386s, 40 million 286s, 30 million 8088/8086s. That implies a similar number of PCs were shipped, but let's assume that, on average, only those shipped in the last four years are still in use. Of those 196 million PCs, we'd estimate some 23% are second PCs, leaving about 150 million PC users in the world.

We ramble on about these numbers for a purpose: Spreadsheets, word processors, and games are cool, useful, and important, but there ain't nothing like communicating with a PC (whether via e-mail; transferring a file; interacting with someone who shares your interest in migration patterns of Canadian Geese; or obtaining information on anything from the weather to the best beer halls in Munich). Or yes, conducting good old-fashioned commerce in a new way.

How Big? How Fast? How Much?

Of those 150 million estimated worldwide PC users, we estimate 35 million (23%) have used e-mail in their businesses, 9 million (6%) have used the Web, and only 8 million (5%) have used an online service. We feel that e-mail, online/Web access may be ubiquitous for PC users within a decade. Intel shipped about 60 million x86 chips for PCs in 1995 (up 20% Y/Y) and expects 100 million PCs to ship in a year sometime before the year 2000. This implies more than 250 million PC users by the year 2000 — in short, a big market opportunity for lots of companies. See Chapter 3 for details on our PC and Internet user estimates.

Node counting is one way to size a market; there are others, such as infrastructure revenue. Although not easy to estimate with accuracy, the 1994 data communications market approached roughly $15 billion/year if one includes private line data services ($9 billion/year), local area network and bridge/router equipment ($3 billion/year), wide area network services ($1 billion/year), electronic messaging and online services ($1 billion/year), and proprietary networking software and hardware ($1 billion/year). Some of these markets show 35–50% annual growth rates, and the Internet itself has nearly doubled in size each year since 1990.

What is the Internet?

- The Internet is a network of networks that are both commercial and publicly-owned.

- It has no end and no beginning; as networks are added or removed, or failures occur in parts of the system, the rest of the Internet continues to operate.

- No one owns the Internet; it is a shared resource that grows more useful as more networks — both private and public — are added.

- Growth in connections to the Internet, or hosts, is doubling annually, a rate that should continue for at least the next five years.

The following definition is taken from the archives of the RFC (Request for Comments) by the U.S. government's networking task force:

> "The Internet is a world-wide network of networks with gateways linking organizations in North and South America, Europe, The Pacific Basin and other countries. . . . The organizations are administratively independent from one another. There is no central, worldwide, technical control point. Yet, working together, these organizations have created what to a user seems to be a single virtual network that spans the globe."

> "The networks all use a common suite of networking protocols, TCP/IP. It is because of this commonality of protocols, this commonality of network functionality and interoperability, that the networks provide what may appear to be a seamless, integrated virtual network, regardless of the underlying heterogeneity of the underlying computer hardware or communications transport."

That is just the technical core of what the Internet is. We believe the Internet has taken on many new meanings. The Internet is also:

- No longer for academic, UNIX-gurus;

- Getting easier to use;

- A new shopping paradigm;

- A generational thing;

- An extension of the ubiquitous PC;

- A vast source of information, facts, opinions, and entertainment; and

- Not going to be the same in five years.

A few years ago, the Internet user base was dominated by academics and researchers. Now, most users pay to access it through an Internet Service Provider (ISP) like Netcom or PSINet, or an Online Service Provider (OSP) like America Online. Individual dial-up modem accounts typically cost about $20 per month, depending on use; corporate accounts cost hundreds to many thousands of dollars, depending on the bandwidth purchased.

We believe the most important factor in the Internet's ongoing growth was the Mosaic browser, an easy-to-use graphical interface that allows easy navigation through the World Wide Web, one of many protocols running on the Internet. Improvements in search engines like Yahoo or InfoSeek that let users easily look up information on nearly every imaginable topic have also helped the Web multiply.

As the PC becomes a communications device, an increasing number of PCs are being connected to ISP and OSP networks. Companies have also begun to ramp up Internet software for use on internal networks, called intranets. The motivation for this is put into perspective when you ask yourself the simple question: *Why is it that I can use the Internet to easily find a file in Russia when I can't even find a file I created two months ago on my corporate LAN?*

The Internet now encompasses an estimated 70,000 networks worldwide, about half of which are in the United States. **Users on the Internet are doubling annually, or a rate of about 0.19% per day**. About 10 million computers (hosts) are permanently attached to the Internet, plus at least that many portable and desktop systems only intermittently online. (In 1969, there were only four computers on the ARPANet, and only 200 on the Internet in 1983.) Traffic rates in the recently "retired" NSFNet backbone approached 20 trillion bytes per month and were growing at a 100% annual rate.

As technology analysts, we are used to change. We have witnessed the adoption of the minicomputer, the rollout of the Macintosh, the ramp-up of the PC, the pervasiveness of the spreadsheet, the invasion of the Automatic Teller Machine, the growth in the number of local area networks, and of course, the rapid acceptance of Windows. But we have never seen anything like the recent rapid ramp and scale of the use of online services and the Web. We have a simple approach to calibrating just how big the market opportunities may be. We call it our *less than/more than* perspective. *Less than* describes emerging or rapidly growing things that make us enthusiastic about the potential market opportunities; *more than* shows historical consumer or business buying patterns that also make us enthusiastic about the size of the market opportunity. Confused? Here goes, as of mid-1995...

Figure 1.1
Internet Host Growth, 1969 to 1995

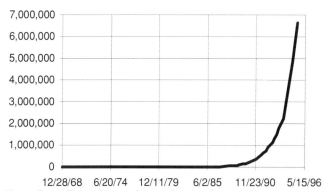

Note: Generally speaking, an Internet host is a device such as a computer or router that is connected to the Internet
Source: Network Wizards

Table 1.2
Perspectives on Market Opportunities

Less Than
Less than 15% of worldwide office workers have PCs;
Less than 10% of U.S. population uses cellular phones;
Less than 10% of worldwide PC users have electronic mail connected to the Internet;
Less than 10% of worldwide PC users have online services;
Less than 9% of worldwide PC users have CD-ROM drives;
Less than 7% of worldwide PC users have real-time Internet access;
Less than 5% of worldwide homes have PCs;
Less than 4% of the U.S. population has real-time Internet access;
Less than 1% of the world population has any kind of Internet access (e-mail included).

More Than
More than 95% of U.S. homes have television sets;
More than 95% of U.S. homes have corded telephones;
More than 85% of U.S. homes have VCRs;
More than 60% of U.S. homes have cable television;
More than 55% of U.S. homes have telephone answering devices;
More than 45% of U.S. homes have videogame software;
More than 45% of U.S. homes have CD-audio players.

Paraphrases, Quotes, and Tidbits From George Gilder

In his book *Life After Television* (Norton: 1992), George Gilder articulates his view of the changing medium being created by the Internet and developing technologies. We offer some of our favorite Gilderisms to help describe what's driving many current/future technology changes.

Data is rapidly approaching a level of 50% of the bits in a telephone network and already comprises 20% of the profits. Data income is growing six times as fast as voice income. As the telephone network becomes a computer network, it will have to change, root and branch. All the assumptions of telephony will have to give way to radically different assumptions. Telephony will die.

Computer networks respond to all the human characteristics that TV networks defy. Computer nets afford peer-to-peer interactivity rather than top-down broadcasts. Rather than a few "channels," computer networks offer as many potential connections as there are machines linked to the web. Rather than a system whereby a few "stations" spray images at millions of dumb terminals in real time, computer networks put the customer in control, not settling passively for what is on the "air" but actively seeking and even shaping the customer's first choices.

The cost-effectiveness of individual computers measured in MIPS (millions of instructions per second) per dollar approximately doubles every 18 months and the value of computers in networks rises as the square of the rise in the number of networked machines. In a top-down network, such as a conventional phone or cable system, attaching a new device may burden the central switch or head end; it is close to a zero-sum economy of communications; in broadcasting over the air, each additional receiver has no effect on the technical power of the system. But in a peer-to-peer computer heterarchy, each new device is a resource for the system, expanding its capabilities and even its potential bandwidth. The larger the network grows, the more efficient and powerful are all its parts.

The computer industry feeds on the explosive advance of semiconductor and networking electronics: (1) The Law of the Microcosm showing that microchip cost-effectiveness rises as the square of the number of transistors crammed on a single chip; and (2) the Law of the Telecosm showing that computer cost-effectiveness rises by the square of the number of computers connected to networks. According to Moore's law, the famous projection of Intel Chairman Gordon Moore, the number of transistors on a single chip will double every 18 months. According to the record of the last five years, the number of computers attached to networks is rising too fast to measure. Only by comprehending the full force of the computer juggernaut can one anticipate the future of the information age.

In 1950, few people could imagine that in a decade or so television would become a peremptory force in American culture, defining the news, reshaping politics, reorienting family life, and remaking the cultural expectations of several generations of Americans. No one predicted that in a few decades 98% of all American households would own a television set, exceeding the level of telephone ownership by five percentage points, and by a far larger margin in the homes of the poor. No one anticipated that the members of an average household would watch the screen some six hours a day, while in poor homes television would become a substitute hearth, glowing constantly day and nights. Few people foresaw that television, more than any other force, would provide the unifying images that would define the national experience and consciousness.

By radically changing the balance of power between the distributors and creators of culture, the teleputer will forever break the broadcast bottle-neck. Potentially, there will be as many channels as there are computers attached to the global network. The creator of a program on a specialized subject — from fly-fishing to quantum physics — will be able to reach with one video everyone in the United States, Europe, and Asia who shares the interest. Artists will be able to command a large audience without worrying about mass appeal. The medium will change from mass-produced and mass-consumed commodity to an endless feast of niches and specialties.

Today, some 70% of the movie dollar goes to distribution [and 68% of magazine revenues are dedicated to manufacturing and distribution]. The masters of the bottleneck charge a toll to the queued-up creators seeking to reach the public and a toll to the public seeking the creators' work. In the fiber-optic network, however, the share of the entertainment dollar going to distribution will drop below 5%. With essentially unlimited bandwidth, the cost of adding another option on a fiber cable will be negligible. The operators of fiber networks will want above all to fill them with programs. A huge variety of suppliers will gain access to audiences and money will pass from the distributors to the creators. But this will not be a zero-sum game. The distributors will do better, too, because of an explosive expansion in the market.

Big-events — the Super Bowl or the election debates or the most compelling mass programs — will still command their audiences, which can be reached by direct-broadcast satellite or broadcasts through fiber-optic cables. But all the media junk food and filler that stretches out toward the horizons of mass culture like so much strip development will tend to disappear. People will order what they want rather than settling for what is there. In the world of the teleputer, broadcasters, educators, investors, and filmmakers, who thought they could never go broke underestimating the intelligence of the American people, are going to discover that they were wrong.

A tablet that looks very much like a newspaper but in fact is a flat-panel screen some nine inches wide, a foot high, and a half inch thick . Weighing a little over a pound, far less than the Sunday edition of your local newspaper, this device — call it a newspanel — might contain a trove of news, graphics, audio, and even video, representing more than a year of Sunday papers. Through fiber-optic lines and radio links it might connect to databases of news and entertainment from around the world.

As Steve Case of America Online puts it: 'Everybody will become information providers as well as consumers. The challenge is to create electronic communities that marry information and communications — thereby creating an interactive, participatory medium. The community aspect is crucial — it is the soul of the new medium.' America Online is uniquely focused on the vital center of the new market: the point of convergence of newspapers, magazines, and computers in new communications of interest and interaction.

This is it, folks, the PC — defined not just by a programmable microprocessor or digital graphics or robust interactivity, but by a culture of adult engagement and invention. Follow the personal computer and you can reach the pot of gold. Follow anything else and you will end up in a backwater. What the Model T was to the industrial era — the teenage training board, the tinkerers' love and laboratory, the technological epitome — the PC is to the information age. Just as people who rode the wave of automobile technology — from tire makers to fast food franchisers — prevailed in the industrial era, so the firms that prey on the passion and feed on the force of the computer community will predominate in the information era.

Generational Combustion?

As in the past, much of the new Internet industry will be created by twenty-somethings just out of college (either before or after graduation) and heading new companies. Marc Andreessen, at the age of 23, was sought out by Silicon Graphics founder Jim Clark to be the technical visionary for Netscape. After a stab at a magazine/newsletter venture, the Gardner brothers of "The Motley Fool" stock forum on America Online, have created one of the hottest interactive forums in the online world. If they keep it up, they (and others) have the potential to shake up the finance and publishing industries.

In short, this generation grew up with PCs, knowing how to use them and knowing how powerful they can be. It's overly simplistic to say that the PC revolution was created by "kids" such as Steve Jobs/Steve Wozniak (Apple), Bill Gates/Paul Allen (Microsoft), Mitch Kapor/Jim Manzi (Lotus), Paul Brainerd (Aldus), Trip Hawkins (Electronic Arts), and Dan Bricklin/Bob Frankston (Software Arts), but they sure had a lot to do with it. There is a lot to be said for how a near-maniacal leader (who lives/breathes his/her business passion) can indeed, with the right idea and a little capital, create big changes, and, yes, make lots of money.

With each step in the evolution of computing (figure 1.2) from mainframe to minicomputer to PC — or from cen- **tralized to decentralized to networked computing — more and more people gained control of their computing capabilities. Smaller, cheaper computing systems also made this control more economical.** From a business perspective, the overriding theme was that no company that dominated one generation of computing managed to dominate the next; each became wedded to its legacy systems and cash flow.

The reason that communications-enabled computing will continue to grow is twofold. First, it allows people to control the way they communicate. Just as e-mail is so much more efficient than voice-mail, when you first speak to someone via your PC and the Internet (watch out, IXCs) you may feel the same sense of epochal breakthrough memorialized by Alexander Graham Bell in 1876 with "Mr. Watson, come here, I want you." Second, it allows them to control the time and manner in which they obtain information (why wait for the current weather forecast on the evening news when you can get it at the click of a mouse anywhere and anytime). No doubt, solutions will arise for problems that we didn't know we had. Just as automatic teller machines eliminated trips to the bank, communications-enabled software products such as Intuit's Quicken will eliminate some of those trips to the ATM and will, no doubt, eliminate lots of check-writing, manual bill-paying and stamp licking.

Figure 1.2
Life Cycles of Mainframe, Mini, PC and Internet Enabled Systems

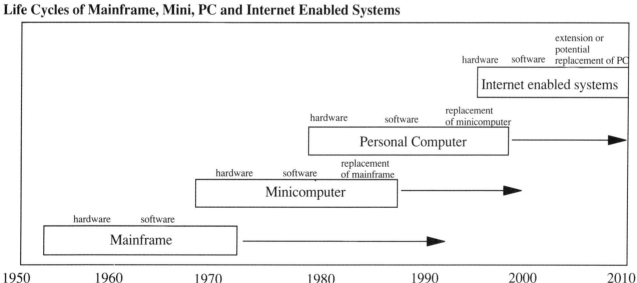

Source: Morgan Stanley Research Estimates

So What's an Investor to Do?

It's simple, go to work for a start-up or become a venture capitalist! :-)

Any public investor who's lived through the development of the PC business knows what rough-and-tumble, volatile investing is all about, knows the thrill of buying Microsoft shares in the IPO and holding on...a single investment that allowed one to make a lot of poor investments and still come out way ahead. No doubt, we will go through periods of investor enthusiasm and depression and periods of capital gains and losses. Concepts and companies will come and go (remember artificial intelligence, Fortune Systems, Kaypro, Daisy Systems, MiniScribe, Eagle Computer, and the first iteration of Activision?) but opportunities will abound.

We will also go through periods of rapid growth in the number of new companies followed by shakeout and consolidation. These sorts of gyrations, too, will provide investment opportunities.

In general, we believe development of the Internet industry will follow a pattern similar to the beginning of personal computers in the early 1980s, with three distinct phases (figure 1.3). In the early years, hardware/**infrastructure** will dominate, but over time, value will shift first to enabling technology (like an operating system and **software** and **services** to manage the interactive environment) and ultimately to programming, **content,** and **aggregation**.

We have a simple investment thesis for the evolution of the Internet industry: Buy stock in companies that have good underlying business/growth fundamentals and be very selective. For these companies, one should use traditional valuation parameters for valuing the core business and use P/E analysis and/or discounted cash flow to value the base case Internet opportunities for the company (as a call option). In fact, some companies, like Netscape, can be considered call options. It is also useful to estimate potential market sizes and attempt to determine what market shares and margins a company may obtain. If a business is subscriber based, estimating lifetime revenue per subscriber is useful. Of course, a portfolio investment approach is key.

Figure 1.3

**Timing and Development
Of the Three Internet Market Segments**

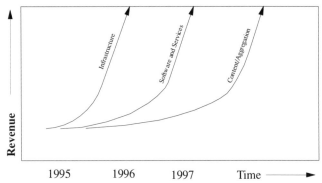

Source: Morgan Stanley Research Estimates

A Few Brief Thoughts from Biotechnology Investors Regarding Internet Investing

Given the euphoria, enthusiasm, and downright investor warp related to the Internet, we thought it wise to converse with our brethren from biotech-land to compare and contrast Internet with biotech frenzy. Lucky for us, many of our fellow analysts are also PC-using Internet cruisers.

Morgan Stanley's emerging growth analyst Mike Sorell and biotech analyst Eric Hecht watched biotech stocks experience explosive growth in 1991. Many issues rose several hundred percent; IPOs were oversubscribed many times and went to quick premiums of 100% or more. Investors were trying to find another Amgen, which went from $0 to about $1 billion in sales in about one year's time.

Although it was predictable that disaster lurked, it took fundamental bad news on three individual stocks in late 1991 and early 1992 (three years after the biotech bull market began) to result in a fundamental reevaluation of the industry's prospects: U.S. Bioscience had a negative review at the FDA for its flagship product, Ethyol. Synergen, which had risen from the low teens to close to $100 a share, failed to confirm its phase II results for Antril (a treatment for septic shock) in a definitive phase III controlled trial. And Centocor saw the FDA give a strong, and almost lethal, turndown to its entry in the septic-shock arena.

The fallout was severe: First-tier stocks fell 30%; second-tier about 60%; and the mass of third-tier names declined

80%. Our analysts have tracked the class of 1991 IPOs and note that while the market capitalization is now, four years later, about double that of the group at the end of 1991, the share price is, on average, the same. This underscores a key difference between biotech and many (though not all) Internet companies: namely, the need for additional capital.

How does all this compare to the Internet arena? In our view, the industry dynamics are very different. The examples cited above point out the tremendous and unpredictable clinical and regulatory risk associated with biotech stocks. On the positive side, most Internet companies are selling products and can do so very quickly after inception — most also do not have an insatiable need for capital (with the exception of the OSPs/ISPs, which are in rapid infrastructure build mode) as they often generate cash quickly. On the negative side, the market sizes, business models, and competitive threats for Internet companies are not yet defined.

What are the similarities? Well, to keep it short, the suspension of disbelief among investors and the triumph of greed over fear. However, when sentiment turns from positive to negative, picking up the pieces will be fruitful and rewarding; with biotech, other than a handful of leaders, this effort took three years to unfold and has just recently proven fruitful.

Table 1.3
Estimated Internet-Related Revenue by Category C1995E-C2000E

($ in millions)	C1995E	C2000E	CAGR	Revenue Sources
Infrastructure (Direct)	**$2,200**	**$14,000**	**45%**	
Data Networking Equipment	1,600	8,000	38	Incremental revenues to companies to build Internet
Internet Security Equipment and Software	200	1,000	40	Firewalls, virtual private networking, transaction/authentication enabling solutions
Internet Service Providers	400	5,000	66	Internet service providers
Infrastructure (Indirect)	**10,950**	**43,000**	**30**	
PC, Server and Semiconductors	10,000	40,000	32	PC and server companies
Telecommunications and Related Services	700	2,000	23	Internet services
Telecommunications Equipment	250	1,000	34	Incremental revenues to companies to build Internet
Software and Services	**900**	**5,100**	**41**	
Application Software	600	2,500	33	E-mail, TCP/IP applications, browsers, authoring tools
Enterprise and Networking Software	200	2,000	58	Enterprise/database/server software sales related to Internet
Internet/Online Services, Consulting and Development	100	600	44	Services and consulting
Content and Aggregation	**1,850**	**17,000**	**56**	
Organization/Aggregation	1,500	6,000	32	Online service providers and search engines
Information	100	5,000	11	Incremental revenues from pay-services and advertising
Publications/Static and Publications/Interactive	50	1,000	82	Magazines (printed and electronic) addressing the Internet
Commerce and Transaction Processing	200	5,000	91	Incremental revenue from related to Internet-based transactions
Total Revenue	**$15,900**	**$79,100**	**38%**	
Revenue Created by/for Internet*	4,950	36,100	49	

CAGR Compound Annual Growth Rate. *includes Infrastructure (direct), Software and Services, and Content and Aggregation.*
Source: Morgan Stanley Estimates

We believe new businesses that are created by or for the Internet marketplace will grow very rapidly, at an estimated CAGR of 38% from now until the year 2000 (see table 1.3). Such businesses include data networking equipment specialized for the Internet, Internet Service Providers, security equipment and software, Internet applications software, transaction processing, segments of the enterprise software market, information provision, information aggregation services, online and offline publications, and online commerce. We also believe growth in some existing markets, namely PCs, servers, semiconductors, and telecommunications service and equipment, will benefit indirectly. This segment should grow at a 30% CAGR, thanks in part to its role in supporting the Internet's growth. Combining directly and indirectly-related markets, we believe the Internet market will grow at a 38% CAGR until the year 2000.

We estimate Internet-related revenues by applying our estimates for the fraction of a company's total revenue in the latest 12 months that is related to the Internet. For new businesses like ISPs, this is easy, 100%. For existing businesses, this is less obvious. Data networking equipment is a good example. We estimate that about 1/5 of all worldwide data networking equipment revenues were derived as a result of sales to ISPs, OSPs, carriers for use on the Internet, or for sales which were incremental as a result of the Internet. Similar logic is applied for other company categories. In Table 1.3 **we put the size of today's Internet market at about $5.0 billion for new markets plus another roughly $11 billion related indirectly to existing infrastructure companies. We believe the 'new businesses' market may grow to $36 billion in the year 2000, and the indirectly-related existing markets will grow to $43 billion.**

In describing some of the more interesting public companies in the communications evolution, one thing is absolutely certain: a host of companies will be key to new developments that no one has heard or thought of yet...and some of the best-and-brightest companies of today will become also-rans. We have created a series of competitive analysis charts (see Chapter 10). Our summary chart (Fig. 1.4) divides the Internet market into 16 subsegments. We compare the value-added of various companies' products with growth opportunities relative to the Internet. The sweet spot is high and to the right.

Figure 1.4
Competitive Analysis Internet Industry Over Next 2 to 3 Years

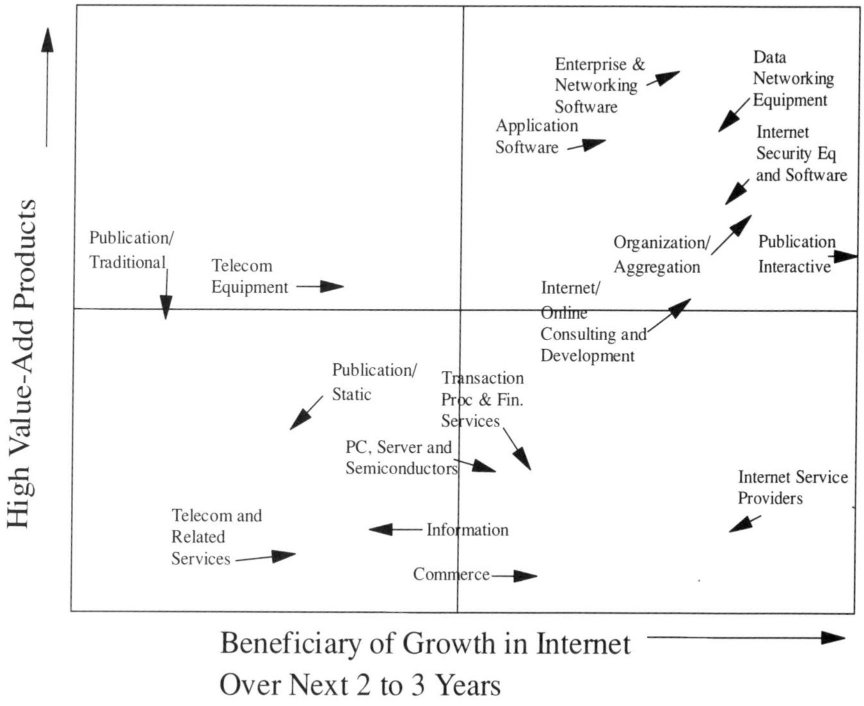

Note: Arrows indicate direction of competitive position over time.

Infrastructure

Data Networking Equipment (Bridges, Routers & Hubs)

Right now, development of the connected community is just beginning, and a simple analogy would compare it to the rollout of the railroad system in America in the 1860s. Let's say that it's 1865 and railroad track/ties are just beginning to be deployed (at its peak in 1928, America had over 260,000 miles of railroad track in operation) and you have the option of investing in (a) a group of five companies that have a near monopoly on railroad ties, or (b) one of 20 capital-intensive start-ups that want to control railroad traffic in different regions. Which would you pick? We would invest in the railroad tie companies: They are not particularly capital-intensive, they have market leadership, and the demand for their products is bound to grow dramatically with the rollout of the train system.

We believe that the railroad-tie equivalents for the rollout of today's PC communication systems are Cisco, Ascend,

and Cascade, and possibly U.S. Robotics. In the IPO prospectuses of Netcom, PSINet, and UUNET, Cisco is identified as a sole source provider in the risk section of each, and Cascade and Ascend are identified in two. Once one of the brands/products is installed, more of the same are likely on the way. These are as close to proprietary 'railroad ties' as you can get. In general, to build a small- to medium-sized Point of Presence (POP), which gives subscribers local call access to their ISP or OSP network, you need one router, one switch (though mainly in large networks), and one or more call aggregators. One way to assess the potential market size for data networking equipment related to ISP and OSP networks is to estimate the number of POPs necessary to allow local access calls to most users in the U.S. and in the rest of the world. Today, each of the largest ISPs has 200–300 or more POPs worldwide, mostly in the U.S. and in the same cities as their competitors (New York City, Los Angeles, San Francisco, Chicago, etc.).

Cisco's routers comprise an estimated 80% of the Internet backbone. The ISPs are standardized on the product, for the prevailing TCP/IP technology needs routing to work. Cisco's yearly growth has chugged along at rates of almost 100% for FY1992 to FY1994, 59% for FY1995; Morgan Stanley analyst George Kelly estimates 74% annual growth over the next year and 45% the year after. Cisco has grown from a $340 million company in fiscal 1992 to nearly $2 billion in FY1995. Cascade and Ascend, two companies that went public in 1994, are big beneficiaries of growth in the Internet. Both have leads in incorporating features needed by the ISPs into their products, and both have substantial installed bases in the ISPs, OSPs, and other carriers.

Because Cisco, Ascend, and Cascade equipment is necessary to build the Internet, we believe these stocks are the safest and cleanest way now to invest in its evolution.

Internet Security Equipment and Software

In surveys over the past year, the No. 1 concern of network managers considering a connection of their corporate networks to the Internet is security. There are many forms of security to be concerned with.

First, **external threats of hackers** from the outside. Once connected to the Net, a system may need some degree of firewalling and/or packet filtering. Applications-layer firewalling, considered more advanced than packet filtering, is being addressed by many privately-held and publicly-traded companies, including Raptor, Secure Computing, Border Networks, Trusted Information Systems, and CheckPoint Software.

Second, meeting the **threat of messages being intercepted.** Once they are on the Internet, messages require some kind of transmission and/or transaction security (encryption). Transmission security is being addressed using on-the-fly encryption by companies such as Raptor and TimeStep, an affiliate of Newbridge Networks. Transaction security is being addressed by software encryption technology built into browser and other software by Terisa (a joint venture between EIT and RSA Data Security), RSA Data Security, Netscape, VISA International, Microsoft, Spyglass, and many others.

Third, **the threat of unwanted users** being authorized access to ISP networks or to corporate networks through the

Internet. This is being combated by more advanced passwording and user authentication. Security Dynamics, maker of the SecurID card, and CryptoCard, are making extended user authentication challenge/response token cards that generate one-time passwords.

The market for Internet security is small today but has the potential for strong growth over the next several years. Over time, it's likely that many of the small security companies will be acquired by larger companies wishing to enhance or extend product lines.

Internet Service Providers (ISPs)

With 1995 year-end public valuations in the range of 20, 25, and 6 times latest 12-month sales, companies such as UUNET, PSINet, and Netcom have certainly captured the enthusiasm of investors. Together, the three have an aggregate public market capitalization of $3 billion but only $176 million in latest 12-month revenue and $57 million in latest 12-month losses. These companies are helping create the backbone for the Internet by providing interconnections. While this market is growing very rapidly, large companies such as MCI, Sprint, AT&T, IBM, CompuServe, America Online and many others (remember, there are more than 3,000 ISPs worldwide) are competing in this space or soon will.

The growth/business model dynamics of this business can be compared with that of the cellular business in the 1980s and '90s. Companies are investing lots of capital to build regional POPs (points-of-presence) as quickly as possible to secure users around the country and worldwide. While this business is growing rapidly, over time it will likely experience considerable pricing pressure as new entrants fight for traffic. In addition, in time it's likely that we will see an industry shakeout, and the better-capitalized may acquire the smaller pioneers.

ISPs are moving fast to find ways to enhance their revenue streams, ranging from using their own interfaces/browsers, search engines and soon, bundling (in cable-model fashion) basic and premium services for Web access/membership to certain sites. For example, Microsoft would like to bundle (for a fee) MSN and NBC news with every ISP's offerings.

ISPs were first to market in providing Internet access to customers. We expect many RBOCs to begin offering limited service by 2Q96; PacBell and US West already do;

some of the IXCs are already offering service. As it stands now, the ISPs' infrastructure and customer base are growing as rapidly as their people can purchase, install and maintain network equipment; ISP and OSP network infrastructures have been growing more slowly than customer usage. ISP and OSP networks are not as reliable as telephone users have become accustomed to. We have seen the ISPs come to market for more capital many times, and the valuations on these stocks look high relative to sales. The telcos will either miss the market; buy into the market; or successfully enter it on their own.

Bandwidth expansion will be an ongoing issue for the ISPs. As Internet usage increases and bandwidth requirements expand, the infrastructure will need to ramp as well. In time, cost increases will have to be passed on to users, and it is likely that structural bottlenecks may occur.

PCs, Servers, and Semiconductors

Anyone who wants to communicate digitally needs a communication device, a PC (or a pager or a set-top box). As indicated earlier, we expect PC growth to remain reasonably strong (though the rate of growth will likely continue to slow) as the market for PCs expands globally and as functionality (largely communications features) increases. The most play in this space is the company with an 80% market share in PCs, Intel. We feel it is clearly positioned to be the primary beneficiary (at least, based on microprocessor units shipped; revenues may be another story) as end-users continue to ramp up their PC processing power.

Of course, PC vendors such as Compaq and Dell profit from PC growth. However, their relatively low, though leading, worldwide market shares (10% and 3%, respectively) indicate just how competitive this space of the market is. Microsoft, naturally, benefits from PC growth as well.

You want to set up a home page or a stable communications infrastructure for internal/external digital communications? You need a server plus software. Companies such as Compaq, Hewlett-Packard, Sun Microsystems, and Silicon Graphics have indicated that server sales have picked up due to the Internet. We believe there is a trend to make servers, and the software that runs on them, easier to use and less expensive.

Telecommunications and Related Services

Telecom service providers should benefit from increased utilization of the Internet in two important respects, increased network usage and new access services, and new retail service offerings.

Increased activity on the Internet will increase demand for access to Internet points of presence (POPs). This could benefit local exchange carriers by stimulating demand for second access lines (for use with modems) and — depending on calling plans and POP locations — increasing local usage revenues. Current Internet applications are also very graphics-intensive, which requires faster connections and should facilitate both high-speed business-line and residential ISDN sales. More Internet activity will also stimulate demand for backbone capacity, of which the long-distance carriers, primarily AT&T, Sprint, and MCI, are already supplying a large portion.

The telecom service providers hope the real revenue opportunity will be through retail product offerings.

Telecommunications Equipment

Many (but not all) telecommunications equipment vendors are significant beneficiaries of increasing Internet activity. Since much of the Internet's allure stems from its heavy use of graphics and often sound, high-speed digital connections are required, at the very least, between major nodes comprising the Internet. Ideally, digital connections should also exist between Internet Service Providers' points of presence and their subscribers' access equipment, though admittedly most Internet connections today are being made over slower, analog phone connections.

Much of the Internet is composed of multiprotocol routers linked by high-speed data lines. These leased connections, operating at 1.5 megabits/second in the case of T1 lines, or 45 megabits/second in the case of less ubiquitous but higher capacity T3 connections, are supplied by carriers using digital cross-connects manufactured by companies such as Tellabs and DSC Communications. Cross-connects serve to trunk and groom digital signals between the endpoints of leased connections.

While routers play an important role in Internet infrastructure, larger ISPs are increasingly choosing to establish private frame relay networks to aggregate subscriber traffic from their many points of presence and to manage the flow of that traffic onto the Internet. Major ISPs and OSPs have purchased frame relay switches from Cascade and StrataCom for this purpose. Subscribers can connect directly to Internet Service Providers' frame relay networks, attracted by high throughput (generally 56 kilobits/second to 1,544 kilobits/second) compared with the tens of kilobits on conventional analog connections. When accessing the Internet using frame relay, subscribers often need FRADs (frame relay access devices) manufactured by companies such as Digital Link, the Kentrox division of ADC Telecommunications, and Motorola to interface with the frame relay service.

Another increasingly attractive method of accessing the Internet is Integrated Services Digital Network. ISDN, long the "Rodney Dangerfield of digital connectivity," is beginning to gain respect given its high bandwidth (up to 128 kilobits/second for a BRI connection, with throughput several times that with compression) and attractive pay-as-you-go nature. Companies that supply ISDN connections or make equipment to access ISDN include Ascend Communications, ADTRAN, U.S. Robotics, Premisys, and Motorola.

Telecommunications carriers offering or planning to offer video services may ultimately harness one of the most promising means of increasing bandwidth to the home and office. CATV operators are conducting trials of high-speed data communications over an upgraded broadband plant. Success in this endeavor hinges on more widely upgrading plant to accommodate two-way communications and manage communications over a combination of fiber and copper. Several companies have cable modems under development, including CATV equipment leaders General Instrument and Scientific-Atlanta, a host of other large companies such as Intel, Digital Equipment, Hewlett-Packard, and Zenith, as well as several smaller companies such as @Home, LAN City and Com21. While architectures differ widely — is the upstream/downstream bandwidth equal or primarily broadcast in nature? Will Ethernet, ATM, or some other protocol be employed? — this product segment will likely remain an area of intensive trials and investment over the next few years.

Software and Services

Application Software

There will likely be four key areas for Internet software development: (1) **Browser** software; (2) **Server** software; (3) Internet software **development/authoring tools**; and (4) software for back-end processes and databases. The Web is about software; heretofore, lots of Internet software has been distributed freely. Many companies today are spending heavily to develop software to make the Internet easier to use. To date, we think the biggest success story is Netscape Communications, which will likely end C1995 as the fastest growing software company in history (based on first year sales). By using the Mosaic web browser software as its guide, Netscape created and freely distributed its browser software across the Internet. We believe more than 60% of web surfers use the Netscape browser. Through licensing arrangements with Spyglass, companies such as Microsoft are also rapidly rolling out other browser products, for free.

Many other companies want to be in the browser game (including America Online, CompuServe, Prodigy, Oracle, Sun, Lotus and AT&T). We believe that over time, the market will standardize on one or two browsers — the most likely winners are Netscape and Microsoft. Both companies will likely end up receiving very little money per browser as they build critical mass in an attempt to control the front-end software for the Web. The company that controls the web's front-end will likely be best positioned to control the server and development tool markets. For now, Netscape has the lead in the browser market, but it's still too early to tell whether it can dominate the market on an on-going basis. Microsoft's edge with Windows 95 and Windows NT, combined with its own browser, over time can be a powerful challenge.

Scott McNealy of Sun Microsystems has been saying for years that "The Network is the Computer," and with the rapid ramp-up in Internet usage, he's starting to look spot on. The success of the mainframe created IBM's market dominance, the argument goes; the rise of the minicomputer gave power to Digital Equipment and Hewlett-Packard; and the success of the personal computer made Microsoft, Compaq and Apple dominant. If indeed, the Internet/network is the next computing platform, a host of new dynamic companies will capitalize on it. The reason for the massive investor appetite for shares of Netscape, in our opinion, is that at least for now, it appears that Netscape could be the leader in creating the software platform for the Internet.

The dominant players in this emerging industry are making strategic bets, building proprietary Internet applications and giving them away to users to gain mass acceptance and try to become the de facto system. Such attempts include Microsoft's often changing efforts; Adobe's Acrobat; Macromedia's ShockWave; Netscape's proprietary HTML extensions and SSL/Secure Courier; Sun's Java; electronic payment systems from DigiCash, First Virtual, and CyberCash; Xing Technology's StreamWorks, Progressive Networks' RealAudio, VocalTec's Internet Phone, Paper's VRML, World's VRML+. This type of positioning by software companies is what creates long-term opportunities for "annuities" as proprietary implementations become standards. We will watch carefully as these "standards" emerge.

Enterprise and Networking Software

The Internet's potential for fundamentally restructuring the computing industry is more apparent and imminent in the enterprise space than in others. In short, the Internet represents the next application development platform and ubiquitous access to applications regardless of location.

The impact on the enterprise will be as significant, if not more so, than the previous platform shifts (mainframe to mini to PC). What's at stake is a battle for application developers. For the first time, developers will have a standard, cross-platform GUI with fairly well-defined programming interfaces. Universal access to the Web and an uncharacteristically uniform desktop environment in the form of Web browsers have created an attractive volume market for developers that, heretofore, has only been matched by Microsoft DOS and Windows environments.

The volume market for developers has been controlled by Microsoft for nearly a decade. HTML, Java, and related families of emerging development tools based on these standards represent a chance to break away from the Micro-

soft stranglehold and still reach the Windows market. HTML is a cross-platform page description language in the public domain. Enhanced scripting language with sophisticated logical constructs that complement HTML will emerge from another generation of tools companies. Likewise, many existing development tools vendors will license Java and incorporate HTML generation into their current tool sets.

No doubt, for the Web, Microsoft will revert to its proven formula of creating proprietary extensions and programming interfaces tied to Windows. Every company in the computing industry, with the possible exception of Microsoft, wants to see the Internet become a critical platform in the enterprise since it reduces the role of the desktop and weakens Microsoft. The openness of the Internet throws a wrench into Microsoft's one-stop shopping plans and makes a Windows-everywhere strategy look a little dated.

The enterprise use of the Internet doesn't require a major cultural shift in consumer behavior or a major uptick in computing infrastructure. Enterprise users already have the problem of remote and mobile access, and the Internet simply represents a better solution. Many corporations already have experience with internal Web sites over "Intranets," and opening up some applications to external users is not a large technological leap. So while excitement over "hot Web pages" is capturing attention for now, the enterprise use of the Internet will likely capture the dollars in the near term, because there is an immediate problem to be solved by buyers who have budgets. The perfunctory list of hot Web pages that most users view for two minutes will be old news next year, and consumers will demand more useful content. One near-term use of the Internet that could keep consumers interested is an ability to tie into their office environments easily.

Internet/Online Consulting, Services and Development

Not all users of the Internet will be experts. Today, for the most part, power users and early adopters built their networks, connected them to the Internet, and developed web sites. We believe there is an opportunity for vendors to do the same, as an outsourcing agreement, for corporations connecting in the future. Sprouting up all over are advertisements for web development, consulting, and other such arrangements. It would not be surprising if larger consulting and computer services companies such as Electronic Data Systems addressed this in the future.

Because it is impossible to accurately count the number of Internet users, we believe there is a small opportunity to perform the service for advertising purposes, such as in marketing studies. Find/SVP is one such company doing this today. Nielsen, of Dun+Bradstreet, recently completed a study of the Internet marketplace as well.

Content and Aggregation

For now, the information on the Internet is called content. In the future, it will probably be called programming. As can be evinced by a quick perusal of our "cool sites" (Chapter 12), the Internet is about information and information sharing. And it's not just for external information, it can be about internal corporate information; like many enterprises, Morgan Stanley has put its corporate information and communications stuff up for internal access via Web browsers. The 'Net was created so academics in semi-arcane fields could share information with hard-to-find colleagues. In fact, in the early days, we venture that the more arcane an area of interest, the easier it was to find out about it on the Internet. Subsequently, some great information access tools have been created; such as InfoSeek, Yahoo!, Lycos and WebCrawler. These search engines, available freely on the Web, are basically massive databases resulting from periodic automated searches of the Web.

The Web has been dubbed a massive virtual disk drive, and its beauty is not only that there is lots of information available, but also that it's getting easier to access. However, organizing the massive, rapidly growing, and infinitely distributed data on the Internet is a service that will always be valuable to consumers. For now, no company, in our opinion, does a better job of making general information available for a mass market audience than America Online. In our view, its online service is a superset of the Internet; AOL should be viewed as a consumer media/entertainment company and a content aggregator/programmer. With its large subscriber base and its ability to point to data and garner advertising, annuity revenue streams should be significant. Microsoft is also adopting a content aggregator model for its Internet/online efforts; its recently announced relationship with NBC is a clear indicator of its long-term plans.

A lot of the information that's available on the Web is worth its price (free). Although many organizations use the Web only as a means of distributing marketing material, entrepreneurs are creating more interesting material. Re-member the early days of television, when the hosts got up on stage and read from a script in the same way that they did on radio? It wasn't until Milton Berle and his *Texaco Star Theater* came along and started interviewing and interacting with people in a variety-show style that the new medium of television began to leverage its strengths and gain broader acceptance. Truly dynamic, sophisticated use of the Internet's full capabilities is still relatively rare.

Again, since anyone with a PC and a modem can become a publisher, predicting the eventual winners is all but impossible. At this stage it appears that, as with traditional media, advertising will eventually provide most of the revenue for content providers/aggregators on the Web. Over time, this should be augmented by revenues from subscriptions and transactions. Companies with high-traffic sites today collect revenue from advertisers in exchange for a logo or banner ad (with hyper-text links to more details). Yet the infrastructure for Web "narrowcasting" (distinct from traditional broadcasting) — educating media buyers, creating usage statistics, ad rate cards, etc. — has just begun to emerge.

While a large portion of traditional media revenue is typically generated from advertising (100% for television; 80% for newspapers; and 50% for magazines), similar occurrences should occur on the Internet. Remember how Procter & Gamble funded the soap operas? We will see similar developments again; in fact, we already are.

We have divided the various content and aggregation companies into several subsegments.

A Sampling of Advertisements on the Internet*

Advertiser	Home Page
Gatorade	ESPN
Saturn	America Online
Callaway Golf	iGOLF on America Online
IBM	Magellan/McKinley Group
AT&T	InfoSeek
Hewlett-Packard	HotWired
NBC	Yahoo

*circa 12/95

Organization/Aggregation

In concept, the function of an online service interface and a web database site are similar; they allow quick retrieval of vast amounts of information. Good web databases, like Yahoo!, Infoseek, Lycos, and WebCrawler and others, are invaluable for users — they make the web worth using. The same is true with OSP interfaces such as America Online, Microsoft's MSN, CompuServe, Prodigy and others. Users like America Online because it has an easier interface, making it easy to quickly get at information. OSPs are paid for their service on a per hour and/or monthly charge; a web database service is usually paid for by advertiser revenue.

Information/Publications

There are "**static**" pages, "**dynamic**" pages, "**interactive**" pages, and combinations of all three on the Web today. Static areas include text-based information; Dynamic areas include text-based information with moving images/data; and Interactive areas include chat features where users interact. Traditional media companies such as *Time*; ESPN; *Business Week*; *The New York Times*; *The Wall Street Journal*; *The San Jose Mercury News*; *The Chicago Tribune*; Ziff-Davis; and ABC have offered impressive static and dynamic pages, while start-up companies like Motley Fool and clnet are taking advantage of the new medium and offering great interactive services. America Online is actively funding emerging companies such as The

Motley Fool, NetNoir, and iGOLF to provide content. Over time, one of the hot areas of interactive excitement on the Web will be in the area of online multiplayer gaming and gambling.

Newspaper companies spent millions in the late 1970s and early 1980s developing new, electronic-based news services that readers ultimately rejected, such as Knight-Ridder's Viewtron, a two-way interactive information service. Consequently, newspaper companies have in general approached the new wave of online mania more cautiously and with much less up-front capital commitment. But they are not sitting on their hands. Both alone and in partnership, newspapers are jumping into the online arena and generally achieving much better results than they had in the past: distribution channels are much more fully developed, the public is much more computer literate, and the demand for online services is strong.

As newspapers attempt to create critical mass in the online arena quickly and dramatically, there is some standardization for media content on the Internet through the New Century Network, a cooperative effort among eight newspaper companies (Knight-Ridder, Gannett, Times Mirror, Tribune, Washington Post, Advance Publications, Cox Newspapers, and Hearst Newspapers). NCN is developing standards for 'Net publishing, exploring distribution arrangements for the digital marketplace with wire services and others, and focusing on content sharing. Eventually,

Check Out This Business Model

Our favorite example of a low-cost business model is Robert Seidman's. Robert started a newsletter 14 months ago called *In, Around and Online* (recently changed in what was probably a marketing effort to *Seidman's Online Insider* (available at http://www.clark.net/pub/robert). Word (and e-mail) of his newsletter spread quickly. He distributes this 5-10 page newsletter to over 10,000 subscribers weekly, for free, spending, by his admission, 15-20 hours per week gathering information and creating the product, and we estimate that his capital equipment cost to run the business is a nice 486 PC (say $3,000) and that his monthly Internet/online bills are gratis. Within about a year he has become somewhat of a cult figure in the Internet community.

We believe that at some point in the next year, when we get some glimmers of secure financial transactions on the Internet, or even if we don't, Mr. Seidman may begin charging for his newsletter. Let's say he charges his 10,000 subscribers a whopping $20 per year (we would pay a lot more), then suddenly he's grossing more than $200K per year (all for less than $100 in annual COGS, a $3,000 PC and about 18 hours a week).

We'll take that business model, thank you. All by himself, Robert could have profits that exceed those of many of the Internet Service Providers. Now, that's a business model. It's also good news for the next *Rolling Stones* and *MTV*, and maybe not such good news for companies with high costs!

NCN expects to offer its capabilities to virtually any newspaper.

Another major joint venture is a national employment service on the Internet called CareerPath, being developed through six major newspapers including *The Boston Globe, Chicago Tribune, Los Angeles Times, The New York Times, San Jose Mercury News,* and *The Washington Post.* Beyond these significant joint efforts, most major newspaper and publishing companies are busy developing and selling a host of company-specific services for both the Internet and other online systems.

Transaction Processing and Financial Services

It is easy to see how companies that service this industry can readily exploit the virtues of the Internet. In general, as the trend accelerates from a paper-based to electronically based transaction environment, the more vibrant the business of transaction processors will be. With a virtually cashless society's financial transactions consummated on varying forms of credit, debit, or smart cards, the demand for secure and efficient processing capability is hard to overstate. Companies such as First Data Corporation, with the scale to be truly a dominant player, are poised to benefit from this secular trend. Similarly, HNCS, with leading-edge fraud detection products, is positioned nicely in specialized applications such as transaction securitization and data interpretation. Companies that own data bases of transaction and user profile data stand to benefit tremendously.

Commerce

A complaint about the Internet today is that it's tough for publishers to make money from it, there aren't enough users, and there isn't a secure way to transfer funds. It seems like the only folks making much, if any, money are the networking equipment companies, the organizations that sell Internet publications and host conferences, and, yes, the investment bankers that bring Internet-buzz companies public.

Over time this will change. More users will come as ease of use and access improves (this Christmas should bring lots of consumer users), and security on the Internet will happen someday (though it will probably take longer than the bulls hope). Two key areas for improvement: encryption technology and public trust.

In the short term on the commerce front, we are most excited about developments in electronic commerce over non-Internet, private (allegedly secure) networks, such as:

- transactions over America Online, which in fact is kind of like a cyberspace shopping mall;

- the rollout of Intuit's electronic commerce products linked with financial institutions; and

- purchases of items made over the Internet where items are chosen/ordered over the 'Net, but the actual funds transfer is made via credit card with phone confirmation, or via a coded account with a company like DigiCash, First Virtual or CyberCash.

We believe the benefits of choice and selection for consumers via the Internet will make the medium a key way of conducting commerce. The sooner it can become more secure, the better, but that's not critical to the evolution of the medium for purposes of commerce. For now, it's important for companies to nab customers and keep improving product offerings: mind share and market share will be crucial. While skeptics like to say that America Online loses money on a cash flow basis (excluding subscriber acquisition costs), once it obtains 5-10 million subscribers, it will be able to harvest the cash flow. If a company can build subscribers in a small but rapidly growing market with a compelling economic model and maintain that share when the market gets bigger, it should reap good profit margins.

Once you have purchased your first audio CD, CD-ROM, flowers, or book electronically, there's a good chance that you will do it again and again. And companies like CUC International, the Internet Shopping Network (owned by Home Shopping Network), and 1-800-FLOWERS are making it even easier via the Internet and online services. Companies like 1-800-FLOWERS and pcflowers have popularized the electronic purchase of flowers and gifts, offering items consumers don't feel the need to inspect (or even see) before unloading their cash. Both CUC International and ISN provide fairly comprehensive Web shopping services that allow members to buy things through a member number rather than placing the customer's credit card information out on the Net with each purchase.

Some Data for the New Media World from the Old

Stats from today's media world offer a sense of how this new medium may develop. It's important to understand what U.S. consumers are willing to pay today via various media in order to understand what they may pay for the same information (but better packaged) via the Internet. We attribute lots of our data to Shirley Biagi's *Media/Impact*.

- About 62% of all adults read a daily newspaper; 75 % of all adults read a newspaper at least once per week.

- U.S. adults read an average of ten magazines a month.

- On weekdays, adults listen to the radio an average of 3 hours and 20 minutes per day.

- Each household leaves the TV set turned on for an average of 7 hours and 15 minutes a day; adults watch TV on average 4 hours per day.

- One out of four American adults goes to the movies once a month; adults with a VCR rent an average of one video-cassette a week.

- Each American spends an average of $55 per year on recorded music.

- Half of all Americans buy at least one book a year; the average library user borrows 15 items a year.

- The average American spends $60 on telephone usage per month.

According to Veronis Suhler & Associates, the relative size of the US media industries in 1994 was $175 billion in revenue (a lot of which comes from advertising). This breaks down as follows: newspapers, $47 billion; televi-

sion, $35 billion; book publishing, $26 billion; magazines, $23 billion; movies, $21 billion; recordings, $12 billion; and radio, $11 billion. These are all mass-media markets in which communication is one-way (or what the publisher wants the consumer to hear/read/see or believes the consumer wants to hear/read/see). With the Internet and on-line services, communication is two-way; for the most part, this same stuff can be delivered to consumers, who can choose what they want.

The newspaper chain with the largest average daily (not including Sunday) circulation is Gannett with 6.3 million via 83 daily newspapers including *USA Today,* which comprises about 1/3 of the total. Among the top 300 magazines in the U.S., the magazine company with the largest circulation is Time Warner, with approximately 26 million copies. The cable company with the most subscribers is TCI, with just over 12 million subscribers (plus another 3.1 million in non-consolidated affiliates). The highest grossing film of all time, *Jurassic Park,* grossed $913 million in box office sales and (at an average ticket price of about $6.50) was seen by over 140 million movie goers and, to date, by an estimated 45 million videophiles. The most successful single recording of all time, "Rock Around the Clock," performed by Bill Haley & the Comets, was purchased by 25 million consumers, and the most successful album recording of all time, *Thriller,* performed by Michael Jackson, was purchased by 25 million consumers.

America Online currently has about 5 million subscribers, up from 1 million a year ago. We think it could hit 10 million within a year or so. And the number of consumers with direct Web access, though small now, will continue to grow rapidly. That's powerful.

Where We Have Been and Where We May be Going

America Online offers a perspective on where we have been with content/aggregation/programming in the online line space and where we may be going in the online/Internet space. We buy into this perspective.

New Media Programming Evolution

1) 1985+

Iron Age
(text-based; low speeds; small audience)

- Member-generated content
- Branded, repackaged ("repurposed") content areas
- Reference database materials
- Icons for information areas and logos for ads
- Rudimentary transactions

2) 1994+

Bronze Age
(text/picture-based; higher speeds; niche audiences)

- Channel creation and new media programming
- Packaging of multiple content streams
- Shopping malls for commerce (with text and photos)
- Interactive marketing areas as information providers
- Celebrity events and vertical communities
- Connected properties
- Pointing to Web sites

Source: America Online

3) 1996+

Silver Age
(multiple media; higher speeds; critical mass audience)

- Original content
- Less "repurposed" content
- Commerce as a programmed area
- New channels to serve new markets
- Network initiated, purchased or produced shows
- Member-generated content via home pages, personal Web sites, road trips, intelligent message boards
- New HTML original content areas
- Few partners; better service and increased promotion

4) 1999+

Gold Age
(full-motion video; speed not an issue; mainstream media)

- The next thing: cable and telephony and datacom and Hollywood blended together
- Advertisers/marketers pay the freight
- More consumers using PCs in prime time than TVs
- Promise of interactive services achieved

Chapter 2: The Internet — Past, Present, and Future

Summary

- The Internet began as a U.S. Department of Defense experiment to demonstrate the feasibility of interconnecting computing devices.

- Stimulated by the need for fault-tolerant, wartime communications, the predecessor to the Internet began as four interconnected computers in 1969. There were 1,000 in 1984 and 6.6 million by mid-1995. Following a decision in 1989 to stop funding commercial traffic, in April 1995, the U.S. government began a two-year phase-out of Internet backbone support.

- Future user demand should increase following the arrival of more killer applications like Mosaic, such as real-time audio and video, as well as telephony.

Throughout military history, superior communications has been the strategic key to winning wars. After World War II, computation devices and transistors began to create a new era in technology that proved decisive for the military. In the 1960s, computers began to allow multiple users to share the resources of one processor simultaneously. Time sharing was one in a string of technologies that would contribute to the concept of the Internet. But the Department of Defense wanted a more robust network, one that would allow communications across the U.S., even if a nuclear attack destroyed telecommunications lines.

In 1968, Bolt Beranek and Newman won the competition to develop a communication system based on a set of small, interconnected computers that the DoD's Advanced Research Projects Agency (ARPA) called Interface Message Processors. These specifications were met by a self-healing, packet-switched, routed network. Following a decade of study, the packet-switched ARPANet began as four interconnected computers (hosts) in September 1969 (three in California and one in Nevada).

ARPANet was highly experimental, but the number of computers seeking to connect to the network grew rapidly. In 1972, the first documented e-mail message was sent across the ARPANet, and in 1973, ARPA developed other, non-terrestrial networks, including SATNET, which used synchronous satellites to contact ships at sea, and PRNET, which used packet radio to contact ground mobile units. However, differences in networking capabilities made it essential to devise a software-based packet-switched proto-

col that allowed the various systems to interconnect. In 1973 and 1974, a standard networking protocol emerged that became known as transmission control protocol and Internet protocol, or TCP/IP, for which Vint Cerf and Bob Kahn are credited.

TCP/IP enabled every ARPANet computer to communicate regardless of its operating system. Ethernet LAN technology was another offshoot of ARPA funding. By mid-1975, when there were about 100 computers on the ARPANet, ARPA decided that its experiment was successful and robust enough to move to a separate agency for operations, the Defense Communication Agency (now the Defense Information Systems Agency).

While most of the funding for the ARPANet came from military sources, the project was largely developed at universities and research-oriented government contractors. Some aspects of the network remained classified, but most of the network had to be open to ensure that it was as stable, robust, and useful as possible. By 1977, a four-network demonstration using TCP/IP connected ARPANet, SATNET, Ethernet, and PRNET successfully.

AT&T Bell Labs had introduced UNIX in 1969, and by its 1977 revision TCP/IP had been integrated into the operating system. By 1980, TCP/IP had advanced sufficiently so that ARPA decided to require all computers on the ARPANet to use it (another TCP/IP version came in 1983). UNIX and VMS multi-user operating systems had already gained widespread acceptance and captured a large in-

---

stalled base at academic and research facilities, and in 1979–80, academia was allowed to connect to the ARPANet. Host growth accelerated as the TCP/IP-capable academic systems, as well as the Department of Energy and NASA, plugged in.

Most of the applications for the Internet from the late 1970s until 1995 were developed by non-commercial interests who posted their programs on the Internet as freeware or shareware. Many were developed collaboratively, in the sense that users who developed applications would usually allow others to improve their source code. Basic services for remote connectivity, file transfer, and electronic mail appeared in the mid- to late-1970s. Usenet news, a bulletin-board-like network, appeared in 1981, and was soon followed by the Gopher file search and transfer system in 1982. Open discussions over the Internet continue today about how to optimize the technology; they are posted for public comment as RFCs (request for comments).

At least five companies and individuals each claim to have coined the term "Internet" around 1979, but the term didn't stick until the mid 1980s. In 1986, the National Science Foundation initiated the NSFNet, a series of high-speed (56 kbps) networks connecting the NSF's supercomputers. With the NSFNet in place, and the military using a separate Defense Data Network, the dismantling of the ARPANet was nearly complete. The new NSFNet backbone connected the various regional networks, and with that the term "Internet" was formally adopted. In 1988, NSF selected Merit, at the University of Michigan, to lead a contract with IBM and MCI to develop a 1.5 mbps NSFNet backbone upgrade (Figure 2–1).

In 1989 and 1990, Internet use became obviously more commercial, which was inconsistent with NSF policies. As NASA and the U.S. Department of Energy contributed additional backbone facilities in the form of the NSINet and ESNet, respectively, the NSF began planning to withdraw funding of commercial traffic. In 1988, MCIMail was granted permission to connect to the Internet, followed in 1989 by CompuServe, ATTMail, and Sprintmail (Telemail), which, together with NSFNet, formed the major backbone communications service for the Internet.

To allow commercial networks to connect to the Internet, the Commercial Internet Exchange (CIX), a universal commercial connection point to the Internet, was formed in

Figure 2.1

Internet Backbone (NSFNet) and Regional Networks Service Connections, September 1991

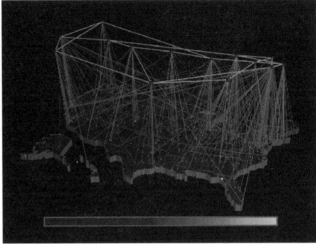

Source: Donna Cox and Robert Patterson, National Center for Supercomputing Applications/University of Illinois. This image is a visualization study of inbound traffic measured in billions of bytes on the NSFNet T1 backbone. It represents data collected by Merit Networks, Inc.

1990. In April 1995, NSFNet began a two-year phased withdrawal from its funding role, although it continues to support vBNS, a backbone intended primarily for academia. Connected to the vBNS are four commercial network access points, to which the "Group of Six" commercial backbone providers (PSINet, UUNET, ANS/AOL, Sprint, MCI, AGIS-Net99) connect. The dismantling of the NSFNet and the transition to the commercial Group of Six backbone was nearly transparent to users, yet it clearly marks the moment of the Internet's commercialization.

The World Wide Web made its debut in 1989 at CERN *(Conseil Europeen pour la Recherche Nucleaire),* based in Geneva. It was developed for scientists (primarily by Tim Berners-Lee) at CERN's nuclear supercollider facility to facilitate research by allowing authors to reference other documents (hypertext), all of which are available on the Internet. At its inception, the system was text-based; CERN did not start publicizing the development until about 1992.

Just two years ago, most of those on the Internet were university users or ex-university users at computer-related corporations. Today, demographics have changed, largely because of the availability of graphical user interfaces like Mosaic, PC-based access, and increasingly robust cataloging and searching resources, such as Yahoo, Infoseek, and Lycos. Mosaic, developed in 1993 at the University of Illinois/National Center for Supercomputing Applications (NCSA) by a team of students, was posted on FTP servers connected to the Internet and made available for free download during its test stages.

Today, Netscape and many others carry on the tradition of letting others use the software for free testing during beta stages. However, to get software that is not a test version, current practice is that users must pay for it. This trend is a reminder that the future of the Internet looks increasingly commercial in terms of content and the user base.

Over the next decade, we believe, the Internet could become as ubiquitous as telephone service. Also, penetration of about 50% of the population will occur more rapidly than it did for the telephone, we believe. However, with 20 times the addressable market outside the U.S. than inside (a reasonable estimate based on population), the Internet should see even more rapid growth as non-U.S. participants demand greater connectivity. There may well be a trend toward convergence of broadcast media into the Internet, if Internet appliances, $500 set-top boxes, and "Internet on a chip" products come to force. In our judgment, the following enablers will accelerate the rate of Internet use as they become more robust and standards-based:

- Internet telephony (available today);

- real-time audio playback (available today);

- real-time video playback (available today);

- PCS (personal communications services [wireless]);

- PDAs (personal digital assistants);

- speech recognition (not ready for prime time); and

- near-synchronous TCP/IP video and voice applications (television quality — not available).

Two years ago, the Internet consisted of a group of users who were homogeneous and decidedly not business-oriented. In the months and years ahead, we should expect the Net to become a closer reflection of the society in which we live, complete with retailers, advertisers, consultants, manufacturers, and people of all types — except it will be global and more accessible.

Social

1964 - Civil
Rights Act Passed

1969 - Woodstock

3/17/76 - Stock Market
tops 1,000

1968 - *The Graduate*
Saturday Night Live Starts

1975 - *One Flew Over
the Cuckoo's Nest*

1979 -
Star Wars

1972 -*The Godfather*

1977 -*Saturday Night
Fever*

1967 - The Doors,
Light My Fire

1973 - Oil Prices
Skyrocket

1978 - US
"dollar crisis"

Political

1968 - Martin Luther
King, Jr.Assassinated
RFK Assassinated
Nixon elected

1975 - Vietnam
War ends

1963 - JFK
Assassinated

1962 - Cuban
Missile Crisis

1972 - Nixon re-elected
Watergate break-in

1976 - Carter elected
U.S. 200th Birthday

Cold War

1979 - Margaret
Thatcher
elected
Prime Minister

1961 - The Berlin
Wall is Built

1974 - Nixon
resigns

Technology

1978 - Intel introduces the 8086
Philips and Sony unveil the CD

1969 - Apollo II
moon landing

1976 - Wang introduces first
computerized WP for $30K
Matsushita introduces the VCR
Jobs & Wozniak market Apple I for
$666

Internet

1957 - U.S. forms the ARPA
USSR launches Sputnik.

1967 - NPL Data Network
developed in England

1974 - TCP defined
Telnet protocol revised

1979 - USENET
established

1973 - First international
connections

1962 - Paul Baran (RAND)
outlines concepts of packet-
switching

1969 - ARPA Net commissioned and 4
nodes set: UCLA, SRI, UCSB, U of Utah

1977 - First TCP
for UNIX

1968 - PS-network
presented to ARPA

1972 - Public demo of
ARPA Net. INWG formed w/
Vint Cerf as Chairman
First E-mail message sent

1976 - First Internet routers
X.25 protocol defined
UUCP developed

1965 - ARPA-sponsored study
on "cooperative networks of
time-sharing computers"

1970 - Hosts start using NCP

1975 - >63 IMPs
Defense Comms. Agency becomes
responsible for ARPA Net

DARPA Experiment | ARPANet

1955　1960　1965　1970　1975

Internet Hosts Semilog Scale

Internet Hosts Normal Scale

1955　1960　1965　1970　1975

Forty Years of Development

Social

1981 - Premiere of MTV
Prince Charles marries Lady Di
War Games

1982 - *ET*
First artificial heart transplant

1987 - Launch of "Just
Say No" to drugs

1989 - Student revolt in China makes
use of Internet

1991 - Russian electronic networks carry
Soviet coup news before TV

1994 - *Schindler's
List*

1995 - *The Net*

2000 - *Rocky
XIX*

Political

1980 - Reagan elected

1981 - Reagan shot

1983 - U.S. invades Grenada

1987 - Irangate
hearings

1988 - Bush elected.
Unrest in USSR.

1989 - Fall of the Berlin Wall.

1991 - The Gulf War

1992 - Clinton elected

Technology

1980 - Sony launches Walkman
in Japan

1984 - Macintosh introduced

1982 - Intel introduces the 286
Time names the computer
"Machine of the Year"

1985 - First personal laser writer
from Apple for $7,000
Intel introduces the 386
Space shuttle explodes

1986 - Challenger accident

1989 - Intel introduces the 486

1993 - Intel introduces the
Pentium processor

1994 - 33% home
PC penetration

1995 - Intel introduces the P6

1996 - Speech recognition
moves to mainstream
50% home PC penetration

1998 - Intel
introduces the P7

2000 - Intel
introduces the P8

Internet

1980 - >400 hosts connecting
>10,000 people

1982 - Defense Data
Network built by DOD

1983 - Split to ARPANet/Milnet
TCP/IP established
MCIMail launches

1981 - CSNet started. ARPANet
links computers at >200 sites
Change from NCP to TCP
mandated.

1984 - DNS established.
Hosts >10,000

1986 - NSFNet
implemented

1987 - 4,000 BBSs linked by
hobbyist networks

1988 - Beginning of
dismantling of ARPANet
Avgs. About 77.5MM
packets per day

1989 - ARPANet ceases to
exist. >100K hosts
Requests for online files
averages. 1,000/month

1990 - EFF founded
Archie released

1991 - CIX formed
Gopher introduced
WAIS released

1992-93 -Internet Society
established
WWW launched

1993 - NPNet
dismantled

1994 - Mosaic

1996 - Elvis becomes AOL's
6MMth Subscriber

100,000
Web Sites

150,000,000
Internet Users

20,000,000
Web Sites

ARPANet/Internet	The Internet

1980	1985	1990	1995	2000

Internet Hosts Semilog Scale

Internet Hosts Normal Scale

1980	1985	1990	1995	2000

	JANUARY	FEBRUARY	MARCH	APRIL	MAY	JUNE
Social	Kobe earthquake Rose Kennedy dies	Dow tops 4000 for first time (2/16) SF wins Superbowl XXIX vs. Chargers		Michael Jordan returns to basketball (vs. Indiana) 234-day long baseball strike ends	Oklahoma City bombing	Time Warner/Turner announcement
Political	[Newt Gingrich becomes Speaker of the House]		World Summit for social development 1995 G7 Ministerial conference			
Technology		U.S. District Court Judge Stanley Sporkin rules against consent decree DOJ reached previously w/MSFT		MSFT's Bob avail. in stores	First E3 conference Sega launches Saturn in U.S. INTU/MSFT merger called off MSH Index begins trading on AMEX	IBM announces cash tender offer for Lotus
Internet	Mark Lotter's count of # of networks = 71,000/4.852MM hosts.	GMGC IPO	AMER/Bertelsmann AG joint venture PSIX IPO UUNT IPO WWW surpasses ftp-data in March as service with greatest traffic on NSFNet based on packet count. WWW surpasses ftp-data in April as service with greatest traffic on NSFNet based on byte count.	NSFNet retired	AMER announces acquisitions of Medior and WAIS	SPYG IPO

Where We Are Today

	JULY	AUGUST	SEPTEMBER	OCTOBER	NOVEMBER	DECEMBER
Social	*The Net*	Jerry Garcia dies / ABC/Disney announcement	Chemical/Chase announce merger	OJ Simpson acquitted / Atlanta Braves win World Series		Dow tops 5000
	Westinghouse/CBS announcement					
Political		First woman admitted to Citadel / 50 yrs after Hiroshima	Unabomber's manifesto published by Washington Post		UN's 50th Anniversary / Election Line Web site introduced by ABC/CapCities and Digital Ink/Newsweek / Yitzhak Rabin assassinated / Powell says no to Presidential race	U.S. Govt. Shutdown
Technology	Tech stocks hit highs / AT&T restructuring announced	Barton vs. Byron / Long awaited release of Windows 95	Sony launches Playstation in U.S.	Tech stocks volatile -- fears of poor earnings / Internet World, Boston, MA	Cisco completes Grand Junction acquisition	
Internet	Mark Lotter's count of # of networks = 61,538/6.642MM hosts / AMER reaches 3MM subs / NSCP IPO / CompuServe reaches 3.4MM subs / French hacker cracks NSCP code	MSN debut	AMER completes Ubique acquisition / AMER reaches 3.5MM subs / $50 fee now charged for domain name registration	UUNT announces Unipalm acquisition / Edgar lives / CompuServe unveils Spryte / VISA Interactive unveils remote banking software / NETC announces 232,800 subs / NETC opens 200th POP	Internet World 95 in Boston - attended by 32,000 / INTU's Quicken offers Internet access/QFN / AMEX Internet Index begins trading / AMER launches GNN	NSCP completes Collabra acquisition / AMER reaches 4MM+ subs / AT&T plans to offer Internet access in schools / Nielsen survey - nearly 37MM w/Internet access; 24MM online users in North America; 17.6MM Web users; and @2.5MM purchased products over Web

Chapter 3: Internet Market Size

Summary

• Though the numbers of Internet and online service users cannot be measured with certainty, we estimate that as of year-end C1995 there were 9 million users of the Internet's World Wide Web, with 75% of them in the U.S. This figure represents about 3% of the U.S. population.

• We estimate there are more than 35 million users of e-mail.

• With the increasing use of the PC as a communications device and the growing need for global information access, we estimate that e-mail users could number 200 million worldwide by the year 2000, and that about 150 million of these could access the Internet/Web, with slightly less than half representing U.S. users. These numbers would represent 35% and 30%, respectively, of the projected U.S. population. While we doubt that our estimates are entirely accurate, we believe they have directional significance. There are currently about 150 million PC users in the world, and over the next one to four years many PCs should be replaced by more powerful, communications-enabled PCs. In our opinion, a factor that might preclude these PCs from accessing the Web would not be lack of demand but rather lack of bandwidth.

• We have used the ramp of Microsoft's Windows operating system (which went from an installed base of 3 million users in 1990 to about 115 million today) as a sanity check in creating our Internet growth estimates.

• In short, we believe that Internet market growth has just begun, and that it will prove to be big.

Summary of Market Estimates

We believe that, within a decade, there is a good chance the PC and the Internet will become ubiquitous in the U.S., with other industrialized countries following within five years. While many companies are eager to get a handle on the actual and projected size of the Internet, unfortunately there is currently no precise, direct method of counting users. Even the foremost experts on sizing the Internet, Network Wizards, said in July 1995, "No one has any clue how many Internet users there are."

Nonetheless, we have joined the fray, and made what we feel are conservative estimates of the current and future Internet user base, based primarily upon observable growth rates of hosts, domains, and networks, and to a lesser degree on market research. We have correlated these results with the counts of subscribers to online services and Internet services, correlated those with user surveys, and cross-checked the results to ensure that they are consistent with governing factors to growth, such as the PC installed base, demographics, and regional populations.

To summarize, we estimate there are currently about 9 million interactive Internet users and about three times that number who use e-mail (Table 3.1). We estimate that the number of Internet/Web users could grow to about 150 million by the year 2000. By then, we expect most users to have real-time graphical user interface access and to use e-mail. For the record, we define a user as an individual who uses the service at least two or three times per month — anything less probably means the user is borrowing someone else's account, which implies no revenue generation.

Table 3.1
Worldwide Connectivity Market 1995E–2000E

(Millions)	1995	1996	1997	1998	1999	2000
Users of:						
PCs	144	167	184	203	217	225
E-Mail	35	60	80	130	180	200
Net/Web	9	23	46	81	122	152
Online/ Hybrid	8	13	18	23	27	30

Source: Morgan Stanley Research Estimates.

Sizing the Market

By all counts, the number of Internet users is growing rapidly, at a historical sustained rate of approximately 100% per year for the past five or ten years. Similar growth is occurring in the online services market. However, there is a distinct difference between the ways user growth can be measured for each of the two segments of cyberspace.

In the online service provider (OSP) market, there are a few key players (e.g., America Online, CompuServe, and Prodigy), and each has a proprietary system that can be accessed only by subscription. This allows the relatively simple measurement of *number of subscribers*. However, there is not necessarily a one-to-one relationship between the number of subscribers and the number of users of OSPs, as there can be multiple users accessing a single account or an individual who has multiple accounts. We estimate a 25% overlap in online service users — that is, on average, one of every four users have two accounts. Thus, in estimating the number of OSP users, we have factored in the likelihood that some users have multiple accounts.

On the other hand, it is impossible to count the number of Internet users, due to the various ways people access the Internet. Today, it carries much less meaning to count the number of Internet service provider (ISP) subscriber accounts, as there are generally two types of accounts: individual and commercial. For purposes of counting users, individual ISP accounts are much like those of OSP accounts. For commercial users, anywhere from one to 100,000 or more users could be served through one account. Therefore, with no means to directly count Internet users, only estimates can be made.

Figure 3.1

Estimated Numbers of Internet, E-Mail, PC Users In the U.S. and Worldwide, 1986–2000E

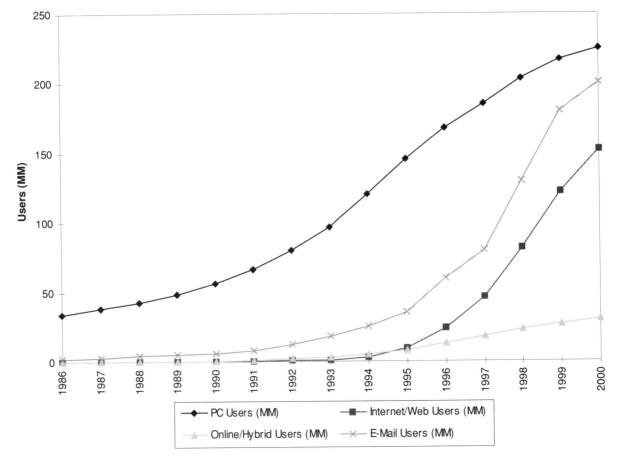

Source: Morgan Stanley Research Estimates.

Figure 3.2
Internet Growth Drivers 1990–2005E

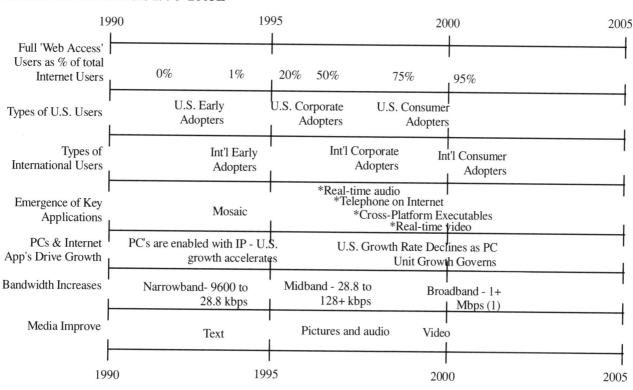

Source: Morgan Stanley Research Estimates. (1) Many corporate users currently have T-1 (1.5 Mbps) connections.

As an example, corporate accounts typically connect their network to an ISP through a permanent leased line, usually a T-1 line (1.5 mbps), although 56K frame relay and ISDN connections are also popular. Though certain applications may exceed the capacity of a T-1, common applications used on the Internet require considerably less bandwidth; therefore, a T-1 connection would allow simultaneous users to access the Internet through the same corporate account. So, as many as ten — or even several hundred — people could gain access to the Internet via a corporate local-area network (LAN) connected to the Net by a T-1 line. By contrast, it is relatively easy to estimate the number of users per modem/dial-up account because, typically, only one user (or perhaps two or three) would connect through such an account, as it would not provide adequate bandwidth for more users (even if the account used a high-speed 28.8 kbps modem connected to a LAN).

People use the Internet for many reasons, and they usually establish a degree of connectivity that suits their needs and budget. Generally, there are three such degrees of Internet connectivity today, listed below from least expensive to most expensive:

- E-mail and Usenet news only;
- Partial Internet access; and
- Fully-interactive, Web Internet access.

By the end of 1994, there were about ten times as many e-mail users as Web users. Each of the three types of access represents a unique user class on the Internet. We believe the type of Internet access is an important factor for estimating the future of the Internet market segment. So we considered the factors that affect users' decisions to use one type of access over another.

We believe that, in about five years, the growth in Internet-connected computers will be strongly correlated with the rate of growth in the installed base of PCs. However, initially we expect the existing installed base to connect to the Internet rapidly. In addition, we expect other phenomena over the next 15 years. To back up for a moment: In the early 1990s and before, Internet users generally were in the class of "early adopters," defined in this context as the research, academic, and corporate beta-test community. Then, beginning about 4Q94, corporate America began adopting the Internet as a means of marketing and of serving customers. Now, we anticipate a period of two or three more years where corporate America's demand for Internet connectivity will continue at an accelerating rate, followed by a more modest pace that's more correlated with the growth in corporate America itself.

Second, although a small number of consumers started connecting to the Internet in 1Q95, we believe they will begin connecting in earnest during 1996–97, and that the rate of growth in American Internet connectivity will continue at a near-100% annual rate until the late 1990s.

Third, we believe that each user class (early, corporate, or consumer adopter) outside the U.S. will follow about three to five years behind the respective U.S. adopter classes. There are two good explanations for this lag: 1) Most applications are written first in English and later translated, and 2) PCs and connectivity tend to cost more in geographies that have low per-user density. We have observed a similar lag in adoption of the PC. In fact, Europe, which tends to adopt PCs quicker than most other non-U.S. areas, is still buying 486s in earnest. In 1994, a large number of international Internet connections were established by those whom we would characterize as early adopters.

Once corporate non-U.S. connections accelerate, we expect the overall growth rate of international connections to surpass the U.S. rate in the late 1990s. We would then expect international consumers to connect in earnest around the turn of the century. In general, we expect the adoption cycle for the international market to be slightly more compressed than for the U.S., as many of the technical issues that prevailed during the U.S.'s early adopter phase (1969 to the early 1990s) probably will have been addressed.

We looked at installed-base figures for other electronics products, such as the telephone, television, and, of course, the PC, as "sanity checks" when calculating the Internet market size figures. It seems the PC is reaching, or has recently reached, critical mass by achieving a penetration rate of nearly one-third of the U.S. home market, just as television in the U.S. did in the late 1950s (TV is now in about 99% of homes.) The availability of relatively easy-to-use, fully interactive, graphical user interface software, such as Mosaic and later Netscape, that allows PCs (not just UNIX minicomputers and mainframes) to communicate globally is driving a fast-growing industry — the OSP/ISP market. One hurdle to more mass appeal for the Internet is the cost of connectivity, including capital costs (PC and software) and monthly subscriber fees (the OSP/ISP charge).

In the rest of this chapter, we detail our calculation methods for the analysis of the Internet and online service market sizes. After defining the degrees of connectivity and the types of users, we present a summary of the market size — past, present, and future. Next, we present measurable and reportable facts that are available on the growth of the Internet. Then we present surveys on user demographics, hardware usage, and service usage, as well as an abridged version of others' Internet sizing estimates. Later, we offer our opinions on the surveys and relate them to the facts, and, finally, we lay out our projections and rationale for the future of the market.

Degrees of Connectivity

We have presented historical Internet user data to reflect three degrees of Internet connectivity: E-mail and Usenet news only, partial Internet access, and fully interactive, Web/Internet access. In the vast majority of cases, users with full Web access also have the capabilities of the partial-Internet and e-mail/Usenet users. Likewise, users with partial Internet access usually have e-mail/Usenet access. Looking at it the other way, e-mail/Usenet-only users don't have partial Internet or full Web access, and partial Internet users do not have full Web access.

The first group, and the largest, is e-mail/Usenet users, who are defined as having the capability of obtaining Internet e-mail and Usenet information only. Such users work on computers that may or may not be "hosts" on the Internet, meaning they will not necessarily be counted in the Internet host numbers presented in the following section, and thus may not necessarily be directly connected to the Internet. Rather, these users may be connected to systems that get regular "batch feeds" from Internet-connected computers that contain e-mail or Usenet news for users on that particular system. For example, if you receive e-mail via an internal corporate mail system, then you're one of these users. Or, for instance, up until 1995 CompuServe users were only counted as e-mail/Usenet users because the CompuServe system only received batch feeds of Internet mail. Many corporate networks have this degree of connectivity. Another example is the FidoNet network, used frequently by bulletin board services (BBSs).

Second, partial Internet access comprises a class of users who have real-time access (in contrast to the delayed batch-feed method) to other Internet hosts but lack the degree of graphics capability or connectivity needed to interact on the Web. In most cases, this type of connection is a UNIX shell account, which users have access to through a terminal-emulation software package. Therefore, the user's computer is not technically a "node" on the Internet, and as such cannot run many fully-interactive programs, including a Mosaic-based Web browser.

This deficiency is usually due to a lack of computational power required to run graphics programs such as Mosaic, limitations imposed on the network, or limitations on the type of connection. An example of the second deficiency may be that the management at a company has decided that users should have only FTP capabilities, evidently assuming employees will waste too much time on the service or that the service is not necessary. An example of the third deficiency, a connection limitation, may be that the computer is not IP-enabled (i.e., is not a true host) but has limited access to a host that allows the remote computer to issue certain (non-Web) commands. This can be accomplished with terminal-emulation software, which is how Delphi offered Internet access in 1994. Typically, this type of account has a command-line, text-based interface. Another example of this type is one who uses a Unix-shell-only account.

Third, full Web access implies that the user is working on an IP-enabled computer (with some exceptions) that has graphics capabilities, such as Mosaic-type Web software. The full Web access computer usually has either a permanently registered Internet address or a temporary Internet address (where the computer is only considered a host during an active session). Once this type of connection is established, full Web access is achieved, and users can run Web browser software. Many OSPs (such as AOL, CompuServe, and Prodigy) offer full Web access — although only a fraction of subscribers, perhaps 20% or 30%, use it. ISPs such as Netcom, PSINet, UUNET, BBN Planet offer full Web access to users, except those with shell accounts.

Who Are 'Users'?

We believe many previously published online/Internet user and subscriber measurements have been somewhat misleading. Subscriber data can over- or under-represent the number of real users, as users often have more than one OSP or ISP account. For example, a fair number of corporate users of the Internet also have personal OSP or ISP subscriber accounts. On the other hand, corporations frequently enable large numbers of their networked computers with either IP or Internet e-mail capabilities. Not all of these computers are registered on the Internet, and users of the enabled computers often do not otherwise use the Internet. Perhaps five years ago, there were ten users per host. This is no longer the case, and the ratio is changing rapidly. In addition, users commonly share computers that are on the Internet, and increasingly common protocols, such as PPP, allow the sharing of IP addresses.

We define a user as an individual who accesses a service at least two or three times per month. Any less than that, and the user probably is borrowing someone else's account.

What Are Hits, Visits, and Caching?

Other means of assessing Internet usage have been adopted by various Internet content and service providers. One such method is by counting *"hits"* to a Web server. Essentially, a hit represents the number of files that have been uploaded from the server to the client. A count of files sent, or "hits," is entered into the log file of a server. A hit is generated by every request made to a Web server, and thus has little predictable relation to users, visitors, or pages.

A Web server responds to a client's request to upload files most frequently when a client requests a page, such as a home page. However, the number of files that make up a particular page depends on the number of graphics files used to construct the page, as well as other factors related to the way the page was designed.

The second means of counting Internet site usage is to count user *"visits."* Technically, a visit is a sequence of hits made by a single user at a single time. Several software/service companies, such as I/Pro and Netcount, have developed relatively sophisticated applications to count visits.

Measurement of user counts and Web usage is often distorted by *caching*, which is the storing or buffering of data in a temporary location. The data (e.g., a home page) can then be retrieved quickly, which makes an application, like a Web browser, run faster. On the Internet, caching occurs in two different places: at OSP networks, where content from Internet sites is cached on servers, and on the hard drives of local PCs or workstations, where graphics files from frequently visited sites are stored so that they can be retrieved locally when sites are revisited.

The second, local type of caching does not distort Internet usage counts, but the first, OSP caching, does, because the cached files are duplicates that reside in locations other than the original Web site. Thus, an OSP subscriber requesting a particular Web page might actually receive the OSP's cached version, resulting in fewer hits to the original Web site, or none at all. This creates problems for advertisers on the Web, which can't be sure how many people they're actually reaching (refer to the Glossary later in this report for definitions of hit, page, media objects, visit, unique users, AdViews, AdClicks, AdClick Rate, and Qualified Hits). Netscape may have a solution with its http "cookies," files that track more accurately individuals' use of the Internet.

Intranet versus the Internet

An intranet is a network (or internetworked system) that uses TCP/IP but is not available to Internet users outside the network. Intranets are commonly used by corporations to allow employees connected to the system to "browse" through corporate information, such as schedules, company events, employee manuals, technical standards, and so forth. In the future, intranets probably will be used to allow collaborative work-sharing among users in the same corporation, even if they're in different locations.

There seems to be a lot of confusion in the marketplace about the difference between Intranet and Internet users. Both use browsers, servers, workstations, routers, bridges, call-aggregating (remote-access) devices, and other similar software and hardware. The difference, however, is that the Internet is public, while Intranets are private. Nonetheless, because both systems are based on the same protocols, corporations with Intranets can relatively easily connect their networks to the Internet. In fact, Netscape estimates that half of its browser users are part of Intranets.

Facts — Past and Present

Any new user must register with his or her ISP or OSP prior to connecting to the Internet, to avoid duplicate Internet addresses. As a result, government contractors responsible for the collection of this publicly available information have been able to track trends in the number of hosts, domains, and networks, as well as the types and locations of organizations. In the following paragraphs we present the raw data, which identify growth trends in:

- Hosts, domains, and networks; and
- Hosts by country and domain types (.com, .gov, and so forth).

In addition, we have compiled information on some commercially oriented services related to the Internet. This information includes:

- The number of ISP subscribers of UUNET, PSINet, Netcom, and BBN Planet; and
- The number of OSP subscribers and the percentage of OSP users on the Internet.

Put simply, hosts are devices permanently connected to the Internet. Registered with the government contractor that maintains such lists, the devices include computers and routers. "Domains" are unique names for Internet connections, which are hierarchical in nature. For instance, the (fictitious) Net address "mary@morgan.com.uk" represents a few things. The last phrase, "uk", represents the geographical top-level domain, in this case, the United Kingdom. The "com" shows the type of organization, in this case commercial. The sub-domain "morgan" represents a network (or computer) name, typically corresponding to a company, organization, or person's name (in this case, "Mary," who is at "Morgan," a commercial organization in the U.K.). Domains correlate roughly with the number of companies and organizations on the Internet.

Table 3.2
Internet Host Growth Rate 1990–95E

Begin Date	End Date	Annual Host Growth Rate
July 1994	July 1995	107%
July 1993	July 1994	81%
July 1992	July 1993	79%
July 1991	July 1992	85%
July 1990	July 1991	90%+/-

Source: Merit Networks

In the context of the Internet, networks represent groups of computers that are connected to one another, usually in one location, and are also connected to the Internet. In Figures 3.3 and 3.4, note that the rate of growth, represented by the semi-log graph's slope, has remained fairly steady, with two inflection points:

• The first inflection point came in the early 1980s, when ARPANet (the precursor to the Internet) began allowing the U.S. university system to link itself to the Net in a widespread manner.

• The second inflection occurred in 1989, when commercialization of the Internet began.

During the July 1990 to July 1995 period, the host compound annual growth rate was 93%. Yearly growth rates varied from 79% to 107%. Domains and networks have experienced similar growth.

As measured on the NSFNet Internet backbone, the type of data sent across the Internet between January 1993 and April 1995 changed significantly. In that two-year period, WWW traffic overtook FTP and gopher — in a sense, legacy applications — as the dominant percentage of data.

Figure 3.3
Internet Host Growth (Normal Scale) 1969–95E

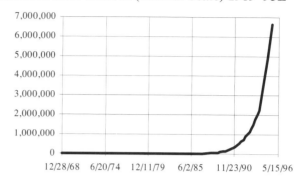

Source: Network Wizards

Figure 3.4
Internet Host Growth (Semi-Log Scale) 1969–95E

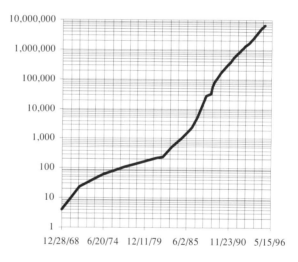

Source: Network Wizards. Note: In the early 1980s there is an increase in the rate of growth attributable to the connecting of universities to the Internet.

Figure 3.5
Internet Traffic Usage on the NSFNet Backbone, January 1993 to April 1995

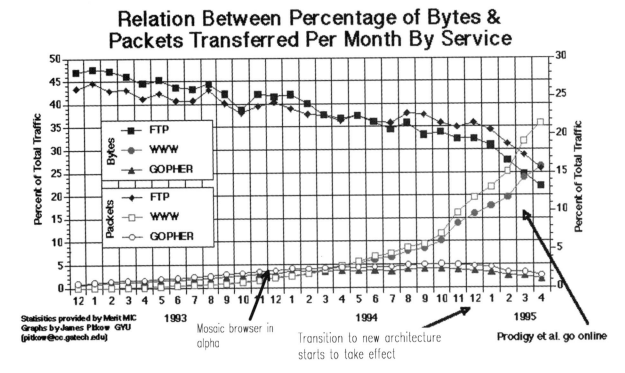

Recently, online service providers have begun to provide Internet access services to their subscribers; in most cases, this is not direct access via an IP connection, which can hinder performance. A small fraction, about one-quarter, of OSP subscribers currently use these services; however, the number of OSP Internet users as a percentage of total

OSP subscribers is growing rapidly, as GUI (graphical user interface) Internet connectivity through OSP accounts has been available only since 1Q95. Data for four large publicly traded ISPs — Netcom, PSINet, UUNET, BBN Planet — have been compiled by growth in subscriber base over time.

Table 3.3
OSP Subscribers, August 1994 to December 1995

		8/94	9/94	10/94	11/94	12/94	1/95	2/95	3/95	4/95	5/95	6/95	7/95	8/95	9/95	10/95	11/95	12/95
Total	Subscribers	4.2	4.5	4.7	5.0	5.4	5.8	6.3	6.9	7.3	7.7	8.3	8.5	8.8	9.6	10.5	11.2	11.5
	Subscribers (x75%)	3.1	3.3	3.5	3.7	4.0	4.3	4.7	5.2	5.5	5.8	6.2	6.4	6.6	7.2	7.9	8.4	8.6
	IISR Subscriber Count		5.5			6.3									9.9			11.3
	Internet Users (x75%)	0.0	0.0	0.0	0.0	0.0	0.2	0.4	0.6	0.7	0.8	1.2	1.4	1.4	1.6	1.8	2.0	2.2
	Rev/Subscr ($/mo) (1)	15.0	15.0	15.0	15.0	15.5	15.5	15.5	15.5	15.5	16.0	16.0	16.0	16.0	16.0	16.0	16.0	16.0
	Industry Revenue ($)	62	67	70	74	83	90	98	107	113	123	133	136	141	154	168	179	184
AOL	Subscribers	1.0	1.2	1.3	1.4	1.6	1.8	2.0	2.3	2.5	2.7	3.0	3.0	3.1	3.9	4.2	4.4	4.6
	Internet Users (%)	--	--	--	--	--	--	--	--	--	2%	5%	8%	12%	15	15	17	19%
Compuserve	Subscribers	2	2.1	2.2	2.3	2.4	2.5	2.7	2.9	3	3.1	3.2	3.3	3.4	3.54	> 3.8	4.3	4.5
	Internet Users (%)	--	--	--	--	--	--	--	--	--	--	2%	5%	10%	15	15	17	20%
Prodigy	Subscribers	1	1	1	1.1	1.2	1.3	1.4	1.5	1.6	1.7	1.9	2	> 2.0	≥ 1.7	> 2.0	1.8	1.6
	Internet Users (%)						10	25%	35%	40%	40%	45%	45%	50%	50%	50%	50%	50%
MSN	Subscribers	--	--	--	--	--	--	--	--	--	--	--	0.05	0.15	0.2	0.3	0.5	0.6
	Internet Users (%)	--	--	--	--	--	--	--	--	--	--	--	5%	25%	25%	25%	30%	35%
Delphi	Subscribers	0.1	0.1	0.1	0.1	0.1	0.1	0.1	0.1	0.1	0.1	0.1	0.1	0.1	0.125	0.125	0.1	0.07
	Internet Users (%)			5%	10%	15	20%	25%	30%	40%	50%	55%	55%	55%	55%	55%	55%	55%
eWorld	Subscribers	0.05	0.055	0.06	0.065	0.07	0.085	0.1	0.09	0.08	0.08	0.09	0.08	0.09	0.115	0.09	0.1	0.126
	Internet Users (%)	--	--	--	--	--	--	--	--	--	--	5%	10%	15	15	15	16%	17
GEnie	Subscribers	0.03	0.04	0.05	0.06	0.07	0.08	0.09	0.1	0.1	0.1	0.1	0.1	0.1	0.1	0.1	0.09	0.07
	Internet Users (%)	--	--	--	--	--	--	--	--	--	--	--	--	--	--	--	--	--

Source of **boldfaced** entries are from each company.
Source of <u>underlined</u> entries are from Information & Interactive Services Report (and include 64 services). Others are estimated by Morgan Stanley.
Internet users (%) - OSP users who use the OSP to access the Internet. Percentages estimated by Morgan Stanley.
(1) Overall industry rate. Estimated by Morgan Stanley. Industry Revenue is estimated as subscribers times Rev/Subscr.
Note that CompuServe, as of October 1995, is about 50% business users.
As of October 1995, CompuServe had 130K Canadian, 460K European and 100K Japanese subscribers. Another 900K to 1,000K were Japanese NiftyServe subscribers.

Table 3.4
ISP Subscribers, September 1994 to December 1995

		9/94	10/94	11/94	12/94	1/95	2/95	3/95	4/95	5/95	6/95	7/95	8/95	9/95	10/95	11/95	12/95
Total	Commercial Subscribers	6,400	7,350	7,750	8,110	8,500	8,750	9,240	9,500	11,600	12,774	14,150	17,000	18,504	19,900	21,800	23,407
	Individual Subscribers	85,200	102,500	123,500	149,920	167,000	194,000	247,840	251,000	325,000	366,500	393,000	435,000	505,600	527,000	615,000	690,000
	POPs	147	155	170	183	197	220	254	290	330	904	951	1020	1042	--	--	1241
	Service Revenue ($mil)*	11.0	--	--	--	--	--	--	--	--	35.3	--	--	49.5	--	--	N/AV
Netcom	Total Subscribers																
	Commercial Subscribers	0	0	0	0	0	0	0	0	0	0	0	2,000	2,000	2,500	2,700	3,000
	Individual Subscribers	41,500	50,000	60,000	72,500	80,000	90,000	114,200	115,000	150,000	168,500	180,000	200,000	232,800	240,000	280,000	307,500
	POPs	32	40	45	51	60	75	89	110	130	171	175	190	200	203	207	210
	Service Revenue ($mil)	3.3	--	--	5.2	--	--	7.5	--	--	10.5	--	--	14.7	--	--	19.7
PSI	Total Subscribers																
	Commercial Subscribers	3,500	3,750	3,850	3,910	4,100	4,250	4,440	4,500	4,600	4,700	4,850	5,100	6,200	6,800	7,500	8,200
	Individual Subscribers	2,200	2,500	3,500	4,920	7,000	14,000	19,440	21,000	25,000	29,500	33,000	35,000	40,000	47,000	55,000	75,000
	POPs	75	75	75	82	87	95	105	110	120	135	150	153	159	170	180	241
	Service Revenue ($mil)	4.5	--	--	4.3	--	--	5.9	--	--	7.7	--	--	11.0	--	--	--
UUNet	Total Subscribers																
	High speed dedicated connections										439						
	Commercial Subscribers	2,900	3,000	3,300	3,600	3,800	3,900	4,000	4,000	6,000	7,074	8,000	8,500	8,704	9,000	10,000	10,607
	Individual Subscribers	0	0	0	0	0	0	0	0	0	0	0	0	0	0	0	0
	POPs	40	40	50	50	50	50	60	70	80	98	106	112	118	130	140	290
	% Rev from MSN										21%			33%			33%
	Service Revenue ($mil)	3.182	--	--	4.117	--	--	6.48	--	--	10.47	--	--	16.4	--	--	33.14
BBN Planet	Total Subscribers																
	Commercial Subscribers		> 600	< 600	600	600	> 600	800	> 1000	> 1000	> 1000	> 1300	1400	1600	1600	1600	1600
	POPs										> 500	> 520	565	565			> 500
	Service Revenue ($mil)		--	--	--	--	--	--	--	--	6.6	--	--	7.4	--	--	9.1

Four of the largest, publicly-traded ISP companies are included on this table.
*Source of **boldfaced** entries are from each company. Others are estimated by Morgan Stanley.*
* Netcom, PSI and UUNet only.
Netcom estimates its CQ495 quarter consisted 20% permanently connected customers (commercial).
1) BBN owns 65 POPS and leases approximately 500 POPS.

Table 3.5

Regional Host Growth on the Internet 1Q–4Q95

	Jan-94	Jul-94	Oct-94	Jan-95	Last qtr Growth
North America	1,685,715	2,177,396	2,685,929	3,372,551	26%
Europe, West	550,933	730,429	850,993	1,039,192	22%
Pacific	113,482	142,353	154,473	192,390	25%
Asia	81,355	111,278	127,569	151,773	19%
Europe, East	19,867	27,800	32,951	46,125	40%
Africa	10,951	15,595	21,041	27,130	29%
CC&S America	7,392	11,455	14,894	*	*
Middle East	6,946	8,871	10,383	13,776	33%
Total	**2,476,641**	**3,225,177**	**3,898,233**	**4,851,873**	**24%**

* Accurate Latin American host counts were not obtained.

Source: Network Wizards

Looking at countries with registered networks on the Internet, Table 3.5 shows that, in 1Q94–1Q95, Eastern Europe grew most rapidly, from a relatively small base, while Asia grew most slowly; other regions grew close to the average quarterly rate of 24%. There were 93 countries with active hosts on the Internet as of May 1995, and over 200 by the end of summer 1995. Between 10 and 30 new countries

Table 3.6

Top 20 Internet Geographic Domains May 1995

Rank	Domain Code	Country	Total No. Networks	Pct. of Total
1.	US	United States	28,470	56.08%
2.	CA	Canada	4,795	9.45
3.	FR	France	2,003	3.95
4.	AU	Australia	1,875	3.69
5.	JP	Japan	1,847	3.64
6.	DE	Germany	1,750	3.45
7.	GB	United Kingdom	1,436	2.83
8.	FI	Finland	643	1.27
9.	TW	Taiwan	575	1.13
10.	IT	Italy	506	1.00
11.	KR	Korea, South	476	0.94
12.	CZ	Czech Republic	459	0.90
13.	ZA	South Africa	419	0.83
14.	SE	Sweden	415	0.82
15.	AT	Austria	408	0.80
16.	NL	Netherlands	406	0.80
17.	RU	Russian Fed.	405	0.80
18.	NZ	New Zealand	356	0.70
19.	CH	Switzerland	324	0.64
20.	ES	Spain	257	0.51
		Others		5.77

Source: Merit Networks. Note: As of August 1995, there were 208 countries on the list. Rate of growth is approximately 10–30 per month.

have been added each month, although each of the new countries represents an insignificant number of networks as a proportion to the total.

Figure 3.6
Worldwide Distribution of Computers 1994

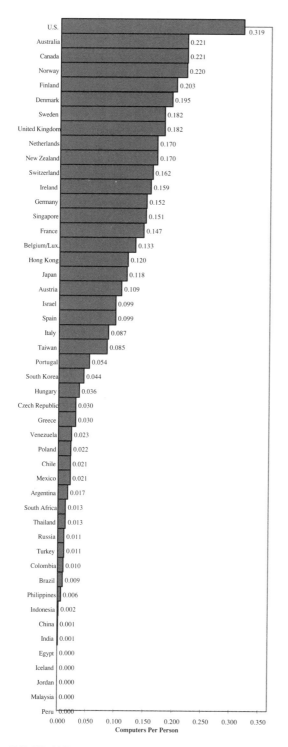

Computers Per Person

Sources: IMD, World Economic Forum

Figure 3.7
Share of Total Worldwide MIPS 1994

Sources: IMD, World Economic Forum

Bulletin Board Services (BBSs)

There are groups of online users who are not connected to the Internet. Of the roughly 50,000 to 70,000 bulletin board services (BBSs) in the world, which are mainly located in the U.S., most are not connected to the Internet, although many are connected to one another. We estimate that only 1–2% are connected in varying degrees to the Net, with most of those having e-mail/Usenet connectivity but only 1% having partial Internet access. Currently, BBSs are not Web-capable. The larger BBSs tend to be the ones connected to the Net; an estimate of the average subscriber base of the larger BBSs who use the Internet functions is about 500 per BBS. Therefore, of the roughly 0.5 million e-mail/Usenet-capable BBS users, only about half, or 0.25 million, have partial Internet access.

Trends in User Types

Table 3.7 is based on information gathered from a Web site that features searches of compact disks by title. Although these statistics clearly may not represent the Internet as a whole, they compare favorably to data at other sites and to published statistics based on surveys. The table identifies three general categories: 1) the percentage of users accessing the home page from a commercial site, 2) the type of Web browser used, and 3) the type of user operating system.

The number of commercial (.com) domains visiting this site is generally rising, and the Netscape Navigator browser is noticeably dominant. At the same time, a considerable market-share loss was recorded for the freeware NCSA Mosaic and Lynx browsers, while in August the Microsoft Internet Explorer browser surged from almost nothing to a 25% share. In addition, the Windows/DOS environment has become increasingly popular and is now the dominant operating system on the Web, going from the high-30% to high-50% range. In the same period, the UNIX share dropped from 30% to 20% and the Mac share fell from 16% to 11%. We identify these trends simply to point out that the character of the Internet user is changing drastically, from a UNIX/Mac, freeware-oriented, non-commercial user to a Windows/PC, payware-oriented commercial user.

Table 3.7

Browser and Operating System Statistics from a Typical 'For-Pleasure' Web Page

	Mar-95	Apr-95	May-95	Jun-95	Jul-95	Aug-95	Sep-95	Oct-95
Retrieval information								
.com retrievals	--	--	24%	30%	33%	31%	29%	28%
Average Traffic to Site (hits/day)	800	300	400	600	1,000	1,000	1,300	1,400
Browsers								
Netscape	47%	50%	62%	65%	64%	61%	58%	56%
MS Internet Explorer	--	--	--	0.0	0.3	11	19	25
Lynx	15	16	12	11	8	6	4	3
NCSA Mosaic	21	17	12	10	7	6	4	3
Air Mosaic	1	1	1	3	3	3	2	2
User Operating Systems								
Windows/DOS	37%	40%	46%	47%	48%	57%	62%	65%
UNIX/X11	30	40	33	30	24	21	14	15
Macintosh	16	13	14	15	14	12	13	13

Note: Statistics reflect information from browsers hitting the Craig Knudsen CD Search page only. His page has a search engine to identify album titles by song, and other related searches. The data are reflective only of users who visit this page, not others on the Internet, and are used as an example only. Mr. Knudsen's site was taken out of commission at the end of October but is now up and running at another location, and we have collected six days of data: Netscape is still dominant, and it appears that the MS Internet Explorer share is lower (single digits) than it was in October.

Surveys — Past and Present

Demographics: Gender and Age The most common Internet user is a young, educated male. However, the profile of the typical Internet user is slowly becoming more reflective of the entire population. According to Georgia Tech's GVU Fourth WWW Survey, conducted over the October 10 through November 10 period of 1995, 29% of all users were female and 71% were male. This difference is more striking in Europe, where 90% are male and 10% female.

The GVU survey also indicates that 12% of users were 16–20 years of age; 18% were 21–25; 16% were 26–30; 13% were 31–35; 11% were 36–40; and 10% were 41–45. The rest of the age ranges amounted to less than 10% each.

Commercial Organizations There are a few large organizations and companies with thousands of hosts on the Internet, but most Internet-connected organizations have far fewer. According to the MIDS results, the average number of hosts per organization is 279, with a median of about 40. A TIC/MIDS survey for October 1994 showed: <10 hosts, 25%; <100 hosts, 37.6%; <1,000 hosts, 30.9%; <10,000 hosts; 6.5%; and <100,000, 0.1%.

There are many more privately held organizations on the Internet than publicly owned ones. This is consistent both with the greater number of small private companies in general and with the large number that have connected to the Internet lately.

Location In the GVU study, 76% of the respondents were from the U.S.; 10% from Canada and Mexico; and 8% from Europe. Compared to a prior GVU study — 81% from the U.S.; 10% from Europe; 6% from Canada and Mexico — this represents a shift away from U.S. dominance of the Web. To put it all into perspective, though, 11% of Web users are located in California.

Educational Organizations According to TIC/MIDS, as a percentage of total users on the Internet, 22% were educationally related in October 1994. As a percentage of total educational users, higher education is dominant.

According to a Mika Rissa & Co. survey conducted in January 1995, 23% of users were university and other ".edu" classifications; 8% were students (unspecified); 19% were in computer-related organizations; 11% were in industrial companies; 9% were in professional service organizations; and 8% were in government and local administration. The rest of the responses were less than 5% each.

OSP Entry versus ISP Entry In the past several months, there seems to have been a drastic shift away from using OSPs to access the Internet and toward using ISPs. According to the GVU study, the three main kinds of primary Internet providers are local online providers (ISPs), at 42%; educational providers, 32%; and the workplace, 10%. Compared to the previous GVU study, local online providers gained an additional 14% share, while the OSPs went to 8% from 28%.

Early Adopters/Corporate Adopters The GVU Fourth WWW Survey lends support to our theory that early adopters use the Internet first, followed by corporate users. In addition, we theorize elsewhere in this report that international users follow U.S. users. In the GVU study, European users were heavier users of Unix (14% in Europe versus 7% in the U.S., and 7% of overall responses). Slightly over one in five (21%) were using Windows 95, which lends support to the "early adopters" profile of the Web users sampled.

Means of Connection Popular methods of linking to the Internet are T-1 (corporate and academic users) and dial-up/modem connections (mainly consumers and small offices). In the GVU study, 2% of all users accessed the Internet at speeds below 14.4 kbps; 34% at 14.4%; 27% at 28.8 kbps; 4% at 56 kbps; 2% at 128 kbps; 5% at 1 mbps; 2% at 4 mbps; 9% at 10 mbps; and 1% at over 45 mbps. (Some 14% were not sure.)

The most popular Internet connection speeds in 1994 were T-1 leased, 56–64 kbps leased, and 14.4 kbps dial-up. Since then, two things have changed: the 28.8 kbps modem has flourished, and dial-up access has become more convenient, with the spreading availability of Internet service from OSPs and the rapid buildup in POPs from ISPs.

According to the Mika Rissa survey, from December 1994 to January 1995, 69% of Internet connections were direct connections, while 32% were dial-ups. Now, after a little less than a year has gone by, about 62% of users access through dial-up connections.

Opinions and Observations

There is a wide disparity among other estimates of Internet usage, most likely caused by the various time frames involved. Small inconsistencies in reporting the dates of the data can cause wide differences in estimates, because the Internet grows so quickly. It is hard to keep track. There are, of course, upper limits on growth in the number of Internet users, due to the following factors, in our view:

• The number of households;
• A commercial entity's inability to expand its Internet service networks much more quickly than 100–200% per year (as evidenced by MSN's and AOL's growing pains);

- The lack of reasonably priced wireless Internet technology;
- The difficulty in using online and Internet services;
- The cost of hardware, software, and connectivity;
- Alternative media, such as interactive- and cable-TV;
- The relative lack of "things to do on the Internet" (you can't exercise or eat there); and
- The lack of an ability to physically move anything but electrons from one location to another.

On the other hand, PCs are becoming communications devices — perhaps a necessary communications device that may supersede television, radio, and, who knows, maybe even the newspaper. There is still tremendous demand from potential users who want to get online.

Going forward, we expect certain dynamics to prevail as the Internet continues to grow:

Demographics should become more reasonably representative of a cross section of the world population.

Non-domestic use will grow rapidly.

Ease-of-use will increase — graphical interfaces will rule, connectivity will become trivial.

Vast arrays of services will migrate to the Internet and online, such as retailing, consulting, news, entertainment, and just about anything else that can be viewed in two or three dimensions.

PCs, and variants thereof, will become far-and-away the dominant platform, as well as the driver for Internet/online growth.

The **cost of connectivity**, as it decreases, should boost mass appeal and stimulate demand.

Use will become more interactive, as more e-mail-only users decide to go for full Internet access.

Communications over the Net will become commonplace, and necessary, for business as well as pleasure.

Bandwidth requirements will increase at an expanding rate, due to greater use of graphics, sound, and, ultimately, video.

Commercialization of the Internet will be extremely rapid.

Separate networks, perhaps akin to today's BBSs, may again proliferate a few years from now, as users' concerns about security and government control increase.

There are 95 million households in the U.S., according to the U.S. Census Bureau. As Table 3.8 shows, installed bases of most widespread communications devices is nearly 100%. For instance, color television is found in 97% of U.S. homes, and the telephone is in 96%. The VCR has an 85% U.S. household penetration rate, while the PC has a 30% rate.

These figures demonstrate simply that once a communications technology becomes widespread, nearly everyone uses it. There are limitations to the use of communications devices, usually due to money or lack of connectivity. Urban regions have been getting local-call, dial-in access to online services and Internet service providers' networks first, so it is important to identify the most likely candidates to receive convenient wired access. Currently, there is no reasonable wireless technology to enable nonurban users remote from POPs. If such connectivity were made widely available, consumers and business users might rapidly adopt it.

Table 3.8
Consumer Electronics Sales and Units to U.S. Household Market 1985–94

	Color Televisions (1, 4)			Corded Telephones (1, 4)			VCRs (2, 4)			Cordless Telephones (1, 4)			CD Audio (2)			Home PCs (1, 3)		
	Units ('000s)	Cum. Units (5) ('000s)	Sales ($ MM)	Units ('000s)	Cum. Units (5) ('000s)	Sales ($ MM)	Units ('000s)	Cum. Units (5) ('000s)	Sales ($ MM)	Units ('000s)	Cum. Units (5) ('000s)	Sales ($ MM)	Units ('000s)	Cum. Units (5) ('000s)	Sales ($ MM)	Units ('000s)	Cum. Units (5) ('000s)	Sales ($ MM)
Date of Introduction	1939 - 1st B&W for sale in US 1953 - color TV stds. approved			1930's in quantity			1975 - VCRs introduced 1984 - VHS 8mm introduced			early 1980's - introduction			1983 - CD audio introduced			1981 - IBM PC introduced		
1983	na	na	na	na	na	na	na	na	na	na	na	na	na	na	na	na	na	na
1984	na	na	na	na	na	na	na	na	na	na	na	na	na	na	na	na	na	na
1985	16,995	16,995	$5,522	21,000	21,000	$630	11,336	11,336	$4,173	4,000	4,000	$280	na	na	na	na	na	$2,175
1986	18,204	35,199	5,836	18,100	39,100	561	12,005	23,341	3,978	4,100	8,100	295	na	na	na	na	na	3,060
1987	19,330	54,529	6,147	15,900	55,000	461	11,702	35,043	3,442	6,400	14,500	435	na	na	na	na	na	3,100
1988	20,216	74,745	5,908	15,200	70,200	441	10,748	45,791	2,848	8,200	22,700	681	na	na	na	na	na	3,340
1989	21,706	96,451	6,421	19,000	89,200	532	9,760	55,551	2,625	10,000	32,700	830	na	na	na	na	na	3,711
1990	20,384	116,835	6,197	22,003	111,203	638	10,119	65,670	2,439	10,148	42,848	842	9,155	9,155	$2,016	4,000	4,000	4,187
1991	19,474	136,309	5,979	20,872	132,075	605	10,718	76,388	2,454	13,232	56,080	1,125	11,595	20,750	2,391	3,900	7,900	4,287
1992	21,056	157,365	6,591	23,964	156,039	575	12,329	88,717	2,947	14,944	71,024	1,091	16,134	36,884	3,005	4,875	12,775	5,573
1993	23,005	180,370	7,316	27,080	183,119	617	12,448	101,165	2,851	16,183	87,207	1,046	20,425	57,309	3,552	5,850	18,625	6,921
1994	24,715	**205,085**	7,225	23,664	**206,783**	610	13,087	**114,252**	2,869	16,772	**103,979**	1,106	26,544	**83,853**	4,368	6,725	**25,350**	8,070
Households with units (6)	97%	91,882		96%	90,935		85%	80,515		52%	49,256		44%	41,679		33%	31,259	

(1) Source: "The U.S. Consumer Electronics Industry," Electronic Industry Association, 1995
(2) Source: "1994 Electronic Market Data Book," Electronic Industry Association - Data not available before 1990
(3) Does not include Corporate PC Sales
(4) 1984 to 1989 data from source (2) , 1991 to 1994 from source (1)
(5) Cumulative Units which are displayed include only data under column, "Units ('000s)"
(6) % household penetration from source (1). U.S. households of 94,724,000 based on American Housing Survey, 1993 source. Note: MS estimate is 30%.
(7) Source: International Data Corp (IDC). Worldwide Inst. base est. 172,194,000 at 1994.
(8) Home PC shipments presumably exceed cumulative shipments because data are unavailable prior to 1990.

Figure 3.8
Household Penetration of Consumer Electronics Products

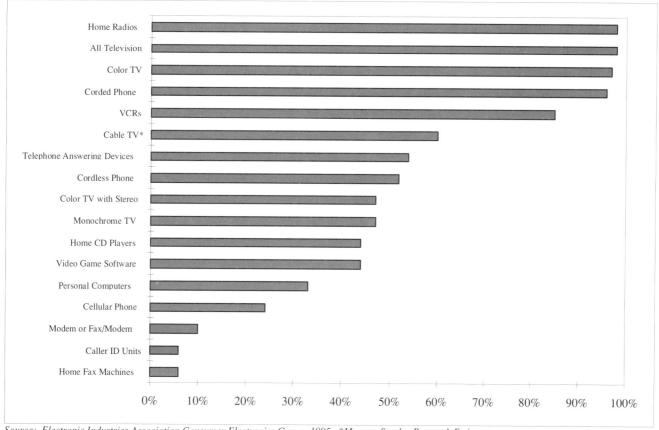

*Source: Electronic Industries Association Consumer Electronics Group, 1995. *Morgan Stanley Research Estimate.*

3 – 16

Table 3.9

Number of PCs, Modems, and Internet Users 1984–2000

	1984	1985	1986	1987	1988	1989	1990	1991	1992	1993	1994	1995	1996	1997	1998	1999	2000
Worldwide																	
PC Unit Shipments (MM)	9	9	10	12	14	16	19	25	34	43	51	60	69	77	85	94	102
Y/Y Growth	--	2%	12%	17%	17%	14%	19%	32%	36%	25%	20%	18%	14%	12%	11%	10%	9%
PC Lifetime Shipments (MM)	23	32	42	54	68	84	103	128	162	205	256	316	384	461	546	640	742
PCs in Use (MM) (a)	23	28	35	40	45	52	61	74	94	121	153	188	222	256	290	324	358
Pct. with Two PCs (b)	2%	2%	3%	5%	6%	7%	8%	10%	15%	20%	22%	23%	25%	28%	30%	33%	37%
Actual # of PC Users (MM)	23	27	34	38	43	49	56	67	80	96	119	144	167	184	203	217	225
Y/Y Growth	--	22%	24%	13%	11%	14%	16%	19%	20%	21%	23%	21%	15%	11%	10%	7%	4%
U.S.																	
PC Unit Shipments (MM)	6	6	6	7	7	7	8	10	13	16	20	23	25	28	31	33	36
Y/Y Growth	--	-6%	3%	8%	6%	0%	12%	23%	37%	24%	21%	15%	11%	11%	10%	8%	9%
U.S. Pct. of PC Unit Shipments	70%	65%	60%	55%	50%	44%	41%	38%	39%	38%	39%	38%	37%	37%	36%	35%	35%
PC Lifetime Shipments (MM)	16	21	25	30	34	37	42	49	63	79	99	120	141	169	197	227	263
PCs in Use (MM) (a)	16	18	21	22	23	23	25	28	36	46	59	71	82	94	105	115	127
Pct. with Two PCs (b)	5%	6%	7%	8%	10%	15%	20%	22%	23%	25%	28%	30%	33%	37%	42%	48%	50%
Actual # of PC Users (MM)	15	17	20	20	20	19	20	22	28	35	43	50	55	59	61	60	63
Y/Y Growth	--	12%	14%	5%	0%	-5%	3%	11%	27%	24%	22%	17%	10%	8%	3%	-2%	6%
Worldwide Connectivity Estimates																	
# of PC Users (MM)	23	27	34	38	43	49	56	67	80	96	119	144	167	184	203	217	225
# E-Mail Users (MM) (c)	1	1	2	3	4	5	6	8	12	18	25	35	60	80	130	180	200
Pct. PCs with E-Mail Access	4%	4%	6%	8%	9%	10%	11%	12%	15%	19%	21%	24%	36%	43%	64%	83%	89%
# Internet/Web Users (MM)	<1	<1	<1	<1	<1	<1	<1	<1	1	1	3	9	23	46	81	122	152
Pct. PCs with Internet Access	1%	1%	1%	1%	1%	1%	1%	1%	1%	1%	3%	7%	14%	25%	40%	56%	68%
# Online/Hybrid Users (MM)	<1	<1	<1	<1	<1	<1	<1	1	2	3	5	8	13	18	23	27	30
Pct. PCs with Online/Hybrid Access	1%	1%	1%	1%	1%	1%	1%	2%	3%	3%	4%	6%	8%	10%	11%	12%	13%
Windows Installed Base (MM) (d)	<1	<1	<1	<1	<1	<1	3	8	23	44	77	115	--	--	--	--	--
	1000																
# Web Servers (MM)(e)	--	--	--	--	--	--	--	<1	0.00	0.00	0.02	0.10	0.60	1.20	2.20	3.30	4.00
U.S.																	
# of PC Users (MM)	15	17	20	20	20	19	20	22	28	35	43	50	55	59	61	60	63
# Internet/Web Users (MM)	<1	<1	<1	<1	<1	<1	<1	<1	1	1	2	6	14	25	41	58	67
Pct. PCs with Internet Access	--	--	--	--	--	--	--	--	2%	2%	5%	12%	25%	43%	67%	98%	106%
									76%	74%	70%	64%	59%	55%	50%	48%	44%
U.S.																	
Homes with PCs and Modems																	
Installed Base (MM)	--	--	--	--	--	--	--	--	4	6	10	20	25	30	32	35	
Y/Y Growth										50%	67%	100%	25%	20%	7%	9%	

(a) Assumes that PCs have average useful life of 4 years. *(b) Estimated Number of PC users that use second PCs: home, office, and portables.*
(c) Estimates of all e-mail accounts. We estimate that 50% of 1995 e-mail users could be connected to the Internet.
(d) Estimated legal (non-pirated/copied) shipments of Microsoft Windows. Arrows added to compare Windows ramp with Internet ramp.
(e) Source: Lycos, Web Crawler, and Morgan Stanley Research estimates. Note: There are more Web sites than servers.
Source: Morgan Stanley Research estimates.

This kind of rapid adoption occurred recently, for example, with pagers. The number of pagers for personal and business use has grown from 9.9 million in 1990 to an estimated 34 million in 1995, according to the Personal Communications Industry Association/MAT-EMCI.

Mass appeal and high penetration rates are correlated with a low cost of participation for a particular device. We believe devices other than the PC may stir additional demand for Internet connectivity if they are competitively priced. Based on a pretax average U.S. household income of $32,000, the following are the relative costs of ownership for dominant communications devices: color television

0.78% ($250), VCR 1.09% ($350), telephone 0.08% ($25), and PC 7.8% ($2,100). The PC is a relatively expensive device, but such alternatives as low-priced Internet boxes could, over time, come to market.

Education also represents an area of growth, in our view. According to Higher Education Publications, of Falls Church, Va., there are 3,616 accredited institutions of higher education.

Two observations can be made regarding Internet use and enrollment in school: students represent a new generation of Internet users, and the educational market still represents a significant and likely target for growth in Internet use.

Projections

The most important and dynamic aspect to the acceptability of online service and Internet usage is that the software interfaces to cyberspace are becoming easier to use. We believe the primary reason for the continued growth in the number of Internet users was the introduction of the Mosaic browser. Underlying the strong overall increase in the number of Internet users, we believe, is a dramatic shift in the use of applications on the Internet, from text-based e-mail and partial FTP/telnet/gopher use to full WWW access (which includes the former applications).

The second most critical driver for growth in the Internet user base should come from the non-U.S. market. Access to the rest of the world's information will be the reason that other nations' users will come to the Internet, in our view. We believe that by the end of the decade, fully 50% of Internet users will be non-domestic.

The typical Internet user is in his or her mid-30s. The average age is growing steadily. Internet users who graduated from college in the 1980s are still online, and the Internet is being used not only for academic purposes but also for business reasons, so people in business are using it more.

Further, the user base is becoming more reflective of the population in general, as its offerings become more diverse.

By and large, academia and corporate concerns should still dominate the user base. However, we believe that, with the proliferation of consumer-oriented offerings and the necessity of online communication, consumers will represent a faster-growing group of users by the end of the decade. In the short term, corporations are expected to expand their presence more quickly, followed by consumers.

Perspective Check

As a check on our perspective, we note that the 1994 total U.S. and worldwide populations were about 250 million and 5.5 billion, respectively. There are 21 million employees of Fortune 500 companies. Currently, the total number of full-Web-access users is about 9 million, while all e-mail users are about 35 million. According to the GVU study (conducted 10/10–11/10/95), about 75% of users are from the U.S. This means that about 3% of the U.S. population are Web users and 10% are e-mail users. In the year 2010, we project, the number of U.S. Internet users will represent somewhat below 50% of the total U.S. population.

Worldwide full-Web access users and worldwide e-mail users thus represent about 0.2% and 0.6%, respectively, of the total worldwide population. In the year 2010, we project, the number of worldwide Internet users should reach about 7% of the global population.

As another check on our perspective, we can estimate the number of users connected to the Internet through major ISPs. According to the TIC/MIDS' October 1994 survey, the average number of hosts per organization was 279. Using 279 hosts per commercial subscriber, and assuming a 1:1 relationship between "user" and "host" (because most corporate users have dedicated workstations for each user), the number of users per commercial subscribers in September 1995 can be estimated at 5.16 million. Estimated December 1995 commercial users would be about 45% more, assuming the same quarterly growth rate, or 7.47 million.

That number would include many, but probably not all, of the other 3,000 or more ISPs in the world, as most ISPs connect to the larger ISPs (MCI, Sprint, Net99, and ANS are also players, but this is an estimate). Therefore, the estimated number of Internet users at December 1995 (38% more than September), adding in individual users of 700,000, presumably with full-Web access, was 8.2 million. We believe these user counts are fairly consistent with our reported 9 million full-Web access worldwide Internet users estimate, when the estimated 2.6 million Internet users accessing the Web through OSPs (36% more than 1.9 million in October) are added in. This would yield 10.8 million; however, we believe there is some overlap between the OSP and ISP Internet users.

Section II
Features and Uses of the Internet

Chapter 4: How to Use the Internet

- There are multiple ways to access the Internet today: commercial Internet Service Providers (ISPs), Online Service Providers (OSPs), and selected telecommunications carriers. Connections can be made by using dial-up (analog or digital ISDN) or leased-line connections.

- The Internet is already the vehicle for a broad array of services: communication, education, broadcast-like media, daily news, reference and book-like materials, advertising, want-ads, magazine and direct marketing retailing. In the future, it may be used for broadcast-like media, taxes, banking, and more.

- To exploit the Internet's current capabilities, users today turn most often to the World Wide Web, e-mail, File Transfer Protocol, Usenet, and many legacy Internet features (such as Gopher, IRC). There are many new applications already in beta test (video, audio, telephony, 3D), and in the future we expect more robust systems exploiting video, audio and telephony, Internet faxing, conferencing and collaborative work. There will also be highly-integrated, automated features incorporating commercial back-end applications with the Web and other features, perhaps supported by Java or other languages.

Many newcomers think the World Wide Web is all there is to the Internet. In fact, the web is just one of its features, enabling browsers to view graphics and text stored on web servers. It coexists with other protocols such as FTP (file transfer protocol), all of which run simultaneously over the same Internet infrastructure. This chapter describes how to connect to the Internet, its existing and contemplated resources, and the applications and protocols needed to allow the use of those resources. Although it is not intended to be a technical guide to surfing the Web, the overview is fairly detailed, so experienced webmasters can skip to the next chapter and skim this one as needed.

Making an Internet Connection

In general, connecting to the Internet occurs through either a dial-up or a permanent, leased line connection. Most consumers connect through dial-up or modem connectors, while corporate users usually connect with permanent connections (remote corporate uses, of course, require a dial-up connection). It's important to remember the customary distinction today between two basic classes of users, software and equipment: the client and the server. In general, clients use network resources, while servers are repositories of content and information. Nearly all consumers are clients; corporate users tend to be clients and servers. About 80% of servers have permanent connections to the Internet, so information on the server is almost always available to clients.

Dial-Up Connections

Gaining access to the Internet has become easier over the past year and a half. A full, interactive, graphical-based, TCP/IP Internet connection is possible with an inexpensive PC (even a 386) running Windows, a modem (28.8 kbps or 14.4 kbps is preferable), inexpensive or free software (many service providers give it away), and a contract agreement with an Internet service provider that costs about $20 per month. Two years ago, that degree of connectivity was for the elite power-user, predominantly a UNIX user with a workstation. Now, common PCs can inexpensively access the Internet. Other non-PC devices are being tested or are already in limited distribution that hold promise as client connectivity devices. These could potentially include a $150 device by Philips that lets television users connect, the $500 Internet terminal being touted by Oracle, Microsoft's ITV set-top box, Sun Microsystem's Internet box, LSI Logic's Internet-on-a-chip system, Digital Equipment's StrongARM chip, and others. We believe these devices may coexist with the PC; though offering less functionality, they could expand and perhaps accelerate the trend towards worldwide connectivity. Time will tell...

There are currently four dial-up connectivity options that consumers, mobile users, and small corporations might consider for Internet access with PCs or workstations: 1) a SLIP (Serial Line Internet Protocol) or PPP (Point to Point Protocol) account with an Internet service provider; 2) an online service provider; 3) a bulletin board service with an Internet gateway; or 4) a shell account with a dedicated Internet service provider (UNIX). Below, we discuss these four options:

SLIP or PPP Account with an ISP

There are more than 3,000 Internet service providers with local, regional, nationwide, or worldwide networks connected to the Internet. A user dials into the ISP's network using a modem or ISDN adapter, connects using a TCP/IP-enabled SLIP or PPP software, and conducts a real-time, interactive, graphical interface Internet session. This is the most common means of consumer access to the Internet; companies such as PSINet, Netcom, and Concentric offer this service.

There are two major advantages to using a SLIP or PPP account with an ISP, compared with a BBS gateway or shell account. First, a large ISP usually has a nationwide network that allows local-number dial-in access to the Internet (this is also the case with online service providers with Internet access). Second, an ISP's graphical interface and TCP/IP enabled connections allow the use of the World Wide Web (another service that OSPs allow). ISPs also generally charge less than an online service provider. The drawback is that ISPs generally offer less content than what's available from OSPs, because online service providers charge a premium to let subscribers access their proprietary networks as well as access to the Internet. ISPs only allow the latter.

Online Service Providers

For about a decade, online service providers have offered easy connections to their proprietary networks. Each provider's network is different, and many have had only limited offerings. E-mail access through the OSPs has been available for about a decade, but not until autumn 1994, did a major online service provider (Delphi) offer Internet Web access, though its service was text-based. Delphi was followed by Prodigy, which debuted Internet access with a graphical service in C1Q95, and then the other OSPs.

Today, nearly all major OSPs — America Online, Compu-Serve, Microsoft MSN, and Prodigy — allow full, interac-

tive access through their networks to the Internet. Most OSP networks have dial-up access servers throughout the country. These interconnected servers comprise a national (or even global) proprietary and private network operated by the online service provider.

Bulletin Board Services with Internet Gateways

Bulletin board services (BBSs) are dial-up computer services typically operated by individuals who have a zeal for computers. BBSs are much like online services, except they generally are not as well funded and the user interface is often a command-line, text-based system. Few, if any, BBSs have their own, proprietary networks, which would allow a user to connect to the BBS from various geographical locations. About 98% of BBS users connect via modem; however, some BBSs have Internet gateways, which allow users to telnet to the BBS (such as through Concentric's server), log on, and interact as if they had dialed in directly. In addition, an Internet gateway usually allows dial-in users access to the Internet. BBSs usually do not allow real-time graphical Internet access, due to the requirements of the software needed to access the Net.

Perhaps 10% of the thousands of U.S. BBSs are connected to the Internet, via e-mail and newsgroups, and subnetworks of the Internet, such as Fidonet; about 1–2% of BBSs have real-time, text-oriented Internet access, including FTP, Gopher, and telnet features. There are currently few BBSs on the Web, and we believe it may be another year or so before robust software that enables them to connect becomes widespread. Currently, at least one of the well-known BBS operating systems is being upgraded to allow such access to whom we spoke with on the promise of anonymity. In addition, San Francisco-based The WELL is developing its own HTTP software with help from Netscape. Concentric has also recently developed a Web-based software that allows connection to BBSs through its service.

Shell Accounts with Dedicated ISPs (UNIX)

One option that is losing popularity is an Internet-connected UNIX client using a text-based interface (i.e., the kind of terminal emulation software one would use to connect to a BBS.). Once connected, common UNIX commands, such as FTP or telnet, are used to access resources on the Internet. Although this allows real-time, interactive connection to the Internet, it does not easily allow graphical

Web access unless a shareware program, called SlipKnot, is used.

Leased-Line Connections

In contrast to dial-up service to the Internet, leased-line connections are aimed at large corporate, institutional, or government organizations, and typically connect two or more users to the Internet. Permanent connections to the Internet are used because:

• Higher-speed connections are available (9.6 kbps or 56 kbps to 45 mbps) than with dial-up connections;

• There is zero connect time, compared with 4-second ISDN connects or 30-second analog modem connects;

• More reliable connections are made with unswitched, leased lines than switched analog (modems) or switched digital (ISDN) connections;

• Dial-up connections are more expensive to keep open all the time (such is the case with ISDN connections kept "off the hook" at all times);

• Applications relying upon the connection require a permanent connection, for example, if the site operates a WWW server.

To set up a permanent Internet connection, one would need a leased-line connection from a telecom provider, as well as an IP router, which is a dedicated networking device. These two components would most likely connect the organization to the Internet through an ISP or ISP hosting. A domain name, such as "bigcompany.com", and a corresponding IP address, such as "123.456.789.123", would be obtained through an Internet registration process coordinated either by the company connecting to the Internet or by the ISP. The most common permanent connection speeds are 56 kbps and 1.54 mbps. A dedicated connection to the Internet usually links to a campus-wide or corporate-wide network, with several hosts and workstations.

Historically, academic, government, and scientific institutions, most of whose connections are funded by the government, bypass some of the commercial requirements for connecting to the Internet. With the dismantling of the NSFNet, however, these institutions are being forced to connect through commercial providers. Costs for 56 kpbs, excluding the leased lines, are about $300-$400 per month and for T-1 access, $1,000 to $2,500. Costs for the leased line are above and beyond the costs to the ISP, and vary significantly from telco to telco with distance and RBOC tariffs.

Resources of the Internet and their Uses

When the Internet first emerged, about all you could do was remote computing (telnet). New applications slowly emerged, like e-mail in early 1970s, FTP in late 1980s, and so on. In the future, we believe the Internet may converge with — or even supplant — television, radio, telephone, and other communications media we use today. At the very least, it will complement these older media. As more robust applications appear on the Internet, many other social and business functions may follow suit.

The table on the following page describes many of today's personal, corporate and governmental activities that we believe will be conducted over the Internet in the next 5 to 10 years, first in industrialized countries, then in emerging regions. The table also generally identifies software necessary to enable these functions.

Table 4.1
Internet Resources and Enabling Applications

Function/Use	Internet Replacement Application	Software/Internet Protocols
Communication (including for educational purposes)	E-mail Telephony Video conference Text chat	Many VocalTec, Camelot, Quarterdeck, Pulver CuSeeMe, Connectix Videophone IRC
Fax	Faxing from the Internet to a Fax E-mail	Various services E-mail
Broadcast Media	E-mail Web sites Video on demand Audio on demand Sound and video playback	Many Web server software Xing Tech, MBONE, VDONet Progressive Networks, DSP Group Store first, then play
Daily News	Personalized newspapers (intelligently filtered news)	E-mail via services Browser via newspage
Books, reference materials	For-charge publishing (web pages) Free-of-charge publishing (web page)	Web server, authoring tools Web server, and authoring tools
Advertising, want-ads	Zero-cost publishing (personal web pages)	Web server (or rented space on a web server) and authoring tools
Magazine and direct marketing retailing	Web-based retailing	Web server software
Banking	Web-based electronic banking	Internet banking software on web server and on client station
Taxes	Electronic tax filing	Tax software
Retailing	Web-based retailing	Web server software

Communication

E-mail is the most common means of communication on the Internet. Using e-mail, a permanent and easily duplicated text record is transmitted from the sender to the recipient. Files may be attached to e-mail messages using the MIME standard.

Multi-user, text-based conversations also take place on the Internet, such as IRC (Internet Relay Chat). Other so-called chat services are becoming available, including World's and Microsoft's avatar-based 3D chat systems.

It is technically feasible to transmit speech in real time over the Internet as well. This Internet telephone service is enabled by inexpensive software available from several companies (VocalTec and Camelot's Third Planet division, Quarterdeck, and Electric Magic), a Sound Blaster card, and a microphone. Various technical issues such as latency and delay must still be resolved; these systems also require the use of dedicated servers.

Sound files may be transmitted as a file download for later playback or as a real-time broadcast. Files for later playback must be completely downloaded before the sound can be sampled. Real-time broadcast is similar in principle to Internet telephony. RealAudio, Xing, I-Wave, True Speech and others, are being developed to allow one-way real-time broadcasts over the Internet. There are drawbacks to both methods. The first requires the user first to download relatively large files (about 1 megabyte per 10 to 20 seconds) before playing back the sound using software that comes standard with sound playback hardware (a $150 sound card and speakers, for example). Therefore, a user with a 14.4 kbps modem would wait through a download of 10 minutes or so to listen to a 10 to 20 second playback. The second method, in which files can be played back simultaneously with the download, requires either large amounts of bandwidth or diminished sound quality (fewer digital samples per unit time).

Video can also be transmitted in the same two ways. Video of TV-quality transmitted or broadcast in real-time across the net requires considerable bandwidth, say 1.5 mbps. The

MBONE, a network within the Internet which has been deployed for several years, enables large video files to travel on the Internet. Currently, other software solutions (Xing Technologies) allow real-time playback with low bandwidth requirements (28.8 kbps) of video files transmitted across the Internet (not on the MBONE). Two-way videoconferencing has been enabled by CuSeeMe, developed at Cornell University, though commercial software, such as Connectix Videophone, has recently become available.

Information (News Media) Access

Considerable information from traditional news media can be found on the Internet, mainly the World Wide Web. These include electronic newspapers, trade and other magazines, news feeds, and audio and video broadcasts. Innovative information sources include nontraditional news media such as search engines and catalogued databases. Financial and government information also abound on the 'Net. In general, and consistent with the heritage of the Internet, most information that is available is on the subjects of computing, medicine, and on current news topics.

Examples of traditional-news-media-gone-Internet are newspapers like *The San-Jose Mercury News* (Knight Ridder), *The Wall Street Journal*, and *The New York Times*; trade magazines from Ziff-Davis (*PC Week*, *PC Magazine*) and CMP Publications (*Communications Week* and *Computer Shopper*); other magazines like *HotWired* and *Time*; news feeds from PR Newswire and Reuters; audio broadcasts from clnet, ABC, and National Public Radio; and video broadcasts like NBC Pro. There are literally hundreds of traditional news media sources available on the Internet, and we estimate the growth in availability of these services is growing more rapidly than the growth of the Internet.

Nontraditional news media information sources on the Internet range from search engine/catalogued databases like Yahoo and Lycos to news aggregation services with searchable databases, such as Infoseek and Individual Inc.'s NewsPage. We believe the search capabilities of the Infoseek and Newspage pay services are very powerful resources, but as with other traditional news media products on the Internet, they have not replaced paper-written media information sources. Only when handheld, wireless devices can be substituted for paper media will the new media challenge the mass market, in our view.

Financial information such as free stock quotes with 15-minute delay are available on the Web as well as by e-mail. The Edgar database contains SEC filings for many companies (those that have volunteered to file electronically). Thousands of government servers dedicated to the purpose of public dissemination contain vats quantities of information. One excellent government database is the IRS Home page, from which tax forms formatted in Adobe Acrobat can be downloaded.

Entertainment

Hundreds of thousands of shareware and freeware games can be downloaded from Internet sites. There are hundreds of MUDS (Multiple User Dimensions, Multiple User Dungeons, Multiple User Dialogues) and MOOs (MUD, Object Oriented), multi-user chat sessions (Worlds Inc.), Usenet discussion groups on entertaining subjects (alt.fan.elvis), and new places and new countries and cultures to explore (such as on the China Home Page).

Education/Research

A common use of the Internet for some 15 years has been posting and sending academic papers for review by peers, using FTP, gopher and more recently the Web. Searching libraries worldwide, then contacting the library to request to borrow books or other materials, has come into widespread use. In nonacademic settings, corporate web pages offer abundant information, ranging from entire product catalogs, in full detailed graphics, available for browsing, to sound bites of the CEO. Such audio and video content may soon find growing applications in education and research.

Marketing/Advertising

Corporate web pages have become the most popular means of distributing corporate information to Internet users. Developed by a company or an agency on its behalf, a corporate web page can offer varying levels of detail and sophistication, depending entirely upon what the company wants the public to see, from simple one-page text-oriented web pages to multi-paged, interactive multi-media (video, sound, text and graphics). Most corporate web pages are somewhere in between, and feature a company description, markets addressed, product specifications, and ordering information. Although most corporate web pages are technology-related, other companies are quickly joining in.

Corporate web page advertising designers who have been prominent on the Internet include: Modem Media (customers include Zima, AT&T, CBS and MasterCard), CKS Interactive, Free Range Media (The NFL), and Einstein and Sandom. Companies that maintain their own sites for the purpose of promoting others' products include On Ramp, Inc. (Metaverse, Planet Reebok), Fry Multimedia (Ragu Pasta Sauces), and Cybersight (Stolichnaya Vodka).

As with Nielsen ratings for television, for business reasons advertisers and corporations want to be able to count viewers of advertisements. This is a controversial topic on the Internet; as many have observed, it is not as simple as counting "hits" per web page, that is, the number of times files are downloaded from a home page during a user's visit. Hits are counted in different ways, pages with many single graphics images cause more hits to be recorded, and that users may often hit a site numerous times while browsing, even though they only visit there once during a session.

More sophisticated and accountable means of counting visitors to home pages have been developed and offered to the Internet marketplace by two companies, I/PRO and Netcount. The I/PRO System consists of I/COUNT, I/AUDIT and I/CODE. With I/COUNT, site owners monitor aspects of site usage such as number of user-sessions, most frequently accessed files, and geographic and organization origin of users. I/AUDIT is a third party audit report of web site activity that site owners can provide to advertisers and potential advertisers. I/AUDIT is commercially available. The I/CODE Universal Registration System allows site owners to learn more about the demographics of their visitors. The I/CODE System will be commercially available on August 1. Netcount is a competing system that relies upon Netcount's servers to track visits to the site owner's page. Netcount has tried to differentiate itself I/PRO by providing more service to the site owner.

Customer Service

A good example of how a company can use the Internet to improve customer service is Federal Express, which offers package tracking through its interactive web page. FedEx can meet its customers' desire for faster and more accurate access to information and, at the same time, control its own costs more efficiently. Cisco Systems has CIO, Cisco In

formation Online, a web-based trouble-shooting database containing network failure symptoms and possible solutions. This service has helped Cisco's business and overall customer satisfaction, because most user questions can be answered very quickly without having to contact Cisco engineers on the customer service line.

Retail/Wholesale/Commerce

A count of Yahoo's directory shows over 40,000 companies use the web to advertise, to offer service, to communicate, or to sell products and services directly through the Internet. The latter includes companies that display product specifications and pictures, expecting consumers to pay for a product which will then to be shipped to them using a common carrier. The services and products available on the Internet range from flowers, sneakers, and business supplies to business opportunities, music, real estate and travel.

Shopping centers (malls) are becoming popular on the web, numbering in the hundreds. Many of the images on the screen use the analogy of walking into the mall, entering through doorways, and so on. Excellent "malls" or marketplaces on the Internet are Internet Shopping Network (ISN), MarketplaceMCI, Wholesaler's Worldwide Marketplace, and CUC International's site.

There are even ways to make shopping more expedient and to find the lowest prices for products and service publicized on the Internet. One option consists of data bases of prices and specifications, in which a web site will display a searchable compilation of prices and product specifications from various retailers and wholesalers. Web users will typically enters a key word or search by subject to find the lowest prices for various items. One example of this type of Internet shopping database is Fido: the Shopping Doggie (http://www.continuumsi.com/cgi-bin/Fido/Welcome), which shows a comprehensive list of competitive prices. Another example of such a site is shareware.com, a site created by clnet. It is becoming a definitive source for finding shareware of all types.

A second option is an active agent. A software agent would be launched from a client station, and would go from one site to another, seeking the lowest prices for standardized goods. AT&T has announced it will produce one, and Andersen Consulting had introduced a limited-capability beta version of a shopping agent (unfortunately, it was immediately blocked from accessing the sites it was programmed to survey, because the sites didn't want their prices to be compared with others'). FTP Software has developed software agents to perform remote computer configuration using a high-level script language, which could possibly evolve into a software shopping agent.

Internet Features and Applications

Exploiting the various resources on the Internet and enabling communication, news delivery, and other services requires some familiarity with protocols and applications of the 'Net.

World Wide Web and Browsers

The de facto desktop application for Internet use is the Web browser, which has been likened to the word processor or spreadsheet in the early days of the PC revolution. Just as with the PC desktop applications and the Microsoft Office platform, the browser is being enhanced with newer revisions to include an ever-expanding feature set of "plug-in" applications.

The Web runs on the http protocol, which runs atop other Internet protocols. We believe the browser is an "eye" into the Internet, the front end that sees the result of considerable "back end" processes such as content development, databasing, collaborative workgroup efforts, and multimedia becoming available on the Internet.

E-mail

Suffice it to say, e-mail is here to stay and will complement other means of human (and computer) communications well into our future. This system is also being embraced by the U.S. Postal Service, such that proof-of-delivery systems are maintained.

E-mail is an economical, easy way to communicate electronically. It is a competing service to mail delivery services and faxing and has the advantages that it is quick (it takes minutes to transfer a message across the world), does not require paper, and is less expensive than faxing. An e-mail message can be sent from one computer to another on the Internet if each is connected to an e-mail 'gateway' (a specialized Internet connected device which stores, forwards and routes mail). Compared to other services on the Internet, e-mail messages can experience a slight delay, because most gateways collect and store messages, then process them in batches. Gateways are configured according to the needs of the e-mail using organization, the costs of the service, and priority of messages being sent and received. A typical delay in sending an e-mail message from one organization to another, when each is connected to a large, well-funded Internet Service Provider, would be about 10 minutes. On the other hand, a small corporation with an analog dial-up connection to the Internet may decide to collect e-mail and send it out every hour or two.

File Transfer Protocol (FTP)

FTP was developed to allow users to connect to remote systems, log on, move and search through the file system, and upload and download files. Two types of interfaces are available: command line and graphical user interfaces. With the command line interface, once the user has logged on to the host system, the user's screen displays the host machine's operating environment file system. Using the command line FTP interface therefore requires some knowledge of the host machine's filing and operating system. Graphical user interfaces hide operating systems differences and display a consistent, easy-to-use interface capable of interpreting a variety of different operating system filing systems.

Usenet

Usenet is a service carried over the Internet that has been available since 1979. The service allows millions of users to share their thoughts on a variety of topics by posting messages (uploading messages to discussion groups) for public comment, reading and reviewing other's thoughts, and responding to other's comments. It is characterized by rich and consistently varying content, similar to the user forums or discussion groups found on AOL, CompuServe or other online services. Users will join or subscribe to Usenet groups that interest them; there are about 17,000 active Usenet discussion groups, ranging on topics from

U.S. Robotics modems, to ISDN terminal adapters, to pets and hobbies. A unique culture has arisen in the use of Usenet. Peculiarities include the use of emoticons, such as the smiley face :) and use of abbreviations like IMHO (in my humble opinion), and the well-publicized flame wars, where users insult one another. Usenet posts are typically updated on the same time frame as e-mail, that is it might take 10 minutes, 1 hour, or 12 hours, depending upon the UUCP (Unix to Unix Copy Protocol) gateway connection.

Legacy Internet Features

Several features of the Internet that are in declining use today are Gopher, Archie, Veronica, Jughead, WAIS, telnet, IRC, Finger and WhoIs. The first five have essentially been supplanted by the functionality of the Web and its applications. telnet is an interface that emulates a dumb terminal connection to a mainframe or minicomputer. It is still in use today, but few applications are being developed to use this technology. IRC (Internet Relay Chat) is a text-based multi-user chat system that allows real-time communications in various chat discussion groups — not a small business, since about 1/3 of AOL's and 1/4 of CompuServe's revenues derive from catering to proprietary services like this. Finger and WhoIs are in most cases inef-

fective user location systems: There are too many different network systems on the 'Net today, and many administrators of networks do not allow Finger-ing of their sites for security reasons (hackers can use this information to breach security networks).

New Applications in Beta Test

Several new applications exploiting various features of the Internet are in beta testing now. Each has serious implications for future use of the Internet. Four such are depicted in a simultaneous Windows 95 session in Figure 4.1, entitled StreamWorks, RealAudio, Internet Phone and Worlds Chat Session.

In the upper left-hand corner is Xing Technology's StreamWorks software running a real-time playback of an NBC broadcast of a Charles Kurault monologue. In the upper right-hand corner is Real Audio software, which enables real-time playback of radio and music. Next is the Worlds Chat, a real-time, interactive chat software. In the lower left-hand corner is VocalTec's Internet Phone software, which is connecting to an Internet Phone server to see what other users have logged in and can speak using the two-way voice system (telephony) enabled by the software card.

Figure 4.1

StreamWorks, RealAudio, Internet Phone and Worlds Chat Session

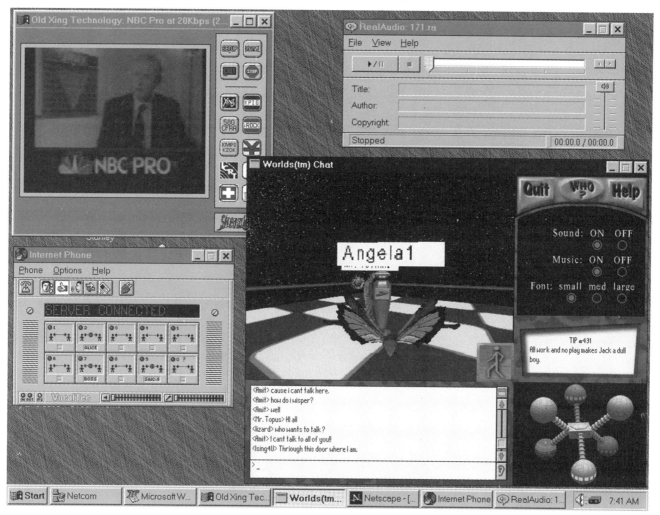

Section III:
Infrastructure

Chapter 5: Worldwide Internet Infrastructure

- Telecommunications carriers, in general, own the physical plant consisting of wires, fiber-optics, and switching equipment. They lease access to portions of their network to Internet service providers (ISPs) and online service providers (OSPs), which resell a value-added service — the Internet.

- The infrastructure consists of many ISPs' networks, which are cooperatively connected to allow the sharing of traffic, enabling customers on different providers to exchange information.

- Server and client computers are interconnected to a worldwide network infrastructure.

- Server computers connected to the Internet store "content," while client computers retrieve it. About 80% of traffic today flows from the server to the client as a result of client information requests.

The Internet is the largest interconnection of networks in the world, and today exists mainly for the purpose of communicating and sharing information among network users. The reason that networks can communicate with one another is because each uses a common network protocol suite called TCP/IP. The types of networks on the Internet include those for college campuses, government agencies, the military, corporations, and service companies (such as America Online, CompuServe, or UUNET). But just because a network is internetworked, or connected together, does not necessarily mean that it is on the Internet. Numerous internetworks exist on their own. Examples of private networks (in this context, "network" is used interchangeably with "internetwork") include the Reuter news service, AOL and CompuServe (except for those portions connected to the Internet), and the thousands of corporate networks.

There are four key components to a typical internetworked system: server computers, client computers, the networks, and the internetwork. All of these components communicate with each other mostly over leased lines provided by the telecom carriers.

Infrastructure

Servers Servers are computers of various sizes and capabilities on which information resides and from which other computers, called clients, can retrieve data. The importance of servers on the Internet is that they store information and send it when a request is made by client computers. Servers can be mainframes, microcomputers, or personal computers; it is not the size, power, or operating system that makes a computer a server or client, it is the

manner in which it is used. UNIX, the predominant computer operating system on the Internet, allows multiple tasks to occur simultaneously as well as multiple users to access computer resources. Thus, the multitasking, multi-user capabilities of UNIX blur the distinction between server and client somewhat, and also allow many clients to simultaneously retrieve information from a single server.

Clients Clients are computers used for performing work, displaying images, and inputting data. A typical client computer is used by an office worker for word processing, sending and receiving e-mail, Web-surfing, and transferring files from hosts. A client computer must be networked to a host, or must be a host connected directly to the Internet, to communicate on the Internet.

Given the way the Internet is being used today, which might be described as "mildly interactive," most information flows from servers to clients, as clients request information. By our estimate, 80% of Internet traffic flowed from server to client in mid-1995, while 20% flowed the other way (e-mail "sends," Usenet postings, and file uploads account for approximately 15%, with the remaining 5% occurring when, for instance, a user responds to an interactive Web questionnaire or requests specific data via gopher or Archie searches).

Networks Wires, network adapters, hubs, switches, and various connectors comprise most of the networking equipment that connects servers and clients and allows sharing of computing resources. A typical network, such as one used for a small office, is shown in Figure 5.1. A local-area network (LAN) connects computers in a building or

5 – 2

nearby buildings using wires or fiber optics installed by the owner of the facilities. In general, it is possible to connect any type of network to the Internet, although data sent and retrieved from the Internet must be in IP (Internet protocol) format, which is the common networking software protocol that enables disparate networks to converse.

Networks that do not support the TCP/IP protocol must have a means of converting the network's protocol to IP. This can be done at the server, or host, connecting to the Internet; however, some complications do occur. Therefore, the most popular operating system for computers and networks on the Internet is UNIX, which has native IP support. Other computer operating systems have been upgraded recently to include IP support, including Windows NT and Windows 95, and many network operating systems support many networking protocols, such as Novell's Netware, which supports IP, IPX (Internet packet exchange), and others.

Networks may be connected to form their own internets. The example shown in Figure 5.2 is not connected to the Internet, but it does demonstrate how the Internet is built — by connecting networks to one another.

Internetworks   Routers, bridges, and switches are the primary internetworking equipment used to connect networks. Multiprotocol routers represent the majority of internetworking equipment used in building the Internet, because they decide which direction to send network data. Bridges and switches, which are in general faster than routers because they do less computing, are used in conjunction with routers because they cannot handle multiple protocols

Figure 5.1
A Corporate Network

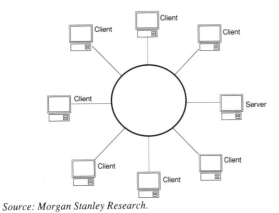

Source: Morgan Stanley Research.

Figure 5.2
A Corporate Internetwork

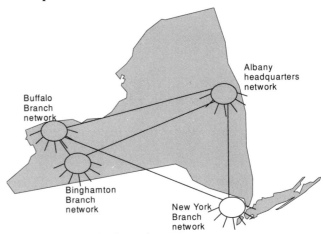

Source: Morgan Stanley Research.

and cannot protect networks using security techniques such as firewalling. Using the three types of equipment, but mainly routers today, enables the exchange of information from computers on one network to another.

Routers perform two primary functions relating to the Internet. First, if a non-IP network, such as a Novell IPX, is connected to the Internet, a multiprotocol router is needed to interpret the other protocol and package the data into IP "packets" (chunks of information) with destination addresses. Large pieces of data are packetized into multiple packets. Second, once in packet form, the router directs the data packets through wire or telecommunications carrier's lines, toward the destination. The packets might not be sent directly to the final destination, depending upon traffic patterns, equipment failure, or line speed, but may instead go through many different midpoints, most likely more routers, before reaching the final destination network. Once at the routing device of the destination network, packets are combined and sent via the destination network to the destination computer.

The Internet has a hierarchical system of naming and numbering that uniquely addresses computers and networks. For example, in the e-mail address billg@microsoft.com, the domain is microsoft.com. Each data packet sent along the Internet has unique addressing information attached, and routers use that information to direct the data toward their destination.

Unless a network can be linked to the Internet via another, nearby network (e.g., one several hundred feet away), it probably would be connected to the Internet through either leased, or dedicated, lines or dial-up lines provided by a telecom carrier.

Telecommunications Carriers Leased lines, which are dedicated, or permanent, connections provided by the telecom carriers and linking one physical location to another, carry most data traffic on the Internet. Leased lines connect at each point along the Internet to equipment such as switches or routers. Dial-up lines, on the other hand, are more frequently used by small corporations or individuals to connect small networks or individual computers to the Internet using modems and ISDN connections.

Telecom carriers play a variety of roles in operating the Internet. In some cases, they lease dedicated lines and let others operate the network over the line, while in other cases the carrier operates a portion of the Internet using its own lines.

What Does the Internet Look Like? Who Owns It?

Basically, the Internet is a complex, highly redundant network of telecom circuits connected together with routers. Today, most of the Internet is owned by commercial interests and has been functioning independently from the U.S. government backbone since April 1995. The primary backbone of the Internet, called the NSFNet (National Science Foundation Net) and in existence from 1986 until April 1995, was federally funded and intended for non-commercial use. Merit Network, Inc., operated the NSFNet over a seven-year period, ending April 1995, in partnership with Advanced Network Services (ANS; now part of America Online), IBM, MCI, and the State of Michigan.

Figure 5.3

Organization of Internet, 1986 through April 1995

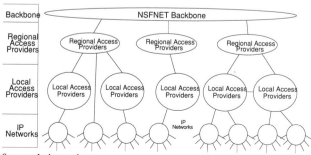

Source: Industry data.

Figure 5.4

Internet Backbone (NSFNet) and Regional Networks Service Connections, September 1991

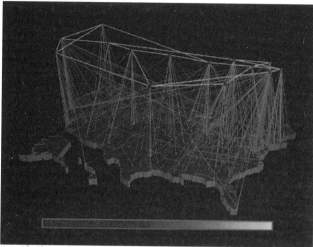

Source: Donna Cox and Robert Patterson, National Center for Supercomputing Applications/University of Illinois. This image is a visualization study of inbound traffic measured in billions of bytes on the NSFNet T1 backbone. It represents data collected by Merit Networks, Inc.

The NSFNet operated at a speed of 56 kbps in the mid-1980s, was upgraded to T-1 (1.5 mbps) in the late-1980s, and was boosted to T-3 (45 mbps) in the early 1990s. As Figure 5.3 shows, the NSFNet spanned the country; various regional access providers, which covered regions such as New England (NEARNet) and the Bay Area (BARNet) were connected to NSFNet; local access providers, such as local dial-up firms, were connected to regional providers; and IP networks were connected to local shops. A characteristic of the build-up of the Internet was the lack of a strong central authority; hence, some IP networks connected directly to the NSFNet or to regional access providers.

Technical decisions related to the Internet are made by the Internet Engineering Task Force (IETF), a committee of scientist and experts, and connections to the Internet are governed by the Internet Architecture Board (IAB) through a public "request for comment" (RFC) process, whereby proposal are posted on various Usenet groups and FTP servers (such as ftp.internic.net). Management of the Internet is separate from the IETF, and in April 1993 the NSF awarded three five-year contracts to manage Network Information Services, which collectively include the administrative requirements to run the Internet. Collectively, the three contracts are for managing the InterNIC (Internet Network Information Center), with the primary responsi-

Figure 5.5
Worldwide Internet Connectivity, 6/15/95

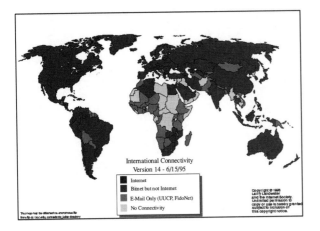

bility of providing information about getting connected to and using the Internet. Network Solutions was chosen to provide Internet registration services, including assignment of IP addresses. AT&T, meanwhile, publicly maintains a variety of databases on the resources available to Internet users, such as FTP sites, yellow-page directories, and data archives.

Seeing the steady growth of the Internet, the U.S. government decided to get out of the business of funding commercial networking; so, in 1993, the NSF proposed a new architecture, composed of an experimental very high-speed network (vBNS) operating at OC-3 (155 mbps), to which the commercial backbone connects at network access points (NAPs). The routing arbiter (RA) and many network service providers (NSPs) carry traffic nationwide and do not depend upon the vBNS; rather, they share traffic among themselves, independent of the vBNS.

As Figure 5.6 shows, the new architecture began operation in April 1995, coincident with the termination of NSFNet. The NSF directly funds the vBNS, which is operated by MCI and restricted to organizations requiring high speeds for scientific computing and visualization, and the RA, operated by Merit under a five-year award from the NSF that began in July 1994. The NAPs, which interconnect the vBNS and other backbone networks, both domestic and foreign, are operated by PacBell in San Francisco (a subsidiary of PacTel), Ameritech in Chicago, Sprint in New York, and MFS in Washington, D.C. The larger network service providers include PSINet, UUNET, and ANS.

Besides the decommissioning of the NSFNet and its replacement with the vBNS, the major difference between Figures 5.3 and 5.6 is that the commercial providers are now interconnected directly and can share traffic without needing the vBNS. This means the commercial Internet no longer requires a government backbone.

Figure 5.6
Organization of Internet, April 1995 Through 1998

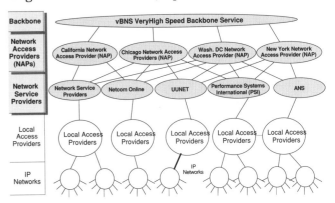

Source: Industry data.

Figure 5.7

The New NSFNet Service, 1995

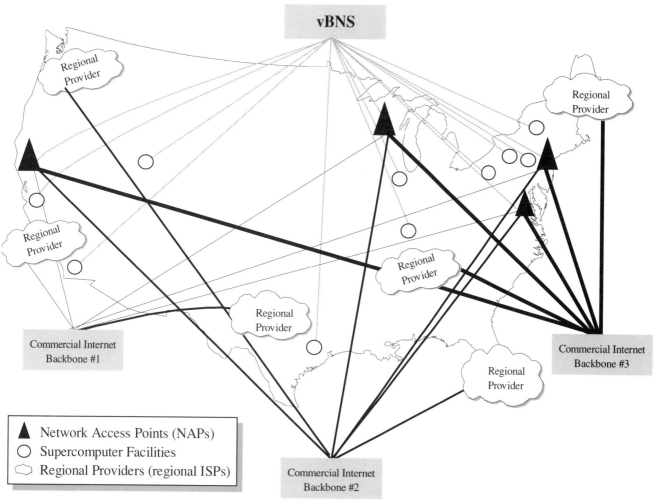

Source: Morgan Stanley

Description: Separate networks — VBNS, commercial Internet backbone provider #1, #2, and #3 — all connect at common data-sharing locations, such as at NAPs (network access points). Customers connect to their regional provider, which is connected to a backbone provider, each of which shares traffic with the others. Regional provider networks (or ISPs) may be owned by the same commercial entity as the backbone provider. Note the similarity between the above diagram, with its multiple commercial backbones, and Figure 5.4, with its one government-funded backbone.

The switchover has caused universities and other institutions that were dependent upon the NSFNet to use commercial service providers like AT&T Network Services, MCI, Sprintlink, BBN Planet, and others. In addition, the commercialization has created pricing pressure; according to Glenn Fleishman, a principal at the Point of Presence Web of Seattle, prices for obtaining a T-1 connection have dropped to $1,650 per month, from $3,000–4,000. Other NSPs that have come into existence recently include Chicago's Net99, a private company. BBN Planet has also recently announced $995 T-1 lines.

Chapter 6: Internet Service Provider Infrastructure

- Large Internet service providers (ISPs) offer local Internet access to customers by building out their own networks, which consist of hundreds of points of presence (POPs) connected by high-speed dedicated lines leased from telecom providers (or alternatively by connecting POPs together with frame relay or ATM service connections).

- POPs, the building blocks of an ISP network, consist of routers (typically Cisco's), digital/analog call aggregators (typically Ascend's), servers (typically Sun's), and, as the network grows larger, frame relay or ATM switches (typically Cascade's).

- Smaller ISPs may commonly lease IP-connectivity service, as well as POPs, from larger ISPs, rather than build out their own networks.

Internet Service Provider Networks

ISPs maintain IP networks, connected to the Internet through network access points (NAPs), at key locations — currently California, Chicago, Washington, D.C., and New York, or by connecting to other ISPs. NAPs are the entry points to the Internet, where ISPs share information. There are other means of sharing such data between networks, such as the Commercial Interexchange (CIX). In Figure 6.1, Netcom's star-shaped points of presence and telecommunications backbone are centered on the NAPs' hookups. Note that the ISP network is a 45 mbps backbone of T-3s that connect the major points, as well as to the Texas area, where there is no NAP (also see UUNET's backbone network topology in Figure 6.2).

The purpose of the ISP network is to establish a presence in many localities, so that customers have local dial-in (no toll) access, or short leased-line access to the ISP network. Users access the ISP network at a so-called point of presence (POP), which consists of call aggregators, routers, frame relay and/or ATM switches and multiplexers. POPs, commonly located within an existing telecom carrier's facilities in rented space, are being rapidly deployed across the country and the world, as ISPs build out their Internet access infrastructure.

Typically, larger ISP networks are cell-switched and frame-relay-based. For reliability, ISPs usually depend on more than one interexchange carrier (IXC) to provide time-division multiplexing (TDM) point-to-point (or permanent leased line) T-1 and T-3 circuits, which interconnect the POPs. ISPs provide two types of service: leased line and dial-up. We have seen the emergence of another class of ISP, those which interconnect POPs by leasing frame-relay service directly from IXCs, which reduces somewhat the capital an ISP must make to its own network.

Figure 6.1

Netcom Points of Presence (POP) And Telecommunications Backbone

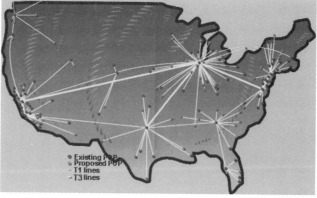

Source: Netcom

Figure 6.2
UUNET DS-3 Backbone Network

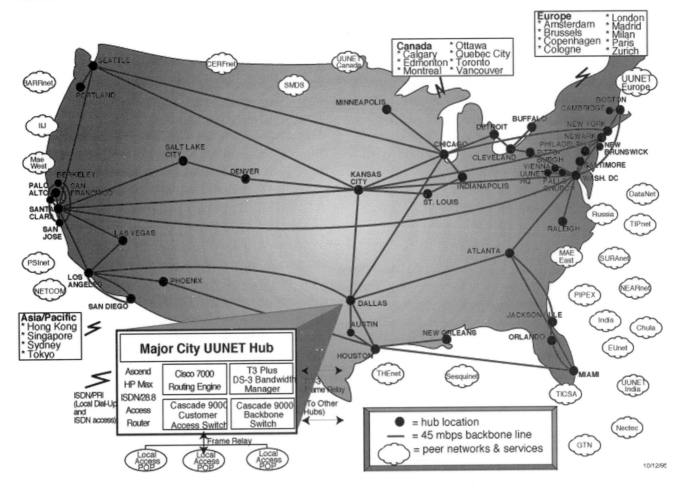

Source: UUNET

Figure 6.3
PSINet Leased and Dial-Up Connections

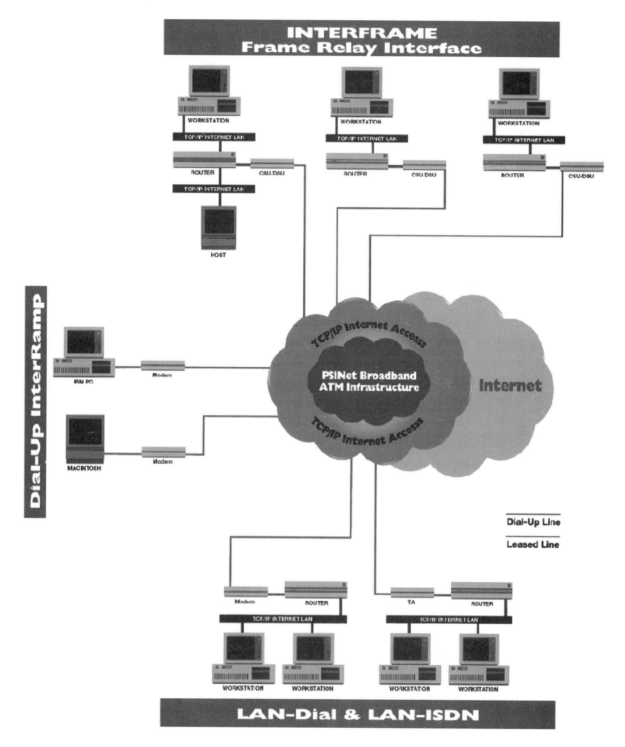

Source: PSINet

Leased line service is sold to ISP customers that need to be permanently connected to the Internet. These connections typically require corporate customers to have a router on site to perform Internet routing frame-relay interfaces between the ISP and the corporate customer. Dial-up connections, on the other hand, are handled by call aggregators that pick up the incoming call from the dial-up telephone system. Call aggregators are connected to routers that send traffic to the Internet via the ISP's network. Figure 6.3 depicts commonly available client and server connections to the PSINet Internet service, which is typical of large ISPs.

POPs

Direct and online service providers are building up their respective networks in various metropolitan areas, so that users and corporations can connect with local dial-up numbers or leased lines provided by regional exchange carriers. POPs are built-in, secure, rented facilities, consisting of telecommunications and internetworking equipment that allows dial-up access to a direct service provider's network, which in turn accesses the Internet. A typical POP is shown in Figure 6.4. According to PSINet, constructing a small to medium-sized POP costs about $70,000 to $150,000, and contains routers, ATM switches, T-3 or T-1 DSUs, dial-up ISDN and analog modem devices, and 1–20 workstations. The networks that a direct service provider operates connect POPs together and allow connected users to access the Internet. A typical DSP's network is depicted in Figure 6.1 and shows how the POPs are connected together by leased telecommunications lines.

Multiplexers

Time-division multiplexing (TDM) devices are used to connect leased lines to other TDM devices. A MUX (multiplexer) aggregates many different calls or data streams and combines them in slices of data sequenced with time, then channels the combined data through the leased line. A MUX on the other side uncombines the signals. MUXs, when connected to the Internet, are used with other devices to route the data packets through the Internet.

Frame Relay Switches

Frame relay is a packet-based interface standard optimized for the transport of protocol-oriented data, such as IP. Protocol-less network services, such as frame relay or ATM, are very efficient and use less overhead than protocol-dependent transport services. Frame relay service performs statistical multiplexing, which means that all paths across the network are defined; however, no bandwidth is allocated to the paths until actual data need to be transmitted. Therefore, instead of keeping open many paths, or channels, full time when they are transmitting no data, frame relay transmits other data across the available bandwidth. If the aggregate amount of data to be transmitted across a frame relay link exceeds the available bandwidth, the frame relay device, for a short period of time, may store the data for later transmission. In general, the use of frame relay in the buildout of large ISP networks is becoming increasingly common, because in many circumstances it increases the performance of the system.

Routers

The router is the basic building block of the Internet. At every branch, or connection of three or more routes, in the Internet, there must be a routing device that decides which direction to send data. Routers may be located at the customer premise or at the ISP (or other Internet connection point). A router is connected to two or more networks and appears to each of these networks as a connected host. Routers can be located at the ISP's location or on the customer's premise. Routers are discussed in this chapter, rather than Chapter 7, "Customer Premise Infrastructure," because we believe more new users connect through routers which are located at the ISP's site.

The function of a router is to direct data efficiently. When routing is implemented, it usually brings together two or more networks. Maps of the Internet generally depict dots connected by lines. Each dot generally represents a network, and, for the most part, at each dot is a router. The lines are telecommunications lines, either leased or switched, and digital or analog; most are leased digital lines. The routers constantly chat electronically to each other over the lines, and when a request from a host is made to send data from one point to another, the routers, having gathered the latest information about the status of the routes available through the Internet, send the data in packets along an optimum path. This optimum path from one host to another may include passing through several, or dozens of, routers on the way.

Figure 6.4

Typical PSINet Point of Presence (POP)

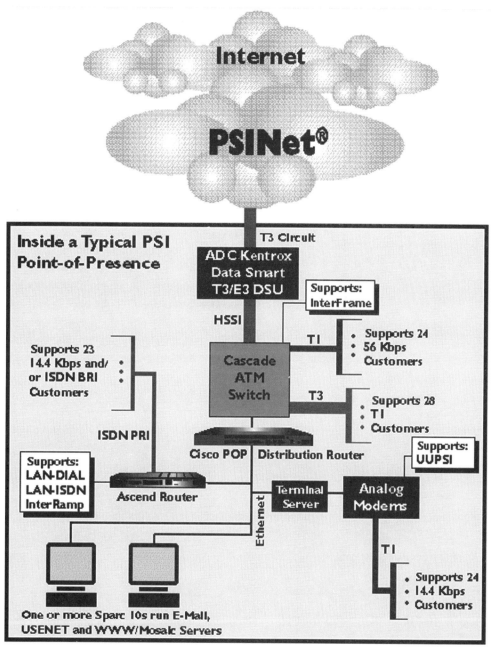

Source: PSINet home page on the WWW.

Router operation involves several processes. First, the router creates a routing table to gather information from other routers about the optimum path to each packet. Routing tables may be static or dynamic; the latter is considered a better technique because it adapts to changing network conditions. Next, when data are sent from a net-work host to a router enroute to its destination, the router will break open the data packet and look at the destination address to determine the most efficient path between two end-points. Factors considered in this determination include distance and cost. In identifying the most efficient path, the router plugs the factors into algorithms. Popular open-standard algorithms include Distance Vector and Link State. The former is choice-based on the distance of the remote node; the latter algorithm includes, in addition to distance, information about the status of the various links connecting the nodes and the topology of the network.

The term "gateway," used in the context of the Internet, is almost always synonymous with "IP router" or "router." The term gateway began to be used in the 1970s, when routers as we know them did not exist. About 95% of the Internet's routing devices are routers; the remaining 5% consist of computers running routing code. Typically, the computers are dedicated to performing the routing function, although they could perform other functions, too, with the disadvantage that they are less efficient than routers.

Recent Internet documentation discourages the use of computers for the purpose of routing because of a number of hidden pitfalls. It is possible to embed router functions within a host operating system that supports connections to two or more networks. The best-known example of an operating system with embedded router code is the Berkeley BSD system. The coming "Cairo" version of Windows NT, now in development, is expected to include Bay Networks' enterprise routing code.

Dial-Up Call Aggregators (Remote Access Hubs)

To handle multiple incoming dial-up calls at POPs, ISPs typically use remote access hubs that concentrate the calls. Supported devices typically include digital dial-in (ISDN) and analog dial-in (via modem), as well as leased-line and frame relay traffic.

Dial-up call aggregators are an alternative to external modem pools, which use multiple modems cabled together to servers. State-of-the-art remote access hubs would typically have up to 100 ports and include support for ISDN, 28.8 kbps analog modems, and possibly leased lines and frame relay traffic; they also would have router and terminal server capabilities all in one box.

Chapter 7: Customer Premise Infrastructure

- Client-side consumer equipment for connecting to the Internet consists of PCs and modems for typical consumers.

- Client-side small-office/home-office (SOHO) equipment consists of PCs, modems or ISDN routers, and possibly hubs and network interface cards (NICs).

- Client-side corporate and large-organization equipment consists of PCs and workstations, NICs, hubs, routers, and, although not required for Internet access, as bandwidth requirements dictate, more high-performance local-area network (LAN) equipment, such as LAN switches.

- Server-side equipment, consists of PC-based or workstation-based computer equipment, such as NICs, hubs, switches, and routers.

- The bare minimum required to store content ("make a Web site") is a PC server and a connection (preferably permanent) to an ISP.

Client Hardware

Client Computers   Nearly all personal computers, whether IBM-compatible, Macintosh, or other — running DOS, Windows (3.1, NT, or 95), MacOS, Linux, or another operating system — can connect to the Internet if equipped with the proper client software and hardware and if linked through a network or carrier connection to an Internet service provider.

Workstations   Workstations, frequently running UNIX or Windows NT, are microcomputers that are generally more powerful than PCs. These likewise can connect to the Internet through the same means as PCs.

Client Communications

Network Connections   If a client computer is connected to a network that's connected to the Internet, then it is not necessary for that client computer to be connected directly to an Internet carrier line. By virtue of the client computer's connection to the network, any applications it's running should be able to use the resources of the Internet. Of course, this depends upon they way the server is configured and the degree to which the network is connected to the Internet. With rare exceptions, the only client equipment that is required for a network is a network adapter.

Carrier Connections   If a client computer isn't connected through a network and server to the Internet, then the client computer must connect through telephone service or, possibly in the future, cable-TV service.

Network Adapters

The most common means of connecting a computer to a network is by using a network interface card (NIC), which, via wire or fiber optics, interconnects using a loop or, more commonly, links to a concentrator or hub using a star pattern. Wireless network adapters can also be used, but these are slower and less reliable.

Figure 7.1

Client PC or Workstation Connection to a Network

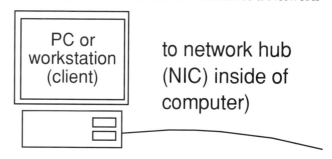

Client Carrier Connections

At the client side, common alternatives to connecting to the Internet using carrier lines are, in order of increasing cost and bandwidth:

- **Ordinary switched (dial-up) analog telephone lines, also known as plain old telephone service (POTS),** which is the same service used by telephones and fax machines.

- **Switched digital telephone lines, referred to as ISDN** (integrated services digital network), which use the existing copper wire infrastructure installed in most homes and businesses. ISDN service uses an NT-1 (network terminator 1) device, which performs a conversion of signals to allow the many ISDN channels run over the two pairs of wires.

• **Leased analog or digital (permanent) lines,** which are uncommon and for power users, who must always be connected to the Internet. This type of client is probably continually surfing the Web and checking e-mail, so it would be less expensive in this case to connect permanently with a leased line, than to keep an ISDN line open at all times.

Figure 7.2

Client PC or Workstation Connection to an ISP

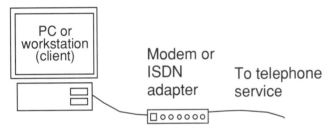

An alternative means of connecting to the Internet is by linking a computer to the cable-TV network. However, wholesale infrastructure changes must first be made to the existing cable networks, which today are one-way, broadcast-based systems; a small percentage of the networks have been made two-way. An issue that has been identified, although not widely publicized, during testing is that the performance of cable modem transmissions based on proprietary implementation of the broadcast Ethernet networking architecture decreases inversely as the number of users on the cable system increases. To counteract this, the cable networks could be segmented more and more, using routers or router-like devices. The cable operators would have to weigh the benefits of microsegmenting the networks to overcome these issues. ATM technology, currently being developed for cable, promises to address some of these issues. Despite the challenges of retrofitting the existing cable network, the technology of cable modems looks promising due to the inherent superiority of the higher-capacity coaxial wire installed nationwide for CATV, versus the thin copper-wire infrastructure of the telecommunications providers.

Client Modems

Analog modems allow the transfer of data across ordinary switched telephone lines. Modems, which are used at the client side (workstation, desktop, or laptop), are available in five form factors: external, internal, PCMCIA, parallel port, or built onto the motherboard. Each performs the same thing but connects to computers differently. Modems connected to POTS, can dial up any other modem connected to the worldwide telecommunications system.

A modem functions by converting digital signals from the computer to analog signals. The analog signals are transmitted over the telephone service and received by another modem, which unconverts analog to digital. State-of-the-art modems run at speeds of 28.8 kbps, although 14.4 kbps modems are common. Software upgrades from some modem manufacturers can update certain 28.8 kbps modems to 33.6 kbps speeds.

The theoretical speed limit for modems is around 40 kbps and will never exceed 64 kbps, which is the true capacity of an analog phone line. In practice, average connect rates of modems over typical phone lines peak at somewhat less than the 28.8 kbps (or 33.6 kbps) nominal ratings of a modem, say 24 or 27 kbps, due to noisy lines, grounding, loose connections, or other factors. As a reference point, transferring a compressed file containing a 3.5-inch floppy disk's data (1.44 megabytes) would take about 10 minutes using a 14.4 kbps modem; transmission time would be half that at 28.8 kbps. One weakness in communicating with modems is that most take about 20–30 seconds to connect (negotiate) with other modems before beginning to transmit data. A key strength with analog modems is that they can be connected to nearly any telephone jack, at home, in a hotel, or at a pay phone.

Client ISDN Equipment

Digital "modems" allow the transfer of data across switched digital telephone lines, or ISDN. From an operational standpoint, ISDN adapters are available in two form factors: external and internal. The PCMCIA and parallel-port form factors should soon be available on a widespread basis; so far, no manufacturer has announced publicly whether ISDN will be built onto a motherboard.

ISDN for the client side is called ISDN BRI (basic rate interface) and is characterized by the number of channels available: two "B" and one "D," with corresponding speeds of 64 kbps per B channel and 16 kbps per D, for a total of 128 kbps (asynchronous) or 144 kbps (synchronous). Some Internet service providers offer 64 kbps only, but there is an ongoing, rapid transition to 128kbps (and beyond) via the Multilink PPP protocol supported by Microsoft, 3Com, and others.

A key ISDN advantage is that it requires perhaps one second to connect to another ISDN device. A weakness of ISDN is that the service is not widely used, even though the majority of telecom providers' lines in the U.S. are ISDN-ready (ISDN is far more widespread in Europe and Japan). Another weakness of ISDN is the RBOCs' general lack of support for residential and business applications. It is not strongly marketed, and tariffs in different BOC regions vary widely. Ahead of the curve, however, are PacBell and Bell Atlantic.

Client Cable Modems

Cable modems are not widely available for commercial use today on the Internet, though trials exist for these devices. In late 1995, TCI, Comcast, and others have announced their intentions to purchase these devices by the hundreds of thousands. It is anticipated that cable modems will be well-suited for high-bandwidth, multimedia applications; currently, they are being used in trials with a few thousand cable-carrier subscribers in North America. The nominal speeds for two-way, interactive cable systems using cable modems are about 10 mbps (in the downstream direction) — about 78 times faster than an ISDN connection and 350 times faster than a 28.8 kbps modem. Most cable modems being discussed today are of asymmetrical design, meaning the "upstream," or "return path" channel would be considerably less than downstream. Most return paths are around one-tenth the downstream speed.

Server Hardware

Server Computers PCs have been used as file servers for more than a decade. Equipped with a network operating system with IP capabilities, a file server can be made to perform as a communications server to other stations (clients) on the network and allow access to the Internet. Many software programs can enable a PC-based server to properly connect to the Internet; a server, though, must

connect to the network using a NIC. A PC server may have communications functions built into the PC itself, or these functions may be located on another server dedicated to communications. Built-in communications equipment may include modem(s) or DSU/CSUs (to connect to leased lines). Externally connected devices may include routers or bridges.

Workstations can have integrated server and client capabilities, a virtue of the multitasking, multiuser UNIX operating system. Mainframes, on the other hand, and in the context of this report, are considered server devices. For mainframes to communicate on the Internet, they must have application gateways that convert the mainframe communications protocols to TCP/IP, such as an IBM SNA gateway.

Server Communications On the server side of the client/server model, communications are generally characterized as more complex and as having higher bandwidth capacity. In this context, clients connect to the servers and related equipment. The latter includes communications (data networking) equipment, such as modems, ISDN adapters, cable modems, carrier leased lines, hubs, other servers, routers, and bridges. All of the equipment identified in this section is intended for installation at the customer premise location — that is, in the building where the server and most likely the client are located. Clients that do not connect to a network would not need to use the equipment described in this section; rather, they would connect directly to an ISP. (The ISP's equipment, although similar to some of this equipment, is somewhat different.)

On the server side, common options for connecting to the Internet using carrier lines are, in order of increasing cost (assuming four hours of dial-up use per day) and bandwidth:

• Ordinary switched (dial-up) analog telephone lines, up to 28.8–33.6 kbps;

• Switched 56 kbps service, which is similar to ISDN;

• Switched digital telephone lines, which is called ISDN BRI service, up to 128–144 kbps;

• Switched digital telephone lines, which is called ISDN PRI service, when operating at speeds up to 1.5 mbps;

- A 56 kbps leased line, which is an unswitched, permanent, point-to-point telecommunications line that has a connection to the customer premise equipment and to the ISP — it uses either a DSU/CSU/leased-line box, a frame-relay access device, or an ATM switch;

- T-1 and fractional T-1 service, which are leased-line connections, like 56 kbps, but operating at 1.5 mbps and fractions thereof — it uses either a DSU/CSU/leased-line box, a FRAD, or an ATM switch; and

- T-3 service, which is a leased-line connection operating at 45 mbps — there are about 2,000 of these connections in the entire U.S., and they are not very common on the customer premise site. T-3 uses either a DSU/CSU/leased-line box, a FRAD, or an ATM switch.

In addition, cable modems may become available some time in the future.

On the customer premise side of a networked system, modems can be used to connect to an Internet service provider. On the client side, modems come in different form factors than for the server side. Groups, or pools, of modems can be combined and connected to a server using serial cabling, which allows the server to call out to the ISP when a client requests information from the network server. Modems used for this purpose are more full-featured, and typically are the modem manufacturer's top-of-the-line model. These tend to be about double the price of a manufacturer's client-side modem.

Another option is to connect modems to proprietary communications servers (such as the Shiva or U.S. Robotics Communications servers product), separate from the computer-based server. Multiport modem cards (ISA, PCI, or another form factor, such as Xircom's product) may be used to construct devices similar in function to Prosperity communications servers, which are based on PCs. In these cases, the communications server allows clients connected to the network to effect a call to the ISP.

Server ISDN Equipment

At the customer premise, client network side, ISDN equipment is available in all of the modem configurations. ISDN equipment, likewise, calls out to the Internet when a network client makes a request for Internet access.

PRI (primary rate interface) ISDN is occasionally used at the server side, differing from the BRI ISDN used at the client level. PRI ISDN offers 23 B channels and 1 N in the U.S. (30 in Europe and Japan). The sum of these B channels and N add to 1.5 mbps, equivalent to a T-1 leased line. Thus, if many simultaneous outgoing ISDN calls are made, they each consume one or two B channels only, and there is a cost savings if PRI is ordered in lieu of many BRI lines.

Servers, Hubs, Bridges

There are file servers, communication servers, print servers, and terminal servers. In the context of the Internet, servers are network devices that perform a centralized function, rather than having the function of distributing throughout a network or being tied to particular hosts. The term "server" in this context differs somewhat from its meaning in the client/server context. The term "appliance" is used synonymously here with "server" and means a specialized device, or box. Servers in general contain a lot of software to communicate with other networked devices and perform their specific function.

File servers store files, programs, or both. Files may be retrieved from and stored on file servers from clients that are networked with the file server. An example of a file server would be a departmental Novell Netware server that stores many individuals' files. Communications servers are devices that operate with data-communications-related products, such as modems or ISDN communications devices. Communications servers contain considerable software to allow clients connected to the same network to call out, or for various dial-in connections to call in and access the network. Communications servers provide communication-related functions, depending upon the type: These include modem pools, remote-access servers, and asynchronous LAN gateways. Print servers perform the administrative tasks of storing print jobs and spooling them to printers as the printers become available. Terminal servers allow connected devices to view data on other servers. Terminal servers allow the connection of multiple "dumb terminals" to large computer systems.

Network hubs interconnect the wiring that is connected to workstations and are a building block of most networks. There are many types of hubs, categorized by the network architecture and wiring media they support: Ethernet, ARCNET, token ring, FDDI, ATM.

Bridges are used to connect networks together; however, unlike routers, they do not perform data-path optimization. In addition, they are commonly used to connect networks so that the collective network shares the same IP network number (they logically form a single IP network). Bridges

Figure 7.3

Corporate Network Connected to the Internet

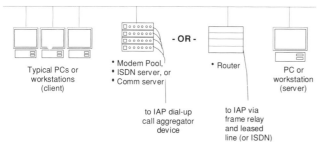

Typical PCs or
workstations
(client)

• Modem Pool,
• ISDN server, or
• Comm server

- OR -

• Router

PC or
workstation
(server)

to IAP dial-up
call aggregator
device

to IAP via
frame relay
and leased
line (or ISDN)

perform forwarding, filtering, and learning functions: In forwarding, data are passed to their destination; in filtering, data are discarded before reaching the final destination; in learning, a bridge receives data from a host but does not have the address of that device in its table, whereupon the table is updated. In general, bridges are used in connecting smaller numbers of similar networks.

The advantages of bridges are that they generally can link networks of different speeds, can be managed easily, and can be adapted during network expansion. Disadvantages are that they can be difficult to troubleshoot, problems can occur with fast protocols because of delay factors, and they can occasionally impede the use of some applications over the Internet, such as when multiple copies of an application are operating and using the same naming or addressing scheme.

Section IV:
Software

Chapter 8: Software

- **Client/browser software** runs on users' PCs/workstations and enables either the retrieval of information or the use of a communications service. Netscape's client/browser software is the market-share leader today in enterprises (for both the Internet and intranets) — Netscape's biggest competitive threat is Microsoft. America Online is the share leader in the consumer market, and its biggest competitive threats are Microsoft and Netscape. Ultimately, the company that controls the front-end software for the Internet (by obtaining the largest number of users) will have a key role in the market for server software and development/authoring tools. Netscape is approaching this goal as a technology company, Microsoft is using a technology/media approach, and America Online is taking a media approach.

- **Server software** enables either dedicated computer resources to store information for retrieval on demand, or enables communications sessions. Today, server software market shares are dominated by such freeware products as NCSA httpd and CERN httpd on the UNIX platform. Emerging competitors include Netscape and Microsoft (for Windows NT).

- New **development/authoring tools** such as Sun's Java, Netscape's LiveWire, Macromedia's ShockWave, Microsoft's Internet Studio (and, if the merger is approved, Vermeer), and Adobe's Acrobat, among others, are emerging to exploit and assist the growth in the Internet. Two classes of products are emerging — one for content creators/authors and one for programmers.

- Opportunities will arise for **back-end process and database** companies, such as Oracle, Informix, Sybase, and Computer Associates, as demands for distributing data and information increase.

- **New applications** that are under development (in "beta") or nearly ready for beta are Java-enabled browsers, VRML (3-D) browsers, intelligent agents, Internet-based telephony (computer-to-computer and, later on, computer-to-telephone), real-time audio playback, real-time video playback, easy-to-use file transfer over e-mail, secure mail, notarized mail, and collaborative-work enabling applications. Much of this (and other) software will increasingly be downloaded by users over the Internet.

- In this chapter we describe four key areas of Internet software development: client/browser software, server software, development/authoring tools, and back-end process and database products. In addition, we detail the Internet strategies of some of the larger, key companies: Netscape, Microsoft, America Online, Sun Microsystems, Adobe, and Macromedia.

- In general, the software area should be one of the most fertile areas of growth for new companies targeting the Internet — we have profiled many of these companies elsewhere in this report.

The market for Internet software has been around for a long time, but it wasn't until the debut of Mosaic that growth and product improvements began to accelerate. The market is developing so rapidly that the browser downloaded just six months ago looks lethargic and short on features. In this dynamic marketplace, though, market share can be misleading. Still, the mind share created in the beginning of such a market is important. It is clear that Netscape developed its dominant position by giving away its software early in the game.

Since the Net's inception, most Internet software has been free. This began to change by the second half of 1994, as Windows-based and easy-to-use graphical programs, especially Web browsers, made it easier for mainstream corporate and consumer users (i.e., non-programmers) to access the resources of the Internet. Freeware or shareware software written by researchers, academics, and hackers has been the driving force behind much of the innovation and progress of the Internet. But this software comes with little or no guarantee that it will work much the same as today's free beta browsers and development tools from leading companies. Worldwide connectivity's appeal and the Internet's consumer reach have forced corporations to use the Internet. In the course of adopting the Internet, however, IT managers at these companies are staking their careers on the software they choose for their corporate users (clients) and for their corporate Internet infrastructure (servers) subsequently, these managers, with increasing frequency, **have begun to develop strategic, paying relationships with vendors**.

It's important to note, too, that many of the capabilities offered by freeware or shareware (or for that matter, for-pay-ware like FTP's and Netmanage's) have been added to the Windows 95 operating system, such as a TCP/IP stack, a Web browser, and an e-mail client. As we have seen before, though, premium utilities and software are now available to enhance or replace operating system utilities or applets.

The **first stage of Internet software development was dominated by text-based, less-interactive applications, geared for power users.** These applications were developed by researchers who **freely distributed** their software over the Internet with permission for others to modify it. There was little perceived business opportunity. Some pioneers made higher-quality Internet applications beginning about the early 1990s, such as FTP Software and Netmanage. These companies made various suite packages for sale, which included TCP/IP stacks and modem dialers, as well as applications for e-mail, FTP, and Gopher.

Traditional IP-stack vendors — Netmanage, FTP Software, and Frontier Technologies — have been caught somewhat off-guard by the adding of the IP stack (and browser, mail, ftp and telnet) into the Windows 95 operating system (and OS2 Warp). Though both sell extremely robust IP stacks, and products that are complementary to the stacks, such as FTP clients, mail clients, browsers and such, these companies have been forced to react, because the primary value they added to customers has been basic functionality, which has recently been added to the O/S. They must now come up with new product lines as well as more fully-featured utilities that are far superior to the basic functionality of the new O/S's. The companies' strategy seems to focus on the corporate customer, and this may be succeeding to a degree. The jury is still out as to whether they can survive the onslaught of Microsoft, Netscape, and AOL, however, especially at the consumer level.

We believe we are in **the second stage of Internet software development** based on the Mosaic WWW browser. These applications were available first for the UNIX X/Windows platform, then Windows 3.1, and then the Macintosh. The mass appeal has been great, and mice clicked in unison worldwide.

Netscape and Spyglass have developed competing browsers, the former a rewrite and the latter an enhanced version of the NCSA Mosaic browser, which has been available since late 1994. In August 1995, Windows 95 included many underlying software utilities required to use Internet client software, such as a TCP/IP stack, winsock.dll (for Windows only), and a PPP dialer. Beginning in late 1994, online service providers (OSPs) began incorporating browsers and the complementing utility software, such as TCP/IP, winsock.dll, and PPP dialers, while Internet service providers (ISPs) gave software away (e.g., Pipeline and Netcruiser) or distributed others' (Netmanage through PSINet).

Table 8.1
Third-Generation Applications Available Today

Technology	Comments
VRML 3D browser	Enables modeling of 3-D space
Java and other cross-platform applications	Runs on more than one operating system
Intelligent Agent	Professional shopper. Remote software installer. Replaces workers.
Internet-based telephony	Internet is becoming more competitive with regular telephony
Real-time audio playback	Internet is becoming more competitive with radio, and at greater distances
Real-time video playback	Internet is becoming more competitive with broadcast TV & at greater distances
MIME-enhanced mailer	Allows transfer of files that are coded and decoded automatically upon sending or receipt
Secure mail applications	Like insured mail
Notarized mail	Like a notarized letter
Collaborative-work enabler	Simultaneously work on documents from remote locations

The **third generation of software** (Table 8.1) is bound to include new features that are highly interactive and easy-to-use, and enable users to perform more useful information-gathering tasks on their machines, as well as others' machines. In beta, or made recently available, in this category are **VRML** (virtual reality modeling language) browsers, **HotJava** (Sun's scripting language application viewer), **intelligent agents** (FTP's utility agent and General Magic and Andersen Consulting's shopping agents), highly integrated systems using the client-server model on the "winsock operating system," and communications applications such as **Internet phone** (like the telephone system), **real-time audio** (like the radio), **and video playback** (like broadcast television), MIME-enhanced mailers, secure mailers (like insured mail), and notary mail (like a notarized letter).

In the context of commercial sales to corporate and consumer markets, client software is that which runs on users' machines and enables them to interact with other host machines (typically servers) and other users (typically clients through the use of servers). **Client software includes browsers, mailers, intelligent agents, phone-software, chat software, and similar applications.** In the same context, **server software is installed on machines permanently connected to the Internet that are used to store, and allow distribution of, data and information to clients.** Server software include the many types of WWW servers (commerce, publishing, communications, and so forth), FTP servers, gopher servers, terminal servers, and IRC servers (as well as phone servers).

Except for a few proprietary or non-SLIP software packages, client computers, in order to run browsers, need several critical utilities programs: 1) winsock.dll (for Windows only), 2) a TCP/IP stack, and a 3) PPP (or SLIP) dialer or LAN protocol drivers. These utilities are usually distributed with client software, such as Netscape's Navigator, or with operating systems like Windows 95 or UNIX.

The following is a discussion of browser software, server software, development/authoring tools, and back-end process and database products.

Browser Software

Browsers are used to access information on the Internet and enterprise intranets. There are hundreds of different Web browsers, with most distributed for free or at very low prices. The dominant commercial browsers on the Internet are from Netscape, Spyglass, America Online, and Microsoft (Table 8.2). By most counts, Netscape has the majority of the Internet browser market, followed by the Spyglass-licensed browsers, such as Spry/CompuServe and Microsoft, and America Online's browser. The browser vendors are vying for market leadership, as the winner may be able to control industry standards in the future. All browsers are descendants of Mosaic, the first graphical Web browser, and thus have similar feature sets. Over time, though, the leaders will diverge in terms of features in their attempts to set standards. For example, many Web pages state that they are "enhanced" for the Netscape browser, meaning they were created to work best with Netscape Navigator. Microsoft is attempting to create the same kind of environment for its browser.

To date, a lot of the browser/server usage has been ad hoc and assisted by the trials of free software. However, as companies are leaving their "trial" phases and entering "deployment," the need for reliable, consistent software is increasing.

Table 8.2
The "Big Four" Web Browsers

Browser	Company	Compatibility	Comments
Netscape Navigator	Netscape	Mac, Win, UNIX	Version 1.1, and now Version 2.0 with Java support, is in our view vastly superior to the software it was intended to compete with, NCSA Mosaic. This is the premium browser today, although others have been developing competitive browsers like version-1.1. It is basically a nonproprietary browser.
Enhanced Mosaic	Spyglass	Mac, Win, UNIX	Spyglass, through a licensing agreement with NCSA/University of Illinois, has enhanced the NCSA Mosaic browser. The browser has not been made available to the public; rather, it is being licensed to companies to be bundled with their software. Licensing companies include: Microsoft, Spry/CompuServe Internet Div., Quarterdeck, Netmanage, Ventana, and many others. It is a nonproprietary browser.
Internet Explorer	Microsoft	Win95	Microsoft's Windows95-compatible browser provides strong competition to the rest of the browsers on the market. Via its relationship with Spyglass, Microsoft has begun to release versions of Internet Explorer for Windows 3.1 and Macintosh.
AOL browser	America Online	Mac, Win	Running on the America Online service, AOL's browser is activated from within the America Online service's proprietary graphical interface while the subscriber is online. The browser has a unique appearance, and is highly tailored to the America Online interface. Its drawbacks are probably overlooked, considering the convenience this browser offers to online service users who want to occasionally access the WWW. America Online also sells the GNN Internet Navigator.

Proprietary Browsers

Several large Internet Service Providers supply their own software to users, which can only be used with the provider's system. For users who don't want the hassle of manually configuring a SLIP or PPP connection, this software can make life easier. There is, however, a trend away from proprietary browsers. Prodigy announced it will support the use of Netscape's browser. Over time, we expect the vendors of proprietary browsers to migrate to industry-standard browsers from the Big Four companies.

Table 8.3
Proprietary Web Browsers

Browser	Company	Compatibility	Comments
AOL browser	America Online	(See previous table)	
Air Mosaic	CompuServe	Win	CompuServe Browser - The CompuServe browser is the Air Mosaic browser, packaged with its PPP dialer, and therefore is not really a proprietary browser. However, the browser and the IP stack and dialer are available for use on the CompuServe network, and available for free download. Unique to CompuServe's Internet offering, however, is that other software, such as the Netscape browser, can replace the Air Mosaic software (after issuing a few DOS commands) and still work on the CompuServe network. CompuServe recently announced that it will include a customized version of Microsoft's Internet Explorer with its products.
Prodigy WB	Prodigy (IBM and Sears)	Win, Mac	Prodigy must be applauded for being the first major online service (1Q95) with a browser offering. The browser allowed online users to gain access to the WWW. Its use is dwarfed, however, by most measurements of browser use on the Internet today by other browsers. This browser is being pushed aside by Prodigy's endorsement of the Netscape browser.
Internaut	Pipeline (PSINet)	Win, Mac	Internaut is the Web-browsing component of Pipeline's tightly integrated suite of Internet programs. The Pipeline offering has Winsock compatibility and, as such, its browser can easily be supplanted by a nonproprietary offering.
NetCruiser	Netcom	Win	In Netcom's suite of Internet tools, the Web browser is easy to use and, in some ways, too simple. It probably has enough features to keep most casual users happy, but don't expect anything fancy. The overall NetCruiser suite is a breeze to work with, although it doesn't have the sort of system integration you'd find with Pipeline's.

Server Software

The following diagram (available at www.compaq.com) outlines the various components that could be used to build an Internet server software system. The diagram focuses on the server platform, network operating system components, and Web components. Usually, many of these functions are spread across multiple servers that are connected to the Internet. However, many of these functions and services can be combined into one server in environments that do not place a significant demand on any one function or Internet service.

Figure 8.1

Components of an Internet Server

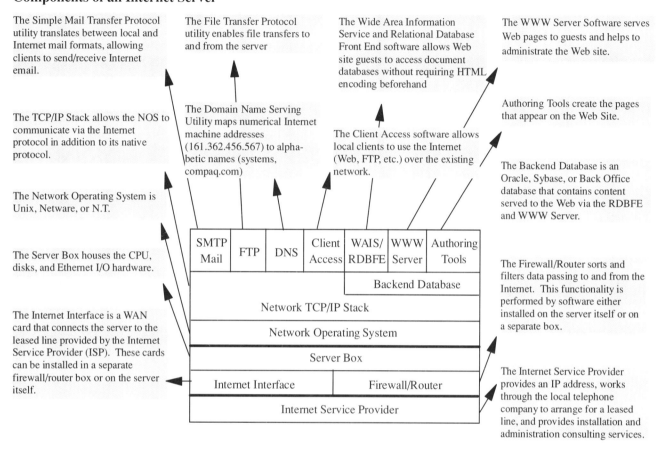

The Simple Mail Transfer Protocol utility translates between local and Internet mail formats, allowing clients to send/receive Internet email.

The File Transfer Protocol utility enables file transfers to and from the server

The Wide Area Information Service and Relational Database Front End software allows Web site guests to access document databases without requiring HTML encoding beforehand

The WWW Server Software serves Web pages to guests and helps to administrate the Web site.

The TCP/IP Stack allows the NOS to communicate via the Internet protocol in addition to its native protocol.

The Domain Name Serving Utility maps numerical Internet machine addresses (161.362.456.567) to alphabetic names (systems, compaq.com)

The Client Access software allows local clients to use the Internet (Web, FTP, etc.) over the existing network.

Authoring Tools create the pages that appear on the Web Site.

The Network Operating System is Unix, Netware, or N.T.

The Backend Database is an Oracle, Sybase, or Back Office database that contains content served to the Web via the RDBFE and WWW Server.

The Server Box houses the CPU, disks, and Ethernet I/O hardware.

The Firewall/Router sorts and filters data passing to and from the Internet. This functionality is performed by software either installed on the server itself or on a separate box.

The Internet Interface is a WAN card that connects the server to the leased line provided by the Internet Service Provider (ISP). These cards can be installed in a separate firewall/router box or on the server itself.

The Internet Service Provider provides an IP address, works through the local telephone company to arrange for a leased line, and provides installation and administration consulting services.

Source: Compaq

Most of the commercial server software applications available for the Internet are Web servers (Table 8.4). Gopher and FTP servers are also available but have considerably less commercial importance, as consumers and corporations will more than likely focus on the Web as a vehicle to exploit the Internet. The CERN and httpd servers are free, the others are not.

Table 8.4
Web Server Software

Server	Company	Comments
Netscape Servers (NetSite)	Netscape	Netscape Communications has four offerings: Netscape Commerce Server, Netscape Communications Server, Netscape News Server, and Netscape Proxy Server. The Commerce Server enables secure commerce to be conducted over global networks with the open Secure Sockets Layer (SSL) protocol for Internet security, using RSA Data Security technology. Communications Server, available for UNIX and Windows NT platforms is high-performance software that enables organizations to publish rich hypermedia information. News Server enables companies to create their own public and private discussion groups for information exchange among employees, customers, or any other audience. Proxy Server provides secure Internet access and dramatically increased network performance for users behind a firewall. Mail Server is a client/server messaging system.
WebSite	O'Reilly & Assoc.	A 32-bit World Wide Web server that combines the power and flexibility of a UNIX server with the ease of use of a Windows application. Its intuitive graphical interface and easy installation make it a natural for Windows users. WebSite provides a tree-like display of all documents and links on a server, with a simple solution for finding broken links. Using CGI, users can run a desktop application like Excel or Visual Basic from within a Web document on WebSite, and its access security lets users control who has access to different parts of their Web server.
Web Server	Open Market	A 32-bit Web server that provides strong competition to the Netscape servers. The Secure Web Server offers simultaneous support for both SSL and S-HTTP. To complement the servers, Open Market has the Open Market WebReporter tool for analyzing Web Server access activity and generating customized reports.
NCSA httpd	NCSA	Available for UNIX systems, NCSA httpd features include server scripts to support forms, indexes, and image maps per directory access control based on user names and passwords or the host of the remote user server side "include" files for dynamic changes to WWW pages. The server is available via anonymous FTP from "ftp.ncsa.uiuc.edu" in the directory "/Web/httpd". This product is free.
Internet Information Server	Microsoft	Pending. This NT-based Web server will support Internet Studio and HTML. The product is expected to ship for free with Windows NT in C1H96.
CERN httpd	CERN	Providing a feature set very similar to the NCSA daemon, the CERN server can be used as a WWW gateway for systems that are behind firewalls. This server is available for UNIX and VMS systems via anonymous FTP from "ftp.w3.org". This product is also free.

There are other Web servers. For Windows 3.1, there are: 1) Windows httpd, 2) WebSite, 3) EMWAC. For Macintosh, there is: MacHTTP/WebSTAR Home Page. For UNIX, there are: 1) Netscape, 2) SafetyWEB, 3) NCSA, 4) CERN HTTP, 5) Apache.

Historically, the dominant TCP/IP server software has been UNIX. Recently, Windows NT has been making inroads in the market, as it's easier to use and runs on less-expensive Intel-based servers. Web server market share estimates are elusive, as they can be estimated only by surveys. A C1Q95 survey conducted by Mirai categorizes market share by operating system, HTTPd server, and CPU (Figures 2–4).

In the survey, Web operating system market share for all servers broke down as follows: UNIX at 69% (with Sun at 31%), which says something about power requirements for Web servers; Macintosh at 17%, which says something about Apple's presence in the publishing/graphics markets; and Windows at 14% (9% Windows and 5% Windows NT), which says something about UNIX and Macintosh. Still, we estimate that Windows NT share is now closer to 10%, and rising.

Web server software market share for all servers broke down as follows: NCSA HTTPD at 46%; Mac HTTPD, 17%; CERN HTTPD, 17%; other, 20%. We estimate that Netscape has been gaining share and is closer to 5–10%.

Our Internet server thesis has two elements: 1) Server growth will accelerate, and 2) Intel/Microsoft will take commodity economics into the enterprise, eventually threatening traditional UNIX server vendors. The need for servers to access both the Internet and host Web pages should translate into continued server strength. For example, about 10% of server sales for Sun and SGI are Internet-related.

The rise of the PC transferred the burden of storage and computation from centralized mainframes to localized desktops. The Internet's explosive development reverses this trend. With the Internet, a client's operating system and hardware setup become less important as content shifts back to server repositories. Harkening back to the days of dumb terminals, there is talk of "thin" clients — stripped down PCs sporting little local storage and just enough computational horsepower to run Internet access software.

Figure 8.2
Web Server Market Share by Operating System

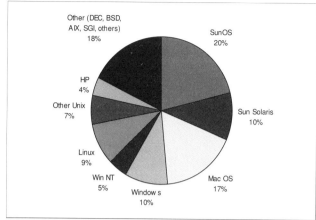

Source: Mirai.com survey, 1/95 to 3/95.

Figure 8.3
Web Server Market Share by CPU

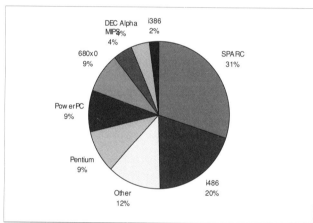

Source: Mirai.com survey, 1/95 to 3/95.

Figure 8.4
Web Server Market Share by HTTPd Server

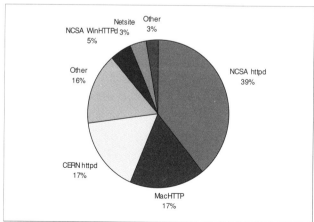

Source: Mirai.com survey, 1/95 to 3/95.

The Internet may represent another fundamental shift, perhaps the embodiment of network computing, following the mainframe, minicomputer, and PC waves. Sun's motto that "the network is the computer" may finally be true. The Internet is also an open architecture, which could threaten the closed architectures championed by Microsoft and Intel.

Finally, the Internet continues the increase in computing complexity. Server vendors such as IBM, Digital, and HP know more about systems and network management than those companies born of the desktop-driven 1980s. The pendulum swing away from a PC-centric world to enterprise computing could improve the outlook for previous PC losers, like IBM and Digital.

Development Tools

Traditionally, the development tool environment for the Web has been dominated by HTML tools, which are used to create hypertext-based Web pages. At the same time, online services have offered platform-specific development systems to their content creators.

As the Web evolves from a text-only format to a more dynamic interactive environment — including images, audio, video, chat, and live hookups to structured and unstructured data — demand increases for more powerful development tools. In addition, Web authors typically have been computer-savvy folks that were unafraid of programming — but this is changing. On one hand, experienced programmers are adopting Sun's high-level Java technology. On the other hand, word-processing amateurs are being called on to become Web authors, and these people need tools that are easy to use.

While the market for new Web development tools will grow rapidly, it should take several years before the winners become apparent. In the short term, it's likely that everyone wins: HTML for the masses; Java for power users; LiveWire for Netscape; RainMan for America Online users; Macromedia ShockWave for publishers; Adobe Acrobat for publishers; Adobe Photoshop for photos; Internet Studio for Windows 95; and so forth. Over time, though, the market should consolidate.

Finally, over the next couple of years, the progress in development tools should outpace the increases in bandwidth — i.e., no matter how cool that Java applet looks, your mother's 14.4 kbps modem will download it like it's molasses.

How to Create a Home Page Using HTML

To have a home page on the Web, one must first have access to a Web server connected to the Internet and then create content in the form of HTML-coded files and upload those files to the server. Once the files are on the server, an Internet user with a browser can visit the Web site and view the HTML files.

A Web server is a computer that runs Web server software and is connected to an ISP using a permanent leased-line connection, so that information stored on it is available for others to access. It is also possible to lease space on someone else's Web server, called Hosting.

Generally, there are three ways to create "content" for a web site:

- manually coding HTML (hypertext markup language) using a text-editor;
- using HTML authoring software (such as Vermeer's FrontPage, Microsoft's Internet Assistant for Word, or an online service offering);
- having HTML code generated automatically coinciding with events, such as breaking news or database updates.

Our observation is that the latter two methods are becoming more popular, as more tools are developed and as the Web becomes a more popular means of communicating information.

Under the first option, the content developer (a new media publisher) uses a simple text editor, as well as a graphics program, to create Web pages in a three-step process: First added is the information to be published, such as the text of a press release. Second, the text is formatted on the page using HTML commands enclosed in angled brackets (for example, <strong> for bold text), which tell the Web browser software to display the text as in a certain way. Third, images may be added to the page by using HTML commands that refer to graphics files located elsewhere on the Web server. Graphics files may be created or modified with many standard computer drawing and painting programs, such as Adobe Illustrator.

The second option is to use an HTML authoring software application that automates the HTML coding process, so that the author doesn't have to deal with HTML code. The author positions the document text and graphics on the screen, then the application generates an HTML-coded file.

The third content-generating option would be to use a system that is developed to automate the generation of HTML-coded files after significant events, such as news events. Custom applications like this have been developed for several well-known Internet web-sites. Most have been developed in-house, and most right now are related to automated updates corresponding to news stories.

Back-end Process and Database Products

The Web will affect every company in the enterprise sector. Development tool vendors will have to decide whether to license Java or wait for Internet Explorer from Microsoft. An early decision could provide a time-to-market advantage or commit a vendor to a dead-end path.

Enterprise application vendors will have to determine how aggressively to re-architect their applications to run across the Web and what tools to use. Most of these vendors have proprietary development tools and will have to decide whether to update them with Java. Also, some application vendors have tied their logic to the interface and will have more difficulty in separating interface code from application logic and database management. The issue in this segment will be execution, just as it was in the rush to client/server: Who can get there first with fully functional product?

The systems management vendors should enjoy new opportunities, since greater complexity and distributed processing give them more things to monitor, manage, schedule, connect, and restore. These vendors will have to rethink management solutions to a new implementation of the traditional functional requirements of systems management.

Finally, the database vendors should profit from the move to Web-based computing. If the Web generates more electronic transactions and commerce, these transactions will drive database usage and deployment.

A new model of pricing will be needed for the database and application vendors, since the current model is user-based. If the number of users is unknown because the users are external to an organization and the firewall, then some new scheme will be needed.

Strategies and Descriptions of Key Companies
With Products for Clients, Servers, and Development Tools

Netscape

Background

Netscape offers a broad line of cross-platform Internet software that enhances the exchange of information and allows users to conduct commerce over the Internet and other TCP/IP-based private intranet networks. We estimate as much as 50% of Netscape's sales are for "commercial" Web use, with the remainder for internal corporate intranets. In C4Q95, 58% of Netscape's sales were derived from browser sales, while server products accounted for 29% of revenue, and services (including consulting, support, and training) represented about 13% of revenue.

While actual usage numbers are difficult to obtain (largely because Netscape traditionally gave away its browser for free to expand its installed base), our research indicates that many companies and individuals (Netscape estimates at least 15 million users) have already standardized on the Netscape browser and are just beginning to pay for the software. We believe that the rollout/deployment of Netscape's browser software may be ramping more quickly than that of any previous software product. At this juncture in the development of its core markets, Netscape is in a potential standard-setting position.

Netscape's four product lines are as follows: the Netscape Navigator client/browser (a graphical network navigator); the Netscape server line (for setting up and maintaining servers for publishing data and conducting commerce); Netscape development tools (allow users to create, manage, and assemble entire online application systems); and Netscape Internet applications (turnkey software that enables electronic commerce).

Products

Browsers — The Netscape Navigator browser software products, available for Windows, Macintosh, and UNIX, provide access to Internet/intranet resources. The Navigator family includes: Navigator (for users on enterprise networks or with an Internet connection); Navigator Personal Edition (for home or small-office users requiring simple Internet access); Navigator Gold (with other features for creating, editing, and navigating live documents online);

and Netscape Power Pack (a set of add-on applications for Navigator, including SmartMarks, Chat, Acrobat Reader, QuickTime, and RealAudio Player). An upgraded version of Navigator, 2.0, shipped in C1Q96 and includes enhanced performance, integrated e-mail and newsgroups, increased security, editing tools, in-line plug-ins, support for Java applets, and Netscape scripting language. Significant enterprise users of Netscape's browser (for use on intranets and the Internet) include General Electric, Hewlett-Packard, Bank of America, Wells Fargo, AMD, Rockwell, the U.S. Postal Service, and JC Penney.

In addition, in C4Q95, Netscape acquired Collabra Software. That company's core product, Collabra Share, is a groupware product that features user collaboration and messaging capabilities. While Collabra Share will remain a stand-alone product, Netscape has begun to integrate some of the product features into Navigator.

In 1Q95, Netscape announced its intention to acquire In-Soft, a network-based communications/enterprise multimedia software firm, for 1.96 million NSCP shares. NSCP said that, over time, it would use InSoft's technology (specifically, Communique for desktop collaboration and video conferencing; Network Television — or INTV — for distributed digital video; and CoolTalk and CoolView for Internet audio, video, and data communications on Windows, Windows 95, and UNIX-based platforms) to create the framework for Netscape's LiveMedia, which will bring real-time audio-video to NSCP's platform. NSCP plans to make the LiveMedia framework a standard component in future NSCP clients, servers, and tools, and will provide users with easier access to new Internet applications, such as audio/video-on-demand, real-time video conferencing, and Internet telephony. LiveMedia's framework will be based on the Internet Realtime Transport Protocol (RTP), as well as other open audio/video standards, including MPEG, H.261, and GSM. In the short term, we expect NSCP to include standard features such as streaming audio, video, and Internet telephony in a browser to be shipped before year-end. InSoft had estimated software revenue near $5 million in C1995 and a $2 million loss. The deal will likely be dilutive by about 10%. In February, 1996, NSCP announced its intention to acquire Paper Software, a developer of 2-D and 3-D user interface technology.

Servers — The Netscape server software line comprises four products: 1) Netscape Communications Server for UNIX and Windows NT, which is designed for publishing HTML-based hypermedia documents and information; 2) Netscape Commerce Server, which offers the Communications Server features plus SSL open protocol for conducting secure electronic commerce; 3) Netscape News Server, which enables the creation of secure forums and discussion groups for confidential or proprietary information exchange; 4) Netscape Proxy Server, which provides increased performance and secure Internet access for corporate users behind firewalls; and 5) Netscape Mail Server, which is a client-server messaging system. Users of Netscape server software include AT&T, Electronic Arts, Eli Lilly, McDonnell Douglas, Mobil, National Semiconductor, and Silicon Graphics.

Integrated Applications — Netscape's Internet applications are turnkey, high-end software solutions targeted at business that create sophisticated online services and large-scale businesses on the Internet by integrating high-volume transaction processing, real-time data management, and secure communications. The product line includes: 1) Netscape Merchant System, which allows users, such as mail-order catalogers, online mall operators, and retailers, to market and sell products — for example, MCI uses the Merchant System for its marketplaceMCI Web site; 2) Netscape Community Systems, which allows users to create bulletin boards, Usenet news, online chat, and electronic mail — e.g., The Discovery Channel uses Community System for its Web site; 3) Netscape Publishing System, which allows users to distribute publications, services, and information — SportsLine USA uses Publishing System for its site; and 4) Netscape IStore, which is targeted at small-business owner (SOHO market) and is an entry-level merchant product — MacZone uses IStore for its Web site.

Development/Authoring Tools — Netscape is aggressively launching its Internet/intranet development and authoring tools called LiveWire. LiveWire components include Site Manager (a Web site management tool that allows drag-and-drop control of Web pages, links, and targets). LiveWire and LiveWire Pro allow developers to create live online applications that combine multimedia content with application logic and database connectivity. The applications allow the use of most key multimedia datatypes, such as Adobe Acrobat files, Macromedia Director/ShockWave movies, VRML, and SGML documents. They also incorporate Java and JavaScript applets and provide connections to SQL databases.

General Comments

In our opinion, Netscape's strengths include:

• some of the best software developers in Internet-land;

• 15 million, or more, browser users (most of whom are in corporations that are in various stages of deploying the browser company-wide), with a 65%+ share of the browser market;

• shipping/stable software products across product lines (browsers and servers) and key computing platforms (Windows, Macintosh, UNIX) — the average corporation, with a heterogeneous computing environment, needs products for all three platforms (Microsoft's strategy is largely Windows 95/NT based, and while these products have lots of momentum, for now they have less than 10% shares in their respective client/server markets);

• market-leading, first-to-market products — the reviews continue to favor Netscape's browser over Microsoft's (the latter's server products aren't shipping yet, so it's too early to tell in that area);

• relatively low-priced products — as Intuit has demonstrated repeatedly, sub-$40 price points (where Netscape's browser falls), aren't terribly invasive for customers that want products and support that are "mission-critical";

• mind share, plus Netscape's home page, which continues to be one of the most-visited sites on the Net; and

• great revenue momentum — Netscape's first-year revenues (C1995) exceeded $80 million, which made Netscape one of the fastest-growing software companies in history, based on first-year revenue growth.

We believe Netscape's weaknesses include:

• a financial/business model with very little history;

• emerging product and price competition from Microsoft; and

• a stock price that may have lost its momentum, and a lock-up that ends in February, 1996.

Microsoft

Microsoft revealed its latest Internet plans at a full-day "Internet Strategy Workshop" on Thursday, December 7, in Seattle. The strategy clearly is aimed at Netscape and, to a lesser degree, America Online. It should be an interesting couple of years — it's been a while since Bill Gates and crew had serious, pending, rapidly growing competition (in what should be a huge market) to get jazzed up about. (A transcript of Gates's keynote presentation is available at www.microsoft.com.)

The event basically went as expected, but with a few twists:

- Microsoft announced plans to ship the **final version of Internet Explorer for Windows 3.1 in C1Q96** — this represents an attempt to target the 15 million or more users of Netscape's Navigator (who are mostly Windows 3.1 users). Internet Explorer will be free via Net downloads and other means. Someday, Microsoft will ship Internet Explorer for the Macintosh, but we don't think the company plans to ship a browser for UNIX — Microsoft has offloaded these efforts to Spyglass.

- Microsoft intends to **license Sun's Java Runtime for playing Java applets in a future release of Internet Explorer** (our best estimate for integrated final shipment is C3Q96) — this is a move to appease potential Java developers and an attempt to more closely match the features of Netscape's Navigator browser. In addition, in what could be a "head fake" move, this licensing allows Microsoft access to Java developers, which it then can attempt to attract to Microsoft's own development tools.

- Microsoft will **cross-license technology with Oracle** to deliver standard scripting and programming features in their respective Internet software products. Oracle will license Visual Basic Script from Microsoft and include it in its PowerBrowser Web products, and Microsoft will license PowerBrowser OCX and distribute it to third-party developers. For now, in our opinion, this relationship is largely symbolic;

- Microsoft spent a lot of time talking about *free* **browsers and server software** — no doubt, the company's products will likely benefit from this airtime. We wonder if the Department of Justice will take notice . . . it's a tricky situation. Interestingly, the history of free software versus entrenched competition is in favor of entrenched competition; however, the history of "free" software bundled in the operating system, versus entrenched competition, favors the operating system. In the Internet space, over time, Microsoft's operating system dominance (combined with the its software expertise) should give the company a very large competitive advantage.

In short, Microsoft is clearly taking the Internet very seriously (it's mimicking parts of Netscape's strategy and is adopting Internet industry standards such as HTML extensions and SSL security), and while most of the company's products are in beta test, they will likely ship in C1996. Microsoft's entry into this market will likely accelerate the growth in Internet adoption. Microsoft's challenge will be to slow down Netscape's heady momentum in the enterprise.

Regarding **Netscape,** while the entry of Microsoft (with "free" products) into Netscape's core markets is a scary concept (as it should be), in our opinion Netscape has a lot going for it (still, the company must move quickly to gain a better position before Microsoft enters the market full-scale some time in late C1996). **Time will tell if Netscape vs. Microsoft is David vs. Goliath, or David vs. Big David.**

General Overview of Microsoft and the Internet

Microsoft was late to the Internet market (especially with Windows 3.1, UNIX, or Macintosh products — lots of stuff still in beta stage). There are millions of browsers in use and millions of Web pages have been created using HTML (a format that Microsoft will try to augment and ultimately bypass) without the use of Microsoft products. And the winners in the Internet space may well be the companies that gain critical mass early (we believe that we will know within one year if Netscape has critical mass in the browser and server markets).

No doubt, Microsoft, as it has done for stand-alone PCs, would like to control the standards for online services and Internet software (including the browser, the development tools, and the server — and there are lots of synergies in controlling all three of these software products). Microsoft will aggressively attempt to leverage its positioning/pricing flexibility with Windows 95, with PC OEM operating system bundles, and acceptance of Windows NT/servers to pull out yet another come-from-behind victory for the company. Been there, done that.

The big-picture view is that Microsoft's biggest asset is its software expertise. On a lower level, on one hand, Windows 95 is Microsoft's biggest asset/Trojan horse, because its Internet products currently are maximized for the platform, and Microsoft can, and will, bundle lots of stuff with the operating system that it owns. **(Microsoft would love nothing more than for MSN/Internet Explorer just to seep into your life the way Windows 3.1 and Office did).** On the other hand, Windows 95 is Microsoft's biggest liability, because it's not yet widely deployed (especially within corporations, where Netscape-based intranets are expanding like crazy) — however, we have little doubt that Windows 95 (in standard Windows or Windows NT flavor) will become the standard desktop PC operating system over the next few years. Another thing working against Microsoft is that the company wants to control the Internet, yet lots of companies would prefer that the Internet remain as open and uncontrolled as possible.

In short, though, the proliferation of Internet users has just begun. We estimate that there are at least 10 million Web users on a base of 150 million PC users — the Fat Lady hasn't even begun to open her mouth. Thus, it would be crazy to count Microsoft out of the game. Its competitors certainly aren't.

In the long run, we believe that major networks and companies will be created that capitalize on the growth of the Web — the growth in interactive capabilities and the power of the Web leave little doubt about this, in our opinion. **No company brings as many resources or links to the opportunity as Microsoft does — e.g., an operating system, e-mail, an online service, an Internet browser, Internet authoring/development tools, online/Internet server software, content, investments and strategic relationships, and, simply, power and brand-name recognition.**

So What About Microsoft and the Internet?

"What it is, what it was, what it shall be." If Walter Cronkite's words were a question applied to Microsoft's Internet strategy, the answer would be different every time. (For example, per its white papers on its Web page, Microsoft's Web authoring tool strategy has changed four times in the last six months.)

The growth in the Internet has kind of taken Microsoft by surprise, and the company's competitors are praying that the Internet will define the demise of Microsoft's near monopoly in the software business. Oracle is shouting about Internet x-terminals *uber alles;* Sun Microsystems is hoping that its Java programming language will become the development tool of choice for the Net; America Online is rapidly bringing Americans online; Netscape appears to be developing critical mass in the Internet browser and server software market; and Internet start-ups are popping up like flowers in spring. And in the view of most of these companies, they have a universal enemy — Microsoft, even though the company is hardly in their markets. Yet.

The factors in Microsoft's favor are many:

- Microsoft owns the PC operating system (a 90%+ share), with Windows in one form or another (3.1, 95, NT);

- Microsoft is gaining share in server operating systems (and the enterprise) with Windows NT;

- Microsoft has leadership in development tools (with Visual Basic and C++);

- Microsoft has clear (75%+) market share leadership in PC applications software with Office and its components;

- Microsoft has leading consumer software products (including Flight Simulator, Works/Bookshelf, Encarta, Automap Streets, Publisher, Magic School Bus) and has the ability, with its cash position, to own lots of content (it already has baseball, basketball, wines, foods, animals, film, photos, and so on);

- Microsoft has MSN and Internet Explorer (an online service and Internet browser);

- Microsoft has 18,000-plus employees and something like 4,000 software developers;

- Microsoft has the highest name-brand recognition in the computer industry;

- Microsoft had $6 billion in fiscal 1995 (June) revenue, a $1 billion-plus annual R&D budget, and a 25% net margin, and ended C4Q with $6 billion in cash;

- Microsoft has an only 40-year-old Bill Gates; and

- Microsoft has the goods associated with being a software company for 20 years.

Microsoft's Internet Chronology/Facts

Microsoft has dubbed its Internet strategy "Embrace and extend" — meaning that every product the company offers will be maximized for use with the Internet and that the operating system will become a front-end to the Internet.

Windows 95

Whatever you may think about Windows 95, it's a great operating system if you give it the power it needs — and it's far easier to use than Windows 3.1 for those interested in communicating via a PC. Installing new modems is a snap, as is installing new software. And in anticipation of the growth in the Internet, Microsoft integrated TCP/IP drivers and stacks plus dial-up networking protocols (PPP/SLIP).

E-Mail

Microsoft has been in the e-mail business for quite some time, but it has really ramped up its efforts recently with its universal e-mail client in Windows 95 and its Microsoft Mail Server for centralized management of large e-mail networks.

For now, Microsoft's competitors in this area are Lotus cc:Mail/Notes, Netscape (version 2.0, which shipped in February, includes e-mail, and the next version, to ship in C3Q/C4Q, will offer more groupware functions from Collabra), and the e-mail functionality built into the online services. For years, Microsoft has had a very difficult time unseating Lotus's cc:Mail and Notes products in the enterprise. We believe that it may prove equally difficult for Microsoft to unseat Netscape's browser base in the enterprise intranet markets.

Online Service

Microsoft entered the online service space by bundling *MSN* with Windows 95 in August, 1995. The bundle provides Microsoft with a huge marketing and cost savings advantage versus its competitors (the Department of Justice has clearly taken note of this). In mid-C1995, when Microsoft realized how rapidly the Internet was ramping up, it began to expand MSN's feature set to include Internet hooks and routing (Microsoft is now calling MSN an

"Internet online service," and the company is trying to become more of an Internet front-end/assistant than a traditional online service).

While MSN has some nice technical features, the product is generally slow (improvements are promised) and is a bit me-tooish in relation to America Online. In addition, while the graphics look good, the system lacks the activity and captivation level found in the more seasoned America Online service. MSN membership (at an estimated 600,000 users as of 12/7/95) is impressive for three months' of effort, but it's well below America Online's lifetime effort of 5 million users (note that AOL added 500,000 subscribers in January and is doing just fine). While Microsoft has shipped more than 15 million copies of Win95 (with about 6 million at retail), Windows 3.1 should continue to be the dominant PC operating system for the installed base of 150 million Windows users for the next few years, and MSN works only with Windows 95, not Windows 3.1. This gives competitive online services that have Windows 3.1 products a near-term (note, near-term) market advantage.

Additionally, Microsoft has a Web page that focuses solely on MSN and the Internet (http://www.msn.com); this site does an excellent job of aggregating such Internet tools and information as search engines, cool sites, and reference material. Microsoft is attempting to make MSN access available for both Internet and online users, thereby creating a hot site and boosting recognition for its MSN brand.

Ultimately, Microsoft wants to own a "front-end" to the Internet (via MSN, its home page, or Internet Explorer) with which it will be able to generate advertising and transaction revenue — for example, if Microsoft is able to create a "hot" Web site, then advertisers would be willing to pay to get exposure at the site (similar to traditional advertising schemes in television and print media). Further, Microsoft potentially could get a cut of transactions that are routed through its front-end. In addition to offering MSN via Windows 95 and the Web, Microsoft plans to offer the service through multiple Internet service providers by using à la carte or menu groupings (like NBC, Star Trek, Microsoft News, and Microsoft MSN) — similar to the tiered pricing structures offered by cable-TV providers.

Finally, Microsoft, through its *Virtual Worlds Group,* has just begun testing shipment of an avatar-based 2-D/3-D chat service for MSN.

For now, Microsoft's competition is America Online, CompuServe, and the Internet.

Internet Browser

Microsoft included its enhanced Spyglass Web browser, called *Internet Explorer,* with its Plus Pack software for Windows 95. The browser can also be downloaded for free (and it will remain free) from Microsoft's home page on the Web. And, if possible, Microsoft will bundle Internet Explorer with Windows. The Internet Explorer connects users to the Internet via MSN and takes advantage of Windows 95 features such as Shortcuts, Drag and Drop, OLE, Favorites, and the use of the right mouse button. Like MSN, Internet Explorer is easy to use with Win95.

Internet Explorer 2.0 shipped in late November. Final features include 32-bit code; new HTML Extensions, such as marquees, font specifications, table colors, watermarks, and background sounds; improved multi-threading and progressive rendering; support for all standard Internet HTML tags, such as right align, centering, and tables; and support for VRML. Most competitive comparisons between Internet Explorer 2.0 and Netscape Navigator 2.0 favor Navigator for its speed/performance; integration of e-mail, news posting, and Web browsing; user interface; and plug-in capability.

For now, Microsoft's competition in the browser arena is Netscape. While Netscape is ahead on features, Microsoft is narrowing the gap. Netscape's key advantages include: installed base (in excess of 15 million); an early market lead; and cross-platform efforts, especially in the enterprise. A recent Dataquest survey of 100 information technology decision-makers from medium-size to large organizations in the U.S. found that all departments within 60% of the organizations had access to the Internet. At the same time, it is estimated that Netscape has at least 65% of the Web browser market; subsequently, the company could already have critical mass — we expect to know for sure within a year.

Online/Internet Authoring/Development Tools

Microsoft's authoring tool for MSN, code-named Blackbird/MSN, entered beta test in July 1995 — until January, Microsoft intended to broaden the focus of Blackbird, so that it would become an Internet (not just MSN) authoring tool. Beta testing of Blackbird/Internet (now called Internet

Studio) was expected to begin in C1Q96, with the final product to ship later in the year. But with the announcement of its intent to purchase Vermeer, creator of the FrontPage web authoring software, Microsoft has shelved these plans. Now, it appears that Microsoft has changed its online/Internet authoring tool strategy for the fourth time in six months. According to the company, Microsoft will focus on two development tools (based on HTML) for the Internet: 1) Internet Studio (formerly Blackbird), in development by Microsoft, for high-end commercial publishers and professional developers that want to create sophisticated interactive Web applications; and 2) Vermeer's FrontPage, which will be a complementary product to Microsoft office and will target lower-end users, making basic Web document publishing and site management easy for people who are not full-time Web publishing professionals.

Vermeer's FrontPage is shipping and is a solid product. Internet Studio is not shipping yet. Note that it appears that the Department of Justice is taking a close look at Microsoft's proposed merger with Vermeer.

While Microsoft had previously targeted proprietary technologies for its online/Internet strategies, the company, by more fully embracing HTML, is focusing more on industry standards. Time will tell if the strategy changes again.

In late C1996, Microsoft intends to include *Visual Basic,* called *VBScript,* as the scripting language for Internet Studio (Microsoft claims that there are 5 million developers using Visual Basic). Microsoft is hoping to establish OLE custom controls (OCXs) as alternatives to Sun's Java applets — both would execute Internet client functions (Java betas already do), like incorporating real-time information updates for Web pages.

Like Netscape, Microsoft has bundling "plug-in" deals for Internet Studio with providers of various multimedia players, including Adobe (Acrobat ".PDF" format), Macromedia (Director), and Caligari (VRML editing). Microsoft recently announced that it will license Sun's Java Runtime for Internet Explorer. In addition, in an effort to become a standard-setter for 3-D on the Web, Microsoft proposed a new standard for VRML, called ActiveVRML.

In addition, Microsoft's latest versions of Word have plug-in code (called Internet Assistant for Microsoft Word, licensed from America Online's Booklink unit) that allow users to easily convert Word documents to HTML format for the Web. In addition, Microsoft is offering a Microsoft Word Viewer for free that will allow users to read Microsoft Word documents on the Web without having Word installed on their PCs. And in C1Q96, Microsoft plans to offer a feature in its browser called DocObjects, which could allow a user accessing an enabled Web page, for example, to access financial information and, via the browser, access his or her copy of Excel to manipulate the data.

Finally, Microsoft is in the process of making all of its applications software products "Net-aware," allowing users to launch into the Internet/intranet while in an application and then easily find and integrate Net information into the application. Microsoft knows that the majority of content creators for the Web are not programmers, and the company will attempt to target these folks with tools that are easy to use. Note that there are more than 10 million users of Microsoft Office.

For now, Microsoft's competition is Netscape, America Online, Sun Microsystems, Adobe, Macromedia, and lots of small start-up companies.

Internet/Online Server Software

In C1H96, Microsoft plans to ship a commercial low-price Web server product, called Internet Information Server (formerly code-named Gibraltar), for free as a part of Windows NT Server — the product, a part of the BackOffice product line, entered beta test in November 1995. Internet Information Server, based on Windows NT, is intended to be maximized when the Microsoft web-authoring tools are used for creating content and when the content is viewed using Microsoft's Internet Explorer browser. In addition, in C1996, Microsoft plans to release a server security product called *Catapult*, plus media, proxy, and merchant servers.

For now, Microsoft's competition in this area is Netscape, OpenMarket, NCSA httpd, CERN httpd, MacHTTP, and, simply, UNIX and Apple Macintosh hardware, which together dominate the hardware in the server space.

Content

With its wide breadth of consumer *CD-ROM titles,* which focus on themes such as encyclopedias, baseball, film, music and wine, Microsoft has created a beachhead of useful content for its online/publishing efforts. Over time, expect to see more of this CD-ROM content appear on the Web — for example, observe what Microsoft has done with its encyclopedia product (first a book, then a CD-ROM, then online). Microsoft's new Windows 95 CD-ROM products are extremely easy to use. For example, to use Microsoft's Music Central 96, you simply put the CD-ROM in your CD-ROM drive and it auto-installs. If you have a modem, it can auto register you via MSN, and you have the option of receiving monthly music updates via MSN or via the Internet to stay current with new music releases. Like others, Microsoft wants home PC users to increase their Internet bandwidth (moving up from 14.4 kbps modems, to 28.8 kbps and ISDN and cable modems) before it can really send this stuff (and offer really-cool multi-player games) over the Internet. And over time, the content will become NBC News...

Investments/Strategic Relationships

Microsoft has a number of investments/strategic relationships that may benefit its Internet efforts over time: *SoftImage* (MSFT purchased this imaging software company); *Rendermorphics* (purchased this creator of a 3-D rendering engine); *Mobile Telecommunications Technology* (invested in this paging company); *DreamWorks* (invested in this upcoming Hollywood studio); *UUNET* (owns 13% of this Internet service provider, which is the non-exclusive builder of MSN's online/Internet connectivity); *Individual* (invested in this Internet-based news/content aggregator); *Automap* (purchased this mapping software company); *Stac Electronics* (invested in this compression software company); *Netwise* (database connectivity); *Citrix* (Windows NT-based products); *Wang* (imaging, workflow, and service); *Digital Equipment* (has a strategic relationship regarding deployment of enterprise computing systems); *TeleCommunications, Inc.* (collaborating on MSN, with TCI purchasing a 20% stake in MSN); *VISA International* (collaborating on developing protocols for conducting credit card transactions on the Internet); and NBC (collaborating on developing Internet/online products, set-top box products, and a 24-hour all-news cable-TV channel called MSNBC). And, as previously indicated, Microsoft recently announced its intention to buy Vermeer (a Web authoring tool company).

As evinced by its failed attempt to acquire Intuit, Microsoft will continue to use its clout (and $5 billion in cash) to expand its relationships and franchise. We find it noteworthy that *Michael Kinsley* (the former editor of "The New Republic" and co-host of CNN's "Crossfire") has joined Microsoft to produce an electronic magazine for Microsoft.

Microsoft's hiring of a top-notch journalist for the appropriately named "Microsoft Network" is a sign of things to come, in our view.

America Online

America Online is the mother of all consumer online services. The company was created ten years ago as a "new media" company — well before anyone knew what that term meant. With more than 5 million members/subscribers, America Online is the largest U.S. consumer online service and has just begun its international expansion efforts. The fundamental tenet for the company since Day One has been the importance of providing an easy-to-use online service to consumers. The company consistently focuses on offering great content, context, community, commerce, connectivity, at a low cost — in short, AOL is a product even your mom can use. America Online offers its members a broad range of features, such as e-mail, online conferences, entertainment, software, computing support, an extensive "newsstand" of electronic magazines and newspapers, access to the Internet, and original and informative programming and content.

AOL presents its online information in "channel" style; within each channel are lots of programs. For example, programs in the personal finance channel include Motley Fool (the coolest interactive stock area, in our opinion) and Company Research (offering brief stock research reports and First Call earnings estimates). In the news channel, there are options to search news stories or set up a targeted news profile (which sends news stories to a subscriber's AOL e-mail address — how 'bout that little news agent that sends current news stories on one's competitors!). Other channels are Today's News, Personal Finance, Clubs & Interests, Computing, Travel, Marketplace, People Connection (Chat), Newsstand, Entertainment, Education, Reference Desk, Internet Connection, Sports, and Kids Only. We see AOL as one big consumer-oriented programming interface for the online/Internet world — in our opinion, America Online does a better job of programming than any other company, by a long shot.

There are more than 350 companies that provide content or services on America Online's channels. A sizable number of AOL's subscribers have contributed stuff in chat forums and interactive services. In addition, in our view, the company has done a great job of integrating the offerings of Internet Web pages into its channels. Some of America Online's key content/marketing partnerships with traditional companies include: Warner Brothers, New Line Cinema (a 50/50 venture in The Hub program for young adults), *The New York Times,* Viacom (MTV, VH1, and Nickelodeon), American Express, Intuit, Bertelsmann, Hachette, Capital Cities/ABC (a 50/50 venture in interactive fashion and lifestyle programming), Time Inc. (a 50/50 venture in health and fitness), and Simon & Schuster. America Online's key content/marketing/investment relationships with new, emerging companies include: The Motley Fool (investment/stock program), NetNoir (afrocentic culture program), and iGOLF (golf program).

While there have been fears that the rapid ramp of the Internet (plus Microsoft's MSN efforts) would cause mass defections of publishers from AOL, the service actually has seen a resurgence of interest from publishers. The reasons are simple:

- More than 5 million users excites almost any provider of anything.

- Making money on the Internet for publishers is not easy — having a Web page doesn't mean anyone will visit it, or that it will generate revenue (as a data point, 600 of the top print publications that offer information on the Web generate more than 20,000 new articles per day, which is a lot of stuff to find or filter). If America Online can route its users to the best stuff, then those providers can make money via royalty payments from AOL.

- Microsoft/MSN/Blackbird hasn't lived up to publishers' expectations.

America Online has focused on aggressively building its subscriber base by freely giving away its access software on new PCs and modems, aggressively mailing it to slews of mailing lists, and co-marketing with groups and organizations. The company's view has been that the online medium, given the low penetration among PC users, has the potential for significant growth — and that building a subscriber base (or critical mass) early on would provide the potential for significant cash flow (from subscriber fees, advertising, and transactions) as the business began to stabilize and mature. At 5 million users (and 110% year-over-year net new subscriber growth in C4Q), we believe the company is getting closer to harvest time — we estimate that AOL may have 9 million subscribers by C4Q96 (at $17 in revenue per subscriber per month, that implies a $1.8 billion annual revenue run rate). The good news about America Online's business is that it is an annuity/subscription business; the larger the subscriber numbers, the more likely it is that advertisers and content providers will want to participate in the service, which should enhance AOL's revenue and profits.

As the lines separating the Internet, multimedia, and online began to blur, America Online, in order to increase its flexibility in a changing market, has made a slew of acquisitions (to the tune of $255 million, largely in AMER stock), such as: Redgate Communications in August 1994 (2Market/shopping catalogs); BookLink Technologies, December 1994 (Web browser); NaviSoft, December 1994 (high-end publishing and development tools); Advanced Network & Services (ANS), January 1995 (commercial Internet service provider); Wide Area Information Servers (WAIS), May 1995 (Internet search engine); Medior, May 1995 (multimedia product studio); Global Network Navigator (GNN), June 1995 (Web information service); Ubique Ltd., September 1995 (real-time Internet interaction and joint navigation); and Johnson-Grace, February 1996 (data compression technologies).

America Online is many things:

It is   a consumer online services company (AOL);

It is   an Internet company (AOL-embedded and stand-alone GNN offerings);

It is   an online/Internet service provider (through ownership of ANS, which provides a network connection for AOL and the Internet);

It is   content aggregation/programming company (or new media publishing company), via its relationship with content providers/partners;

It is   a venture capital holding company (through its $6 million-plus in investments in 20, and rising, "Greenhouse" companies);

It is   a development/authoring tool company (with its Rainman product line for creating AOL content);

It is   a proprietor of 5 million-plus sets of online "eyeballs," which can provide lucrative advertising and transactions businesses;

It is   an awesome brand name . . .

The company's business strategy gives it lots of flexibility in a rapidly changing market environment. So let's look at investors' biggest concerns about America Online, and offer a response to each issue:

• Issue: negative cash flow. Argument: 5 million-plus subscribers, combined with emerging revenue opportunities from advertising and transactions, plus structural critical mass, should allow America Online to become cash-flow positive in C1996/C1997.

• Issue: the open Internet will make proprietary systems like America Online obsolete. Argument: as long as the average consumer doesn't have ISDN and T-1 connections to the home, using America Online will remain a much more pleasurable experience, simply because of the relative speed of the service. In addition, we believe that AOL is well positioned as a great editor/aggregator/programmer of the volumes of stuff on the Internet — we think America Online is the interactive equivalent of *USA Today*.

• Issue: Microsoft will make America Online obsolete. Argument: Microsoft is a technology company, while America Online is a media company. Online is about entertainment and information-gathering, not technology. While Microsoft has a huge advantage in the online/Internet world, due largely to its ability to bundle or link its products with Windows, the company still has a Windows 95 strategy, and most consumers won't have Win 95 for a couple of years. Meanwhile, the Department of Justice continues to monitor Microsoft's business practices.

We suggest that America Online doomsayers ponder the following estimated worst-case business scenario for the company. The Internet totally unseats the online companies when America Online has something north of 10 million subscribers. America Online converts these customers to standardized Internet access (via Netscape Navigator or

Microsoft Explorer) on its AOLnet backbone. AOL continues to provide content aggregation and programming, continues to collect advertising and transaction fees, and takes a handful of its new media Greenhouse investments public (America Online's talent scouts are funding some, in our opinion, very interesting interactive media start-ups that could be the next MTV or *Rolling Stone* magazine). This scenario is a different business model than the one America Online has today, but it's not a bad one.

The America Online service is deployed in over 750 U.S. cities, representing potential access to 90% of all domestic households. The company's AOLnet offers higher access speeds (28.8 kbps and ISDN-capable) in over 250 cities, and is scheduled to be in 400 cities by spring 1996.

America Online is expanding its efforts overseas and has entered into a substantial joint venture with Bertelsmann AG, Deutsche Telekom, and Axel Springer to offer online services in Europe — AOL Germany launched in November. The combination of publishers (Bertelsmann has more than 40 million members in its book and music clubs), a telco, and America Online looks like a nice way to enter a new market, in our view.

Bottom line, we think America Online is very well positioned to continue to lead the evolution of the online/Internet markets for consumers. When we first looked at Quantum Computer Systems (America Online's former name) as an investment idea in 1989, we thought the entrenched leaders at the time — Prodigy and CompuServe — would toast America Online. We learned a lot over the next couple of years. Steve Case and his team have been key catalysts in this market — 5 million or more users, up from 500,000 in C4Q93!

In summary, America Online has the customers, the programming, the pipes, the leading market share, and the mind share in a rapidly expanding market. Just think back to the rollouts of broadcast TV and cable TV.

Sun Microsystems

Sun, maker of the leading Internet server and popularizer of the concept, "The Network is the Computer," has been developing over the course of nearly five years a programming language called Java. The Java programming language environment (version 1.0) first became available on January 23, 1996, via download from Sun's Web site. Java marries Web browser technology and a programming language to extend Web functionality. It promises to enable the transfer and execution of interactive executables called "applets" from a Web server to a client, regardless of the type of computer or its configuration. For instance, a Java program retrieved from a Web server would execute on a Windows client exactly as it would on a UNIX client.

Corporate programmers may realize the efficiency of programming in Java due to its capability to run on computes in heterogeneous environments. A company's intranet could enjoy cost savings and shorter development times by writing code in Java. A typical Java application might consist of a front end to an Oracle database distributed to Windows, UNIX, and Macintosh clients. Moreover, Java would facilitate software management, the installation of bug patches, and version updates. Managers could use Java apps to monitor how people in an organization work with software. MIS professionals could thus determine software utilization and manage their efforts accordingly.

The Interaction of the Browser and Java

Netscape's decision to include Java in version 2.0 of Netscape Navigator (Microsoft will include Java and JavaScript runtime in the next release of Internet Explorer, probably in C3Q96) could provide the standards, technology, and sheer momentum to lift distributed applications design to a new level. Netscape's scripting language to build applications will include a version of Java, allowing developers, using new features in Navigator 2.0, can build dynamic applications. Navigator 2.0 provides several new features that give developers more control over the screen.

Java can provide a dynamic aspect to HTML, which is fundamentally a static page-description language. Java is an execution environment based on C++, except with the fangs removed. Since Navigator 2.0 has a Java execution engine built in, Netscape browser users can execute any applet (an object-oriented application written in Java) locally on their machines regardless of hardware platform. The combination of Java and Navigator 2.0 also means that competing execution environments could have a tough time breaking into the market. Since customers need a Java-aware browser to execute a growing inventory of Java applets, the drawback to using a non-Java-aware browser will increase as more Java applets become available on the Web.

Web sites are already increasingly exploiting the power of Navigator 2.0. With version 2.0, Web sites provide much livelier pages once they detect a Navigator 2.0 browser. In other words, many Web sites provide extra enhancements to their pages for Navigator 2.0 that don't appear if the user has a non-Navigator 2.0 compliant browser. As developers begin to take advantage of these advanced features, they would force users to stay within the Netscape/Java camp, or miss out on the advanced graphics and more sophisticated page displays.

Java as a Development Tool

Java is a C++-based programming language that removes pointers, powerful but dangerous shortcuts that often lead to memory leaks and security breaches. Through a mechanism called automatic garbage collection, Java re-duces memory errors by automatically freeing memory after an operation, when possible. Another major difference between Java and C/C++ is that Java eliminates pointers that can overwrite memory and corrupt data. The absence of pointers makes it improbable that applications can access private data in objects that they do not have security rights to. This closes the door on most of today's viruses.

On the negative side, Java is a very new technology and is still in the development stages in many respects, not least of which is security. Any time a program is run during a download there is the possibility of a security risk. Java provides help in this area, but throughout the history of computing, hackers have found ways, usually through original programming glitches, to exploit weakness and breach security. Running the applets on the server could alleviate some of these concerns. At its current state of development, Java is immature in such areas as transaction processing, still in the research phase. In addition, Java is an interpreted, not a compiled, language. This means that after it is downloaded, it must be processed on the client computer, which can hinder somewhat the performance of the Java applet.

Adobe

Adobe is the kingpin of desktop publishing, now dubbed authoring tools. The company's key products include: *Photoshop* photo design and production software; *Illustrator* illustration and page-design software; *PageMaker* desktop publishing software; *Premiere* video production software; *Adobe Acrobat* electronic document file format; and *Postscript* page-description language for printers. Bolstering its product line, Adobe recently purchased Frame Technology's *FrameMaker* and has invested in several Web authoring products. More than 75% of Adobe's desktop application software sales are to graphics professionals; about 60% of sales are based on Apple Macintosh software, followed by Windows at 30% and UNIX at 10%. Adobe's self-proclaimed mission is "to be the premier supplier of information authoring and management tools that enable people to create, send, find, view and print information."

The market share positions of the company's products are significant: We estimate that Photoshop carries 80% or more of the PC-based digital imaging market; Illustrator has at least 60% of the PC-based illustration and design market; PageMaker has 42% of the PC-based desktop publishing market; FrameMaker has a dominant share of the high-end desktop publishing market for UNIX; and PostScript is used on the majority of high-end monochrome and color printers.

In its efforts to focus on the growth in the Internet, Adobe has made a series of strategic moves and investments, including:

• integration of the Acrobat Reader into browsers from Netscape, Microsoft, and Spyglass;

• introduction of PageMaker 6.0 software, which allows users to output files in HTML and PDF formats;

- acquisition of Frame Technology, producer of Frame-Maker high-end desktop publishing software, which converts documents into SGML and HTML;

- acquisition of Ceneca Communications, a developer of Web publishing (PageMill) and Web site management (SiteMill) tools;

- made an $8.5 million investment in mFactory; and

- investment in Netscape Communications, buying a 4% stake, pre-IPO.

From a positioning perspective, Adobe is approaching growth related to the Internet from three angles:

Content Creation/Authoring Tools

Abobe is hoping to leverage its strengths in static document content creation tools (with Photoshop, Illustrator, Page-Maker, and FrameMaker) into the emerging markets for dynamic document creation.

Adobe enjoys several advantages: a large base of desktop publishing professionals knows how to use its products (which now can convert documents into HTML and PDF file formats); second, most photos integrated into the Web are likely processed using Photoshop; third, we believe that many content providers, with large volumes of documents with lots of graphics, will use Adobe's Acrobat technology to place those documents in electronic form on the Web (while users cannot "interact" very much with Acrobat PDF files, content providers such as the Internal Revenue Service don't want interaction); fourth, there are the investments in some hot, new online-oriented development tools from Ceneca and mFactory.

Adobe's disadvantages may include the company's heritage as a printing company. Adobe was created for the purpose of introducing the PostScript printer page-description language, which allowed nice-looking stuff on PC screens to remain nice-looking when it comes out of printers. Adobe then invested in PC application software products that allowed great-looking documents to be created on PCs and then printed. However, all of these documents are "static" and are intended to be displayed on paper. In the world of the Internet, documents are "dynamic" and are intended to be interacted with. The most exciting thing about the Web is obtaining information via hypertext linking and interactive chat. Finding and creating information on the Web in the most efficient way is more important than the presentation of that information, we believe.

Adobe has key tools for Internet content developers with Photoshop and Illustrator, but the rest of its main products are not yet maximized for interactive Internet development. No doubt, lots of content developers will use PageMaker, Illustrator, FrameMaker, and Acrobat for displaying static documents on the Web. Over the next several months, we expect Adobe to begin to articulate the next steps in its strategy for creating interactive content area for the Web. Expect smaller, faster, more interactive versions of Adobe's Acrobat tools.

Adobe's biggest competitors in the content creation/authoring tool space are likely to be Netscape, Microsoft, Sun Microsystems, Macromedia, America Online, and a host of smaller, new companies.

Content Delivery

Adobe was one of the first companies to grasp the vision and market opportunity for the electronic distribution of documents. Its efforts with the Acrobat products have been impressive: Acrobat is a line of Adobe software products that allow fully formatted electronic documents — containing distinctive typefaces, color, graphics, and photographs — to be easily distributed, accessed, and reused, regardless of the hardware platform, operating system, or application used to create the originals. Receivers of Acrobat PDF files, using the freely available Acrobat Reader software can view, search, navigate, print, and store the documents.

We believe that Acrobat, like PostScript, has a solid chance to become a standard-setter in a niche of the Internet market for the delivery of graphics-rich static documents.

High-Quality Printed Output

If our personal Web use is an example of things to come, demand for high-end color printers (PostScript's sweet spot) is destined for strong growth, as demand rises for users to print the cool-looking (and getting cooler) stuff on the Web.

Macromedia

Macromedia is a leading provider of cross-platform tools for the creation of multimedia content. Its products allow multimedia content to be built simply, and without an extensive knowledge of programming languages. Macromedia tools — Director, Authorware, FreeHand, Extreme 3D, SoundEdit, xRES, and Fontographer — enable developers to create output that has traditionally been delivered on CD-ROMs, in interactive training products, or on the printed page. Macromedia increasingly is taking advantage of the Internet as a conduit for dynamic content delivery. The company recently aligned with two important Internet players: Netscape and Sun Microsystems. Further, Macromedia has a very active Website that it uses to communicate with current and potential clients.

Early in November 1995, Macromedia announced a new toolset for the delivery of dynamic Director content to the Internet — its ShockWave and Afterburner products. Essentially, ShockWave allows small Director movies (and eventually other Macromedia-built content) to be condensed and viewed over the Internet via an imbedded viewer in the Netscape Browser (and possibly others as Macromedia rolls out the technology). Windows 3.1 and Windows 95 versions of ShockWave for Netscape's Navigator 2.0 are available on Macromedia's home page now, with a Macintosh version under development. Also of note, ShockWave movies will be playable in Web browsers offered by Microsoft (Internet Studio), America Online/Navisoft (NaviPress), and Silicon Graphics (WebForce).

Already, a number of Web sites are utilizing the technology, including MTV online, Disney, and Sony Music.

Further, Macromedia is addressing Sun's Java technology by adding compatibility within Macromedia's tools and by the potential development of an easy-to-use Java front-end.

Section V:
Company-Related

Chapter 9:
The Internet: Technology and Administrative Issues

Internet users and providers alike face many technical and administrative issues, including the following:

• **Bandwidth requirements and server capacities** are increasing rapidly, perhaps more rapidly than infrastructure buildout.

• **Security** is needed to protect corporate resources.

• **Authority is distributed.**

• **Competing standards** exist, such as IPng, ATM, HTML and others.

• **Censorship** threatens the openness of the system. Other social and national concerns may also emerge as issues.

• **Old Media Resistance** will come from publishers, retailers, radio and television broadcasters, and telephony carriers, in the form of lobbying and cost cutting.

• **Competing Networks** such as Online Service Provider and news delivery networks will cause some dislocation.

Many issues have arisen since the commercialization of the Internet. We believe there are none that would cause the system to stop working altogether, but some developments could slow progress. The practical nature of the Internet community is such that if there are problems, technical or administrative, users will demand that they be fixed. If technical solutions are needed, as we have seen recently, companies will likely develop profitable solutions. The Internet's distributed architecture requires less administration than a centrally-architected system. Therefore, if there are administrative issues, committees will likely be formed and solutions will appear, slowly. Currently, in our opinion, the biggest issues facing the practical use of the Internet, and its future applications, are discussed below.

Bandwidth

Next-generation applications require more data bandwidth, from the desktop to the backbone. Cable modems could be the Holy Grail, and consumers could embrace new "killer apps" if more bandwidth were available. By all means, a step increase in bandwidth would correspondingly boost demand for Internet connectivity. But who pays for this increasing level of bandwidth is an open question...

A central issue, made obvious from the use of Mosaic-based browsers, is the increased bandwidth demands created by

transmitting graphics files on the Internet. As a result of the launch of Mosaic, we estimate that bandwidth demands for a typical user cruising the Net have increased 16–55 times in the past two or three years. As more applications such as 3-D graphics, audio, video, and telephony go on the 'Net, the demand for bandwidth will increase considerably.

We estimate a patience threshold for retrieving information at about 10 to 30 seconds. The next wave of Internet applications will include real-time sound and limited real-time 3-D graphics capabilities. **Bandwidth requirements of this next wave of Internet technology far exceed the bandwidth capabilities of today's communications devices.** New products will also be more expensive than most users can afford, although as volume and competition grow, prices will decline. A reasonable benchmark for the Internet to be perceived as useful and efficient, in our view, would require retrieval times for web pages and other semi-interactive Internet applications of 10 seconds or faster.

On the client side, we believe that except for e-mail and text-only applications, the 14.4 kbps modem is near death, and the 28.8 kbps modem has about 1 or 2 years left before online and Internet applications demand more bandwidth. Table 9.1 shows four phases of bandwidth demand for Internet applications. The first was text-based and used the

9.6 and 14.4 kbps modems, sufficient for client-side devices to connect to text-based online services. The second, with graphical user interfaces and massive graphics downloads enabled by Mosaic technology, requires a 28.8kbps modem or up to an ISDN 64 to 128 kbps BRI (Basic Rate Interface) line. Even these, however, are unlikely to be enough for satisfactory use of the third wave of real-time sound and close to real-time 3D graphics.

Without significant advancements in compression technology, ISDN BRI adapters operating at 64 kbps or 128 kbps, corresponding to the third wave of bandwidth are likely to be a transition technology available from the telcos. The ISDN BRI technology will only support Web applications that are text; graphics (still photos, JPEG/GIF); mildly interactive games and forms; and fair quality sound. We do not believe ISDN, at 128 kbps (2 B channels), can handle real-time full-screen MPEG video, 3-D graphics (other than relatively simple images), highly interactive applications, and other Internet technologies and applications that are being tested on leased line connections and LANs operating at T-1 (1.5 mbps) and Ethernet speeds (10 mbps), respectively. For the fourth wave of highly interactive applications, a T-1 line or cable modem would be needed.

Therefore, unless ISDN is implemented at a competitive cost at higher data rates, using "rubber bandwidth", or variable on-demand bandwidth, ranging from 64 (1 B channel) to 256 kbps (4 B channels) to 768 kbps (12 B channels), we believe competing technologies will substitute, such as affordable T-1, T-3, HFC and cable modems, and fiber optics.

Table 9.1
Four Waves of Bandwidth to the Client Station

Minimum Acceptable Technology*	File type	File size per page**	Times more than ASCII text	Time to download at 14.4 kbps***	Comments
First Wave					
14.4 kbps modem	B&W ASCII text (or e-mail)	4 kbyte	1	2.2 sec	- approximately a 1:1 ratio between characters and bytes
14.4 kbps modem	Color ASCII text	6 kbyte	1.5	3.3 sec	- requires ASCII control characters to identify following characters' color
Second Wave					
14.4 kbps modem	Typical web page	64 kbyte	16	35.2 sec	- with four 2"x2" .GIF/JPEG images (10% of screen graphics, rest text)
28.8 kbps modem	Complicated interactive web page	220 kbyte	55	122 sec (2 min 2 sec)	-75% of image is detailed graphics
28.8 kbps modem	Sound file attached to web page (e.g. 3Com)	220 kbyte	55	122 sec (2 min 2 sec)	- using RealAudio, 60 second playback, barely discernible AM radio sound quality****
64 or 128 kbps ISDN BRI adapter	Sound file attached to a web page*****	1 MB	250	556 sec (9 min 16 sec)	- 10 to 20 seconds of AM radio sound quality
Third Wave					
128 kbps ISDN BRI adapter	Video clip attached to a web page	3.2 MB	800	1,778 sec (29 min 38 sec)	- low quality, 2" x 2" image, choppy playback, 16 colors video clip, 60 sec playback
fractional T-1 line/ multi-plexed ISDN	Stereo sound file of music	3.7 MB	925	2,056 sec (34 min 16 sec)	- CD quality (digital) playback song of 2 min 30 sec length
T-1 line/PRI ISDN/ADSL	Full screen video (compressed)	11 MB	2,750	6,111 sec (1 hr 42 min)	- TV quality, full screen image, medium playback quality, 256 colors video clip, 60 sec playback
Fourth Wave					
T-1 line/ADSL/ CableModem	Next-generation highly interactive applications	20 to ??? MB	5,000 to ???	11,111 sec (3 hr 5 min)	- TV quality, full screen image, medium playback quality, 256 colors video clip, 60 sec playback

*uncompressed or nominal data rate   **based on typical file sizes   ***with 14.4 kbps modem
****considerably better with a 28.8 kbps modem   *****or a typical 2-3 page Microsoft Powerpoint slide show.
Morgan Stanley Research Estimates.

Figure 9.1

Bandwidth Technology Adoption to Client Station

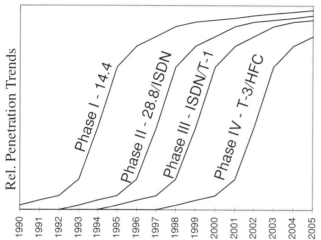

Source: Morgan Stanley Research Estimates.

Transmission technology tends to be adopted at two year intervals by three groups of users in turn: early adopters, corporations and consumers. We believe this relationship will continue, although there will be some anomalies, principally due to advances in compression technology. Applications developed for the Internet should drive demand for increased bandwidth, not the converse.

The RealAudio system is an exceptional example of how to overcome bandwidth issues. It has impressive compression abilities, which can take a 15MB .au file (.au files are UNIX sound files) down to 2 MB .ra file (.ra files are RealAudio files). This technology enables real-time playback of AM-radio quality sound over a 14.4 kbps modem.

Is ISDN Really Available? The RBOCs/CAPs attest that ISDN service is available to most customers, as follows: U.S. West 59%, Southwestern Bell 66%, Pacific Bell 87%, NYNEX 76%, GTE 18%, Bell South 64%, Bell Atlantic 90%, and Ameritech 80%. Yet we believe this technology, unlike the ubiquitous POTS/analog system, is ferociously difficult to obtain in most places. For consumers and small corporations the process may have become easier over the past year, but to outfit a residence with ISDN, typical installation lead times are 3–4 weeks (with a range of possibilities from 1 week to 6 months depending upon RBOC/CAP); they require the consumer to take a day off from work to supervise installation and install an NT-1. We still have yet to see national advertising that ISDN is available in hotels, and it is definitely not available at payphones.

Cable Modems: Cable modems, and the eventual cable systems to which they would connect, have been demonstrated to transmit at up to 10 mbps (up to 30 mbps), or about the same nominal speed as shared-media Ethernet LAN technology. Digital cable-transmission is still in the testing stage, with perhaps 30,000 users in North America on such services.

Several issues must be addressed, we believe, before this technology becomes a serious competitor to ISDN and other telco digital services. First, the 10 mbps rate is a nominal rate, which decreases considerably with an increasing number of subscribers; the Ethernet LAN suffers from the same drawback. Second, the CATV infrastructure is analog and one-way; cable modems need digital, two-way (though asymmetrical is OK) interactive systems which will be expensive to operators to deploy massively, estimated at $1,000 per subscriber (within a wide range of estimates). Third, while several tests of digital interactive cable systems have been announced, few have actually met their goals. Ultimately, however, the issues will be addressed, in our view, because customers will pay up for more bandwidth.

Security

The Internet is an open and inherently non-secure public system that requires the application of practical security solutions to keep intruders from entering corporate networks via the Internet (firewalls), to keep information which may be intercepted indecipherable (encryption), to allow commercial transactions (encryption and identification), to grant access to corporate network resources judiciously (token security and user authentication). Over time, security scares will come and go. Our perception is that there is a need for only a few solutions in this arena as users begin to standardize on secure communications protocols. This trend may squeeze the little companies.

The Internet connects many resources together, but there are no inherent, built-in security protocols, and few ways to stop messages from being intercepted. Several types of security concerns are being commercially addressed.

Security against external threats to networks connected to the Internet is being addressed with *firewalls* and *packet-filtering* software and devices.

Security against message interception on the Internet is being addressed by software and hardware devices that encrypt data in real time before they are sent to the Internet.

Transaction security, required when sending credit card and other sensitive information across the Internet, is addressed by encryption systems in software. Our discussion of competing standards below reviews various security schemes (SST, SSL, S-HTTP, etc.) being built into browsers and servers by competing server software makers (Microsoft, Netscape, Open Market).

User Authorization security protects the network by allowing only authorized users access to parts of the network by using extended user authentication challenge/response token cards that generate one-time passwords and other systems not based on hardware.

The external threat of hackers may require some degree of *firewalling*. Firewalling deters intruder attacks to corporate networks connected to the Internet by a gateway leased-line connection (a router connecting a network permanently to the Internet). Firewalling may be incorporated into a router, typically using an older technology called packet-filtering (which stops packets from certain destinations), or it may be implemented on a server using a newer and more secure system called applications-layer firewalling (which allows only information from 'allowed' sites to enter the secured network). The latter, considered more advanced than packet filtering, is being addressed by many companies, including Raptor Secure Computing (SCUR), Border Networks, Trusted Information Systems, and CheckPoint Software.

The threat of messages being intercepted on the Internet requires some kind of transmission and/or transaction security (encryption). Transmission security uses on-the-fly encryption at the computer by companies such as Raptor and TimeStep (an affiliate of Newbridge Networks). The same type of security is being addressed by other companies, but only for servers — these are Sun, DEC, and the firewalling companies mentioned above.

Transaction security is being addressed software encryption built into browsers and other software by Terisa (a joint venture between EIT and RSA Data Security), RSA Data Security, Netscape (NSCP), VISA International, Microsoft (MSFT), Spyglass (SPYG), and many others.

Encryption technology and key-lock identification algorithms have been available for decades and are widely in use at government agencies. Companies such as RSA Data Security (encryption experts), Terisa, Enterprise Integration Technologies (owned by VeriFone), and Verisign are developing practical encryption and identification systems. Services that permit online transfers of electronic cash, such as DigiCash and CyberCash, offer alternatives to secure-transaction systems. Elegant, simple solutions, such as implementation of automated telephone-based transactions, can also complement Internet commerce (InfoSeek).

More advanced passwording and user authentication are being deployed on networks to reduce the threat of unwanted users entering ISP or corporate networks. Security Dynamics (SDTI), maker of the SecurID card, CryptoCard, VASCO Data Security, and Digital Pathways, are making extended user authentication challenge/response token cards that generate one-time passwords.

Authority

This distributed, shared system has a collaborative, committee-based leadership and lacks a strong central authority (the government is backing out over the next 1-1/2 years); new mechanisms will therefore have to be enforced. It is unclear who will step in here; it could be a dominant player offering de facto software (perhaps Netscape or Microsoft); it could be the government (perhaps via censorship and encryption bullying); it could be access providers with overwhelming market share (perhaps AT&T).

Partnership among many networks — glued together by U.S. federal government funding — was the rule of the Internet until April 1995. Without that tacit central authority, we believe there will be some decline in the cooperative nature of the Internet, driven by any number of potential factors, such as security, competing networks, and profits.

Thousands of private IP networks exist at corporations for the very reason that companies do not want others to gain access. This fragmentation is necessary to attempt to keep a secure system (see below). Networks such as AOL, CompuServe, MCI mail, MSN, and many others also have a clear incentive to try to keep as many users on their networks as possible. Proprietary network operators (OSPs) have historically been able to charge higher monthly subscription fees because of a lack of competitive offerings from ISPs. Now, the WWW allows ISPs to offer a competitive service, but if the 'Net were proprietary or enough users used a single proprietary system, then user fees, or advertiser fees, could theoretically be raised.

While no one owns the Internet, companies, governments, and other entities own the networks that connect to the Internet. The 'Net thrives as a result: tens of thousand of networks and millions of users have been connected at very little cost. But there have been shortcomings as well: relatively long turnaround times for technology advances due to the committee-nature of decision making and the traffic bottlenecks created by lack of concentrated funding.

Competing Standards

Emerging standards such as *IPng* (the new, pending version of the Internet Protocol); *ATM* (asynchronous transmission mode, hardware-based networking system); *HTML* standards versus proprietary extensions; enhanced proprietary browser features; cross-platform application languages such as *Java* (Sun), *Blackbird* (Microsoft) and others; *VRML* (3D potential successor to HTML), audio (GSM), and video (*MPEG*) standards; and security-standards (*SST, SSSL, S-HTTP*). We project that IP will run over ATM but that ATM will not replace IP. HTML is here to stay, but it could be transformed through the addition of proprietary extensions (Netscape) or strong complementary features available in other languages (Java) or by near-replacment (Blackbird). We see so much turmoil in the marketplace it is difficult to tell, but we would give a slight handicap to the close-to-open-standard approach of HTML.

New standards in the works that will affect the Internet include IPng; ATM; HTML; Transaction security; enhanced proprietary browser features; Java and Blackbird; VRML; RealAudio/Xing and Internet Phone.

IPng: IPng is intended to improve the current version of IP (version 4) by adding additional address space, support for video transmission, and several other improvements. The current version of IP is predicted to run out of unique ad-

dresses for hosts in a couple years, and so a new numbering scheme is needed. Others (Network Translation Inc., which Cisco just purchased) are trying to correct this problem by fooling the Internet number system and performing a translation such that large networks require only a few network addresses.

Video transmission across the Internet typically involves latency and delay, unless the available bandwidth between two points is very large. While it is true that buffering (temporary storing of information) and other technologies can improve video over IP version 4, transmission support for video and voice may be integrated into IPng.

ATM: This emerging standard may also affect the Internet. The ATM forum, a collection of hundreds of individuals representing asynchronous transfer mode companies, has been actively developing standards since 1992. These standards should be completed in about 2 or 3 years, but successful implementation of fully-compliant products may be available a year earlier or sooner. This hardware based networking architecture promises unprecedented scalability (from desktop to worldwide networking) and extremely fast speeds (155 mbps at the desktop).

In order to implement ATM from the desktop to Internet, most of the installed base of networking and internetworking hardware in existence today would need to be replaced — an unlikely prospect. ATM is being successfully implemented in new backbones because it is extremely fast. We believe that ATM may become the underlying Internet networking architecture in 5 to 10 years. In this scenario, we believe TCP/IP routing will very likely continue to be used in conjunction with ATM.

HTML: The WWW is based on the hypertext transport protocol (HTTP), which runs over the Internet infrastructure. Data transmitted over the Web is formatted to a standard called hypertext markup language (HTML). Currently, the IETF is in the final stages of accepting HTML version 2.0 (it is waiting for an RFC number). A proposed HTML version 3.0 is under discussion in the IETF's HTML working group. It includes HTML enhancements including tables, wraparound and centered text, and background colors.

A separate set of HTML tags, including <FONT> and <CENTER>, intended as an enhancements to HTML version 2.0, have been supported by Netscape Navigator versions 1.0 and above as early as late 1994. Netscape browsers as of August 1995 enjoyed the vast majority of the browser market share (about 60% to 75%). However, the proposed HTML version 3.0 standards do not currently include all of the Netscape HTML tags. This means that if a user is using a non-Netscape browser, such as a Spyglass version 2.1, which allows users to view the proposed HTML version 3.0 features, not all the HTML tags will be recognized. In short, a non-Netscape browser user who visits a Web site using Netscape server software may not be able to properly or completely view the page on his browser.

Proprietary Browser Standards: Open standards are the key to making the Internet an attractive platform for developers. Netscape has begun adding proprietary extensions to HTML that render Web pages less attractive for users of competing browsers. Microsoft will do the same. A journey too far down the proprietary extensions path could recreate the problem of UNIX "flavors" all over again.

Transaction Security: Browsers and servers are being offered in new revisions with key/lock encryption capabilities to enable secure commerce over the Internet. This means credit card information will be indecipherable if data are intercepted over the Internet. Each team of companies wants its proprietary encryption algorithm and user identification implementation to become the de facto standard.

• *Microsoft and Visa.* Secure Transaction Technology (STT) is expected in 1Q96.

• *Netscape and MasterCard.* Secure Socket Layer (SSL) is secure channel system, now enabled as part of the Netscape browser, which makes whatever is sent during a session encrypted. Secure Courier, also Netscape's, encrypts only a field within a document such as a credit card number.

• *IBM and MasterCard.* Under development is IBM's Internet Keyed Payments protocol (iKP).

• *Terisa.* SSL/S-HTTP toolkit creator Terisa enables the browser companies to develop products with security in their product. S-HTTP encrypts http documents only. Open Market's servers support both.

• *VeriSign.* A joint venture with many partners including Security Dynamics, Microsoft, and RSA Data Security, to create Digital ID, a technology to allow clients to be identified with a digital signature.

• Visa and MasterCard announced in late summer, though, that they would collaborate in their efforts to create a new standard.

Electronic Cash: Three companies are getting the most press about their electronic equivalents to cash, or anonymous electronic cash: DigiCash, of Amsterdam, CyberCash (VeriFone has a minority investment), of Reston, Va., and First Virtual.

Acrobat, Blackbird/Internet Studio, HTML: Web/online authoring standards from Adobe, Microsoft, Netscape, Spyglass and others are currently being debated by the open market now. A lot is at stake. Remember the mid- to late-1980s, when converting word processing formats (WordPerfect to Word, for instance) would create massive delays and reductions in office productivity?

Java: Sun Microsystems developed a web browsing technology called HotJava. It adds support for Java applets, executable programs written in Java, a new object oriented language designed to solve a number of problems of modern programming. With Java, you can create interactive

Figure 9.2
HTML Code Sample

```
<HTML>
<HEAD>
<Title> China Internet Home Page</Title>
</HEAD>
<p><center>
<body bgcolor="#ffffff" text="oooooo">
<img src="logo.gif">
<P>
<H1>ChinaNet - China Internet Home Page</H1>
<h3>(Computer Network Center of Chinese Academy of Sciences)</h3>
<P>
<img src="images/rainbow.gif" >
</center>
<p>
<h3><dd>ChinaNet is a nation-wide Internet in<strong> <A HREF="china.html"> China
(china home page)</strong> </A>, based on the World Bank
supported project NCFC (The National Computing and Networking
Facility of China). A 64Kbps dedicated link connects the ChinaNet, via
Sprint International's router, to The NSFNET which is the main body
of The Internet. Therefore, The ChinaNet is the China portion of The
Global Internet.</h3>
<P>
<center><A HREF="http://www.cnc.ac.cn/china.html"><h2>Great China (
Da4 Zhong1 Guo3) Home Page </h2>
<img src="hong/images/chinamap.gif" ></a></center><p>
<hr size=6><P>
```

Source: Computer Network Center of Chinese Academy of Sciences

programs, independent of the server software, that run on any client computer. Netscape LiveWorks is a scripting language available in Navigator 2.0 based on Java intended to create interactive multimedia applications on-line.

Virtual Reality Modeling Language: VRML is a standard similar to HTML which is used to allow development of 3-Dimensional multi-user "Web" sites. Leaders in VRML authoring include Caligari Corp., Silicon Graphics, Virtus Corp., and Chaco Communications, Inc. Just as Netscape's early lead in browsers allowed it to offer enhanced HTML tags, Worlds is attempting to offer the development community its own version of VRML called VRML+. Currently, World's VRML+ can be seen in action on the Worlds Chat service available on the Web for free.

Until the past quarter, delivering **real-time audio and video** over modems has been impossible. About three months ago, Progressive Networks made available for Internet downloading a product called RealAudio. This proprietary software system consists of server software and client software. Sound files are converted to RealAudio file format and put on to the server, which can be retrieved over the Internet and listened to using the client software. The effect is that using modems as slow as 14.4 kbps, AM-radio quality broadcasts can be listened to in conjunction with a sound card as they are being downloaded on the client station. Xing Technologies has also released StreamWorks, which allows real-time playback of audio and video. Xing uses an enhanced MPEG digital compression system to permit real-time video playback.

Computer-to-Computer Telephony: Telephone-like capabilities over the Internet are also emerging. VocalTec makes software called Internet Phone; CyberPhone was first released on April 13, 1995 by Matt Krokosz and Greg Foglesong (now known as CyberScience); Camelot makes NetPhone; and Electric Magic makes a Macintosh telephony software called NetPhone. Several other individuals and companies, Camelot and Quarterdeck, have developed similar software. Generally, two callers using the same client phone software can use a sound card with a microphone to conduct voice conversations with each other. In most cases they must be connected to an IRC or functionally similar server or a specialized Internet phone server. Voice quality is considerably worse than a regular tele

phone, but not that bad. This technology is in its formative stages, but is very appealing because there is no time limit or distance charge, only a connect charge from an ISP.

Computer-to-Telephone Telephony: New technologies also enable computers to initiate calls to regular telephone. One service by IDT, a company with Internet access in most states in the U.S, allows a long distance call at about 1/10 the cost charged by the traditional carriers. Its service works by leveraging a call-back feature in its network centers and integrating telephony switching. The Free World Dialup Project (FWD) is a non-commercial venture now in beta testing. It expects to offer full service in early 1996, available for free but restricted to non-commerical use. Though few details are available, the group will enable computer-to-telephone communications.

Censorship

Governmental mandates such as censorship may increase the overhead required to operate an ISP and OSP. If censorship, in any form, is mandated, costs may rise, and the attractiveness of the system may diminish. It seems certain this issue will come up over and over again, and it will be argued in court after laws have been tested.

Controversy surrounds the issue of pornographic images and "indecent" material on the Internet. The Senate's telecommunications reform bill contains a rider that prohibits on-line distribution of "indecent" material to minors, and it is punishable with fines up to $100,000 and jail terms. The House version of telecommunications reform bill makes strong recommendations that technology shall be developed to ensure that indecent material does not make it to the eyes of minors. It is not clear exactly which bill will pass, or what the compromise will be when the two are melded together, but any bill addressing indecent material is likely to create new business opportunities. There may, however, may be a slight slowdown in the growth rate of the Internet as ISPs and OSPs grapple with how to comply with the mandates.

Other social issues involving community standards, social policy, privacy, and other legal issues will also arise? How will the emergence of a new anarchistic medium affect society? How will government deal with equal access to Internet facilities? How will the law deal with the "big brother" aspects of the Internet?

Old Media Resistance

In general, existing players that distribute *products* (publications, retailers), *information* (radio, television), and *connectivity services* (telephony, carrier-based data connections, X.500 systems, Lotus Notes systems) through traditional means may attempt to thwart the activities of newer players using the Internet. Resistance may come in the form of lobbying (especially for telephony and television), and cost-cutting (retailers, publications). We would expect new, large-scale retailers or distributors to cut out the middle-man, so to speak. Information flow will change in favor of the Internet distribution model and the individual.

Competing Networks

Proprietary online services compete with the services available from the Internet. These services are integrating IP-based content on their sites, but the OSPs are likely to continue to provide significant competition (in part, as they embrace the Internet). Eventually, we believe all services will offer IP-only service. Microsoft's announcement that MSN will be available from anywhere on the Internet was a strong step in this direction. We believe that down the road, ISPs and OSPs will not be fighting among themselves too much; rather, we expect them to do battle with the traditional telecom providers who own the physical plant.

Administration of the Internet is now shared between the government and companies. As the government pulls funding almost completely by April 1997, commercial entities will be picking up the slack. Internet operation is shared between the companies that operate the backbone (MCI, Sprint, PSINet, UUNET, ANS, Net99/AGIS), the CIX, NAPs, and some government-funded operations centers. As the NSF reduces funding, private companies should have near-complete control over operational decisions by 1997.

Technical issues are handled in two ways. First, the Internet Engineering Task Force (IETF) is the technological entity that attacks problems that face operation and construction of the Internet, such as the new version of Internet protocols, IPng. Other technology forums, such as the ATM forum, also represent commercial interests by allowing company representatives to participate. Second, a single company may innovate with more effective networking and computing products. Vendors may introduce products which revolutionize certain aspects of the Internet. Many technical issues are addressed by the security products and more efficient networking devices made by such companies.

Chapter 10: Competitive Analysis

- In this chapter, we analyze the competitive positioning of various companies, and their Internet product offerings, specifically, in 16 key business segments related to the Internet. While the Internet market is still very new, we have attempted to identify the companies that appear to be in the strongest positions, for now.

Data Networking Equipment: *Cisco, Ascend, Cascade, U.S. Robotics, Livingston*
Internet Security Equipment and Software: *Terisa, RSA Data Security, Raptor, Verisign*
Internet Service Providers: *ANS/AOL, Concentric Network, @Home*
PC, Server and Semiconductors: *Sun Microsystems, Intel*
Telecommunications and Related Services: *MCI Communications*
Telecommunications Equipment: *Cascade, Stratacom, Premisys*
Applications
Software: *Netscape, Microsoft, Intuit, Open Market, Worlds, Vermeer, Progressive Networks, Paper Software*
Enterprise and Networking Software: *Oracle, Informix*
Internet/Online Consulting and Development: *I/Pro*
Organization/Aggregation: *America Online, Microsoft, Starwave*
Information: *[None yet]*
Publication/Static: *Wired Ventures*
Publication/Interactive: *Motley Fool, c/net*
Publishing (Traditional): *Knight-Ridder, Dun+Bradstreet*
Transaction Processing and Financial Services: *CyberCash, DigiCash, First Virtual Holdings*
Commerce: *CUC International*

Our analysis of the competitive forces and strategies tries to identify companies that will be the strongest beneficiaries of Internet growth, businesses that have emerged or will emerge as a result of the Internet's commercialization, and companies that have converted part or all of their operations to the online/Internet world. Initially, we believe, the infrastructure stocks will benefit, followed by software and services, then content and aggregation.

Table 10.1
Estimated Internet Market Subsegment Trends Over Next 5 Years

Internet Market Subsegment	CAGR Rev. Growth	Subscriber Based	Capital Intensity	Net Margin. Levels	Annuity, Replacement or New Business Characteristics
Data Networking Equipment	40%	No	Medium	10%-25%	Accelerating bandwidth demand
Internet Security Equipment and Software	85%	No	Medium	10%-15%	Little except software upgrades
Internet Service Providers	100%	Yes	High	2%-10%	Monthly subscribers
PC, Server and Semiconductors	25%	No	High	5%-15%	Processor-related upgrades
Telecommunications and Related Services	20%	Yes	High	2%-7%	Monthly subscribers
Telecommunications Equipment	30%	No	Medium	8%-18%	Accelerating bandwidth demand
Application Software	50%	Maybe	Low	10%-25%	Yearly upgrades, perhaps
Enterprise and Networking Software	60%	No	Low	20%-25%	Revisions
Internet/Online Services, Consulting, and Development	60%	No	Low	--	As needed or on contract
Organization/Aggregation	40%	Yes	Medium	3%-10%	Monthly subscribers
Information	135%	Yes	Low	--	Monthly subscribers
Publications/Static and Publications/Interactive	110%	Yes	Low	5%-12%	Monthly subscribers
Transaction Processing and Financial Services	80%	No	Medium	10%-20%	Per transaction
Commerce	65%	No	Low	5%-20%	Per transaction

Source: Morgan Stanley Estimates

Infrastructure

Data Networking Equipment

The Internet market for data networking equipment consists of the server side (ISPs, large corporate) and the client side (consumers and small offices). Dominant suppliers on the server side are Cisco (routers), and Ascend (call aggregators). Challengers include U.S. Robotics, a leader in the client side with modem pools and call aggregators; 3Com, a LAN market leader with Primary Access call aggregators and Sonix ISDN products; and Livingston, a leader in remote-access port shipments last year. On the client side, the dominant supplier is U.S. Robotics (modems and ISDN), challenged by Hayes Micro (modems), Boca Research (modems), Zoom (modems), Xircom (ISDN and PCMCIA modems). U.S. Robotics' competitive strategy on the client side has been cost leadership in the modem.

Internet Security Equipment and Software

Internet security is a rapidly developing, yet small, market. On a small revenue base, market shares may swing wildly over the next year or two as new companies enter the market and ramp up revenues. We believe market demand for security products will begin at the enterprise level, implemented primarily at the server, and then move to the desktop. As this shift occurs, distribution of security products will change. Ideally, security would be implemented at every computer connected to the Internet, and more ideally, basic security functionality would be integrated into an operating system. Big players not cited in this chart include Cisco, Oracle, Microsoft, Digital Equipment, IBM, and Sun Microsystems, although all of these companies would lie on the far left-hand side of the chart because their Internet security-related revenues are dwarfed by other lines of businesses' revenues.

Companies that, for now, appear well positioned include Terisa, RSA Data Security, Raptor, Verisign, Trusted Information Systems, and Secure Computing. Over time, many will likely consolidate. Companies can also develop de facto Internet security standards; Livingston's RADIUS is one such standard being adopted by other companies. Livingston is depicted in Figures 10.1 and 10.2 for its involvement in both security (RADIUS) and remote access.

Internet Service Providers

Three types of ISPs are in the market today:

• **Pure-plays** who provide the service exclusively (e.g. UUNET, PSINet, Netcom, Concentric Network).

• **OSPs** that have begun to offer Internet access through their existing proprietary networks (America Online, CompuServe, MSN, IBM/Prodigy).

Figure 10.1
Data Networking Equipment
Competitive Analysis for 2–3 Year Time Horizon

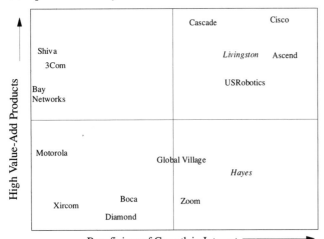

Figure 10.2
Internet Security Equipment & Software
Competitive Analysis for 2–3 Year Time Horizon

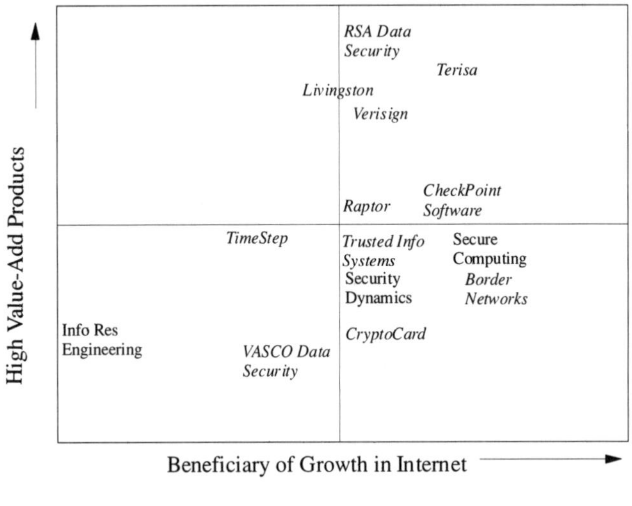

• **Existing telecom companies** that have begun to address this market (AT&T, MCI, Sprint, RBOCs).

Efforts are also under way to provide **cable-based connections** to the Internet. Cable Internet providers, like the start-up company, @Home, seek to provide megabit per second range speeds at consumer level costs. If this performance is achievable, then leading cable-based systems have a distinct advantage over more traditional, lower performance offerings. Concentric is unique among the larger ISPs because it leases frame relay service from telco carriers, not leased lines. We estimate that frame relay-based Internet services operate at a higher margin, say 10% better, than the publicly traded ISPs using leased lines. However, they will be considerably disadvantaged if they sell frame-relay (protocol-less) service. Concentric also has an advantage in its ability to connect the largest, most popular bulletin board services in North America together.

The larger pure-plays, Netcom, UUNET and PSINet, have similar financial models. Their goal is to build a nationwide or global network faster than their competitors. In the future, today's pure-play ISPs may be viewed as long-distance telephone service resellers are today. There have been some viable resellers in many markets, especially those that are nimble and efficient.

Over the short term (2–3 years) the ISP marketplace will be characterized by relatively low barriers to entry, implying a relatively high threat of new entrants. There is strong rivalry among existing firms in the industry; in the near absence of significant signup fees, customers can switch providers readily. There will also be competition from powerful substitute services, such as OSPs like America Online, CompuServe, and MSN, that package Internet access. The ISPs also face suppliers with very strong bargaining power, though much more from data equipment vendors than from telecommunications services providers.

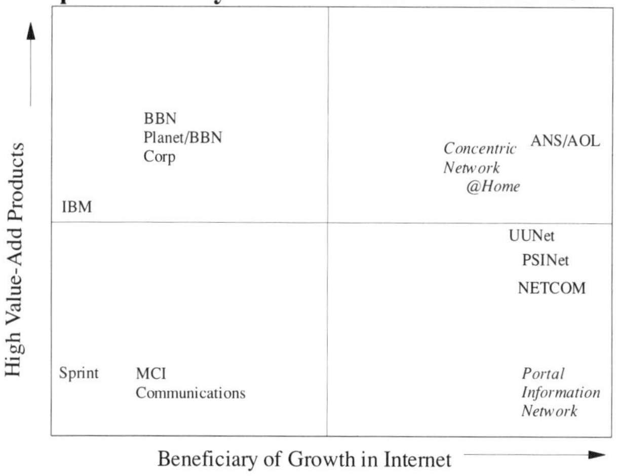

Over the long term (7–10 years), the ISPs must survive a concerted challenge from online service providers (OSPs), such as America Online, CompuServe, and MSN. The OSPs' offering of Internet access is a threat to, and a strategic bet against, the ISPs, such as PSINet, Netcom, AT&T (BBN), UUNET (to a lesser degree because of the MSN affiliation), and others that offer access to the Internet only. The issues surrounding this competition involve primarily the following strategic issues: 1) **proprietary versus nonproprietary content** and network, 2) **billing methods**, 3) **faster network access**, 4) **ubiquitous network access**.

Users may well access all cyber-services, OSP content and Web content, via one of the following models:

• **ISP-based system where all dial-ins occur through one provider** (IP dialtone available from an ISP or what we call today a traditional telecommunications service provider) and content is viewed at various sites that we know now today as OSPs and Web pages, or

• **OSP-based system where multiple dial-ins occur to various providers** of proprietary content, who also provide access to other systems such as the Internet and perhaps those of other OSPs.

The implications for "Internet-only companies" of this possibility are life-and-death, depending on which scenario ultimately prevails —will users access the online services and the Internet, the ISP or the OSP? The financial and strategic implications are farther-reaching than just for the ISPs and OSPs themselves; they apply to companies that have bet on or against ISPs or OSPs (like the exclusive media deals), and on or against single OSPs. It is in this context that we have chosen to categorize the OSPs as organization/aggregation companies (see below). Whatever scenario prevails, we believe these networks perform the task of presenting massive amounts of information in a coherent way to users.

Figure 10.3
Internet Service Providers
Competitive Analysis for 2–3 Year Time Horizon

BBN Planet/BBN Corp		*Concentric* *Network* ANS/AOL *@Home*
IBM		
		UUNet PSINet NETCOM
Sprint MCI Communications		*Portal* *Information* *Network*

(vertical axis label: High Value-Add Products)

(horizontal axis label: Beneficiary of Growth in Internet →)

PCs, Servers, and Semiconductors

Beginning three years ago, we argued that the server side of client-server had been underappreciated and that growth would return to large systems. Servers took off in 1995, with roughly a 30–35% sales gain. The pendulum has swung away from the PC dominating the industry and back toward enterprise computing. The level of computing complexity is rising, which is good for large-system vendors, which usually have solutions expertise.

The Internet is proof that the network is the computer. The Internet and its corollary, private Intranets, allow more work to be pushed onto the network, potentially resulting in a fat-server/thin-client world. Sun and SGI have made waves with servers for Internet access and to host Web pages. We believe larger servers will be required to support commerce and download applets as the Net matures. Currently, Sun leads the market for Internet servers and commands mindshare. We estimate that Sun's machines comprise 32% of the Internet server base.

We expect that Sun will continue to benefit from Internet-driven growth over the next 2-3 years. Sun's Java language has cemented the company's association with the Internet.

We see, however, two potential threats to Sun's Internet franchises.

Increased competition from other server hardware vendors. Digital, IBM, and Hewlett Packard have aggressively

moved to make their product lines web-enabled. Any of these companies could pose formidable competition. Microsoft NT (along with Compaq servers) is gaining lots of momentum in the enterprise and the Internet server spaces.

Commodity economics moving into the enterprise could begin to pressure server hardware vendors. Our long-term scalable computing thesis is that commodity technology, specifically Intel's Pentium Pro and Microsoft's NT, will be accepted as the building blocks of enterprise systems. One result could be an explosion in server unit growth as prices decline; another might be margin pressure on UNIX/RISC server vendors. NT is gaining acceptance, and Intel's quad-board should become the new hardware building block.

Telecommunications and Related Services

The traditional telecom carriers today provide the base infrastructure on which others build Internet value-added service. AT&T uses BBN Planet's service, for example, which runs over several carriers, including AT&T and MCI.

MCI carries much of the Internet traffic through its Internet backbone service. It connects regional networks, such as BBN's SURANet and NEARNet, and in general forms much of the commercial Internet backbone. It also runs the vBNS, the very high speed backbone that connects major supercomputing centers in the U.S.

Figure 10.4

PCs, Servers, and Semiconductors
Competitive Analysis for 2–3 Year Time Horizon

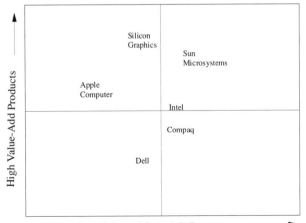

Figure 10.5

Telecommunications and Related Services
Competitive Analysis for 2–3 Year Time Horizon

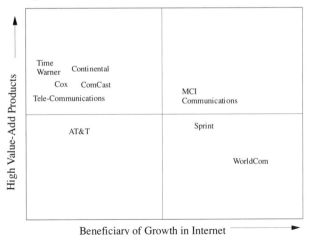

Sprint's SprintLink service is second to MCI in traffic percentage. Sprint is strong in international connections. Other players, competitive access providers such as MFS, provide some backbone service, such as Network Access Points, and also provide backbone service to the ISPs. RBOCs are expected to enter the market in 2Q96.

Cable operators, typically more leveraged than their telecom peers, may be more constrained in capital spending on new projects. Cox has one of the strongest balance sheets in the CATV industry, allowing it to aggressively deploy data services.

Telecommunications Equipment

For the traditional telecommunications carriers to build more value-added service, more equipment will be purchased. These value added services include frame relay, ATM, SMDS (Cascade and Stratacom) and dial-up services (Premisys and Ascend). For non-traditional carriers such as the cable multi-service operators (MSOs) and wireless/PCS operators to enter the market, hybrid fiber coax(HFC) and digital cable products may be needed (General Instrument and Scientific Atlanta).

Though Cascade could easily have been placed under the data networking hardware section, it sells mainly to the telco service companies. Relative to its traditional telecom equipment peers, more of Cascade's products are Internet-related — about 10–15% of revenues. Its products are also for high value-added technologies, frame-relay and ATM

(in 1Q96). Stratacom has a solid relationship with AT&T, and should benefit from AT&T's Internet infrastructure spending; it is also making inroads with other buyers in the frame relay and the ATM carrier markets as well as the OSP/ISP market. Premisys also looks positioned to benefit as the carriers move to provide Internet services. Introduction of PRMS's integrated telecom service provider access has been well timed to benefit from infrastructure build as networks allow more powerful Internet connections.

Figure 10.6

Telecommunications Equipment
Competitive Analysis for 2–3 Year Time Horizon

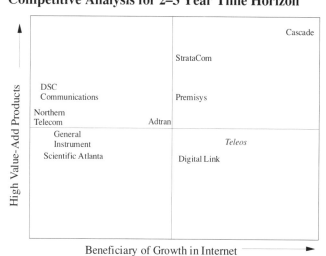

Software and Services

Application Software

The potential for developing Internet software is huge, and the market is crowded. Three types of companies are now developing such software:

• **existing non-Internet software companies** that have begun to develop Internet applications (Microsoft, Quarterdeck, Spyglass, Adobe),

• **existing Internet software companies** (FTP Software, Netmanage, Frontier Technologies, Intuit), and

• **new Internet software companies** (Netscape, Open Market, Vermeer, Worlds, Progressive Networks, InterVista, Paper Software, Connect).

Many companies with established lines of non-Internet software have been rather slow in responding to the threat of the Internet, we believe. New companies that have incorporated solely to develop Internet software appear to have taken the early lead.

We believe one of the keys to owning this market is the Internet server platform. Microsoft has demonstrated that in the PC world, to own the operating system is to be king. There is technically no operating system analogous to the PC O/S, but in the Internet software market, the server software will be the basic building block, with which all other applications presumably must be compatible. Netscape is attempting to wrangle the same type of stronghold as it becomes clear that the World Wide Web and other Internet applications are becoming more useful.

Netscape has an early lead; its useful proprietary HTML extensions appeal to Web content developers, which encourages the use of these servers. Microsoft's Internet Server initiative is similar to the Netscape approach, although much less subtle, and its advantages in bundling its products with Windows NT could, over time, prove insurmountable for competitors. Much as we have seen with DOS and Windows, an early lead in an operating-system may last as long as a decade if others standardize on the application.

Areas of software development focus on: **Browsers, Servers, Development Tools, and specialized applications** (like agent software). We expect development of Internet software parallel the course of PC software, and furthermore would not be surprised if there were only a few key players towards the end of the improvement cycle. We also see signs that the evolution may not take as long, at least in

Figure 10.7
Application Software
Competitive Analysis for 2–3 Year Time Horizon

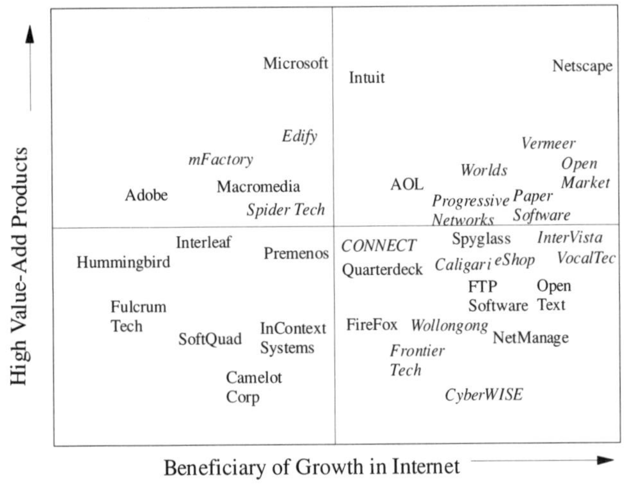

Figure 10.8
Enterprise and Networking Software
Competitive Analysis for 2–3 Year Time Horizon

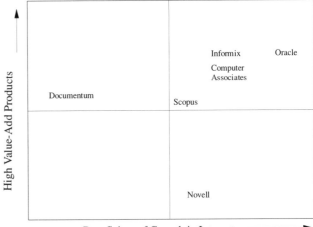

part due to the openness of the Internet, which combines the best of most computing platforms (DOS, Windows, Mac, UNIX, and even mainframes).

Enterprise and Networking Software

We believe Oracle has shown leadership in the enterprise software market segment. As shifts in computing move in favor of servers and networking, as we are seeing with the wide acceptance of the Internet and intranet models, this larger company should benefit. Oracle has identified itself with the Web and has gained more mindshare, announced more products, and poses more a threat to the traditional companies in the applications software segment than its traditional competitors. Oracle has demonstrated that it has a high value-add product, and its product announcements strongly imply its revenues will benefit as the Internet and intranet phenomena grow. The Internet server market appears to be all incremental opportunity, allowing Oracle to manage unstructured data as well as its traditional structured data. Informix has done almost as much technology work but doesn't have the marketing boost; we expect this to change soon, however. Sybase seems further behind the curve in this area.

Some enterprise software companies (e.g., systems management companies like CA or BMC software) should profit from the incremental complexity of distributed computing. Development tool vendors could be more at risk as popular development tools get distributed freely over the Web by vendors looking to create a standard and sell back-end services. The burden will be on development tool vendors to add value around Java for Web-based apps.

Packaged application vendors like PeopleSoft or SAP are in neutral territory initially, but we expect those slow to exploit the Web, just as those that were slow to client/server, will begin to lose some market share this time next year. The database vendors stand to profit from a shift to more server- and network-based applications; intranet applications normally access internal business systems already running on relational databases.

Figure 10.9

Internet/Online Consulting and Development Competitive Analysis for 2–3 Year Time Horizon

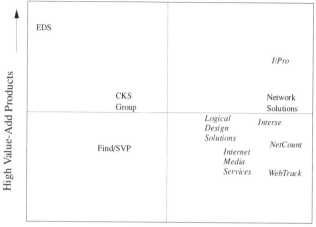

Internet/Online Consulting and Development

Although this is a rather small market today, we believe that as more companies embrace the Internet as a critical means of doing business, the demand for Internet (and networking) consultants and developers of Internet content will blossom. Historically what we have seen in this market is an opportunity for small groups of consultants, not sizable enough for public investment. However, the opportunity is sizable. Currently, two public companies are doing this type of work, and neither is a pure play. Another interesting company, Network Solutions, which has developed a strong knowledge-base by running the InterNIC domain-name registration system, is beginning to leverage its core strengths in Net management to perform corporate intranet consulting. For small-to-medium sized businesses attempting to generate advertising revenues from their web sites or generally trying to quantify site usage for marketing purposes, we like the focus I/Pro has on the question, "How can we know the number of visitors to a home page?" The solution works, in our view, because I/Pro is establishing itself as a credible third party with its affiliation to Nielsen.

Content and Aggregation

Organization/Aggregation

When boiled down to the most common denominator, OSPs do something very similar to the top Web search sites: they organize and aggregate vast amounts of information. We believe that Yahoo, Infoseek and Lycos compete with America Online, CompuServe and Microsoft for this function, and it is the Web search sites that make the Web, and hence the Internet, tolerable and semi-navigable. Also in this space are the software engines that allow Web search sites to be developed. The Web needs better search, organization and aggregation tools and sites.

Strategically, the OSPs have an advantage, because they are already organizing information that has been filtered. The Web is cluttered with useless information, and unfortunately the current Web search sites only assist in mining the useful from the useless information. We have a long way to go.

Like Web search sites, each of the OSPs has differentiated itself. America Online is known as the friendly, easy-to-use service; CompuServe is known as the "power user" service. Microsoft's MSN will be available on the Internet shortly but will likely retain many of its online service characteristics: customizable information, unique content, and pointers to worldwide content. Prodigy is in the process of reinventing itself with a new web-oriented interface, while Delphi was rolled into MCI/News Corp. Internet Ventures in late 1995. Further complicating matters, in February MCI announced a partnership with Microsoft. Several forces affect the competitive environment:

- **Threat of New Entrants**. MSN (and Microsoft generally) represents the big threat.

- **Threat of Substitute Products or Services**. Internet Service Providers and Web search sites pose a threat as customers want to explore the Internet. Online service providers are responding by offering links within their services to the Internet and direct Internet service.

- **Bargaining Power of Suppliers**. Online service providers deal with dominant suppliers, many as sole-source suppliers. Servicing the equipment of multiple manufacturers in an ISP network may be expensive.

- **Bargaining Power of Customers**. While customers can switch providers readily, they become familiar with keystrokes and offerings of a proprietary interface.

- **Rivalry Among Existing Firms Within the Industry** is strong, but the common threat from Microsoft has caused some cooperation among the leading providers.

America Online's strategic focus is on service differentiation, as befits the easiest service to connect to and to use. CompuServe's focus is also on service differentiation, power users and business users who need premium services such as obscure news feeds and databases. Microsoft is going after new users who would not have otherwise attempted to go online. We anticipate a shift in strategic focus in the future that will be on service differentiation, namely on providing Blackbird-compatible content produced by strategic providers.

Prodigy seems to be differentiating its service as the open platform, one that is HTML-based. Users can view Prodigy content and Internet content using a non-Prodigy browser such as Netscape. It appears the Delphi strategy is to drop the Delphi name, repackage as an all-HTML system, and rename together with MCI and News Corp.'s service and content. In doing this, the service will be differentiated as

Figure 10.10

Organization/Aggregation
Competitive Analysis for 2–3 Year Time Horizon

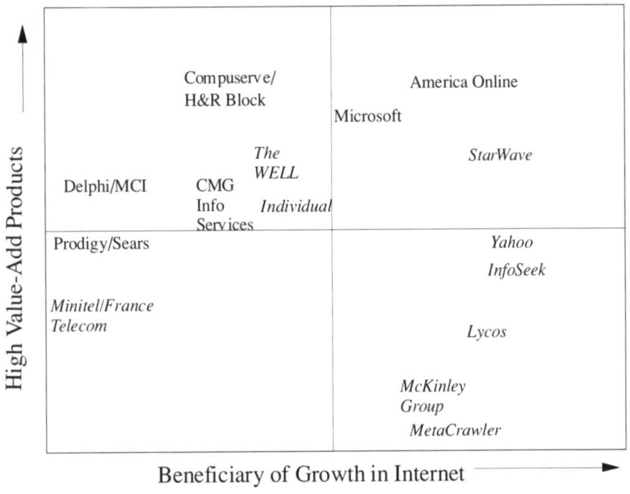

Figure 10.11
Information
Competitive Analysis for 2–3 Year Time Horizon

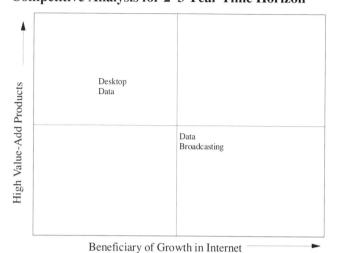

Figure 10.12
Publications/Static
Competitive Analysis for 2–3 Year Time Horizon

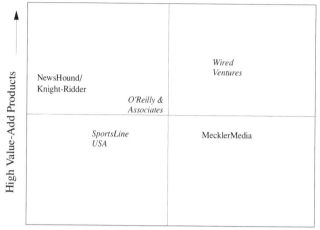

an open platform to which Internet users can access vast amounts of content.

AOL is the leader in the OSP space, in our opinion, as it has the greatest number of users, has been attracting users at a faster rate than others, and has a broad blend of content easily accessible from the service. Starwave, a developer and maintainer of content, holds a leading position in the Internet-based organization/aggregation space. Starwave is benefitting by affiliating itself with early adopters and is gaining mindshare as a content aggregator. It now has ESPN signed up, and including its other sites, it is among the busier sites on the 'net.

Information

There are few "pure" information providers devoted exclusively to the Internet. Two companies feeding information that is not particularly formatted or sorted are Data Broadcasting Corporation and Desktop Data. DBC's strategy appears to be tied very directly with the Microsoft Network, where it has a site where users can get financial information and news. Desktop Data provides feeds to corporate accounts. Considerable market development is necessary before we can identify the leaders.

We have placed Individual, Inc. in the Organization/-Aggregation category because its search engine is a slightly more value-added system that utilizes a more sophisticated (and patented) search engine, resulting in a more reliable and valuable display of information.

Publications/Static

Static publications, as we have defined them in this report, are those that do not change after initial publication or on-line posting. This would include magazines and online magazines. An interactive "publication," by contrast, is constantly changing, like a valuable and highly-moderated chat session.

Currently, we believe Wired Ventures has established strong mindshare in its online product, *HotWired*, and in its printed product, *Wired* magazine. *Wired*'s focus is oriented toward cutting-edge applications, trends in the technology industry, and in its editorial style captures the attitude — and attention span — of the demographic bulge on the Internet: the young and the technology-oriented. Over time, we believe more popular subjects such as sports and news will become more compatible as demographics change, but for now *Wired* has the market.

Publications/Interactive

Interactive publications are those that are available in an online or Internet environment only. These often highly original, specialized publications offer rich content available only in a service, like a chat forum, that is moderated. Thus far, we have only seen one that we consider useful and differentiated from other chat groups: Motley Fool on

Figure 10.13
**Publications/Interactive
Competitive Analysis for 2–3 Year Time Horizon**

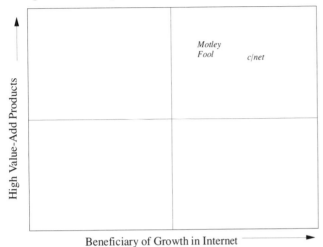

Figure 10.14
**Publishing (Traditional)
Competitive Analysis for 2–3 Year Time Horizon**

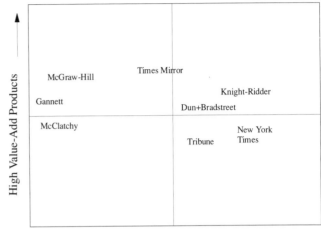

America Online. Coming in second in our ranking is c|net, which, though somewhat less interactive than Motley Fool, is clearly taking a leadership position focusing on the computing industry. It is heavily promotional of its 'Net offering through other media, including the sides of city buses, on billboards, and everywhere else.

Publishing (Traditional)

These companies are in such early stages in the development of online and Internet content that it is very difficult to tell which have a competitive edge. Low-cost publishing, in fact, permits consumers to construct their own Web sites at about $5 per month (see CompuServe's pending service).

Dun+Bradstreet has shown some corporate interest in its Nielsen service by surveying the 'Net. Among newspapers, in our view Knight-Ridder is one of the furthest along in developing an Internet strategy. It is developing online/Internet-oriented offerings including its Mercury News Center and NewsHound, as well as the Internet-availability of many of its regional newspapers such as the Detroit Free Press and Miami Herald. It also has a joint venture with Landmark Communications called InfiNet, which should make newspaper-oriented offerings available in mid-1996.

Transaction Processing and Financial Services

A very young industry is forming as a result of the demand for remote purchasing, transaction processing, and new financial services generated by the Internet and online services. According to an October survey by the Times Mirror Center for the People and the Press, only 8% of Internet users made an online purchase within the last month. Of those who shop online, 90% purchase with credit cards. Those buying on the 'Net spent little time fretting over the security debate: 42% said they were "not at all" concerned about security risks associated with their purchases, 40% were concerned "a little," and 17% said they worried "a lot." Considering these results and how few people are making regular purchases on the 'Net, a major incident is probably needed for this market subsegment to take off.

We believe it will in time, but currently only a few companies have succeeded in gaining mindshare. These are DigiCash, CyberCash and First Virtual. Though each enables cyberpurchasing in a slightly different way, we perceive their opportunities to be roughly the same — they are all in a race to become the de facto standard. Time will tell.

Commerce

Commerce is in its early stages on the Internet and online services. Flowers have sold the best because they're easy. Setting up shop is getting easier and cheaper. Those who master the model early and become frequently visited sites may have some advantage versus other competitors. These appear to be CUC and Internet Shopping Network/Home Shopping Network.

Competitive threats to all commerce companies include intelligent agents: remotely operating software code that can be launched to seek products on the Internet, find low prices, and report back to the computer that initiated the request. Currently there are no robust applications of this type. Andersen Consulting demonstrated one such on the Internet, and the sites to which it was programmed to go (eleven Compact Disk Internet retailers) blocked its access a few days after it was released. We anticipate this technology will have a strong effect on commerce in the future.

Figure 10.15

Transaction Processing and Financial Services Competitive Analysis for 2–3 Year Time Horizon

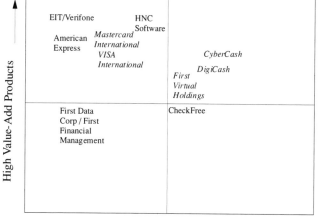

Figure 10.16

Commerce Competitive Analysis for 2–3 Year Time Horizon

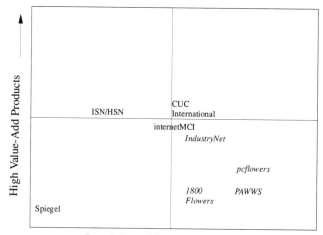

The Internet Report

Section VI:
Supporting Documentation

Chapter 11: Company Descriptions

- Existing and emerging companies, both public and private, are embracing the Internet as a new means of accelerating growth and brand equity.

- We have identified 16 unique Internet market subsegments, comprising three major categories:

- *Infrastructure* — Companies involved in data networking equipment; Internet security equipment and software; Internet service providers; PCs, servers, and semiconductors; telecommunications and related services; and telecommunications equipment.

- *Software and Services* — Companies in application software; enterprise and networking software; and Internet/online consulting and development.

- *Content and Aggregation* — Companies in organization/aggregation; information; publications, whether static, interactive, or traditional; transaction processing and financial services; and commerce.

In this chapter, we list a variety of companies that are in businesses that are, or will be, affected by the ramp-up of the Internet. Our presentation follows the format in our introduction: companies involved with Internet infrastructure, Internet software and services, and Internet content and aggregation (companies are listed in the following table).

Many of the companies in this section don't yet have significant businesses related to the Internet, although all of them are vying to develop Internet-related sources of revenue. **While our company list and write-ups can't be comprehensive (especially for the rapidly growing list of information and content providers), we have attempted to list companies that have a lot to gain or lose from the development of the Internet. We've also included a lot of Internet-specific start-up companies.** One thing is certain: the companies that seem appropriate for the following list today will look very different one year from now (we have also included other interesting companies in our "Cool Sites" chapter). We list the URLs for all companies, and stock tickers are given for those that are publicly traded.

Table 11–1

A. Internet Infrastructure Companies

1. Data Networking Equipment

Public Companies
3Com
Ascend Communications
Boca Research
Cisco Systems
Diamond Multimedia
Global Village
Motorola
Shiva
U.S. Robotics
Xircom
Zoom Telephonics

Private Companies
Hayes Microcomputer Products
Livingston Enterprises

2. Internet Security Equipment and Software

Public Companies
Information Resource Engineering
Secure Computing
Security Dynamics
TimeStep/Newbridge Networks
VASCO Data Security/VASCO Corp.

Private Companies
CheckPoint Software
Livingston Enterprises
RSA Data Security
Raptor Systems
Terisa Systems
Trusted Information Systems
VeriSign

3. Internet Service Providers

Public Companies
Advanced Network Services/America Online
BBN Planet/BBN Corp.
IBM Global Network
iSTAR Internet
MCI Communications
Netcom Online
PSINet
Sprint
UUNET

Private Companies
@Home
Concentric Network Corp.
Demon Internet
IDT
InfiNet
Network 99, Inc./AGIS
Portal Information Network

4. PC, Server, and Semiconductors

Public Companies
Apple Computer
Compaq Computer
Dell Computer
Digital Equipment Corporation
IBM
Intel
Silicon Graphics
Sun Microsystems

5. Telecommunications and Related Services

Public Companies
AT&T
Cox Communications
MCI Communications
Sprint
Tele-Communications Inc.
Time Warner

A. Internet Infrastructure Companies *(continued)*

6. Telecommunications Equipment

<u>Public Companies</u>
Adtran
Cascade Communications
DSC Communications
Digital Link
General Instrument
Northern Telecom
Premisys Communications
StrataCom

B. Internet Software and Services

7. Application Software

<u>Public Companies</u>
Accent Software International
Adobe Systems
Camelot Corporation
FTP Software
Firefox Communications
Fulcrum Technologies
Hummingbird Communications
InContext Systems
Interleaf
Intuit
Macromedia
McAfee Associates
Medior/America Online
Microsoft
Navisoft/America Online
NetManage
Open Text
Netscape Communications
Premenos
Quarterdeck
SoftQuad Inc.
Spyglass
Ubique/America Online
Verity
WAIS/America Online

Private Companies
Ceneca Communications
CONNECT
CyberWISE
Edify Corporation
eShop
Frontier Technologies
InterVista Software
mFactory
Open Market
OpenConnect Systems
Paper Software
Progressive Networks
Spider Technologies
Vermeer Technologies
VocalTec
Wollongong Group/Attachmate
Worlds Inc.

8. Enterprise and Networking Software

<u>Public Companies</u>
Computer Associates
Documentum
Informix
Novell
Oracle Systems
Scopus Technology

9. Internet/Online Consulting, and Development

<u>Public Companies</u>
CKS Group
Find/SVP

Private Companies
I/PRO
Internet Media Services
Intersé
Logical Design Solutions
NetCount
Network Solutions
Web Communications
WebTrack/Caddis International

C. Content and Aggregation

10. Organization/Aggregation

Public Companies
America Online
CMG Information
CompuServe/H&R Block
MCI/News Corp. Internet Ventures (including Delphi)
Lycos, Inc./CMG
Microsoft/MSN
Prodigy/Sears and IBM
WebCrawler/America Online

Private Companies
Architext Software, Inc.
Individual, Inc.
InfoSeek Corporation
The McKinley Group
MetaCrawler
Minitel/France Telecom
Starwave
The WELL
Yahoo Corporation

11. Information

Public Companies
Data Broadcasting
Desktop Data

12. Publication/Static

Public Companies
Mecklermedia
NewsHound/Knight-Ridder
ZDNet/Softbank

Private Companies
iGOLF
NetNoir
O'Reilly & Associates
SportsLine USA
Wired Ventures Ltd.

13. Publication/Interactive

Private Companies
c|net, Inc.
Motley Fool

14. Publishing (Traditional)

Public Companies
Dun & Bradstreet
Gannett
Knight-Ridder
McClatchy
McGraw-Hill
New York Times
Times Mirror
Tribune

15. Transaction Processing and Financial Services

Public Companies
American Express
CheckFree Corporation
Electronic Data Systems/General Motors
Enterprise Integration Technologies/VeriFone
First Data Corp./First Financial Management
HNC Software
VeriFone

Private Companies
CyberCash
DigiCash
First Virtual Holdings
MasterCard International
VISA International

16. Commerce

Public Companies
CUC International
Internet Shopping Network/Home Shopping Network
Spiegel

Private Companies
1-800-FLOWERS
The Electronic Newsstand
IndustryNet
PAWWS
PC Flowers

Infrastructure

Data Networking Equipment

- **Data networking equipment companies supply the building blocks for the Internet, as well as for other data networks**. Simply, this equipment connects computers using wire, fiber, and telecommunications lines. There aren't any large data networking companies that supply only Internet equipment because, in general, the equipment can be used for a variety of applications. Several types of equipment are essential to the building of the TCP/IP Internet system.

- First, there are **routers**, which direct incoming data traffic generated on networks toward its eventual destination and account for many factors, including outgoing line status, traffic patterns, and cost of transmission.

- Second, when a user connects to an ISP or OSP via a modem or ISDN, another device, **a call aggregator, or remote access device**, answers the user's call and switches the session to a router or a switch, which allows the eventual connection to the Internet.

- Third, primarily for larger ISPs and OSPs, **switches** allow a provider to expand its network while still offering fast transmission speeds with few delays between information requests.

- Fourth, **modems** allow remote callers to use the existing analog phone system to connect to an ISP or OSP.

- Other data networking equipment, such as local-area networking (LAN) products (e.g., NICs, or network interface cards, hubs, and LAN switches), have less applicability to the Internet space.

3Com (COMS; Santa Clara, CA; www.3com.com) — 3Com is a leading networking hardware manufacturer, with a diverse product line that includes LAN hubs, LAN network interface cards, switches, routers, and remote access devices. Historically, the company's core competency has been in LANs and corporate internetworking; however, the recent Primary Access and Sonix acquisitions have positioned 3Com to compete in the remote access and Internet marketplace. Although 3Com's remote access and Internet-related products represent a relatively small part of total revenue, they are important to the company's strategic positioning with customers, as corporations rely more upon 3Com to provide a complete networking solution.

Primary Access remote access products are used by carriers, ISPs, and corporations to allow remote users to connect to networks, including the Internet. There is a reasonably solid installed base of Primary Access products at several major carriers that provide dial-up access to data networks, including the Internet. Recent product introductions from Primary Access include a high-density chassis-based call aggregator, which is being marketed to ISPs and carriers. We anticipate that routing and advanced switching capa-

bilities will be announced for Primary Access products in 1996. Sonix products are primarily client-side devices that allow branch offices and small offices to connect to corporate networks and the Internet. Most Sonix products are digital dial-up (ISDN) devices. 3Com's router products historically have been used in non-Internet installations, such as corporate LAN-to-LAN connectivity, but it is likely some routing functionality will be integrated into Primary Access and Sonix products.

Ascend Communications (ASND; Alameda, CA; www.ascend.com) — Ascend manufactures and markets a line of access equipment for network connectivity over switched public digital data services. The company's products also support leased lines. The common denominator of the many application areas served by Ascend's products is bandwidth management — making the most of switched communications links while minimizing costs. Ascend makes access equipment that allows connectivity for a variety of applications, including Internet access, remote access, small-office/home-office, and video conferencing. Ascend's newer products include central-site (MAX) and remote-site (Pipeline) products, which allow LAN interconnection, or single-user to remote network interconnection, over a variety of digital carrier services.

Ascend's MAX has been deployed by 28 of the top 30 Internet access providers (IAPs) to concentrate their subscribers' incoming dialed connections onto the Internet. The MAX has been particularly popular for this application, since it can handle a large number of incoming connections (96), aggregate both analog and digital communications, and convert subscriber traffic into frame-relay packets for transport onto the increasingly popular private frame-relay networks of the IAPs. Ascend's remote-site Pipeline, the SOHO counterpart to the MAX, not only complies with digital communications standards but also links with the MAX. The Pipeline is also well-suited for use by Internet subscribers connecting to their ISP.

Boca Research (BOCI; Boca Raton, FL; www.boca.org) — Boca designs, manufactures, and markets data communications, multimedia, and networking products to enhance the transmission of information on personal computers and computer networks. Hardware products are augmented with software for use in such markets as corporate, consumer, and small office/home office. Current product categories are: 1) data communications — fax/data/voice modems; 2) multimedia peripherals for video, telephony, sound, voice, and data; 3) networking — Ethernet hubs and network interface cards; 4) videographics; and 5) input/output, interface device enabler (IDE), and multiport products.

Boca recently signed an agreement with Asian-based MBF Group to gain access to market opportunities in that region. In addition, the company announced a licensing agreement with Midisoft, whereby Boca will bundle Midisoft's MediaWorks collection of audio- and telephone-related software with its own products. Similarly, Boca's products will be bundled with VocalTec's version of Internet Phone software. Boca also plans to develop ISDN drivers for Windows 95.

Cisco Systems (CSCO; San Jose, CA; cio.cisco.com) — Cisco is the leading supplier of backbone routers on the Internet, with an estimated 80%-plus market share. An estimated 35%–45% of all of Cisco's revenue is related to the Internet infrastructure build-out. Cisco is also positioning itself to capture leading market shares in several other Internet markets, including remote access and Internet

(server) software. Traditionally, Cisco has been regarded as a router company; however, the company recently announced a new organizational structure consisting of the following business units: Core (routers); Workgroup (hubs, switches); InterWorks (IBM); Access; ATM; and Internet (software).

Cisco's mission statement is to: "1) sell networks; and 2) do anything else that promotes #1." The company's three most recent acquisition announcements are: Grand Junction, a supplier of Fast Ethernet and Ethernet desktop switching products; Internet Junction (announced August 1995), a software company specializing in Novell LAN connectivity to the Internet; and Network Translation (October 1995), a developer of low-maintenance network address translation (NAT) and Internet firewall software and equipment. These three acquisitions should stimulate Cisco's growth in the end-market for Internet connectivity by supporting growth in Cisco's sales of network equipment and software. In addition, Cisco's acquisition of Combinet (August 1995) increases its offerings to the small-office/home-office (SOHO), branch office, and Internet access markets with ISDN products. Cisco also announced a strategic alliance with Nokia to provide ATM-based voice/data networking solutions to Internet Service Providers.

Diamond Multimedia (DIMD; San Jose, CA; www.diamondmm.com) — Diamond Multimedia is a designer, manufacturer, and marketer of multimedia hardware solutions for the personal computer, Power PC, and Macintosh professional and consumer markets. Products include accelerators, sound cards, audio/telephony subsystems, and multimedia accelerators and upgrade kits. The company recently announced a line of integrated 3-D multimedia accelerators and believes its product to be the only single-board solution offering such a complete set of features. Additionally, Diamond is one of 24 vendors that plans to develop ISDN drivers for Windows 95.

In mid-October, Diamond bid to acquire Hayes Microcomputer Products, a well-known modem maker, for $158 million. Subsequently, U.S. Robotics bid $7 million more for Hayes, and the pending deals are still outstanding. As of December 7th, Diamond Multimedia bid more for the company, and on December 18, confirmation hearings are expected in court. This is not a done deal. Shortly before the Hayes acquisition attempt, Diamond acquired Supra

Corp., a lesser-known modem maker, for $56 million. Diamond's strategy is to compete with modem market-share leader U.S. Robotics.

Global Village (GVIL; Sunnyvale, CA; www.globalvillag.com) — Global Village markets modems and communications software, and provides Internet access. The company is the market-share leader in Macintosh-compatible fax/modems and software. Recently a number of the company's products have been ported to Windows- and OS/2. Finally, the company is an Internet Service Provider — its offering, called GlobalCenter Internet, is focused toward small and medium-sized businesses. With GlobalCenter Internet, Global Village is basically a reseller of UUNET's service to consumers. By tapping into UUNET's network, Global Village expects to offer customers increased local dial-up services by the end of 1995. Global Village recently signed an agreement with UUNET Technologies, allowing GlobalCenter Internet customers faster and more sophisticated dial-up options.

Global Village acquired KNX Limited in October 1995, a U.K.-based provider of ISDN remote access products, to address the demand for high-speed Internet access.

Hayes Microcomputer Products (Atlanta, GA; www.hayes.com) — Hayes, a leading modem maker, filed for Chapter 11 bankruptcy in late 1994 and has been involved in three separate merger discussions over the past year, with Boca Research in August, Diamond Multimedia in early October, and U.S. Robotics in late October. Each time the bids have gone up, and as of December 7, Diamond had raised its bid.

Hayes' product line comprises modems, software, WAN products, and connectivity products. The company was founded in 1978 and, after the PC emerged in 1981, Hayes was about the only modem maker around. By the mid-1980s though, competition had heated up, and the pressure grew strong by the end of that decade. In 1989, Hayes acquired modem maker Practical Peripherals, and in 1990 Hayes underwent a corporate restructuring consisting mainly of lay-offs. In 1994, the company experienced difficulty with manufacturing its products, leading to a shipping stoppage from chip supplier Rockwell in early 1995.

Livingston Enterprises (Pleasanton, CA; www.livingston.com) — See discussion in the "Internet Security Equipment and Software" section of this chapter.

Motorola (MOT; Schaumburg, IL; www.mot.com) — Motorola has conveyed a vision that it plans to be a major developer and supplier of system solutions for network switching equipment over the next several years. Currently, Motorola offers several Internet-related products, such as external and PCMCIA modems, leased-line CSU/DSUs, ISDN terminal adapters, and cellular modems. The company expects ATM communication protocol to be the catalyst for a variety of future consumer services, such as switched digital video, interactive multimedia, and telecommuting.

ATM switches, configured as "edge" or "access" switches, will combine the functions of a Digital Loop Carrier, Add/Drop multiplexer, and ATM switch router, serving as a gateway between the local- and wide-area networks. The next-higher layer of the network is the backbone of the system, very large switches configured as virtual path cross-connects. At the highest level, connections between switches traverse optical fiber. Motorola offers OPTOBUS parallel optical links for this purpose. It also offers a wide selection of specialized communications chips for switch control, signal processing, and the 100VG-AnyLAN next-generation, high-speed LAN protocol. Motorola takes a big-picture view of the requirements of the telecommunications infrastructure of the future, and it plans to have a technical solution to meet challenges on every link in the system. Finally, the company will continue to offer and expand a comprehensive array of wireless components and devices so that laptop, cellular phone, pager, and personal digital assistant users can effortlessly go online and make convenient timely use of a seamless communications infrastructure. Motorola also recently made an equity investment of an undisclosed amount in Terisa Systems, and will take a seat on Terisa's board of directors.

Shiva Corporation (SHVA; Burlington, MA; www.shiva.com) — Shiva develops analog and digital remote access server products. These products allow remote users access, via dial-up modems or ISDN terminal devices, to centralized networks such as corporate LANs. Shiva offers a variety of product lines, including NetModem, LanRover, and Integrator. These remote access servers operate under MS-DOS, Windows, Macintosh, and UNIX environments and can be configured and managed using Shiva's Net Manager software. Shiva also operates an OEM business, and recently announced the production of frame relay software intended to allow equipment suppliers to easily add frame relay functionality to their products. In a move to offer a broader range of remote access products, Shiva acquired Spider, an ISDN networking company, in August 1995.

Shiva's partners include Hewlett-Packard, IBM, Microsoft, and Nortel. The company recently announced a strategic alliance with XcelleNet, a provider of connection-deferred remote enterprise computing, intending to simplify and improve the way remote and mobile computer users access centralized information.

U.S. Robotics (USRX; Skokie, IL; www.usr.com) — U.S. Robotics, the leading supplier of analog modems, has been rapidly expanding its product offerings to include all aspects of remote network connectivity, including digital dial-up capabilities (ISDN), multi-user shared access communications servers, and enterprise WAN server hubs. Unlike many of its modem competitors, the company manufactures many of its products. Modem offerings include: 1) the Courier, the high-end analog modem line; 2) the Sportster, the low-end analog modem line; 3) ISDN-enabled versions of the same modems, dubbed I-modems; and 4) Megahertz PCMCIA modems. Shared access products allow multiple users on networks to use the same resource, such as a fax or modem. USR has two such product lines: the Shared Access Com Server; and the Shared Access Fax Server. These products allow users on a network to call out to other networks, such as the Internet.

Every product that U.S. Robotics sells could be used at some place on the Internet. Due to the indirect nature of product distribution, it is unclear what percentage of its products are used on the Internet. USR's Total Control products, which in the early days would have been called "modem pools," are becoming a larger percentage of total revenue; when connected to a network, these products allow remote, modem-using callers to call in to the Total Control product, which then connects the user to the network. Total Control products are typically installed at larger corporate LANs and at Internet Service Providers' data centers. The products include: 1) the Security Server, a PC-based dial-up platform that provides secure remote access to the Total Control Enterprise Network Hub Chassis; 2) Enterprise Network Hub/6, a modular, software-configurable integrated access platform for smaller hybrid networks; 3) Integral X.25 PAD, which allows asynchronous dial-up access to X.25 networks (like an OSP network) without

cabling modems to an external PAD, which is perhaps most applicable to an Internet Service Provider; and 4) The Total Control Enterprise Network Hub chassis, which is used for dial-up local- and wide-area data networking applications and can be configured with variations of channelized T1 cards, analog or digital modem cards, or gateway cards for connections to Ethernet/Token.

Recent announcements by the company include: a letter of intent signed with Bell Atlantic to bring an ISDN product to retail markets in the next month; a bid to acquire Hayes Microcomputer Products; the acquisition of Palm Computing, the maker of operating systems and application software for hand-held computers and communications devices; and the acquisition of ISDN Systems, a developer of board-level ISDN and frame relay-based client-server products. U.S. Robotics bid in late 1995 to acquire Hayes and withdrew in February 1996.

Xircom (XIRC; Thousand Oaks, CA; www.xircom.com) — Xircom is a manufacturer and marketer of networking equipment. Xircom's core business includes: 1) parallel port LAN adapters; 2) PCMCIA LAN adapters; and 3) combined LAN and modem adapters. Other product lines include PCMCIA modems, ISDN client products such as ISA cards (and soon external terminal adapters), ISDN server PRI products, wireless LAN adapters, and multiport modem cards for remote access.

Over the past year, the company has expanded its product line beyond the core business, LAN adapters, and in the past two quarters has begun manufacturing operations in Malaysia. Expectations are that Xircom will come to market with new products in early 1996, such as PCMCIA ISDN/analog modems, PCMCIA 10/100 mbps ASIC-based Ethernet adapters, and ISDN terminal adapters.

Zoom Telephonics (ZOOM; Boston, MA; www.zoomtel.com) — Zoom markets modems and fax/modems for Macs and PCs. The company produces a number of variations on its products, including internal, external, pocket, and PCMCIA models, available as both landline and cellular send-and-receive devices. Zoom's products are distributed by retailers, distributors, and OEMs, and are also integrated into personal computer products by PC manufacturers. Zoom is developing distribution markets in Europe, Asia, and Africa and plans to further develop and expand its product line.

Internet Security Equipment and Software

- **The No. 1 concern for information technology managers considering a corporate connection to the Internet is security.** Despite the hype that surrounds this general phrase, the issue is real. There are many types of security to be concerned about when connecting a network to the Internet. No single company currently addresses all of these Internet security concerns, and there are more security concerns to be addressed that are not related to the Internet, such as internal security breaches to sensitive corporate information. We believe there will be rapid consolidation in this industry after an initial introductory phase where products compete for market share, such that vendors develop or aggregate products to create solutions that address most, if not all, security concerns for Internet connections as well as enterprise networks. Offerings in the Internet security market are focused on the following key issues:

- First, **transmission security,** which can be resolved through encryption and virtual private networking;

- Second, **transaction security,** which can be addressed through encryption — typically bundled in software;

- Third, **external security breaches through the Internet connection,** which can be prevented through firewalling;

- Fourth, **external security breaches from dial-up systems for remote users,** which are averted through user authentication schemes and one-time passwording that can be enabled with token cards; and

- Fifth, **user authorization breaches,** which are solved in similar manner to external security breaches from dial-up systems for remote users.

CheckPoint Software (Rabin Gan, Israel; Redwood City, CA; www.checkpoint.com) — CheckPoint Software, primarily a firewalling company, offers a family of software products designed to provide integrated, secure solutions for the Internet. The company's FireWall-1 product was introduced in mid-1994. Primarily due to CheckPoint's lead in bringing the firewall to market, the company has established substantial relationships with resellers and other technology companies, notably Sun. Features of FireWall-1 include: router control management (through the FireWall-1 gateway, which controls network traffic to and from the Internet and a company's internal network); full Internet connectivity with security; a dynamic Stateful Multi-Layer Inspection Module (the system that controls access to a company's network while providing users secure access to all Internet resources and IP-based services); user authentication; address translation; complete control over all network communication; adaptability; transparency; and protocol-independent software tools.

Information Resource Engineering (IREG; Baltimore, MD; www.ire.com) — Information Resource Engineering (IRE) designs, manufactures, and markets secure remote access and ISDN systems, which encrypt data transmissions on computer networks and ISDN products used for high-speed digital dial-up access to networks. In effect, its primary product line is modems that perform encryption. IRE is a leading supplier of secure dial-up access products that allow secure transactions and communications over a remote network link. Products include: the AX400, a secure modem used by financial institutions, government organizations, and recently Internet commerce companies; SafeNet, a family of products that began shipping in C4Q95 that combines public and private key encryption technology for secure communications on the Internet; and other secure remote access and ISDN devices. SafeNet, through the combination of data encryption and firewall technology, allows organizations to use the Internet as a "private" network, saving on the costs of leased telecommunications lines. The SafeNet product has three components: 1) SafeNet/LAN, an encrypting firewall that combines encryption technology with firewall filtering; 2) SafeNet/DIAL, a portable, pocket-size encrypting 28.8 Kbps modem, which generates a new, complex password for each Internet session and serves as a conventional modem when contracting unprotected sites; and 3) SafeNet/CERTIFICATE CENTER, which manages SafeNet security products and services. Both public and private keys are managed on a single high-performance workstation and conform with banking, government, and IETF standards. Currently, the ISDN products have no encryption capabilities, but the company expects these capabilities by the first half of 1996.

In September 1995, IRE announced that MCI had purchased over $10 million of the company's SafeNet Secure Internet products, to be delivered over a two-year period. On October 10, IRE announced that Intuit Services Corp. would use its secure remote access products to protect financial transactions in a state-of-the-art electronic commerce application available through Intuit's Quicken software.

Livingston Enterprises (Pleasanton, CA; www.livingston.com) — Livingston makes dial-in communications servers (remote access), Internet firewall routers (packet filtering), and RADIUS (remote authentication dial-in user service) security. The company's products include dial-in and dial-out communications servers (some with integrated routing), dial-up routers, and access routers. It also offers PC client software, security software, and management utilities to support these products.

As of December 1995, Livingston's customers included 1,363 Internet service providers. Livingston's most popular product remains the PortMaster Communications Server. In 1995, the company shipped 230,050 access ports. Using a typical ratio of 10 subscribers to 1 port, Livingston's products were used to connect over 2 million users to the Internet last year. This user count excluded sales of IRX Access Routers sold through ISPs to Lan-to-Internet customers.

In October, Livingston announced an ISDN product line, using a new ISDN chip from AT&T that significantly reduces cost. The company's work in developing the chip with AT&T allowed it to receive quantities of the chip months ahead of the general market. The ISDN product line includes:

- a 5-port BRI module for the PortMaster 2E and 2ER;

- an ISDN office Router with BRI and an integrated NT-1 for $1,195; and

- an ISDN PC ISA card with BRI (and NT-1) for $299.

Livingston's remote access products address both corporate and Internet connectivity. These include: 1) dial-in/dial-out communications servers with 10, 20, or 30 ports; 2) communications servers with integrated router functions that support TCP/IP and IPX routing over leased lines, frame relay, ISDN, switched 56, and public switched telephone networks (PSTN); 3) dial-up routers, which consist of the Office Router, which provides TCP/IP or IPX connectivity from small-office LANs to corporate headquarters or the Internet, with one Ethernet port and two ISDN ports and support for V.34 modems; 4) access routers for LAN-to-LAN internetworking at T-1 or fractional T-1 speeds with or without packet-filtering firewalling capabilities; 5) network management software, included with all hardware products; and 6) security software (or RADIUS), which is a standard remote dial-up security technology jointly developed by Livingston and Cisco.

RSA Data Security (Redwood City, CA; www.rsa.com) — RSA, a maker of encryption-enabling software, develops platform-independent cryptographic software. This software is a de facto standard that enables many other vendors to implement encryption technology within their products. Although there is other encryption software available, such as the data encryption standard (DES), millions of copies of RSA's encryption and authentication software are in use worldwide. Since the 1970s, RSA has made encryption software for software packages, hardware, and most recently for Internet message encryption. RSA's product lines include: *BSAFE*, a comprehensive cryptographic toolkit for software developers; *TIPEM*, a toolkit for interoperable privacy-enhanced messaging, such as local encryption, electronic forms routing and approval, authenticated software licensing and distribution, network authentication, and secure TCP/IP- or X.400-based applications; *CIS*, Certificate Issuing System, which is RSA's secure, hardware-based certificate generation and tracking system; *RSA Secure*, for disk and file encryption; and *MailSafe*, a security overlay for DOS-based e-mail systems. RSA's technology is incorporated in many of the products from companies described in this report.

At the end of October 1995, RSA announced that its authentication and encryption technology had been incorporated into Aquila Technologies Group's Gemini product, a fully authenticated digital video surveillance system for secure, unattended monitoring. The International Atomic

Energy Agency plans to install the Gemini system by the end of 1995 at nuclear sites across the globe to enforce the Non-Proliferation Treaty.

Raptor Systems (Waltham, MA; www.raptor.com) — Raptor, primarily a firewalling software company, provides network security products for the Internet through its integrated firewall security management software and services. The company's products allow networks (or even single computers) to be connected to other networks, including the Internet, providing high levels of security for network resources and information. Using Raptor firewalling and encryption software, Virtual Private Networks (VPNs) can be effectively set up "inside" the Internet, which allow companies to use the public Internet to securely interconnect branch offices and mobile users as if they were the only ones using it — a significant connectivity cost savings.

The company's Eagle family of real-time network security products is based on an application-level firewall architecture that comprises a suite of modular software components and offers comprehensive Internet and LAN security for corporate enterprises and small businesses. Raptor's products are based on its Five Domains of Security model. This model describes how the products provide network security for Internet, workgroup, mobile computing, and remote office domains within the enterprise. Eagle products include the Eagle Firewall (Internet security), the Eagle LAN/EagleDesk (workgroup security), EagleNomad (mobile PC security), and EagleRemote (remote site security). Raptor's products are compatible with Sun, Hewlett-Packard, and IBM workstations. In addition, Raptor has teamed up with Edify to deliver secure online interactive services. Raptor filed to go public in December 1995.

Secure Computing (SCUR; Roseville, MN; www.sctc.com) — Secure develops and markets: 1) firewall software and hardware servers; 2) one-time challenge-response authentication servers; and 3) secure network servers, which allow computer networks at different levels to exchange information in a secure manner. The company markets to government and corporate users and employs over 160 engineers. The company's firewall server package is called SideWinder. It allows corporate users to connect LANs or corporate internetworks to the Internet, but adds a level of security unavailable in non-secure servers. The SideWinder offers users on corporate LANs access to Internet services; at the same time, using rule-setting and filtering mechanisms and active defense capabilities, it does not allow unauthorized access from persons trying to access the corporate LAN from the Internet. The SideWinder product is complementary to packet-filtering (firewalling) routers. The company has partnerships with Oracle, Cylink, Digital Pathways, and Net One Co. Ltd. (a Mitsubishi corporation).

Security Dynamics (SDTI; Cambridge, MA; www.securid.com) — Security Dynamics develops and markets remote access security products used to restrict access to networks. The products employ a patent-protected combination of smart card technology (SecurID Card) and software or hardware access control products (ACE/Server and ACM) to authenticate the identity of users accessing networked or stand-alone computing resources. The company has a long list of licensees, as many hardware and software companies have standardized upon SDI's remote access authentication products.

The SecurID Card and server software solution enforce the use of one-time passwording each time a remote user logs into a network. Because the password is used only once, even if an eavesdropper has obtained the password, reusing the log-in information will not allow network access. Each remote network user must carry a SecurID card, about the size of a thick credit card, which displays a new number each minute. When logging into the network, which is running the ACE/Server software, the user enters a combination of log-in identification codes coupled with the one-time passcode displayed on the SecurID card. The server then reviews this entry and allows or denies access. The market for this type of product is potentially large, because people are increasingly working remotely.

Terisa Systems (Los Altos, CA; www.terisa.com) — Terisa Systems is a developer of security software toolkits and transaction security technology for application developers, allowing secure transactions over the Internet. The toolkit employs RSA, SSL, and S-HTTP encryption technologies, which enable others to design these security features into their software. Terisa's SecureWeb product family provides secure Web applications for commercial transactions over the Internet. SecureWeb toolkits support S-HTTP, and Terisa has integrated SSL into its toolkits, which support transaction security, payment modules, and certification products. Customers include Bank of America, CyberCash, First Data, MasterCard, OpenMarket, Spyglass, Spry, and Sybase.

Terisa, formed as a joint venture between EIT and RSA Data Security, announced in September the completion of its reorganization, in which America Online, CompuServe, EIT, IBM, Netscape Communications, and RSA Data Security have all become equity holders in Terisa to form a business to develop a unified and consistent approach to Internet security. Under the reorganization, the six shareholders have contributed investments or technology to Terisa for the development of a suite of Internet security products designed to make it easier to provide and access secure information on the Internet. The online service providers will also adopt and implement Terisa's technologies. Terisa's SecureWeb toolkit products support both S-HTTP and SSL. Most recently, Motorola made an equity investment of an undisclosed amount in Terisa, filling a seventh seat on Terisa's board of directors.

TimeStep (affiliate of Newbridge Networks/NN; Ontario, Canada; www.newbridge.com) — As a maker of transmission security products, Time Step has developed hardware- and software-based encryption products that allow the secure transmission of data from desktop to desktop across networks, including the Internet. TimeStep's primary product family is called PERMIT, which, when installed on workstations or network nodes, allows encrypted (secure) communications from the desktop or across the enterprise network, independent of the underlying network media, bridges, or routers. At the workstation, PERMIT provides access control, file integrity for virus protection, and transparent disk encryption. All PERMIT secure node components contain an industry standard SNMPv2 agent for in-band secure management, and can be controlled and monitored by the TimeStep Secure Network Management System (SNMS). Products generally come in two types: 1) hardware systems, complete with processors; and 2) software applications, which run on the workstation. Depending upon the workstation capabilities and network configuration, either software or a hardware "box" is installed at each workstation, or a secure bridge is installed on the LAN, which is to be secured from other LANs. PERMIT uses standards-based encryption, including ANSI Data Encryption Standard (DES) and the de facto RSA Public Key Cryptography. Newbridge Networks owns a minority equity stake in TimeStep.

Trusted Information Systems (Glenwood, MD; www.tis.com) — Trusted Information Systems (TIS) is a maker of The Gauntlet firewall, which is sold both by Trusted and many other partners. Other products include multi-level secure (MLS) e-mail guards and e-mail security products. Trusted's MLS e-mail guard (TMEGTM-200) is the second product in a series of e-mail guards being developed by TIS to meet Department of Defense requirements for multi-level secure (MLS) e-mail guards. These guards aim to achieve affordability, flexibility, ability to upgrade with ease, and DMS compatibility. TIS/MOSS is Trusted Information Systems' implementation of MIME Object Security Services (MOSS). It is a security toolkit that provides digital signature and encryption services for MIME objects. TIS/MOSS can be used to protect sensitive and unclassified e-mail for personal, administrative, logistics, procurement, finance, personnel, and medical communications.

VASCO Data Security (subsidiary of VASCO Corp./VASC; Lombard, IL; www.vdsi.com) — VDSI develops and markets hardware and software products used to protect networks from external security breaches. These products can be used to protect a network connected to the Internet, or a network with remote access devices and/or call aggregators. The company's hardware and software security products manage and protect access to a range of computer-based information resources. VDSI's patented and proprietary products provide computer security, extended user authentication (EUA), and virus protection capabilities. VDSI's product line includes Access Key II, a "one-time" password generator that authenticates users before granting access to a computer system or network. ABN-AMRO Bank in the Netherlands has utilized the company's products since 1987 to authenticate users of its Cash Management System, which allows bank customers to perform sophisticated transactions, including wire transfers unattended by bank officials. Other features of the company's product line include comprehensive virus protection and hard disk encryption, with simultaneous multi-level data security, and access control. SCRAMBLE, an optional feature, allows data encryption for file transfers of sensitive data over any network or public telecommunications system. To date, VDSI has shipped over 250,000 software and hardware access control products worldwide.

VeriSign (Mountain View, CA; www.verisign.com) — A leader of digital authentication services and products for electronic commerce and other forms of secure communications, VeriSign's offerings are divided into three lines of business: 1) Public Certificate Services (also known as Digital ID Services — an authenticated electronic "credential" or "letter of introduction" that certifies the connection between a public key and its owner); 2) Private-Label Certificate Services; and 3) Certificate Management Products. VeriSign, founded in 1995 as a spin-off of RSA Data Security, is working with its investors — including Ameritech and VISA International — and its partners — such as Netscape, Open Market, and IBM — to open the digital marketplace to all consumers. VeriSign's goal is to provide consumers, merchants, and corporations with the confidence to conduct electronic commerce worldwide.

VeriSign is best known for its Digital ID technology, and in September it announced the Web's first Online Digital ID Issuing Service. The initial service allows Netscape Navigator 2.0 users to enroll and receive a unique Digital ID. VeriSign also announced a classification system for its brand of public identification certificates, defining four available levels of identity assurance. Investors in Verisign include: Ameritech, Bessemer Venture Partners, Fischer International, Mitsubishi Corporation, RSA Data Security, Security Dynamics, Terisa, and VISA International.

Internet Service Providers

- Narrowly defined, an Internet Service Provider (ISP) is a company that offers consumers and corporations dial-up or permanent access to the Internet. More broadly, we can include the "bulk carriers" of traffic, either Internet traffic or just data. In the broader view, ISPs may also include Internet backbone providers, or companies that connect smaller ISP networks and may also provide access on the consumer or corporate level. Even more broadly defined, network (or data) service providers are companies that lease telecommunications lines, such as T-1s and T-3s, or data network services, such as frame relay or ATM. Looking ahead, it is likely that the three groups of providers will offer similar services, such as when AT&T begins providing dial-up access to consumers, or when PSINet offers network service.

- **In general, an ISP allows consumers, corporations, and other network service providers to connect to the ISP networks, which are in turn connected to an Internet backbone provider. ISPs include Netcom, PSINet, UUNET, and Concentric — there are more than 3,000 ISPs worldwide.** An ISP may be a small regional network with, say, one to twenty points of presence (POPs), or it may be a collection of large nationwide or worldwide regional networks interconnected by others' Internet backbones. **The primary value an ISP provides to a customer is local-call access (for dial-up accounts) or short-distance leased-line access (for corporate/dedicated accounts).** Significant capital is being expended by major ISPs to establish numerous POPs in major local-call areas to compel users to connect to the ISP networks. Many ISPs lease their networks for non-Internet traffic as a public network service, including such services as frame relay and X.25. The ISP networks may be owned or leased.

- Internet backbone providers connect ISPs' regional networks using their high-speed (usually optical-based) networks. **Today, there are six major Internet backbone providers, of which MCI is the largest. The others are Sprint, PSINet, UUNET, ANS (owned by America Online), and Network 99**.

- **Network service providers** lease "bulk" network capacity to the ISPs. ISPs, using their own networks or others', in turn interconnect with one another through peering and transit agreements. ISP interconnections are enabled by Internet backbone providers. **Data network service providers** offer customers use of their network infrastructure. There are many types of networks available on this basis; the most common Internet-related network types include X.25, frame relay, and ATM. Network usage is measured in a variety of ways. Other leasable network resources include POPs, network operations centers, and maintenance. Network service providers are dominated by the traditional telecommunications providers, such as MCI, Sprint, and AT&T, as well as competitive access providers Wiltel and WorldCom/LDDS. Non-Internet data network service providers are described under the heading "Telecommunications and Related Services."

@Home (Mountain View, CA; www.home.net) —
@Home, a joint venture between cable giant TCI and venture capital firm Kleiner Perkins Caufield & Byers, plans to provide high-speed data services to homes, businesses, and schools via hybrid fiber coaxial (HFC) technology to PCs. HFC technology delivers both cable television signals and data over a combined fiber-optic and coaxial infrastructure. The company announced at the beginning of November 1995 that Sunnyvale, CA, will be the initial market for the launch of its services in early 1996. @Home will operate its own global network infrastructure that connects to the Internet at multiple locations. This backbone will connect information providers to regional data centers via a multi-megabit, switched data system. The @Home services will be offered via a high-speed modem attached to the user's computer through high-volume cable connections delivering information at speeds of 10 Mbps. The result is expected to be a vivid and fluid impression — received without waiting for the downloading of images.

@Home is also expected to feature a multimedia home page (a high-bandwidth media-like set of pages with the ability to guide the system into the Internet and to online services, such as America Online, CompuServe, Prodigy, and MSN), as well as a wide variety of local content from third parties, including news, information, and community networking.

@Home also plans to provide users with a customized browser developed by Netscape.

Advanced Network Services (subsidiary of America Online/AMER; Ann Arbor, MI; www.ans.net) — ANS is a major Internet backbone provider in the U.S. It was established by IBM, MCI, and Merit (a consortium of Michigan universities), and later joined by Northern Telecom. The company develops proprietary technology for the design, development, and deployment of large-scale, high-performance WANs and private data network services, providing Internet connectivity. As the principal architect of the NSFNet, ANS uses its expertise to deliver high-speed (45 Mbps), value-added internetworking solutions that meet the mission-critical requirements of a wide range of businesses and organizations.

Committed to advancing TCP/IP technology, ANS designs, engineers, installs, manages, monitors, and maintains nationwide private corporate data networks over AOLnet, a high-speed, large TCP/IP network. Customers can attach their networks to the AOLnet (formerly ANSnet) backbone infrastructure to communicate with users on other networks. ANS offers services in four general areas: 1) Connection Services; 2) Professional Services; 3) Enabling Services; and 4) Security Services. ANS was acquired by America Online in January 1995 and is working closely with Global Network Navigator (GNN) to beta test America Online's dial-up Internet service. Currently, a large portion of ANS's traffic is being used for Internet access via America Online's users through their access to AOLnet. Note that in C4Q95, 40% of America Online's traffic was on AOLnet. ANS has 250 POPs.

AGIS (Apex Global Information Services; Phoenix, AZ; www.net99.net) — AGIS is a global Internet backbone provider based in the Chicago area. Net99 was recently acquired by AGIS and competes with about five other backbone providers: MCI, Sprint, ANS, PSINet, and UUNET. Net99's competitive focus is price leadership, as its costs for leased-line connections to its backbone network are less than half of the historical rate for connections. The company estimates it carries 15% of domestic and 12% of global internet traffic. Through arrangements with other carriers, such as LDDS/World Com, the company has over 200 POPs for permanent connection (non-dialup) customers. The company has 300 T-1 plus customers, including Demon Internet and ATM Net.

Concentric Network Corp. (Cupertino, CA; www.cris.com) — Concentric is a nationwide data network service provider offering: 1) Internet access; 2) a proprietary information service (CRIS); 3) a nationwide bulletin board system (BBS) network; and 4) access to Intuit's Quicken Financial Network (QFN). The Concentric network is frame-relay based and uses AT&T's InterSpan backbone. There are currently 100 POPs to the network; the company also offers an 800 service.

Concentric provides connectivity for a wide variety of information and entertainment services, including: *BBS Direct* — which offers links to dozens of bulletin boards nationwide; *CRIS (Concentric Research Information Service)* — offering network games, forums, file libraries, and conferencing; and *Internet Services* — providing complete Internet functionality (via UNIX shell or dial-in SLIP), including e-mail, USENET news, telnet, FTP, IRC, and Web access and authoring tools. Concentric recently announced an alliance with Intuit to provide Internet access to users of Quicken for Windows through an upgrade route, with pricing at $1.95 per month for one hour of use and $1.95 for each additional hour for low-use customers; for high-use customers, the price is $9.95 per month for 7 hours of access, plus $1.95 per each additional hour. Concentric also has announced a strategic alliance with Ameritech to help local telephone exchange carriers (LECs) in the U.S. provide Internet access to rural customers, thereby allowing rural LECs to become ISPs.

BBN Planet (division of BBN Corp./BBN; Cambridge, MA; www.bbnplanet.com) — BBN (formerly Bolt Beranek & Newman) is a research and development company with several operating divisions. Most of its efforts are focused on government-funded research. BBN Planet, a division of BBN, is an Internet service provider. BBN Planet represents a small portion (less than 10%) of the overall company revenue and has become well-known for connecting many major universities to the Internet. BBN Planet consists of the recently acquired SURANET (Southeastern regional network), BARRNET (Bay Area regional network), and NEARNET (New England regional network). BBN Planet, thus far, has focused on corporate and university accounts and does not provide Internet access to consumers through dial-up connections. BBN Planet is leading a cable-TV Internet access trial in the Boston suburbs. BBN is also focusing on vertical markets, such as the educational market, through its relationship with Competitive Curriculum Corp., a division of Simon & Schuster Educational Multimedia Publishing.

BBN Systems and Technologies, BBN's largest division, performs contract research for corporate and government accounts. In 1969, BBN was selected to develop and build the ARPANet; as such, BBN lays claim to being one of the oldest Internet companies around. Ongoing projects involve advanced networking, speech recognition and language understanding, distributed collaborative systems, educational technologies, sensor systems, and acoustics. This division also builds large data networks for private companies and develops customized software and hardware. For instance, BBN recently developed a commercial video router that works over IP networks. But BBN's core business is R&D, and occasionally its new products and software become the basis for a new operating division. This was the case with all of the current noncore operating divisions: BBN Planet; BBN Hark (speech recognition); and BBN Domain (industrial process control software). The company owns 65 POPS and leases approximately 500 more.

Demon Internet (London, U.K.; www.demon.co.uk) — Demon Internet is the largest Internet service provider in the U.K. As of October 1, 1995, Demon had over 45,000 dial-up customers (a 65% share of that market), including consumers, corporations, and government agencies, and it is acquiring subscribers at a rate of about 8% per month. Demon also has one of the largest commercial Web sites in Europe, with over 75,000 files and more than 3.5 million accesses per month. The company offers: full, direct access to the Internet via local dial-up from over 800 locations throughout the U.K.; a unique Internet address for each user's computer (allowing users to create multiple user names); access to all Internet newsgroups (currently over 14,000) via a local news server; access to files and other information worldwide via high-speed international links and an FTP server; and hundreds of lines for dial-up usage around the U.K., plus private international leased lines to the U.S.; and interconnections with all other U.K. providers.

In October 1995, Demon announced that the Conservative Party had become a customer (www.conservative-party.org.uk), posting daily press releases, details of Party policy, and campaign news. The Conservative Party has a leased line to Demon and operates a dial-up service for Party members via the company. Demon also uses a RealAudio server. Demon completed a private stock issue in October to a number of private investors and U.K. institutions, including Apax Partners & Co., raising £5.5 million (US$8.64 million) of new capital. Following the issuance of the shares (at £20 each, or US$31.40), the company is valued at £26.7 million (US$41.9 million).

IBM Global Network (division of IBM; Armonk, NY; www.ibm.com/globalnetwork) — IBM Global Network is the world's largest integrated data, voice, and video network. Approximately 25,000 businesses and over 2 million individuals (including Prodigy subscribers) use the Global Network as their Internet connection. IBM plans to offer local dial-up access points to over 450 cities in over 40 countries by the end of 1995, and access speeds are planned to be increased to 28.8 kbps soon.

"Local access points," which are not the same as POPs, can include POPs and VPOPs (the latter are the functional equivalent to a "real POP" but require somewhat less capital investment through a provider's arrangement with its network service carrier). The carrier enables users in the VPOP location to call a phone number, which is paid for by the user as if it were local service (i.e., there is no toll). Once the call is initiated, it is switched to an actual POP at another location that has equipment, where the call is completed (the modem is picked up). Another type of VPOP is leased, in part or in whole, from another service provider. We estimate the number of IBM's VPOPs at about 200 to 250, bringing its actual POP count more in line with IBM's competitors. In 1996, IBM plans to integrate ATM technology into the Global Network. IBM also offers client access through its "Internet Connection" interface bundled with OS/2 Warp (see the "PC, Server, and Semiconductors" section of this chapter).

IDT (Hackensack, NJ; www.idt.com) — IDT is an Internet service provider with 272 POPs in 44 states that has leveraged its security call-back infrastructure to enable Internet-connected computers to contact telephones located in the local call areas of IDT POPs. This value-added service gives IDT a temporary market advantage, as other ISPs decide whether they want to invest in a similar infrastructure. The company has focused on providing low-cost Internet access. IDT filed to go public in January 1996.

InfiNet (Norfolk, VA; www.infi.net) — InfiNet, a joint venture between Knight-Ridder and Landmark Communications, provides Internet access in local markets nationwide and focuses on bringing newspaper publishers to the Web to help businesses, governments, and others create an online community. For consumers, InfiNet offers Internet access through a dial-up connection (via SLIP/PPP) or terminal access through InfiNet's menuing system (for systems prior to the 386 on PCs or the '030 on Macintosh). InfiNet offers Eudora (e-mail), Usenet newsgroups, FTP, Gopher, Telnet, WWW (Mosaic), and IRC. Its Basic surfer pricing plan includes 10 hours for $9.95 per month and $2 for each additional hour; the Standard surfer plan includes 100 hours for $24.95 per month and $2 for each additional hour. For businesses, InfiNet provides wide bandwidth connections, ISDN, dedicated SLIP/PPP accounts, dial-up accounts, dedicated servers, domain registration and service, UUCP, free technical support, home pages, network management, and training.

InfiNet's Web site also offers: links to a number of newspapers and news sites online (including the "San Jose Mercury News," CBS Eye on the Net, the "Philadelphia Inquirer," the "Philadelphia Daily News," "Washington Magazine," and the "Roanoke Times"); a complete marketplace area with links to numerous business, finance, shopping, and travel-and-leisure sites; the ability to search or explore the Net; and a "cool site of the day." Recently, InfiNet signed a licensing deal with Spyglass, where the newspapers that work with InfiNet on their Web sites will distribute copies of Spyglass' Mosaic to readers.

iSTAR Internet (WWW; traded on Toronto Exchange; Ontario, Canada; www.istar.ca) — Canada's iSTAR Internet, a late-November 1995 IPO that recently purchased three companies, claims to be the largest Internet access provider in Canada. Purchases of several more companies are supposed to close in the next few months. According to iSTAR, the company has about 35% of the Canadian access provider market.

iSTAR Internet was created in July through the merger of NSTN with I*Internet Inc. of Ottawa. The merged company is maintaining operations at NSTN's former headquarters in Dartmouth, Nova Scotia, and has been increasing staff there since the merger. iSTAR now has a base of 20,000 customers, including Toronto-Dominion Bank, Digital Equipment Corp., and Molson Breweries. IStar is developing a system with Okanagen Skeena Group, Ltd., a major broadcasting and cable company in British Columbia, to make Internet access available via cable lines.

Netcom Online (NETC; San Jose, CA; www.netcom.com) — Netcom is a worldwide Internet Service Provider with a proprietary TCP/IP network. The company is differentiated from most other companies focusing on consumer dial-up accounts by its competitive pricing and easy-to-use proprietary interface called NetCruiser. NetCruiser offers a suite of Internet resource tools, such as e-mail, a Web browser, Usenet newsgroups, Gopher, and Telnet. The company has traditionally focused on providing access to the individual consumer, but recently entered the small-business market.

Netcom entered into a partnership with Artisoft, a provider of networking solutions to small businesses. In addition, the company recently purchased PICnet, a Dallas-based ISP. In July, Netcom announced an agreement with LDDS WorldCom, the fourth-largest U.S. long-distance carrier, to provide WorldCom's customers with Internet access services. Also in July, Netcom formed Netcom Business Services Group, further underscoring its intent to increase market share in the corporate sector. Netcom recently agreed to support NetManage's Automatic Internet protocol for online sign-up of new Internet users. The company plans to expand its operations into Canada and is considering providing service in Europe, Asia, and the Americas. Netcom has 210 POPs.

Portal Information Network (Cupertino, CA; www.portal.com) — Portal is an ISP offering its Selector software technology, an integrated suite of Internet applications. The software can be easily customized to support a variety of applications. Portal's technology focuses on: 1) customer management (an account manager, registration manager, billing system, marketing intelligence module, trouble tracking, and external interfaces that allow third-party systems to be integrated with Portal's internal systems); 2) data and information management (for content storage and maintenance); 3) communications (connectivity through existing relationships with SprintNet and CompuServe Packet Network); and 4) client software (for easy integration of network access). Portal's partners include Apple, eShop, InterCon, MKS, NetManage, Netscape, Qualcomm, and Quarterdeck. Portal claims that The Portal Information Network has the best worldwide coverage of any Internet Service Provider. According to Portal, it is accessible through a local phone call by an estimated 95% of the U.S. population because of its connections to a nationwide network of 1,100 local access numbers and 200,000 modems. In addition, Portal is accessible from the public data networks of about 100 countries. The company's coverage is accomplished by using eight of its own POPs, leasing about 400 of CompuServe CPN network's POPs, and by letting users connect to up to 700 city locations using SprintNet.

PSINet (PSIX; Herndon, VA; www.psi.net) — PSINet is a worldwide Internet service provider to businesses and, more recently, individuals. The company has differentiated itself by providing a unique frame-relay network that allows PSINet to offer services beyond traditional TCP/IP services. The company is also an Internet backbone provider and leases network services from about ten different providers, thus limiting its dependence upon any one supplier and affording the network considerable redundancy. Connectivity services include 28.8 kbps modem access, 128 kbps ISDN access, and dedicated high-speed circuits for corporate connectivity. PSINet offers varied Internet access solutions for businesses, ranging from full-time dedicated Internet connections (InterFrame), to low-cost, basic Internet e-mail and news services (UUPSI). The company also offers InterRamp, which is open Internet access for the individual. ISDN connectivity is available for PSINet's users, and the company claims to be the only national Internet service provider to offer this service to individual users. Another unique, semi-proprietary interface is PSINet's Pipeline. Pipeline's pricing has tracked Netcom's offering. Therefore, PSINet offers two consumer Internet connectivity options: Pipeline (low-priced, fewer features, easier to use); and InterRamp (higher-priced, more feature-rich, and focused on the "power user").

PSINet has a new distribution agreement with Creative Labs, under which PSINet's InterRamp service will be packaged with Creative Labs' communication equipment. The company recently made two acquisitions: 1) Software Ventures, a developer of Internet and general communications software for Macintosh users; and 2) InterCon Systems, a producer of Internet Mac connectivity and application software for businesses. Clients include VocalTec, CivNet, IntelliCom, Positive Response, U.S. Digital, and

Tripod. Additionally, the company has expanded Internet service into Canada and the Pacific Rim; the latter will be done through a joint venture with CLEAR Communications, an Auckland, New Zealand-based telecommunications company, which will build an extension of the PSINet network and provide Internet access services in New Zealand. Service has also been added through a joint venture in Korea. PSINet will own a 45% stake in the resulting company, tentatively called CLEAR PSINet Ltd., with service expected to be available in the first quarter of 1996. PSINet has 241 POPs.

UUNET (UUNT; Fairfax, VA; www.uu.net) — UUNET is an ISP and consulting company focused mainly on business accounts, the largest of which is Microsoft. As a subcontractor to Microsoft, UUNET provides dial-up access over its network for Microsoft Network. UUNET focuses on two types of customers, MSN and corporations, because each group tends to access the network at different times of day: During the day, corporate customers, primarily through leased lines, access the UUNET service, but their activity slows considerably at the end of the business day. As that usage slows, MSN customers, after they've arrived home from work or school, begin accessing the UUNET network. Thus, the UUNET network's capacity is used efficiently.

At the beginning of its relationship with UUNET, Microsoft made a cash equity investment in the ISP, enabling UUNET to expand its network. Further expansion, apparently influenced by MSN's intention to become more global, occurred in October 1995, when UUNET announced its plan to acquire Unipalm Group, the largest U.K. provider of corporate Internet services. Unipalm has a large presence in Europe as well. UUNET is also an Internet backbone service provider, and in July announced a deal with Global Village, whereby the latter would tap into UUNET's backbone and offer smaller customers more local dial-up services nationwide. UUNET also produces a family of Internet security products, and through its Web hosting service provides all of the hardware, software, facilities, maintenance, and Internet connectivity required to establish a Web site. About six months ago, UUNET began building a frame-relay network similar to PSINet's; however, it is differentiated in that UUNET has a 45 MB backbone. UUNET has 290 POPs.

- **If growth in the Internet ramps as we expect it likely will, PC hardware and semiconductor companies should benefit from healthy unit growth**. PCs, RISC-based workstations, minicomputers, and mainframes can connect to the Internet, either as servers or as clients (except mainframes).

Apple Computer (AAPL; Cupertino, CA; www.apple.com) — Apple's Internet strategy is to leverage its market share in three key Internet development areas: schools (where we estimate the Mac has a 23% share); publishing (we estimate a 24% share); and multimedia developers (we estimate a 60% share). It might be easy for business PC users to write off the Macintosh, but the fact is that Apple carries an impressive market share in the creative communities. It's our view that, despite its current problems, Apple may be able to retain its strength in the publishing/multimedia developer areas (which, combined, should account for about 30% of the company's estimated calendar 1995 revenue) as creators for the Web continue to look for the easiest and most familiar ways to create new content. In addition, Apple is aggressively marketing its Internet features/product solutions in the educational channel.

Compaq Computer (CPQ; Houston, TX; www.compaq.com) — In 1994, Compaq generated 17% of its revenue (and a much higher percentage of profits) from server sales. For 1995, servers may have driven 20–25% of Compaq's sales. Based on unit shipments and revenue, Compaq is the clear leader in the server space, and the company carries a 20–40% market share depending on how you cut the numbers. To date, we believe the portion of Compaq machines being used as Internet servers has been reasonably low, but it's our view that as Microsoft NT gains share in the Internet server space over the next several years, Compaq's contribution from this area will rise. Note that we estimate the operating system mix for Compaq servers has been 45% Netware, 25% UNIX, 15% OS/2, and 15% Windows NT.

Given Compaq's high market share in servers (combined with its relationship with Cisco and the recent purchase of NetWorth), it's our view that the company, as well as its resellers, should be able to leverage this positioning to drive incremental growth related to the Internet growth. And it's clear that Compaq intends to be very aggressive about this

opportunity. To date, UNIX-based servers, especially from Sun Microsystems, have dominated the Internet server market. As Windows NT continues its creep into corporations, more users may begin to consider Windows NT on the Intel platform as an Internet server solution.

Dell Computer (DELL; Austin, TX; www.us.dell.com) — Like Compaq, Dell is relying on the Intel platform and Windows NT to gain share in the Internet server space. To date, servers have been a small contributor to Dell's revenue (accounting for 3% of revenue in the October quarter of 1995). But given the above-average profitability of servers (versus desktop and portable PCs), Dell is focused on raising the company's profile in the server market. Dell recently introduced its PowerEdge Web Server product line, which is being marketed as a Pentium server with pre-installed software (including Windows NT, Netscape Communications Server, and SoftQuad's HoTMetaL Web authoring tool) that provides a ready-to-run Web information server. We think Dell's marketing message, combined with its direct-selling/support infrastructure and loyal customer base, should assist the company in building an Internet server business. The message: "With the tools provided, you can easily create Web pages to disseminate information to customers, clients, or employees. Using the Internet allows you to not only gain customer awareness and disseminate information at a low cost, but also generate sales leads and improve customer satisfaction by offering timely product support and related information on a worldwide, around-the-clock basis."

Digital Equipment Company (DEC; Maynard, MA; www.digital.com) — Digital has made connectivity an important strategic focus related to its Internet development. The company recently formed a new group called the Connectivity Systems Businesss Unit. CSBU will sell hardware, software, and services to help customers unify disparate hardware platforms into a coherent "intranet" that can communicate with the Internet. Like IBM, Digital wants to become a comprehensive vendor of Internet software, hardware, and related services (see sidebar below).

IBM (IBM; Armonk, NY; www.ibm.com) — IBM intends to offer a broad range of Internet services, providing customers with one-stop shopping for Internet solutions. The three main thrusts of IBM's efforts include Internet access, network and systems integration, and enablement (see sidebar).

Intel (INTC; Santa Clara, CA; www.intel.com) — Intel, the world's largest semiconductor manufacturer and the inventor of the semiconductor memory and microprocessor, focuses on supplying the building blocks for the "new computer industry," where the majority of key products are built around the PC architecture standard. Intel supports the computing industry's needs for strategic products that provide performance, mobility, conductivity, and digital video computing (see sidebar).

Silicon Graphics (SGI; Mountain View, CA; www.sgi.com) — SGI is a high-end hardware manufacturer and software developer. On the hardware side, it offers a full line of workstations and scalable Web server hardware under the WebForce brand, ranging from small desktop machines to high-end servers. The base WebForce Indy workstation, costing $11,000, offers the MIPS RISC architecture bundled with digital-media software and a keyboard and monitor. Key features include CD-quality audio output and digital video peripheral interfaces. At the high-end, SGI offers the WebForce Indigo2 Extreme workstation, designed to render and manipulate 3-D graphical content for Web site construction. On the software side, Silicon Graphics offers Netscape server and browser products. SGI also publishes its proprietary WebMagic software, an HTML editor that simplifies the creation of Web content through an easy-to-use editor with a WYSIWYG interface. Other software tools help Web programmers create and edit digital images and sounds.

The success of Silicon Graphics' high-performance Web server and authoring systems represents a major marketing opportunity for the company. Its WebForce products have helped SGI achieve penetration at accounts that had previously been loyal to workstation offerings from Sun or HP.

Customers who had previously dismissed SGI machines as specialty graphics boxes are giving the products a second look. The company recently announced an alliance with Avid to jointly deliver all-digital and distribution products to the broadcast and post-production markets.

Sun Microsystems (SUNW; Mountain View, CA; www.sun.com) — Sun, a hardware and software company, recently has become strongly identified with the Internet, the UNIX operating system, and cutting-edge applications, such as its Java software. Sun's current Netra Internet server line is an integrated software and hardware solution that features scalable processors based on Sun's SPARC architecture, along with proprietary software that permits easy administration and integration into a customer's existing information infrastructure. Additional software products include firewall protection and Solstice SunScreen SPF-100, which protects data transfers with external Internet sites from tampering.

Sun intends to center its Internet strategy center on its Java object-oriented programming language. Java enables the transfer and execution of applets from a Web server to a client, regardless of the client's setup, allowing for the portability of programs. Sun has licensed Java technology to Netscape, which is bundling it with its Netscape browser and Web server software. Sun also plans to permit free usage and distribution of its coming Java browser and compilers. The company intends to sell Java development tools in the first half of 1996. Java currently is based on code interpretation, which translates high-level Java code into low-level instructions understandable by a CPU. Interpretation takes place during Java code execution and slows program operation. The company plans to aggressively develop Java compiler technology that would perform all of the necessary translation before Java code execution, yielding executables that run more quickly. Nevertheless, compilation is time-intensive for complex applications, and we believe Sun needs to focus on efficient Java applet compilation technology to ensure Java's viability. Thanks to its strong presence in academia, though, Sun has built the largest Internet server installed base of any company. While we believe Sun still leads the server market, we think its share has dropped from 50% to closer to 33% as the Internet expands.

DEC

The key parts of Digital's Internet portfolio include:

Server Hardware On the hardware side, Digital has created a line of Internet/Web servers based on its leading high-performance 64-bit Alpha chips. These scalable AlphaServer products come pre-loaded with Internet software and are ready to run out of the box. In addition, Digital has introduced a line of Intel-based Internet/Web servers. Additional hardware offerings include data networking equipment.

In April 1995, Digital announced its enVISN (Enterprise Virtual Intelligent Switched Networks) architecture for corporate networking. enVISN is based on a concept called "virtual networking," an architecture that allows companies to build networks that can be customized through software rather than physical modification, resulting in significant cost savings. With virtual networking, an administrator can optimize network topology regardless of the underlying network's hardware composition or physical location.

Security Digital has developed tunneling software that allows secure data transactions between networks over the Internet. This tunneling software is based on RSA encryption technology that uses large prime numbers as encryption keys and is compatible with any firewall product. A company can thus use Digital's tunneling to tie its remote LANs together or permit individuals to access its intranet without interference from firewall software. Individuals can also use Digital's tunneling technology to create secure links with corporate intranets from a local desktop. Digital offers other security software, too, including firewall products from Border Network Technologies.

Consulting Services Digital offers consulting services to help customers integrate the Internet into their existing business practices and infrastructure. The company can assist companies with tasks such as basic setup to comprehensive Internet-based marketing strategies.

Digital faces some tough competition in the Internet arena. Market leaders Sun and Silicon Graphics already sell similar hardware and software products and command Internet server mindshare. IBM markets its own tunneling software and has aggressively moved to Web-enable its entire server line, including its RS/6000 workstations, AS/400 minicomputers, and mainframes as part of its newfound network-centric computing focus. Further, IBM has made Internet consulting an important component of its efforts to integrate the Internet with its large installed base. Cisco, Bay Networks, and 3Com already dominate the market for virtual LAN products.

IBM

Access IBM operates the IBM Global Network, the world's largest integrated data, voice, and video network. Approximately 25,000 businesses and over 2 million individuals use Global Network as their connection to the Internet. (See the "Internet Service Providers" section in this chapter for more detail on this service.)

Integration IBM offers Internet consulting services, including Web site construction, and can custom-design Internet solutions around a customer's existing information infrastructure. IBM plans to enable all of its major hardware platforms for use as Web servers to give customers maximum flexibility. The company also offers IBM Web server software for AIX on the RS/6000 and OS/2 on the PC side, and intends to unveil Web server software for AS/400 minicomputer and mainframes running MVS. Other offerings include software tools, firewall software, Web page authoring tools, and DB2/WWW (a Web interface for the DB2 relational database). Through its Lotus subsidiary, the company offers InterNotes, intended to unite a company's internal information resources, through Lotus Notes, with the Internet. Products include InterNotes Web Publisher for OS/2 and Windows NT, and programs that allow Lotus Notes to filter Usenet news.

Enablement IBM publishes Infomarket Search, a software tool that can query a customer's private database as well as Internet resources, such as the Web and Usenet. To enhance its ability to assist commerce on the Internet, IBM, along with Prodigy, made equity investments in Terisa Systems.

IBM management hopes to position the Lotus Notes groupware product as complementary to the Internet. The company plans to use Notes as the connectivity glue between the Internet and the various platforms in a corporate intranet. An integrated server software bundle, code named "Spike," will play an integral role. Spike is based on a Lotus Notes infrastructure and will permit information transactions between the Internet and legacy platforms, such as IBM MVS mainframes and AS/400 minicomputers. Spike is scheduled for release sometime in 1996 and will include IBM's gateway security software as well as the Lotus InterNotes line. InterNotes translates Notes documents into HTML format accessible by Web browsers. InterNotes Web Publisher also can take information from Web forms and translate it into Notes data.

The challenge for Notes is to differentiate its offerings from less-expensive Web technology. Netscape's acquisition of Collabra, a company specializing in groupware, seems to be a clear sign that the Web will increasingly compete in Notes' domain. In a recent survey of corporate MIS directors, we found that one-third viewed Internet technology as a potential Notes replacement. Lotus backers point to the product's robust security, replicated database capability, and workflow management as key Notes advantages over Web technology. However, the Web could limit Notes' upside, in our view.

Intel

Intel is reticent about stating its strategic intentions in any market in which it participates. However, recent product announcements show that Intel views its role as a computing hardware supplier to the Internet in three primary areas:

The Personal Computing Platform of Choice for the Internet Intel is the world's largest supplier of PC microprocessors (its market share is estimated at over 80%) and motherboards (market share estimated at over 15%). To solidify its position in the home and office markets, and thereby remain the supplier of the "subscriber unit" for the Internet, Intel has begun to articulate a vision of the PC as a communications, rather than computing, tool. Its view is that the PC is the single, flexible, adaptable device that every Internet user should use, and that Intel eventually will provide features such as hardware multimedia support for graphics and sound that will support the Internet multimedia environment as it evolves. Essentially, Intel is saying that most people already have the ideal Internet subscription device (their current PC), and that Intel is working to make it even better.

Internet Servers The Pentium Pro is targeted at the server market in either uni-processor or multi-processor configurations. Intel has demonstrated several systems that offer performance similar to low-end and mid-range workstations but at lower price points. By doing this, Intel has demonstrated the ability to deliver an Internet server with hardware compatibility and one-stop shopping for both subscriber and server hardware. To the IT department looking to construct an intranet, this seems highly appealing. To the Internet access provider, the argument maybe even more compelling, given the dominant installed base of Intel architecture machines. Intel recently announced the development of a turnkey Web server. Scheduled to hit the market in the second half of 1996, the server is expected to include: Pentium Pro processors running faster than 200Mhz (and possibly as fast as 300 Mhz); intelligent agent software for ease of set-up and use; an integrated router; and a dedicated I/O subsystem (expected to be based on the Intel 1960 RP RISC chip architecture). The server will be configured as a Windows NT-based plug-and-play machine and should be priced in the $4,000–6,000 range. At the Pentium Pro product rollout, one Intel executive said he envisioned an integrated Intel/Cisco Internet CPE box that would be sold by Internet solutions providers. This combination could prove unbeatable, in our view.

Hardware is only part of the Internet server story. Software is an important component, and Intel is focusing on this, too. The company has demonstrated (admittedly, at the alpha-level) software tools that help Webmasters rapidly build home pages, set up security systems, and perform other routine but time-consuming server construction and maintenance functions. In our view, this is just an ancillary service that will help Intel considerably in its real mission of selling hardware.

NSP or Equivalent   The NSP rumblings coming out of Intel appear to be dying down. However, the concept must still be alive and well if Intel is to execute its strategy of positioning the PC as the ideal multimedia subscriber unit for the Internet. The demands for graphics and sound processing capability will only accelerate, and Intel must provide application-specific hardware processing functions (perhaps, DSP functions for sound and hardware graphics support for visual support) to wrest control of this function from the group of companies that control this space. It appears that Intel has chosen to move slowly during the current period of uncertainty but undoubtedly will enter forcefully once the definition of multimedia on the Internet solidifies.

- Without the use of the traditional telecommunications services' infrastructure, the Internet could not exist. "Value-added" service providers, such as ISPs and OSPs, lease telecommunications lines and run IP or X.25 data over them. In fact, the ISPs and OSPs are resellers of services from interexchange carriers (IXCs), competitive access providers (CAPs), and, to a lesser extent, the regional Bell operating companies (RBOCs).

- Long-distance companies (the IXCs), such as AT&T, MCI, and Sprint, historically have provided the majority of the underlying infrastructure of the Internet. Increasingly the major IXCs are expanding their role from providing transmission to directly providing value-added services to the end-user. In particular, AT&T and MCI have made substantial investments in establishing their own portfolios of Internet and online services. With the exception of Sprint, the major IXCs have limited presence in the local telecommunications market. This is widely expected to change, given pending regulatory events, which may further increase the presence of the IXCs in this market.

- Local telephone companies, also called local exchange carriers, or LECs, provide the actual connection to customer premises and carry telecommunications traffic within a specific region. Historically, LECs, in particular the seven RBOCs, which constitute the bulk of the market segment, have been prevented by law from providing services across regions. Consequently the RBOCs have been somewhat reluctant to provide Internet services, particularly Internet backbone services, on a large scale. Now, however, regulatory changes and the explosive growth of the Internet market are combining to speed the RBOCs' entry into the market. Over time, it is expected that the RBOCs will develop a substantial Internet presence, though individual strategies may vary from providing traditional Internet access (Pacific Bell) to offering content-based services (NYNEX's Interactive Yellow Pages).

- Cable television companies have substantial networks that connect to two-thirds of U.S. homes. Although these networks currently do not support IP data applications, they present a tremendous opportunity because they can operate at 10Mbps (although large-scale deployment of such a system has yet to be demonstrated). This rate is much faster than a typical 28.8 Kbps modem or a 128 Kbps ISDN line.

- Competitive Access Providers, or CAPs, are in the process of constructing competitive networks and leasing existing facilities to provide alternative local access to end-users and IXCs. The larger facilities-based CAPs, such as MFS and Teleport, have nationwide fiber-optic networks capable of providing backbone service equivalent to that of the IXCs'.

AT&T (T; Basking Ridge, NJ; www.att.com) — AT&T's strategy for the Internet and online market has expanded somewhat over the past year, where previously the company sought to provide proprietary online services (AT&T Interexchange). Last year, the company announced an alliance with BBN Planet to provide corporate Internet connectivity. In addition, as the dominant U.S. IXC, AT&T has historically played a role in managing the Internet infrastructure as a government contractor. AT&T currently has 80 million customers (10 million business), as well as a significant share of the 800 business.

Cox Communications (COX; Atlanta, GA; www.cox.com) — Cox is one of the five largest cable television companies in the U.S., serving approximately 3.3 million subscribers. Through the use of cable modems, the company expects to offer Internet access to subscribers beginning in 1996. The company is part of the Sprint Telecommunications Venture, whose partners include Sprint, Tele-Communications, Comcast, and Cox. The partners plan to bundle cable TV and telephony services at a discount, and in the future may include access to the Internet via a cable modem. Cox recently announced a partnership with the Rhode Island Secretary of State's office to use Cox's telecom infrastructure to access the Internet.

MCI Communications (MCIC; Washington, DC; www.mci.com) — MCI is the second-largest IXC in the U.S. and plays a key role in the Internet market as the largest Internet backbone provider. Its role is also expanding in this market as it grows to provide Internet service to individuals. MCI and Microsoft recently announced an alliance that signaled two strategic changes from a previous alliance with NewsCorp/Delphi. MCI will market a custom version of MSN for the MCI Network, and MCI licensed Microsoft's Internet Explorer Web browser and will sell Microsoft's server software. In addition, MCI has a well-known shopping site on the Net called Marketplace MCI.

MCI's relationship with News Corp. should provide MCI with unique access to programming content and software. (MCI invested $2 billion in News Corp. in exchange for preferred securities. In addition, MCI and News Corp. have seats on each other's boards.)

Sprint (FON; Westwood, KS; www.sprint.com) — In 1992, Sprint, through its SprintLink service, became the first major U.S. interexchange carrier to provide commercial Internet transport services. Today, the company remains a major provider of Internet backbone capacity and has over 1,200 SprintLink customers, including America Online. Sprint also handles about 50% of all international Internet traffic through Global Link, which extends SprintLink to Europe and Asia via international frame relay and dedicated line access.

Although Sprint was the first interexchange carrier to offer Internet services, it is still primarily a "wholesale" player. Sprint is in the process of formulating its retail Internet strategy and has not yet rolled out any strong end-user Internet services. Sprint is close to finalizing its strategy (and alliances) and should make some significant product announcements over the next several months.

Tele-Communications Inc. (TCOMA; East Lansing, MI; www.tcinc.com) — Tele-Communications is the largest cable television operator in the U.S., serving approximately 12.1 million subscribers as of September 30, 1995. The company expects to offer subscribers access to the Internet through the use of a cable modem. TCI has formed a joint venture with Sprint, Cox Communications, and Comcast called Sprint Telecommunications Venture, which will enable the cable TV partners to bundle cable television and telephony services under the Sprint brand name. TCI also has a 20% interest in the Microsoft Network and recently partnered with Kleiner Perkins Caulfield & Byers to offer a new Internet service called @Home, which offers customers high-speed access to the Internet via TCI's hybrid fiber/coax cable system.

Time Warner (TWX; New York; pathfinder.com) — Time Warner provides international, sports, entertainment news, and promotional material on its Internet site, Pathfinder. Time Warner products are also available on commercial services such as America Online and CompuServe. Time Warner offers its current stable of weekly magazines on the Internet, and it offers daily updates for *Time, Money,* and *People* that are available only online. Recently, the company switched *Time* from America Online, where it received approximately $500,000 per year, to CompuServe, in a deal valued at several million dollars. CompuServe also publishes online versions of *People, Fortune,* and *Sports Illustrated. Entertainment Weekly* has a site on America Online.

Time Warner promotes its movies on the Internet, setting up sites for many film and video releases that offer trailers, information on "the making of the movie," and profiles of the actors. These sites also link users to sites with movie-based video games and to sites for ordering movie-related merchandise. Time Warner's pending merger with Turner Broadcasting brings to it CNN Interactive, an online news information and video provider.

AT&T

In its Internet strategy, AT&T created three separate businesses — access, hosting, and content services. AT&T envisions offering access to the Internet as yet another communications option to its existing long-distance customers as well as to new customers.

AT&T recently unveiled EasyWeb, a site-hosting and development service marketed under AT&T's strategy to migrate its business customers to the Web. Vermeer's FrontPage HTML document creation product will be the site manager for EasyWeb.

In October 1995, AT&T's WorldNet division announced it had begun beta testing its consumer-oriented Internet service, establishing dial-up POPs in 110 cities. The company has also established separate European (called AT&T Internet Services) and Asian (called Spin) Internet business units. On October 10, Spin activated TCP/IP backbone linking Hong Kong, Japan, and Australia.

AT&T plans to divide its services into business (with connections largely handled by BBN, of which AT&T purchased a minority stake in early 1995) and consumer connections. The company expects to have consumer POPs in about 650 cities by early 1996, with dial-up connectivity available at speeds of up to 28.8 kbps. Pricing should be announced in 1996, but is expected to be about $20 per month for about 20 hours and $2 for each additional hour.

WorldNet currently accesses the POPs available from AT&T's InterSpan service and AccuNet (a global packet network operated by InfoNet). AT&T plans to create its own content tailored for customers, which will be handled by the Personal Online Services (POS) division. The first partner to sign on with AT&T's POS is IVI, a CD-ROM publisher of medical information.

AT&T's family of services include the following:

AT&T Interchange Online Network   This offering hosts a collection of specialized online information services that are developed by independent content partners and that share the same network and user interface. The network currently has Ziff-Davis Interactive's ZDNet, the *Washington Post's* Digital Ink, the Minneapolis/St. Paul-based Star Tribune Online, and Gartner Group's @vantage. The AT&T Interchange network also provides access to Internet e-mail and features integrated Web-browsing capabilities.

AT&T NetWare Connect Service   This product makes use of the AT&T Network and Novell NetWare to connect local-area networks while providing directory services and access to the Internet. Customers of AT&T Netware Connect can expand their existing Novell LAN environments into wide-area networking.

AT&T Network Notes   This product enables businesses to use custom-developed Lotus Notes-based applications to electronically collaborate with remote partners, suppliers, customers, and employees. AT&T Network notes is an open platform that can connect to directory and messaging services via SMTP, including the Internet.

AT&T EasyLink Services   This is a family of electronic messaging offerings, including Internet messaging connectivity via SMTP and domain name services.

Telecommunications Equipment

- Traditional telecommunications is predominantly related to voice calls. Recently, telecommunications carriers have been deploying data communications services, which, based on anecdotal evidence, may be nearly-doubling annually. Telecom Equipment companies that have responded to the needs of carriers building the infrastructure for these data networks have had exceptional financial results. The most successful are those that have provided the best "edge switches," which functionally reside outside of the core network that historically has switched voice calls.

- The ISPs and OSPs purchase much of the same equipment that the traditional telecommunications carriers have bought — for instance, frame relay switches (like Cascade's). The following are summary descriptions of the companies that provide the building blocks to the multi-billion-dollar telecommunications carriers' networks.

Adtran (ADTN; Huntsville, AL; www.adtran.com) — Adtran was established in 1985 as a producer of advanced transmission products for high-speed digital communications. Adtran's role in the telecom equipment industry is threefold: 1) as a supplier of DDS and ISDN digital-loop products to RBOCs; 2) as a provider to customers of devices that allow them to connect applications systems to the digital data connections provided by the RBOCs; and 3) as a distributor of Adtran's own products to OEMs. The company uses two rapidly growing technologies to advance its products: 1) ISDN, a dialed digital service used in remote LAN and Internet access; and 2) HDSL, high-speed data transmission over existing copper cables. In addition, Microsoft's recently announced addition of the ISDN telephone system to Windows 95 should have the effect of increasing the demand for this technology.

Cascade Communications (CSCC; Westford, MA; www.casc.com) — Cascade develops and sells multi-service data-optimized edge-switches to telecommunications and Internet carriers. In recent years, Cascade's switches, configured for frame relay service, have sold very well. These switches are being deployed by the carriers and the ISPs, and are considered by many ISPs to be on the "bleeding edge." Cascade's frame relay products are being deployed at larger Internet service providers to allow the networks to "scale up," and as such their purchase appeals to the larger ISPs. Smaller, router-only networks carry traffic efficiently, but as the networks grow in size, a switching, non-protocol (e.g., without routed traffic) fabric may be used to carry traffic across large network spans rapidly. Currently, the largest ISPs are in various stages of adding these switches to their networks: PSINet's network has had Cascade switches for over two years; UUNET re-

cently announced that it is in the process of adding the switches; in September, Netcom announced it will begin purchasing Cascade's switches for deployment in its network. An estimated 10–15% of Cascade's sales are to ISPs (including traditional carriers like Sprint and MCI for their Internet backbone services) for this purpose. The STDX 6000 is a lower-end switch, while the B-STDX 8000/9000 family is higher-end switches.

The remainder of Cascade's sales are to traditional carriers like MCI and Sprint. The switches are being deployed at these carriers for several purposes. First, carriers sell frame relay service to others on a primarily usage basis, mainly as a substitute to leasing T-1 lines, so that a corporate LAN and branch offices may be connected using frame relay service. The motivation for using the service is mainly cost savings, but it depends upon usage patterns. Second, some ISPs are using carriers' frame relay service instead of leased lines to connect their POPs, and, again depending upon usage patterns, can therefore save costs in allowing users to connect to their Internet service. In C1Q96, Cascade will begin selling an ATM switch, the Cascade 500 High-Scalability Multiservice ATM Switch, which may be deployed in a similar fashion to the frame relay switches at ISPs and carriers.

DSC Communications (DIGI; Plano, TX; www.indra.com) — DSC manufactures a line of communications products addressing the needs of telecommunications carriers (e.g., telcos, CATV companies, competitive access providers) and private networks. The majority of the company's sales consists of digital switches that provide the transport for, and manage the traffic of, long-distance and wireless communications networks. Other significant products include: transmission gear, which provisions high-speed digital circuits; access products, which connect customers to carrier networks; and private networking products, which allow end-users to connect their networking and communications equipment to the public network.

Since DSC's equipment is used to provision high-bandwidth services, it's not surprising that the company is a direct beneficiary of Internet activity. For example, the company's digital cross-connects are used to deploy the basic building blocks of Internet connectivity, T1 (1.5 megabits/second) and T3 (45 megabits/second) leased lines. Also, the company's Litespan access product family, which bridges the span between the telco central office and customer site, is used to provision both plain old telephone service (POTS) as well as high-speed ISDN data lines.

Digital Link (DLNK; Sunnyvale, CA; www.dl.com) — Digital Link addresses the high-speed data connectivity market, developing products that connect data devices such as workstations, computers, mainframes, and LANs to high-speed phone lines. The company's customers include AT&T, MCI, and Sprint, as well as the RBOCs, which use Digital Link equipment in their networks and resell it to users of their services. The company's customer base also includes Fortune 500 companies in the industrial and high-technology fields, as well as utilities, universities, governmental agencies, and CAPs. Digital Link maintains a strong focus on customer satisfaction and offers technical support through domestic and international offices. Its suite of products spans the spectrum of global high-speed transmission speeds, including 56K/64K, T1, fractional T1, E1, fractional E1, T3, E3, OC-3c, and STM-1, providing access to such worldwide services as ATM, SMDS, and frame relay. Digital Link products provide the protocol conversion needed to transport data over high-speed phone lines, monitor and report the performance of these expensive lines, and provide the ability to efficiently use these lines by gathering data from multiple data devices to send over one line. The company's products are also used in ISPs' networks.

General Instrument (GIC; Chicago, IL; www.gi.com) — General Instrument is a world leader in developing technology, systems, and product solutions for the interactive delivery of video, voice, and data. The company's Communications Division is the No. 1 global provider of addressable systems and subscriber terminals for the cable

television industry. It is also the pioneer and market leader in satellite television encryption and broadband digital compression technologies, as well as a major player in radio frequency and fiber-optic distribution electronics. GI's CommScope division is a leading supplier of both coaxial and fiber-optic cable to the cable television industry. The company's Power Semiconductor Division sells power rectifiers and related transient voltage suppression components.

GI's enabling technology for high-speed access to the Internet over CATV networks is the company's PCLinX architecture. PCLinX was designed for full ATM compatibility and seamless integration with conventional hybrid fiber/coax networks. The first-generation PCLinX technology supports downstream data rates of up to 27 megabits/second over a single cable TV channel. Information rates scalable up to 1.5 megabits per second are supported from the home. The PCLinX system features dynamic bandwidth allocation for both downstream and upstream transmission, providing flexible and efficient network operation. An advanced modulator/demodulator transmission system ensures robust and reliable upstream communications required for real-time interactivity.

Northern Telecom (NT; Ontario, Canada; www.nortel.com) — Northern Telecom is a leading supplier of central office switching equipment, telco and CATV transmission equipment, broadband data switches, wireless communications equipment, PBXs, and telephone handsets. Nortel benefits broadly from Internet usage, as its products enable the deployment of analog and high-speed digital data lines. Nortel is specifically addressing demand for Internet infrastructure with a series of products known as Rapport. Its first offering is the Rapport Dialup Switch (Rapport DS), which will be used by large and small service providers for Internet dial-up access, wholesale Internet access, enterprise remote access outsourcing, and service bundling. The DS combines functions of the modem, terminal server, access router, and ATM or frame relay switch of the ISP's POP into a single, easily managed device. Other members of the Rapport portfolio of Internet products and services are planned — these should address other offerings for ISPs, users, and enterprises.

Premisys Communications (PRMS; Fremont, CA; www.premisys.com) — Premisys is a pioneer in integrated access products for telecommunications service providers.

The company's IMACS products enable public carriers to provide business customers with cost-effective, reliable access to telecommunications services, such as ATM, ISDN, frame relay, voice, and digital data. Premisys's products are also used in wireless applications. The company benefits from Internet activity because its products are used to provision high-speed digital services such as frame relay and ISDN in an integrated, cost-effective manner.

In October, Premisys announced an agreement with Fore Systems to sell Premisys access products as part of a line of Fore Systems' ATM access products.

StrataCom (STRM; San Jose, CA; www.stratacom. com) — StrataCom is a developer of cell switching technology and a leading supplier of high-performance wide-area network switching systems in both the frame relay and ATM markets. The company manufactures and markets a variety of cell-based modular switches and network access devices, as well as call processing and network management products, for use by private enterprise and public carriers.

StrataCom's switches have heretofore not been employed in the networks of Internet access providers. However, the company counts among its customers CompuServe, which has selected StrataCom's BPX and IGX ATM switches as the foundation for a worldwide broadband ATM network. Though financial details of the agreement were not disclosed, CompuServe said it plans to spend $30 million over the next two years on StrataCom switches to build a production-quality ATM network.

Software & Services

Application Software

- The Internet application software market has developed into two market segments: client application software and server application software. The market for Internet application software has grown into one of the largest portions of the overall software market, with a large number of players.

- In general, **client application software** has been developed to: 1) **access information** on Internet servers (e.g., browsers, FTP clients); 2) assist in **viewing information** accessed from servers (e.g., Postscript viewers, Acrobat viewers); 3) **make content** for placement onto servers (e.g., HTML "home page" development packages); and 4) **allow client-to-client communications** (e.g., e-mail, chat, Internet telephony).

- **Server application software** has been developed to allow computers, which typically are connected permanently to the Internet, **to grant access for retrieval to client computers upon request**. Examples are software for Web servers, FTP servers, e-mail servers (which store e-mail messages sent from one client to another until retrieved), Internet telephone servers (which identify to other users who is currently online), name servers (which translate domain names to numerical IP addresses), and other, more specialized servers.

Accent Software International (ACNTF; Jerusalem, Israel; www.accentsoft.com) — Accent develops advanced multilingual technology, allowing users to create documents in more than 30 languages for Windows and on the Internet. Formerly known as Kivun Computers, Accent partnered with Microsoft in 1991 to develop the technology currently used in bidirectional versions of Windows, enabling users to enter characters into a word-processing document right-to-left for languages such as Hebrew and Arabic, or left-to-right for European languages. The company has worked in development and distribution with such companies as AT&T, Hewlett-Packard, Lotus, Corel, and Berlitz.

In relation to the Internet, Accent has developed an Accent product line: Multilingual Publisher (which allows users to create documents for the Web in over 30 languages); Multilingual Mosaic (which correctly displays Web pages in over 30 languages, supports HTML, and can be used as a stand-alone browser or installed as a helper application); Multilingual MailPad (which installs itself as a helper application to MAPI-based mail programs); and Multilingual Viewer. Accent recently announced full support for Japanese Web pages as part of its Internet suite. Under agreement with Digital, Accent will bundle its multi-lingual word processor on selected Digital PCs and laptops for a worldwide market.

Adobe Systems (ADBE; Mountain View, CA; www.adobe.com) — Adobe is the kingpin of desktop publishing, now dubbed authoring tools. The company's key products include: 1) Photoshop photo design and production software; 2) Illustrator illustration and page-design software; 3) PageMaker desktop publishing software; 4) Premiere video production software; 5) Adobe Acrobat electronic document file format; and 6) Postscript page description language for printers. Bolstering its product line, Adobe recently purchased Frame Technology (FrameMaker) and has invested in several Web authoring products. More than 75% of Adobe's desktop application software sales are to graphics professionals, and about 60% of sales are based on Apple Macintosh software, followed by Windows at 30% and UNIX at 10%. Adobe's mission is to be "the premier supplier of information authoring and management tools that enable people to create, send, find, view, and print information."

Camelot Corporation (CAML; Dallas, TX; www.planeteers.com) — Camelot, a holding company with a focus on CD-ROM software, publishes DigiPhone software through its Third Planet Publishing subsidiary.

DigiPhone allows real-time, full duplex communications over the Internet. The product has a Mosaic-like interface and six systems, including DigiPhone Phone System, DigiPhone Web Browser, DigiPhone Configuration System, Telnet, FTP, and e-mail. In addition to the ability to place long-distance phone calls, DigiPhone supports voice encryption, conference calling, call screening, and voice messaging.

Ceneca Communications (subsidiary of Adobe/ADBE; Palo Alto, CA; www.ceneca.com) — Ceneca develops software tools to create Web sites. Ceneca recently announced its new suite of Web authoring and site-management tools, which simplify the process of Web authoring. PageMill is a Macintosh-based integrated authoring tool that lets Web site managers quickly and easily create and edit Web pages using normal word-processing tools, without having to learn HTML. It also enables users to work in a single environment, without having to switch between an editor and a browser. The tools match the capabilities of HTML, duplicating a page's appearance in browsers and eliminating the risk of losing data when converting text and graphics into HTML. The software also supports advanced HTML features, such as clickable image maps and fill-in forms. SiteMill includes all the functionality of PageMill but adds a site-management function that includes the ability to find and fix errors in existing sites, move files, and find unused resources with point-and-click functionality. In September 1995, Adobe signed a letter of intent to acquire Ceneca.

CONNECT, Inc. (Mountainview, CA; www.connectinc.com) — CONNECT provides enterprise client-server software and services for creating online, interactive electronic marketplaces and services on the Internet as well as private data networks. Products include: 1) the *OneServer Platform* for branded online services and the Web — an online application platform for rapid development of commercial business solutions, with a retrieval system and API's that link to enterprise business systems; 2) the *OneServer Digital Product Distribution System (DPDS)* — an online distribution solution, with a flexible product search and merchandising system and complete back-office capabilities; 3) the *OneManager Administration System* — a control console for flexible content and user management; 4) the *CONNECT Online Corporate Server for Virtual Private Networks* — an online application plat-

form for private services, with searchable news services, financial quotes and information, e-mail, bulletin boards and chat forums, and content and user administration; and 5) *Online Application Support Services* — which provides training and support for developers, integrators, customers, and content managers. CONNECT has entered into a wide variety of strategic alliances, partnerships, and reseller agreements with a mix of leading companies, including: systems integrators (CONNECT PSD — the company's Professional Services Division — and AVCOM); technology companies (Fulcrum, Hewlett-Packard, Oracle, RSA Data Security, and Sun Microsystems); and creative design companies (Clement Mok Designs, CyberSight, Interse, and R.M. Dudley Corp.).

CyberWISE (Saratoga, CA; www.cyberwise.com) — CyberWISE, a division of The Saratoga Group, is a provider of PC-based Internet learning software products with step-by-step explanations. With the ability to download and store products on a computer's hard drive, users are provided the opportunity for complete interaction (with control of topics and pace), simulations (real screens for Internet comprehension), and graphics (to "see" the Internet). CyberWISE products include "How to Get Started on the Internet" (a free offering), "How to Use the World Wide Web," "How to Find Things on the Internet," "How to Use Email on the Internet," and "The Internet Reference Desk." "The Internet Master Pack" includes the latter four products at a discounted rate.

Edify Corporation (Santa Clara, CA; www.edify.com) — Edify develops software for interactive service applications, providing direct access to corporate information and services for customers and employees. Edify's Electronic Workforce is an interactive service platform that offers an environment, managing and supporting a variety of Web, voice response, fax, and e-mail applications. The three components of Electronic Workforce are: 1) software agents, which are the underlying technology for providing interactive services; 2) the Agent Supervisor, which manages and delivers interactive services; and 3) the Agent Trainer, a visual development environment for defining interactive services performed by software agents. As of November 20, 1995, Edify began shipping Release 4.0 of the Electronic Workforce, which offers companies a rapid, cost-effective way to deploy interactive service applications via standard Web browsers. The Electronic Workforce is installed at over 500 sites within a wide range of industries; customers include Chevron, Comerica, Commonwealth Gas, DHL Worldwide Express, Fidelity Investments, First Union Bank, Ford, Frito Lay, Hewlett-Packard, IBM, Kodak, Kraft Food Services, MCI, Oracle, Pitney Bowes, Penn State, Prudential, PSE&G, Reebok, Signet Bank, University of California, and VISA International. In early November 1995, Edify completed a $7.4 million private round of financing, including an investment from Michael Dell, founder and CEO of Dell Computer.

eShop (San Mateo, CA; www.eshop.com) — eShop develops an interactive electronic commerce software system, including client, server, and tools, that allows vendors to set up interactive shopping sites that customers can access through the Internet, as well as a variety of online and cable services. The eShop technology connects over a network, with three main product groups: the eShop Builder allows vendors to construct and manage their visual shops, on a daily basis; the eShop Warehouse is the central depository for all product information, store imagery, merchandising programs, and customer information; and the eShop Browser allows shoppers to browse and view the aisles and departments on their PC or PDA screens. eShop is working with a number of retailers, including Tower Records, Spiegel, The Good Guys, and 1-800-Flowers.

FTP Software (FTPS; Andover, MA; www.ftp.com) — FTP Software provides Internet-based internetworking software products that enable users to access resources across LANs, enterprise-wide networks, and global networks. Based on the industry standard TCP/IP protocol, the company's principal product, PC/TCP, provides remote access and file/resource sharing across a number of different operating systems, platforms, and network environments. FTP's products cover a range of offerings, including: 1) Internet Browsers (FTP Explorer, Explorer 2.0, and Explore Anywhere); 2) E-Mail (FTP provides OnNet support of NNT, MIME, and MAPI protocols); 3) File and Print services (PC/TCP and OnNet support for NFS resource sharing); 4) Workgroup Servers (UNIX Web Server 1.1, UNIX Secure Web Server 1.1, UNIX Web reporter); and 5) Desktop Management (provides support for terminal emulation, remote file transfer, and tape backup). The company is also developing next-generation applications, such as intelligent agents that can execute on remote

TCP/IP-equipped workstations, and has an affiliation and is joint developing products with Open Market.

On November 30, 1995, FTP announced a strategic alliance with Firefox to jointly develop and market client-based (FTP's *OnNet*) and server-based (Firefox's *NOV*IX* TCP/IP products) networking software, incorporating enterprise, NetWare, Windows NT, and Internet-oriented technologies. Products are expected to be available in the first half of 1996. FTP also recently announced an agreement with Vermeer Technologies, whereby FTP will gain worldwide distribution rights to Vermeer's publishing software, and the two companies will jointly develop publishing tools for Website creation. In addition, FTP entered into a product licensing and technology development partnership with Relay Technologies. FTP and Firefox recently announced they would merge. The merger is still pending.

Firefox Communications (FFOX; San Jose, CA; www.firefox.com) — Firefox develops software that allows Novell Netware LANs to be connected to the Internet. The software is installed on the server only, and workstations do not have to be individually modified to allow network users to access Internet resources. The company's products give workgroups local and remote access across a variety of operating systems and internetworking protocols. Firefox's products are also compatible with a number of third-party client applications, offer system configuration and maintenance, centralize security, and offer multi-server support for alternate routing. On November 30, 1995, Firefox announced a strategic alliance with FTP Software to jointly develop and market client-based (FTP's *OnNet*) and server-based (Firefox's *NOV*IX* TCP/IP products) networking software, incorporating enterprise, NetWare, Windows NT, and Internet-oriented technologies. Products are expected to be available in the first half of 1996. Firefox and FTP recently announced they would merge. The merger is still pending.

Frontier Technologies Corporation (Mequon, WI; www.frontiertech.com) — Frontier Technologies provides TCP/IP- and Internet-based solutions and is currently using its SuperTCP product family as the foundation for a set of Internet access products for both the Windows 95 and Windows NT operating systems. Frontier's products include: the *SuperTCP suite* of products, providing CD-ROM-based Internet, X-Windows, NFS, and TCP/IP networking applications software, which has been structured specifically for mobile, office, and home use; the *SuperTCP/NFS*, a 32-bit VxD (TCP/IP, NFS, and NetBIOS), offering a set of network applications, requiring no DOS memory; *SuperHighway Access*, featuring a complete Internet browser package for Web, Gopher, Gopher+, WAIS, and CSO Phone Book; *SuperX*, offering 32-bit PC-to-UNIX integration software; and *SuperWeb*, an all-purpose Web server for publishing information and conducting commerce over the Internet. Frontier has partnerships with a variety of Internet-related companies, including PSINet, Lycos, RSA Data Security, CyberCash, CyberWISE, Online Access, OpenConnect Systems, and *LAN Magazine*.

Fulcrum Technologies (FULCF; Ottawa, Canada; www.fultech.com) — Fulcrum develops indexing and text retrieval software used in a variety of document formats and in various computing environments, including multiple operating systems, networks, and GUIs. Fulcrum's software conforms with open systems standards, such as X/Open Call Level Interface (CLI) and Microsoft's Open Databse Connectivity (ODBC), and is easily suited for client/server computing. Fulcrum's products include: the *Fulcrum SearchServer*, the core of the product family, a powerful, multi-platform indexing and retrieval server engine that uses an SQL-based query language for full-text retrieval applications; the *Fulcrum SearchBuilder* toolkit, which is easily integrated with popular graphical development tools to build client/server text retrieval applications that access the Fulcrum SearchServer; and *Fulcrum Surfboard*, which allows information providers to search-enable their Internet sites by combining the SearchServer text retrieval engine with Internet access protocols. Microsoft has licensed the Surfboard software for MSN. Fulcrum recently agreed to license its SearchServer software to Compaq for use in customer support applications.

Hummingbird Communications (HUMCF; Ontario, Canada; www.hcl.com) — Hummingbird is a developer of PC X-server software products that provide easy PC-to-UNIX and X Window system integration within corporate networks. Hummingbird's product designs are based upon open systems and accepted industry standards that offer PC networks easy access to corporate information systems and graphical applications residing on mini- and mainframe host computers. The company's eXceed software family offers X servers for all major PC operating systems and user environments, as well as X Development Toolkits for Windows, Windows NT, and OS/2, and serial connectivity PC X server software that enables access to X Window host computers over telephone lines. Hummingbird recently acquired Beame & Whiteside Software, developer of NFS technology. In September, the company announced Columbus, a Windows-based Internet application designed to provide access to the Internet and enterprise intranets.

InContext Systems (VSE:INI; Ontario, Canada; www.incontext.com) — InContext is a developer for easy-to-use Internet software and electronic publishing. The company's inaugural Internet software program, InContext Spider, lets users create their own home page for publishing on the Worldwide Web. InContext Spider Version 1.1 offers the following: a Web Manager for insertion/manipulation of hypertext links; drag-and-drop for insertion of images; 28 home page templates; 200 clip-art images; built-in browser; online help; and support for all versions of HTML, including Microsoft Internet Explorer and Netscape extensions.

Through key distribution agreements, InContext Spider is marketed worldwide by Ingram Micro, in the U.S. by Micro Central, in Australia by Creative Pacific, and in Canada by Beamscope. Other significant strategic partnerships are with CompuServe and Quarterdeck, whereby CompuServe's Web Publishing tool will be integrated into the InContext and Quarterdeck Web publishing products. Users will be able to post Web pages to CompuServe with a single mouse click.

InContext 2 creates documents based on the standard generalized markup language (SGML), an ISO standard. InContext 2 makes it easy for anyone to build SGML documents without having to learn the technical details of the standard. SGML technology has been formally adopted for critical applications in aerospace, automotive, defense, and other information-intensive industries. An API (application program interface) is also available — enabling software developers to customize InContext Spider and InContext 2, and integrate with other software products, such as document management systems and information databases.

Interleaf (LEAF; Waltham, MA; www.ileaf.com) — Interleaf is a provider of open, integrated document management technology. The company's Avalanche technology offers a complete set of solutions that enable the preparation, creation, management, and distribution of corporate information. The company's products are compatible with major applications, including word processors, PCs, graphic packages, spreadsheets, and database managers. Interleaf's products include: 1) *WorldView* and *Cyberleaf* — Interleaf's electronic distribution products providing online document distribution and retrieval applications that assemble diverse types of data, turning them into document collections that can be searched and accessed quickly, with hyperlinks and full-text retrieval tools. The products offer a comprehensive production environment for publishing information on the Web, transferring word-processing applications into Internet-ready information that's capable of being viewed with standard Web browsers; 2) *Interleaf 6* — this electronic publishing product enables users to manage and assemble large volumes of electronic data, reuse and package it, and deliver it to end-users; 3) *Intellecte, RDM,* and *Interleaf Liaison* — Interleaf's document management products provide organizations with timely point-and-click access to documents within a dynamic and secure repository and manage documents from author, to viewer, to reader. The company's products can be easily integrated with other applications, so that document management systems can be built using accustomed tools, such as C++ and Visual Basic; and 4) *Avalanche FastTAG, Avalanche SGML,* and *Avalanche SureSTYLE* — Interleaf's document conversion and structure products add structure to documents and prepare them for conversion into multiple formats, including SGML, HTML, Interleaf, Frame, Word, and WordPerfect.

InterVista Software (San Francisco, CA; www.intervista.com) — InterVista was founded by Tony Parisi, one of the designers of VRML, the emerging standard for 3-D scene description on the Web, which allows users to see the Internet as a 3-D space rather than a network of hyperlinks. The WorldView product, a VRML-based Internet software solution, is a 3-D Web navigator for Windows and runs on all 32-bit Windows platforms, including NT, Windows 95, and 3.11 with Win32s. The beta version is available via download. WorldView can operate either in stand-alone mode or in conjunction with a Web browser — WorldView seamlessly interoperates with Netscape and can be configured as a helper application with Spyglass's Enhanced Mosaic 2.0. Although it has not been tested, any other browsers should be able to start WorldView. WorldView offers support for LOD node,

texture mapping (including GIF, JPG, BMP, and PPM formats), UV texture coordinates, collision detection, nested WebInline nodes, clipping plane adjustment, and GZIP compression, as well as providing a simple navigation interface and memory management.

Intuit (INTU; Menlo Park, CA; www.qfn.com) — For Intuit, owing to its user base of 8 million Quicken users, the online medium offers a number of marketing and product-enhancement possibilities. Intuit began offering online functionality to its flagship product, Quicken, with Quicken for 96, which shipped on October 26 (see sidebar).

Macromedia (MACR; San Francisco; www.macromedia.com) — Macromedia provides cross-platform tools that allow multimedia content to be built simply and without an extensive knowledge of programming languages. The company's products — Director, Authorware, FreeHand, Extreme 3D, SoundEdit, xRES, and Fontographer — enable developers to create output that typically is delivered via CD-ROMs, interactive training products, or the printed page. Increasingly, the company is taking advantage of the Internet as a conduit for dynamic content delivery, and it recently aligned with two key Internet players: Netscape and Sun Microsystems. Macromedia also has aggressively used the Internet as its own marketing and corporate information tool, maintaining one of the most dynamic and popular Web sites, and has stayed ahead of the market in bringing information to the Web (last year, Macromedia simultaneously published its annual report on paper, CD-ROM, and the Internet).

In early November 1995, Macromedia announced a new toolset — ShockWave and Afterburner — for the delivery of dynamic Director content to the Internet. Essentially, ShockWave allows small Director movies (and eventually other Macromedia-built content) to be condensed and viewed over the Internet via an embedded viewer in the Netscape browser (and possibly others as Macromedia rolls out the technology). ShockWave recently began shipping for Netscape Navigator. ShockWave has also been adopted by Microsoft (Internet Studio), America Online/Navisoft (NaviPress), and Silicon Graphics (WebForce). Macromedia is also addressing Sun's Java technology by adding compatibility within its tools and by the potential development of an easy-to-use Java front-end.

McAfee Associates (MCAF; Santa Clara, CA; www.mcafee.com) — McAfee manufactures both anti-virus and network-management software products. Its product offerings include: anti-virus software (VirusScan for Windows 95, VirusScan, WebScan, RomShield, and NetShield); asset management software (BrightWorks, LAN Inventory, SiteMeter, and SiteExpress); configuration management software (NetTools); help desk software (LAN Support Center); remote control software (NetRemote); system management software (Saber LAN Workstation); and storage management software (ImageStor, FileStor, and ServerStor). McAfee recently announced WebScan, an anti-virus software utility to prevent Internet users from downloading virus-infected files and e-mail. The product detects traditional virus types, as well as macro viruses (like the Winword.concept virus, which can hide within Internet e-mail attachments). WebScan utilizes McAfee's Code Matrix Scanning and Code Trace Scanning technology, which are specially adapted virus scanning technologies. WebScan performs a two-step process on all downloaded files: automatically placing the files in a special holding area, where they're scanned for viruses; if the file is found to be virus-free, the user is allowed to permanently copy the file onto the hard disk, but if the file is infected, WebScan alerts the user and provides the option to immediately delete the infected file. WebScan accurately detects over 5,800 viruses of all types and can scan Microsoft Word files and compressed file formats, such as ZIP, self-extracting EXEs, ARC, and ARJ. The product integrates a full-featured browser and e-mail package, and can be used with a wide range of leading Web browsers, including CompuServe's Spry browser, Netscape's Navigator, Netcom's Net-Cruiser, and other browsers based upon the Mosaic browser engine.

WebScan's browser also features support for Internet newsgroups, FTP file transfers, SHTTP security, and Gopher sites. WebScan's full-featured e-mail module supports MIME-compliant file attachments; encrypted messaging; a built-in spell check; and multiple address books with support for aliasing, distribution lists, and sorting. WebScan also features an automated installation routine that allows users to choose an Internet access account with CompuServe's InterServe division. Users can also configure WebScan for use with any other Internet access provider. The product supports Windows 3.x, Windows 95, and Windows NT. All of McAfee's products, upgrades, and documentation are available via Internet FTP (ftp.mcafee.com), the Web (www.mcafee.com), McAfee's BBS, and online services, including America Online (MCAFEE), CompuServe (GO MCAFEE), and The Microsoft Network (GO MCAFEE). McAfee has strategic relationships with Compaq, Hewlett-Packard, Novell, Desktop Management Task Force, Microsoft, AST Research, NCSA, and Network Professional Association (NPA).

Medior (subsidiary of America Online/AMER; San Mateo, CA; www.blue.aol.com) — Medior is a recognized leading developer of interactive CD-ROMs. Medior has developed over 150 products covering a wide range of applications, including entertainment, publishing, education, and electronic commerce. The company has successfully developed an asset management-type of production process that rivals Hollywood movie-type development systems and handles all aspects of interactive development and design, such as research and development, engineering, quality assurance, screen interface, 3-D texturing, and video and production services. This new class of technology and services should allow America Online to offer capabilities that push the multimedia development envelope. AOL acquired Medior in May 1995 for about $30 million.

mFactory (Burlingame, CA; www.mfactory.com) — mFactory is a provider of multimedia development tools. Its primary product is mTropolis, an object-oriented authoring environment for the development of multimedia CD-ROMs and online content. A developer's release of mTropolis was shipped in July 1995, and a full product release is expected by the end of the year. mTropolis is an object-oriented, cross-platform (the final version will target Macintosh, Windows 3.1, and Windows 95) tool that supports extensions and is highly compatible with content produced with products from Adobe and other creative software providers. Finally, mTropolis allows for drag-and-drop construction of content. The tool will be priced at $4,995 and will likely compete with Macromedia Director and, to a greater extent, with raw multimedia programming languages. mFactory expects to develop extensions to its tools that enable content to be distributed and viewed over networks and the Internet. Adobe Ventures made an $8.5 million strategic investment in mFactory in October 1995.

Microsoft (MSFT; Redmond, WA; www.microsoft.com) — Microsoft was late to the Internet market, and it's still without Windows 3.1, UNIX, and Macintosh Internet products (and has lots of stuff still in beta stage). There are millions of browsers in use and millions of Web pages that have been created using HTML (a format Microsoft will attempt to augment and ultimately bypass) — all without the use of Microsoft products. The winners in the Internet space may well be those companies that gain critical mass early (we believe we'll know within a year if Netscape has critical mass in the browser and server markets). No doubt Microsoft, as it did in the stand-alone PC arena, would like to control the standards for online services and Internet software (including the browser, the development tools, and the server, which would offer lots of synergies). Microsoft will aggressively attempt to leverage its positioning and pricing flexibility with Windows 95, PC OEM operating system bundles, and Windows NT/servers to pull out yet another come-from-behind victory.

Microsoft's biggest asset is its software expertise. Specifically, its Internet products are maximized for Win95, and Microsoft can bundle lots of stuff with the operating system that it owns (the company would love it if MSN/Internet Explorer seeped its way into your life, the way Windows 3.1 and Office did). On the other hand, however, Win95 may be a big liability because it's not yet widely deployed (especially within corporations, where Netscape-based intranets are expanding like crazy). Another problem Microsoft faces is that it wants to control the Internet, but many other companies would prefer that the Internet remain as open and uncontrolled as possible. In the long term, we believe, major networks and companies will be created that capitalize on the growth of the Web — the growth we've seen so far in interactive capabilities and the power of the Web leave little doubt about this, in our opinion. We think no company brings as many resources or links — operating system; e-mail; online service; Internet browser; on-line/Internet authoring and development tools; online/Internet server software; content; investments and strategic relationships; and, simply, power and brand-name recognition — as Microsoft does to the Internet opportunity.

NaviSoft, Inc. (subsidiary of America Online/AMER; Vienna, VA; www.naviservice.com) — NaviSoft, acquired by AOL in December 1994, develops high-end publishing and development tools for the Internet. NaviSoft offers a publishing, hosting, and maintenance solution for content creators, personal publishers, software developers, and businesses that want to create a commercial or personal

presence on the Web, placing the whole Web site in the hands of the content producer. The company's products and services provide an integrated, client-server environment for creating, posting and managing applications on the Web. NaviSoft's products, including NaviPress and NaviServer, provide AOL with a core set of tools, enabling the development of a wide range of Internet content and services.

NetManage (NETM; Cupertino, CA; www.netmanage.com) — NetManage is a developer and marketer of TCP/IP software applications, servers, and development tools for Windows, Win95, and Windows NT. Using Internet technology, NetManage's products facilitate the sharing and communicating of information between workgroups. Products include Chameleon variations, Internet Chameleon, ECCO, and NEWT development tools. In June, NetManage demonstrated ISDN connectivity to the Windows PC, which should allow for faster connectivity and sharing of data on the Internet or among workgroups.

NetManage recently agreed to have Netcom Online Communication Services support NetManage's Automatic Internet protocol for online sign-up of new Internet users. In addition, the company has joined forces with Creative Labs, whereby the Chameleon Internet starter kit will be packaged with Creative Labs' communication equipment. Also, NetManage recently announced the launch of WinPCT, a Windows implementation of the newly proposed Private Communication Technology protocol standard for Internet security.

Netscape Communications (NSCP; Mountain View, CA; www.netscape.com) — Netscape offers a broad line of cross-platform software that enhances the exchange of information and provides users with the ability to conduct commerce over the Internet and other TCP/IP-based networks, like company intranets. We estimate that 50% of Netscape's sales are for "commercial" Web use, with the remainder for deployment of internal corporate intranets. In C4Q95, browsers accounted for 58% of Netscape's sales, server products accounted for 29% of revenue, and services (including consulting, support, and training) represented about 13% of revenue. Netscape's four product lines are Netscape Navigator (a graphical network client/browser); server products (allows users to set up and maintain servers for publishing data and conducting commerce); development tools (allow users to create, manage, and assemble

entire online application systems); and Internet applications (turnkey software that enables electronic commerce).

While actual usage numbers for Netscape products are difficult to obtain (largely because Netscape traditionally gave away its browser to expand its installed base), our research indicates that many companies and individuals (we estimate at least 15 million users) have standardized on the Netscape browser and are just beginning to pay for the software. We believe the rollout and deployment of the Netscape browser software may be ramping more quickly than that of any previous software product. At this juncture in the development of its core markets, Netscape is in a potential standard-setting position.

Open Market (Cambridge, MA; www.openmarket.com) — Open Market is the only company to offer a full spectrum of software products for secure, mission-critical business on the Internet. Benchmarked at high performance levels, Open Market's Web servers and software products enable companies to reinvent the way they do business in the information economy. Open Market's software products bring a full range of business capabilities to the Internet, and make it possible for companies to implement powerful, enterprise-wide solutions and to conduct secure, transaction-intensive electronic commerce.

Commerce Products include: Merchant Solution (allows users to open a "store" on the Internet); Transaction Management System (provides back-office operations — including hosting an electronic marketplace, enabling business-to-business transactions, and offering home banking or bill-payment services — for transaction-based business on the Internet); and Integrated Commerce Service (Open Market's own "marketplace," based entirely on its Transaction Management System, which gives merchants access to a wide variety of back-office and other services).

Server and Enterprise Products include: WebServer and Secure WebServer, which are complemented by WebReporter (which enables data to be gathered from the WebServer and Secure WebServer, providing information on traffic patterns in order to manage performance and provide marketing information about "hits" to a Web site).

Open Market recently introduced version 1.1 of its Secure WebServer software that unifies SHTP and SSL. This enables the Secure WebServer, which uses SecureWeb technology from Terisa Systems and secure software from RSA Data Security, to support requests from any of the multiple browsers available that communicate using HTTP, S-HTTP, or SSL. The Secure WebServer can also support all three simultaneously.

The company recently agreed to license its electronic commerce software to IBM. In addition, Hewlett-Packard plans to ship and support Open Market's Internet server and software products on its UNIX- and MPE/IX-based platforms. HP intends to use Open Market's technology as the basis for its electronic commerce offerings.

Open Text (OTEXF; Ontario, Canada; www. open-text.com) — Open Text markets software products for full-text indexing, searching, retrieval, and display. Its software, set up in a complete client-server system, offers a set of APIs, with an SGML parser that builds structure indices to support structure-based retrieval (although retrieval can also be done on non-SGML data such as word-processing files). Open Text products and services include: TextSearch (a full-text search engine/database); TextQuery (a query client); TextView (a display client); Open Text marketing literature; Open Text Training Services; and Open Text Consulting Services. In September 1995, Open Text teamed with Yahoo! Corporation, forming a partnership to incorporate the Open Text Web Search Server OEM technology into Yahoo!'s online guide. Open Text has also announced a merger with Odesta Systems, a developer of document management systems. Open Text recently filed a registration statement for an initial public offering in the U.S.

OpenConnect Systems (Dallas, TX; www.mitek.com) — OpenConnect develops TCP/IP-to-SNA connectivity software products. Its products are enterprise-wide, vendor-independent, bi-directional, and offer protocol conversion, file transfer, printing, terminal emulation, and inter-program communications capabilities. OpenConnect's products enable companies to easily integrate SNA systems with TCP/IP networks, without applying additional software or processing demands on the host. The company's product solutions include both software and hardware server/gateway products; host products; workstation/client products; print products; and internetwork servers/gateway products.

Paper Software (Woodstock, NY; www.paperinc.com)
— Paper Software has developed 2-D and 3-D user interface technologies and toolkits for a variety of operating systems. The company recently released the beta version of its WebFX Plug-in software which, based on the VRML standard, allows users to view and interact with 3-D images inside HTML documents, creating the experience of virtual worlds, 3-D chat rooms, and 3-D special effects on the Web. The software acts as a high-performance add-on for Netscape's Navigator 2.0 running on Windows 3.1, Windows NT, and Windows 95. The beta version is available free for educational and non-profit charitable use (expiring around March 1996) and can be freely downloaded from www.paperinc.com for commercial evaluation. Bundled with WebFX Plug-in is WebFX Explorer, a 3-D Internet viewer that provides stand-alone HTTP communications, object-oriented drag-and-drop, sorting and customization shortcuts, and foldering, which are integrated into the Windows 95 interface but will also run with Windows 3.1 or NT. WebFX Explorer runs independently of any Web browser. In February 1996, Netscape announced its intention to acquire Paper Software.

Premenos (PRMO; Concord, CA; www.premenos.com)
— Premenos is a midrange computer EDI software developer; its Templar product is a secure Internet e-mail software solution for PCs and UNIX workstations. In 1992, Premenos introduced QMAIL, the first open systems, e-mail product designed for the AS/400. Premonos has more than 3,500 businesses that use the company's EDI translation software. Its products include: 1) EDI/400 for the AS/400, which handles large volumes of data. Premenos recently unveiled *PremeView*, a new optional GUI for EDI/400 that replaces the existing character-based AS/400 screens; 2) EDI/e V2 is an easy-to-use EDI solution for UNIX; 3) QMAIL is an AS/400 e-mail solution; and (4) Templar, provides the software and services necessary for secure transmission of EDI documents over the Internet and other TCP/IP networks. Templar runs over IP-networks, including the Internet. Premenos recently joined forces with UUNET, combining Premenos' Templar EDI software with UUNET's broad range of business-class Internet services, to provide an integrated solution for businesses interested in conducting EDI over the Internet.

Progressive Networks (Seattle, WA; www.prognet.com)
— Progressive Networks provides software and services that enable audio-on-demand over the Internet. The company's RealAudio system offers a set of tools that make it possible for news and entertainment providers to make broadcasts available, live or downloaded, over the Internet. Progressive Networks maintains a RealAudio Web site that enables broadcasts of real-time and recorded news services and information. The RealAudio Player provides users with the capability of downloading or live playing of audio. The company also maintains the RealAudio Studio, where users can speak in real-time over the Internet, and the RealAudio Server, which enables users to set up their own online radio stations. Progressive Network's RealAudio Server has been purchased by leading media companies, including Dow Jones, ABC News, CBS, and MCI Communications.

Quarterdeck (QDEK; Marina Del Rey, CA; www.qdeck.com) — Quarterdeck is a developer of software utilities that enhance the performance of computers by maximizing the usefulness of existing PC software, hardware, and networking systems. In early 1995, Quarterdeck realigned its software product development into three strategic business areas: utilities; remote computing; and the Internet. Quarterdeck's product line offers a complete solution of tools for users to access, view, share, distribute, author, and publish on the Internet. The company's Internet products include: WebTalk (a Web phone; additionally, Quarterdeck's Connect and Play Location Manager allows instant account sign-up with major Internet Service Providers, including Netcom, CERFnet, Portal, PSINet, and UUNET. WebTalk was co-developed by partners Intelligence At Large, Inc., Prospero Systems Research, Inc., and Lernout & Hauspie*);* IWare Connect (provides Internet access for Novell Netware LANs, installing quickly onto a single, central Netware server using resident TCP/IP. It allows administrative control of Internet access by users, groups, applications, or destinations and creates a security firewall to protect a NetWare network from hackers); QMosaic (Quarterdeck's "rebuilt" version of the original Mosaic, offering speed, simplicity, easy information management, and an intuitive user interface); WebAuthor (allows users to create Web documents in Word for Windows, with little or no knowledge of HTML); WebServer (allows users to set up a direct Internet connection with an ordinary 486-class, or better, PC without the need for UNIX hardware or programming skills); Quarterdeck InternetSuite (includes Quarterdeck Mosaic, Quarterdeck Message Center (provides instant access and easy management of electronic mail and newsgroup communications, both on and off-line), QTERM (Telnet), QFTP, and Quarterdeck Location Manager). Quarterdeck InternetSuite includes integrated Windows SLIP/PPP support for easy dial-up connections to the Internet.

Quarterdeck also recently introduced WebCompass Personal Edition, its new PC-based Web search system. WebCompass, developed by Limbex Corp. and marketed by Quarterdeck, is the first PC-based meta search engine for the Web, allowing users to send a single query to multiple Web search engines, such as Yahoo and WebCrawler, so users can perform the widest search for information, and then have it summarized, organized, and stored on the desktop.

SoftQuad Inc. (SKI; Ontario, Canada; www.sq.com) — SoftQuad provides a variety of software tools based on a "write once, publish anytime/anywhere" principle. With the company's multi-platform SGML and HTML software, users can create information once and publish it any number of times across a variety of platforms, including on screen, on paper, on CD-ROM, and on the Internet. SoftQuad's product categories include Web Products, SGML Authoring Tools, Electronic and Desktop Publishing Tools, and Reference Materials. The Web Products (HoTMetaL PRO and Panorama PRO), which are publishing and viewing technologies, allow users to create hypertext documents and browse SGML documents on the Web. SGML Authoring Tools (Author/Editor, RulesBuilder, and Sculptor) provide users with the ability to quickly create valid SGML documents and compile DTDs (Document Type Definitions). Additionally, Sculptor can customize and integrate Author/Editor with other applications. Electronic and Desktop Publishing Tools (Explorer, SGML Enabler for QuarkXPress, and Enactor for Microsoft Word) give the user the ability to import and convert documents, as well as organize and deliver SGML documents. Reference Materials (SGML World Tour and SGML Printer) provide an overview of SGML, including its history, an introduction to getting started, its uses, and its future role.

SoftQuad recently announced an agreement with Ventana Communications whereby Ventana will be the exclusive distributor of SoftQuad's HTML publishing tools.

Spider Technologies (Palo Alto, CA; www.w3spider.com) — Spider develops graphical software tools that integrate communication between a Web browser and a database, allowing developers to link Web pages without programming or coding. The company's product consists of two modules: Spider Development and Spider Deployment. Spider Development, used to create applications, is a graphical user interface for defining relationships between the fields in an HTML form and database tables and information. The applications are built in a four-step process: 1) selecting a database and tables; 2) linking the HTML form to the database (with drag-and-drop performance); 3) defining the SQL statement; and 4) choosing the output fields and format. Changes can then be made through editing the specified links. Spider Deployment performs the Spider Development applications from input received from the Web server after it is transformed into an HTML document.

Spyglass (SYPG; Naperville, IL; www.spyglass.com) — Spyglass develops and licenses Web application software, including the Mosaic browser. The company licenses a variety of software developers, OEMs, VARs, and integrators to use its products; it currently does not retail or wholesale the product. The company, therefore, identifies its software as embedded-technology. The company's technologies are licensed by many large corporations, such as AT&T, Microsoft, DEC, Oracle, IBM, and Vanguard. In addition to its client (browser) product, the company develops a server product, Spyglass Server. Mosaic is an Internet browser that provides graphical point-and-click access to the Web. Enhanced Mosaic technology is developed and distributed under a joint development and licensing agreement with the University of Illinois, which developed NCSA Mosaic. Spyglass Server is a fast HTTP server that manages and controls access to information stored at individual Web sites. Spyglass Server is also expandable, adaptable, easily integrated with applications, secure, and client-compatible.

Recent announcements include: a letter of intent with Microsoft as the developer and prime licensee of STT for Windows, Macintosh, and UNIX; an agreement to license its Mosaic Web client to InfiNet, a joint venture between Knight-Ridder and Landmark; an alliance with Sun Microsystems to integrate Java with Spyglass's Mosaic Web client technology; and agreements with Accent Software and Quarterdeck for Spyglass's Mosaic technology.

Ubique, Ltd. (subsidiary of America Online/AMER; Rehovot, Israel; www.ubique.com) — Ubique develops software designed for real-time interaction and collaboration over the Internet. The company's Virtual Places product line and client/server architecture create virtual communities on the Internet by delivering human presence and live interaction on the Web. The Virtual Places architecture is composed of the Virtual Places Server and Virtual Places Client. The server manages real-time connections among the inhabitants of a virtual space. The client, a Web browser extension, includes a GUI for interaction and an audio engine for voice communication. AOL recently acquired Ubique for $14.6 million in stock to use the Virtual Places technology to expand its existing online communication service, as well as its coming Internet brand service.

Verity (VRTY; Mountain View, CA; www.verity.com) — One of two organization/aggregation software companies featured in this section, Verity is a developer of software tools that enable users to search, filter, and distribute textual information on a variety of electronic media, including the Internet, online services, and enterprise networks. Verity's product line, the Topic family, is designed to address the needs of individuals, enterprises, and publishers by performing rapid and timely searches, as well as real-time monitoring and filtering of information. Users can also perform personalized searches across information previously stored within multiple sources and formats. The Topic technology has been deployed within Verity's suite of applications, as well as an embedded feature within distributed third-party software applications, such as Lotus Notes and Adobe Acrobat. Verity has also begun licensing Topic technology to providers of Internet products and online services, including Netscape, Quarterdeck, and Delphi Internet (MCI). Topic software, licensed to over 650 corporations, government agencies, software developers, online service providers, and Internet publishers, has approximately two million end-users worldwide. Topic products include: the Developer's Kit; the Enterprise Server; the Internet Server; the Client; the CD Publisher; the Agent Server; and the News Server.

Vermeer Technologies (Cambridge, MA; www.vermeer.com) — Vermeer Technologies, which recently announced its intention to be acquired by Microsoft, provides a suite of production-strength Web authoring tools that require no programming or coding. Its core product, FrontPage, has helped develop the concept of "Webtop publishing." In order to eliminate the need for programming/coding, Webtop publishing incorporates client/server development tools and authoring environments designed for easy deployment and maintenance of Web services. FrontPage features include WebWizards (smart templates), WebBots (drop-in, interactive objects), hyperlink browsing, full-text indexing/search/retrieval, and visual application and management tools.

VocalTec (Northvale, NJ; www.vocaltec.com) — VocalTec develops the Internet Phone software and other voice communications and messaging software products for multimedia and workgroup computing; these products are designed to improve productivity, reduce communications costs, and maximize investments in technology. The company's primary product, the Internet Phone, permits users to speak over the Internet in real-time, supporting full-duplex audio. VocalTec has also developed the Internet Wave (or IWave), a helper application that brings audio-on-demand to Web pages. IWave enables organizations and individuals to broadcast shows, discussions, and events via the Internet. The company also markets an external parallel-port adapter sound card. The company filed to go public on January 8, 1996.

WAIS (subsidiary of America Online/AMER; San Francisco; www.wais.com) — WAIS develops a publishing software system that is focused on tools and services for distributing information over the Internet and improving the quality of the information published. WAIS develops the WAISserver and WAIS Production Services, which create custom online services for such familiar faces as Encyclopedia Britannica and Dow Jones, and provides Internet users with access to books, magazines, news, product data sheets, technical overviews, company information, and many other services. The WAISserver allows content providers to index and publish large databases to the Internet and automatically creates HTML documents as it indexes content databases. WAIS Production Services implements WAISserver technology and can custom integrate modules for, among others: user registration and feedback; transaction-based and subscription-based billing; personalized invoicing for online shopping; archived searching for back issues; automatic content expiration; and new content alerting.

In May 1995, WAIS was acquired by America Online for about $15 million. The move provides an advance in AOL's strategic imperative to provide its partners with the ability to simply and easily create an integrated strategy and "best of breed" presence in the converging mediums of on-line, multimedia, and the Internet.

Wollongong Group/Attachmate (Palo Alto, CA; www.twg.com) — Wollongong provides TCP/IP-based internetworking software that offers users object-oriented desktop access to data and information on the Internet, as well as on private, TCP/IP-based corporate networks. Wollongong's PathWay products provide corporate intranet access and are being integrated into the framework of the company's latest product, the Emissary line, which has received strong reviews. The Emissary line provides: 1) transparent network access, by separating users from the complex structures behind the Internet and corporate net-works; 2) the ability to access all resources via one inte-grated application, including sending mail, copying files, accessing remote applications, receiving news updates, and browsing the Web; 3) a Windows desktop environment; 4) extensible architecture; and 5) integrated intranet access.

Attachmate has signed a letter of intent to acquire Wollon-gong, with the deal expected to close before the end of the year. Attachmate plans to integrate its host access software products with Wollongong's Emissary software, providing corporate users with a complete "intranet" solution. Other recent announcements include a partnership with A&I

Technologies, a systems integrator for the healthcare Indus-try, and a strategic alliance with Netcom to develop a cost-effective turnkey solution for Internet/intranet access.

Worlds Inc. (San Francisco; www.worlds.net) — Worlds Inc. is a developer of 3-D Internet software. The company offers consumer and commercial networked software that provides interactive virtual experiences. Through its WorldsWare interface, the company creates virtual spaces that it populates with online users, represented as 3-D Digital Actors. Positioned in a unique and interactive envi-ronment, Digital Actors enable users to assume a personal-ity, enter a shared space, and communicate with one an-other. WorldsWare's communications layer also permits connection of multiple worlds across the Internet, or any other network.

The company was the first to launch a 3-D online chat en-vironment, Worlds Chat. As opposed to traditional text- and icon-based interfaces, Worlds Chat is based on a model of social computing and is an excellent demonstration of how exceptional 3-D graphics can be used interactively by multiple users connected on the Internet using low-speed modems. Worlds Inc.'s software is also being used by sev-eral organizations, such as the Starbright Foundation, to create STARBRIGHT World (a virtual playground for seri-ously ill children), and Visa International, to create a vir-tual banking environment. Worlds has also teamed up with VISA International and has designed a software system that provides a 3-D experience for retail operations and banking on the Internet, called Electronic Courtyard. Worlds Inc. is a spin-off of an entertainment and educational software developer, Knowledge Adventure.

Intuit

• First, online banking and bill-paying developments will be assisted by Intuit's financial services partners, which, so far, include 37 institutions, ranging from banks (such as Chase and Wells Fargo) to a financial services company (American Express) and brokerage (Smith Barney). Intuit and these partners will provide customers with the ability to access and transact with certain accounts at those institutions. The online backbone for this service will be an Intuit-administered pro-prietary network through Intuit subsidiary, Intuit Services. The network hub will allow PC/modem-equipped customers to dial into the Intuit network using local phone numbers (via AT&T's 950 network) and connect with their financial institu-tions.

• Second, via Intuit Services, Intuit will offer Investor Insight, an online investment information module (accessible from Quicken), which will, at the click of a button, update consumers' portfolios with stock prices, news, analyst estimates, re-ports and other investment information. Intuit will offer Investor Insight directly for approximately $9.95 per month.

- Intuit has announced a number of initiatives to integrate the Internet as a communications tool within its products. First, Intuit announced the debut of its Website which will provide financial information, product support, and material on Intuit's financial service partners. Second, Intuit announced that it will bundle the Netscape Navigator Internet Browser with Quicken for 96 — the browser will be launchable from within Quicken, thus providing easy Internet/information access. Third, Intuit announced that access to its Web page would be free through a Quicken/Navigator bundled product, and access to other Internet services would be offered at competitive prices through Concentric's Network Services Division.

- On November 8, Intuit announced that it had signed a letter of intent to purchase GALT Technologies (a provider of mutual fund and financial information on the Internet through the NETworth Web site).

- On November 13, Intuit and America Online announced a strategic alliance to jointly provide electronic banking to America Online members. The alliance will include: 1) electronic banking through participating financial institutions (to be announced over the next few months); 2) the revamping of Intuit's America Online area, providing greater service to Intuit customers; 3) links to the Quicken Financial Network; and 4) Intuit's software products available for sale on America Online. The two companies plan to sponsor joint promotions to introduce their products to each other's customer base. The new electronic commerce service, expected to launch in the spring of 1996, will allow users to directly access checking, savings, money market, and credit card account data and bill payment services from the financial institutions via America Online and Intuit Services Corporation (ISC) — the same facility linking Quicken users to their financial institutions. Users will be able to check account balances, download complete account statements, transfer funds, and pay bills from within their America Online account. The electronic banking services available on America Online, using the same procedures required via Quicken, will require access with a PIN number (for user identification/verification) and include high-level RSA Data Security encryption to secure the transactions while in transit between the America Online subscriber's PC and the bank.

• The Web will affect every company in the enterprise sector. Development tool vendors will have to decide whether to license Java or wait for Visual Basic to evolve. An early decision could provide a time-to-market advantage, or commit a vendor to a dead-end path.

• Enterprise application vendors will have to determine how to aggressively re-architect their applications to run across the Web and what tools to use. Most of these vendors have proprietary development tools and will have to decide whether or not to update them with Java. Also, some application vendors have tied their logic to the interface and will have more difficulty in separating interface code from application logic and database management. The issue in this segment will be execution, just as it was in the rush to client/server: Who can get there first with fully functional product?

• The systems management vendors should enjoy new opportunities, since greater complexity and distributed processing give them more things to monitor, manage, schedule, connect, and restore. These vendors will have to rethink management solutions to a new implementation of the traditional functional requirements of systems management.

• Finally, the database vendors should profit from the move to Web-based computing. If the Web generates more electronic transactions and commerce, these transactions will drive database usage and deployment.

• A new model of pricing will be needed for the database and application vendors, since the current model is user-based. If the number of users is unknown because the users are external to an organization and the firewall, then some new scheme will be needed.

Computer Associates (CA; Islandia, NY; www.cai.com)
— The systems management issues associated with the Web will be complex, since systems integrity must now span multiple companies and network segments. Computer Associates has been working on a systems management infrastructure to manage Web sites as part of a broader computing infrastructure at a customer site.

CA has announced partnerships with Netscape and Microsoft to provide systems management infrastructure around each company's Web server offering. Unicenter/ICE (Internet commerce enabled) is a version of CA's flagship systems management product tailored for the Web. It addresses the management needs of Web servers and Web clients by providing security, event management, help-desk, storage management, resource accounting, and database monitoring. The need for systems management should escalate as the number of servers explodes, since the resulting complexity can only be managed with automated software utilities. Key areas that CA is focusing on as Web opportunities are:

Security — CA-Unicenter/ICE secures data and program resources on Web servers from unauthorized access over

the Web. By securing TCP/IP ports, it prevents hackers from breaking into systems by writing their own TCP/IP clients. CA-Unicenter/ICE can take automated actions in response to attempted security violations, as well as provide auditing and reporting of user activity.

Intranet-Specific Capabilities — 1) Web clients: CA-Unicenter/ICE manages Web client desktops by providing software distribution and configuration management, monitoring and management of events on the client, and user-based secure access to multiple applications. 2) Configuration: CA-Unicenter/ICE keeps client configurations in its database, allowing the help-desk staff to answer user questions and resolve problems. 3) Monitoring: Advanced monitoring capabilities watch for events on Web clients and other resources, which improves Web system availability. CA-Unicenter/ICE agents can read error logs, track system and network events, and monitor memory and disk resources. 4) Administration: CA-Unicenter/ICE provides auditing and reporting of data access, attempted security breaches, and security policy modifications. 5) Storage: Hierarchical storage management capabilities reduce the storage driver requirements of a Web server. By automatically offloading infrequently used information, CA-

Unicenter/ICE optimizes the use of storage. 6) Reliability: To facilitate recovery from disasters, CA-Unicenter/ICE supports automated backup and recovery of data. 7) Database Monitoring: CA-Unicenter/ICE monitors and manages databases used for Web applications and enables administrators to identify and correct performance and availability problems. It tracks CGI requests to databases such as CA-OpenIngres/ICE, Microsoft SQL Server, Oracle, Informix and Sybase, and provides event and availability management. 8) Resource Monitoring: Administrators can monitor usage and resource consumption on Web servers by components and user classification. They can track Web site availability, data access counts, transactions least utilized, and usage patterns by geography, user-class, or department.

Given the company's large installed base and cross-platform management tools, the heterogeneous environment of the Web plays to CA's strengths. CA also dominates the market for mainframe security and has a solid position in security administration with the UNIX market via Unicenter. As security concerns grow, CA can leverage its security products as initial justification for Unicenter in customer sites. Moreover, we expect the company to extend its security product line, given the plethora of small companies working on Internet security products.

Documentum (DCTM; Pleasonton, CA; www.documentum.com) — Documentum markets the Enterprise Document Management System, a product designed to managed documents of multiple formats across the enterprise. The product's document management capabilities extend to word processing documents, CAD/CAM files, spreadsheets, video, audio, and many types of unstructured data. The company has large installations of its products in several document-intensive vertical markets (such as aerospace, pharmaceuticals, and chemical engineering). Those customers are likely to demand access to business-critical documents over the Web.

Documentum recently unveiled Accelera, an extension of its document management functionality to the Web. Search-and-retrieval tools for the Web are still fairly rudimentary, and Documentum should be able to provide more sophisticated searching and archiving of documents to be displayed over the Web. Moreover, the company can provide a repository for the documents and automatically update Web servers as the source documents are changed

anywhere in the network with appropriate security rules. Documentum is in the business of managing, distributing, and displaying documents across the enterprise; the Web brings a wider audience of users for the company's product line.

Informix (IFMX; Menlo Park, CA; www.informix.com) — Informix is furthest along in extending relational database technology to address non-structured data. The company has the most recently architected database in the industry, which includes modular extensions for multimedia-oriented data. Informix is also the development platform for Netscape server applications. Silicon Graphics has selected Informix for several initiatives in the Web server arena, as well as some in the entertainment industries. Informix has taken a partnering approach to the Web and will look to provide robust database engine technology to multiple partners. The company also recently licensed Java from Sun to include in Informix's object-oriented tool, NewEra.

Informix has accelerated the focus on nonstructured data types (such as text, video, audio, spatial data, images) that might be housed and displayed across the Web. The Web provides a convenient distribution and display infrastructure for unstructured data types. By acquiring Illustra, the premier object relational database focused on unstructured data, Informix can exploit the Web should unstructured data grow in importance and variety. If network bandwidth evolves as quickly as we suspect, and users start to demand more dynamic and entertaining Web pages, then storing these data types in volume becomes critical. Just as important, searching and retrieving these data types could become essential. Illustra uses technology that understands the contents of unstructured data to allow, for example, searches of all images in the database for match with a particular photo.

Novell (NOVL; Orem, UT; www.novell.com) — If Novell can reposition Netware as a gateway to the Internet by providing simple connectivity to the Web supported by robust management and administration software, it can move its installed base toward networked-based applications. Moreover, the heterogeneous nature of the Web environment probably means customers retain a myriad of server architectures, and Novell can provide internal connectivity between these sources. ANCS (AT&T Netware Connect Services) is a joint service from Novell, AT&T, the

RBOCs, and several foreign telecommunications companies. Customers will be able to outsource their local-area networks to AT&T and Novell and obtain wide-area networking functionality transparently. ANCS is being positioned as a subset of the Internet for customers looking for a more secure means to outsource applications (Web and non-Web based) over the Internet without administration overhead or maintaining the infrastructure themselves. ANCS is the key initiative for Novell's future, in our view, but the service is just now reaching production status.

Novell's first Web server offering was developed by a third party and in our opinion is difficult to set up and lacks differentiating features. Given the volume of servers that are likely to be deployed over the next two years, it's not too late for Novell to add some polish to the product. The company's large installed based of networked file servers is still an attractive potential captive market, as their customers may be reluctant to bring a second operating system into their environment. We also think Novell could address the dearth of applications on Netware by porting Java to the Netware environment, as opposed to hoping that developers will write to Novell's proprietary API, Net2000.

Oracle Systems (ORCL; Redwood Shores, CA; www.oracle.com) — Oracle has aggressively pursued a one-stop-shopping strategy for Internet servers. The company offers its own browser and Web server software. The company will announce a server suite in late December that incorporates Internet connectivity, systems management, and software distribution under a single server suite, tentatively called BusinessServer. Since half of the client/server systems in production are drawing data from an Oracle database, and given the likelihood that customers will want to expose some of the data to Web applications, Oracle looks well positioned to market Internet-related products to its installed base. Oracle applications (financials, manufacturing, and human resources) are particularly server-centric — a design which lends itself to Web access. Consequently, we expect Oracle applications to become available as Web applications. Finally, Oracle's 5,500 consultants can help implement Web-based servers and applications for those customers looking to outsource Web development.

Scopus Technology (SCOP; Emeryville, CA; www.scopus.com) — Scopus has a family of applications addressing customer information systems (customer support, product management, help desk, and sales force automation). The product line has been architected in a way to generate HTML pages from the meta data. The company's customers include Sun and Netscape, and Scopus should make its product line Web-aware fairly quickly. Given the architecture and relationships with key Web development vendors, Scopus may be well positioned to migrate its enterprise applications to the Web, and the applications are such that distributed access to customer information is already a requirement.

Internet/Online Consulting

- **Internet consultants provide services to companies that are using or attempting to use the Internet**. Typically, there are two varieties of consultants: 1) pure consultants that bill by the hour or by the job; and 2) companies that offer products that must be coupled with a service, such as auditing. Internet consultants today perform one of three tasks: **general Internet guidance; Web-page building;** and/or **counting of Web-page usage**.

- The need for expert consultants is fairly obvious — connecting to the Internet is still fairly complicated. As a result, several entities have emerged to give companies and individuals **general Internet guidance** as well as more specific aid, such as Web-page building and counting Web-page usage.

- The first consulting service is **Web-page building**. Although software to automate Web-page building is coming on stream quickly, the process of producing a "quality" Web-page is still fairly technical. However, numerous companies, organizations, schools, and others want to get on the Internet soon with exciting home pages that draw an audience. These trends have created a new business opportunity for talented technicians to create Web pages for others.

- Today, a common type of service company focusing on the Internet provides independent, unbiased **counting of Web-page usage**. There is a strong perceived need for this type of service or product, as many Web pages are now offering services that pull in large audiences for which advertisers will pay to gain access. Specifically, advertisers want to accurately quantify how many people have visited a particular site, as advertising dollars are allocated based on the potential number of impressions or visits. The second type of consulting firm provides the same service of counting of Web-page usage, but does so through the use of auditing software, which typically resides on the Web page server and independently records usage.

CKS Group (Cupertino, CA; www.cks.com) — CKS Group, Inc., specializes in offering a wide range of integrated marketing communications services that help companies market their products, services, and messages. The integrated marketing communications services provided by the company include strategic corporate and product positioning, corporate identity and product branding, new media, packaging, collateral systems, advertising, direct mail, consumer promotions, trade promotions and media placement services.

The company believes that it is a leading provider of integrated marketing programs that utilize advanced technology solutions and new media, which the company defines as media that deliver content to end users in digital form, including the Worldwide Web, the Internet, proprietary online services, CD-ROMs, laptop PC presentations, and interactive kiosks.

Since the first CKS company, CKS Partners, was founded in 1987, the CKS Group has grown from two employees in a single office to 185 employees in six offices billing more than $130 million in 1994. Headquartered in Cupertino,

Calif., CKS Group locations currently include Campbell, Cupertino, and San Francisco, California; Portland, Oregon; New York, N.Y.; and London, England.

Find/SVP (FSVP; New York, NY; www.findsvp.com) — Find/SVP provides a number of consulting and research services that address the multitude of needs and questions for business information. Such services range from the American New Small Business Survey to the American Internet User Survey. Find/SVP's primary business is its Quick Consulting & Research Service, which, through its base of consultants, offers fast, confidential, and cost-effective answers to questions posed by the company's individual "Cardholders" (about 15,000 individuals in over 2,250 firms). Typically, requests through this division take no more than a few hours of research. For longer requests, the company's Strategic Research Division performs custom assignments, such as market analyses, surveys, extensive and complex information collection, and benchmarking and customer satisfaction studies. Find/SVP's Customer Satisfaction Strategies Division works with clients to determine customer needs and expectations.

For market and industry studies, the Published Products Division generates over 120 syndicated market intelligence reports on an annual basis. Additionally, the Emerging Technologies Research Group performs multi-client studies information demand and use. Other Find/SVP businesses include: the Information Catalog (featuring proprietary research, books, directories, reference materials, software, and videos); Newsletters ("The Information Advisor," "The Ice Cream Reporter," "InterActive Consumer," and "The LowFat Monitor"); and Seminars and Conferences (offering a number of professional development seminars and conferences, in conjunction with Strategic Research Institute, or SRI).

I/PRO (San Francisco, CA; www.ipro.com) — Internet Profiles Corporation is a provider of services and software for independent measurement and analysis of Web site usage. I/PRO's offerings provide a more accountable, accurate, and unbiased means of measuring Web Page usage than methods such as counting hits, a practice that has come under fire due to its potential for under- and over-counting usage depending upon the complexity of the Web page. The I/PRO system has three components: I/CODE, I/COUNT, and I/AUDIT. I/CODE registers users and provides site owners with demographic information; I/COUNT monitors and analyzes aspects of Web site usage; and I/AUDIT compiles a third-party report of Web site activity which can be provided to advertisers. The system fills a marketplace need for an accurate assessment of Web site audiences, which has in turn helped organizations to determine the value of their Web site as a marketing medium. I/PRO's success in meeting this demand has made the company a leader in providing measurement standards on the Internet.

I/PRO recently formed a strategic partnership with Nielsen Media Research, an established leader in television audience measurement. The company is also working with Enterprise Integration Technologies (EIT), a developer and marketer of electronic commerce initiatives that was recently acquired by VeriFone. In addition, I/PRO was selected by Microsoft to track Web site usage relating to the launch of Windows 95. Other I/PRO customers include CompuServe, CMP Publications, Individual Inc., Internet Shopping Network, Netscape Communications, Yahoo!, Playboy Enterprises, and Ziff-Davis Publishing. In addition, the recent announcement of a Web Partner Program

will have the effect of bringing the I/PRO system of measurement tools to more Web sites.

Internet Media Services (Palo Alto, CA; www.netmedia.com) — Internet Media Services (IMS) builds interactive hi-tech Web sites. The company produces its own software for use in designing and implementing clients' Web sites. Its products and services include: 1) Wander, a Web server enhancement that allows for advanced interactivity between the site visitor and the online service; 2) Open Forum Messaging System, a technology that allows Web users to join in both moderated and unmoderated discussion groups specific to the client's Web site; 3) Web Development tools, including WebBuilder and Sweep, which assist in the rapid development and modification of Web sites; 4) InterCat Online Ordering System, a virtual online store that caters to any market of customers and enables merchants to convert traditional print catalogs into online catalogs; and 5) IMS Consulting Services, which assists in the entire Web site development process.

IMS has designed Web sites for such companies as Hewlett-Packard, Adobe Systems, Sun Microsystems, UB Networks, and Harvard University. In addition, the company has formed strategic partnerships with UB Networks and Tandem Computers to strengthen its ability to provide companies with solutions to Web problems.

Intersé (Sunnyvale, CA; www.interse.com) — Intersé develops and markets products and services that help users market on the Internet and develop Web sites, as well as analyze usage of a site. Rather than counting hits, Intersé's market focus software provides users with a precise tally of Web site users. The software also translates Internet addresses into actual organization names and filenames into document titles, making it easier to understand a Web site. Market focus includes the Intersé Internet database, which contains most U.S. Internet domains indexed by city, state, and zip code, combined with other Internet demographic information. Intersé's market focus combines this information with a company's or an organization's files to develop detailed, professional-looking reports. The software provides an easy-to-use tool for on-site analysis, as well as an intuitive graphical user interface.

Logical Design Solutions (Murray Hill, NJ; www.lds.com) — Logical Design Solutions (LDS) designs and provides strategic interactive communications solutions for corporate clients. Through LDS, corporations are able to use interactive media to market products and services, as well as educate and inform employees. LDS's products and services include: 1) WebTrac, a tool to monitor and analyze Web site usage; 2) TeleTrac, a telecommunications data processing software; 3) StyleMinder, a Windows-based style enforcement software package that lets customers design their own style rules and apply them to documents; and 4) Internet/Web applications, which includes customized interactive business communications solutions.

LDS Partners include Electronic Book Technologies (EBT), a provider of comprehensive electronic publishing solutions, and MC2, a provider of long-term network solutions using LAN/WAN design, implementation, and support. Clients include Ameritech, AT&T, Bell Atlantic, Checkfree, Dun & Bradstreet, Telecom Australia, Novell, Phoenix Technologies, The Vanguard Group, and WorldPartners Company.

NetCount (Los Angeles; www.netcount.com) — NetCount is a third-party Web-site tracking and verification service that has gained more than 100 customers since its commercial launch in October 1995. NetCount's mission is to provide accurate measurement of the Worldwide Web, including user counts and demographic collection, without violating user privacy. NetCount is the technology leader in Web measurement using true census-based tracking techniques, auditable systems, and timely reporting practices. NetCount fills a marketplace need with a suite of products and services designed to meet the measurement requirements of Web sites, media research professionals, advertisers, and media buyers.

Through its AdCount service, advertisers and media buyers can accurately determine and compare the effectiveness of their online advertisements. Combined with NetCount's user-counting service HeadCount, AdCount facilitates the tracking of users from an advertisement on one Web site to a purchase on another site. This enables a new form of electronic commerce advertising rates that is based on online sales commissions.

NetCount recently announced its Marketing Alliance Partner (MAP) program, which provides channel distribution of NetCount's products and services through major Web-site development agencies and Internet service providers. Potomac Interactive, Media Circus, Digital Planet, and

Whirlwind Interactive join BBN Planet as the first companies to sign on. BBN Planet has bundled NetCount's services into its Web Advantage hosting services since November 1995.

Network Solutions, Inc. (NSI; Herndon, VA; www. netsol.com) — Under contract with the NSF, Network Solutions is the company that handles domain-name and IP address registration, as well as other administrative tasks, for the Internet. NSI runs the centralized InterNIC Web site (http://rs.internic.net/). The company's contract with the NSF began in 1993 and is scheduled to end in 1998. In September 1995, NSI, with permission from the NSF, began charging a $50 per year registration fee for each domain name. Prior to authorization to charge each domain-name holder separately, the NSF funded all of NSI's work. In addition to its responsibility to maintain Internet registration, NSI has leveraged its networking expertise and performs corporate network consulting.

Web Communications (Santa Cruz, CA; www. webcom.com) — WebCom provides organizations and individuals with software tools, services, and resources to quickly and easily establish a Web site. Users have full control over the content and maintenance of their Web site, with service offerings that include: 5 Megabytes of online disk storage; 200 MB (400 MB for corporate accounts) of network traffic; the option to register a personal domain name; a site activity report; the ability to easily use extended Web functionality (like fill-out forms, secure encrypted Web transactions, clickable image maps, access authorization, and full-text searching); a personal access log; mail forwarding; free technical support; guides for getting the site indexed on other major indexing services; and online help and tutorials. WebCom's Instant Site tool lets users create Web pages without needing to know HTML code. To establish an account, users must already have Internet access with a non-WebCom e-mail address. The company has over 1,320 customers.

WebTrack/Caddis International (New York, NY; www.webtrack.com) — WebTrack, a subsidiary of Caddis International, is an information service that tracks advertising, publishing, and usage on the Internet and other online services. WebTrack's WebStat division offers site traffic verification services to provide an objective standard by which companies can track online activity. Other products and services offered by WebTrack include: 1) InterAd and

"InterAd Monthly," a database and newsletter that track online corporate advertising; 2) WebTrack 500, a monthly ranking of the 500 most popular Web sites; 3) Web Advertising Database, a searchable database of Web sites published by U.S. advertisers, organized by industry; 4) Ad Space Locator, a directory that lists sites that accept advertising and sponsorship; and 5) Marketing Directory, a listing of companies and professionals involved in Web and interactive marketing.

WebTrack also provides Internet development services, and is currently working with the Audit Bureau of Circulations (ABC) to manage the technical process of online auditing and to further develop auditing software.

Content & Aggregation

- Thanks to a broadening reach, low cost, and easy-to-use Internet access, **near-zero-cost publishing has arrived.** For example, e-mail newsletters can be distributed to millions of users worldwide for no more than the cost of a $5–10 monthly membership; beginning in December 1995, CompuServe intends to offer its subscribers $5-per-month home pages.

- Given the **new, low barriers to entering the publishing and information distribution markets**, new companies are entering the markets traditionally dominated by paper-based publishing companies. The Internet is allowing users to **quickly obtain large volumes of information** about topics of interest and to **quickly disseminate information.**

- In this section, we describe various types of content and aggregation companies. Given the sheer volume of information on the Internet, opportunities have arisen for companies and products that can **organize and aggregate** and filter information, and companies that provide **information** and newsfeeds are finding lots of opportunities on the Internet.

- The following are four groups of "content" that can be put onto servers on the Internet or on online services. First, there are the **organization/aggregation** companies, which comprise today's OSPs and Internet search services. These two types of businesses are categorized together because they functionally perform something similar: they allow users to rapidly obtain information about a particular subject, or allow a user to go to a certain place quickly. Next are the **information providers**. **Publications/static** are third, a category intended to describe information that stays constant or static. The fourth category is **publications/interactive,** which explains a type of publication that can be altered by a reader or a user action, such as a moderated chat group.

- Content and aggregation providers' revenues are based on advertising and usage charges.

America Online (AMER; Vienna, VA; www.blue.aol.com) — America Online is the mother of all consumer online services. The company was created ten years ago as a "new media" company — well before anyone knew what that term meant. With more than 5 million members/subscribers, America Online is the largest U.S. consumer online service and has just begun its international expansion efforts. The fundamental tenet for the company since Day One has been the importance of providing an easy-to-use online service to consumers — the company consistently focuses on offering great content, context, community, commerce, and connectivity, at a low cost — in short, AOL is a product even your mom can use. America Online offers its members a broad range of features, such as e-mail, online conferences, entertainment, software, computing support, an extensive "newsstand" of electronic magazines and newspapers, access to the Internet, and original and informative programming and content. AOL presents its online information in "channel" style, and within each channel are lots of programs. The channels are Today's News, Personal Finance, Clubs & Interests, Computing, Travel, Marketplace, People Connection (Chat), Newsstand, Entertainment, Education, Reference Desk, Internet Connection, Sports, and Kids Only. We see AOL as one big consumer-oriented programming interface for the online/Internet world — in our opinion, America Online does a better job of programming than any other company, by a long shot.

America Online is many things: 1) a consumer online services company (AOL); 2) an Internet company (AOL-embedded and stand-alone GNN offerings); 3) an online/Internet service provider (through ownership of ANS, which provides a network connection for AOL and the Internet); 4) a content aggregation/programming company (or new media publishing company) via its relationship with content providers/partners; 5) a venture capital holding company through its $6-million-plus investments in 20, and rising, "Greenhouse" companies; 6) a development/authoring tool company with its Rainman product line for creating AOL content; and 7) a proprietor of 5 million-plus sets of online "eyeballs," which can provide lucrative advertising and transactions businesses.

Architext Software, Inc. (Mountain View, CA; www.architext.com) — One of two organization and aggregation software companies featured in this section, Architext Software develops a search-and-retrieval software engine called Excite that scans documents on the Internet (or any network) to help users locate information. The service includes hypertext linking and dynamic subject grouping to help condense large lists of documents into subgroups of related topics. Architext's search engine, rather than doing textual searches, performs "concept" searches. Its software, based on the idea that words often found near each other tend to be conceptually related, regularly scans the networks it searches and updates its statistical analysis of the relationships between words within a huge number of documents. The program then delivers all references arranged under subject headings, ranked by relevance to the initial query. Recently, Excite was averaging 600,000–700,000 hits per day, and the software is complemented by Excite for Web servers, adding media navigation capabilities to local Web sites. The Excite media navigation service, launched on the Internet in October 1995, features over 40,000 professionally written reviews of Web sites.

Architext recently announced the acquisition of City.Net, which provides local and regional information about restaurants, civic and cultural events, entertainment, business, government, and travel on the Internet. From about August through November 1995, City.Net serviced, on average, about 3 million requests per month.

CMG Information (CMGI; Wilmington, MA; www.cmgi.com) — CMG is a direct marketing company that has made five strategic Internet-related investments or acquisitions, through CMG@Ventures, its Internet investment and development arm, positioning the company to expand products and services into the online arena. The first is Lycos, an 80%-owned unit, which maintains and continually updates a Web catalog using Lycos Spider Technology. Second is NetCarta (formerly NICE Technologies), which develops and markets Web management, navigation, and design tolls that make the Web easier to use and more practical for corporate MIS departments.

Third is Black Sun Interactive which develops tools that allow Internet users to interact with electronic information and each other in three dimensions. Fourth is FreeMark Communications, which develops advertiser-supported e-mail concepts via the Internet. Fifth is Ikonic Interactive, which develops interactive software and is a leading provider of interactive television applications and easy-to-use graphical user interfaces for interactive TV, the Web, and commercial and private online services.

CompuServe/H&R Block (subsidiary of H&R Block/HRB; Columbus, OH; www.compuserve.com) — CompuServe, a division of H&R Block, and the second-largest consumer online service behind AOL, has been an online service provider of computer-based information and communications services to businesses and individuals for over 20 years. The company develops services that provide access to host server and data communications services and the Internet. As of November 1995, the CompuServe Information Service had over 3.8 million consumer users and over 900 corporate customers in 150 countries accessing over 3,000 databases, via modem. Several financial and business connectivity services are also sold to companies. During October 1995, CIS had over 13 million hours of traffic (doubling from the previous year), of which 2 million was Internet-related. Features of the service include communications, bulletin boards, weather, sports, travel, health, electronic shopping, money and markets, entertainment and games, research, and reference (see sidebar below).

MCI/News Corp. Internet Ventures (MCIC; Washington, D.C.; www.delphi.com) — Delphi was acquired by News Corp. in September 1993 and in early 1995 announced plans for a relaunch. In February 1996, News Corp. announced that it would lay off half of Delphi's 515 employees and focus on Internet-related products rather than a relaunch of Delphi's online service. Now, as best as we can tell, News Corp. will focus on Internet-based services for businesses and consumers developed jointly by News Corp. and non-affiliated companies. The venture plans a variety of interactive products and services, including a guide to the Internet, a news service, games, an online area for children, and specialized programming developed with News Corp. companies, such as "TV Guide," Fox Broadcasting, Twentieth Century Fox, fX, Harper Collins, and the company's worldwide news organizations. Many of these features can be accessed now at the Web site listed above.

Individual, Inc. (Burlington, MA; www.newspage.com) — Individual developed and maintains the NewsPage site on the Web. This is not the company's only offering, as it is a provider and distributor of news and other current information. The company developed a patent-pending technology, SMART, which searches thousands of news sources for relevant information and sorts and customizes findings for clients. The distilled information is automatically fed into a newsletter format and distributed electronically. Individual's three types of customized services include First! for corporate workgroups, HeadsUp for individual executives, and iNews for business professionals. Information is delivered via e-mail, Internet/Web, fax, and through enterprise-wide groupware platforms, such as Lotus Notes.

NewsPage is a fee-based Internet newsletter on the Web that offers a vast amount of information categorized by topic. The company considers itself the first company with a Web site to offer a broad spectrum of customized news on the Internet, and it promotes one-stop current news shopping through its service. NewsPage receives up to 20,000 news stories each day from over 500 news sources, which are sorted into over 1,000 user topics. Individual recently acquired BookWire, an Internet resource for book readers and the publishing industry. BookWire will use Individual's SMART technology to filter book lists according to personal interest. Other Individual alliances are with Knight-Ridder, Lotus, Motorola, Apple, Prodigy, Gartner Group, and AT&T. In addition, a newly announced bid for an equity investment by Microsoft would deliver Individual's iNews product to MSN. The company filed to go public on January 31, 1996.

CompuServe

In March 1995, CompuServe acquired Spry to form the CompuServe Internet Division. The service's Mosaic Direct provides easy Internet access worldwide. Key benefits include the "Internet Made Easy" features, including "one button" installation of Spry's Mosaic software. Additionally, the CompuServe Network Services Division provides global network communications services to over 750 companies and government agencies, with features including e-mail, frame relay, WAN/LAN services, and software. Mosaic Direct provides Internet access to over 90,000 individuals and corporate accounts. CompuServe also announced that, as of November 1995, over 1 million CompuServe customers had downloaded the Mosaic browser through the online service. While CompuServe has maintained steady subscriber growth over the last few years, it has lost market share to America Online (currently, AOL has over 4.1 million members).

CompuServe plans to launch its new consumer online service, WOW!, in early spring 1996. The strategy behind WOW! is to offer a user-friendly online service that users can design to accommodate their needs. WOW! will offer intuitive navigation and common terminology without the need for an instruction manual. CompuServe plans to support a heavy national advertising campaign combined with special events to promote the service, distributing it exclusively on CD-ROM. The company expects to announce its pricing strategy closer to the time that the service becomes available.

CompuServe recently launched its Internet In A Box (I-Box) for Kids. It's the first complete Internet software package that includes filtering mechanisms designed to protect children from inappropriate content on the Internet. I-Box for Kids targets the specific interests of 8–14 year olds, while also giving adults, teachers, and guardians control over Internet content and usage, offering a "Surf Watch" service that keeps kids out of areas they shouldn't be in. CompuServe also recently announced Spryte, a low-cost Internet access service, which it's planning to launch in December 1995. At $4.95 per month (including three hours of online usage time, with each additional hour costing $1.95), Spryte will include the Spry Mosaic browser, Spry Mail (an e-mail program), and CompuServe's Home Page Wizard (a home page designer).

InfoSeek Corporation (Santa Clara, CA; www.infoseek.com) — InfoSeek developed and maintains the InfoSeek Web site, which provides no-fee and for-fee services, receiving over 5 million information requests per day. The no-fee service offers a powerful, Internet full-text search service with a point-and-click interface, which is compatible with a variety of Web browsers, including Netscape, Mosaic, and Lynx, and allows the user to find information on the Web by searching on key words to find sites with the requested information or by searching pre-sorted subjects on the InfoSeek home page. The for-fee service provides access to a database that stores over 80 computer periodicals in real-time, over 10,000 Usenet newsgroups, over 400,000 Web pages, and a wide range of other resources and publications, including newswires (such as Reuters, AP, Businesswire, PR Newswire, Newsbytes, and News Network), and business, health, and entertainment publications.

Lycos, Inc. (80% owned by CMG Information Services/CMGI; Marlboro, MA; www.lycos.com) — Lycos was formed in June 1995 as a subsidiary of CMG@Ventures (the strategic investment and development company of CMG), following CMG's purchase of the exclusive rights to the Lycos Spider Technology. The Lycos home page offers a high-speed Web search engine that uses key words. The recently redesigned site offers: a new user interface (with a navigation/status bar, a new search form, and a "backlink" feature); new content (hot lists, FAQs, help search access, the ability to add Lycos to a user's browser); and increased performance (availability and responsiveness — thanks to improvements in bandwidth utilization and systems — at speeds up to 8 times faster than for previous searches). At the end of October 1995, Lycos was serving more than 30 million queries per month.

Lycos' business partners include CMG@Ventures; Frontier Technologies, incorporating The Lycos Catalog into its SuperHighway Access CyberSearch product (which allows users to perform a Lycos search offline via CD-ROM, and connect to the Internet after a relevant Internet resource has been identified); Microsoft, which is incorporating the Lycos Catalog of the Internet within MSN; and NlightN, which incorporates the Lycos Catalog into its NlightN Universal Index (the world's largest table of contents, where users can retrieve information from various databases and news sources). At Internet World 1995, Lycos announced that it had catalogued more than 10 million sites, representing nearly 92% of the Web. Lycos recently acquired Point Communications, publisher of an online review and rating guide, which will become a wholly-owned subsidiary of Lycos.

The McKinley Group (Sausalito, CA; www.mckinley.com) — The McKinley Group developed and maintains a Web page. It also delivers an online directory of Web sites, providing a comprehensive navigational and informational directory for the Internet. The company's online Internet directory, Magellan, contains listings for more than a million Internet sites, of which 30,000 are fully described, reviewed, and rated (receiving anywhere from one to four stars) by the McKinley Group's in-house team of high-level subject-matter specialists (in coordination with the McKinley Editorial Advisory Board — a panel of international experts). Magellan enables Internet users to navigate the vast resources of the Internet and have the ability to preview rated resources and access descriptions about the sites before viewing them. Magellan, available at no cost to users via the Internet, is also available through licensed ISPs, such as AT&T, IBM, Netcom, and NYNEX. In June 1995, Netcom made a "strategic" investment in the McKinley Group.

MetaCrawler (Seattle, WA; www.metacrawler.cs.washington.edu:8080) — The MetaCrawler is a search service developed for and maintained as a Web page. It allows users to search through multiple search crawlers at once. The MetaCrawler queries a number of existing, free search engines and organizes and displays the results. Users also have the option of scoring the hits, which allows the list to be sorted any number of different ways, such as by locality, region, and organization. The MetaCrawler takes in a search string, along with some optional parameters used for sorting results, and queries all of its known search engines simultaneously. The MetaCrawler currently accesses six services: Galaxy, InfoSeek, Lycos, Open Text, WebCrawler, and Yahoo!.

Minitel (subsidiary of France Telecom; France; www.minitel.fr) — In the early 1980s, France Telecom recognized that society could benefit from widespread use of a data network. Since then, Minitel has grown in usage and content. About 14 million users, all in France, are connected via proprietary terminals. An estimated 23,000 content providers offer services on the Minitel system. For instance, the yellow and white phone book pages are on Minitel. France Telecom customers can book plane, train, and dinner reservations; they can also shop online at large retailers; find out what is on TV; and so forth.

Several problems exist with the system, unfortunately: It is proprietary, character-based, doesn't use the client/server model, and is not interoperable with the Internet. Despite these shortcomings, the Minitel system has far more content than AOL, CompuServe, or any other collection of Web or online services today. Despite Minitel's impressive content and large installed base, the Internet and online services pose a serious threat to its long-term viability. Already, France Telecom has announced it will begin offering Internet services.

Prodigy (jointly owned by Sears (S) and IBM (IBM); White Plains, NY; www.prodigy.com) — Prodigy, co-owned by Sears, Roebuck and IBM, and the third-largest consumer online service, recently announced a series of strategic initiatives and projects to offer, in addition to the current service, an Internet-only service. Prodigy, the first online service to offer Web access, has transferred about 30% of the service's content to its newly developed graphical user interface (the P_2 Windows GUI, of which, after two days of availability without on-screen promotion, the company recorded over 40,000 downloads) and to the Web-standard HTML coding, integrating Web listings into proprietary Prodigy content. The company converted its backbone network to TCP/IP from its closed platform recently, and by 1H96 the "last mile" should be converted to an IP system as well. The Internet-only service will use IBM's high-speed Advantis network, as well as Prodigy's own network backbone (consisting of about 320 file servers). Each server will operate as a stand-alone Internet server. The new service will also offer a new Web browser and the ability to use any other browser on the market. Prodigy is also offering its new Net Names program, a complex e-mail service that transitions user names to full, proper names from the subscriber ID numbers previously used. Largely due to its clunky interface, Prodigy has been ceding market share to America Online — we do not expect this trend to reverse.

Prodigy recently acquired an interest in SonicNet, a division of Sunshine Interactive Network that provides a rock and alternative music Web site. SonicNet will provide Prodigy with exclusive content, including celebrity chats and a direct link to the SonicNet Web site.

Starwave (Bellevue, WA; www.starwave.com) — Starwave creates interactive consumer content services for use on the Internet. Starwave launched its online service on the Internet in March 1995. The company was founded by Microsoft co-founder and new media investor Paul Allen. In addition to ESPNET SportsZone (a multimedia sports information service co-developed with ESPN Enterprises), Mr. Showbiz (an online entertainment news and features magazine), and Outside Online (a service for outdoor enthusiasts co-developed with "Outside" magazine), Starwave launched The Family Planet in July 1995. The Family Planet is an online service that focuses on family life and family-related matters. Featured areas include news, advice, "fun stuff," resources, and reviews (of books, toys, software, and videos). At the end of May 1995, Starwave reported that its online services (at the time, ESPNET SportsZone, Mr. Showbiz, and Outside Online) had recorded more than 1 million users worldwide, logging more than 283,000 hours of total viewing time. The company also reported that its combined services generated more than 10 million hits per week, with ESPNET SportsZone alone averaging over 1 million hits per day and an average viewing time per user of 15 minutes.

WebCrawler (subsidiary of America Online/AMER; Vienna, VA; www.webcrawler.com) — WebCrawler is a Web site that AOL maintains for visitors to perform Internet searches. The WebCrawler Project began as a research project at the Department of Computer Science and Engineering at the University of Washington in Seattle. The company participates in a number of services, including operating the service itself, publishing research in Internet resource discovery, and helping build Internet standards. In June 1995, WebCrawler was acquired by America Online; it continues to operate as a public service available to the Internet and as the search tool integrated into AOL's Internet service. The WebCrawler site also provides links to a list of top 25 sites, as well as other cool sites.

The WELL (Sausalito, CA; www.well.com) — The WELL is an online service, considered by many to be the birthplace of citizen-based "virtual communities." The WELL is a full PPP Internet service provider, offering e-mail, Web access, and Usenet news. It is also home to a vibrant online community where people meet to exchange information and ideas. The WELL is divided into over 260 discussion areas, referred to as conferences, on subjects including music, media, health, Generation X, writing, politics, parenting, business, and science. In order to bring high-speed PPP connectivity to The WELL, the company created its Whole Earth Networks (WEN) division. This service provides members with low-cost local dial-up lines. These access lines support speeds up to 28.8 kbps, at no additional charge.

Additionally, the WELL's Web site is open as a self-publishing medium, known as WebExpress, for WELL members to enable public exchange of ideas and tools. The WELL also offers MUSE (multi-user simulation environment), a second kind of interactive communications medium, where members create descriptions of a place for people to meet or play and then connect to that place for real-time interaction.

Yahoo Corporation (Mountain View, CA; www.yahoo.com) — Yahoo developed and maintains the Web site called Yahoo! This extremely popular site provides a highly useful guide for information, resources, and online discovery on the Internet. Yahoo! uses a hierarchical index and search engine, which helps to turn the vast (and overwhelming) amounts of content on the Internet into a more meaningful, easily understandable form. Yahoo!'s search engine enables users to find information about topics of interest through simple keyword queries. Searches can be restricted to titles, URL addresses, or comments (Boolean searches can also be performed), returning results along with their locations within Yahoo!'s hierarchical index. Yahoo! also has access to newsfeeds, as well as other timely content, and a news summary page allows users to quickly scan current news and identify stories of interest. Users can retrieve complete articles by clicking on the related story summaries. Yahoo! also highlights cool and new Internet sites. In September 1995, Yahoo! Corporation teamed with Open Text, forming a partnership to incorporate the Open Text Web Search Server OEM technology into Yahoo!'s online guide.

Information

Data Broadcasting (DBCC; San Mateo, CA; www.dbc.com) — Data Broadcasting Corporation is an international data communications services company that utilizes wireless, cable, and satellite transmission networks to convey news, financial, and other worldwide information for use by online service providers and Internet content providers. The company provides real-time news, sports, and financial information through two media: a hand-held portable device and a Windows-compatible wireless news-feed device; the latter is available for both PC and laptop computers. In addition, the company has the ability to provide the news feeds "raw" to other online services. DBC recently purchased Computer Sports World, an extensive statistical sports database. This acquisition has helped to make DBC the industry leader in real-time odds transmissions and historical sports gaming data. In addition, DBC was recently selected by Microsoft as an independent provider of information for Microsoft's MSN.

Desktop Data (DTOP; Waltham, MA; http://www. newswire.ca) — Desktop Data is an independent provider of customized, real-time news and information delivered to "knowledge workers" over their organizations' local-area networks. Desktop Data's NewsEDGE service delivers over 500 news and information sources in real time to users' personal computers, automatically monitors and filters the news according to pre-established personal interest profiles, and alerts users to stories matching their profiles. NewsEDGE is used by executives, salespeople, marketers, lawyers, accountants, consultants, bankers, and financial professionals.

Publication/Static

iGOLF (Boca Raton, FL; www.igolf.com) — iGOLF is an online, virtual clubhouse for golfers of all levels. Features of the service, available on America Online, include the iGOLF Challenge, an interactive golf game; timely news, live online interviews, and columns from and online discussions with golf writers and personalities (such as Gary McCord from CBS, Steve Hershey from "USA Today," Brad Klein from "Links Magazine," Jim Bartlett from "Golf Week," and Vartan Kupelian from the "Detroit News"); and iGOLFology, filled with golf jokes and one-liners. iGOLF also provides a valuable resource for information about the world of golf, including statistics on pro golfers and tour events, complete overviews of publicly traded golf companies and their stock performances, and news and information from golf organizations. There's also a live chat room to exchange stories, look for golf partners, and ask and answer rules questions.

Mecklermedia (MECK; Westport, CT; www.mecklerweb.com) — Mecklermedia is a provider of Internet-related content (magazines and online publications) and services (trade shows). The company provides information through its various publications and trade shows, including: 1) "Internet World," a magazine with more than 200,000 monthly subscribers, the first magazine devoted to the Internet; 2) "Web Week," a newspaper that provides a variety of information, such as news, product reviews, legislative issues, and product analysis, on Web site development which went to a Web-only platform; 3) "Web Developer," a magazine for commercial Web developers; 4) MecklerWeb's *iWORLD,* a Web site that hosts content about Mecklermedia's products, services, and conferences, as well as information about the Internet with links to other Web sites; 5) Internet-related books (through agreements with IDG Books Worldwide and McGraw-Hill Europe); and 6) VR WORLD, a trade show for the virtual reality market.

NetNoir (San Francisco, CA; www.netnoir.com) — NetNoir, on AOL, digitizes, archives, and distributes Afrocentric information and culture, including literature, music, fashion, history, art, and cuisine. It targets individuals, groups, and organizations of direct, or indirect, African descent. NetNoir has two divisions focused on these efforts. The first, NetNoir New Media Consulting (NNC), focuses on: consulting in the areas of digital formatting, database development, and management, including back-up, storage, and security systems; Web page design and development; methods of distribution and their respective formats; and appropriate distribution platforms. The second, NetNoir Online (NNO), focuses on distribution of content and information; current departments include Music, Sports, Education, and Business. The service plans a total of 18 departments over the following 18 months, including Film, Travel, Games, Health, Women, Politics, Lifestyles, Religion/Spirituality, Comics, News, Literature, The Arts, Communications, and Shopping. Aspects of the service are available in English, French, and Spanish.

NewsHound (subsidiary of Knight-Ridder/KRI; San Jose, CA; www.sjmercury.com/hound.htm) — NewsHound is an Internet-based news "clipping service," run by KRI's "San Jose Mercury News" newspaper, that automatically searches articles from a wide range of newspapers and wire services and sends any relevant documents directly to a subscriber's e-mail address, for $4.95 per month. The system uses Internet mail to receive requests when a member establishes a "profile" and sends back relevant articles and ads from a variety of sources, including the "San Jose Mercury News," the Knight-Ridder/Tribune News Service (with articles from the "Chicago Tribune," "Detroit Free Press," "Miami Herald," "Philadelphia Inquirer," and many other major newspapers), Knight-Ridder/Tribune Business News (with business articles from more than 60 newspapers), the Associated Press, Kyodo News Service, Scripps-Howard News Service, Business Wire (press releases), PR Newswire (press releases), and unpublished articles and documents sent to Mercury Center, as well as classified ads from the "San Jose Mercury News." The software runs on a high-capacity UNIX computer located at the News' newspaper plant using a Verity search engine.

O'Reilly & Associates (Sebastopol, CA; www.ora.com) — O'Reilly & Associates is an Internet publisher, as well as a publisher of information and technical solutions for the Internet and UNIX. In 1992, O'Reilly launched a series of books about the use and administration of the Internet, including "The Whole Internet User's Guide & Catalog" — the No. 1 best-selling Internet guide in the U.S., U.K., and Japan, with sales of around 400,000 worldwide. The company currently publishes over 80 books. O'Reilly is the developer of GNN (owned by America Online), a leading commercial application on the Web, that has successfully organized Internet resources, adding content as well as editorial perspective. O'Reilly has also co-developed, with Enterprise Integration Technologies, the award-winning WebSite — a 32-bit Web server software package for Windows 95 and Windows NT that offers an easy-to-use, complete graphical interface. O'Reilly's Digital Media Group

is also pursuing advanced uses of CD-ROM, online delivery of book-length information, and the development of digital libraries.

SportsLine USA (Ft. Lauderdale, FL; www.sportsline.com) — SportsLine USA, the official online service of the National Football League Players, is an Internet source for sports information, entertainment, and merchandise, with its content available on the Internet. Having teamed up with sports legends Joe Namath, Mike Schmidt, and Bob Costas, SportsLine offers a dynamic and interactive online sports experience with information, chat forums (with Joe Namath and Mike Schmidt), game previews and recaps, up-to-the-minute stats, contests, and strategy games. The company offers the choice of either a General Admission or a Box Seat Membership, both of which provide in-depth coverage of numerous sports associations and leagues, including the NFL, NBA, NHL, MLB, PGA, LPGA, Tennis, Soccer, and NCAA sports.

Wired Ventures Ltd. (San Francisco, CA; www.hotwired.com) — Wired publishes an Internet-based sponsor-supported magazine called "HotWired," which is also distributed electronically on the Hotwired Web page. The publication offers free news and information, and the HotWired home page has become one of the fastest-growing, top-ranked subscriber sites on the Internet. By becoming a member of HotWired (by filling out a form with one's address, name, and other information), users are provided exclusive access to features such as: What's New — a custom real-time report that informs members of new information since their last visit; Your View — customizing capabilities; Club Wired —live events; Threads — a community space where members can participate in and lead ongoing discussions; Coin — a classified/personal ads section; Search — which searches the current site, archives, and back issues of "Wired" magazine (a paper-based publication also published by Wired Ventures); and Help.

ZDNet (Ziff-Davis/now owned by Softbank of Japan; New York, NY; www.zdnet.com) — ZDNet is a Web site, developed and maintained by Ziff-Davis Interactive, that offers access to current headlines and news stories from Ziff-Davis publications, including "PC Magazine," "PC Week," "Computer Shopper," "PC Computing," "MacWeek," "Computer Life," "InternetLife," and more. The site also provides personalized access to news stories once users fill out a profile form that specifies items of particular interest. Users can then access catered news searches on the ZDNet site, from PR Newswire, Business-Wire, and many computer trade publications. ZDNet also offers product reviews, an area dedicated to Macintosh users, a home PC section, an Internet-specific site, as well as

the ability to search just Ziff-Davis publications, either by keyword or by publication. Ziff-Davis Interactive is also creator of ZD3D, a site dedicated to news, information, and product reviews for VRML.

Publication/Interactive

c|net, Inc. (San Francisco, CA; www.cnet.com) — c|net, the provider of perhaps the richest content to the Internet community, has two media outlets: cable TV and the Internet. The company's nationwide television programming service began in April 1995 on the USA Network and the Sci-Fi Channel, with "c|net central," and in June 1995 c|net launched its worldwide Internet site. Content on both media is devoted entirely to computing, multimedia, and online services. c|net's Internet members (over 400,000, and growing at more than 300% per week) have free access to information, education, entertainment materials, and daily e-mail updates. At the Internet site, which is supported mainly by advertising revenue, users can share information and opinions; find out about new products (through c|net's lab-based reviews); catch up on the latest computer and online news; download software; talk to guests, hosts, and producers; participate in contests and polls; get technical help from vendors and other members; and learn about products and trends.

Recently, c|net launched "shareware.com," a Web site that allows consumers to locate and download software from a "virtual library" of over 140,000 software titles from 33 top Internet hardware and software companies. The company has also announced the launch of c|net radio, an original audio "Webcast" using RealAudio's technology. Finally, in January 1996, E! Entertainment Television and c|net joined forces to create a 50/50 venture called E! Online, which will launch a large-scale, advertiser-supported online service devoted entirely to the world of entertainment. The service plans to begin operating in C2Q96. At the end of

1994, c|net received an investment from Paul Allen's Vulcan Ventures. In our view, c|net is positioning itself to become the definitive source for computing and technology information, programming, and opinion.

Motley Fool (Alexandria, VA; keyword Motley Fool on America Online) — Motley Fool is a forum on America Online dedicated to individual investors. Motley Fool's three goals are to inform, amuse, and make money for investors. Created by the Gardner brothers to make investing more fun, Motley Fool was named one of "The 99 Best Hangouts Online," according to "Computer Life" magazine. The site hosts hundreds of active and organized individual stock folders, and a concentration of timely information for everyone from the expert investor to the novice. Motley Fool also holds chats every night for real-time investment discussion, and there's also the Fool's School, which (humorously) explains the "Foolish" approach to investing. The Fools at Motley Fool also run The Fool Portfolio, a real-money online portfolio (which deducts the cost of commissions and accounts for the bid/ask spread in reporting returns). All trades made by the Fools are announced the night before they are made, so anyone can trade along with them. In addition, Motley Fool has launched an e-mail and forum-based service called *The Evening News,* which summarizes key stock market events each day. In our view, Motley Fool has done an outstanding job of creating one of the hottest franchises online. And they haven't stopped there. Their recent book, *The Motley Fool Investment Guide,* has been very well received.

Publishing (Traditional)

Dun & Bradstreet (DNB; New York, NY; www.dnb.com) — Dun & Bradstreet and its Nielsen division have been very active on the Internet front. For example, Nielsen Media Research and I/PRO jointly market two Web services: I/COUNT, which "measures Internet site usage such as total number of visits, sections read within each site, and the geographical and organization origin of visitors," and I/AUDIT, which is the Web's first independent auditing and verification service. Customers receive monthly or quarterly reports detailing Web audience usage and characteristics. The reports are similar to those produced in the print and broadcast media.

Nielsen has joined with ASI Market Research and Yankelovich Partners to form ANYwhere Online, a partnership to develop a wide range of qualitative research services for online media. The company's Information Services division provides the Business Background Report, which offers useful information on the selected company's history, business background of management, special events, recent newsworthy items, and a business operations overview. The Dataquest division provides some of its technology-market research via the Internet.

Dun & Bradstreet recently divided itself into three independent, global companies: Cognizant Corporation for high-growth information markets, The Dun & Bradstreet Corporation for financial information services, and A.C. Nielsen for consumer product information services.

Gannett (GCI; Arlington, VA; www.gannett.com) — Gannett's online strategy so far might best be described as incremental. The company has avoided any major bets on either online services or the Internet. However, it has been aggressive about leveraging its strong local news franchise into online services. Many of the company's newspapers are available online, including: "The Detroit News," "Democrat and Chronicle" (Rochester, N.Y.), "The Times-Union" (Rochester, N.Y.), "Journal and Courier" (Lafayette, Ind.), "North Hills News Record" (North Hills, Pa.), "Tennessean" (Nashville), "The Courier-Journal" (Louisville, Ky.), "The Marietta Times" (Marietta, Ohio), and "The Olympian" (Olympia, Wash.).

In addition, the company's flagship newspaper, "USA Today," is online. In particular, the USA Today Information Network offers access to a wide range of sports statistics, as well as news, weather, and entertainment stories. All of this is available on the Web. In addition, through CompuServe, a user can communicate with "USA Today" reporters and editors or participate in chat lines.

Knight-Ridder (KRI; Mountain View, CA; www.dialog.com) — Of the nation's largest newspaper companies, Knight-Ridder, along with Tribune, are probably the furthest along in developing a large number of online services. Knight-Ridder has been experimenting with online formats for several years, at both its Mercury News Center in San Jose and at a special R&D lab in Colorado. However, in August 1995 the company announced the closing of its Information Design Laboratory (specializing in flat-panel publishing) to concentrate its efforts and resources on the Internet and online publishing (see sidebar).

McClatchy (MNI; Sacramento, CA; www.sna.com/sacbedit/pubs.html) — McClatchy offers its recently acquired "News & Observer" newspaper (Raleigh, N.C.), as well as the "News Tribune" (Tacoma, Wash.), via the Internet. In addition, the company's Nando.Net is an online information service available on the Internet. The "Nando Times" (free access) provides continuously up-dated world, U.S., business, and sports news. In addition, the Nando News Network (monthly subscription) provides premium news and information, including "access to the company's searchable news and magazine archives and access to over 100 news and feature columns not available anywhere else."

McGraw-Hill (MHP; New York, NY; www.mcgraw-hill.com) — McGraw-Hill has been active in developing online products across several of its business units. For example, "BusinessWeek" magazine is available through America Online, while "Aviation Week" is available on CompuServe. The Standard & Poor's unit offers the following on the Internet: "The Corporate Finance Criteria" and "The Municipal Finance Criteria," which outline S&P's rating criteria. F.W. Dodge provides "DataLine2," "Market Leader," and "Dodge Lead Time." Osbourne McGraw-Hill publishes the best-selling "Internet Yellow

Pages," as well as the reference guide, "The World Wide Web." The Publishing Book Group has experienced significant success with its online catalog of over 9,000 titles and descriptions.

New York Times (NYTA; New York, NY; www.nytinfoserv.com) — The New York Times has actually been involved with electronic online services for years through an agreement with NEXIS, a former Mead Data Central service now owned by Reed-Elsivier, to allow access to the "New York Times" newspaper archival information. The arrangement has subsequently been renegotiated several times (see sidebar).

Times Mirror (TMC; Los Angeles, CA) — Times Mirror's new management has dramatically curtailed the company's numerous online start-up projects in an effort to raise profit margins. However, TMC has continued to pursue a bevy of efforts to place its newspapers, magazines, and other services online. For example, the "Los Angeles Times" is available through TimesLink on the Prodigy network. National Journal Washington Online is also available through TimesLink, and provides information from Washington that affects Southern California. The "Hartford Courant" newspaper is available on the Internet. "Yachting" magazine provides an online, multiple listing service for thousands of boats for charter and sale, while Jeppesen provides online weather information and electronic data flight-planning services. Like Knight-Ridder, Times Mirror was an early investor in Netscape and owns approximately 889,000 shares.

Tribune (TRB; Chicago, IL; www.tribune.com) — Tribune has been active in developing online services to broaden its reach and product line. TRB was one of the original investors in America Online. In addition, most TRB newspapers have been online for some time, including: "The Chicago Tribune," "Sun-Sentinel" (Fort Lauderdale), "Orlando Sentinel," and "The Daily Press" (Newport News, Va.). In addition, the "Chicago Tribune" provides an online employment service for the Midwest, while the "Orlando Sentinel" provides its classified ads online (see sidebar).

Knight-Ridder

Currently, many of the company's newspapers are available through the Internet, including: "San Jose Mercury News," "Philadelphia Daily News," "Philadelphia Inquirer," "Detroit Free Press," "Miami Herald," "El Nuevo Herald" (Spanish; Miami), "Tallahassee Democrat" (Tallahassee, Fla.), "Akron Beacon Journal" (Akron, Ohio), and "St. Paul Pioneer Press" (St. Paul, Minn.). The company's goal is to bring all of its newspapers online within two years.

The two Philadelphia newspapers developed Philadelphia Online, which not only offers the text of both newspapers but also an online magazine highlighting the best of both papers, classified ads, and an extensive news retrieval system. Free Press Plus allows users to go online through CompuServe and access the Detroit Free Press through a fax-on-demand service. Destination Florida, available on AOL, is a joint venture with Tribune offering travel information. The company is in the process of putting together a product called ScienceBase, an online search tool for scientists and researchers that will include access to the company's Dialog database. BusinessBase is an online information resource providing quick company information, such as company profiles, financial data, product lists, news, organizational structure, and so forth. Knight-Ridder was an early investor in Netscape and owns approximately 444,500 shares.

KRI's Mercury Center makes the "San Jose Mercury News" and many ancillary services available through the Internet and America Online. Mercury Center offers an electronic version of the day's newspaper, plus additional articles, archival information, classified ads, photo images, video clips, electronic bulletin boards, and a customized online news-clipping service called NewsHound.

Recently, Spyglass agreed to license its Spyglass Mosaic Web client to InfiNet Company, a joint venture between Knight-Ridder and Landmark Communications. InfiNet will offer Spyglass Mosaic to help newspapers establish a presence on the Web, and should be available by June 1996.

In addition to putting many of its newspapers online, Knight-Ridder has developed several services, many through its Information Services division, available for the Internet or other online services. For example, Knight-Ridder Information provides online reference services through Dialog, Data-Star, and Infomart Dialog on the Internet.

New York Times

NYTA's Information Services Group packages and delivers content on the Internet through five divisions: 1) New York Times Syndication; 2) TimesFax (a daily summary of the "New York Times" distributed by satellite and fax but also on the Internet); 3) New York Times New Media (consumer online services, including @times on AOL); 4) New York Times Business Information Services (provides "New York Times" material via online services); and 5) New York Times Custom Publishing.

Besides being available on the Internet through TimesFax, a more comprehensive version of the "New York Times" will be coming online soon. In 1995, the Times began offering online classified advertising for the first time. The "Boston Globe" is available on the Internet as well, and many of the Times' 28 regional newspapers are developing, or have launched, new electronic newspapers.

Boston Globe Electronic Publishing — The "Boston Globe" has launched a new venture that provides interactive news and advertising services for New England, including local entertainment, regional travel and recreation, community news, shopping, and real estate. It is linked to news content from the Globe.

NYTA has reached an agreement with UUNET to create an online sports network, called Sports/Regional Online Network, beginning with the online services of the company's magazines.

Tribune

Besides making newspapers available online, the Tribune has developed other online services. For example, the online "Farm Journal Today" provides selected agricultural articles from its five magazines, and the "Sun-Sentinel" newspaper in Fort Lauderdale provides an online college guide for high school students that focuses on Florida colleges. In addition, the newspaper provides its "XS" magazine (news/entertainment/music) online. The College Press Exchange offers content to college newspapers via the Internet.

The Tribune's Chicago Online (a regionally based information, entertainment, and shopping service), Destination Florida (travel information service; partner with Knight-Ridder), The Orlando Sentinel Online, and TMS TV Source (television listings) are all available on America Online as well. Tribune owns approximately 6% of America Online.

Tribune Media Services TMS provides content and services to America Online, Prodigy, and eWorld, and it develops interactive television listings for online services.

Picture Network International has an online photo and image service, called Seymour, which enables newspapers and information publishers to search, browse, price, and download images by computer.

Transaction Processing and Financial Services

- As a necessary precursor to commerce on the Internet, financial transaction solutions and financial services are necessary to enable secure transactions. The companies we describe below concern themselves with Internet-based transaction solutions (transfer of money) that are secure (i.e., cannot be successfully redirected or intercepted). Generally, there are two types of companies involved in enabling secure Internet commerce, although hybrids of the two types have recently been established:

- Technology companies that develop encryption solutions to enable secure transmission of data across the relatively non-secure public Internet.

- Financial services companies, traditional credit card companies, and banks with new or repackaged offerings, in addition to new companies that enable the electronic-equivalent to cash, checks, debit cards, and credit cards.

American Express (AXP; New York, NY; www.americanexpress.com) — American Express's interaction with the Internet can be divided into two broad categories. One is the use of the American Express Card as a method of payment for transactions conducted over the Internet. The other is the use of the Internet as a means for American Express cardholders to communicate with American Express and conduct a variety of transactions related to their charge-card account. In the first category, American Express has arrangements with four companies that offer Internet services (and are described elsewhere in this report): CyberCash; First Virtual Holdings; Netscape Communications; and Open Market. In each case, users of transaction services offered by these companies are able to pay for purchases using an American Express or Optima card. These arrangements began in July and August 1995, and no data have been disclosed yet about the volume of transactions.

In the second category, American Express launched an arrangement in January 1995 with America Online for the online service to provide a link between American Express and cardholders who want to deal with the company over the Internet. The service, called ExpressNet, allows American Express cardholders to check the status of their accounts, pay their American Express bills, make travel reservations, and enroll in rewards-for-spending programs. Subscribers can download monthly statements into several personal finance programs. AOL subscribers who do not have an American Express card can apply for one through ExpressNet. ExpressNet also offers a service called Global Guide, which searches for travel information across several

databases, including Fodor's Worldview, Frommer's Online Travel Service, "Travel & Leisure" magazine, and American Express Travel Guides. American Express recently established its own home page on the Internet, currently geared mostly to students, which provides information about a variety of American Express products and services. Eventually, the page will also provide information geared to American Express shareholders. At the end of C1Q95, American Express had 36 million cards outstanding worldwide.

CheckFree Corporation (CKFR; Columbus, OH; www.checkfree.com) — CheckFree provides a complete family of electronic commerce products and services for delivery of financial services to consumers, corporations, and financial institutions. Its consumer service is marketed under an exclusive, patented electronic payment processing method. To ensure acceptance of payments, CheckFree offers three payment methods: 1) electronic, where CheckFree debits the user's checking account after paying the payee; 2) electronic-to-check, where CheckFree draws a check from its own account, sends it to the payee, and debits the user's account; and 3) laser drafts which are just like the user's personal checks. After offering the first month of service at no charge, CheckFree offers customers a monthly rate of $5.95 for the first 20 payments, and $2.95 for each additional set of ten payments. Customers include financial institutions, telecommunications companies, and book and software publishers. The company also offers a merchant information file to customize processing for specific merchants, built-in security codes on the processing system, and extensive customer service support.

CheckFree PC software and electronic industry licensees include MECA Software, Computer Associates, Intuit, and SmartPhone Communications. CheckFree also serves the consumer market (through a partnership with AT&T), the business market (providing EFT and EDI services to Dac Easy Corporation, Data Pro Accounting Software, Macola, Peachtree Software, and others), and corporations (including ADP, AT&T, CompuServe, FiServ, Genie, Delphi, Reality Technologies, PSINet/Pipeline, Netcom, Spry, Optigon, and Cellular One). The CheckFree system transfers its electronic money over its own private network.

CheckFree's recent acquisition of Servantis Systems enhances its position with financial institutions and corporations. The company's leadership position in providing electronic transaction solutions for consumers and businesses, combined with Servantis' 25 years of experience in back-office software and remote processing services for banks, results in a complete range of solutions for electronic exchange among financial service providers, consumers, and businesses.

CyberCash (Reston, VA; www.cybercash.com) — CyberCash is focused on providing secure financial transactions and services over the Internet. Its Secure Internet Payment Service is browser-independent, providing a secure purchasing environment for electronic commerce on the Internet and offering instantaneous communications among consumers, merchants, and banks. The company's transactions move among three software programs: a "wallet" (a program that resides on the consumer's PC); a program that operates as part of the merchant server; and a program that operates within the CyberCash servers. The consumer and merchant software is free. Once the consumer selects items for purchase and fills out the merchant's order form, the merchant server presents an invoice, requesting payment. The consumer can then launch the CyberCash Wallet, or go get one if needed, and click on the "Pay" button. A message is then sent from the CyberCash software on the merchant server to the consumer's PC asking that the consumer choose which card he or she wishes to use. The consumer chooses a card, and the rest is a series of encrypted automatic messages that travel between the three programs on the Internet and the credit card networks that are connected directly to the CyberCash server.

CyberCash processes thousands of transactions daily, and there are over 400,000 CyberCash Wallets in the distribution channel. The company, started in August 1994, has developed a number of partnerships with leading companies, including Mastercard, IBM, Netscape, GTE, RSA Data Security, Sun Microsystems, Trusted Information Systems, Enterprise Integration Technologies, Cisco Systems, Terisa Systems, CompuServe, CheckFree, Frontier Technologies, FTP Software, Netcom, Open Market, and Quarterdeck. VeriFone recently announced it would take a 10% equity stake in CyberCash following its $4.0 million investment. CyberCash was founded by technology entrepreneur Dan Lynch and VeriFone founder Bill Melton. CyberCash has several other investors, of whom RSA Data Security is the only publicly announced one. Other owners include venture capital and other public companies. CyberCash filed to go public in December 1995.

DigiCash (Amsterdam, The Netherlands; www.digicash.com) — DigiCash develops electronic payment systems that are functional equivalents to cash, for open, closed, and network systems. Using DigiCash's system, users make an advance lump-sum payment to a bank that supports the DigiCash system and receive "E-cash" in return. Users then make purchases electronically, and the E-cash is debited from their checking accounts. Both the user and merchant must use DigiCash software.

The company's technology is being deployed by a number of companies and organizations in a variety of industries. Examples include: the Dutch government, for the development of a road toll system; Amtech, for use of DigiCash's high-speed digital cash technology for road toll applications; MasterCard, for the development of a demonstration system implementing the first smart-card chip mask technology; Crypto AG, for use of DigiCash's encryption technology; the European Commission Project CAFE, used as an electronic wallet; VISA International; IBM; Siemens; and a number of European telecommunications companies.

Electronic Data Systems (unit of General Motors/GME; Plano, TX; www.eds.com) — Electronic Data Systems has been experimenting with electronic commerce over the Internet for several years. The company is the second-largest processor of credit cards in the country and has an interest in seeing more transactions generated electronically over Internet. The company will also provide outsourcing services for customers looking to offload the management of security, administration, and maintenance of internal and external Web sites. As more customers become comfortable with the Web, the Internet should provide surplus networking bandwidth for EDS, as opposed to the company continuing to build its private network as the business scales.

Enterprise Integration Technologies (subsidiary of VeriFone/VFI; Menlo Park, CA; www.eit.com) — Enterprise Integration Technologies develops software that helps businesses optimize the benefits of the Internet, focusing on the Web, electronic commerce services, and collaboration tools. EIT is a major contributor of open standards and technology for Internet electronic commerce, and is the principal architect of SHTTP. Toolkits for upgrading Web clients and servers to SHTTP are marketed by Terisa Systems (a joint venture between EIT and RSA Data Security). Other EIT toolkits allow easy installation of Web servers and participation in IP multicast conferences. EIT is also the program manager of CommerceNet, a consortium of over 70 businesses and organizations participating in a large-scale market trial of electronic commerce. Additionally, EIT is the system integrator for the ARPA-sponsored program, MADE (manufacturing, analysis, and design engineering) to create a national network of design and manufacturing services on the Internet. In August 1995, VeriFone announced that it was planning to acquire EIT for about $28 million, to be completed by the end of 1995. EIT will become a wholly owned unit of VeriFone, developing technology and products for VeriFone's Internet Commerce Division.

First Virtual Holdings (San Diego, CA; www.fv.com) — First Virtual Holdings is a financial services company that enables users to buy and sell information on the Internet. The First Virtual Internet Payment System provides a secure, easy-to-use Internet payment service in a "try before you buy" environment. Avoiding encryption issues, buyers sign up for a First Virtual account by calling First Virtual to obtain an account number in exchange for the user's credit card number. Then, as the buyer makes purchases with online merchants that accept First Virtual accounts, he or she provides the First Virtual account number. The merchant then contacts First Virtual, which contacts the buyer by e-mail and allows the buyer to approve or disapprove the purchase before the credit card is billed. No special software is required for these transactions.

HNC Software (HNCS; San Diego, CA) — HNC Software develops, markets, and supports intelligent client-server software solutions for mission-critical decision applications in real-time environments. Currently, HNC serves the electronic payments, financial services, and retail markets. HNC's flagship product, Falcon, is used by 18 of the top 20 credit-card-issuing banks to interdict fraud at the point of sale. HNC should continue to benefit on at least two fronts that have special relevance to the Internet: transaction securitization and data interpretation. Some specific applications that HNC offers that could have Internet applicability include HNC's automated consumer lending and real-estate appraisal. These products, called Colleague and AREAS, respectively, would allow for bank customers to apply for home mortgages and consumer loans directly over the Internet.

Intuit (INTU; Menlo Park, CA; www.qfn.com) — We discuss Intuit's Internet strategy in the "Application Software" section of this chapter.

MasterCard International (New York, NY; www.mastercard.com) — MasterCard International is a global payments system company of 22,000 financial institutions that issue MasterCards and make available other MasterCard products and services. By broadening its presence in new and existing markets, MasterCard hopes to obtain global acceptance. The introduction of electronic commerce and financial services over the Internet provides yet another medium for payment, creating a huge potential for cardholder use.

Currently, MasterCard's primary objective is to create a secure environment for credit card transactions. In January 1995, MasterCard and Netscape Communications began working together to develop the technology for authorizing and clearing transactions on credit and debit cards in a secure environment over the Internet. Since then, MasterCard and Netscape have collaborated with IBM, GTE, and CyberCash to develop a single, open industry specification for securing on-line credit card transactions. Their joint efforts have, so far, produced a draft document of the Secure Electronic Payment Protocol (SEPP) Specification, which is now available to the public for comment. The next step toward a single specification is modification of the document and integrating the comments received, followed by final publication. At the end of C1Q95, MasterCard had 247 million cards outstanding worldwide.

VeriFone (VFI; Redwood City, CA; www.verifone.com) — VeriFone designs and sells transaction automation software used by a variety of clients to electronically automate the processing of payments, benefits, and information transactions. VeriFone was the first company to offer low-cost systems for electronic credit card authorization. VeriFone's products include: transaction system platforms, system and application software, peripheral products, communications options for both local- and wide-area networking, and interface options for connectivity and other point-of-sale devices, such as displays, scanners, electronic cash registers, and PCs. In August 1995, VeriFone acquired Enterprise Integration Technology (EIT), a leading independent provider of software and consulting services for electronic commerce on the Internet. In general, VeriFone's strategy is to port the merchant counter-top paradigm to the Internet.

VISA International (San Francisco, CA; www.visa.com) — VISA is leading a project to develop a standard protocol to enable credit and debt-card transactions to be conducted securely over the Internet. VISA recently announced the introduction of Secure Transaction Technology (STT), an enabling technology for assuring the safety of bankcard purchases and other financial transactions over the Internet and other networks. STT is a joint development effort with Microsoft and can be incorporated into all types of software and hardware.

In addition, Visa is developing a specific project with Sony Corp. to provide entertainment services. At the end of C1Q95, Visa had 400 million cards outstanding worldwide.

Commerce

- As in counting Internet users, it is impossible to measure directly the amount of commerce on the Internet. Our observation is that there are several commerce models that have been successful on the Internet: sales of flowers, music, small gifts, computer parts, and other easy-to-identify commodity goods. These businesses have succeeded for the simple reason that online buyers know what they will be getting without having to see it in advance.

- In retail, the key is to focus on a market segment, know it best, and then hit it hard. That is why the online services' gift services are successful. Today, the online user is an experimenter, an early adopter. Small purchases, "to try it out," make sense. The same goes for purchasing compact disks. Another obvious market is the computer shopper. Most computer products are commodities, and as such may be traded easily over the Internet.

- The next phase of commerce on the Internet may well occur when two things happen: First, secure transactions must be enabled sufficiently so that users are comfortable that their credit card information (or digital cash) will not be stolen. Second, a wider audience has to be online — the audience has to be more mainstream. There is evidence, based on surveys, that the second requirement is beginning to happen quickly, while the first issue is being addressed by many companies. Once the market develops, retailers should begin to make money on the Internet.

1-800-FLOWERS (Westbury, NY; www.800flowers.com) — 1-800-FLOWERS, a subsidiary of Teleway, Inc., is the world's largest direct marketer of flowers and gifts, offering 24-hour, 365-days-a-year customer service and same- or next-day delivery. 1-800-FLOWERS features fresh flowers from an exclusive network of hand-picked, local florists, designing custom-crafted arrangements. The company also offers gift and gourmet items via 1-800-GIFTHOUSE. The 1-800-FLOWERS & GIFTHOUSE area consists of a database of products and text documents offering convenient ways to shop (by occasion, gift category, holidays and seasonal suggestions, or by products to be delivered outside the U.S.); a Contests and Special Promotions area; and a free Gift Concierge Service, which includes the Gift Reminder Service, Gift Registry, Sure Winners, and Personal Shopper. The company's Interactive Services Division (ISD) was established in 1993 to capitalize on the growing opportunities in electronic retailing. The ISD is currently involved in computer online services, interactive television,

CD-ROM catalogs, wireless environments, multimedia kiosks, and audiotex services. Key partners include America Online (Keyword: FLOWERS), AT&T PersonaLink, Bloomberg ("Gift Go"), CompuServe (GO FGH), eWorld (Shortcut: FLOWERS), Fourth Network, the Interactive Channel, Interaxx, Contentware, and 2MARKET.

CUC International (CU; Stamford, CT; www.cuc.com) — CUC International is a consumer-services provider, offering approximately 40 million members access to a variety of discount services, including home shopping, auto, dining, travel, insurance, lifestyle memberships, and discount coupon programs. CUC offers its services through both conventional channels, such as affinity relationships with banks, retailers, oil companies, and fund raisers, and interactive media, such as online services and the Internet.

CUC currently offers its home shopping, dining, auto, and travel services through the major online services: America Online, CompuServe, and Prodigy. In September 1995, CUC launched its home shopping service, called Shoppers Advantage, on the Internet. Billed as one of the most comprehensive shopping services to appear on the Web, Shoppers Advantage offers over 250,000 brand-name products at 10-50% below the manufacturer's listed price. Shoppers Advantage also offers its members enhanced security by conducting purchases through a membership number, rather than a credit card. Recently, the company launched its time-share service, Interval International, on the Web. During 1996, CUC plans to launch additional services, such as travel and auto, on the Internet.

The Electronic Newsstand (www.enews.com) — The Electronic Newsstand Web service allows users to browse periodicals and purchase them at a discount. The site includes the world's leading magazines, newsletters, newspapers, and catalogues. Visiting the site is free, and subscriptions are significantly less than newsstand prices. An interesting feature of this site, which is becoming increasingly common, is that it has several sponsoring advertisements, including Lincoln-Mercury. The site lists about 320 publications.

IndustryNet (Pittsburgh, PA; www.industry.net) — IndustryNet, now available as a Web page, is a member organization formed in 1991 to provide electronic methods for the purpose of automating industrial buying and selling. The company provides services and products, including: 1)

"IndustryNet Report," a tri-weekly publication with 150,000 subscribers; 2) The IndustryNet Online Marketplace, available via modem, Telnet, or the Web; 3) "The IndustryNet Regional Buying Guide," a computer-based industrial buying guide available on the Web; and 4) The IndustryNet Continuing Education Group, which are regional seminars conducted for the benefit of IndustryNet's members.

IndustryNet Online Marketplace, which is available free on the Web, offers products such as industrial supplies and mechanical manufacturing services, and business centers that allows access to information on over 400 leading manufacturers. Surplus equipment from various manufacturers is also available. This site is a good example of how geographically dispersed manufacturing companies can offer products, whether first-pass or surplus, at one storefront — a Web page. Jim Manzi, formerly of Lotus, recently joined IndustryNet as president and CEO.

Internet Shopping Network (division of Home Shopping Network/HSN; St. Petersburg, FL; www.internet.net) — The Internet Shopping Network (ISN) is an Internet-based division of the Home Shopping Network, Inc., and is among the first large-scale enterprises to use the medium for conducting commerce. ISN is one of the largest retailing and mall operations on the Internet, offering on-line shoppers access to a broad range of products, including over 25,000 computer products from more than 600 major companies (like Lotus, Symantec, and Microsoft); flowers from FTD; steak and lobster from Omaha Steaks International; gift items from the Hammacher-Schlemmer catalog; a wide variety of name brand merchandise from Home Shopping Network Interactive's Global Plaza; and many other types of merchandise. Membership is free, and prospective members pre-register with a credit card, for use when purchasing items, an e-mail address, and a shipping address (which can be done either over the telephone or by using ISN's secure network communication — the Netscape Commerce Server). A membership code is then issued for future transactions, with credit card information kept off-line, and the shopper's membership code is linked to the shipping address.

PAWWS (Jersey City, NJ; pawws.secapl.com) — PAWWS allows you to enter trade orders via the Web through the company's Net Investor service. Other services include portfolio accounting software, brokerage services quotes, news, fundamental and technical data, and reports. An online, Internet-based trading system allows the user to execute secured transactions (Netscape SSL) directly to The Net Investor trading desk at any time of the day or night. Discount brokerage commissions are available through this service, too. Depending upon the account type, discount rates and free online access to the latest news, research, and analysis are available, as are real-time quotes, current market news, company research, earnings analysis, and price forecasting. In addition, The Net Investor service links the user to the Internet's vast library of data, analysis, and opinion, as well as to many investment bulletin boards. The Net Investor gives the user a choice of three money market accounts, free check writing, and a VISA debit card. The parent company is Howe Barnes Investments, Inc., a brokerage firm based in Chicago and a member of the NYSE since 1915. The firm may also be contacted by telephone.

PC Flowers (www.pcgifts.ibm.com) — PC Flowers was founded in March 1989 to provide floral wire service to customers through interactive networks like Prodigy. Today, PC Flowers is one of the top two FTP members. PC

Flowers is also one of the most successful services on the Prodigy network. Over the past several years, the company has been expanding its distribution reach to other networks and its offerings to include more than flowers. It now distributes through electronic kiosks throughout the U.S., through RBOC gateways, via France Telecom's videotex terminals, and through the Internet. Products include balloons, bears, gift baskets, food, and customized greeting cards. This is one of the more successful online commerce companies in history.

Spiegel (SPGLA; Downers Grove, IL; www.spiegel.com/spiegel) — This traditional magazine retailer has chosen to develop a limited Web site, which consists of a small selection of its magazine offerings. Typically, if an online shopper finds something he or she likes, there is a "click here to order" button. The user would then enter credit card information, shipping address, and so on. However, Spiegel's site, perhaps for security reasons or to keep down costs, has been designed to merely display the company's 800 phone number, along with a brief message, once the button is clicked.

Chapter 12:
Morgan Stanley's Cool Sites — 500 Channels & Everything's On

- Morgan Stanley's research analysts have compiled a list of Web sites that we consider informative examples of what the WWW offers.

Introduction: Getting Started

So you want to "surf the Net," but it's your first time and you're not quite sure if it's legal in this country to have a URL, and the last time you heard the word "Yahoo" was when your grandfather's favorite baseball team won the pennant. It is very likely that somewhere out there on the Internet is everything you wanted to know, plus a whole lot of other stuff that would seem really interesting if you knew it existed. So whether it's your first time, or you've "been there, done that," **we have organized this section into what we consider to be the most important, highly useful, and, simply put, coolest cool sites on the Internet.**

Specifically, our cool site areas include the following categories (screen shots for our cool sites appear on following pages):

- Finance

- Technology/Trade Magazines and Newsletters

- Magazines/Publishing

- Commerce

- Company

- Network

- Sports

- Government/NASA

- Travel/Food

- Entertainment/Games/Art

- Resources/Education

- Kids

- Miscellaneous

Once a browser or online service software is installed on a PC, cruising the Internet or online service is pretty simple. To check out our cool sites via an Internet browser,

just type the URL (uniform resource locator) into the horizontal URL bar (labeled "Location" in Netscape Navigator 1.2) and, after a short wait, the desired Web page will be downloaded into the browser. To find our cool sites on America Online, go to the Menu bar, choose "Go To... Keyword," type in the keyword, and press Enter. AOL's Internet browser is available by double clicking on "Internet Connection" on America Online's Main Menu screen and it operates in a manner similar to Netscape Navigator.

There are a few different ways within Netscape's browser to search for other stuff on the Web. The Net Search button defaults to the InfoSeek search engine — simply type in key search words and InfoSeek will scour its Web database and display some text from relevant Web sites; double-click on an entry's underlined title, and the browser will take you there. Other search engines are available; see the **Company Descriptions: Organization/Aggregation** section of this report. Further, the Netscape browser has its own "What's Cool!" button, which will route you to sites that Netscape likes.

America Online uses a "channel" interface on its Main Menu screen, with easy connections to resources, information, and services via its 14 channels, which include: Today's News, Newsstand, Personal Finance, Entertainment, Clubs & Interests, Education, Computing, Reference Desk, Travel, Internet Connection, Marketplace, Sports, People Connection, and Kids Only. AOL also provides suggestions for recommended Web sites within each channel. AOL also has a Directory of Services and Highlights of Services, which provide a quick tutorial of the service, an overview of What's Hot, and an introduction to What's New on AOL. Clicking on AOL's Internet Connection directs members to the Internet, via the GNN browser, to the WebCrawler search page (AOL's default search engine).

Have fun!

Cool Sites

1. Coolest Finance

<u>Site/Area</u>	<u>URL</u>
American Express' EXPRESSNET (AOL)	AOL Keyword: EXPRESSNET
Bank of America	http://www.bofa.com
Company Research (AOL)	AOL Keyword: COMPANY RESEARCH
E*TRADE	http://www.etrade.com
Fidelity Investments	http://www.fid-inv.com
FinanCenter	http://internet-plaza.net/resources
Morgan Stanley	http://www.ms.com
Morningstar (AOL)	AOL Keyword: MORNINGSTAR
The Motley Fool (AOL)	AOL Keyword: FOOL
Quicken Financial Network	http://www.intuit.com
SEC EDGAR Database	http://www.sec.gov
Security First Network Bank	http://www.sfnb.com
Wells Fargo	http://wellsfargo.com

2. Coolest Technology Trade Magazines/Newsletters

<u>Site/Area</u>	<u>URL</u>
Computer Reseller News	http://techweb.cmp.com/techweb/crn
HotWired	http://www.hotwired.com
Interactive Age	http://techweb.cmp.com/techweb/ia
Interactive Week	http://www.zdnet.com/~intweek
Internet World	http://www.mecklerweb.com/mags/iw
PC Week Online	http://www.zdnet.com/~pcweek
Seidman's Online Insider	http://www.clark.net/pub/robert

3. Coolest Magazines/Publishing

<u>Site/Area</u>	<u>URL</u>
BusinessWeek (AOL)	AOL Keyword: BUSINESSWEEK
CMP Publications	http://techweb.cmp.com
Digital City Washington (AOL)	AOL Keyword: DIGITAL CITY
Individual, Inc.	http://www.newspage.com
Mercury Center Web	http://www.sjmercury.com
NY TimesFax	http://nytimesfax.com
Pathfinder — Time, People, Life	http://www.pathfinder.com
The Wall Street Journal	http://www.wsj.com
ZD Net — Ziff Davis	http://www.zdnet.com

4. Coolest Commerce

<u>Site/Area</u>	<u>URL</u>
1-800-FLOWERS (AOL)	AOL Keyword: FLOWERS
2Market	AOL Keyword: 2Market
Amazon.com Books	http://www.amazon.com
The Electronic Newsstand	http://www.enews.com
The Internet Shopping Network	http://www2.internet.net/directories.html
marketplaceMCI	http://www2.pcy.mci.net/marketplace
Music Boulevard	http://www.musicblvd.com
Tower Records (AOL)	AOL Keyword: TOWER

5. Coolest Company

<u>Site/Area</u>	<u>URL</u>
Adobe Systems	http://www.adobe.com
Eastman Kodak	http://www.kodak.com
Electronic Arts	http://www.ea.com
Global Network Navigator	http://www.gnn.com
I-Phone	http://www.vocaltec.com
Macromedia	http://www.macromedia.com
MCA/Universal Cyberwalk	http://www.mca.com
MCI	http://www.mci.com
Microsoft	http://www.microsoft.com
Netscape Communications	http://www.netscape.com
RealAudio	http://www.prognet.com
Silicon Graphics' Silicon Surf	http://www.sgi.com
Sony Online	http://www.sony.com
StreamWorks	http://www.xingtech.com
Sun Microsystems	http://www.sun.com
TrueSpeech	http://www.dspg.com
Worlds Chat	http://www.worlds.net
WebSpace	http://www.sd.tgs.com/~template/WebSpace

6. Coolest Network

<u>Site/Area</u>	<u>URL</u>
CBS News Up to the Minute Online	http://uttm.com
clnet — The Computer Network	http://www.cnet.com
CNN	http://www.cnn.com
The Discovery Channel	http://www.discovery.com
NBC HTTV	http://www.nbc.com

7. Coolest Sports

<u>Site/Area</u>	<u>URL</u>
ABC Sports	AOL Keyword: ABC SPORTS
Eric Simon's Frisbee Connection	http://www.access.digex.net/~erics/ultimate.html
ESPN SportsZone	http://espnet.sportszone.com

Golf Web	http://www.golfweb.com
Guide to the 1996 Olympic Games	http://www.atlanta.olympic.org
iGOLF (AOL)	AOL Keyword: iGOLF
Inline Online	http://bird.taponline.com/inline
SnoWeb	http://www.snoweb.com
SportsLine USA	http:/www.sportsline.com

8. Coolest Government/NASA

Site/Area	URL
The Department of the Treasury	http://www.ustreas.gov
FBI's Home Page	http://www.fbi.gov
Internal Revenue Service	http://www.irs.ustreas.gov
NASA's Astro-2	http://liftoff.msfc.nasa.gov
U.S. Department of Commerce	http://www.doc.gov
The White House	http://www.whitehouse.gov

9. Coolest Travel/Food

Site/Area	URL
Alamo Rental Car	http://www.freeways.com
City.Net	http://www.city.net
Conde Nast Traveler	http://www.cntraveler.com
Dining Out on the Web	http://www.ird.net/diningout.html
EAASY SABRE (AOL)	AOL Keyword: EAASY SABRE
Hotels and Travel	http://www.webscope.com/travel/homepage.html
INTELLiCast	http://www.intellicast.com
Peter Granoff's Wine Recommendations	http://www.virtualvin.com
Subway Navigator	http://metro.jussieu.fr:10001/bin/cities/english

10. Coolest Entertainment/Games/Art

Site/Area	URL
@the.Movies (AOL)	AOL Keyword: MOVIES
The Art on the Net Gallery	http://www.art.net/TheGallery/the_gallery.html
Buzz Online: The Talk of Los Angeles	http://www.buzzmag.com
Follywood (AOL)	AOL Keyword: FOLLYWOOD
Hollywood Online	http://www.hollywood.com
Hyper-Jeopardy	http://www.hype.com/game_show
Mr. Showbiz	http://showbiz.starwave.com
MTV	AOL Keyword: MTV
NetNoir (AOL)	AOL Keyword: NETNOIR
nVESTOR	http://www.investor-net.com
Online Gaming Forum (AOL)	AOL Keyword: GAMING
Rocktropolis	http://Rocktropolis.com
The Spot	http://www.thespot.com

11. Coolest Resources/Education

Site/Area	**URL**
Better Health (AOL)	AOL Keyword: BETTER HEALTH
Compton's Encyclopedia (AOL)	AOL Keyword: COMPTONS
Consumer Reports (AOL)	AOL Keyword: CONSUMER REPORTS
Deja News Research Service	http://www.dejanews.com
Forrest Stroud's Consummate Winsock Apps List	http://cwsapps.texas.net
NYNEX Interactive Yellow Pages	http://www.niyp.com
Planet Earth Home Page	http://www.nosc.mil/planet_earth/info.html
Ticketmaster Online	http://www.ticketmaster.com
Universal Currency Converter	http://www.xe.net/currency
Yahoo!	http://www.yahoo.com

12. Coolest Kids

Site/Area	**URL**
Blackberry Creek (AOL)	AOL Keyword: BLACKBERRY
Club KidSoft (AOL)	AOL Keyword: KIDSOFT
Kids Web	http://www.infomall.org/kidsweb

13. Coolest Miscellaneous

Site/Area	**URL**
Awesome Sports Site of the Week	http://www.awesomesports.com
Cool Word of the Day	http://www.dsu.edu/projects/word_of_day/word.html
David Letterman's Top 10	http://www.cbs.com/lateshow
Geek Site of the Day	http://chico.rice.edu/~indigo/gsotd
Netscape's FishCam	http://www2.netscape.com/fishcam/fishcam.html
Peeping Tom Homepage	http://www.ts.umu.se/~spaceman/camera.html
Political Site of the Day	http://ross.clendon.com/siteoftheday.html
Question of the Day	http://www.ptown.com/qod

Getting Started

Using Netscape Navigator:

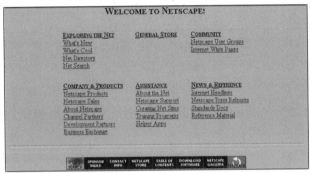

http://www.netscape.com

At Netscape's home page, users are given a variety of choices. Depending on their interests, they can explore the Internet through Netscape's What's New and What's Cool sections, as well as get news and reference information on the Internet, find information on Netscape and its products, and shop the Netscape store.

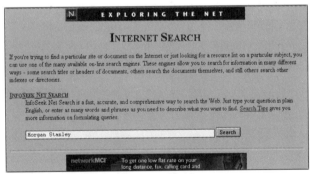

"Net Search" key in Netscape Navigator

InfoSeek search engine in Netscape Navigator.

Using America Online:

AOL keyword: Main

At America Online's Main Menu, users are given the opportunity to search the extensive resources provided within its 14 channels. Additionally, users can enter AOL's features for the month (In the Spotlight), use the fast key to send/access mail (Post Office), or learn more about the service and take a quick tour of AOL's offerings (Discover AOL).

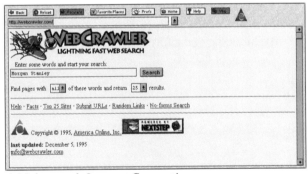

AOL keyword: Internet Connection

WebCrawler search engine in America Online's Internet service, GNN. The URL is http://webcrawler.com.

Coolest Finance

American Express

AOL keyword: EXPRESSNET
Offers a broad array of financial and travel information and services. Cardmembers can perform numerous tasks, including checking status of accounts, paying AMEX bills, and enrolling in rewards programs. ExpressNet Global Guide has a large travel database of over 150 destinations.

Bank of America

http://www.bofa.com
Learn about personal financial services, business banking, and special offers.

Company Research

AOL keyword: Company Research
One-stop searching for public company information. Includes Morningstar research reports, First Call earnings estimates, stock charts, financial statements, news stories (from Reuters, Knight-Ridder, PR NewsWire, and Business Wire), and direct access to SEC financial filings via Edgar.

E*TRADE

http://www.etrade.com
Provides investors with the ability to perform many operations, including: place stock and option orders online; get quotes and symbols on stocks, options, market indices, mutual funds, commodities, and futures; and get timely news alerts through TradeWeb. Also links to E*TRADE's Stock Trading Game.

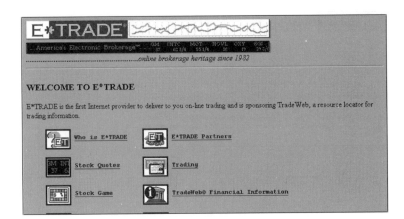

Fidelity Investments

http://www.fid-inv.com
Provides information on Fidelity's mutual fund offerings and services.

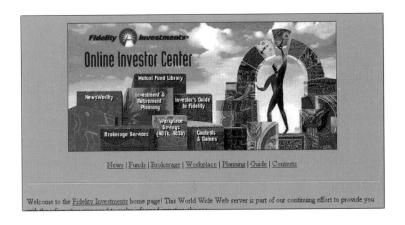

FinanCenter

http://internet-plaza.net/resources
Personal finance resource center with interactive calculations to help users evaluate borrowing and investing options.

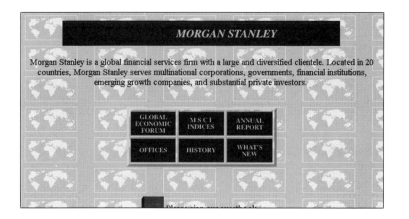

Morgan Stanley

http://www.ms.com
In addition to providing basic information about Morgan Stanley and regular updates of the MSCI global stock indices, economist Steve Roach presents Morgan Stanley's worldwide economics research perspective.

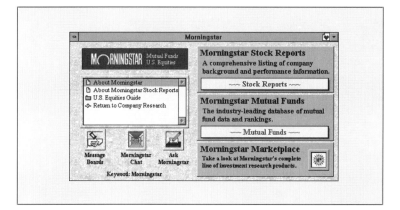

Morningstar

AOL keyword: Morningstar
Includes Morningstar mutual fund statistics/information and stock reports. Provides details on mutual fund performance and detailed fund descriptions, as well as publications and software with data and analysis on over 6,800 mutual funds.

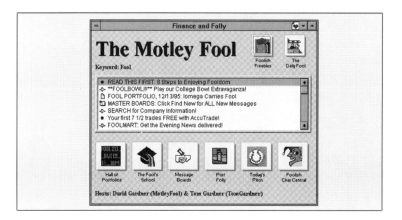

The Motley Fool

AOL keyword: Fool
Probably the best interactive finance service. Provides views/opinions/information from users and hosts about specific stocks in interactive forums. In addition, service features include investor tips, an investment game, and a collectively managed stock portfolio.

Quicken Financial Network

http://www.intuit.com
Offers access to Intuit's technical support and
product information, as well as information and
advice on personal finance topics.

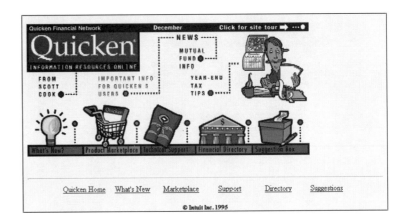

SEC EDGAR Database

http://www.sec.gov
A searchable database providing access to all
electronically filed SEC documents.

Security First Network Bank

http://www.sfnb.com
View account statements, register, pay bills, get
current account balance, and more. Offers
tutorials, product information, rates, fees,
personal financial advisors, and 24-hour
customer service.

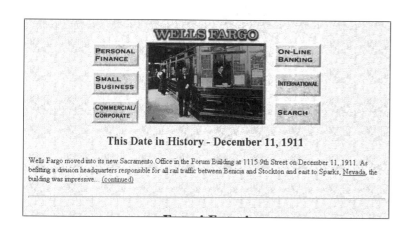

Wells Fargo

http://wellsfargo.com
Vast amounts of information on online banking and more, including personal finance, small business, and corporate accounts.

Coolest Technology Trade Magazines/Newsletters

Computer Reseller News

http://techweb.cmp.com/techweb/crn
Get the latest on CRN's news, special reports, product reviews, opinions, Internet focus, and more. Recently added its Internet Directory with company and product information.

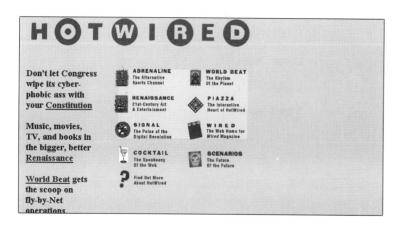

HotWired

http://www.hotwired.com
One of the fastest-growing, top-ranked subscriber sites. This Internet version of *Wired* (and more) magazine offers free news and information. Member benefits include features like What's New, Your View (customization), Club Wired, Thread (ongoing discussions), Coin (personal ads), and Search.

Interactive Age

http://techweb.cmp.com/techweb/ia
Explore the current issue, as well as search the archives. Includes Interactive Age Daily, Daily Media and Marketing Report, and NY Times Syndicate Computer News Daily. Also offers Interactive Age Daily's e-mail service.

Interactive Week

http://www.zdnet.com/~intweek
Combination of online-only information and articles from the print version of *Interactive Week*. Users decide how they want to view content, and the site offers a calendar of industry events as well as a searchable database.

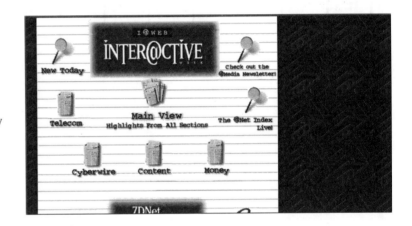

Internet World

http://www.mecklerweb.com/mags/iw
Focuses exclusively on the Internet. Provides extensive up-to-date information on industry news and trends. Also offers commentary, personality profiles, advice, and links to other Web sites. Advertising rates and information for the magazine are available online, as well as an I-site ordering and maintenance service.

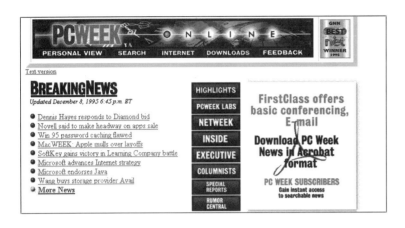

PC Week Online

http://www.zdnet.com/~pcweek
Offers continuously updated industry news and information, with a searchable database, downloads, a personal view — which users set up after filling out an on-screen form, and more.

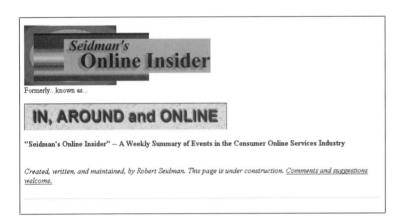

Seidman's Online Insider

http://www.clark.net/pub/robert
Weekly analysis covering the major online services and the Internet. Formerly called "In, Around and Online."

Coolest Magazines/Publishing

BusinessWeek

AOL keyword: BusinessWeek
The electronic version of *BusinessWeek*. Provides the weekly issue plus interaction with editors and reporters.

CMP Interactive Media

http://techweb.cmp.com
Digital publishing division of CMP Publications
whose site, called Tech Web, houses the CMP
publication and business units that maintain
linked home pages.

Digital City Washington

AOL keyword: Digital City
Digital City brings the social life, commerce,
and sense of community and culture of
Washington, D.C., online with its five
components: news; entertainment; people; DC
marketplace; and cityweb. Digital City is all
about our nation's capital, with a variety of
information and resources on restaurants,
weather, politics, personal ads, selling items,
and surfing local Web sites.

Individual, Inc.

http://www.newspage.com
Newspage is a subscription service that compiles
news feeds (such as Reuters, Associated Press,
and PR NewsWire) and various publications
covering all industries (such as *The Economist,
Variety,* as well as a number of CMP and Ziff
Davis publications, including *Computer Reseller
News, Information Week, Interactive Age, PC
Magazine,* and *PC Week*). Users can access
targeted information on the home page.

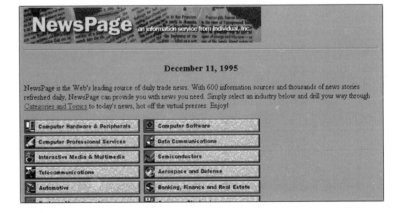

Mercury Center Web

http://www.sjmercury.com
Continuously updated news coverage and the complete text of each day's final edition of the *San Jose Mercury News*.

NY TimesFax

http://nytimesfax.com
A condensed digest of *The New York Times*, including top stories, sports results, editorials, and the crossword puzzle.

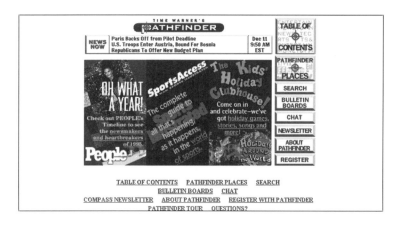

Pathfinder

http://www.pathfinder.com
Created by Time Inc., Pathfinder offers numerous links to many cool publications and Web sites.

The Wall Street Journal

http://www.wsj.com
The electronic version of *The Wall Street Journal.* Provides daily versions of the paper. In addition, for a fee, users can receive, via e-mail, customized news information (Personal Journal) from the resources of Dow Jones Company.

ZD Net — Ziff Davis

http://www.zdnet.com
Created by Ziff-Davis, includes links to a number of magazines, as well as news, stories, downloadable software, product reviews, online columns, and discussions.

Coolest Commerce

1-800-FLOWERS

AOL keyword: Flowers
Offers ability to electronically purchase flower arrangements and gift items (viewable via cool graphics) for delivery by mail.

2Market

AOL keyword: 2Market
Packages products from a variety of vendors (it's like the electronic version of the airline shopping catalog) and markets them electronically. Vendors include 1-800-Flowers, Godiva Chocolates, Hammacher Schlemmer, Starbucks, The Museum of Modern Art, The Nature Company, The Sharper Image, and Windham Hill Records.

Amazon.com Books

http://www.amazon.com
Offers over one million books/titles, with 30% discounts on bestsellers, 10% off both hardcovers and paperbacks, and more discounts on other titles featured in its Spotlight. Also offers Eyes & Editors, a free personal notification service.

The Electronic Newsstand

http://www.enews.com
One-stop shopping — a wide selection of articles from leading worldwide magazines, newspapers, newsletters, and catalogs. Also contains links to news searches.

The Internet Shopping Network

http://www2.internet.net/directories.html
A division of the Home Shopping Network, Inc., ISN offers free membership in one of the largest retailing and mall operations on the net, providing online shoppers access to a broad range of products from more than 600 major companies, including: software from Lotus, Symantec, and Microsoft; flowers from FTD; steak and lobster from Omaha Steaks International; and unique merchandise from Hammacher Schlemmer.

marketplaceMCI

http://www2.pcy.mci.net/marketplace
With over 30 stores offering goods and services, marketplaceMCI also offers: a What's New section (new offerings, updated frequently); a Gift area, with ideas and information for any occasion; a Computer section, with software and hardware, as well as news and views on technology; and a Small Business area, specifically designed to meet the needs of the small business owner with office supplies, information on insurance carriers, and more.

Music Boulevard

http://www.musicblvd.com
Boulevard has over 145,000 listings in stock in rock, country, jazz, classical, folk, bluegrass, world beat, and more. Includes sections for new releases, the latest music news, facts (includes biographies, reviews, interviews, song lists, titles in print, artists/composers, cover art, sound clips, and Billboard charts).

Tower Records

AOL keyword: Tower
Offers descriptions of Tower's database of CDs and records. Also features hot new recordings, artists, and product promotions. Provides ability to electronically purchase for delivery by mail. Also offers features such as "collectors library," which lists top music collections of all time by category (such as Rock and Roll, R&B, and Classical).

Coolest Company

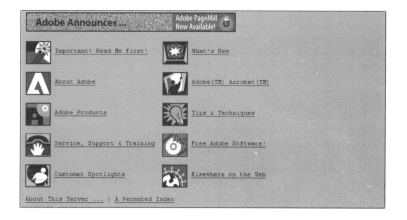

Adobe Systems

http://www.adobe.com
Provides information about Adobe and its products. Access Adobe's service, technical support, and training, as well as download free Adobe software and upgrades. Also provides valuable links to other cool Web sites.

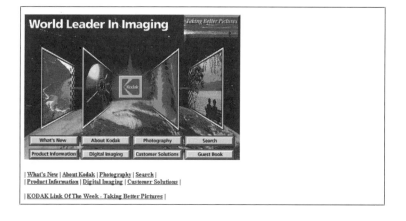

Eastman Kodak

http://www.kodak.com
Offers Kodak company information, detailed customer solution categorized by industry, as well as some really cool digital images.

Electronic Arts

http://www.ea.com
Information on Electronic Arts' products and
platforms (search by brand or platform), with
company press releases, the EA store, and links
to other hot sites.

Global Network Navigator

http://www.gnn.com
Offerings from Internet navigational guides and
reference resources to informative and
entertaining special-interest publications. Areas
of focus include: Navigating the Net (The Whole
Internet Catalog, and the NCSA What's New
Page); Marketplace (GNN Direct, and GNN
Business Pages); and Special GNN Publications
(NetNews, Travelers' Center, Personal Finance
Center, and Sports Center). GNN is owned by
America Online. Parent Soup is a new forum for
parents to talk to other parents about life, sex,
fun, etc.

I-Phone

http://www.vocaltec.com
Provides information on Internet phone software
that allows users to speak with other users over
the Internet.

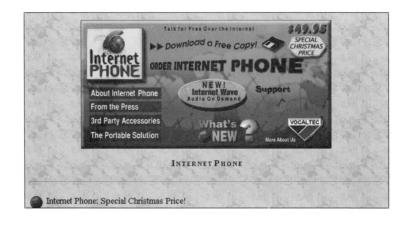

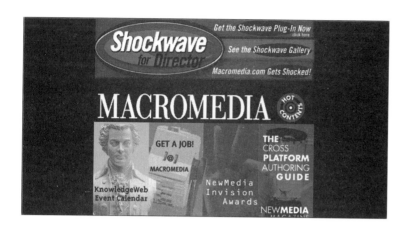

Macromedia

http://www.macromedia.com
Allows users to explore news, resources, and services from Macromedia. Users can register for the company's online newsletters that contain the latest technical information and special offers.

MCA/Universal Cyberwalk

http://www.mca.com
Provides links to various sites within Universal/MCA, including The Ultimate Hollywood Screening Room, Putnam Berkley Online, Universal Channel, Universal VIP, AMP music magazine from MCA Records Online, Winterland Productions, Spencer Gifts, and Universal Studios Hollywood.

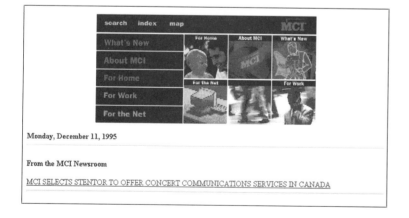

MCI

http://www.mci.com
Provides links to internetMCI, Gramercy Press, MCI Developers Lab, and Small Business Center.

Microsoft

http://www.microsoft.com
Provides information on products and support, as well as current Microsoft news. Microsoft has also done an impressive job of creating a nice front-end for many of the resources on the Internet and MSN.

Netscape Communications

http://www.netscape.com
Lots of hot links, from Netscape's products and services, to its employees and Partners, to numerous resources and guides for traveling the Net.

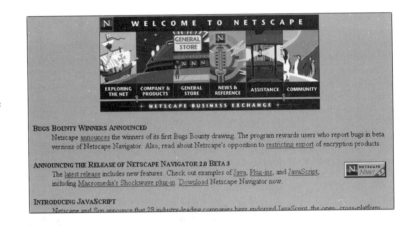

Real Audio

http://www.prognet.com
Download free real-time audio playback software. Site includes links to good content sites.

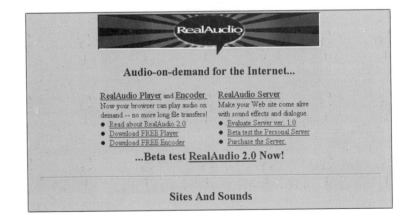

Silicon Graphics' Silicon Surf

http://www.sgi.com
Lets users find information on the company, employees, products, technology, and customer support, while offering links to other cool sites, including the Silicon Studio.

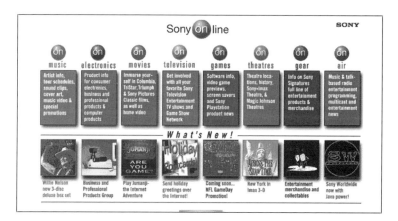

Sony Online

http://www.sony.com
Access to company news and information, with specific categories including Sony Music, Sony Pictures, Sony Electronics, Sony Interactive, Sony Gear, and Sony SW Networks.

StreamWorks

http://www.xingtech.com
Provides ability to download real-time video and audio software. Includes links to NBC Pro (NBC's online news service) and other Xing servers.

Sun Microsystems

http://www.sun.com
Provides a comprehensive overview of Sun, with sections such as Facts at a Glance, Business Units, Community Investment, Environmental Policies, Investor Information, and Employment Opportunities at Sun.

TrueSpeech

http://www.dspg.com
Provides information about and access to DSP Group's real-time audio playback software based on the ".wav" file format.

Worlds Chat

http://www.worlds.net
A multi-user, 3-D VRML-based chat community that allows you to use your own personal "avatar." This application is one of many Worlds applications currently available (such as Alpha World) or under development (other 3-D applications).

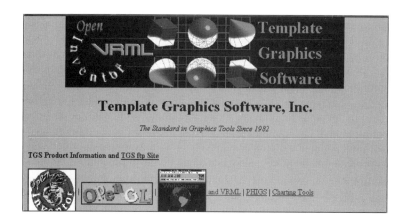

WebSpace

http://www.sd.tgs.com/~template/WebSpace
Provides information about and access to a
VRML (3-D) browser for Windows 95 and
Windows NT.

Coolest Network

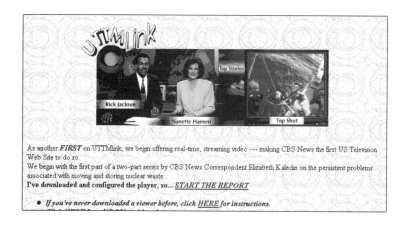

CBS News Up to the Minute Online

http://uttm.com
Updated overnight news coverage with the latest
worldwide news and other information,
including Internet and CD-ROM developments,
movie reviews, women's health reports, and
parenting.

c|net — The Computer Network
http://www.cnet.com
c|net offers a comprehensive online tutorial on
how to build your own Web page, from getting
your idea together to getting it on the Web. Both
a nationwide television programming service
and a worldwide online service, c|net: The
Computer Network also provides its online
members with: Web exploration; information
and opinions about general news and the
Internet; exclusive lab-based computer product
reviews; the latest computer and online news;
downloadable software; chat with guests, hosts,
and producers; contests and polls; technical help
from vendors and other members; and
information on products and trends.

12 – 26

CNN

http://www.cnn.com
Provides the latest in world and U.S. news, as well as information on business, entertainment, weather, food and health, sports, politics, technology, and style.

The Discovery Channel

http://www.discovery.com
Original interactive stories with film, music, photography, and illustration.

NBC HTTV

http://www.nbc.com
Find out more about NBC shows, your local NBC station, sports, news, and various other data.

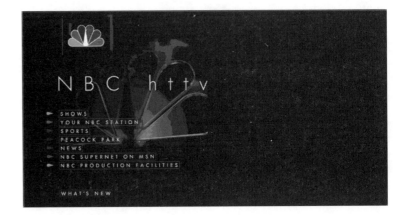

Coolest Sports

ABC Sports

AOL keyword: ABC Sports
Features ABC highlights, updated game and player information, chat room, Monday Night Football highlights, photo clips, scores and stats, ABC sports store, and information on college games.

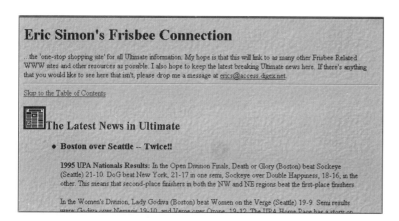

Eric Simon's Frisbee Connection

http://www.access.digex.net/~erics/ultimate.html
The one-stop shopping site for all ultimate frisbee information and news including: league, tournament, rankings, and UPA information; links to other Web sites; and UPA Committees and Materials.

ESPN SportsZone

http://espnet.sportszone.com
ESPN SportsZone includes key features, such as team and player coverage, in-depth news and analyses, AP photos, NFL game recaps, celebrity and subscriber chat, fantasy-league play, The Daily Line, enhanced NFL previews from *Pro Football Weekly*, and college football injury reports and odds.

Golf Web

http://www.golfweb.com
An organization of computer, publishing, and golf professionals, dedicated to serving golf fans around the world.

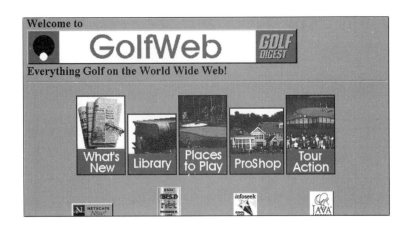

Guide to the 1996 Olympic Games

http://www.atlanta.olympic.org
Established by the Atlanta Committee for the Olympic Games (ACOG, the organization responsible for planning and staging the Centennial Olympic Games), this site provides up-to-date, official information about the 1996 Olympic Games.

iGOLF

AOL keyword: iGOLF
An online golf magazine with coverage of PGA, the LPAG, and the Senior Tours. Also provides information on golf travel, history, equipment, and course architecture. In addition, chat rooms and message boards about golf are a part of the service. Partially sponsored by Callaway Golf.

Inline Online

http://bird.taponline.com/inline
Contains inline hockey news, retailer and industry news, events, clubs, and an offer to subscribe to *Inline Magazine.*

SnoWeb

http://www.snoweb.com
Great Web site for skiers and snowboarders. Provides information on publications and links to everything snow-related, including where and when to go, as well as lift-ticket information and current snow/weather conditions.

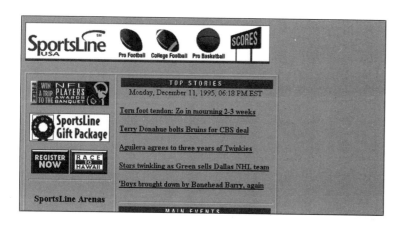

SportsLine USA

http://www.sportsline.com
Devoted to sports information, entertainment, and merchandise, with innovative offerings, such as: proprietary contests; live chats with sports celebrities; a merchandise and memorabilia store; and comprehensive, up-to-the-minute sports scores, highlights, and information. SportsLine is also the online home of the Special Olympics.

Coolest Government/NASA

The Department of the Treasury

http://www.ustreas.gov
Links to all the divisions under the Treasury, including: the IRS; Customs; the Bureau of Alcohol, Tobacco, and Firearms; the Mint; and even the Secret Service. There are also several links to useful economic statistical repositories and listings of the bulletin-board phone numbers for many of the Treasury's own statistical boards.

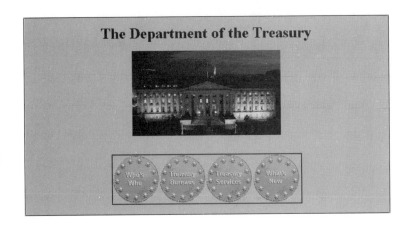

FBI's Home Page

http://www.fbi.gov
Includes links to some other pretty hot spots, including: "Ten Most Wanted Fugitives" Program; Computer Crime Investigations – The National Computer Crime Squad; and recent/ongoing investigations like UNABOM and the Oklahoma City bombing case.

Internal Revenue Service

http://www.irs.ustreas.gov
Gives the mission statement for the U.S. Internal Revenue Service, with links to information on tax forms (and valuable instructions), FAQs, where to file, and where to get help with taxes. Can download copies of IRS tax forms.

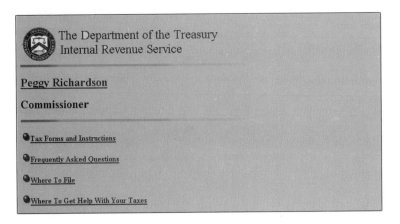

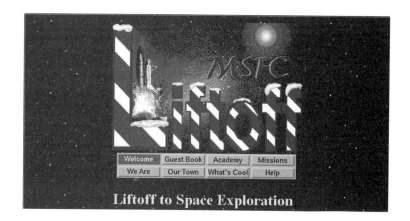

NASA's Astro-2

http://liftoff.msfc.nasa.gov
Visit liftoff at the Marshall Space Flight Center, with information on such topics as the mission plan and operations.

U.S. Department of Commerce

http://www.doc.gov
Provides a valuable starting place for retrieving government and economic data. Includes many services, such as statistics from the census bureau, patent and trademark information, and a search engine (called "Fedworld: a Locator for Federal Government Information").

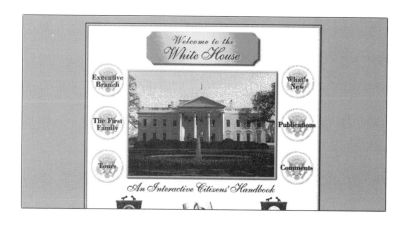

The White House

http://www.whitehouse.gov
Offers information on the First Family, the Executive Branch, publications, tours, and "what's new."

Coolest Travel/Food

Alamo Rental Car

http://www.freeways.com
Offers renting/booking reservations online, travel tips, maps and weather reports, and forums.

City.Net

http://www.city.net
A comprehensive international guide to communities around the world, City.Net is updated daily to provide easy and timely access to information on travel, entertainment, and local business, plus government and community services for all regions of the world.

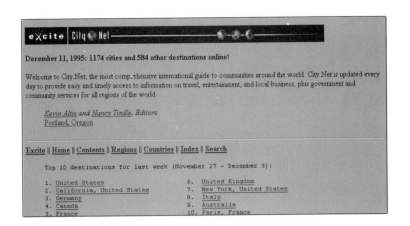

Condé Nast Traveler

http://www.cntraveler.com
Built on the principles behind the magazine, *Condé Nast Traveler*, the site offers a source of worldly, opinionated travel advice in a constantly updated, interactive form. Provides daily dispatches from a global network of correspondents, discussion forums, contests, games, and photos of places from around the world.

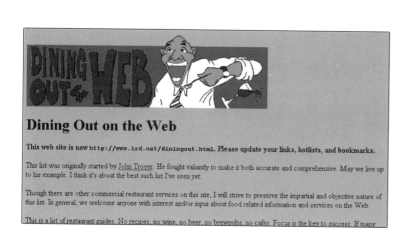

Dining Out on the Web

http://www.ird.net/diningout.html
Offers a comprehensive and extensive list of restaurant guides, sorted by type and by region.

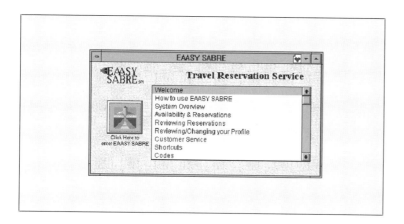

EAASY SABRE

AOL keyword: EAASY SABRE
Consumer version of the American Airlines SABRE Travel Information Network, the world's leading computerized reservations system. Allows users to make reservations on more than 350 airlines, access flight schedule information on more than 682 airlines, and access fares. Also provides access to more than 60 car rental companies and 180 hotel companies.

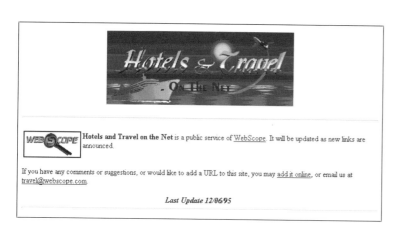

Hotels and Travel

http://www.webscope.com/travel/homepage.html
A public service directory maintained by WebScope, with information on airlines, airports, cruise lines, and hotels around the world.

INTELLiCast

http://www.intellicast.com
Provides weather updates and information from around the world, including valuable information on ski/ocean/boating conditions.

Peter Granoff's Wine Recommendations

http://www.virtualvin.com
A good source for good wines and specialty food stores. Also suggests food/wine combos.

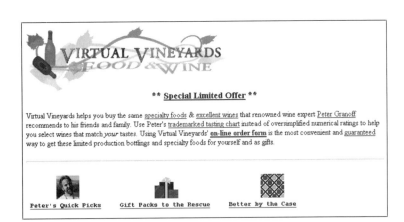

Subway Navigator

http://metro.jussieu.fr:10001/bin/cities/english
Helps users find the best route from one metro station to another, in various cities around the world. Just choose a city, from Amsterdam to Washington, D.C.

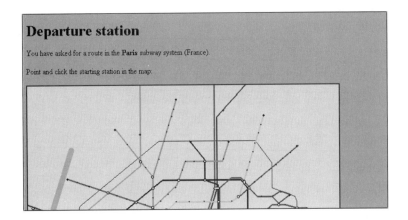

Coolest Entertainment/Games/Art

@the.Movies

AOL keyword: Movies
Great source for information on movies including reviews, interviews, and publications.

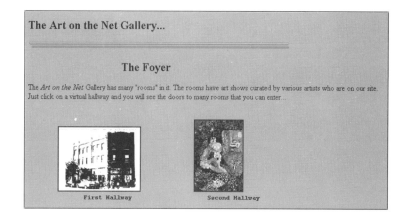

The Art on the Net Gallery

http://www.art.net/TheGallery/the_gallery.html
Contains many rooms with art shows curated by various artists on the site. Enter doors in the virtual hallway to proceed to the different rooms of collections. Currently has 75 artists from around the world, including poets, musicians, painters, sculptors, digital artists, performance artists, and animators.

Buzz Online: The Talk of Los Angeles

http://www.buzzmag.com
Features What's New, What's the Buzz, and Buzz Chat areas with links to many other hot sites.

Follywood

AOL keyword: Follywood
A forum (created by the founders of the Motley Fool) focusing on Hollywood. Includes creativity, criticism, games, and contests that relate to the people, places, events, and products that make Hollywood what it is. Also includes a pretty good interactive movie forum.

Hollywood Online

http://www.hollywood.com
Provides, among others, movie notes, trailers, sneak peeks, clips, and multimedia kits.

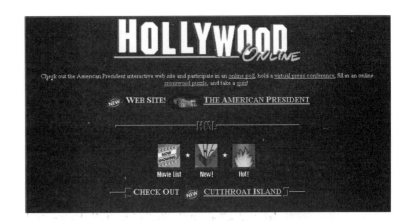

Hyper-Jeopardy

http://www.hype.com/game_show
Designed and produced by Hype! Inc., includes a variety of games to choose from and play , including Hyper-Jeopardy. Also offers news and information on movies, video games, entertainment, music, and more. Hype! is remade and updated frequently.

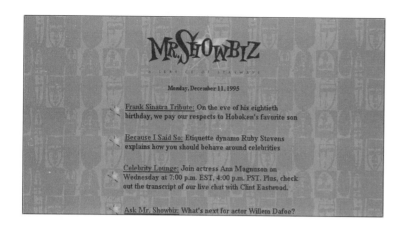

Mr. Showbiz

http://showbiz.starwave.com
Contains gossip, reviews, tabloid headlines, news of the coming millennium, celebrity profiles, TV ratings, a serial novel, celebrity birthday calendar, and many other fun/interesting links.

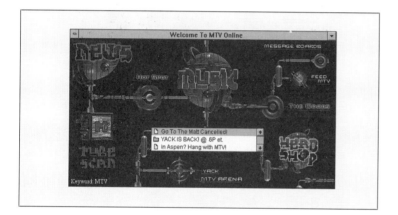

MTV

AOL keyword: MTV
All you would expect from the electronic version of one of Generation X's favorite productions. Includes news, images, interviews, and commentary about the hot players in the current music scene.

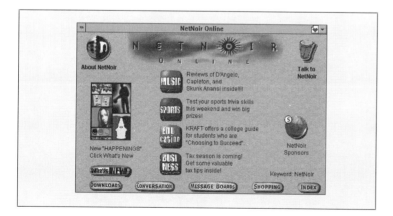

NetNoir

AOL keyword: NetNoir
NetNoir focuses on Afrocentric culture. The mission of the service is to digitize, archive, and distribute Afrocentric culture in cyberspace — this includes literature, music, fashion, history, art, cuisine, and sports. The service includes lots of information, interactive forums, and interviews.

nVESTOR

http://www.investor-net.com
Stock market simulation game, sponsored by the
League of American Investors. Players must go
to the Web site to register for the game, which is
then played via e-mail. Players are given a
starting portfolio of stocks worth $100,000
(financial details of real companies are
available). The League maintains and values
players' portfolios and ranks their success versus
other players. No real money is involved.

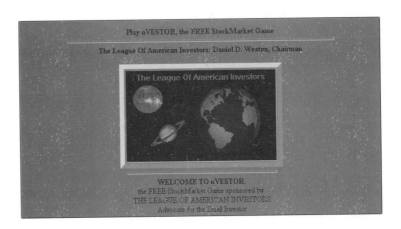

Online Gaming Forum

AOL keyword: Gaming
A forum where users can play AD&D
NeverwinterNights, MasterWord, Casino, and
the Sol III Play-By-Mail game, as well as join in
the Free-Form Gaming Forum, the Strategy
Forum, and Role-Playing Gaming Forum.

Rocktropolis

http://Rocktropolis.com
A rock 'n' roll fantasy theme park, Rocktropolis
is a surreal city landscape inhabited by some of
pop culture's greatest musicians and cult heroes.
It also offers recent entertainment news and
quotes.

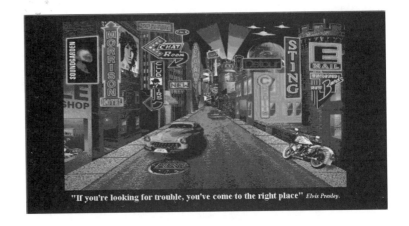

The Spot

http://www.thespot.com
First episodic Web site (very Melrose Place-ish) revolving around the activities and lifestyles of five attractive, twenty-something housemates of a California beach house. Winner of the first "Webby," or "Cool Site of the Year" award, announced 8/29/95.

Coolest Resources/Education

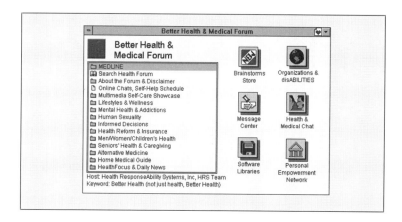

Better Health

AOL keyword: Better Health
Suitable for everyone, from consumers to health professionals, interested in health, providing information and support from fellow users on a specific health topic. Also for health professionals interested in networking with others in a specific field.

Compton's Encyclopedia

AOL keyword: Comptons
Provides valuable reference information. The site also offers access to Compton's online New Media Forum.

Consumer Reports

AOL keyword: Consumer Reports
Provides product and service reviews, ratings, and advice. Also includes specially designed summaries of CR's tests and evaluations, prepared for America Online.

Deja News Research Service

http://www.dejanews.com
Provides access to extensive Usenet news archive, offering a variety of options allowing users to tailor searches, including a "create a query" filter that limits searches by newsgroup, date, or author.

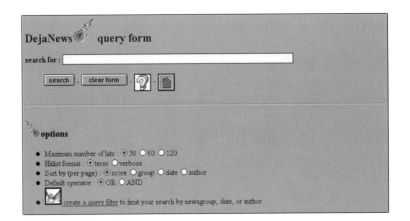

Forrest Stroud's Consummate Winsock Apps List Page

http://cwsapps.texas.net
Forrest Stroud's Consummate Winsock Apps List page contains reviews of the latest freeware, shareware, and demoware for use on the Net. It is the definitive source for identifying the latest Internet software applications.

NYNEX Interactive Yellow Pages

http://www.niyp.com
Search by business name or category, or visit the Top 25 Headings or Latest and Greatest sites, linked.

Planet Earth Home Page

http://www.nosc.mil/planet_earth/info.html
Filled with numbers and facts, including: world/U.S. population; national debt; census; area codes; currency/exchange rates; AT&Ts 800 directory; 800 airline numbers; and the World Factbook.

Ticketmaster Online

http://www.ticketmaster.com
Loaded with information on tens of thousands of upcoming concerts and events nationwide, plus a weekly update on the latest events to go on sale. Includes more than 400 venues around the country. Search the database by category, date, or venue. Other information includes: listing of charge-by-phone numbers and outlet locations; news from live events and personal contributions from entertainers and athletes; and special events and promotions.

Universal Currency Converter

http://www.xe.net/currency
From Xenon, the program uses flat text files as input, then searches on currency type using floating strings. The site currently gets its rates from those prepared by the The Bank of Montreal's Treasury Group for *The Globe and Mail*, Canada's national newspaper. It is currently gearing up for a real-time rate feed.

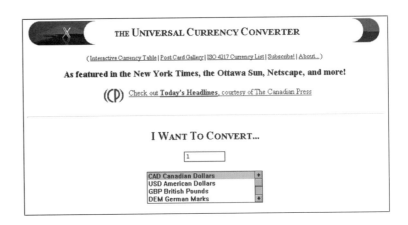

Yahoo!

http://www.yahoo.com
Great guide and search service for information, delivery, and online discovery.

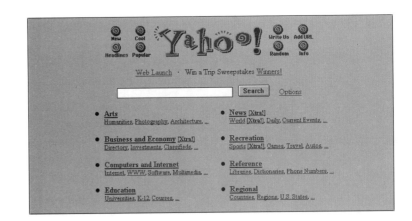

Coolest Kids

Blackberry Creek

AOL keyword: Blackberry
Blackberry Creek is a creativity community for kids ages 6–12. Kids can create stories, drawings, and more on their computer. Also includes Hungry Ear (a comedy club chat area), Party People (make great gifts), Story Teller (great stories by kids, ranging from serious to silly), and The Player (skits and sound effects).

Club KidSoft

AOL keyword: KidSoft
Club KidSoft is filled with special surprises and information for kids 4 to 14, including an art gallery of kids' computer creations, creative multimedia stories, contests, activities, and music. As a Club KidSoft subscriber, users also get deals on software, including two-for-one specials, and free software.

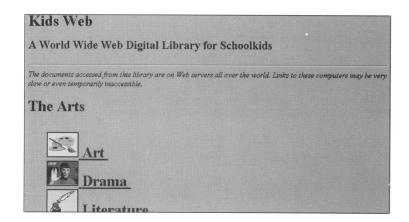

Kids Web

http://www.infomall.org/kidsweb
A digital library for kids, offering information on the arts, sciences, social studies, entertainment, games, reference materials, and sports. Also provides links to other Web sites.

Coolest Miscellaneous

Awesome Sports Site of the Week

http://www.awesomesports.com
When searching the archives list, note that the Site of the Week for 8/16–8/25 was "Mudsluts."

Cool Word of the Day

http://www.dsu.edu/projects/word_of_day/word.html

David Letterman's Top 10

http://www.cbs.com/lateshow.

Geek Site of the Day

http://chico.rice.edu/~indigo/gsotd/

Netscape's FishCam

http://www2.netscape.com/fishcam/fishcam.html

Peeping Tom Homepage

http://www.ts.umu.se/~spaceman/camera.html
The links here (more than 70) are each connected to Internet cameras around the world, such as: Boulder, Colorado; Stockholm, Sweden; and Santa Cruz, California.

Political Site of the Day

http://ross.clendon.com/siteoftheday.html

Question of the Day

http://www.ptown.com/qod/

Chapter 13: Glossary of Internet Terms

- For a quick reference of Internet terminology, we have included this glossary.

56K Line A digital phone-line connection, or leased line, capable of carrying 56,000 bits per second. At this speed, a megabyte of data would take about 3 minutes to transfer, which is four times as fast as a 14,400 kbps modem.

AdClicks[1] The number of "clicks" by an end-user on an in-line ad within a certain period of time.

AdClick Rate[1] AdClicks as a percentage of AdViews, or, the number of clicks by end-users on an ad as a percentage of the number of times that ad was downloaded by end-users.

ADN (advanced digital network) Usually refers to a 56 kbps leased line.

AdViews[1] The number of times an in-line ad (commonly referred to as a "banner") was downloaded (and presumably seen) by end-users within a specific period of time. The actual number of times the ad was seen by end-users may be higher due to "caching."

algorithms A programmed set of mathematical formulas developed for a computer environment to perform a specific function

Archie A software tool for finding files stored on anonymous FTP sites. A user needs to know the exact file name or a substring of it.

ARPANet (Advanced Research Projects Administration Network) The precursor to the Internet. Developed in the late 1960s and early 1970s by the U.S. Department of Defense as an experiment in wide-area networking that could survive a nuclear war.

ASCII (American standard code for information interchange) The de facto worldwide standard for the code numbers used by computers to represent all of the upper- and lower-case Latin letters, numbers, punctuation, and other characters. There are 128 standard ASCII codes, each of which can be represented by a seven-digit binary number: from 0000000 through 1111111.

ATM Asynchronous transfer mode (ATM) is an international ISDN high-speed, high-volume, packet-switching transmission protocol standard. ATM uses short, uniform, 53-byte cells to divide data into efficient, manageable packets for ultrafast switching through a high-performance communications network. The 53-byte cells contain 5-byte destination address headers and 48 data bytes. ATM is the first packet-switched technology designed from the ground up to support integrated voice, video, and data communication applications. It is well-suited to high-speed WAN transmission bursts. ATM currently accommodates transmission speeds from 64 Kbps to 622 Mbps. ATM may support gigabit speeds in the future.

backbone A high-speed line or series of connections that forms a major pathway within a network. The term is relative, though, as a backbone in a small network will likely be much smaller than many non-backbone lines in a large network.

bandwidth Terminology used to indicate the transmission or processing capacity of a system or of a specific location in a system (usually a network system). Bandwidth is usually defined in bits per second but also is usually described as either large or small. Recently, the term bandwidth has evolved into something describing human capacity.

baud (bits at unit density) A unit of transmission speed equal to the number of times the state (or condition) of a line changes per second. Equal to the bit-per-second (BPS) rate only if each signal element represents one bit of information. The baud rate usually refers to the number of bits transmitted each second.

BBS (bulletin board system) A computerized meeting and announcement system that allows people to carry on discussions, upload and download files, and make announcements without all being connected to the computer at the same time. There are thousands (maybe millions) of BBSs around the world, but most are very small and are run on a single IBM clone PC with one or two phone lines. Some are very large, though, and the line between a BBS and a system like CompuServe gets crossed at some point, although it is not clearly drawn.

BinHex (binary hexadecimal) A method for converting non-text files (non-ASCII) into ASCII. This is needed because Internet e-mail can only handle ASCII.

bits A binary digit, either a 0 or 1. The smallest element of a computer program. In the U.S., 8 bits make up one byte. Typically, transmission capacity is measured in bits (kilobits or megabits).

Boolean A descriptor for a specific type of search of two or more words, connected by the operative words AND, OR, NOT, or any combination, to more precisely define a search and minimize extraneous information.

BITNET (Because It's Time Network) A network of educational sites separate from the Internet, although e-mail is freely exchanged between the two. Listservs, the most popular form of e-mail discussion groups, originated on BITNET. BITNET machines are IBM VMSs, and the network is probably the only international network that is shrinking.

bps (bits per second) A measurement of how fast data are moved from one place to another. A 28.8 modem can move 28,800 bits per second.

BRI (basic rate interface) The BRI is the basic ISDN-to-user connection option, using four unshielded normal telephone wires to deliver digital services. It comprises two 64 kbps bearer (B) channels and one 16 kbps data (D) channel that carry both call set-up and user packet data across the network. The BRI interface is also referred to as a 2B+D connection.

browsers Software programs that retrieve, display, and print information and HTML documents from the Worldwide Web. Different browsers support different versions of the HTML standard, sometimes causing illegible information to be displayed. Most browsers also support other network protocols, such as FTP, gopher, and Usenet.

bytes The fundamental unit that a computer uses in its operation. It is a group of adjacent binary digits, usually 8, often used to represent a single character (see "bit"). A

byte is typically composed of 8 bits. Memory and storage capacity usually are measured in bytes (megabytes or gigabytes).

caching Storing or buffering data in a temporary location, so that the information can be retrieved quickly by an application. On the Internet, OSPs cache Web page data on their networks for use by their subscribers to speed up access to commonly accessed Web content.

client A software program used to contact and obtain data from a server software program on another computer, often across a great distance. Each client program is designed to work with one or more specific kinds of server programs, and each server requires a specific kind of client.

cyberspace Term originated by author William Gibson in his novel "Neuromancer," and currently used to describe the whole range of information resources available through computer networks.

daemon A transport agent program that runs in the background on UNIX systems and responds to requests from users. One common daemon is the "sendmail" program, which works behind the scenes to ensure that messages are addressed and transported in an orderly fashion.

digital certificates An encoded document that verifies the connection between a server's public key (known to anyone) and the server's identification. This verification process is similar to that provided by a driver's license, which verifies the connection between the photograph and the personal identification. Cryptographic checks, including a digital signature, ensure that the information within the certificate can be trusted.

DLL (dynamic link library) A set of routines used by Windows software packages as standard functions available for use by other software packages. These functions are loaded when the programs are run.

domain name The unique name that identifies an Internet site, such as "microsoft.com". A domain name always has two or more parts, separated by periods. The part to the left of the period is the most specific, and the part on the right is the most general. A given machine may have more than one domain name, but a given domain name points to only one machine. Usually, all of the machines on a particular network will use the same phrase as the right-hand portion of their domain names: e.g., gateway.gbnetwork.com, mail.gbnetwork.com, or www.gbnetwork.com. It is also possible for a domain name to exist but not be connected to an actual machine. This is often done so that a group or business can have an Internet e-mail address without having to establish a real Internet site. In these cases, some real Internet machine must handle the mail on behalf of the listed domain name.

download   The transfer of a file from a server computer to a client computer. Alternatively, sending a file from one's own computer to any other computer (peer-to-peer transfer, not involving a server). Upload is the transfer of a file in the opposite direction.

EC/EDI System   Business system built around standard EDI formats and re-engineered processes to achieve all-electronic capabilities.

electronic commerce (EC)   Business environment integrating electronic transfer and automated business systems (end-user computing and computer-to-computer capabilities).

Electronic Data Interchange (EDI)   Computer-to-computer exchange of structured transactional information between autonomous computers.

e-mail (electronic mail)   Messages, usually text, sent from one person to another via computer. E-mail can also be sent automatically to a large number of addresses.

encrypt   To scramble the contents of a file or message in such a way as to make it unreadable to everyone except those with a software "key," which makes it possible to unscramble the encrypted file or message.

encryption   Making a file unreadable by everyone not in possession of a special key, with which an encrypted file can be appropriately deciphered.

Ethernet   A very common method of networking computers in a LAN. Ethernet will handle about 10,000,000 bits per second and can be used with almost any kind of computer.

FAQ (frequently asked questions)   FAQs are documents that list and answer the most common questions on a particular subject. There are hundreds of FAQs available on the Internet on subjects as diverse as pet grooming and cryptography. FAQs are usually written by people who grew tired of answering the same questions repeatedly.

FDDI (fiber distributed data interface)   A standard for transmitting data on optical-fiber cables at a rate of around 100,000,000 bps (10 times as fast as Ethernet, about twice as fast as T-3).

file transfer protocol (FTP)   An Internet utility program to obtain files from another system or to move files between systems. These files may contain information or software programs.

finger   An Internet software tool for locating people on other Internet sites. Finger is also sometimes used to give access to non-personal information, but the most common use is to see if a person has an account at a particular Internet site. Many sites do not allow incoming Finger requests, while others do.

flame, flaming, flame war   An occasional feature of the Usenet newsgroups, a flame is an e-mail message, usually a response to someone else's post, that takes a strongly personal and sarcastic, cynical, or angry tone. Often initiates a back-and-forth "flame war" that eventually dies down.

forms   The capability in many browser/navigator software packages to accept input in text-entry fields displayed on the user's screen. Customized forms can be developed easily to request information for company data, including time cards, expense reports, personnel records, and other such corporate information.

gateway   The technical meaning is a hardware or software set-up that translates between two dissimilar protocols; for example, Prodigy has a gateway that translates between its internal, proprietary e-mail format and the Internet's e-mail format. Another, sloppier meaning of gateway is to describe any mechanism for providing access to another system; e.g., AOL could be called a gateway to the Internet.

gopher   An Internet protocol that directly preceded the WWW, created by the University of Minnesota. It is a more basic system than the Web's HTTP.

helper application A program launched by a browser to view a particular type of data.

hit (Web site) Web-speak for a successful access to a file on a Web page. Often used to attempt to compare popularity in the context of getting so many "hits" during a given period. A "newbie" mistake is equating hits with visits. A single visit usually is recorded as several hits, because each file accessed is recorded as a hit.

hit[1] An entry in the log file of a Web server. A hit is generated by every request made to a Web server. It has no predictable relation to users, visitors, or pages.

home page The first HTML (hypertext markup language) page that users generally see on a World Wide Web site. The home page represents the image that a company or individual chooses to project to users on the Internet. Most home pages are structured to also provide links to relevant documents or information at other locations on the Internet.

host Any computer on a network that is a repository for services available to other computers on the network. It is common to have one host machine that provides several services, such as the Web and Usenet.

Hot Java A new generation of browser technology developed by Sun Microsystems which allows users to observe and interact with Java programs.

HTML (hypertext markup language) A simple coding system used to format documents for viewing by World Wide Web clients. HTML can be compared with early word-processing software, in which all special characters, like bold or underline, need to be marked or "tagged" to let the printer know that the character requires special consideration during output. Web pages are written in this standard specification, which is a data type definition (DTD), or subset of SGML (standardized graphics markup language).

HTTP (hypertext transfer protocol) An Internet computer communication encoding standard for the exchange of multimedia documents on the Web.

HTTP linked object A clickable object (text, picture, or both) that provides a path between documents, directing the browser to a new URL.

HTTPD (hypertext transfer protocol daemon) The server that handles Internet and Web protocols.

hyperlink The path between two documents, which allows the user to point-and-click on specific words on the screen and thereby move to the requested location, wherever it is on the Internet.

hypertext Generally, any text that contains "links" to other documents — words or phrases in the document that can be chosen by a reader and which cause another document to be retrieved and displayed.

image map A clickable picture that directs the browser to different links, depending on which part of the image is clicked.

internet (lower-case "i") Any time you connect two or more networks together, you have an internet.

Internet The global network of networks that grew out of a Department of Defense (DARPA) funded research project.

InterNIC A collaborative project of three organizations to offer the Internet community a full scope of network information services, such as providing information about accessing and using the Internet, assistance in locating resources on the network, and registering network components for Internet connectivity. The InterNIC's goal is to make networking and networked information more accessible to researchers, educators, and the public. The InterNIC name signifies the cooperation between Network Information Centers, or NICs. For general information about the InterNIC, send e-mail to info@internic.net.

IP Number Sometimes called a "dotted quad." A unique number consisting of four parts separated by dots, e.g., 165.113.245.2. Every machine on the Internet has a unique IP number — if it doesn't, then it's not really on the Internet. Most machines also have one or more domain names, which are easier to remember.

IRC (Internet relay chat) Basically, IRC is a huge multi-user live chat facility. There are a number of major IRC servers around the world linked to each other. Anyone can create a "channel," and anything that anyone types in a given channel is seen by all others in that channel. Private channels can (and are) created for multi-person "conference calls."

ISDN (integrated services digital network) A digital telephonic system made up of two 64 kbps "B" channels for data and one "D" channel for traffic messaging. While an analog line usually takes up to 10 seconds to dial and make a connection, ISDN typically makes a dial-up connection within 0.5 second, allowing dial-up rates for a leased-line-like connection.

ISP (Internet service provider) A business that allows companies and individuals to connect to the Internet by providing the interface to the Internet backbone.

IXC An Interexchange Carrier (IXC, or also IEC) is a company providing long-distance phone service between Local Exchange Carriers and Local Access Transport Areas. With regards to the Internet, an IXC is known as an Interexchange Circuit, or a circuit that connects PoPs.

Java A new, object-oriented programming language developed by Sun Microsystems that allows Web pages viewed with Java-enabled Web browsers to display applets, which are small programs that can create sound and graphical animations, among other uses.

kbps (kilobits per second) Approximately 1,000 bits per second. An abbreviation for a unit of measure used for gauging the transmission of digital data from one point to another, typically but not necessarily across telephonic networks. Local-area networks (LANs) usually are measured in megabits per second (approximately one million bits per second).

LAN (local-area network) A computer network limited to an immediate area, usually one building or one floor of a single building.

leased lines A permanent physical connection between two locations that forms a private wide-area network (WAN) or links a single computer or a network of computers to packet-switching networks like the Internet. They are called leased lines because they are rented from a telephone company.

Linux An operating system that runs only on 386/486/Pentium machines. Linux implements POSIX, with System V and Berkeley Software Distribution (BSD) extensions (which means it looks like UNIX but does not come from the same source code base). It is copyrighted by Linus B. Torvalds (torvalds@kruuna.helsinki.fi) and other contributors and is freely redistributable under the terms of the GNU public license.

Listserv The most common kind of Internet mailing list. Listervs originated on BITNET.

login Noun or a verb. Noun: The account name used to gain access to a computer system. Not a secret (contrast with "password"). Verb: The act of entering into a computer system; e.g., "Login to the WELL and go to the GBN conference."

Lycos A Web search engine developed by Carnegie Mellon University. It allows one to search for a document by title, content, links, headings, and keywords. Lycos is a system composed of a "robot" that scours the Web in search of new information, which it then catalogs, indexes, and stores.

mail list (or mailing list) A (usually automated) system that allows people to send e-mail to one address, whereupon their message is copied and sent to all other subscribers to the mailing list. In this way, people who have many different kinds of e-mail access can participate in discussions together.

media objects[1] Files, other than HTML documents, which can be displayed or executed within HTML documents, or in a stand alone fashion. Examples include GIFs, JPEGs, video, audio, PDF, and HotJava Applets.

megabyte A million bytes. A thousand kilobytes.

MIME (multipurpose Internet mail extensions) The public domain multimedia standard for Internet SMTP e-mail systems. Graphics, audio clips, or video can be sent along with an e-mail message by using MIME attachments.

modem A contraction for modulation/demodulation. A modem is a device that converts a digital bit stream into an analog signal (modulation) and converts analog signals back into digital signals (demodulation). A modem typically uses telephone lines, and the analog signals are typically sounds. Fax machines have built-in modems.

MOO (MUD, object oriented) One of several kinds of multi-user role-playing environments, so far only text-based.

Mosaic User interface software for navigating, browsing, and accessing files on the Internet. The Mosaic browser was developed at NCSA, the National Center for Supercomputing Applications at the University of Illinois.

MPEG (Motion Picture Experts Group) A proposed international standards organization (ISO) standard for digital video and audio compression for moving images. MPEG-1 was defined with CD-ROM as the primary application. The MPEG-2 concept is similar to MPEG-1 but includes extensions to cover a wider range of applications. The primary application targeted during the MPEG-2 definition process was the all-digital transmission of broadcast-quality video.

MUD (multi-user dungeon or dimension) A (usually text-based) multi-user simulation environment. Some are purely for fun and flirting, others are used for serious software development or educational purposes. A significant feature of most MUDs is that users can create things that stay after they leave, and which other users can interact with in their absence, thus allowing a "world" to be built gradually and collectively.

netiquette Short for "Net etiquette," or the traditional way of doing things on the Internet. For example, sending an e-mail message in all caps is considered rude, as it's the textual equivalent of shouting.

network Any time a computer is connected to two or more other computers, so that they can share resources, creates a network. Connecting two or more networks creates an internet.

newbie A newcomer to the Internet, particularly someone who, through ignorance or indifference, violates the traditional rules of Internet etiquette, or "netiquette."

newsgroups The name for discussion groups on Usenet.

NIC (network information center) Generally, any office that handles information for a network, providing administrative support, user support, and information services for a network.

node Any single computer connected to a network.

open electronic commerce Standard EDI transaction formats enclosed within standard e-mail envelopes and exchanged between Internet and VAN customers using MIME and PEM capabilities.

operating system A computer-system-specific set of programs that interoperate with the computer system to control resources and to process those resources. Examples of operating systems are DOS, Windows 3.1, Windows 95. Windows NT, UNIX, MacOS (System 7.5), and OS/2.

page[1] An HTML document which may contain text, images, and other in-line elements. It may be static or dynamically generated. It may be a stand-alone HTML document, or one which is contained within a frame.

packet switching The method used to move data around on the Internet. In packet switching, all the data coming out of a machine are broken into chunks; each chunk has the address for where it came from and where it is going. This enables chunks of data from many different sources to co-mingle on the same lines and be sorted and directed to different routes by special machines along the way. This way, many people can use the same lines concurrently.

pagemaster A designation for the person responsible for the contents of a Web site. While the Webmaster is responsible for the technical aspects of a Web site, the pagemaster has content responsibility (see "sitemaster").

PEM (privacy-enhanced mail) PEM is the Internet standard for providing authentication, non-repudiation, and privacy via email. POP (post office protocol) e-mail is used by some software packages for e-mail routing.

Perl Perl (Practical Extraction and Report Language) is a compiled scripting language freely available for UNIX, MVS, VMS, DOS, Macintosh, OS/2, Amiga, and other operating systems. Perl has powerful text-manipulation functions and it eclectically combines features and purposes of many command languages. Perl is optimized for scanning arbitrary text files, extracting information from those text files, and printing reports based on that information. It's also a good language for many system management tasks.

POP (Internet access) Points of presence, a term used by Internet service providers to indicate the number or geographical locations of their access to the Internet.

Port First, port means a place where information goes into or out of a computer; e.g., the serial port on a personal computer is where a modem would be connected.

On the Internet, though, "port" often refers to a number that is part of a URL, appearing after a colon at the end of the domain name (e.g., http://www.apple.com:80/). Every service on an Internet server "listens" on a particular port number on that server. Most services have standard port numbers; for example, Web servers normally listen on port 80. Services can also listen on non-standard ports, in which case the port number must be specified in a URL when accessing the server. Thus, one might see a URL like gopher://peg.cwis.uci.edu:7000/, which shows a gopher server running on a nonstandard port (the standard gopher port is 70).

Finally, "port" also refers to the act of translating a piece of software from one type of computer system to another, such as translating a Windows program so that it will run on a Macintosh.

PPP (point to point protocol) This is best known as a protocol that allows a computer to use a regular telephone line and a modem to make a TCP/IP connection, and thus be really and truly on the Internet. PPP is gradually replacing SLIP for this purpose.

protocol A common language between computers over a network, such as hypertext transfer protocol (HTTP), used by the Web, or file transfer protocol (ftp), a quick software method of sending or receiving files over the Internet. Another example is Internet public key cryptography, a security scheme in which a different key is used for encryption and decryption. Key-1 is the public key; that is, everyone knows it. Key-2 is private, so that only the recipient knows it. In this scheme, it is computationally impossible to derive key-2 from key-1.

qualified hits[1] Hits to a Web server which deliver information to a user. Qualified hits exclude error messages (i.e., "URL Not Found" or "Permission Denied"), redirects, and requests by computer programs (as opposed to end-users).

QTVR (QuickTime Virtual Reality) A recent multimedia standard developed by Apple Computer that "stitches" together pictures to give a 360-degree vantage point onscreen.

RAM (random access memory) A specific type of memory in which each element can be individually addressed and accessed with the same speed as any other element. RAM is the predominate type of memory in the main memory of a computer. One of the earliest forms of RAM was called "core," because it consisted of directly addressed cores of feromagnetic material, each of which represented one bit. A faster, more recent form of RAM is dynamic RAM (or DRAM).

RFC (request for comment) The name of the result, as well as the process, of creating standards on the Internet. New standards are proposed and published on line, as RFCs. The Internet Engineering Task Force is a consensus-building body that facilitates discussion, eventually establishing standards, but the reference number and name for a new standard retains the acronym "RFC," such as RFC 822, the official standard for e-mail.

router A special-purpose computer (or software package) that handles the connection between two or more networks. Routers spend all their time looking at the destination addresses of the packets passing through them and deciding which route to send them on.

server Any computer that allows other computers to connect to it. Most commonly, servers are dedicated machines. Most machines using UNIX are servers. Technically, peer-to-peer network nodes are also examples of servers (such as Microsoft's Windows for Workgroups and Windows 95 or Apple's System 7 File Sharing).

SHTTP (secure hypertext transfer protocol) Terisa Systems' implementation of secure information transmission through the Internet.

sitemaster A designation for the person with overall responsibility for a Web site. This definition often is applied to the Webmaster, an individual whose primary responsibility is for the technical aspects of a Web site. But the sitemaster must also deal with content, corporate image, legal issues, and communication methodologies.

SLIP (serial line Internet protocol) A standard for using a regular telephone line (a serial line) and a modem to connect a computer as a real Internet site. SLIP is gradually being replaced by PPP.

SMDS (switched multimegabit data service) A new standard for very high-speed data transfer.

SMTP (simple mail transport [or transfer] protocol) The Internet standard protocol for the exchange of e-mail messages.

SR (search and retrieval) The abbreviated terminology sometimes used for ISO 10162 and 10163, the International Standards Organization's version of ANSI/NISO Z39.50.

SSL (secure sockets layer) Netscape Communications' implementation of secure information transmission through the Internet.

T-1 A high-speed leased line often used by companies for access to the Internet.

T-3 A leased-line connection capable of carrying data at 45,000,000 bps — more than enough to do full-screen, full-motion video (see also: 56K, bandwidth, bit, byte, Ethernet, T-1).

TCP/IP (transmission control protocol/Internet protocol) This is the suite of protocols that defines the Internet. Originally designed for the UNIX operating system, TCP/IP software is now available for every major kind of computer operating system. To be truly on the Internet, your computer must have TCP/IP software (see also: IP number, Internet, UNIX).

terminal A device that allows you to send commands to a computer somewhere else. At a minimum, this usually means a keyboard and a display screen and some simple circuitry. Typically, terminal software is used in a personal computer — the software pretends to be (that is, "emulates") a physical terminal and allows the user to type in commands to a computer that is somewhere else.

terminal server A special-purpose computer that has places to plug in many modems on one side and a connection to a LAN or host machine on the other side. Thus, the terminal server does the work of answering the calls and passes the connections on to the appropriate node.

Most terminal servers can provide PPP or SLIP services if connected to the Internet.

Telnet A software service packaged with most operating systems that allows the user to get onto a system over a network in the same way as if he or she were using a terminal attached to the system.

thread An ongoing conversation on a particular subject in a newsgroup. The initial message and its responses are usually linked by the user's software, so that the thread can be followed more easily.

unique users[1] The number of unique individuals who visit a site within a specific period of time. With today's technology, this number can only be calculated with some form of user registration or identification.

UNIX An operating system developed by AT&T that is widely used by universities. UNIX uses TCP/IP as its standard communications protocol, making UNIX a natural access operating system for the Internet.

upload The transfer of a file from a client computer to a server computer. Alternatively, receiving a file from another computer where neither is a server.

URL (uniform [or universal] resource locator) The URL provides information on the protocol, the system, and the file name, so that the user's system can find a particular document on the Internet. An example of a URL is http://www.sholink.com/, which indicates that "hypertext transfer protocol" is the protocol and that the information is located on a system named "www.sholink.com," which is the Sholink Corporation's Web server. This example does not need a particular file name, since the Web server is set up to point to the company's home page if no file name is used.

usage A program available on the Net that many Webmasters use to track Web site usage by visitors. Usage measures the number of accesses to each Web page at a site and cumulatively reports it for a given period, usually one week.

Usenet A worldwide system of discussion groups, with comments passed among hundreds of thousands of machines. Not all Usenet machines are on the Internet, maybe half. Usenet is completely decentralized, with over 10,000 discussion areas, which are called newsgroups.

VANs (value-added networks) Privately owned and maintained computer networks, in which network bandwidth is leased for use between geographical disparate sites or between autonomous organizations.

Veronica (very easy rodent-oriented netwide index to computerized archives) Developed at the University of Nevada, Veronica is a constantly updated database of the names of almost every menu item on thousands of gopher servers. The Veronica database can be searched from most major gopher menus (see also: gopher).

visit[1] A sequence of hits made by one user at a site. If such user makes no requests from that site during a predetermined (and discretionary) period of time, the user's next hit would constitute the beginning of a new visit. *While the optimal time-out interval is different for each site, I/PRO currently uses 30 minutes for all sites for purposes of comparability.*

VRML (virtual reality modeling language) A three-dimensional interactive Web standard, pronounced *vermul.*

WAIS (wide area information servers) A search capability that locates requested information on the Internet using a keyword or combination of keywords.

WAN (wide-area network) Any internet or network that covers an area larger than a single building or campus (see also: Internet, internet, LAN, network).

Web page An HTML document on the Web, usually one of many that together make up a Web site.

Web server A system capable of continuous access to the Internet (or an internal network) through retrieving and displaying documents via hypertext transfer protocol (http). Files can be audio clips, video, graphics, or text.

Web site The virtual location for an organization's presence on the Worldwide Web, usually made up of several Web pages and a single home page designated by a unique URL.

WebCrawler A search engine that searches the Web by document title and content. It is part of the WebCrawler project at the University of Washington.

Webmaster Generally accepted term for the person responsible for a Web site. However, due to increasing requirements in the development and maintenance of a Web site, Sholink Corp. has suggested segmenting the responsibilities and focusing the responsibilities of Webmaster to just the technical aspects of a Web site (see also: pagemaster and sitemaster).

World Wide Web The mechanism developed by Tim Berners-Lee for CERN physicists to be able to share documents via the Internet. The Web allows computer users to access information across systems around the world using URLs (uniform resource locators) to identify files and systems and hypertext links to move between files on the same or different systems.

WWW Generally accepted shorthand for the World Wide Web. Also called the Web, or W3.

Yahoo Yet Another Hierarchical Officious Oracle. An extremely popular Web site developed and maintained by Jerry Yang and David Filo of Stanford University. Yahoo maintains a list of hypertext-linked Web sites categorized by topics and sub-topics and sub-sub-topics, and so forth. Also available is a point-and-click, user-definable search engine (http://www.yahoo.com/).

Notes:
(1) Source: Internet Profiles Corporation, "An Attempt At Common Vocabulary For Web Measurement, Draft 1.0."

Chapter 14

Internet Basket: Performance, Valuation & Financial Statistics

February 8, 1996

Company	Ticker	Price 2/8/96	1995 Price Change % C1Q Chg%	C2Q Chg%	C3Q Chg%	C4Q Chg%	1995 Chg%	1996 Chg%	52-Wk Price Range High	Low	Disc't & Prem % to the 52 wk High	Low	Mkt Val ($MM)	FirstCall-IBES Mean EPS (a) C95E	C96E	FirstCall-IBES Mean P/E (a) C95E	C96E	IBES Mean% Growth	LTM Financial Data (b) Sales ($mm)	PSR	Op. Mgn.	P/E to IBES Growth	Short Interest (c) Shares (,000)	Days To Cover	% of TSO	Fiscal Year Ends
Internet Basket																										
Netscape Communications Corp	NSCP	66	--	--	7	122	139	(5)	87	23	(24)	190	5,009	(0.05)	0.18	--	--	75	38	131	--	--	4,430	3	6	Dec
Spyglass Inc	SPYG	36	--	--	60	149	320	(36)	61	13	(40)	175	442	--	0.27	--	136	50	9	48.6	26	2.7	1,092	3	9	Sep
UUNET Technologies	UUNT	42	--	6	68	36	142	(34)	99	22	(58)	92	1,258	--	0.23	--	185	50	38	33.5	--	3.7	1,248	2	4	Dec
America Online Inc	AMER	51	33	19	56	9	168	36	51	15	(0)	230	3,852	0.30	0.63	168	81	50	535	7.2	7	1.6	15,216	6	20	Jun
Ascend Communications Inc	ASND	44	59	56	58	103	696	8	47	7	(7)	564	5,263	0.22	0.59	202	75	51	103	51.1	28	1.5	1,918	1	2	Dec
Cascade Communications Corp	CSCC	102	12	25	14	73	176	19	103	30	(1)	234	3,090	0.67	1.30	152	78	50	109	28.4	27	1.6	1,452	2	5	Dec
Cisco Systems Inc	CSCO	89	9	33	36	8	112	19	90	33	(1)	172	25,422	2.11	3.09	42	29	34	2,296	11.1	37	0.9	4,230	1	1	Jul
Sun Microsystems Inc	SUNW	48	(2)	40	30	45	157	6	51	15	(6)	223	9,375	1.94	2.83	25	17	17	6,114	1.5	--	1.0	6,455	1	3	Jun
US Robotics	USRX	102	45	74	56	3	306	16	111	26	(8)	297	4,745	2.23	4.13	46	25	39	728	6.5	--	0.6	2,135	1	5	Sep
Mean:			26	32	43	61	246	(16)			(16)	242				106	78			35.5	25	1.7				
Median:			22	29	56	45	168	(7)			(7)	223				99	76			28.4	27	1.5				
Sum:													58,455						9,970							

Note: This run date is 2/8/96. Some references in the text may be based on earlier run dates (2/2/96)

(a) All estimates are First Call mean or I/B/E/S consensus estimated for calendar years

(b) LTM sales based on latest available data. Other LTM figures based on latest fully reported twelve month period.

(c) Short interest and coverage reflect most recent monthly reporting period and average trading volume for the 30 calendar days prior to this report.

E = Morgan Stanley Research Estimates

14–1

Chapter 15
Internet-Specific Stock Universe: Performance, Valuation & Financial Statistics

February 8, 1996

Company	Ticker	Price 2/8/96	C1Q Chg%	C2Q Chg%	C3Q Chg%	C4Q Chg%	1995 Chg%	1996 Chg%	52-Wk High	52-Wk Low	Disc/Prem % High	Disc/Prem % Low	Mkt Val ($MM)	EPS C95E	EPS C96E	P/E C95E	P/E C96E	IBES Mean % Growth	LTM Sales ($mm)	PSR	Op. Mgn.	Internet % of LTM	Internet Rev's	P/E to IBES Growth	Short Shares (,000)	Days To Cover	% of TSO	Fiscal Year Ends
Data Networking Equipment																												
Ascend Communications Inc	ASND	44	59	56	58	103	696	8	47	7	(7)	564	5,263	0.22	0.59	202	75	51	150	35.2	28	1%	2	1.5	1,918	1	2	Dec
Boca Research Inc	BOCI	21	24	143	(10)	9	194	(23)	37	10	(44)	105	186	1.00	1.32	21	16	20	121	1.5	--	15%	18	0.8	306	1	3	Dec
Cascade Communications Corp	CSCC	102	12	25	14	73	176	19	103	30	(1)	234	3,090	0.67	1.30	152	78	50	109	28.4	27	10%	11	1.6	1,452	2	5	Dec
Cisco Systems Inc	CSCO	89	9	33	36	8	112	19	90	33	(1)	172	25,422	2.11	3.09	42	29	34	2,296	11.1	37	40%	918	0.9	4,230	1	2	Jul
Global Village Communication	GVIL	16	29	33	(12)	41	112	(20)	26	10	(40)	63	259	0.62	0.98	25	16	33	123	2.1	12	30%	37	0.5	289	1	2	Mar
Shiva Corp	SHVA	76	(18)	33	42	19	82	4	78	27	(3)	181	1,089	0.59	1.17	129	65	52	118	9.3	--	10%	12	1.2	685	2	5	Dec
US Robotics	USRX	102	45	74	56	3	306	16	111	26	(8)	297	4,745	2.23	4.13	46	25	39	1,092	4.3	--	60%	655	0.6	2,135	1	5	Sep
Xircom Inc	XIRC	10	(20)	(29)	36	(10)	(30)	(17)	19	9	(46)	15	195	(0.40)	0.29	--	35	25	124	1.6	--	10%	12	1.4	781	4	4	Sep
Zoom Telephonics Inc	ZOOM	19	(10)	0	118	27	151	(4)	21	13	(10)	48	117	0.81	--	23	--	25	80	1.5	9	60%	48	--	78	1	1	Dec
Mean:			14	41	38	30	200	0			(18)	201				80	42			10.5	23	26%	190	1.1				
Median:			12	33	36	19	151	4			(8)	180				44	32			4.3	27	15%	18	1.0				
Sum:													40,367						4,212				1,712					
Internet Security Transaction Software																												
Raptor Systems	RAPT	31	--	--	--	--	--	(48)	69	31	(55)	0	351	--	--	--	--	--	4	90.1	--	70%	3	--	--	--	--	Dec
Secure Computing Corporation	SCUR	29	--	--	--	--	16	10	42	10	(31)	202	170	--	0.55	--	53	48	--	--	--	100%	0	1.1	112	1	1	Dec
Security Dynamics Tech Inc	SDTI	60	81	33	6	128	485	(19)	65	12	(8)	403	789	0.41	0.74	145	80	33	34	23.4	22	20%	7	2.4	153	1	1	Dec
Mean:			81	33				(19)			(31)	202				145	67			56.7		63%	3	1.8				
Median:			81	33				(19)			(31)	202				145	67			56.7		70%	3	1.8				
Sum:													789						38				9					
Internet Service Providers																												
BBN Corp	BBN	31	32	39	37	10	176	(25)	49	16	(37)	98	546	(0.98)	(0.93)	--	--	18	236	2.3	--	5%	12	--	2,366	9	13	Jun
Netcom	NETC	29	(19)	10	73	(18)	27	(20)	92	19	(69)	51	260	(1.54)	(1.81)	--	--	113	38	6.8	--	100%	38	--	880	9	10	Dec
PSINet	PSIX	16	--	(0)	42	36	27	(30)	29	12	(45)	33	517	--	(1.32)	--	--	50	30	17.5	--	100%	30	--	1,031	2	3	Dec
UUNET Technologies	UUNT	42	--	6	68	36	142	(34)	99	22	(58)	92	1,258	--	0.23	185	185	50	38	33.5	--	100%	38	3.7	1,248	2	4	Dec
Mean:			7	14	55	9	99	(27)			(52)	69				185	185			15		29%	29					
Median:			7	8	55	8	96	(27)			(51)	72				185	185			12		100%	34					
Sum:													2,581						341				117					
PC, Server and Semiconductor Equipment																												
Sun Microsystems Inc	SUNW	48	(2)	40	30	45	157	6	51	15	(6)	223	9,375	1.94	2.83	25	17	17	6,390	1.5	--	10%	639	1.0	6,455	1	3	Jun
Application Software																												
Camel Corp	CAML	3	93	(19)	270	(40)	244	(16)	8	1	(61)	216	43	--	--	--	--	35	1	66.9	13	5%	0	--	464	1	3	Apr
Firefox Communications Inc	FFOX	12	--	(8)	(4)	(5)	(16)	(48)	30	9	(59)	44	86	--	0.58	--	21	34	20	4.3	13	100%	20	0.6	107	1	2	Dec
FTP Software Inc	FTPS	13	0	(6)	(8)	5	310	(56)	41	10	(69)	35	356	0.98	0.82	13	13	33	132	2.7	34	100%	132	0.4	2,806	3	10	Dec
Macromedia Inc	MACR	37	32	28	32	83	9	(29)	64	14	(42)	168	1,477	0.50	0.86	75	46	33	97	15.2	--	5%	5	1.4	588	1	1	Mar
Netmanage Inc	NETM	12	4	(19)	40	(2)	15	(49)	34	4	(65)	190	517	0.60	0.18	20	14	40	125	4.1	10	100%	125	0.3	3,641	3	8	Dec
Netscape Communications Corp	NSCP	66	--	--	--	122	168	(5)	87	23	(24)	190	5,009	(0.05)	--	--	--	75	38	131.4	--	100%	38	--	4,430	3	6	Dec
VocalTech	VOCLF	15	--	--	--	--	--	(36)	25	5	(40)	175	132	(0.14)	0.11	--	136	50	2	88.0	26	100%	2	2.7	1,092	3	1	Sep
Spyglass Inc	SPYG	36	--	6	60	149	320	(36)	73	13	(51)	168	442	0.38	0.69	96	52	--	12	36.3	26	84%	10	--	--	--	9	Sep
Mean:			32	57		45	143	(34)			(51)	119				36	46			43.6	24	74%	42	1.1				
Median:			18	32		5	139	(36)			(59)	168				20	21			25.8	26	100%	15	0.6				
Sum:													8,061						427				332					
Organization/Aggregation																												
America Online Inc	AMER	51	33	19	56	9	168	36	51	15	(0)	230	3,852	0.30	0.63	168	81	50	535	7.2	7	100%	535	1.6	15,216	6	20	Jun
CMGI Information Services	CMGI	34	(16)	47	49	226	499	(27)	50	6	(32)	518	325	(0.11)	(0.66)	--	--	--	0	--	--	100%	0	--	738	4	8	Jul
H&R Block	HRB	38	16	(5)	(7)	(15)	9	(6)	49	32	(22)	21	3,976	1.63	1.73	24	22	15	1,446	2.7	13	38%	550	1.5	1,263	1	1	Apr
Mean:			11	20	33	81	225	1			(18)	257				96	52			5.0	10	79%	362	1.5				
Median:			16	19	49	9	168	(6)			(22)	230				96	52			5.0	10	100%	535	1.5				
Sum:													8,153						1,981				1,085					
Information																												
Data Broadcasting Corp	DBCC	11	18	23	28	61	200	(13)	15	4	(28)	187	341	0.26	0.37	41	29	13	83	4.1	13	25%	21	--	204	1	1	Jun
Publications/Static and Publications/Interactive																												
Mecklermedia Corp	MECK	13	64	236	(1)	(15)	365	(17)	24	3	(46)	342	105	--	--	72	52	--	14	7.2	--	1%	0	--	155	9	2	Sep
Overall Universe Mean:			21	31	41	39	182	(14)			(33)	173				72	52			22.9	20	53%	131	1.3				
Overall Universe Median:			17	24	36	13	154	(17)			(38)	173				42	32			7.2	18	50%	19	1.2				

Universe Totals (million) $69,771 $13,487 3,916

Note: This run date is 2/8/96. Some references in the text may be based on earlier run dates (2/2/96)

(a) All estimates are First Call mean or I/B/E/S consensus estimated for calendar years.

(b) LTM sales based on latest available data. Other LTM figures based on latest fully reported twelve month period.

(c) Short interest and coverage reflect most recent monthly reporting period and average trading volume for the 30 calendar days prior to this report.

Chapter 16
Internet-Related Stock Universe: Performance, Valuation & Financial Statistics

February 8, 1996

Company	Ticker	Price 2/8/96	C1Q Chg%	C2Q Chg%	C3Q Chg%	C4Q Chg%	1995 Chg%	1996 Chg%	52-Wk High	52-Wk Low	Disc't & Prem High	Disc't & Prem Low	Mkt Val ($MM)	EPS C95E	EPS C96E	P/E C95E	P/E C96E	IBES Mean% Growth	LTM Sales ($mm)	PSR	Op. Mgn.	P/E to IBES Growth	Short Shares (,000)	Days To Cover	% of TSO	Fiscal Year Ends
Data Networking Equipment																										
3Com Corp	COMS	49	10	18	36	2	81	5	54	24	(9)	105	8,618	1.33	1.88	37	26	28	1,789	4.8	19	0.9	4,717		3	May
Ascend Communications Inc	ASND	44	59	56	58	103	696	8	47	7	(7)	564	5,263	0.22	0.59	202	75	51	150	35.2	28	1.5	1,918	1	1	Dec
Bay Networks Inc	BNET	46	25	12	29	16	109	12	50	20	(8)	128	9,227	1.19	1.76	39	26	30	1,728	5.3	26	0.9	1,576	0	1	Jun
Boca Research Inc	BOCI	21	24	143	(10)	9	194	(23)	37	10	(44)	105	186	1.00	1.32	21	16	20	121	1.5	16	0.8	306			Dec
Cascade Communications Corp	CSCC	102	12	25	14	73	176	19	103	30	(1)	234	3,090	0.67	1.30	152	78	50	109	28.4	27	1.6	1,452	2	5	Dec
Cisco Systems Inc	CSCO	89	9	33	36	8	112	19	90	33	(1)	172	25,422	2.11	3.09	42	29	34	2,296	11.1	37	0.9	4,230	1	3	Jul
Diamond Multimedia Sys Inc	DMD	23		6	6	11		(37)	43	15	(47)	52	729	1.29	1.79	18	13	29	468	1.6	14	0.4	838	1	3	Dec
Global Village Communication	GVIL	16	29	33	(12)	41	112	(20)	26	10	(40)	63	259	0.62	0.98	25	16	33	123	2.1	12	0.5	289	2	2	Mar
Motorola Inc	MOT	57	(6)	23	14	(25)	(2)		83	45	(31)	27	34,895	3.05	3.06	19	19	19	27,037	1.3	12	1.0	9,683	2		Dec
Network Equipment Tech Inc	NWK	33	(14)	8	75	(34)	14	19	42	20	(22)	65	692	1.27	1.72	26	19	22	329	2.1	13	0.9	744	3	4	Mar
Newbridge Networks Corp	NN	51	6	(6)	(17)	41	8	24	53	25	(4)	105	4,221	1.57	1.91	33	27	25	628	6.7	13	1.1	2,226	1	3	Apr
Penril Datacomm Networks	PNRL	7	65	9	69	11	240	(6)	11	4	(37)	159	66						55	1.2	33		149	2		Jul
Proteon Inc	PTON	6	19	(6)	60	(29)	26	76	11	6	(42)	14	98	0.45		14			84	1.2	12		2			Dec
Retix	RETX	4	16	(22)	28	(54)	6	9	6	2	(32)	107	67	(0.53)					46	1.5			38	0	0	Dec
Shiva Corp	SHVA	76	(18)	33	42	19	82	4	78	27	(3)	181	1,089	0.59	1.17	129	65	52	118	9.3		1.2	685	2	5	Dec
Telebit Corp	TBIT	5	44	(39)	17	43	47	(22)	9	2	(43)	105	66	(0.27)	(0.06)			20	60	1.1			31	1	0	Dec
U S Robotics Corp	USRX	102	45	74	56	3	306	16	111	26	(8)	297	4,745	2.23	4.13	46	25	39	1,092	4.3		0.6	2,135	1	5	Sep
Xircom Inc	XIRC	10	(20)	(29)	36	(10)	(30)	(17)	19	9	(46)	15	195	(0.40)	0.29		35	25	124	1.6		1.4	781	4	4	Sep
Zoom Telephonics Inc	ZOOM	19	(10)	0	118	27	151	(4)	21	7	(10)	180	117	0.81		23		25	80	1.5	9		78	1		Dec
Mean:		16		20	37	13	127	3			(23)	141				55	33			6.4	19	1.0		19		
Median:		14		12	36	11	96	4			(22)	105				33	26			2.1	14	0.9		14		
Sum:													99,046						36,436							
Internet Security, Transaction software																										
Information Res Engr Inc	IREG	21	24	77	45	29	308	(17)	29	7	(29)	204	80					48	5	16.2			55	1	1	Dec
Secure Computing Corporation	SCUR	29				16		(48)	65	29	(55)	0	170		0.55		53	48	34			1.1	112			Dec
Security Dynamics Tech Inc	SDTI	60	81	33	6	128	485	10	65	12	(8)	403	789	0.41	0.74	145	80	33	153	23.4	22	2.4	153	1	1	Dec
Mean:		52					397	(19)			(31)	202				145	67			19.8		1.8			
Median:		52					397	(17)			(29)	204		0.41	0.74	145	67			19.8		1.8			
Sum:													1,039						39							
Internet Service Providers																										
BBN Corp	BBN	31	32	39	37	10	176	(25)	49	16	(37)	98	546	(0.98)	(0.93)			18	236	2.3			2,366	9	13	Jun
Netcom	NETC	29	(19)	10	73	(18)	27	(20)	92	19	(69)	51	260	(1.54)	(1.81)			113	38	6.8			880	1	10	Dec
PSINet	PSIX	16		(0)	42	6		(30)	29	12	(45)	33	517		(1.32)			50	30	17.5			1,031	2	3	Dec
UUNET Technologies	UUNT	42		6	68	36		(34)	99	22	(58)	92	1,258		0.23		185	50	38	33.5		3.7	1,248	2	4	Dec
Mean:		7		14	55	9	102	(27)			(52)	69					185			15.0					
Median:		7		8	55	8	102	(27)			(51)	72					185			12					
Sum:													2,581						341							
PC, Server and Semiconductor Equipment																										
Apple Computer Inc	AAPL	28	(10)	32	(20)	(14)	(18)	(13)	50	27	(44)	4	3,428	2.12	0.48	13	58	13	11,378	0.3	6	4.6	3,448	1	3	Sep
AST Research, Inc	ASTA	8	9	(2)	(35)	(15)	(42)	6	19	8	(58)	7	357	(3.02)	(1.68)			13	2,348	0.2			724	5	2	Jun
Compaq Computer Corp	CPQ	51	(13)	32	7	(1)	22	6	57	31	(10)	64	14,076	3.74	4.55	14	11	18	14,755	1.0	11	0.6	4,930	2	1	Dec
Dell Computer Corp	DELL	32	7	37	41	(19)	69	(8)	49	20	(35)	62	3,202	2.57	3.43	12	9	22	4,790	0.7	8	0.4	2,751	3	3	Jan
Hewlett-Packard Co	HWP	91	21	24	12	0	68	9	97	51	(6)	79	47,957	4.76	5.69	19	16	16	31,519	1.5	12	1.0	2,973	1	1	Oct
Intl Business Machines Corp	IBM	114	12	17	(2)	(3)	24	24	115	74	(1)	54	62,697	9.62	12.42	12	9	11	71,940	0.9	13	0.9	5,515	1	1	Dec
Intel Corp	INTC	58	33	49	(5)	(6)	78	5	78	37	(26)	59	51,335	3.97	4.39	15	13	19	16,202	3.2	34	0.7	8,064	2	3	Dec
Silicon Graphics Inc	SGI	29	14	13	(14)	(20)	(11)	5	46	21	(36)	37	5,142	1.44	1.61	20	18	27	2,497	2.1	15	0.7	4,309	2	1	Jun
Sierra Semiconductor Corp	SERA	18	69	23	55	(44)	82	31	29	9	(37)	97	549	0.70	1.22	26	15	24	189	2.9		0.6	196	0	2	Dec
Sun Microsystems Inc	SUNW	48	(2)	40	30	45	157	6	51	15	(6)	223	9,375	1.94	2.83	25	17	17	6,390	1.5		1.0	6,455	1	3	Jun
Mean:		14		26	3	(8)	43	6			(26)	68				17	18			1.4	14	1.2			
Median:		10		28	7	(10)	46	5			(31)	60				15	15			1.2	11	0.7			
Sum:													198,119						162,008							

Note: This run date is 2/8/96. Some references in the text may be based on earlier run dates (2/2/96)

(a) All estimates are First Call mean or I/B/E/S consensus estimated for calendar years

(b) LTM sales based on latest available data. Other LTM figures based on latest fully reported twelve month period.

(c) Short interest and coverage reflect most recent monthly reporting period and average trading volume for the 30 calendar days prior to this report.

16–1

Internet-Related Stock Universe: Performance, Valuation & Financial Statistics

February 8, 1996

Company	Ticker	Price 2/8/96	C1Q Chg%	C2Q Chg%	C3Q Chg%	C4Q Chg%	1995 Chg%	1996 Chg%	52-Wk High	52-Wk Low	Disc't&Prem High	Disc't&Prem Low	Mkt Val ($MM)	EPS C95E	EPS C96E	P/E C95E	P/E C96E	IBES Mean% Growth	LTM Sales ($mm)	PSR	Op Mgn	P/E to IBES Growth	Short Int Shares (000)	Days To Cover	% of TSO	Fiscal Year Ends
Telecommunications and Related Services																										
Airtouch Communications Inc	ATI	32	(6)	5	7	(8)	(3)	15	36	24	(9)	35	15,967	0.27	0.42	118	77	30	1,511	10.6	9	2.6	1,466	1	0	Dec
AT&T Corp	T	67	3	2	24	(2)	29	4	69	48	(2)	40	107,735	3.46	3.97	19	17	12	79,609	1.4	17	1.5	7,722	3	0	Dec
Cox Communications -Cl A	COX	23	(4)	16	5	(4)	-	15	24	14	(7)	61	6,078	(0.15)	-	-	-	11	1,124	5.4	12	1.4	97	1	0	Dec
MCI Communications	MCIC	30	12	7	18	0	42	14	30	19	(1)	56	20,511	1.54	1.73	19	17	12	14,529	1.4	12	1.4	2,024	4	4	Dec
MFS Communications	MFST	62	7	(8)	36	22	63	16	68	29	(9)	115	4,001	(4.58)	(5.59)	-	-	25	514	7.8	15	-	2,575	2	4	Dec
Sprint Corp	FON	44	10	11	4	13	43	11	45	28	(1)	59	15,466	2.78	2.97	16	15	12	13,324	1.2	11	1.3	1,779	4	1	Dec
Tele-Communications Inc	TCOMA	21	(3)	12	(25)	14	(9)	7	26	17	(19)	28	6,454	(0.20)	(0.22)	-	-	11	7,992	2.7	11	-	8,873	3	1	Dec
Time Warner Inc	TWX	44	7	10	(4)	(5)	8	7	46	34	(4)	28	16,909	(0.42)	(0.47)	-	-	13	7,992	2.1	11	1.1	4,065	4	1	Dec
Worldcom Inc/Ga -Cl A	WCOM	40	20	16	19	10	81	12	40	20	(1)	98	7,727	1.36	1.80	29	22	19	3,266	2.4	15	1.1	7,344	5	4	Dec
Mean:			5	8	9	4	32	12			(6)	58				40	30			3.9	12	1.6				
Median:			7	10	7	0	36	14			(4)	56				19	17			2.4	12	1.4				
Sum:													211,881						128,323							
Telecommunications Equipment																										
Adtran Inc	ADTN	39	22	20	4	56	137	(28)	56	25	(29)	59	1,553	0.69	0.99	57	40	33	181	8.6	15	1.2	214	0	1	Dec
Digital Link Corp	DLNK	11	14	(8)	(9)	(45)	(47)	(20)	34	8	(67)	45	107	0.50	0.50	22	23	35	44	2.4	21	0.6	29	1	0	Dec
DSC Communications	DIGI	33	(9)	43	27	(38)	3	(11)	64	22	(49)	50	3,878	1.61	1.79	20	18	25	1,422	2.7	21	0.7	3,350	8	3	Dec
General Instrument Corp	GIC	27	16	10	(22)	(22)	(22)	17	42	18	(35)	49	3,388	1.49	1.27	18	21	21	2,324	1.5	15	1.0	7,987	4	6	Dec
Northern Telecom Ltd	NT	50	13	(4)	(2)	21	29	16	50	32	0	58	12,668	1.87	2.43	27	21	14	10,672	1.2	6	1.5	1,885	4	1	Jun
Premisys Communications Inc	PRMS	52	84	25	(23)	39	-	(7)	57	11	(9)	230	1,367	0.29	0.70	180	75	50	50	27.2	6	1.5	805	3	3	Jun
Scientific-Atlanta Inc	SFA	17	11	(6)	13	(11)	(29)	15	25	11	(31)	52	1,318	0.61	0.82	28	21	20	1,140	1.2	23	1.1	1,070	2	2	Jun
Stratacom Inc	STRM	81	23	13	13	33	110	11	83	32	(2)	154	3,286	1.21	1.65	67	49	38	332	9.9	23	1.3	680	0	2	Dec
Mean:			13	19	2	4	26	(1)			(28)	87				52	33			6.8	17	1.1				
Median:			14	12	1	5	3	2			(30)	55				27	22			2.6	18	1.1				
Sum:													27,564						16,166							
Application Software																										
Adobe Systems Inc	ADBE	39	66	17	(11)	20	108	(38)	74	29	(48)	16	2,808	1.94	2.06	20	19	21	762	3.7	-	0.9	1,884	1	3	Nov
Camelot Corp	CAML	3	93	(19)	270	(40)	244	(16)	8	1	(61)	216	43	-	-	-	-	-	1	66.9	15	-	464	1	3	Apr
Firefox Communications Inc	FFOX	12	-	(8)	(4)	(5)	-	(48)	30	9	(59)	44	86	0.98	0.58	13	21	35	20	4.3	13	0.6	107	1	2	Dec
FTP Software Inc	FTPS	13	0	(6)	(8)	5	(8)	(56)	41	10	(69)	22	356	0.53	1.01	13	13	34	132	2.7	34	0.4	2,806	3	10	Dec
Fulcrum Technologies Inc	FULCF	35	71	9	6	39	174	8	37	13	(4)	164	239	1.15	0.71	66	49	19	26	9.4	19	-	3	0	1	Dec
Hummingbird Comm Ltd	HUMCF	42	2	41	27	6	99	7	61	17	(30)	153	576	1.15	1.68	37	25	23	56	10.4	54	1.3	142	1	0	Sep
Interleaf Inc	LEAF	7	39	51	36	1	189	(31)	13	4	(45)	65	132	(0.12)	0.24	144	30	30	91	1.4	-	2.1	150	2	1	Mar
Intuit Inc	INTU	64	17	(3)	24	66	134	(19)	89	30	(29)	113	2,796	0.44	1.02	144	62	30	424	6.6	-	1.4	1,815	4	4	Jul
Macromedia Inc	MACR	37	32	28	32	83	310	(19)	64	14	(42)	168	1,477	0.50	0.82	75	46	33	97	15.2	-	2.1	588	1	1	Mar
Microsoft Corp	MSFT	99	16	27	0	44	44	13	109	60	(9)	66	63,082	2.74	3.55	36	28	22	7,419	8.5	34	1.2	6,784	1	8	Jun
Netmanage Inc	NETM	12	4	(19)	40	(2)	15	(49)	34	10	(65)	19	517	0.60	0.86	20	14	40	125	4.1	-	0.3	3,641	3	6	Dec
Netscape Communications Corp	NSCP	66	-	-	-	122	-	(5)	87	23	(24)	190	5,009	(0.05)	0.18	-	-	75	38	131.4	-	0.5	4,430	3	4	Dec
Quarterdeck Corp	QDEK	17	29	188	67	42	780	(40)	40	3	(58)	389	474	0.38	0.76	44	22	45	93	5.1	-	2.7	1,018	0	4	Sep
Spyglass Inc	SPYG	36	36	6	60	149	-	7	61	13	(40)	175	442	-	0.27	-	136	50	12	36.3	26	-	1,092	3	9	Sep
Mean:			34	24	39	35	190	(24)			(42)	130				51	39			21.9	30	1.1				
Median:			29	9	26	14	134	(30)			(43)	133				37	27			7.5	30	1.1				
Sum:													78,037						9,296							
Enterprise and Networking Software																										
Informix Corp	IFMX	32	7	48	28	(8)	87	7	34	17	(7)	94	4,499	0.71	0.97	45	33	33	642	7.0	22	1.0	2,582	1	2	Dec
Novell Inc	NOVL	14	11	5	(8)	(22)	(17)	1	23	12	(38)	20	5,397	0.87	1.14	17	13	17	2,041	2.6	22	0.7	8,293	1	1	Oct
Oracle Systems Corp	ORCL	50	6	24	(1)	10	44	19	51	28	(1)	79	22,469	1.11	1.55	45	32	33	3,479	6.5	22	1.0	3,293	1	1	May
Mean:			8	25	6	(6)	38	9			(15)	64				36	26			5.4	22	0.9				
Median:			7	24	(1)	(8)	44	7			(7)	79				45	32			6.5	22	1.0				
Sum:													32,364						6,162							

Note: This run date is 2/8/96. Some references in the text may be based on earlier run dates (2/2/96)

(a) All estimates are First Call mean or I/B/E/S consensus estimated for calendar years
(b) LTM sales based on latest available data. Other LTM figures based on latest fully reported twelve month period.
(c) Short interest and coverage reflect most recent monthly reporting period and average trading volume for the 30 calendar days prior to this report.

Internet-Related Stock Universe: Performance, Valuation & Financial Statistics

Company	Ticker	Price 2/8/96	C1Q %	C2Q %	C3Q %	C4Q %	1995 Chg%	1996 Chg%	52-Wk High	52-Wk Low	Disc Prem High	Disc Prem Low	Mkt Val ($MM)	EPS C95E	EPS C96E	P/E C95E	P/E C96E	IBES Mean% Growth	Sales ($mm)	PSR	Op. Mgn.	P/E to IBES Growth	SI Shares (,000)	SI Days To Cover	SI % of TSO	Fiscal Year Ends
Internet/Online Services, Consulting, and Development																										
FIND/SVP	FSVP	2	6	0	14	(20)	(3)	3	3	2	(21)	22	14	--	--	--	--	--	27	0.5	4	--	1	0	0	Dec
General Motors Cl E	GME	55	1	12	5	14	36	6	57	38	(4)	47	26,604	1.96	2.27	28	24	15	11,711	2.3	12	1.6	13,237	15	3	Dec
Mean:			4	6	9	(3)	16	4			(13)	34				28	24			1.4	8	1.6				
Median:			4	6	9	(3)	16	4			(13)	34				28	24			1.4	8	1.6				
Sum:													26,617						11,738							
Organization/Aggregation																										
America Online Inc	AMER	51	33	19	56	9	168	36	51	15	(0)	230	3,852	0.30	0.63	168	81	50	535	7.2	7	1.6	15,216	6	20	Jun
CMG Information Services	CMGI	34	(16)	47	49	226	499	(27)	50	6	(32)	518	325	(0.11)	(0.66)	--	--	--		--	--	--	738	4	8	Jul
H&R Block	HRB	38	16	(5)	(7)	7	9	(6)	49	32	(22)	21	3,976	1.63	1.73	24	22	15	1,446	2.7	13	1.5	1,263	1	1	Apr
MCI Communications	MCIC	30	12	11	18	0	42	14	37	19	(1)	56	20,511	1.54	1.73	19	17	12	14,529	1.4	12	1.4	2,024	1	0	Dec
Sears Roebuck & Co	S	45	16	11	(38)	6	(15)	15	61	30	(27)	47	17,721	3.46	2.94	13	15	13	39,697	0.4	--	1.2	2,386	2	1	Dec
Mean:			12	16	16	50	141	7			(17)	175				56	34			3.0	11	1.4				
Median:			16	11	18	7	42	14			(22)	56				21	20			2.1	12	1.4				
Sum:													46,385						56,207							
Information																										
Data Broadcasting Corp	DBCC	11	18	23	28	61	200	(13)	15	4	(28)	187	341	0.26	0.37	--	29	--	83	4.1	13	--	204	1	1	Jun
Desktop Data Inc	DTOP	26	--	--	40	(29)	--	8	38	17	(31)	53	209	--	0.34	--	78	67	21	10.1	4	1.2	15	0	0	Dec
Mean:			18	23	34	16	200	(3)			(29)	120				--	53			7.1	8	1.2				
Median:			18	23	34	16	200	(3)			(29)	120				--	53			7.1	8	1.2				
Sum:													550						104							
Publications/Static and Publications/Interactive																										
Mecklermedia Corp	MECK	13	64	236	(1)	(15)	365	(17)	24	3	(46)	342	105	--	--	--	--	--	14	7.2	--	--	155	9	2	Sep
Transaction Processing and Financial Services																										
American Express	AXP	47	18	1	26	(7)	40	15	48	32	(1)	50	23,371	3.05	3.52	16	13	13	15,841	1.5	--	1.1	1,409	1	0	Dec
Checkfree Corp	CKFR	22	--	--	(7)	8	--	1	29	16	(26)	36	587	--	(0.05)	--	--	40	46	12.7	0	--	109	1	0	Dec
First Data Corp	FDC	72	9	10	9	8	41	7	73	51	(1)	42	8,734	2.20	2.75	33	26	20	1,884	4.6	21	1.3	17,783	22	15	Dec
Trnsactn Sys Archtcts -Cl A	TSAI	36	17	23	4	26	29	6	37	18	(3)	101	436	0.81	1.17	44	31	25	108	4.0	--	1.2	11	0	0	Sep
Verifone Inc	VFI	37	10	0	14	3	37	31	41	20	(8)	89	941	1.36	1.61	27	23	20	387	2.4	--	1.2	242	1	1	Dec
Mean:			14	9	9	7	37	12			(8)	64				30	23			5.1	11	1.2				
Median:			13	5	9	8	40	7			(3)	50				30	25			4.0	11	1.2				
Sum:													34,069						18,267							
Commerce																										
CUC International	CU	38	17	8	24	(2)	54	11	39	23	(4)	65	7,148	0.85	1.11	45	34	26	1,262	5.7	--	1.3	5,164	10	3	Jan
Home Shopping Network	HSN	10	(20)	6	9	(3)	(10)	6	11	7	(13)	46	861	0.07	0.25	--	38	20	1,032	0.8	--	1.9	1,687	9	2	Dec
Spiegel Inc -Cl A	SPGLA	8	(10)	40	(15)	(37)	(32)	15	14	7	(43)	15	848	(0.01)	0.41	--	19	18	3,116	0.3	--	1.1	316	5	0	Dec
Mean:			(4)	22	6	(14)	4	10			(20)	42				45	31			2.3	--	1.4				
Median:			(10)	12	9	(3)	(10)	11			(13)	46				45	34			0.8	--	1.3				
Sum:													8,858						5,409							
Universe Mean:			16	22	22	13	102	(2)			(25)	107				45	35			8.3	17	1.2				
Universe Median:			12	12	17	6	46	5			(26)	64				26	24			2.8	14	1.1				

Universe Totals (million): $767,217 | $450,511

Note: This run date is 2/8/96. Some references in the text may be based on earlier run dates (2/2/96).

(a) All estimates are First Call mean or I/B/E/S consensus estimated for calendar years

(b) LTM sales based on latest available data. Other LTM figures based on latest fully reported twelve month period.

(c) Short interest and coverage reflect most recent monthly reporting period and average trading volume for the 30 calendar days prior to this report.

Chapter 17
Media Stock Universe: Performance, Valuation & Financial Statistics

February 2, 1996

Company	Ticker	Price 2/2/96	1995 Price Change % C1Q Chg%	C2Q Chg%	C3Q Chg%	C4Q Chg%	1995 Chg%	1996 Chg%	52-Wk Price Range High	Low	Discn't & Prem % to the 52 wk High	Low	Mkt Val ($MM)	FirstCall-IBES Mean EPS (a) C95E	C96E	FirstCall-IBES Mean P/E (a) C95E	C96E	IBES Mean % Growth	LTM Financial Data (b) Sales ($mm)	PSR	Op. Mgn.	P/E to IBES Growth	Short Interest (c) Shares (.000)	Days To Cover	% of TSO	Fiscal Year Ends
Diversified Entertainment																										
News Corp Ltd -Adr	NWS	22	22	18	(3)	(3)	37	1	25	16	(14)	34	15,429	1.27	(0.47)	17	—	15	8,993	1.7	33	—	10,307	22	1	Jun
Time Warner Inc	TWX	44	7	10	(4)	(5)	8	16	46	34	(4)	28	16,909	(0.42)	1.11	—	38	13	7,992	2.1	7	1.8	4,065	4	1	Dec
Viacom Inc -Cl B	VIA.B	43	10	4	7	(4)	16	(10)	54	37	(21)	15	16,078	0.41	—	105	22	21	11,401	1.4	13	—	—	—	—	Dec
Disney (Walt) Company	DIS	64	16	4	3	3	28	8	64	51	(1)	26	33,976	2.50	2.91	25	22	18	12,112	2.8	19	1.2	45,165	29	8	Sep
TV/Cable Programming																										
BET Holdings	BTV	28	15	5	10	14	51	24	29	15	(0)	89	559	—	1.38	—	21	18	121	4.6	33	1.2	13	1	0	Jul
Clark (Dick) Prod Inc	DCPI	10	16	(3)	11	(5)	19	3	10	8	(7)	23	79	—	—	—	—	—	47	1.7	11	—	0	0	0	Jun
Gaylord Entertainment -Cl A	GET	27	15	1	7	2	28	(2)	29	21	(6)	27	2,537	0.83	1.01	33	27	14	706	3.6	18	2.0	259	2	0	Dec
Intl Family Entertain -Cl B	FAM	15	22	3	21	(14)	30	11	17	10	(12)	42	624	0.44	3.49	33	12	16	262	2.4	12	1.1	7	0	0	Dec
King World Productions Inc	KWP	42	14	3	(10)	6	13	8	45	33	(7)	29	1,577	3.10	—	14	—	11	589	2.7	28	—	254	1	—	Aug
Kushner Locke Co	KLOC	2	22	(7)	(19)	(9)	(17)	53	1	0	(7)	93	29	—	—	—	—	30	28	1.0	6	—	25	0	1	Sep
Spelling Entertmnt Grp Inc	SP	13	(5)	(5)	36	6	16	2	14	9	(9)	38	1,154	—	—	—	—	30	752	1.5	20	—	138	4	—	Dec
Turner Broadcasting Sys Inc	TBS.A	28	4	18	38	5	58	7	34	17	(17)	68	1,896	5.17	5.90	25	22	12	—	—	28	1.9	71	3	—	Dec
Capital Cities/ABC Inc	CCB	128	17	22	9	17	45	4	129	81	(0)	59	19,733	0.79	1.26	60	38	26	6,796	2.9	27	1.5	1,128	3	—	Dec
Clear Channel Communications	CCU	48	14	8	13	(2)	74	8	48	26	(1)	80	1,667	—	0.27	—	38	12	228	7.3	3	3.2	427	9	16	Dec
Granite Broadcasting	GBTVK	10	47	21	1	(15)	73	(4)	13	7	(23)	58	59	—	—	—	—	20	85	0.7	34	—	910	5	4	Dec
New World Comm Group -Cl A	NWCG	19	76	27	23	2	49	6	25	14	(26)	32	1,276	—	—	—	—	—	542	2.4	34	—	2,462	3	0	Dec
Outlet Communication -Cl A	OCOMA	47	16	4	4	(5)	182	(0)	47	20	(0)	140	321	—	1.03	—	23	13	66	4.9	28	1.8	4	0	0	Dec
Renaissance Communicatns Cp	RRR	24	13	15	26	1	20	(3)	26	17	(10)	37	729	—	—	—	—	—	175	4.2	33	—	12	1	0	Dec
United Television Inc	UTVI	88	25	25	13	(10)	66	12	91	58	(4)	52	849	4.03	—	22	—	—	165	5.2	33	—	3	0	0	Dec
Young Broadcasting -Cl A	YBTVA	32	46	18	9	(2)	59	12	36	20	(12)	59	357	—	1.37	—	26	16	116	3.1	18	1.6	10	0	1	Dec
Lin Television Corp	LNTV	35	54	12	24	0	31	18	40	27	(11)	29	1,048	—	—	—	—	—	199	5.3	19	—	29	3	0	Dec
Ackerley Communications	AK	20	3	6	12	4	126	32	20	7	0	178	317	1.65	2.00	22	18	15	204	1.6	18	1.2	51	3	0	Dec
AH Belo Corp	BLC	36	7	0	7	9	23	4	44	28	(2)	29	1,402	1.65	—	26	—	12	717	2.0	21	—	117	1	0	Dec
E W Scripps	SSP	43	(4)	12	5	23	30	9	33	24	(1)	55	3,431	1.45	—	22	—	19	1,013	3.4	11	—	36	0	0	Dec
Heritage Media Corp -Cl A	HTG	32	20	11	21	(14)	(3)	23	33	31	(2)	34	564	2.56	—	18	—	14	406	1.4	17	—	30	0	—	Dec
Pulitzer Publishing	PTZ	45	(3)	12	(25)	8	49	(5)	53	31	(15)	47	739	(0.20)	(0.22)	—	—	11	475	1.6	4	—	4	3	0	Dec
Tele-Communications Inc	TCOMA	21	(4)	16	9	14	(9)	7	26	17	(19)	28	17,487	(0.15)	—	—	—	—	6,454	2.7	8	—	8,873	3	—	Dec
Cox Communications -Cl A	COX	23	1	17	5	(11)	11	15	24	14	(7)	61	6,078	—	—	—	—	—	1,124	5.4	33	—	97	0	0	Dec
Comcast Corp Cl A	CMCSA	19	5	20	(6)	9	15	8	23	14	(16)	38	4,557	—	—	—	—	10	—	1.4	25	—	199	1	0	Dec
Cablevision Systems -Cl A	CVC	59	32	(5)	8	(21)	7	9	70	50	(15)	19	1,411	1.27	1.40	24	6	16	1,033	1.3	—	0.4	944	11	4	Dec
Century Commun -Cl A	CTYA	8	20	3	6	8	7	(2)	11	8	(25)	5	580	(5.57)	—	—	—	15	436	4.2	—	—	54	1	0	May
TCA Cable TV	TCAT	31	16	(13)	3	3	27	11	33	23	(5)	34	756	—	—	—	—	—	178	0.5	—	—	34	9	0	Oct
Adelphia Commun -Cl A	ADLAC	7	32	(2)	(22)	(22)	(19)	0	12	6	(39)	12	184	—	—	—	—	—	381	—	—	—	184	9	1	Mar
Jones Intercable Inc	JOIN	13	32	(2)	18	(15)	5	0	18	12	(29)	6	391	—	—	—	—	—	—	—	—	—	65	6	—	May
Newspaper Publishing (Pure Play)																										
Gannett Co	GCI	67	0	2	1	12	15	8	67	51	(0)	30	9,322	3.37	3.69	20	18	11	3,909	2.4	21	1.6	1,201	5	1	Dec
New York Times Co -Cl A	NYT.A	28	5	2	16	8	8	(4)	31	20	(8)	41	2,734	1.23	1.55	23	18	15	2,360	1.2	10	1.2	943	6	1	Dec
American Publishing Company	AMPC	10	(3)	1	16	(16)	34	(8)	13	9	(26)	4	225	0.37	—	26	—	16	—	—	15	—	2	0	—	Dec
Central Newspapers -Cl A	ECP	34	(7)	13	3	3	(5)	7	34	24	0	39	893	1.96	2.30	17	15	14	557	1.6	13	1.0	18	0	0	Dec
McClatchy Newspapers	MNI	22	9	(6)	(1)	5	6	(2)	24	19	(7)	17	672	1.13	1.20	20	19	13	507	1.3	13	1.4	37	6	0	Dec
Harte Hanks Commun Inc	HHS	22	3	25	18	(1)	52	10	23	12	(6)	75	684	0.97	1.28	22	17	22	537	1.3	14	0.8	13	1	0	Dec

(a) All estimates are First Call mean or I/B/E/S consensus estimated for calendar years

(b) LTM sales based on latest available data. Other LTM figures based on latest fully reported twelve month period.

(c) Short interest and coverage reflect most recent monthly reporting period and average trading volume for the 30 calendar days prior to this report.

Media Stock Universe: Performance, Valuation & Financial Statistics

Company	Ticker	Price 2/2/96	1995 Price Change % C1Q Chg%	C2Q Chg%	C3Q Chg%	C4Q Chg%	1995 Chg%	1996 Chg%	52-Wk Price Range High	Low	Discn't & Prem % to the 52 wk High	Low	Mkt Val ($MM)	FirstCall-IBES Mean EPS (a) C95E	C96E	FirstCall-IBES Mean P/E (a) C95E	C96E	IBES Mean % Growth	LTM Sales ($mm)	PSR	Op. Mgn.	P/E to IBES Growth	Short Interest (c) Shares (000)	Days To Cover	% of TSO	Fiscal Year Ends
Newspaper Publishing (Diverse)																										
Dow Jones & Co Inc	DJ	40	22	(3)	0	8	29	(1)	40	34	(2)		3,837	1.98	2.21	20	18	12	2,238	1.7	14	1.5	233	2	0	Dec
Knight-Ridder Inc	KRI	67	12	1	3	7	24	8	68	51	(2)		3,323	2.64	3.34	25	20	11	2,714	1.2	10	1.8	1,962	11	4	Dec
Times Mirror Company -Ser A	TMC	36	(39)	24	20	18	8	6	36	17	(1)		4,011	0.77	1.16	47	31	13	3,439	1.2	–	2.4	1,457	7	1	Dec
Tribune Co	TRB	66	1	11	8	(8)	12	8	69	54	(4)		4,297	3.36	3.85	20	17	14	2,283	1.9	18	1.2	295	1	0	Dec
Washington Post -Cl B	WPO	291	6	2	19	(9)	16	3	315	244	(8)		3,201	15.19	18.16	19	16	13	1,707	1.9	16	1.3	37	6	0	Dec
Lee Enterprises	LEE	21	3	7	14	6	33	(9)	23	17	(10)		1,014	–	–	19	–	12	435	2.3	22	–	139	3	0	Sep
Publishing & Information																										
Scholastic Corp	SCHL	73	7	(0)	16	24	52	(6)	79	50	(7)		1,181	2.39	3.06	31	24	15	839	1.4	9	1.5	238	3	1	May
Readers Digest Assn -Cl A	RDA	50	(2)	(8)	7	9	4	(3)	52	38	(5)		5,360	2.34	2.68	21	19	11	3,088	1.7	12	1.7	1,080	10	1	Jun
McGraw-Hill Companies	MHP	90	7	6	8	7	30	3	90	68	(1)		4,473	4.53	5.06	20	18	11	2,883	1.6	14	1.6	217	2	0	Dec
Dun & Bradstreet Corp	DNB	66	(4)	(0)	10	12	18	2	69	50	(4)		11,202	3.83	4.24	17	16	9	5,269	2.1	16	1.8	823	1	0	Dec
Meredith Corp	MDP	48	12	(2)	57	0	80	13	48	24	(1)		1,344	1.37	–	35	–	–	879	1.5	–	–	176	2	1	Jun
Harcourt General Inc	H	40	11	9	(1)	(1)	19	(4)	46	34	(13)		2,975	2.40	2.41	17	17	16	2,994	1.0	–	1.1	264	1	0	Oct
Houghton Mifflin Co	HTN	42	2	13	(12)	(8)	(5)	(3)	55	40	(24)		577	2.97	2.52	14	17	15	509	1.1	12	1.1	250	5	2	Dec
Mean:			12	7	9	9	30	6			(9)					27	21			2.4	18	1.5				
Median:			10	5	8	(1)	23	6			(7)					22	18			1.7	17	1.5				
Sum:													216,111						100,942							

(a) All estimates are First Call mean or I/B/E/S consensus estimated for calendar years

(b) LTM sales based on latest available data. Other LTM figures based on latest fully reported twelve month period.

(c) Short interest and coverage reflect most recent monthly reporting period and average trading volume for the 30 calendar days prior to this report.

Technology Stock Universe: Performance, Valuation & Financial Statistics

February 8, 1996

Company	Ticker	Price 2/8/96	5-day Chg%	1996 YTD Chg%	1995 Chg%	1994 Chg%	52-Wk Price Range High	52-Wk Price Range Low	Discn't & Prem % to 52wk High	Discn't & Prem % to 52wk Low	Mkt Val ($MM)	FirstCall-IBES Mean EPS (a) C95E	FirstCall-IBES Mean EPS (a) C96E	FirstCall-IBES Mean P/E (a) C95E	FirstCall-IBES Mean P/E (a) C96E	IBES Mean% Growth	LTM Sales ($mm)	PSR	Op. Mgn.	P/E to IBES Growth	Short Int. Shares (,000)	Days To Cover	% of TSO	Fiscal Year Ends
Computer Services - Mark Wolfenberger																								
Analysts International Corp	ANLY	30	3	1	46	14	33	20	(8)	51	224	1.48	-	20	-	20	243	0.9	19	-	8	0	0	Jun
Automatic Data Processing	AUD	42	5	13	27	6	42	30	0	38	12,060	1.48	1.68	28	25	15	3,019	4.0	-	1.7	3,249	5	1	Jun
Bisys Group Inc	BSYS	31	(2)	1	39	28	32	18	(3)	77	765	1.02	1.43	30	22	20	207	3.7	-	1.1	1,517	13	6	Jun
Cambridge Technology Partner	CATP	45	5	(22)	158	41	61	26	(26)	74	769	0.75	1.18	60	38	45	119	6.4	-	0.8	110	1	1	Dec
Ceridian Corp	CEN	46	0	11	53	41	48	29	(3)	57	3,040	1.66	2.24	28	21	18	1,273	2.4	20	1.1	5,419	17	8	Dec
Cerner Corp.	CERN	25	4	20	(7)	1	36	17	(32)	42	790	0.82	0.93	30	26	25	179	4.4	-	1.0	2,496	4	8	Dec
Computer Horizons Corp	CHRZ	29	8	14	322	72	30	6	(3)	366	483	0.58	0.85	50	34	20	187	2.6	6	1.7	89	2	1	Mar
Computer Sciences Corp	CSC	78	0	11	38	54	79	47	(2)	68	4,483	2.34	2.79	33	28	17	3,817	1.2	6	1.7	442	2	1	Mar
Cycare Systems Inc	CYS	28	1	8	72	78	40	18	(30)	57	145	0.85	1.19	33	23	26	61	2.4	9	0.9	37	0	1	Dec
Electronic Data Systems	GME	55	(3)	6	36	31	57	38	(4)	47	26,604	1.96	2.27	28	24	15	11,711	2.3	12	1.6	13,237	15	1	Dec
Equifax Inc	EFX	20	5	(8)	62	(4)	35	15	(12)	35	2,933	0.96	1.14	21	17	15	1,604	1.8	15	1.2	2,427	5	3	Sep
Fair Isaac & Company Inc	FICI	28	(0)	7	(8)	150	31	17	(10)	63	354	1.06	1.32	26	21	23	114	3.1	17	0.9	67	1	2	Dec
First Data Corp	FDC	72	(1)	7	41	16	73	51	(1)	42	15,999	2.20	2.75	33	26	20	-	-	-	1.3	17,783	22	1	Dec
Fiserv	FISV	31	16	2	40	12	31	21	(1)	46	1,404	1.12	1.35	27	23	19	664	2.1	18	1.2	92	0	0	Dec
Gartner Group Inc -Cl A	GART	53	(5)	10	146	126	58	19	(10)	179	2,556	0.59	0.99	89	53	31	245	10.4	-	1.7	1,297	4	3	Sep
HBO & Company	HBOC	90	6	17	123	49	90	35	(1)	158	3,727	1.28	1.89	70	47	31	455	8.2	18	1.5	1,097	3	3	Dec
HNC Software	HNCS	50	(10)	5	120	-	59	20	(16)	153	391	-	0.47	-	106	38	23	17.3	12	2.8	51	0	1	Dec
Hogan Systems Inc	HOGN	12	19	(13)	114	(19)	14	5	(14)	157	185	0.46	0.67	26	18	20	101	1.8	13	0.9	96	1	1	Mar
Keane Inc	KEA	27	16	20	(7)	32	31	18	(14)	45	435	1.17	1.56	23	17	33	368	1.2	9	0.9	25	0	0	Dec
Medaphis Corp	MEDA	37	20	(0)	59	41	43	20	(14)	82	1,952	0.79	1.06	47	35	26	440	4.4	15	1.1	779	0	0	May
Paychex Inc	PAYX	58	10	15	85	10	58	26	(0)	123	2,617	0.96	1.27	60	45	16	280	9.3	19	1.7	169	2	0	May
Reynolds & Reynolds	REY	39	(0)	0	56	10	40	24	(5)	59	1,654	1.88	2.19	21	18	14	911	1.8	10	1.1	182	2	0	Sep
Shared Medical Systems Corp	SMED	55	(3)	2	66	32	58	32	(5)	73	1,311	1.68	1.94	33	28	18	624	2.1	18	2.1	573	2	2	Dec
SPS Transaction Services Inc	PAY	32	3	6	13	(13)	36	25	(11)	27	853	1.67	1.95	19	16	16	380	2.2	16	0.9	30	0	0	Dec
Sungard Data Systems Inc	SNDT	35	13	23	48	(7)	36	19	(2)	83	1,374	1.31	1.53	27	23	20	499	2.8	16	1.4	37	7	0	Dec
Total System Services Inc	TSS	28	0	(9)	78	30	32	13	(12)	108	1,802	0.42	0.55	67	51	25	232	7.8	17	2.6	97	7	0	Dec
Transaction Systems Architect	TSAI	36	2	6	89	-	37	18	(3)	101	436	0.81	1.17	44	31	20	108	4.0	-	1.2	11	0	0	Sep
VeriFone Inc.	VFI	37	(2)	31	29	16	41	20	(8)	89	941	1.36	1.61	27	23	20	362	2.6	-	1.2	242	1	0	Dec
Mean:			2	7	69	33			(9)	89				37	31	31		4.2	15	1.4				
Median:			0	7	54	29			(6)	70				30	25	25		2.6	15	1.2				
Sum:											90,286						28,226							
Technical Software - Alkesh Shah/Steve Milunovich																								
Autodesk Inc	ACAD	37	21	7	(14)	76	53	28	(31)	32	1,832	1.80	2.20	20	17	19	549	3.3	27	0.9	1,535	2	3	Jan
Avant Corp	AVNT	17	(3)	(14)	(27)	-	51	13	(68)	33	308	-	0.70	-	24	38	-	-	-	0.6	1,048	5	6	Dec
Cadence Design Sys Inc	CDN	43	4	2	205	77	44	15	(2)	179	2,630	1.16	1.78	37	24	19	506	5.2	20	1.3	1,412	1	2	Dec
Computervision Corp	CVN	13	1	(18)	294	7	16	5	(19)	170	763	0.46	0.76	27	17	15	514	1.5	14	1.1	302	2	1	Dec
Epic Design Technology Inc	EPIC	34	7	63	87	8	37	9	(7)	281	468	0.37	0.65	93	53	43	21	22.7	21	1.2	283	1	2	Sep
Evans & Sutherland Cmp Corp	ESCC	22	7	25	68	(31)	25	12	(12)	85	193	(0.43)	-	-	-	15	119	1.6	-	-	22	0	0	Dec
Intergraph Corp	INGR	20	7	25	94	(24)	20	10	(2)	96	915	-	0.89	-	22	12	1,093	0.8	-	1.9	256	0	1	Dec
Integrated Measurmnt Sys Inc	IMSC	13	(4)	(14)	9	(3)	17	12	(23)	10	89	-	0.73	-	18	40	38	2.3	-	0.4	5	0	0	Jan
Landmark Graphics Corp	LMRK	20	(5)	(14)	29	6	29	18	(30)	10	140	1.24	1.48	16	14	19	181	0.8	11	0.7	240	2	2	Sep
Mapinfo Corp	MAPS	13	(6)	(38)	(22)	(22)	18	10	(69)	32	73	0.54	0.52	23	24	25	40	1.8	-	1.0	271	7	5	Jan
Macneal-Schwendler Corp	MNS	14	(10)	(10)	54	20	23	11	(27)	36	194	1.12	1.35	13	11	-	127	1.5	18	-	896	33	7	Jan
Mentor Graphics Corp	MENT	15	9	(19)	20	11	23	11	(36)	36	843	0.83	1.18	18	13	15	373	2.3	-	0.8	2,086	2	4	Dec
Parametric Technology Corp	PMTC	70	7	5	93	(11)	73	36	(4)	96	4,653	1.67	2.52	42	28	28	394	11.8	42	1.0	1,062	0	1	Sep
Quickturn Design Systems Inc	QKTN	10	(1)	0	(27)	10	13	7	(21)	54	147	0.59	0.76	17	13	25	77	1.9	14	0.5	205	1	0	Dec
Structural Dynamics Research	SDRC	30	1	1	447	(69)	31	6	(4)	396	904	0.36	0.98	82	30	18	187	4.8	-	1.7	630	1	2	Dec
Synopsys Inc	SNPS	35	13	(9)	74	(3)	39	23	(10)	54	1,447	0.97	1.31	36	27	30	247	5.8	23	0.9	32	2	0	Sep
Softdesk Inc	SDSK	15	12	(25)	2	34	29	11	(48)	34	87	0.87	1.09	17	14	32	32	2.7	6	0.4	20	0	0	Dec
Viewlogic Systems Inc	VIEW	11	2	9	(46)	(19)	15	8	(28)	30	189	0.50	0.70	22	16	16	120	1.6	18	1.0	23	0	0	Dec
Wind River Systems Inc	WIND	34	18	18	238	35	36	9	(23)	265	358	0.51	0.69	67	50	33	41	8.8	8	1.5	11	0	0	Jan
Mean:			5	(2)	83	5			(23)	101				35	23	23		4.5	17	1.0				
Median:			2	0	54	6			(21)	54				23	20	20		2.3	18	1.0				
Sum:											16,232						4,661							

Note: The run date is 2/8/96. Some references in the text may be based on earlier run dates (2/2/96). Where applicable, for companies which became public during a calendar year, the stock performance percentage change is calculated on the price from the close on the first day of trading.

(a) All estimates are First Call mean or I/B/E/S consensus estimated for calendar years.
(b) LTM sales based on latest available data. Other LTM figures based on latest fully reported twelve month period.
(c) Short interest and coverage reflect most recent monthly reporting period and average trading volume for the 30 calendar days prior to this report.

Technology Stock Universe: Performance, Valuation & Financial Statistics

Server Software - Chuck Phillips

Company	Ticker	Price 2/8/96	5-day Chg%	1996 YTD Chg%	1995 Chg%	1994 Chg%	52-Wk High	52-Wk Low	Disc't % to High	Prem % to Low	Mkt Val ($MM)	FirstCall-IBES EPS C95E	EPS C96E	P/E C95E	P/E C96E	IBES Mean% Growth	LTM Sales ($mm)	PSR	Op. Mgn.	P/E to IBES Growth	Short Shares (,000)	Days To Cover	% of TSO	Fiscal Year Ends
Advent Software	ADVS	19	(11)	7	(16)	-	25	14	(23)	36	146	0.42	0.57	46	34	30	-	-	-	1.1	13	0	0	Dec
American Software -Class A	AMSWA	5	(8)	(29)	117	(50)	9	3	(47)	61	110	0.02	0.15	-	-	17	83	1.3	-	-	28	0	0	Apr
Arbor Software	ARSW	41	4	(14)	20	-	49	29	(16)	42	123	-	0.33	-	125	55	35	17.0	-	2.3	44	1	-	Mar
Atria	ATSW	39	20	(0)	172	-	43	16	(9)	139	591	0.38	0.59	103	67	53	35	13.6	18	1.3	217	1	1	Dec
BMC Software	BMCS	56	1	30	50	18	57	28	(1)	102	2,897	2.30	2.81	24	20	20	369	7.9	40	1.0	942	1	2	Mar
Baan Company	BAANF	53	21	17	77	-	53	21	(0)	149	2,483	-	0.63	-	85	40	183	13.6	-	2.1	50	2	2	Dec
Banyan Systems	BNYN	23	1	(24)	(43)	19	19	6	(58)	30	131	(0.15)	0.02	-	-	23	143	0.9	-	-	291	1	2	Dec
Boole & Babbage	BOOL	8	1	(8)	40	57	26	18	(15)	24	269	1.23	1.51	18	15	15	149	1.8	-	1.0	129	4	1	Sep
Business Objects	BOBJY	55	9	14	32	25	61	29	(10)	92	464	0.82	1.41	68	39	48	51	9.0	14	0.8	70	1	1	Dec
Cognos	COGNF	47	14	4	150	-	48	17	(2)	176	644	0.98	1.93	48	24	38	141	4.6	4	0.6	111	1	1	Feb
Computer Associates	CA	73	21	29	76	21	74	35	(1)	110	17,740	2.56	3.36	29	22	24	3,196	5.6	37	1.2	1,426	1	1	Mar
Compuware	CPWR	22	19	18	(49)	44	39	16	(44)	40	946	1.65	1.84	13	12	18	566	1.7	19	0.5	382	1	1	Mar
Comshare	CSRE	24	(2)	(7)	174	-	27	10	(11)	147	210	0.66	0.96	37	25	22	113	1.9	9	0.8	3	0	0	Jun
Datalogix	DLGX	12	5	(9)	(47)	-	27	8	(57)	44	140	-	0.36	-	32	30	46	3.0	-	0.9	16	3	2	Jun
Gupta Corporation	GPTA	6	(1)	(14)	(54)	-	12	5	(52)	21	72	(0.60)	-	-	-	35	74	1.0	-	-	221	3	2	Jun
Hyperion Software	HYSW	18	15	7	8	55	28	14	(35)	31	318	0.72	1.02	26	18	15	147	2.2	22	0.5	37	0	0	Jun
Informix	IFMX	32	0	(7)	87	51	34	17	(7)	94	4,520	0.71	0.97	45	33	33	642	7.0	11	1.0	2,582	1	2	Dec
Intersolv	ISLI	12	19	(10)	(29)	42	26	9	(54)	37	232	0.80	1.11	15	11	33	131	1.8	18	0.5	56	1	0	Apr
MacNeal-Schwendler	MNS	14	(2)	(11)	54	(22)	20	8	(27)	25	194	1.12	1.35	13	11	23	127	1.5	-	-	896	33	7	Jan
Marcam	MCAM	14	(1)	16	51	4	21	8	(35)	74	153	0.11	0.33	-	41	-	202	0.8	-	1.8	373	8	3	Sep
Mercury Interactive	MERQ	21	1	15	38	(23)	29	12	(27)	73	331	0.49	0.66	43	32	22	34	9.6	18	0.7	119	1	3	Dec
Micro Focus	MIFGY	10	(1)	1	(33)	(15)	13	8	(25)	17	145	-	-	-	-	43	132	1.1	-	-	4	2	1	Jan
Novell	NOVL	14	8	19	(17)	(17)	23	12	(38)	20	5,397	0.87	1.14	17	13	17	2,041	2.6	22	0.7	8,293	1	2	Oct
Oracle	ORCL	50	6	22	44	53	51	28	(1)	79	22,469	1.11	1.55	45	32	33	3,479	6.5	22	1.0	3,293	2	1	May
PeopleSoft	PSFT	52	11	(31)	128	142	54	16	(2)	224	2,918	0.47	0.82	110	64	46	190	15.4	19	1.4	1,784	1	3	Dec
Platinum Software	PSQL	4	(21)	(35)	(57)	(49)	17	3	(77)	24	52	(0.22)	-	-	-	18	54	1.0	-	-	143	3	3	Jun
Platinum Technology	PLAT	12	(14)	(27)	(19)	110	26	11	(54)	6	435	0.37	0.66	32	18	32	213	2.0	13	0.6	749	1	2	Dec
Policy Management	PMS	51	8	0	13	35	54	42	(6)	23	994	2.31	2.85	22	18	18	523	1.9	14	1.0	60	2	1	Dec
Progress Software	PRGS	27	(2)	(13)	99	(14)	38	20	(28)	40	378	1.36	1.69	20	16	21	167	2.3	19	0.8	79	1	1	Nov
Project Software	PSDI	35	(3)	26	267	63	38	13	(7)	166	339	0.64	1.02	55	34	31	43	7.9	14	1.1	41	1	0	Sep
Pure Software	PRSW	28	10	(17)	0	-	44	25	(36)	14	480	-	0.38	-	75	50	36	13.2	19	1.5	30	0	0	Dec
Remedy Corp.	RMDY	75	(3)	14	74	-	78	32	(5)	137	725	0.64	1.07	117	70	47	32	22.4	-	1.5	202	3	2	Dec
SPSS Inc.	SPSS	16	(2)	(1)	51	41	20	6	(19)	42	125	0.86	1.09	19	15	21	61	2.1	16	0.7	0	0	0	Dec
Santa Cruz Operation	SCOC	7	4	70	(33)	39	15	6	(53)	30	235	0.42	0.39	17	18	12	199	1.2	6	1.5	99	1	0	Sep
Sterling Software	SSW	62	13	14	70	30	63	33	(2)	87	1,457	2.92	-	21	-	18	588	2.5	23	-	0	1	0	Sep
System Software Associates	SSAX	25	(2)	(1)	107	3	31	12	(20)	99	1,029	0.42	0.98	33	22	22	377	2.7	10	1.3	3,703	16	16	Oct
Sybase	SYBS	33	4	(8)	(31)	24	48	20	(30)	67	2,547	0.81	1.02	80	34	27	944	2.7	11	0.8	2,622	9	6	Dec
Systems & Computer Tech.	SCTC	19	0	(8)	(5)	16	30	14	(37)	39	284	0.19	0.48	23	18	24	174	1.6	11	2.1	997	15	7	Sep
Tivoli Systems	TIVS	47	27	39	10	-	48	24	(1)	97	774	-	0.11	-	99	47	42	18.2	8	-	635	1	4	Dec
Walker Interactive	WALK	10	-	40	10	(29)	11	5	(3)	126	137	0.18	-	-	-	30	63	2.2	-	-	57	0	0	Dec
Mean:		4	2	40	25				(24)	72				38	37			5.3	17	1.1	17		
Median:		3	1	35	25				(21)	52				30	29			2.4	17	1.0	17		
Sum:											73,633						15,794						

Note: The run date is 2/8/96. Some references in the text may be based on earlier run dates (2/2/96). Where applicable, for companies which became public during a calendar year, the stock performance percentage change is calculated on the price from the close on the first day of trading.

(a) All estimates are First Call mean or I/B/E/S consensus estimated for calendar years.

(b) LTM sales based on latest available data. Other LTM figures based on latest fully reported twelve month period.

(c) Short interest and coverage reflect most recent monthly reporting period and average trading volume for the 30 calendar days prior to this report.

Technology Stock Universe: Performance, Valuation & Financial Statistics

Company	Ticker	Price 2/8/96	5-day Chg%	1996 YTD Chg%	1995 Chg%	1994 Chg%	52-Wk High	52-Wk Low	Disc't & Prem % to 52 wk High	Low	Mkt Val ($MM)	FirstCall-IBES Mean EPS (a) C95E	C96E	FirstCall-IBES Mean P/E (a) C95E	C96E	IBES Mean % Growth	LTM Sales ($mm)	PSR	Op. Mgn.	P/E to IBES Growth	Short Shares (,000)	Days To Cover	% of TSO	Fiscal Year Ends
PC Software & New Media - Mary Meeker																								
Acclaim Entertainment	AKLM	11	4	(11)	(14)	(32)	29	10	(61)	12	627	0.80	0.61	14	18	22	567	1.1	13	0.8	4,757	7	8	Aug
Activision	ATVI	12	(12)	13	120	(62)	20	6	(39)	125	188	(0.03)	0.62	-	20	40	55	3.4	-	0.5	279	1	2	Mar
Adobe Systems	ADBE	39	13	(38)	108	34	74	29	(48)	36	2,808	1.94	2.06	20	19	21	727	3.9	-	0.9	1,884	1	3	Nov
America Online	AMER	51	12	36	168	91	51	15	(0)	230	5,384	0.30	0.63	169	81	50	535	10.1	-	1.6	15,216	6	14	Jun
Avid Technology	AVID	18	4	(5)	(41)	50	51	17	(63)	8	369	1.18	1.47	15	12	26	364	1.0	9	0.5	1,827	8	9	Dec
Borland	BORL	19	(1)	14	169	(59)	21	7	(8)	165	624	(0.71)	0.35	-	53	11	209	3.0	-	4.7	1,951	2	6	Mar
Broderbund	BROD	44	(10)	(27)	30	171	79	42	(44)	5	960	1.64	1.95	27	23	27	189	5.1	32	0.9	4,857	4	22	Aug
Corel	COSFF	12	(2)	(11)	(6)	6	20	8	(41)	38	567	0.56	0.32	21	37	18	185	3.1	17	2.1	2,636	14	5	Nov
Davidson & Associates	DAVD	18	1	(17)	35	81	39	12	(54)	47	654	0.34	0.58	54	32	34	133	4.9	-	0.9	310	1	1	Dec
Edmark Corp	EDMK	38	3	21	205	51	51	13	(24)	206	282	0.39	0.65	97	59	35	26	11.1	-	1.7	224	2	1	Jun
Electronic Arts	ERTS	26	9	(0)	36	(36)	42	20	(38)	33	1,420	0.82	1.00	32	26	24	500	2.8	11	1.1	3,304	2	6	Mar
Electronics For Imaging	EFII	35	(3)	(21)	218	67	50	17	(31)	104	938	1.32	1.83	26	19	25	174	5.4	27	0.8	169	0	1	Dec
H&R Block/CompuServe	HRB	38	2	(6)	9	(9)	49	32	(22)	21	3,976	1.63	1.73	24	22	15	1,446	2.7	13	1.5	1,263	1	1	Apr
Intuit	INTU	64	4	(19)	134	57	89	30	(29)	113	2,796	0.44	1.02	144	62	30	424	6.6	-	2.1	1,815	2	4	Jul
Macromedia	MACR	37	(3)	(29)	310	52	64	14	(42)	168	1,477	0.50	0.82	75	46	33	80	18.5	-	1.4	588	4	7	Mar
Maxis	MXIS	25	(2)	(33)	90	-	50	18	(49)	43	291	0.49	0.90	52	28	33	48	6.1	-	0.9	781	2	2	Mar
McAfee Associates	MCAF	50	5	13	225	170	53	11	(6)	364	1,131	0.95	1.57	52	32	28	77	14.7	-	1.1	367	9	2	Dec
Mecklermedia	MECK	13	2	(17)	365	-	24	3	(46)	342	105	-	-	-	-	-	14	7.2	-	-	155	1	1	Sep
Microsoft	MSFT	99	5	13	44	52	109	60	(9)	66	63,082	2.74	3.55	36	28	22	6,706	9.4	34	1.2	6,784	1	10	Jun
Netcom On-line	NETC	29	1	(20)	27	-	92	19	(69)	51	260	(1.54)	(1.81)	-	-	113	38	6.8	-	-	880	3	5	Dec
Netscape	NSCP	66	(12)	(5)	139	-	87	23	(24)	190	5,626	(0.05)	0.18	-	-	75	41	138	-	-	4,430	2	3	Dec
Performance Systems	PSIX	16	19	(30)	50	-	29	12	(45)	33	517	-	(1.32)	-	-	50	30	17.5	-	-	1,031	2	6	Dec
Sierra On-Line	SIER	26	4	(11)	68	86	49	17	(48)	55	543	0.63	1.05	40	24	28	119	4.6	-	0.9	1,234	4	16	Mar
Softkey International	SKEY	18	14	(22)	(9)	91	52	13	(65)	34	507	1.42	1.80	13	10	26	151	3.4	-	0.4	4,515	1	4	Dec
UUNet	UUNT	42	14	(34)	142	-	99	22	(58)	92	1,329	-	0.23	-	185	50	-	-	-	3.7	1,248	6	6	Dec
Symantec	SYMC	14	8	(41)	33	(4)	33	10	(59)	38	724	0.94	0.88	14	16	20	417	1.7	-	0.8	3,024	2	3	Mar
3DO	THDO	10	5	4	0	(55)	18	9	(42)	20	267	(1.15)	-	-	-	58	35	7.7	-	-	646	-	-	Mar
Mean:			3	(10)	98	38			(39)	98				49	39			11.5	20	1.4		20		
Median:			4	(11)	68	51			(42)	51				32	27			5.2	15	1.0		15		
Sum:											97,451						13,288							

Note: The run date is 2/8/96. Some references in the text may be based on earlier run dates (2/2/96). Where applicable, for companies which became public during a calendar year, the stock performance percentage change is calculated on the price from the close on the first day of trading.

(a) All estimates are First Call mean or I/B/E/S consensus estimated for calendar years.

(b) LTM sales based on latest available data. Other LTM figures based on latest fully reported twelve month period.

(c) Short interest and coverage reflect most recent monthly reporting period and average trading volume for the 30 calendar days prior to this report.

Technology Stock Universe: Performance, Valuation & Financial Statistics

Data Networking/Telecom Equipment - George Kelly/Neil Danziger

Company	Ticker	Price 2/8/96	1996 YTD Chg%	5-day Chg%	1995 Chg%	1994 Chg%	52-Wk High	52-Wk Low	Disc't High	Disc't Low	Mkt Val ($MM)	EPS C95E	EPS C96E	P/E C95E	P/E C96E	IBES Mean% Growth	Sales ($mm)	PSR	Op. Mgn.	P/E to IBES Growth	Short Shares (,000)	Days To Cover	% of TSO	Fiscal Year Ends
ADC Telecommunications	ADCT	40	10	(1)	46	40	49	24	(19)	68	2,506	1.01	1.35	40	30	26	586	4.3	14	1.1	779	1	1	Oct
ADTRAN	ADTN	39	(28)	29	137	101	56	25	(29)	59	1,553	0.69	0.98	57	40	33	168	9.2	–	1.2	214	0	1	Dec
Alantec	ALTC	64	9	14	82	115	64	25	(1)	159	756	0.86	1.35	74	47	36	45	16.8	21	1.3	165	–	1	Dec
Andrew	ANDW	49	27	4	10	104	65	28	(24)	73	1,931	1.68	2.21	29	22	22	626	3.1	18	1.0	1,181	2	3	Sep
Artisoft	ASFT	7	10	16	(19)	(47)	14	6	(50)	18	100	(0.04)	0.29	–	24	10	70	1.4	–	–	494	1	3	Jun
Asante Technologies	ASNT	8	2	2	91	(66)	15	3	(49)	152	74	(0.18)	–	202	–	–	61	1.2	–	–	66	–	–	Sep
Ascend Communications	ASND	44	(3)	12	696	172	47	7	(7)	564	5,263	0.22	0.59	202	75	51	103	51.1	28	1.5	1,918	4	2	Dec
Aspect Telecommunications	ASPT	41	8	10	100	(21)	41	16	0	151	913	1.02	1.43	40	28	31	179	5.1	19	0.9	1,207	–	5	Dec
Banyan Systems	BNYN	8	22	1	(43)	19	19	6	(58)	30	131	(0.15)	0.02	–	–	23	143	0.9	–	–	291	5	2	Jun
Bay Networks	BNET	46	1	6	109	(9)	50	20	(8)	128	5,678	1.19	1.76	39	26	30	1,515	5.7	–	0.9	1,576	5	3	Dec
Cabletron Systems	CS	79	(24)	6	74	3	88	38	(10)	107	9,227	2.73	3.56	29	22	26	999	6.1	29	0.9	2,421	5	5	Feb
California Microwave	CMIC	17	(3)	0	(54)	31	35	14	(51)	26	274	1.22	1.23	14	14	18	469	0.6	–	0.8	773	2	5	Jun
Cascade Communications	CSCC	102	19	20	176	153	103	30	(1)	234	3,124	0.67	1.30	152	78	50	109	28.7	27	1.6	1,452	2	5	Jun
Centigram Communications	CGRM	17	(14)	7	41	(26)	25	13	(32)	34	113	0.05	–	–	–	21	70	1.6	–	–	78	3	1	Sep
Cheyenne Software	CYE	22	(16)	9	90	(56)	28	12	(21)	78	856	0.89	1.19	25	18	30	145	5.9	32	0.6	2,012	1	5	Jun
Cincinnati Microwave	CNMW	4	(3)	52	16	9	22	2	(80)	133	64	(0.51)	–	–	–	30	78	0.8	–	–	698	2	3	Dec
Cisco Systems	CSCO	89	19	4	112	–	90	33	(1)	172	25,422	2.11	3.10	42	29	34	2,296	11.1	37	0.8	4,230	1	5	Jul
CrossComm	XCOM	11	(5)	(2)	(1)	–	15	9	(26)	23	98	(0.89)	(0.26)	–	–	20	48	2.0	–	–	137	2	2	Dec
Digital Link	DLNK	11	(20)	0	(47)	–	34	8	(67)	45	107	0.50	0.50	22	23	35	45	2.4	15	0.6	29	0	0	Dec
Digital Microwave	DMIC	10	0	(8)	(52)	–	17	9	(41)	7	158	(0.22)	–	–	–	22	164	1.0	–	–	463	5	3	Mar
DSC Communications	DIGI	33	(11)	7	3	17	64	22	(49)	50	3,878	1.61	1.79	20	18	25	1,360	2.9	21	0.7	3,350	3	1	Dec
FORE Systems	FORE	64	8	15	76	186	68	26	(5)	152	2,214	0.43	0.81	150	79	47	118	18.7	15	1.7	2,709	3	8	Mar
FTP Software	FTPS	13	(56)	18	(8)	6	41	10	(69)	22	355	0.98	1.01	13	13	34	132	2.7	34	0.4	2,806	3	10	Dec
General Instrument	GIC	27	17	17	(22)	(7)	42	18	(35)	49	3,388	1.49	1.27	18	21	21	2,324	1.5	15	1.0	7,987	8	6	Dec
Harris	HRS	65	18	4	29	(21)	65	44	(1)	48	2,522	4.13	4.92	16	13	12	3,454	0.7	8	1.1	362	2	0	Jun
LanOptics	LNOPF	10	(48)	(6)	140	170	21	7	(52)	53	63	0.68	0.90	15	11	20	14	3.1	–	0.6	14	1	1	Dec
Madge Systems	MADGF	43	(4)	1	279	44	49	13	(12)	19	1,688	1.04	1.62	41	26	40	347	4.9	–	–	266	3	0	Dec
NetManage	NETM	12	(49)	(3)	15	345	34	10	(65)	20	517	0.60	0.86	20	14	22	118	4.4	–	0.3	3,641	3	8	Dec
Network Equipment Tech.	NWK	33	19	15	14	(30)	42	20	(22)	65	692	1.27	1.72	26	19	28	318	2.2	13	0.9	744	3	4	Mar
Network General	NETG	39	18	(5)	30	(25)	47	23	(16)	73	904	1.37	1.78	29	22	20	161	5.6	13	0.8	165	1	2	Mar
Network Peripherals	NPIX	11	(5)	1	(57)	112	27	8	(59)	35	130	0.59	0.28	19	39	25	48	2.7	–	2.0	228	1	2	Dec
Newbridge Networks	NN	51	24	11	8	7	53	25	(4)	105	4,221	1.57	1.91	33	27	14	608	6.9	33	1.1	2,226	3	3	Apr
Northern Telecom	NT	50	16	11	29	(11)	50	32	0	58	12,668	1.87	2.43	27	21	20	9,925	1.3	6	1.5	1,885	4	0	Dec
Octel Communications	OCTL	37	0	0	55	(59)	43	18	(14)	103	955	1.42	2.04	26	18	15	481	2.0	10	0.9	704	2	3	Jun
Olicom	OLCMF	12	13	(3)	49	40	16	9	(28)	35	172	0.92	1.05	13	11	20	114	1.5	15	0.7	106	2	3	Dec
Optical Data	ODSI	22	(24)	15	73	318	43	13	(49)	73	373	0.69	1.15	32	19	31	111	3.3	15	0.6	487	3	3	Dec
Ortel	ORTL	14	(13)	11	(57)	(33)	27	9	(49)	59	165	0.50	0.62	27	22	35	54	3.0	18	0.6	20	0	0	Apr
Premisys	PRMS	52	20	14	220	136	57	16	(9)	230	1,367	0.29	0.70	180	75	50	39	34.8	23	1.5	805	2	3	Jun
Proteon	PTON	6	(7)	(4)	26	25	11	6	(42)	14	98	0.45	–	14	–	–	84	1.2	17	–	38	3	0	Dec
Retix	RETX	4	(6)	36	76	(1)	6	2	(32)	107	67	(0.53)	–	–	–	–	46	1.5	–	–	1,070	2	0	Dec
Scientific-Atlanta	SFA	17	76	6	25	4	25	11	(31)	52	1,318	0.61	0.82	28	21	20	1,149	1.1	–	1.1	336	2	2	Jun
Standard Microsystems	SMSC	17	15	(4)	(45)	119	31	13	(45)	34	223	0.71	–	24	–	–	364	0.6	–	–	680	2	3	Feb
Stratacom	STRM	81	2	5	110	318	83	32	(2)	154	3,286	1.21	1.65	67	49	38	301	10.9	23	1.3	61	2	1	Mar
Summa Four	SUMA	11	(18)	(6)	(50)	–	33	8	(67)	106	69	0.77	0.60	14	18	23	41	1.7	17	0.8	2,705	3	3	Dec
Tellabs	TLAB	49	31	3	33	136	53	24	(8)	105	4,451	1.11	1.60	44	30	26	602	7.4	24	1.2	2,135	4	5	Dec
US Robotics	USRX	102	306	15	306	25	111	26	(8)	297	4,745	2.23	4.13	46	25	39	728	6.5	17	0.6	881	4	9	Sep
Wall Data	WALL	15	(10)	(6)	(58)	(1)	56	14	(73)	14	145	0.26	0.62	56	24	15	109	1.3	8	1.6	781	4	4	Dec
Xircom	XIRC	10	(17)	(4)	(30)	4	19	9	(46)	15	195	(0.40)	0.29	–	35	25	127	1.5	–	1.4	4,717	1	3	Sep
3Com	COMS	49	5	5	81	119	54	24	(9)	105	8,618	1.33	1.88	37	26	28	1,789	4.8	19	0.9				May
Mean:			7	1	56	40			(30)	95				45	29			6.1	20	1.0				
Median:			4	2	29	8			(28)	65				29	23			2.9	19	0.9				
Sum:											117,834						32,991							

Note: The run date is 2/8/96. Some references in the text may be based on earlier run dates (2/2/96). Where applicable, for companies which became public during a calendar year, the stock performance percentage change is calculated on the price from the close on the first day of trading.

(a) All estimates are First Call mean or I/B/E/S consensus estimated for calendar years.

(b) LTM sales based on latest available data. Other LTM figures based on latest fully reported twelve month period.

(c) Short interest and coverage reflect most recent monthly reporting period and average trading volume for the 30 calendar days prior to this report.

Technology Stock Universe: Performance, Valuation & Financial Statistics

February 8, 1996

Company	Ticker	Price 2/8/96	5-day Chg%	1996 YTD Chg%	1995 Chg%	1994 Chg%	52-Wk High	52-Wk Low	Disc/Prem % to 52wk High	Disc/Prem % to 52wk Low	Mkt Val ($MM)	EPS C95E	EPS C96E	P/E C95E	P/E C96E	IBES Mean% Growth	LTM Sales ($mm)	PSR	Op. Mgn.	P/E to IBES Growth	Short Shares (000)	Days To Cover	% of TSO	Fiscal Year Ends
Distribution, Contract Manufacturers, and Connectors - Shelby Fleck																								
AMP, Inc	AMP	41	7	8	5	15	46	35	(11)	17	8,959	2.09	2.46	20	17	13	5,120	1.7	17	1.3	2,612	3	1	Dec
Amphenol Corp	APH	24	9	(2)	1	45	30	19	(22)	27	1,124	1.26	1.59	19	15	22	780	1.4	17	0.7	228	1	0	Dec
Arrow Electronics	ARW	42	1	(3)	20	(14)	60	35	(30)	19	1,999	3.94	4.76	11	9	17	5,614	0.4	7	0.5	572	2	1	Dec
Augat	AUG	19	6	10	(9)	3	25	15	(23)	26	376	1.16	1.51	16	13	13	538	0.7	7	0.9	202	2	1	Dec
Avnet	AVT	44	3	(1)	21	(5)	56	36	(20)	22	1,935	3.75	4.67	12	9	14	4,536	0.4	6	0.7	240	1	0	Jun
CompuCom	CMPC	8	4	(15)	204	(23)	11	5	(24)	158	354	0.39	0.52	21	15	20	1,384	0.3	3	0.8	3,516	7	16	Dec
CompUSA	CPU	36	7	2	108	31	44	18	(19)	105	782	1.47	-	24	-	28	2,966	0.3	2	-	7	0	0	Jun
Egghead	EGGS	7	(2)	10	(45)	(25)	14	5	(54)	31	115	(0.21)	0.19	-	-	10	840	0.1	-	0.6	83	0	0	Mar
Inacom	INAC	16	7	2	102	31	17	8	(6)	97	160	1.08	1.50	14	10	17	2,078	0.1	1	0.6	16	0	0	Dec
Intelligent Electronics	INEL	6	(2)	10	(25)	(48)	15	4	(58)	75	208	(0.22)	0.70	-	9	15	3,475	0.1	2	1.1	154	1	0	Jan
Kent Electronics	KNT	65	5	11	121	(71)	67	27	(18)	138	813	1.82	2.79	36	23	22	304	2.7	9	1.1	57	2	1	Mar
Marshall Industries	MI	31	5	(3)	20	39	38	25	(18)	27	548	2.30	3.07	14	10	15	1,062	0.5	7	0.7	96	2	1	May
Merisel	MSEL	4	0	(14)	(45)	(56)	8	3	(55)	36	112	0.14	0.41	-	9	17	5,802	0.0	1	0.5	294	1	0	Dec
MicroAge	MICA	10	16	26	(31)	(54)	15	7	(32)	41	148	0.59	-	17	-	17	2,814	0.1	-	-	44	0	0	Oct
MicroWarehouse	MWHS	43	(2)	(2)	24	68	57	27	(25)	56	1,341	1.32	1.89	32	23	30	1,155	1.2	6	0.8	2,400	3	8	Dec
Molex	MOLX	31	(2)	(2)	15	21	37	25	(16)	25	3,121	1.35	1.61	23	19	17	1,267	2.5	17	1.1	319	4	7	Jun
Sanmina	SANM	55	2	25	90	2	58	27	(4)	105	492	2.08	2.89	27	19	27	168	2.9	16	0.7	624	4	7	Sep
SCI Systems	SCIS	39	5	(10)	72	2	41	17	(4)	128	1,164	1.85	2.45	21	16	21	2,932	0.4	3	0.4	619	8	4	Jun
Software Spectrum	SSPE	19	3	8	43	(32)	27	15	(27)	29	82	1.86	2.28	10	8	19	368	0.2	3	-	179	3	0	Mar
Solectron Corp	SLR	48	3	8	60	(3)	50	22	(5)	115	2,424	1.69	1.02	28	29	24	2,250	1.1	6	0.7	1,058	3	2	Aug
Tech Data Corporation	TECD	15	9	(2)	(12)	(6)	18	8	(17)	79	563	0.51	1.69	28	14	22	2,846	0.2	5	0.7	49	0	1	Jan
Wyle Electronics	WYL	34	9	(5)	80	1	47	20	(28)	68	428	2.61	3.67	13	9	16	1,003	0.4	5	0.6	144	1	1	Dec
Mean:			6	3	37	(5)			(23)	65				20	14	16		0.8	6	0.7				
Median:			5	0	21	(1)			(21)	49				20	14			0.4	5	0.7				
Sum:											27,245						49,301							
Server Hardware - Steve Milunovich																								
Amdahl	AMH	8	3	(9)	(23)	83	14	7	(43)	15	923	0.79	0.32	10	24	7	1,599	0.6	6	3.3	801	2	0	Dec
Auspex Systems	ASPX	18	5	(4)	170	(29)	19	8	(7)	109	446	0.58	0.84	30	21	27	125	3.6	13	0.8	77	0	0	Jun
Comdisco	CDO	22	1	(2)	47	20	24	16	(6)	36	1,202	1.78	2.05	12	11	12	2,240	1.0	-	0.9	181	2	0	Sep
Cray Research	CYR	25	1	3	58	(39)	29	15	(13)	65	648	(0.41)	1.24	-	20	9	677	0.7	-	2.3	791	7	3	Dec
Data General	DGN	19	17	39	36	7	19	7	(1)	181	766	0.68	0.68	28	28	12	1,159	0.7	-	2.4	1,281	4	3	Sep
Digital Equipment	DEC	76	5	18	93	(3)	77	32	(1)	140	11,668	2.43	4.75	31	16	10	13,962	0.8	3	1.5	4,687	3	3	Jun
Hewlett-Packard	HWP	91	5	9	68	26	97	51	(6)	79	47,957	4.76	5.69	19	16	16	31,519	1.5	11	1.0	2,973	1	0	Oct
IBM	IBM	114	4	17	24	30	115	74	(1)	54	62,697	9.62	12.42	12	9	11	69,916	0.9	13	0.9	5,515	1	0	Dec
Lexmark	LXK	21	13	17	(16)		22	16	(4)	38	2,050	1.54	-	14	-	19	2,050	0.8	9	0.7	245	1	1	Dec
Network Computing	NCDI	6	(4)	(19)	68	(37)	12	4	(52)	31	99	0.18	1.18	-	11	16	149	0.7	10	0.5	112	1	3	Dec
Sequent Computer	SQNT	12	3	(17)	(27)	30	12	4	(54)	7	414	1.13	1.44	11	10	19	515	0.8	-	0.7	1,187	2	2	Dec
Silicon Graphics	SGI	29	3	5	(11)	26	46	21	(36)	37	5,142	1.44	1.61	20	18	27	2,375	2.2	8	0.8	4,309	2	2	Jun
Stratus Computer	SRA	28	6	(20)	(9)	21	36	23	(23)	21	653	1.63	2.74	17	10	13	571	1.1	8	1.0	510	2	2	Dec
Sun Microsystems	SUNW	48	5	6	157	22	51	15	(6)	223	9,375	1.94	2.83	25	17	17	6,114	1.5	-	1.0	6,455	1	3	Jun
Tandem Computer	TDM	10	8	(5)	(38)	57	19	9	(45)	9	1,189	0.84	0.64	12	16	12	2,285	0.5	5	1.3	1,826	3	2	Sep
Unisys	UIS	7	(2)	34	(36)	(32)	12	6	(37)	34	1,264	(0.53)	0.44	-	17	9	6,113	0.2	-	1.8	3,139	3	1	Dec
Xerox	XRX	131	4	(5)	38	11	145	107	(10)	23	14,409	8.73	10.56	15	12	11	17,977	0.8	-	1.1	1,088	1	1	Dec
Mean:			4	4	35	12			(20)	65				18	16			1.1	8	1.3				
Median:			4	3	36	21			(10)	37				16	16			0.8	8	1.0				
Sum:											160,453						159,346							
PC Hardware - Mary Meeker																								
Apple Computer	AAPL	28	(2)	(13)	(18)	33	50	27	(44)	4	3,428	2.12	0.48	13	58	13	11,062	0.3	6	4.6	3,448	1	3	Sep
AST Research	ASTA	28	(2)	(6)	(42)	(36)	19	8	(58)	7	357	(3.02)	(1.68)	-	-	13	2,376	0.2	-	-	724	5	2	Jun
Compaq Computer	CPQ	51	8	6	22	60	57	31	(10)	64	14,076	3.74	4.55	14	11	22	13,305	1.1	8	0.6	4,930	2	2	Dec
Dell Computer	DELL	32	14	(8)	69	49	81	20	(35)	62	3,202	2.57	3.43	13	9	21	4,790	0.7	7	0.4	2,751	0	3	Jan
Gateway 2000	GATE	27	5	12	13	10	38	16	(27)	71	2,166	2.14	2.84	13	10	10	3,255	0.7	7	0.5	423	1	1	Dec
Radius	RDUS	2	4	(21)	(77)	(44)	14	1	(89)	9	27	(0.22)	-	-	-	-	308	0.1	-	-	105	1	-	Sep
Mean:			5	(5)	18	6			(44)	36				13	22			0.5	8	1.5				
Median:			5	(7)	22	2			(40)	35				13	10			0.5	7	0.5				
Sum:											23,257						35,096							

Note: The run date is 2/8/96. Some references in the text may be based on earlier run dates (2/2/96). Where applicable, for companies which became public during a calendar year, the stock performance percentage change is calculated on the price from the close on the first day of trading.

(a) All estimates are First Call mean or I/B/E/S consensus estimated for calendar years.
(b) LTM sales based on latest available data. Other LTM figures based on latest fully reported twelve month period.
(c) Short interest and coverage reflect most recent monthly reporting period and average trading volume for the 30 calendar days prior to this report.

18-5

Technology Stock Universe: Performance, Valuation & Financial Statistics

Semiconductor Capital Equipment, Wireless & Peripherals - Robert Maire

Company	Ticker	Price 2/8/96	5-day Chg%	1996 YTD Chg%	1995 Chg%	1994 Chg%	52-Wk High	52-Wk Low	Disc't & Prem % to 52 wk High	Disc't & Prem % to 52 wk Low	Mkt Val ($MM)	FC-IBES Mean EPS C95E (a)	FC-IBES Mean EPS C96E (a)	FC-IBES Mean P/E C95E (a)	FC-IBES Mean P/E C96E (a)	IBES Mean% Growth	LTM Sales ($mm) (b)	PSR	Op. Mgn.	P/E to IBES Growth	Short Int Shares (,000) (c)	Days To Cover	% of TSO	Fiscal Year Ends
ASM Lithography (o,p)	ASMLF	47	2	41	48	—	59	20	(20)	141	1,410	0.84	1.68	56	28	24	308	4.6	29	1.2	42	0	0	Dec
Adaptec	ADPT	50	12	21	74	19	51	29	(2)	71	2,719	2.38	2.99	21	17	21	541	5.0	28	0.8	1,121	1	2	Mar
Applied Materials	AMAT	41	2	3	86	9	60	21	(32)	95	7,492	2.76	4.09	15	10	27	3,062	2.4	23	0.4	4,889	0	3	Oct
Brooks Automation	BRKS	14	6	4	33	(35)	25	11	(44)	25	108	0.75	1.15	18	12	25	46	2.4	14	0.5	26	0	0	Sep
Conner Peripherals	CNR	26	0	1	121	(10)	26	9	(2)	178	1,445	0.84	1.59	31	16	10	2,532	0.6	3	1.6	2,606	4	5	Dec
Creative Technology	CREAF	9	9	23	(39)	34	14	6	(38)	49	771	0.73	0.99	12	9	18	1,251	0.6	5	0.5	1,218	1	1	Jun
Credence Systems	CMOS	23	(8)	(17)	46	33	40	16	(44)	46	509	1.54	2.16	15	11	25	157	3.2	—	0.4	250	1	2	Oct
Electroglas	EGLS	20	1	19	47	21	42	15	(49)	36	372	1.84	2.57	11	8	21	149	2.5	—	0.4	385	1	3	Dec
EMC	EMC	18	(5)	19	(30)	26	27	13	(33)	40	4,524	1.34	1.68	14	11	23	1,833	2.5	—	0.5	7,929	4	3	Dec
Exabyte	EXBT	14	1	(5)	(32)	(7)	19	10	(28)	39	306	0.80	0.88	17	16	20	381	0.8	—	0.8	670	2	3	Dec
FileNet	FILE	59	(1)	25	74	33	61	30	(4)	96	826	1.58	2.18	37	27	26	205	4.0	—	1.1	171	5	1	Dec
General Signal	GSX	35	2	9	2	77	43	28	(17)	26	1,738	2.34	2.57	15	14	11	1,778	1.0	28	1.2	700	—	—	Dec
Glenayre	GEMS	48	19	17	143	47	49	17	(2)	185	3,074	1.07	1.58	45	31	28	271	11.3	10	1.1	1,257	1	2	Dec
Hutchinson Technologies	HTCH	51	5	20	71	50	91	26	(44)	93	285	4.47	5.76	11	9	20	300	1.0	10	0.5	443	2	8	Sep
KLA Instruments	KLAC	32	7	23	6	15	37	21	(34)	51	1,676	1.90	2.58	17	12	25	508	3.3	25	0.5	1,652	1	3	Jun
Komag	KMAG	31	6	36	77	17	49	11	(17)	173	1,652	1.83	2.88	17	11	29	457	3.6	23	0.4	1,182	1	2	Dec
Kulicke & Soffa	KLIC	23	2	0	121	0	45	10	(49)	130	462	2.45	3.36	9	7	20	305	1.5	18	0.3	844	2	4	Sep
Lam Research	LRCX	46	11	1	23	26	73	32	(37)	44	1,302	3.66	5.37	13	9	27	912	1.4	15	0.3	3,239	2	11	Jun
Mattson Technology	MTSN	14	7	(10)	56	46	32	8	(57)	64	208	0.58	1.09	23	12	25	43	4.8	22	0.5	111	1	1	Dec
Maxtor	MXTR	7	0	0	20	—	7	4	(9)	71	352	(0.59)	0.24	—	28	10	1,111	0.3	—	2.7	52	21	0	Mar
Motorola	MOT	57	2	0	(2)	6	83	45	(31)	27	34,895	3.05	3.06	19	19	19	26,192	1.3	12	1.0	9,683	2	2	Dec
Novellus Systems	NVLS	54	(2)	0	8	(9)	87	44	(38)	23	930	4.49	6.33	12	9	32	336	2.8	30	0.3	1,534	1	9	Dec
Network Appliance	NTAP	36	15	(10)	96	7	42	17	(13)	110	576	—	—	—	—	—	49	—	—	—	49	0	—	Apr
PRI Automation	PRIA	28	2	(21)	118	24	46	15	(40)	85	211	1.16	2.03	24	14	38	64	3.3	—	0.4	32	0	0	Sep
Qualcomm	QCOM	48	4	12	79	—	55	24	(12)	99	3,321	0.56	0.92	86	52	55	387	8.6	5	1.0	2,112	3	3	Sep
Quantum	QNTM	19	3	15	7	1	29	14	(35)	35	979	1.49	2.50	12	7	17	3,891	0.3	4	0.4	3,765	4	7	Mar
ReadRite	RDRT	20	1	(16)	25	109	50	14	(61)	39	947	2.72	3.37	7	6	24	911	1.0	15	0.2	1,782	1	4	Sep
SanDisk	SNDK	19	(8)	27	(10)	(9)	31	14	(39)	41	434	0.40	—	48	—	30	148	—	—	1.6	148	—	—	Dec
Seagate	SEG	60	2	26	98	73	62	24	(3)	153	4,530	4.41	5.95	14	10	17	5,060	0.9	10	0.6	20,940	15	28	Jun
Silicon Valley Group	SVGI	30	7	18	22	208	49	18	(40)	69	908	1.56	2.28	19	13	21	462	2.0	11	0.6	93	0	0	Sep
Storage Tek	STK	28	6	19	(18)	22	30	18	(6)	59	1,506	0.97	2.61	29	11	15	1,953	0.8	—	0.7	6,404	9	12	Dec
StorMedia	STMD	29	2	(21)	95	107	55	18	(48)	64	355	—	3.17	—	9	35	133	2.7	—	0.3	32	0	0	Sep
SyQuest Technology	SYQT	5	(35)	(49)	(44)	50	20	5	(74)	4	57	0.13	—	—	—	18	300	0.2	—	—	1,221	3	11	Sep
Tencor Instruments	TNCR	22	(12)	(10)	27	84	49	19	(55)	18	701	1.97	2.66	11	8	27	293	2.4	32	0.3	579	1	2	Dec
Teradyne	TER	22	(2)	(11)	48	66	43	17	(48)	33	1,909	1.94	2.82	12	8	17	1,030	1.9	—	0.5	1,851	1	3	Dec
Ultratech Stepper	UTEK	26	(12)	(0)	36	—	48	19	(46)	39	547	1.10	1.78	23	14	32	139	3.9	—	0.5	228	0	1	Dec
Watkins-Johnson	WJ	42	3	(5)	47	—	57	35	(27)	20	377	3.29	4.20	13	10	11	372	1.0	10	0.9	38	1	0	Dec
Western Digital	WDC	20	6	10	7	—	22	13	(11)	50	951	1.55	1.90	13	10	18	2,224	0.4	5	0.6	1,041	2	2	Jun
Zenith	ZE	7	4	2	(41)	—	12	6	(42)	19	328	(0.29)	—	—	—	—	1,333	0.2	—	—	1,184	8	3	Dec
Mean:			1	5	40	35			(32)	68				21	15			2.4	16	0.7				
Median:			2	2	36	25			(35)	50				15	11			2.0	15	0.5				
Sum:											85,694						61,229							

Note: The run date is 2/8/96. Some references in the text may be based on earlier run dates (2/2/96). Where applicable, for companies which became public during a calendar year, the stock performance percentage change is calculated on the price from the close on the first day of trading.

(a) All estimates are First Call mean or I/B/E/S consensus estimated for calendar years.

(b) LTM sales based on latest available data. Other LTM figures based on latest fully reported twelve month period.

(c) Short interest and coverage reflect most recent monthly reporting period and average trading volume for the 30 calendar days prior to this report.

Technology Stock Universe: Performance, Valuation & Financial Statistics

Semiconductors - Alan Rieper

Company	Ticker	Price 2/8/96	5-day Chg%	1996 YTD Chg%	1995 Chg%	1994 Chg%	52-Wk High	52-Wk Low	Disc'n't & Prem % to 52 wk High	Disc'n't & Prem % to 52 wk Low	Mkt Val ($MM)	FirstCall=IBES Mean EPS C95E	FirstCall=IBES Mean EPS C96E	FirstCall=IBES Mean P/E C95E	FirstCall=IBES Mean P/E C96E	IBES Mean% Growth	LTM Sales ($mm)	PSR	Op. Mgn.	P/E to IBES Growth	Short Shares (000)	Days To Cover	% of TSO	Fiscal Year Ends
Advanced Micro Devices	AMD	20	(2)	22	(34)	40	39	16	(49)	25	2,149	2.97	1.76	7	11	16	2,382	0.9	–	0.7	6,989	5	7	Dec
Altera	ALTR	70	5	41	138	28	75	24	(6)	199	3,226	1.73	2.88	41	24	28	335	9.6	31	0.9	2,786	1	6	Dec
Analog Devices	ADI	28	16	18	51	43	28	15	(0)	88	3,340	1.07	1.46	26	19	23	888	3.8	16	0.8	2,275	2	2	Oct
Atmel	ATML	31	5	39	34	94	37	15	(16)	102	3,104	1.05	1.76	30	18	28	542	5.7	25	0.6	4,388	2	4	Dec
Brooktree	BTRE	9	(24)	(25)	43	(19)	22	8	(58)	14	163	0.53	0.59	17	16	30	124	1.3	3	0.5	58	1	0	Sep
Burr Brown	BBRC	30	5	16	183	108	41	8	(28)	277	504	1.65	2.45	18	12	18	249	2.0	12	0.7	62	0	0	Dec
Chips & Technologies	CHPS	10	4	7	29	8	16	6	(39)	54	210	0.57	0.91	17	11	23	122	1.7	10	0.5	302	1	0	Jun
Cirrus Logic	CRUS	25	13	27	76	(39)	61	15	(59)	63	1,738	1.15	1.53	22	16	24	1,120	1.6	11	0.7	2,483	1	4	Mar
Cypress Semiconductor	CY	15	4	8	9	70	28	10	(46)	50	1,334	1.13	1.66	13	9	20	530	2.5	28	0.5	7,424	3	8	Dec
Dallas Semiconductor	DS	23	4	8	25	7	25	16	(10)	42	631	1.30	1.57	17	14	16	218	2.9	22	0.9	513	5	2	Dec
ESS Technology	ESST	18	(5)	(22)	44	–	40	13	(55)	36	686	–	1.20	–	15	38	–	–	–	0.4	971	42	5	Mar
Integrated Device Technology	IDTI	14	4	2	(13)	73	34	9	(59)	51	1,119	1.42	1.40	10	10	20	562	2.0	25	0.5	2,817	1	3	Dec
Intel	INTC	58	3	1	78	3	78	23	(26)	59	51,335	3.97	4.39	15	13	19	14,850	3.5	34	0.7	8,064	1	1	Dec
Lattice Semiconductor	LSCC	33	(1)	2	95	3	43	23	(23)	46	706	1.78	2.26	19	13	24	170	4.2	27	0.6	374	0	2	Mar
Linear Technology	LLTC	48	6	22	59	28	50	26	(5)	85	3,723	1.36	2.01	35	24	27	294	12.7	47	0.9	882	1	7	Jun
LSI Logic	LSI	35	7	5	62	154	63	23	(45)	53	4,586	1.66	2.15	21	16	22	1,174	3.9	24	0.7	8,969	3	7	Dec
Maxim	MXIM	43	16	11	120	46	44	15	(2)	187	3,028	1.01	2.06	42	20	32	295	10.3	28	0.6	1,314	1	2	Jun
Microchip	MCHP	37	7	1	33	59	45	15	(18)	57	1,350	1.28	1.86	29	21	28	249	5.4	25	0.7	470	1	1	Mar
Micron Technology	MU	40	13	1	80	137	95	23	(58)	75	8,661	4.54	5.33	9	7	22	3,604	2.4	44	0.3	10,394	1	5	Aug
National Semiconductor	NSM	18	(1)	(21)	13	20	34	15	(48)	18	2,221	2.17	2.07	8	8	14	2,652	0.8	13	0.6	3,476	1	3	May
S3	SIII	14	10	(23)	124	(7)	22	9	(38)	58	679	0.69	1.16	19	12	30	257	2.6	16	0.4	1,610	1	3	Dec
SGS-Thomson	STM	39	6	31	77	2	58	25	(32)	59	5,424	3.63	4.18	11	9	15	2,639	2.1	17	0.6	61	0	0	Dec
Sierra Semiconductor	SERA	18	(1)	2	82	107	29	9	(37)	97	549	0.70	1.22	26	15	24	168	3.3	–	0.6	196	1	2	Dec
Texas Instruments	TXN	52	11	38	2	18	84	37	(37)	42	10,197	5.32	5.04	10	10	17	12,307	0.8	12	–	3,354	2	2	Dec
Tseng Labs	TSNG	11	7	13	60	(45)	11	6	(6)	80	201	0.15	–	73	–	–	49	4.1	12	0.5	374	2	8	Dec
VLSI Technology	VLSI	15	6	(18)	51	12	39	12	(62)	23	723	1.34	1.56	11	10	21	685	1.1	10	0.5	3,865	3	1	Dec
Vitesse Semiconductor	VTSS	15	19	21	149	32	17	4	(8)	262	271	0.23	–	67	–	25	40	6.7	8	–	111	0	0	Sep
Xilinx	XLNX	44	8	43	54	24	56	20	(22)	114	3,441	1.25	1.87	35	23	28	467	7.4	30	0.8	3,132	1	4	Mar
Zilog	ZLG	38	3	4	24	(3)	54	28	(29)	35	776	2.14	2.55	18	15	21	251	3.1	24	0.7	304	2	1	Dec
Mean:				9	61	36			(32)	81				22	15			3.9	21	0.6				
Median:				7	54	26			(32)	58				18	15			3.0	23	0.6				
Sum:											116,075						47,223							
Universe Mean:			4	2	55	27			(27)	81				33	25			4.6	16	1.0				
Universe Median:			4	2	41	19			(25)	57				23	19			2.4	15	0.9				

Universe Totals (million): Mkt Val $808,161 ; Sales $447,155

Note: The run date is 2/8/96. Some references in the text may be based on earlier run dates (2/2/96). Where applicable, for companies which became public during a calendar year, the stock performance percentage change is calculated on the price from the close on the first day of trading.

(a) All estimates are First Call mean or I/B/E/S consensus estimated for calendar years.

(b) LTM sales based on latest available data. Other LTM figures based on latest fully reported twelve month period.

(c) Short interest and coverage reflect most recent monthly reporting period and average trading volume for the 30 calendar days prior to this report.

Chapter 19:
Internet/Internet-Related Company Financial Data

Shares outstanding for the following companies are given in thousands: 3Com, Boca Research, Cisco Systems, U.S. Robotics, Xircom, Zoom Telephonics, Security Dynamics, BBN Corp., Netcom, PSINet, UUNET, Dell, Adobe, FTP, Firefox, Intuit, Macromedia, NetManage, Netscape, Spyglass, FIND/SVP, America Online, and H&R Block. Shares for other companies are given in millions.

Data Networking Equipment

3Com — Income Statement

($ Thousands Except Per Share Data)

	F1996E				F1997E						
	8/95A	11/95A	2/96E	5/96E	8/96E	11/96E	2/97E	5/97E	F1995	F1996E	F1997E
Net Sales	497,289	563,544	595,000	660,000	700,000	740,000	770,000	850,000	1,593,469	2,315,833	3,060,000
Cost of Sales	235,550	266,719	280,245	306,240	322,700	340,400	354,200	391,000	738,093	1,088,754	1,408,300
Gross Profit	261,739	296,825	314,755	353,760	377,300	399,600	415,800	459,000	855,376	1,227,079	1,651,700
S&M	102,211	118,920	119,595	130,680	137,900	145,780	150,150	165,750	319,310	471,406	599,580
R&D	51,548	56,082	60,000	66,500	69,000	72,000	76,000	83,000	166,327	234,130	300,000
G&A	20,941	22,902	24,000	26,500	27,000	28,500	30,000	33,000	66,462	94,343	118,500
Total Operating Expenses	174,700	197,904	203,595	223,680	233,900	246,280	256,150	281,750	552,099	799,879	1,018,080
Operating Income	87,039	98,921	111,160	130,080	143,400	153,320	159,650	177,250	303,277	427,200	633,620
Other Income, net	1,253	1,930	550	550	900	1,000	1,100	1,200	4,895	4,283	4,200
Special Items	(1,700)										
Pretax Income	88,292	100,851	111,710	130,630	144,300	154,320	160,750	178,450	308,172	431,483	637,820
Taxes	30,871	(1) 35,600	39,099	45,721	50,505	54,012	56,263	62,458	84,792	151,290	223,237
Income Before Minority Interest	57,421	65,251	72,612	84,910	93,795	100,308	104,488	115,993	223,380	280,193	414,583
Minority Interest											
Net Income	57,421	65,251	72,612	84,910	93,795	100,308	104,488	115,993	223,380	280,193	414,583
EPS	$0.33	(1) $0.37	$0.41	$0.47	$0.51	$0.54	$0.55	$0.60	$1.31	$1.58	$2.20
Shares Outstanding (fully diluted)	174,833	176,396	178,896	181,396	184,096	186,896	189,796	192,796	171,079	177,880	188,396
Growth Rate											
Revenues (yr-yr)	58%	50%	40%	39%	41%	31%	29%	29%	497%	45%	32%
Revenues (seq.)	4%	13%	6%	11%	6%	6%	4%	10%	--	--	--
Expenses (yr-yr)	54%	52%	40%	37%	34%	24%	26%	26%	142%	45%	27%
Expenses (seq.)	7%	13%	3%	10%	5%	5%	4%	10%	--	--	--
Net income (seq.)	-5%	14%	11%	17%	10%	7%	4%	11%			
Net Income (yr-yr)	52%	-5%	29%	41%	63%	54%	44%	37%	-326%	25%	48%
EPS (yr-yr)	45%	-9%	23%	34%	55%	45%	36%	29%	472%	48%	40%
Margin Analysis											
Gross Margin	52.6%	52.7%	52.9%	53.6%	53.9%	54.0%	54.0%	54.0%	53.7%	53.0%	54.0%
Operating Margin	17.5%	17.6%	18.7%	19.7%	20.5%	20.7%	20.7%	20.9%	19.0%	18.4%	20.7%
Pretax Margin	17.8%	17.9%	18.8%	19.8%	20.6%	20.9%	20.9%	21.0%	19.3%	18.6%	20.8%
Net Margin	11.5%	11.6%	12.2%	12.9%	13.4%	13.6%	13.6%	13.6%	14.0%	12.1%	13.5%
Expenses as Pct. of Revenue											
S&M	20.6%	21.1%	20.1%	19.8%	19.7%	19.7%	19.5%	19.5%	20.0%	20.4%	19.6%
R&D	10.4%	10.0%	10.1%	10.1%	9.9%	9.7%	9.9%	9.8%	10.4%	10.1%	9.8%
G&A	4.2%	4.1%	4.0%	4.0%	3.9%	3.9%	3.9%	3.9%	4.2%	4.1%	3.9%
Total Operating Expenses	35.1%	35.1%	34.2%	33.9%	33.4%	33.3%	33.3%	33.1%	34.6%	34.5%	33.3%
Tax Rate	35.0%	35.3%	35.0%	35.0%	35.0%	35.0%	35.0%	35.0%	27.5%	35.1%	35.0%

1Q96 excludes one-time items.
F1995 also excludes $60.796 million purchased in-process technology and $5 million nonrecurring items.
A = Actual   E = Morgan Stanley Research Estimates.

Ascend Communications — Earnings Model 1993-1997E

($ Millions Except EPS)

	1995A				1996E				Full Year			
	Mar	Jun	Sep	Dec	Mar	Jun	Sep	Dec	1994A	1995A	1996E	1997E
Revenue	**$20.4**	**$28.6**	**$40.0**	**$60.6**	**$70.0**	**$76.0**	**$84.0**	**$90.0**	**$39.3**	**$149.6**	**$320.0**	**$540.0**
Cost of Revenue	$7.0	$9.8	$13.8	$20.6	$24.1	$26.1	$29.1	$31.6	$13.2	$51.2	$110.9	$187.9
Sales & Marketing	4.6	6.7	9.4	13.2	15.9	17.1	18.7	19.8	10.5	33.9	71.5	119.9
General & Administrative	1.7	1.9	2.3	2.2	2.9	3.0	3.4	3.4	3.1	8.0	12.8	21.6
R&D	1.9	1.9	2.3	3.5	5.0	5.3	5.7	6.0	3.6	9.6	22.1	36.7
Purchased Technology Write-off			3.0									
Operating Income	$5.2	$8.3	$12.3	$21.1	$22.1	$24.5	$27.0	$29.2	$9.0	$46.9	$102.7	$173.9
Other Income	0.4	0.4	2.1	2.6	3.0	3.3	3.6	3.9	0.9	5.5	13.9	17.0
Effective Tax Rate	38.0%	38.0%	38.0%	38.0%	38.0%	38.0%	38.0%	38.0%	12.2%	38.0%	38.0%	38.0%
Pretax Income	$5.6	$8.6	$14.5	$23.7	$25.1	$27.8	$30.7	$33.1	$9.9	$52.4	$116.7	$190.9
Taxes	2.1	3.3	5.5	9.0	9.5	10.6	11.7	12.6	1.2	19.9	44.3	72.5
Net Income	$3.5	$5.3	$9.0	$14.7	$15.5	$17.2	$19.0	$20.5	$8.7	$32.5	$72.3	$118.3
Earnings Per Share	**$0.03**	**$0.05**	**$0.08**	**$0.12**	**$0.13**	**$0.14**	**$0.16**	**$0.17**	**$0.09**	**$0.30**	**$0.59**	**$0.95**
EPS Fully Taxed at 37.5%	NM	NM	NM	NM	NM	NM	NM	NM	$0.07	NM	NM	NM
Avg. Shares	101.2	102.5	112.6	119.6	120.6	121.6	122.6	123.6	93.3	109.0	122.1	125.0
Margin Analysis												
Total Revenue	100.0	100.0	100.0	100.0	100.0	100.0	100.0	100.0	100.0	100.0	100.0	100.0
Gross Margin	65.6	65.6	65.6	66.1	65.6	65.7	65.3	64.9	66.4	65.8	65.3	65.2
Sales & Marketing	22.6	23.5	23.4	21.8	22.7	22.5	22.3	22.0	26.6	22.7	22.4	22.2
General & Administrative	8.3	6.5	5.6	3.7	4.2	4.0	4.0	3.8	7.8	5.4	4.0	4.0
R&D	9.3	6.7	5.8	5.7	7.2	7.0	6.8	6.7	9.1	6.4	6.9	6.8
Operating Income	25.4	28.9	30.8	34.8	31.5	32.2	32.2	32.4	22.9	31.3	32.1	32.2
Pretax Income	27.4	30.2	36.1	39.1	35.8	36.6	36.5	36.8	25.2	35.0	36.5	35.3
Net Income	17.0	18.7	22.4	24.2	22.2	22.7	22.7	22.8	22.1	21.7	22.6	21.9
Year-Over-Year Growth (%)												
Total Revenue	199	247	289	333	244	166	110	48	143	280	114	69
Cost of Revenue	190	262	304	341	244	165	112	54	136	288	117	69
Sales & Marketing	130	200	249	272	245	154	100	50	91	224	111	68
General & Administrative	244	164	226	92	75	63	49	53	64	163	59	69
R&D	231	175	121	173	167	178	146	73	81	167	130	66
Operating Income	287	339	401	532	326	196	119	38	595	420	119	69
Pretax Income	315	331	409	538	349	223	112	40	634	429	123	64
Net Income	168	197	260	371	348	223	112	40	545	273	123	64
Sequential Quarterly Growth (%)												
Total Revenue	45	40	40	51	15	9	11	7				
Cost of Revenue	50	40	40	49	17	8	12	8				
Sales & Marketing	30	46	39	41	20	8	10	6				
General & Administrative	44	11	21	(1)	31	3	11	2				
R&D	48	1	21	50	45	6	7	6				
Operating Income	55	59	49	71	5	11	11	8				
Pretax Income	50	54	68	64	6	11	10	8				
Net Income	11	54	68	64	6	11	10	8				

3Q95 excludes $3.0 million write-off of purchased technology from Dayna Communications.

A = Actual   E = Morgan Stanley Research Estimates.

Boca Research — Financial Summary F1993–F1995

($ Thousands Except EPS)

	3/94	6/94	9/94	12/94	3/95	6/95	9/95	12/95	F1993	F1994	F1995
		F1994				F1995					
Net Sales	20,698	19,104	20,544	23,248	27,269	33,196	37,350	45,223	64,717	83,594	143,038
Cost of Goods Sold	14,711	14,235	15,096	17,242	19,799	24,769	27,829	35,089	45,142	61,284	107,486
Gross Profit	5,987	4,869	5,448	6,006	7,470	8,427	9,521	10,134	19,575	22,310	35,552
Operating Expenses:											
Research and Development	403	304	363	368	524	723	839	593	1,493	1,438	2,679
General & Administrative/Sales & Marketing	3,441	2,820	3,107	3,023	3,999	4,467	4,951	5,052	12,526	12,391	18,469
Other Expenses									1,938		
Total Operating Expenses	3,844	3,124	3,470	3,391	4,523	5,190	5,790	5,645	15,957	13,829	21,148
Operating Income	2,143	1,745	1,978	2,615	2,947	3,237	3,731	4,489	3,618	8,481	14,404
Non-Operating Income	57	142	95	178	182	174	63	121	320	472	540
Pretax Income	2,200	1,887	2,073	2,793	3,129	3,411	3,794	4,610	3,938	8,953	14,944
Income Taxes	760	713	747	997	1,126	1,228	1,372	1,676	1,204	3,217	5,402
Net Income	1,440	1,174	1,326	1,796	2,003	2,183	2,422	2,934	2,733	5,736	9,542
EPS (fully diluted)	$0.17	$0.14	$0.16	$0.21	$0.23	$0.24	$0.27	$0.32	$0.33	$0.68	$1.07
Shares Outstanding	8,431	8,452	8,450	8,459	8,692	9,047	9,087	9,081	8,316	8,460	8,921
Growth Rate											
Revenues (yr-yr)	--	21%	29%	22%	32%	74%	82%	95%	--	29%	71%
Revenues (seq.)	8%	-8%	8%	13%	17%	22%	13%	21%	--	--	--
Expenses (yr-yr)	--	10%	3%	-53%	18%	66%	67%	66%	--	-13%	53%
Expenses (seq.)	-47%	-19%	11%	-2%	33%	15%	12%	-3%	--	--	--
EPS (yr-yr)	--	-28%	8%	-191%	35%	74%	70%	52%	--	106%	58%
Margin Analysis											
Gross Margin	28.9%	25.5%	26.5%	25.8%	27.4%	25.4%	25.5%	22.4%	30.2%	26.7%	24.9%
Operating Margin	10.4%	9.1%	9.6%	11.2%	10.8%	9.8%	10.0%	9.9%	5.6%	10.1%	10.1%
Pretax Margin	10.6%	9.9%	10.1%	12.0%	11.5%	10.3%	10.2%	10.2%	6.1%	10.7%	10.4%
Net Margin	7.0%	6.1%	6.5%	7.7%	7.3%	6.6%	6.5%	6.5%	4.2%	6.9%	6.7%
Expenses as Pct. of Revenue											
R&D	1.9%	1.6%	1.8%	1.6%	1.9%	2.2%	2.2%	1.3%	2.3%	1.7%	1.9%
S&M/G&A	16.6%	14.8%	15.1%	13.0%	14.7%	13.5%	13.3%	11.2%	19.4%	14.8%	12.9%
Total Operating Expenses	18.6%	16.4%	16.9%	14.6%	16.6%	15.6%	15.5%	12.5%	24.7%	16.5%	14.8%
Tax Rate	34.5%	37.8%	36.0%	35.7%	36.0%	36.0%	36.2%	36.4%	30.6%	35.9%	36.1%

Fiscal Year ends in December.

19 – 6

Cisco Systems — Income Statement

($ Thousands Except Per Share Data)

	F1996E				F1997E				F1995	F1996E	F1997E
	10/95A	1/96A	4/96E	7/96E	10/96E	1/97E	4/97E	7/97E			
Net Sales	710,191	826,482	904,500	1,000,000	1,120,000	1,200,000	1,280,000	1,400,000	1,978,916	3,441,173	5,000,000
Cost of Sales	234,403	277,597	306,626	342,000	387,520	418,800	450,560	497,000	644,152	1,160,626	1,753,880
Gross Profit	475,788	548,885	597,875	658,000	732,480	781,200	829,440	903,000	1,334,764	2,280,548	3,246,120
R&D	62,865	73,262	81,000	92,000	102,000	110,000	118,000	129,000	164,819	309,127	459,000
S&M	129,011	146,895	159,192	177,000	196,000	210,000	224,000	245,000	354,722	612,098	875,000
G&A	25,736	28,826	31,000	34,000	38,000	40,000	44,000	48,000	76,524	119,562	170,000
Total Operating Expenses	217,612	248,983	271,192	303,000	336,000	360,000	386,000	422,000	596,065	1,040,787	1,504,000
Operating Income	258,176	299,902	326,683	355,000	396,480	421,200	443,440	481,000	738,699	1,239,761	1,742,120
Interest Income, net	11,819	14,258	17,000	20,000	23,000	27,000	31,000	35,000	36,107	63,077	116,000
Pretax Income	269,995	314,160	343,683	375,000	419,480	448,200	474,440	516,000	774,806	1,302,838	1,858,120
Taxes	101,248	117,810	128,881	140,625	157,305	168,075	177,915	193,500	294,427	488,564	696,795
Net Income	168,747	196,350	214,802	234,375	262,175	280,125	296,525	322,500	480,379	814,274	1,161,325
EPS	$0.59	$0.67	$0.72	$0.77	$0.85	$0.90	$0.94	$1.00	$1.73	$2.75	$3.70
Shares Outstanding (000)	286,041	292,647	298,000	304,000	307,000	310,000	315,000	322,000	276,858	295,172	313,500
Growth Rate											
Revenues (yr-yr)	81%	82%	77%	61%	58%	45%	42%	40%	59%	74%	45%
Revenues (seq.)	14%	16%	9%	11%	12%	7%	7%	9%	--	--	--
Expenses (yr-yr)	92%	88%	77%	54%	54%	45%	42%	39%	74%	75%	45%
Expenses (seq.)	11%	14%	9%	12%	11%	7%	7%	9%	--	--	--
EPS (yr-yr)	61%	66%	60%	51%	45%	35%	31%	30%	46%	59%	34%
Margin Analysis											
Gross Margin	67.0%	66.4%	66.1%	65.8%	65.4%	65.1%	64.8%	64.5%	67.4%	66.3%	64.9%
Operating Margin	36.4%	36.3%	36.1%	35.5%	35.4%	35.1%	34.6%	34.4%	37.3%	36.0%	34.8%
Pretax Margin	38.0%	38.0%	38.0%	37.5%	37.5%	37.4%	37.1%	36.9%	39.2%	37.9%	37.2%
Net Margin	23.8%	23.8%	23.7%	23.4%	23.4%	23.3%	23.2%	23.0%	24.3%	23.7%	23.2%
Expenses as Pct. of Revenue											
R&D	8.9%	8.9%	9.0%	9.2%	9.1%	9.2%	9.2%	9.2%	8.3%	9.0%	9.2%
S&M	18.2%	17.8%	17.6%	17.7%	17.5%	17.5%	17.5%	17.5%	17.9%	17.8%	17.5%
G&A	3.6%	3.5%	3.4%	3.4%	3.4%	3.3%	3.3%	3.3%	3.9%	3.5%	3.4%
Total Operating Expenses	30.6%	30.1%	30.0%	30.3%	30.0%	30.0%	30.2%	30.1%	30.1%	30.2%	30.1%
Tax Rate	37.5%	37.5%	37.5%	37.5%	37.5%	37.5%	37.5%	37.5%	38.0%	37.5%	37.5%

2Q95 excludes a $96 million one-time charge for purchased R&D and assumes an effective 38.0% tax rate.
A = Actual   E = Morgan Stanley Research Estimates.   Fiscal year ends in July.

Motorola — Income Statement 1994–1997E

($ Millions Except EPS)

	1996E Q1	Q2	Q3	Q4	1997E Q1	Q2	Q3	Q4	Full Year 1994A	1995A	1996E	1997E
Net Sales ($M)	6,725	7,800	8,154	8,736	8,125	9,400	9,620	9,975	22,245	27,037	31,415	37,120
Sequential growth	-8%	16%	5%	7%	-7%	16%	2%	4%		3.4%	5.0%	3.7%
Cost of Sales	3,957	4,555	4,729	4,980	4,704	5,396	5,455	5,651	11,900	15,348	18,221	21,205
Depreciation	477	554	587	629	593	686	693	718	1,525	1,919	2,247	2,690
Gross Profit	2,291	2,691	2,838	3,127	2,828	3,318	3,473	3,606	8,820	9,770	10,947	13,224
SG&A	1,123	1,303	1,362	1,450	1,357	1,570	1,616	1,676	4,381	4,642	5,238	6,219
R&D	558	647	677	725	683	790	808	838	1,860	2,197	2,607	3,118
Interest	40	47	49	52	41	47	48	50	142	149	188	186
Extraordinary Items	0	0	0	0	0	0	0	0	0	0	0	0
Pretax Income	569	694	750	900	748	912	1,000	1,042	2,437	2,782	2,913	3,702
Taxes	199	243	263	315	262	319	350	365	877	1,001	1,020	1,296
Net Income	370	451	488	585	486	593	650	678	1,560	1,781	1,894	2,406
Shares Out.	613	618	622	625	628	632	635	638	593	610	622	633
EPS	**$0.60**	**$0.73**	**$0.78**	**$0.94**	**$0.77**	**$0.94**	**$1.02**	**$1.06**	**$2.65**	**$2.93**	**$3.05**	**$3.80**
Margins:												
Cost of Goods Sold	58.8%	58.4%	58.0%	57.0%	57.9%	57.4%	56.7%	56.7%	53.5%	56.8%	58.0%	57.1%
Gross Profit	34.1%	34.5%	34.8%	35.8%	34.8%	35.3%	36.1%	36.2%	39.6%	36.1%	34.8%	35.6%
SG&A	16.7%	16.7%	16.7%	16.6%	16.7%	16.7%	16.8%	16.8%	19.7%	17.2%	16.7%	16.8%
R&D	8.3%	8.3%	8.3%	8.3%	8.4%	8.4%	8.4%	8.4%	8.4%	8.1%	8.3%	8.4%
Depreciation	7.1%	7.1%	7.2%	7.2%	7.3%	7.3%	7.2%	7.2%	6.9%	7.1%	7.2%	7.2%
Interest Exp.	0.6%	0.6%	0.6%	0.6%	0.5%	0.5%	0.5%	0.5%	0.6%	0.6%	0.6%	0.5%
Pretax margin	8.5%	8.9%	9.2%	10.3%	9.2%	9.7%	10.4%	10.5%	11.0%	10.3%	9.3%	10.0%
Eff. Tax Rate	35.0%	35.0%	35.0%	35.0%	35.0%	35.0%	35.0%	35.0%	36.0%	36.0%	35.0%	35.0%
Net Margin	5.5%	5.8%	6.0%	6.7%	6.0%	6.3%	6.8%	6.8%	7.0%	6.6%	6.0%	6.5%

E = Morgan Stanley Research Estimates   *A = Actual*   *NM = Not Meaningful*

U.S. Robotics — Income Statement

($ Thousands, Except Per Share Data)

	F1994				F1995				F1996			
	12/93	3/94	6/94	9/94	12/94	3/95	6/95	9/95	12/95	F1993	F1994	F1995
Net Sales	108,518	123,139	135,566	131,852	162,455	196,149	237,347	293,396	364,812	242,653	499,075	889,347
Cost of Sales	62,980	73,248	79,761	82,003	95,367	116,376	139,051	170,365	212,196	129,461	297,992	521,159
Gross Profit	45,538	49,891	55,805	49,849	67,088	79,773	98,296	123,031	152,616	113,192	201,083	368,188
Selling & Marketing	N/AV	20,346	23,587	23,524	26,619	33,215	35,996	40,755	47,790	41,857	85,799	136,585
General & Administrative	N/AV	6,867	7,518	8,051	9,303	9,071	10,396	13,844	17,625	18,140	28,734	42,614
Research & Development	N/AV	7,319	7,720	7,885	9,945	11,282	13,835	17,416	23,453	16,888	29,284	52,478
Non Recurring Costs	N/AV				2,111	27,338						29,449
Total Operating Expenses*	N/AV	34,532	38,825	39,460	45,867	53,568	60,227	72,015	88,868	76,885	143,817	231,677
Operating Income	N/AV	15,359	16,980	10,389	19,110	26,205	38,069	51,016	63,748	36,307	57,266	136,511
Interest Income	N/AV	(492)	(602)	0	7,775	(1,275)	(2,208)	1,173	1,220	(792)	(1,305)	5,465
Interest Expense	N/AV	203	631	978	(7,291)	1,417	1,481	(3,307)	(3,271)	377	1,860	(7,700)
Other Income (Expense)	N/AV	216	193	848	488	(210)	190	(91)	218	(673)	1,342	377
Pretax Income	N/AV	15,432	16,758	8,563	18,138	26,273	38,606	53,241	65,581	37,395	55,369	138,369
Taxes	N/AV	5,393	5,736	3,177	6,280	3,922	13,744	19,023	23,936	13,276	19,248	42,969
Net Income	9,668	10,039	11,022	5,386	11,858	22,351	24,862	34,218	41,645	24,119	36,121	95,400
EPS	**$0.26**	**$0.26**	**$0.29**	**$0.14**	**$0.31**	**$0.56**	**$0.59**	**$0.75**	**$0.90**	**$0.71**	**$0.95**	**$2.30**
Shares Outstanding	37,914	38,508	38,184	38,218	38,879	39,694	41,790	45,858	46,467	34,066	38,184	41,555
Growth Rate												
Revenues (yr-yr)	157%	146%	115%	51%	50%	59%	75%	123%	125%	N/AV	106%	78%
Revenues (seq.)	24%	13%	10%	-3%	23%	21%	21%	24%	24%	N/AV	N/AV	N/AV
Expenses (yr-yr)	N/AV	N/AV	N/AV	N/AV	N/AV	55%	55%	83%	94%	N/AV	87%	61%
Expenses (seq.)	N/AV	N/AV	12%	2%	16%	17%	12%	20%	23%	N/AV	N/AV	N/AV
EPS (yr-yr)	-12%	-13%	-22%	-68%	20%	116%	106%	429%	194%	N/AV	34%	143%
Margin Analysis												
Gross Margin	42.0%	40.5%	41.2%	37.8%	41.3%	40.7%	41.4%	41.9%	41.8%	46.6%	40.3%	41.4%
Operating Margin	N/AV	12.5%	12.5%	7.9%	11.8%	13.4%	16.0%	17.4%	17.5%	15.0%	11.5%	15.3%
Pretax Margin	N/AV	12.5%	12.4%	6.5%	11.2%	13.4%	16.3%	18.1%	18.0%	15.4%	11.1%	15.6%
Net Margin	8.9%	8.2%	8.1%	4.1%	7.3%	11.4%	10.5%	11.7%	11.4%	9.9%	7.2%	10.7%
Expenses as Pct. of Revenue												
S&M	N/AV	16.5%	17.4%	17.8%	16.4%	16.9%	15.2%	13.9%	13.1%	17.2%	17.2%	15.4%
G&A	N/AV	5.6%	5.5%	6.1%	5.7%	4.6%	4.4%	4.7%	4.8%	7.5%	5.8%	4.8%
R&D	N/AV	5.9%	5.7%	6.0%	6.1%	5.8%	5.8%	5.9%	6.4%	7.0%	5.9%	5.9%
Total Operating Expenses	N/AV	28.0%	28.6%	29.9%	28.2%	27.3%	25.4%	24.5%	24.4%	31.7%	28.8%	26.1%
Tax Rate	N/AV	34.9%	34.2%	37.1%	34.6%	14.9%	35.6%	35.7%	36.5%	35.5%	34.8%	31.1%

Restated to reflect 2/95 Megahertz merger.
3/95 and subsequent quarters are restated for Megahertz merger.
Fiscal year ends in September.

Xircom — Income Statement

($ Thousands, Except Per Share Data)

	F1995				F1996E						
	12/94	3/95	6/95	9/95	12/95A	3/96E	6/96E	9/96E	F1994	F1995A	F1996E
Net Sales	40,106	39,974	16,474	30,011	37,698	40,500	44,500	48,000	131,580	126,565	170,698
Cost of Sales	20,080	22,357	12,866	30,777	23,944	25,596	28,035	30,096	63,964	86,080	107,671
Gross Profit	20,026	17,617	3,608	(766)	13,754	14,904	16,465	17,904	67,616	40,485	63,027
R&D	3,229	3,186	3,648	3,761	3,007	3,100	3,200	3,350	11,613	13,824	12,657
S&M	8,384	8,625	9,918	11,759	9,121	8,600	8,800	9,400	25,194	38,686	35,921
G&A	1,589	1,734	2,110	2,659	2,365	2,200	2,500	2,600	5,491	8,092	9,665
Total Operating Expenses	13,202	13,545	15,676	18,179	14,493	13,900	14,500	15,350	42,298	60,602	58,243
Operating Income	6,824	4,072	(12,068)	(18,945)	(739)	1,004	1,965	2,554	25,318	(20,117)	4,784
Interest Income, net	376	(142)	291	(86)	(283)	(450)	(400)	(400)	400	439	(1,533)
Pretax Income	7,200	3,930	(11,777)	(19,031)	(1,022)	554	1,565	2,154	25,718	(19,678)	3,251
Taxes	2,664	1,454	(4,340)	(4,578)	(262)	177	501	689	9,895	(4,800)	1,105
Net Income	4,536	2,476	(7,437)	(14,453)	(760)	377	1,064	1,465	15,823	(14,878)	2,146
EPS	$0.27	$0.15	($0.44)	($0.77)	($0.04)	$0.02	$0.05	$0.07	$0.94	($0.79)	$0.11
EPS (including restructuring)			($2.86)								
EPS at 37% Tax Rate			($0.44)	($0.64)	($0.03)	$0.02	$0.05	$0.07			
Shares Outstanding	16,947	16,909	17,018	18,788	18,989	19,400	19,600	19,700	16,825	17,416	19,422
Growth Rate											
Revenues (yr-yr)	52%	32%	-54%	-23%	-6%	1%	170%	60%	60%	-4%	35%
Revenues (seq.)	3.2%	-0.3%	-58.8%	82.2%	25.6%	7.4%	9.9%	7.9%	--	--	--
Expenses (yr-yr)	49%	36%	36%	52%	10%	3%	-8%	-16%	46%	43%	-4%
Expenses (seq.)	10%	3%	16%	16%	-20%	-4%	4%	6%	--	--	--
EPS (yr-yr)	30%	-37%	-276%	-403%	-115%	-87%	-112%	-110%	59%	-184%	-114%
EPS (seq.)	5.6%	-45.3%	-398.4%	76.0%	-94.8%	-148.5%	179.6%	36.9%	--	--	--
Margin Analysis											
Gross Margin	49.9%	44.1%	21.9%	-2.6%	36.5%	36.8%	37.0%	37.3%	51.4%	32.0%	36.9%
Operating Margin	17.0%	10.2%	-73.3%	-63.1%	-2.0%	2.5%	4.4%	5.3%	19.2%	-15.9%	2.8%
Pretax Margin	18.0%	9.8%	-71.5%	-63.4%	-2.7%	1.4%	3.5%	4.5%	19.5%	-15.5%	1.9%
Net Margin	11.3%	6.2%	-45.1%	-48.2%	-2.0%	0.9%	2.4%	3.1%	12.0%	-11.8%	1.3%
Expenses as Pct. of Revenue											
R&D	8.1%	8.0%	22.1%	12.5%	8.0%	7.7%	7.2%	7.0%	8.8%	10.9%	7.4%
S&M	20.9%	21.6%	60.2%	39.2%	24.2%	21.2%	19.8%	19.6%	19.1%	30.6%	21.0%
G&A	4.0%	4.3%	12.8%	8.9%	6.3%	5.4%	5.6%	5.4%	4.2%	6.4%	5.7%
Total Operating Expenses	32.9%	33.9%	95.2%	60.6%	38.4%	34.3%	32.6%	32.0%	32.1%	47.9%	34.1%
Tax Rate	37.0%	37.0%	36.9%	24.1%	25.6%	32.0%	32.0%	32.0%	38.5%	24.4%	34.0%

Fiscal year ends in September.
1Q96 excludes $4,077,000 In-process R&D and other non-recurring charges.
1Q96 includes 8.7 million reserve taken for inventories. If excluded, EPS would be $(0.23)
4Q95 excludes $41,319 restructuring charge related to PRI acquisition. If included, EPS would be $(2.86).
4Q94 excludes a $575,000 one-time (pre-tax) charge and assumes a 38% normalized tax rate.
E = Morgan Stanley Research Estimates.

Zoom Telephonics — Financial Summary F1993–F1995

($ Thousands Except EPS)

	F1994				F1995				
	3/94	6/94	9/94	12/94	3/95	6/95	9/95	F1993	F1994
Net Sales	19,145	16,985	12,853	19,196	20,339	17,122	23,531	55,230	68,180
Cost of Sales	14,694	12,982	10,684	14,932	15,370	12,782	17,494	41,887	53,291
Gross Profit	4,451	4,003	2,169	4,265	4,969	4,340	6,037	13,343	14,888
Operating Expenses									
Sales & Marketing	1,479	1,451	1,561	1,881	1,956	1,719	2,443	4,405	6,372
General & Administrative	541	585	694	895	807	519	737	1,935	2,715
Research and Development	252	255	299	289	358	383	447	964	1,095
Total Operating Expenses	2,272	2,291	2,554	3,066	3,121	2,621	3,627	7,304	10,182
Operating Income	2,179	1,712	(384)	1,199	1,848	1,719	2,410	6,039	4,706
Interest Income (Expense) and Other Income	(10)	(12)	(48)	(4)	21	29	32	89	(75)
Pretax Income	2,169	1,700	(433)	1,195	1,869	1,748	2,442	6,129	4,631
Taxes	868	681	(173)	442	729	686	900	2,342	1,817
Net Income	1,301	1,019	(259)	753	1,140	1,062	1,542	3,787	2,814
EPS (fully diluted)	$0.22	$0.17	($0.04)	$0.13	$0.19	$0.18	$0.25	$0.63	$0.47
Shares Outstanding (fully diluted)	6,014	6,013	6,014	6,013	6,025	6,015	6,238	6,010	6,014
Growth Rate									
Revenues (yr-yr)	40%	16%	15%	22%	6%	1%	83%	--	23%
Revenues (seq.)	22%	-11%	-24%	-61%	6%	-16%	37%	--	--
Expenses (yr-yr)	46%	33%	40%	40%	37%	14%	42%	--	39%
Expenses (seq.)	4%	1%	11%	-57%	2%	-16%	38%	--	--
EPS (yr-yr)	15%	-18%	-168%	-26%	-13%	4%	NM	--	-26%
Margin Analysis									
Gross Margin	23.2%	23.6%	16.9%	22.2%	24.4%	25.3%	25.7%	24.2%	21.8%
Operating Margin	11.4%	10.1%	-3.0%	6.2%	9.1%	10.0%	10.2%	10.9%	6.9%
Pretax Margin	11.3%	10.0%	-3.4%	6.2%	9.2%	10.2%	10.4%	11.1%	6.8%
Net Margin	6.8%	6.0%	-2.0%	3.9%	5.6%	6.2%	6.6%	6.9%	4.1%
Expenses as Pct. of Revenue									
R&D	1.3%	1.5%	2.3%	1.5%	1.8%	2.2%	1.9%	1.7%	1.6%
S&M	7.7%	8.5%	12.1%	9.8%	9.6%	10.0%	10.4%	8.0%	9.3%
G&A	2.8%	3.4%	5.4%	4.7%	4.0%	3.0%	3.1%	3.5%	4.0%
Total Operating Expenses	11.9%	13.5%	19.9%	16.0%	15.3%	15.3%	15.4%	13.2%	14.9%
Tax Rate	40.0%	40.1%	40.0%	37.0%	39.0%	39.2%	36.9%	38.2%	39.2%

Fiscal Year ends in December.

Internet Security Equipment and Software

Security Dynamics Technologies — Financial Summary F1993–F1995

($ Thousands Except EPS)

	F1994				F1995			F1993	F1994
	3/94	6/94	9/94	12/94	3/95	6/95	9/95	F1993	F1994
Net Sales	3,195	4,542	4,225	5,610	6,423	8,174	8,766	12,110	17,572
Cost of Sales	793	966	917	1,197	1,217	1,792	1,804	2,738	3,873
Gross Profit	2,402	3,576	3,308	4,413	5,206	6,382	6,962	9,372	13,699
Research and Development	485	503	593	645	645	762	1,537	1,619	2,226
Marketing and Selling	1,329	1,587	1,546	1,920	2,266	2,666	2,815	4,000	6,382
General & Administrative	323	369	371	573	682	947	922	1,217	1,636
Total Operating Expenses	2,137	2,459	2,510	3,138	3,593	4,375	5,274	6,836	10,244
Operating Income	265	1,117	798	1,275	1,433	2,007	1,688	2,536	3,455
Interest Income	12	13	25	55	384	406	348	37	105
Pretax Income	277	1,130	823	1,330	1,817	2,413	2,036	2,573	3,560
Provision for Taxes	97	395	288	465	700	928	784	900	1,245
Net Income	180	735	535	865	1,117	1,485	1,252	1,673	2,315
Cumulative Effect								564	
Net Income after Cum. Effect	180	735	535	865	1,117	1,485	1,252	2,237	2,315
EPS (before Cum. Effect)	$0.04	$0.17	$0.12	$0.18	$0.18	$0.24	$0.10	$0.37	$0.51
EPS (after Cum. effect)								$0.50	
Shares Outstanding	4,416	4,452	4,476	4,806	6,257	6,264	12,544	4,505	4,540
Growth Rate									
Revenues (yr-yr)	29%	59%	49%	42%	101%	80%	107%	--	45%
Revenues (seq.)	-19%	42%	-7%	33%	14%	27%	7%	--	--
Expenses (yr-yr)	41%	47%	58%	52%	68%	78%	110%	--	50%
Expenses (seq.)	4%	15%	2%	25%	14%	22%	21%	--	--
EPS (yr-yr)	--	90%	28%	35%	338%	44%	-16%	--	37%
Margin Analysis									
Gross Margin	75.2%	78.7%	78.3%	78.7%	81.1%	78.1%	79.4%	77.4%	78.0%
Operating Margin	8.3%	24.6%	18.9%	22.7%	22.3%	24.6%	19.3%	20.9%	19.7%
Pretax Margin	8.7%	24.9%	19.5%	23.7%	28.3%	29.5%	23.2%	21.2%	20.3%
Net Margin	5.6%	16.2%	12.7%	15.4%	17.4%	18.2%	14.3%	13.8%	13.2%
Expenses as Pct. of Revenue									
R&D	15.2%	11.1%	14.0%	11.5%	10.0%	9.3%	17.5%	13.4%	12.7%
G&A	41.6%	34.9%	36.6%	34.2%	35.3%	32.6%	32.1%	33.0%	36.3%
Total Operating Expenses	66.9%	54.1%	59.4%	55.9%	55.9%	53.5%	60.2%	56.4%	58.3%
Tax Rate	35.0%	35.0%	35.0%	35.0%	38.5%	38.5%	38.5%	35.0%	35.0%

Fiscal Year ends in December.

Internet Service Providers

BBN Corporation — Financial Summary F1993–F1995

($ Thousands Except EPS)

	F1994				F1995				F1996				
	9/93	12/93	3/94	6/94	9/94	12/94	3/95(a)	6/95	9/95	12/95	F1993	F1994	F1995
Net Sales	49,930	48,407	48,525	49,242	51,743	51,172	51,957	60,159	61,126	63,200	233,453	196,104	215,031
Cost of Sales	33,043	30,565	32,251	34,226	31,245	32,023	33,515	38,468	40,618	42,940	148,384	130,085	135,251
Gross Profit	16,887	17,842	16,274	15,016	20,498	19,149	18,442	21,691	20,508	20,260	85,069	66,019	79,780
Research and Development	5,304	5,874	5,954	5,319	5,955	6,345	6,662	6,344	5,660	5,423	34,048	22,451	25,306
G&A	13,107	14,496	12,676	11,733	16,035	17,911	17,377	21,965	25,922	24,630	62,874	52,012	73,288
Restructuring Charge										20,470			
Total Operating Expenses	18,411	20,370	18,630	17,052	21,990	24,256	24,039	28,309	31,582	30,053	117,392	74,463	98,594
Operating Income	(1,524)	(2,528)	(2,356)	(2,036)	(1,492)	(5,107)	(5,597)	(6,618)	(11,074)	(9,793)	(32,323)	(8,444)	(18,814)
Interest Income	689	535	494	472	617	593	1,724	1,488	1,585	1,106	1,446	2,190	4,422
Interest Expense	(1,201)	(1,135)	(1,142)	1,128	(1,126)	(1,094)	(1,103)	(1,111)	(1,134)	(1,125)	(4,511)	(4,606)	(4,434)
Minority Interests		585	743	743	296	445	(11,826)	(110)	(69)	(15)		2,071	(11,195)
Other Income (Expense)	89	877	2	(3)	(3)	3,538	105,096	17	(9)	55	3,124	965	108,648
Pretax Income	(1,947)	(1,666)	(2,259)	(1,952)	(1,708)	(1,625)	88,294	(6,334)	(10,701)	(9,772)	(32,264)	(7,824)	78,627
Taxes					100	300	13,827	(444)	(2,050)	(1,882)			13,783
Net Income	(1,947)	(1,666)	(2,259)	(1,952)	(1,808)	(1,925)	74,467	(5,890)	(8,651)	(7,890)	(32,264)	(7,824)	64,844
EPS	($0.12)	($0.10)	($0.14)	($0.12)	($0.11)	($0.11)	$4.11	($0.28)	($0.49)	($0.45)	($2.05)	($0.48)	$3.61
Shares Outstanding	15,978	16,079	16,295	16,179	16,614	16,819	18,118	21,036	17,518	17,694	15,705	16,179	17,984
Growth Rate													
Revenues (yr-yr)	--	--	-11%	-9%	4%	6%	7%	22%	18%	24%	-7%	-16%	10%
Revenues (seq.)	-8%	-3%	0%	1%	5%	-1%	2%	16%	2%	3%	--	--	--
Expenses (yr-yr)	--	--	-23%	-21%	19%	19%	29%	66%	44%	24%	20%	-37%	32%
Expenses (seq.)	-14%	11%	-9%	-8%	29%	10%	-1%	18%	12%	-5%	--	--	--
EPS (yr-yr)	--	--	--	NM	NM	NM	NM	NM	NM	NM	NM	NM	NM
Margin Analysis													
Gross Margin	33.8%	36.9%	33.5%	30.5%	39.6%	37.4%	35.5%	36.1%	33.6%	32.1%	36.4%	33.7%	37.1%
Operating Margin	-3.1%	-5.2%	-4.9%	-4.1%	-2.9%	-10.0%	-10.8%	-11.0%	-18.1%	-15.5%	-13.8%	-4.3%	-8.7%
Pretax Margin	-3.9%	-3.4%	-4.7%	-4.0%	-3.3%	-3.2%	169.9%	-10.5%	-17.5%	-15.5%	-13.8%	-4.0%	36.6%
Net Margin	-3.9%	-3.4%	-4.7%	-4.0%	-3.5%	-3.8%	143.3%	-9.8%	-14.2%	-12.5%	-13.8%	-4.0%	30.2%
Expenses as Pct. of Revenue													
R&D	10.6%	12.1%	12.3%	10.8%	11.5%	12.4%	12.8%	10.5%	9.3%	8.6%	14.6%	11.4%	11.8%
G&A	26.3%	29.9%	26.1%	23.8%	31.0%	35.0%	33.4%	36.5%	42.4%	39.0%	26.9%	26.5%	34.1%
Total Operating Expenses	36.9%	42.1%	38.4%	34.6%	42.5%	47.4%	46.3%	47.1%	51.7%	47.6%	50.3%	38.0%	45.9%
Tax Rate	0.0%	0.0%	0.0%	0.0%	-5.9%	-18.5%	15.7%	7.0%	19.2%	19.3%	0.0%	0.0%	17.5%

Fiscal Year ends in June.

Netcom — Financial Summary F1993–F1995

($ Thousands Except EPS)

	3/94	6/94	9/94	12/94	3/95	6/95	9/95	12/95	F1993	F1994	F1995
		F1994				F1995					
Net Sales	1,589	2,281	3,304	5,185	7,498	10,528	14,724	19,672	2,412	12,360	52,422
Cost of Sales	851	1,138	1,722	2,999	4,997	7,458	10,425	13,761	1,133	6,711	36,641
Gross Profit	738	1,143	1,582	2,186	2,501	3,070	4,299	5,910	1,279	5,649	15,781
Product Development	14	13	119	183	300	539	786	615	69	328	2,239
Sales and Marketing	265	600	867	1,348	1,954	3,825	5,340	7,652	371	3,080	18,771
G&A	375	451	656	862	1,760	1,945	3,174	4,138	596	2,345	11,016
Total Operating Expenses	654	1,064	1,642	2,393	4,014	6,309	9,300	12,405	1,037	5,753	32,026
Operating Income	84	79	(60)	(207)	(1,513)	(3,239)	(5,001)	(6,494)	242	(105)	(16,246)
Interest Income, net	5	(2)	(23)	24	221	361	563	1,052	(3)	5	2,197
Pretax Income	89	77	(83)	(184)	(1,291)	(2,878)	(4,438)	(5,442)	239	(100)	(14,049)
Provision for Taxes	36	31	(33)	(34)			11	4	(12)		15
Net Income	54	46	(49)	(150)	(1,291)	(2,878)	(4,449)	(5,446)	227	(100)	(14,064)
EPS	$0.01	$0.01	($0.01)	($0.03)	($0.19)	($0.37)	($0.49)	($0.55)	$0.04	($0.02)	($1.68)
Pro Forma Data											
Income Before Provision for Taxes									239		
Pro Forma Provision for Income Taxes									(96)		
Pro Forma Net Income									144		
Pro Forma Net Income per Share									$0.02		
Shares Outstanding	6,232	6,224	6,144	5,927	6,731	7,762	9,031	9,892	6,327	5,927	8,350
Growth Rate											
Revenues (yr-yr)	--	430%	400%	457%	372%	361%	346%	279%	--	413%	324%
Revenues (seq.)	71%	44%	45%	57%	45%	40%	40%	34%	--	--	--
Expenses (yr-yr)	--	499%	342%	523%	514%	493%	466%	418%	--	455%	457%
Expenses (seq.)	70%	63%	54%	46%	68%	57%	47%	33%	--	--	--
EPS (yr-yr)	--	103%	NM	NM	NM	NM	NM	NM	N/AV	NM	NM
Margin Analysis											
Gross Margin	46.4%	50.1%	47.9%	42.2%	33.4%	29.2%	29.2%	30.0%	53.0%	45.7%	30.1%
Operating Margin	5.3%	3.5%	-1.8%	-4.0%	-20.2%	-30.8%	-34.0%	-33.0%	10.0%	-0.8%	-31.0%
Pretax Margin	5.6%	3.4%	-2.5%	-3.5%	-17.2%	-27.3%	-30.1%	-27.7%	9.9%	-0.8%	-26.8%
Net Margin	3.4%	2.0%	-1.5%	-2.9%	-17.2%	-27.3%	-30.2%	-27.7%	9.4%	-0.8%	-26.8%
Expenses as Pct. of Revenue											
R&D	0.9%	0.5%	3.6%	3.5%	4.0%	5.1%	5.3%	3.1%	2.9%	2.7%	4.3%
S&M	16.7%	26.3%	26.2%	26.0%	26.1%	36.3%	36.3%	38.9%	15.4%	24.9%	35.8%
G&A	23.6%	19.8%	19.9%	16.6%	23.5%	18.5%	21.6%	21.0%	24.7%	19.0%	21.0%
Total Operating Expenses	41.2%	46.6%	49.7%	46.2%	53.5%	59.9%	63.2%	63.1%	43.0%	46.5%	61.1%
Tax Rate	40.0%	40.5%	40.4%	18.2%	0.0%	0.0%	-0.2%	-0.1%	-5.1%	0.0%	-0.1%

Fiscal Year ends in December.

PSINet — Financial Summary F1993–F1995

($ Thousands Except EPS)

	F1994				F1995				
	3/94	6/94	9/94	12/94	3/95	6/95	9/95	F1993	F1994
Net Sales	3,071	3,336	3,906	4,901	5,887	7,703	11,115	8,665	15,214
Cost of Sales	1,899	2,127	2,419	3,044	4,303	6,732	9,379	5,320	9,489
Gross Profit	1,172	1,209	1,487	1,857	1,584	971	1,736	3,345	5,725
S&M	603	759	919	1,318	1,840	3,526	7,093	1,845	3,599
G&A	699	950	965	991	1,181	2,401	2,799	1,666	3,605
Depreciation and Amortization	679	720	858	926	1,666	2,162	4,899	1,719	3,183
Total Operating Expenses	1,981	2,429	2,742	3,235	4,687	8,089	14,791	5,230	10,387
Operating Income	(809)	(1,220)	(1,255)	(1,378)	(3,103)	(7,118)	(13,055)	(1,885)	(4,662)
Interest Expense	(195)	(179)	166	119	(165)	(378)	(484)	274	645
Interest Income		14				499	549		
Equity in Loss of Affiliate				(35)	(12)	(39)	(60)		(35)
Pretax Income	(1,004)	(1,385)	(1,421)	(1,532)	(3,280)	(7,036)	(13,050)	(2,159)	(5,342)
Income Tax Benefit					65	(65)		(246)	
Net Income	(1,004)	1,385	(1,421)	(1,532)	(3,215)	(7,101)	(13,050)	(1,913)	(5,342)
EPS	($0.05)	$0.07	($0.07)	($0.08)	($0.12)	($0.23)	($0.40)	N/A	($0.26)
Shares Outstanding	20,395	20,395	20,395	20,395	26,857	30,341	32,328	N/A	20,395
Growth Rate									
Revenues (yr-yr)	59%	58%	75%	105%	92%	131%	185%	--	76%
Revenues (seq.)	29%	9%	17%	25%	20%	31%	44%	--	--
Expenses (yr-yr)	131%	117%	108%	67%	137%	233%	439%	--	99%
Expenses (seq.)	2%	23%	13%	18%	45%	73%	83%	--	--
EPS (yr-yr)	--	--	--	--	NM	NM	NM	--	N/AV
Margin Analysis									
Gross Margin	38.2%	36.2%	38.1%	37.9%	26.9%	12.6%	15.6%	38.6%	37.6%
Operating Margin	-26.3%	-36.6%	-32.1%	-28.1%	-52.7%	-92.4%	-117.5%	-21.8%	-30.6%
Pretax Margin	-32.7%	-41.5%	-36.4%	-31.3%	-55.7%	-91.3%	-117.4%	-24.9%	-35.1%
Net Margin	-32.7%	41.5%	-36.4%	-31.3%	-54.6%	-92.2%	-117.4%	-22.1%	-35.1%
Expenses as Pct. of Revenue									
S&M	19.6%	22.8%	23.5%	26.9%	31.3%	45.8%	63.8%	21.3%	23.7%
G&A	22.8%	28.5%	24.7%	20.2%	20.1%	31.2%	25.2%	19.2%	23.7%
Total Operating Expenses	64.5%	72.8%	70.2%	66.0%	79.6%	105.0%	133.1%	60.4%	68.3%
Tax Rate	0.0%	0.0%	0.0%	0.0%	-2.0%	0.9%	0.0%	11.4%	0.0%

Fiscal Year ends in December.

UUNET Technologies — Financial Summary F1993–F1995

($ Thousands Except EPS)

	F1994				F1995						
	3/94	6/94	9/94	12/94	3/95	6/95	9/95	12/95(a)	F1993*	F1994*	F1995*
Net Sales	2,384	2,731	3,182	4,117	6,482	10,470	16,442	33,807	24,019	33,138	94,461
Cost of Revenues	1,364	1,627	2,195	2,376	3,196	6,062	10,583	22,640	13,694	19,631	59,339
Gross Margin	1,020	1,104	987	1,741	3,286	4,408	5,859	11,167	10,325	13,507	35,122
Costs and Expenses											
Network Operations and Support	644	834	986	1,150	1,361	1,878	2,179	3,794	3,850	6,764	13,127
Sales and Marketing	794	974	1,473	1,623	1,906	2,439	2,882	6,142	5,558	9,681	18,762
General and Administrative	617	742	682	1,307	801	901	1,060	2,501	2,248	5,288	12,709
Acquisition Expense	--	--	--	--	--	--	--	11,067			11,067
Operating Expenses	2,055	2,550	3,141	4,080	4,068	5,218	6,121	23,504	11,656	21,733	55,665
Loss from Operations	(1,035)	(1,446)	(2,154)	(2,339)	(782)	(810)	(262)	(12,337)	(1,331)	(8,226)	(20,543)
Interest Income	6	3	15	77	54	374	1,020	927	36	440	2,747
Interest Expense	(18)	(14)	(17)	(27)	(64)	(129)	(151)	(382)	(103)	(76)	(808)
Equity in net loss of affiliates	--	--	--	--	--	--	--	(127)	--	--	(127)
Loss on Sale of Investment	--	--	--	--	--	--	--	--	(433)		
Loss Before Income Taxes	(1,047)	(1,457)	(2,156)	(2,289)	(792)	(565)	607	(11,919)	(1,831)	(7,862)	(18,731)
Tax Benefit	--	--	--	--	--	--	--	53	(197)	(126)	474
Net Loss	(1,047)	(1,457)	(2,156)	(2,289)	(792)	(565)	607	(11,866)	(2,028)	(7,988)	(18,257)
EPS	($0.05)	($0.07)	($0.11)	($0.11)	($0.04)	($0.02)	$0.02	($0.03)	N/A	($0.35)	($0.63)
Operating								($0.37)			
Shares Outstanding	20,030	20,030	20,030	20,030	22,610	23,616	30,122	31,830	N/A	22,946	28,987
Growth Rate											
Revenues (yr-yr)	23%	44%	64%	94%	172%	283%	417%	721%	--	38%	185%
Revenues (seq.)	12%	15%	17%	29%	57%	62%	57%	106%	--	--	--
Expenses (yr-yr)	129%	159%	153%	130%	98%	105%	95%	476%	--	86%	156%
Expenses (seq.)	16%	24%	23%	30%	0%	28%	17%	284%	--	--	--
EPS (yr-yr)	--	--	--	--	NM	NM	NM	NM	--	--	--
Margin Analysis											
Gross Margin	42.8%	40.4%	31.0%	42.3%	50.7%	42.1%	35.6%	33.0%	43.0%	40.8%	37.2%
Operating Margin	-43.4%	-52.9%	-67.7%	-56.8%	-12.1%	-7.7%	-1.6%	-36.5%	-5.5%	-24.8%	-21.7%
Pretax Margin	-43.9%	-53.4%	-67.8%	-55.6%	-12.2%	-5.4%	3.7%	-35.3%	-7.6%	-23.7%	-19.8%
Net Margin	-43.9%	-53.4%	-67.8%	-55.6%	-12.2%	-5.4%	3.7%	-35.1%	-8.4%	-24.1%	-19.3%
Expenses as Pct. of Revenue											
S&M	33.3%	35.7%	46.3%	39.4%	29.4%	23.3%	17.5%	18.2%	23.1%	29.2%	19.9%
G&A	25.9%	27.2%	21.4%	31.7%	12.4%	8.6%	6.4%	7.4%	9.4%	16.0%	13.5%
Total Operating Expenses	86.2%	93.4%	98.7%	99.1%	62.8%	49.8%	37.2%	69.5%	48.5%	65.6%	58.9%
Tax Rate	0.0%	0.0%	0.0%	0.0%	0.0%	0.0%	0.0%	NM	10.8%	1.6%	-2.5%

* Restated for Unipalm Acquisition. (a) Includes $11.1MM in transaction costs for the acquisition of Unipalm Group PLC
Fiscal Year ends in December.

PCs, Servers, and Semiconductors

Apple Computer — Income Statement Comparisons F1994–F1996E

($ Millions Except EPS)

	F1995				F1996E				Annual Data		
	12/94(a)	3/95(b)	6/95	9/95	12/95 (d)	3/96E (e)	6/96E	9/96E	F1994(a)	F1995(b,c)	F1996E(d,e)
Revenue	$2,832	$2,652	$2,575	$3,003	$3,148	$2,600	$2,574	$2,883	$9,189	$11,062	$11,205
U.S.	1,501	1,220	1,313	1,756	1,668	1,430	1,416	1,586	4,990	5,790	6,100
International	1,331	1,432	1,262	1,247	1,480	1,170	1,158	1,297	4,199	5,272	5,105
Cost of Goods	2,018	1,957	1,847	2,382	2,593	2,158	2,136	2,352	6,845	8,204	9,240
Gross Profit	814	695	728	621	555	442	438	530	2,344	2,858	1,965
Operating Expense	547	529	572	549	594	575	550	535	1,948	2,197	2,254
R&D	132	143	168	171	153	155	150	150	564	614	608
SG&A	415	386	404	378	441	420	400	385	1,384	1,583	1,646
Operating Income	267	166	156	72	(39)	(133)	(112)	(5)	395	661	(289)
Interest Income	15	(50)	2	23	10	5	5	5	(22)	(10)	25
Unusual Items	17	50	6	0	(80)	(125)	0	0	127	73	(205)
Pretax Income	299	116	158	95	(29)	(128)	(107)	0	373	668	(264)
Taxes	111	43	61	35	(11)	(47)	(40)	0	142	250	(98)
Net Income	188	73	97	60	(18)	(81)	(68)	0	232	418	(166)
Earnings Per Share	$1.55	$0.59	$0.84	$0.48	($0.56)	($1.30)	($0.55)	$0.00	$2.60	$3.42	($2.40)
Operating	1.46	0.85	$0.80	--	(0.15)	(0.66)	--	--	1.94	3.59	(1.35)
Dividend	0.12	0.12	0.12	0.12							
Shares Outstanding (millions)	122	123	123	125	123	123	123	124	119	123	123
Growth Rate											
Revenue (yr-yr)	15%	28%	20%	20%	11%	(2%)	(0%)	(4%)	15%	20%	1%
Revenue (seq.)	14	(6)	(3)	17	5	(17)	(1)	12	--	--	--
Expenses (yr-yr)	4	14	22	12	9	9	(4)	(3)	(15)	13	3
Expenses (seq.)	12	(3)	8	(4)	8	(3)	(4)	(3)	--	--	--
EPS (Oper.)	327	305	60	(50)	(138)	(252)	(169)	(100)	13	85	(167)
Margin Analysis											
Gross Margin	28.7%	26.2%	28.3%	20.7%	17.6%	17.0%	17.0%	18.4%	25.5%	25.8%	17.5%
Operating Margin	9.4	6.3	6.1	2.4	(1.2)	(5.1)	(4.4)	(0.2)	4.3	6.0	(2.6)
Pretax Margin	10.6	4.4	6.1	3.2	(0.9)	(4.9)	(4.2)	0.0	4.1	6.0	(2.4)
Net Margin	6.6	2.7	3.8	2.0	(0.6)	(3.1)	(2.6)	0.0	2.5	3.8	(1.5)
Expenses as Pct. of Revenue											
Operating Expense	19.3%	19.9%	22.2%	18.3%	18.9%	22.1%	21.4%	18.6%	21.2%	19.9%	20.1%
R&D	4.7	5.4	6.5	5.7	4.9	6.0	5.8	5.2	6.1	5.6	5.4
SG&A	14.7	14.6	15.7	12.6	14.0	16.2	15.5	13.4	15.1	14.3	14.7
Tax Rate	37.1%	37.1%	37.0%	36.8%	37.0%	37.0%	37.0%	37.0%	38.0%	37.4%	37.0%

(a) $126.9MM pre-tax reversal of CQ3:93 restructuring accrual due to changing business conditions and modifications or elimination of some of the original plans.

(b) $17MM pre-tax reversal of CQ3:93 restructuring accrual.

(c) $50MM in realized and unrealized losses on certain foreign exchange hedging activities, primarily a function of the mark-to-market accounting principles.

(d) Reported earnings include $80MM inventory adjustment charge to COGS .

(e) Assumes $125MM charge related to workforce reduction and consolidation, and an associated headcount reduction of 1,300 (approx. 8% of headcount).

E = Morgan Stanley Research Estimates   Fiscal Year ends in September.

Compaq Computer — Income Statement Comparisons 1993–1996E

($ Millions Except EPS)

	1995 3/95	6/95	9/95	12/95(a)	1996E 3/96E	6/96E	9/96E	12/96E	Annual Data 1993	1994	1995(a)	1996E
Revenue	$2,959	$3,501	$3,594	$4,701	$4,137	$4,551	$4,687	$5,390	$7,192	$10,866	$14,755	$18,765
N. America	1,381	1,629	1,882	2,162	1,986	2,230	2,390	2,587	3,670	5,459	6,935	9,193
International	1,578	1,872	1,712	2,539	2,151	2,321	2,297	2,803	3,522	5,407	7,820	9,572
Cost of Goods	2,235	2,675	2,775	3,682	3,206	3,549	3,656	4,204	5,494	8,139	11,367	14,616
Gross Profit	724	826	819	1,019	931	1,001	1,031	1,186	1,698	2,727	3,388	4,149
Operating Expense	388	455	471	550	509	550	566	596	1,005	1,461	1,864	2,221
R&D	60	64	65	81	84	85	86	91	168	226	270	346
Marketing/SG&A	328	391	406	469	425	465	480	505	837	1,235	1,594	1,875
G&A	--	--	--	--					--			--
Operating Income	336	371	348	469	422	451	465	590	693	1,266	1,524	1,928
Interest Income, net	(36)	(30)	(8)	(21)	(20)	(20)	(20)	(20)	(56)	(94)	(95)	(80)
Other Income, net	0	0	0	0	0	0	0	0	(20)	0	0	0
Pretax Income	300	341	340	448	402	431	445	570	617	1,172	1,429	1,848
Taxes	84	95	95	125	121	129	134	171	154	304	399	554
Net Income	216	246	245	323	281	302	312	399	462	868	1,030	1,294
Equity in Affiliate	0	0	0	(241)	0	0	0	0	0	0	(241)	0
Net Net Income	216	246	245	82	281	302	312	399	462	868	789	1,294
Earnings Per Share (Dil.)	$0.80	$0.90	$0.89	$0.30	$1.01	$1.08	$1.11	$1.39	$1.81	$3.23	$2.87	$4.60
Operating	--	--	--	1.17	--	--	--	--	--	--	3.75	
Shares Out. ('000,000)	270.9	273.1	275.2	276.0	278.0	280.0	282.0	286.0	254.7	270.1	275.0	281.5
Growth Rate												
Revenues (yr-yr)	30%	40%	27%	45%	40%	30%	30%	15%	75%	51%	36%	27%
Revenues (seq.)	(9)	18	3	31	(12)	10	3	15	--	--	--	--
Expenses (yr-yr)	26	27	28	28	31	21	20	8	15	45	28	19
Expenses (seq.)	(10)	17	4	17	(7)	8	3	5	--	--	--	--
EPS (Operating)	(0)	15	19	30	27	20	24	19	109	78	16	23
Margin Analysis												
Gross Margin	24.5%	23.6%	22.8%	21.7%	22.5%	22.0%	22.0%	22.0%	23.6%	25.1%	23.0%	22.1%
Operating Margin	11.4	10.6	9.7	10.0	10.2	9.9	9.9	10.9	9.6	11.7	10.3	10.3
Pretax Margin	10.1	9.7	9.5	9.5	9.7	9.5	9.5	10.6	8.6	10.8	9.7	9.8
Net Margin	7.3	7.0	6.8	6.9	6.8	6.6	6.6	7.4	6.4	8.0	7.0	6.9
Expenses as Pct. of Revenue												
Operating Expense	13.1%	13.0%	13.1%	11.7%	12.3%	12.1%	12.1%	11.1%	14.0%	13.4%	12.6%	11.8%
R&D	2.0	1.8	1.8	1.7	2.0	1.9	1.8	1.7	2.3	2.1	1.8	1.8
Marketing	11.1	11.2	11.3	10.0	10.3	10.2	10.2	9.4	11.6	11.4	10.8	10.0
G&A	0.0	0.0	0.0	0.0	0.0	0.0	0.0	0.0	--	--	--	--
Tax Rate	28.0	27.9	27.9	27.9	30.0	30.0	30.0	30.0	25.0	26.0	27.9	30.0

(a) Reported EPS include charge of $241mm (or $0.87 per share) for the acquisitions of NetWorth and Thomas-Conrad.

E = Morgan Stanley Research Estimates.

Dell Computer — Income Statement Comparisons F1994–F1996E

($ Millions Except EPS)

	F1995				F1996E				Annual Data		
	4/94(a)	7/94(b)	10/94	1/95(c)	4/95(d)	7/95	10/95	1/96E	F1995(a,b,c)	F1996E(d)	F1997E
Revenue	$767	$791	$885	$1,033	$1,136	$1,206	$1,416	$1,543	$3,475	$5,300	$6,784
Americas	475	534	620	667	704	784	991	1,018	2,296	3,497	4,206
International	291	277	265	366	432	422	425	525	1,199	1,803	2,578
Cost of Goods	597	622	703	816	900	943	1,125	1,234	2,737	4,202	5,394
Gross Profit	170	170	18	217	236	263	291	309	738	1,098	1,391
Operating Expenses	11	11	122	138	148	172	186	199	489	706	902
Marketing	95	103	105	12	128	147	160	17	423	606	773
G&A	--	--	--	--	--	--	--	--	--	--	--
R&D	15	16	17	17	21	25	26	28	65	100	129
Unusual Charge	--	--	--	--	12	--	--	--	0	12	--
Operating Income	60	51	60	79	88	91	104	11	249	392	488
Interest & Other	(33)	(10)	(1)	7	(1)	1	2	2	(36)	4	(2)
Interest Income	--	--	--	--	--	--	--	--	--	--	--
Interest Expense	--	--	--	--	--	--	--	--	--	--	--
Other Income	--	--	--	--	--	--	--	--	--	--	--
Pretax Income	27	41	58	86	87	92	106	11	213	396	486
Taxes	8	13	17	26	25	27	31	32	64	11	14
Net Income before Prf. Stock Div.	19	29	41	60	62	65	75	79	149	281	345
Preferred Stock Dividends	2	2	2	2	0	0	0	0	9	0	0
Net Income (Operating)	17	26	39	58	62	65	75	79	140	281	345
Earnings Per Share	$0.21	$0.32	$0.47	$0.68	$0.55	$0.66	$0.75	$0.79	$1.68	$2.75	$3.35
Fully Diluted	--	0.31	0.43	0.63	0.53	0.66	0.75	0.78	1.58	2.71	3.32
Operating	--	0.40	--	0.59	0.63	--	--	--	1.63	2.82	--
Shares Outstanding ('000)	80,630	81,240	84,182	85,724	90,508	98,242	100,060	100,500	82,944	97,328	103,000
Shares Outstanding (Dil.)('000)	0	92,094	95,680	96,158	97,544	99,220	100,976	101,500	88,414	99,810	104,000
Growth Rate											
Sales (yr-yr)	14%	13%	17%	39%	48%	52%	60%	49%	21%	53%	28%
Sales (seq.)	3	3	12	17	10	6	17	9	--	--	--
Expenses (yr-yr)	1	-3	3	25	35	45	53	44	9	44	28
Expenses (seq.)	-1	8	3	14	7	16	8	7	--	--	--
Earnings Per Share	65	-132	254	248	166	104	62	16	165	73	18
Margin Analysis											
Gross Margin	22.2%	21.4%	20.5%	21.0%	20.8%	21.8%	20.5%	20.0%	21.2%	20.7%	20.5%
Operating Margin	7.8	6.5	6.7	7.6	7.7	7.5	7.4	7.1	7.2	7.4	7.2
Pretax Margin	3.6	5.2	6.6	8.3	7.6	7.6	7.5	7.2	6.1	7.5	7.2
Net Margin	2.2	3.3	4.4	5.6	5.4	5.4	5.3	5.1	4.0	5.3	5.1
Expenses as Pct. of Sales											
Operating Expenses	14.3%	15.0%	13.8%	13.4%	13.1	14.3%	13.1	12.9%	14.1	13.3%	13.3%
Marketing	12.4	13.0	11.	11.	11.	12.2	11.	11.	12.2	11.	11.
G&A	0.0	0.0	0.0	0.0	0.0	0.0	0.0	0.0	0.0	0.0	0.0
R&D	2.0	2.0	1.9	1.7	1.8	2.0	1.8	1.8	1.9	1.9	1.9

(a) Interest and Other includes after-tax charges of $15.6MM related to interest-rate derivative instruments and $10.7MM for non-temporary declines in the market value of its investment portfolio. Excluding these charges F1Q:94EPS would be $1.07.

(b) Interest and Other includes after-tax charges of $6.2MM related to closure of the company's investment derivatives and short-term investments with principal exposure. (c) Includes 13 months of international operations, to adjust international operations to a January year-end. Note that this had a positive impact of $5.4MM in interest and other, or $0.10 per share. (d) Note that Dell took a $11.6MM unusual charge in F1Q96 related to the conversion of preferred stock to common shares.

E = Morgan Stanley Research Estimates   *Fiscal Year ends in January.*

Digital Equipment Earnings Model

| | 1995A | | | | 1996E | | | | Full Year | | |
	Sep	Dec	Mar	Jun	Sep A	DecA	Mar	Jun	1995A	1996E	1997E
Sales	$1,653	$1,870	$1,961	$2,132	$1,819	$2,347	$2,430	$2,700	$7,616	$9,296	$10,750
Services	1,470	1,603	1,506	1,618	1,452	1,604	1,550	1,667	6,197	6,274	6,560
Total Revenue	**$3,122**	**$3,473**	**$3,467**	**$3,750**	**$3,271**	**$3,951**	**$3,980**	**$4,367**	**$13,813**	**$15,569**	**$17,310**
Cost of Sales	$1,231	$1,300	$1,399	$1,468	$1,257	$1,583	$1,625	$1,795	$5,398	$6,260	$7,050
Cost of Services	949	1,025	953	1,067	961	1,080	1,048	1,132	3,994	4,221	4,485
SG&A	836	869	778	790	734	849	850	866	3,273	3,300	3,442
R&D	288	248	251	253	256	263	268	273	1,040	1,061	1,126
Operating Income	($181)	$31	$86	$173	$63	$176	$189	$301	$108	$728	$1,207
Net Interest Income	(10)	(8)	(7)	(8)	(6)	(5)	(5)	(4)	(32)	(20)	(20)
Special Charge	(65)								(65)		
Effective Tax Rate	NM	16.4%	6.5%	3.1%	15.0%	12.6%	12.5%	14.1	23.7%	13.4%	15.0%
Pretax Income	($191)	$23	$79	$165	$57	$170	$184	$297	$76	$708	$1,187
Taxes	4	4	5	5	9	22	23	42	18	95	178
Net Income	($195)	$19	$74	$160	$48	$149	$161	$255	$58	$613	$1,009
Preferred Dividend	$9	$9	$9	$9	$9	$9	$9	$9	36	36	36
Earnings Per Share	**($1.44)**	**$0.07**	**$0.44**	**$1.01**	**$0.26**	**$0.91**	**$0.98**	**$1.58**	**$0.15**	**$3.75**	**$6.20**
Avg. Shares (Millions)	141.6	145.0	148.0	149.9	151.6	154.3	155.0	155.5	146.3	154.1	157.0
As a % of Revenue											
Total Revenue	100.0	100.0	100.0	100.0	100.0	100.0	100.0	100.0	100.0	100.0	100.0
Cost of Sales	74.5	69.5	71.3	68.8	69.1	67.5	66.9	66.5	70.9	67.3	65.6
Cost of Services	64.5	63.9	63.3	66.0	66.2	67.3	67.6	67.9	64.4	67.3	68.4
Cost of Revenue	69.8	66.9	67.8	67.6	67.8	67.4	67.2	67.0	68.0	67.3	66.6
SG&A	26.8	25.0	22.4	21.	22.5	21.5	21.4	19.8	23.7	21.2	19.9
R&D	9.2	7.1	7.2	6.7	7.8	6.7	6.7	6.3	7.5	6.8	6.5
Operating Income	(5.8)	0.9	2.5	4.6	1.9	4.4	4.7	6.9	0.8	4.7	7.0
Pretax Income	(6.1)	0.7	2.3	4.4	1.7	4.3	4.6	6.8	0.5	4.5	6.9
Net Income	(6.2)	0.5	2.1	4.3	1.5	3.8	4.0	5.8	0.4	3.9	5.8
Year-Over-Year Growth (%)											
Sales	6	13	12	(4)	10	26	24	27	6	22	16
Services	1	1	(0)	(5)	(1)	0	3	3	(1)	1	5
Total Revenue	4	7	6	(4)	5	14	15	16	3	13	1
Cost of Sales	25	17	16	(12)	2	22	16	22	9	16	13
Cost of Services	1	6	1	(2)	1	5	10	6	1	6	6
SG&A	(4)	(4)	(19)	(20)	(12)	(2)	9	10	(12)	1	4
R&D	(9)	(25)	(21)	(25)	(11	6	7	8	(20)	2	6
Operating Income	NM	(146)	(151	(218)	NM	472	120	74	NM	573	66
Pretax Income	NM	(132)	(144)	(205)	NM	654	133	80	NM	834	68
Net Income	NM	(126)	(140)	(200)	NM	688	11	60	NM	965	65
Sequential Quarterly Growth (%)											
Sales	(26)	13	5	9	(15)	29	4	1			
Services	(13)	9	(6)	7	(10)	10	(3)	8			
Total Revenue	(20)	1	(0)	8	(13)	21	1	10			
Cost of Sales	(26)	6	8	5	(14)	26	3	10			
Cost of Services	(13)	8	(7)	12	(10)	12	(3)	8			
SG&A	(15)	4	(10)	2	(7)	16	0	2			
R&D	(15)	(14)	1	1	1	3	2	2			
Operating Income	NM	NM	NM	NM	NM	NM	NM	NM			
Pretax Income	NM	NM	NM	NM	NM	NM	NM	NM			
Net Income	NM	NM	NM	NM	NM	NM	NM	NM			

Fiscal year ends in June.   *E = Morgan Stanley Research Estimates.*   *$ millions except EPS.*

Hewlett-Packard Earnings Model

	1995A				1996E				Full Year		
	Jan	Apr	Jul	Oct	Jan	Apr	Jul	Oct	1994A	1995A	1996E
Sales	$6,285	$6,339	$6,606	$7,895	$8,000	$8,150	$7,950	$9,500	$21,380	$27,125	$33,600
Services	1,019	1,089	1,133	1,153	1,180	1,225	1,250	1,300	3,611	4,394	4,955
Total Revenue	**$7,304**	**$7,428**	**$7,739**	**$9,048**	**$9,180**	**$9,375**	**$9,200**	**$10,800**	**$24,991**	**$31,519**	**$38,555**
Cost of Revenue	$4,547	$4,654	$4,907	$5,906	$6,004	$6,122	$6,011	$7,042	$15,490	$20,014	$25,178
SG&A	1,290	1,343	1,421	1,581	1,510	1,540	1,580	1,800	4,925	5,635	6,430
R&D	535	556	587	624	630	640	655	700	2,027	2,302	2,625
Operating Income	$932	$875	$824	$937	$1,036	$1,073	$954	$1,258	$2,549	$3,568	$4,322
Net Interest Income	(13)	(21)	43	55	25	25	25	25	(126)	64	100
Effective Tax Rate	34.5%	32.4%	33.6%	31.7%	33.0%	33.0%	33.0%	33.0%	34.0%	33.0%	33.0%
Pretax Income	$919	$854	$867	$992	$1,061	$1,098	$979	$1,283	$2,423	$3,632	$4,422
Taxes	317	277	291	314	350	362	323	424	824	1,199	1,459
Net Income	$602	$577	$576	$678	$711	$736	$656	$860	$1,599	$2,433	$2,962
Earnings Per Share	**$1.15**	**$1.10**	**$1.09**	**$1.29**	**$1.35**	**$1.39**	**$1.24**	**$1.62**	**$3.07**	**$4.63**	**$5.60**
Avg Shares	524.0	526.0	527.0	527.0	528.0	529.0	529.0	530.0	524.0	526.0	529.0
As a % of Revenue											
Revenue	100.0	100.0	100.0	100.0	100.0	100.0	100.0	100.0	100.0	100.0	100.0
Cost of Revenue	62.3	62.7	63.4	65.3	65.4	65.3	65.3	65.2	62.0	63.5	65.3
SG&A	17.7	18.1	18.4	17.5	16.4	16.4	17.2	16.7	19.7	17.9	16.7
R&D	7.3	7.5	7.6	6.9	6.9	6.8	7.1	6.5	8.1	7.3	6.8
Operating Income	12.8	11.8	10.6	10.4	11.3	11.4	10.4	11.7	10.2	11.3	11.2
Pretax Income	12.6	11.5	11.2	11.0	11.6	11.7	10.6	11.9	9.7	11.5	11.5
Net Income	8.2	7.8	7.4	7.5	7.7	7.8	7.1	8.0	6.4	7.7	7.7
Year-Over-Year Growth (%)											
Sales	29	18	29	32	27	29	20	20	25	27	24
Services	24	25	24	15	16	12	10	13	13	22	13
Total Revenue	29	19	28	29	26	26	19	19	23	26	22
Cost of Revenue	31	20	30	36	32	32	23	19	28	29	26
SG&A	12	10	17	19	17	15	11	14	8	14	14
R&D	15	11	14	15	18	15	12	12	15	14	14
Operating Income	56	37	52	22	11	23	16	34	36	40	21
Pretax Income	62	40	65	38	15	29	13	29	36	50	22
Net Income	64	41	66	42	18	28	14	27	36	52	22
Sequential Quarterly Growth (%)											
Sales	5	1	4	20	1	2	(2)	19			
Services	1	7	4	2	2	4	2	4			
Total Revenue	4	2	4	17	1	2	(2)	17			
Cost of Revenue	4	2	5	20	2	2	(2)	17			
SG&A	(3)	4	6	11	(4)	2	3	14			
R&D	(1)	4	6	6	1	2	2	7			
Operating Income	21	(6)	(6)	14	11	4	(11)	32			
Pretax Income	27	(7)	2	14	7	3	(11)	31			
Net Income	26	(4)	(0)	18	5	3	(11)	31			

Fiscal year ends in October. *E = Morgan Stanley Research Estimates.* *$ millions except EPS.*

IBM Earnings Model

($ Millions Except EPS)	1995A				1996E				Full Year		
	Mar	Jun	Sep	Dec	Mar	Jun	Sep	Dec	1995A	1996E	1997E
Sales	$7,727	$8,659	$7,745	$11,469	$8,040	$8,870	$8,430	$11,800	$35,600	$37,140	$38,515
Rentals & Financing	869	882	893	916	925	925	925	950	3,560	3,725	3,836
Software	2,873	3,072	3,134	3,578	3,074	3,285	3,285	3,740	12,657	13,384	13,450
Maintenance	1,821	1,877	1,849	1,862	1,840	1,870	1,845	1,855	7,409	7,410	7,200
Support Services	2,445	3,041	3,133	4,095	3,000	3,740	3,850	4,970	12,714	15,560	17,900
Total Revenue	**$15,735**	**$17,529**	**$16,754**	**$21,920**	**$16,879**	**$18,690**	**$18,335**	**$23,315**	**$71,940**	**$77,219**	**$80,901**
Cost of Sales	$4,798	$5,186	$4,957	$6,927	$5,057	$5,542	$5,280	$7,280	$21,869	$23,159	$24,365
Cost of Rentals & Financing	396	391	390	411	416	416	416	427	1,588	1,676	1,726
Cost of Software	1,006	1,066	1,073	1,242	1,075	1,150	1,150	1,310	4,386	4,685	4,842
Cost of Maintenance	900	867	912	972	956	974	950	940	3,651	3,820	3,744
Cost of Support Services	1,973	2,384	2,500	3,182	2,403	2,936	3,022	3,925	10,039	12,286	14,140
SG&A	3,633	3,883	3,858	4,941	3,700	3,899	3,860	4,873	16,315	16,332	16,500
R&D	913	974	1,035	1,248	1,010	1,060	1,118	1,300	4,170	4,488	4,625
Operating Income	$2,117	$2,778	$2,028	$2,997	$2,262	$2,713	$2,539	$3,260	$9,922	$10,773	$10,959
Interest Expense	180	188	159	198	180	180	180	180	725	720	700
Other Income	246	238	208	255	230	230	225	225	947	910	880
Effective Tax Rate	41.0%	39.2%	37.3%	33.7%	38.6%	37.0%	37.0%	36.0%	37.5%	37.0%	37.0%
Pretax Income	$2,183	$2,824	$2,077	$3,054	$2,312	$2,763	$2,584	$3,305	$10,141	$10,963	$11,139
Taxes	895	1,108	775	1,029	892	1,022	956	1,190	3,807	4,060	4,121
Net Income	$1,289	$1,716	$1,302	$2,025	$1,419	$1,741	$1,628	$2,115	$6,334	$6,903	$7,018
Preferred Dividend	$47	$5	$5	$5	$5	$5	$5	$5	$62	$20	$20
Earnings Per Share	**$2.12**	**$2.97**	**$2.30**	**$3.66**	**$2.60**	**$3.25**	**$3.08**	**$4.07**	**$11.02**	**$13.00**	**$14.00**
Avg. Shares (MM)	585.2	575.4	564.6	552.4	543.0	535.0	527.0	518.0	569.4	530.8	500.0
As a % of Revenue											
Revenue	100.0	100.0	100.0	100.0	100.0	100.0	100.0	100.0	100.0	100.0	100.0
Cost of Sales	62.1	59.9	64.0	60.4	62.9	62.5	62.6	61.7	61.4	62.4	63.3
Cost of Rentals	45.6	44.3	43.7	44.9	45.0	45.0	45.0	44.9	44.6	45.0	45.0
Cost of Software	35.0	34.7	34.3	34.7	35.0	35.0	35.0	35.0	34.7	35.0	36.0
Cost of Maintenance	49.4	46.2	49.4	52.2	52.0	52.1	51.5	50.7	49.3	51.6	52.0
Cost of Support Services	80.7	78.4	79.8	77.7	80.1	78.5	78.5	79.0	79.0	79.0	79.0
Cost of Revenue	57.7	56.4	58.7	58.1	58.7	59.0	59.0	59.5	57.7	59.1	60.3
SG&A	23.1	22.2	23.0	22.5	21.9	20.9	21.1	20.9	22.7	21.2	20.4
R&D	5.8	5.6	6.2	5.7	6.0	5.7	6.1	5.6	5.8	5.8	5.7
Operating Income	13.5	15.8	12.1	13.7	13.4	14.5	13.8	14.0	13.8	14.0	13.5
Pretax Income	13.9	16.1	12.4	13.9	13.7	14.8	14.1	14.2	14.1	14.2	13.8
Net Income	8.2	9.8	7.8	9.2	8.4	9.3	8.9	9.1	8.8	8.9	8.7
Year-Over-Year Growth (%)											
Sales	23	13	(0)	8	4	2	9	3	10	4	4
Rentals & Financing	(5)	5	11	6	6	5	4	4	4	5	3
Software	11	13	14	9	7	7	5	5	12	6	0
Maintenance	3	4	2	1	1	(0)	(0)	(0)	3	0	(3)
Support Services	33	33	36	25	23	23	23	21	31	22	15
Total Revenue	18	14	9	10	7	7	9	6	12	7	5
SG&A	3	(1)	(1)	(0)	2	0	0	(1)	0	0	1
R&D	(17)	(11)	(2)	12	11	9	8	4	(4)	8	3
Operating Income	254	159	67	48	7	(2)	25	9	102	9	2
Pretax Income	269	137	73	47	6	(2)	24	8	100	8	2
Net Income	281	150	83	65	10	1	25	4	114	9	2
Sequential Quarterly Growth (%)											
Sales	(27)	12	(11)	48	(30)	10	(5)	40			
Rentals & Financing	1	1	1	3	1	0	0	3			
Software	(12)	7	2	14	(14)	7	0	14			
Maintenance	(1)	3	(1)	1	(1)	2	(1)	1			
Support Services	(26)	24	3	31	(27)	25	3	29			
Total Revenue	(21)	11	(4)	31	(23)	11	(2)	27			
SG&A	(27)	7	(1)	28	(18)	5	(1)	26			
R&D	(18)	7	6	21	(58)	5	5	16			
Operating Income	5	31	(27)	48	(25)	20	(6)	28			
Pretax Income	5	29	(26)	47	(24)	20	(6)	28			
Net Income	5	33	(24)	56	(30)	23	(7)	30			

E = Morgan Stanley Research Estimates.   *A = Actual NM = Not Meaningful*   *Note: Table excludes restructuring charges.*

Intel Earnings Summary 1994–1996E

($ Millions Except EPS)	1995				1996E				Full Year		
	Q1A*	Q2A	Q3A*	Q4A	Q1	Q2	Q3	Q4	1994*	1995A*	1996E
Sales	$3,557.0	$3,894.0	$4,171.0	$4,580.0	$4,580.0	$4,854.8	$5,049.0	$5,452.9	$11,521.	$16,202.0	$19,936.7
Gross Profit	$1,948.0	$2,089.0	$2,163.0	$2,191.0	$2,231.0	$2,395.9	$2,512.4	$2,754.7	$5,944.9	$8,391.0	$9,894.0
Gross Margin	54.8%	53.6%	51.9%	47.8%	48.7%	49.4%	49.8%	50.5%	51.6%	51.8%	49.6%
SGA	$387.0	$447.0	$440.0	$569.0	$540.4	$572.9	$580.6	$627.1	$1,447.0	$1,843.0	$2,321.0
% Sales	10.9%	11.5	10.5%	12.4%	11.8	11.8	11.5	11.5	12.6%	11.4	11.6
R & D	$294.0	$316.0	$334.0	$352.0	$380.0	$405.0	$430.0	$455.0	$1,111.	$1,296.0	$1,670.0
% Sales	8.3%	8.1%	8.0%	7.7%	8.3%	8.0%	8.1%	8.1%	9.6%	8.0%	8.4%
Operating Inc	$1,267.0	$1,326.0	$1,389.0	$1,270.0	$1,310.6	$1,418.0	$1,501.8	$1,672.7	$3,386.9	$5,252.0	$5,903.0
% Sales	35.6%	34.1%	33.3%	27.7%	28.6%	29.2%	29.7%	30.7%	29.4%	32.4%	29.6%
Interest (Exp)	$149.0	$73.0	$94.0	$70.0	$65.0	$65.0	$70.0	$70.0	$216.0	$386.0	$270.0
% Sales	4.2%	1.9%	2.3%	1.5%	1.4%	1.3%	1.4%	1.3%	1.9%	2.4%	1.4%
Pretax Income	$1,416.0	$1,399.0	$1,483.0	$1,340.0	$1,375.6	$1,483.0	$1,571.8	$1,742.7	$3,602.9	$5,638.0	$6,173.0
Pretax Margin	39.8%	35.9%	35.6%	29.3%	30.0%	30.5%	31.1	32.0%	31.3%	34.8%	31.0%
Taxes	$527.0	$520.0	$552.0	$472.9	$502.1	$541.3	$573.7	$636.0	$1,315.0	$2,071.9	$2,253.0
Tax Rate	37.2%	37.2%	37.2%	35.3%	36.5%	36.5%	36.5%	36.5%	36.5%	36.7%	36.5%
Net Income	$889.0	$879.0	$931.0	$867.1	$873.5	$941.7	$998.1	$1,106.7	$2,287.9	$3,566.1	$3,920.0
EPS Incl. AMD, VLSI, ALTR	$1.02	$0.99	$1.05	$0.98	$0.98	$1.05	$1.10	$1.22	$2.62	$4.03	$4.35
EPS Excl. AMD, VLSI, ALTR	$0.96	$0.99	$1.02	$0.98					$3.32	$3.95	$4.35
Avg Shares (MM)	872	888	889	887	887	900	905	910	874	884	900.5

Q1, full year incl $0.06/share gains from AMD legal settlement, sale of VLSI stock. Q3, full year incl $0.03/share from sale of Altera stock

E = Morgan Stanley Research Estimates

Silicon Graphics Earnings Model

($ Millions Except EPS)

	1995A				1996E				Full Year		
	Sep	Dec	Mar	Jun	Sep A	DecA	Mar	Jun	1995A	1996E	1997E
Sales	$395.4	$491.8	$515.8	$587.1	$524.7	$597.5	$647.0	$761.0	$1,990.0	$2,530.2	$3,310.0
Service	53.1	57.8	61.2	66.1	70.6	74.3	81.0	87.0	238.3	312.8	406.7
Total Revenue	**$448.5**	**$549.6**	**$577.0**	**$653.2**	**$595.3**	**$671.7**	**$728.0**	**$848.0**	**$2,228.3**	**$2,843.0**	**$3,716.7**
Cost of Sales	$180.8	$226.1	$232.0	$269.6	$234.7	$291.1	$313.0	$366.0	$908.5	$1,204.8	$1,570.0
Cost of Service	27.1	29.4	31.4	35.7	37.9	40.3	43.7	47.0	123.5	168.9	220.0
SG&A	123.5	145.7	159.8	190.2	172.2	193.2	207.0	232.0	619.3	804.3	1,028.0
R&D	56.2	60.8	61.4	69.2	72.7	80.8	84.5	95.0	247.6	333.0	430.0
Merger-related Expense	0.0	0.0	0.0	(22.0)	0.7	0.6	0.5	0.3	-22.0	-2.0	
Operating Income	$60.9	$87.5	$92.4	$88.5	$77.0	$65.9	$79.3	$107.7	$329.3	$334.0	$468.7
Interest Income & Other	2.9	(3.9)	4.5	6.0	6.3	6.7	4.0	4.0	9.4	21.0	16.0
Effective Tax Rate	29.3%	29.4%	29.6%	20.9%	30.0%	27.9%	29.0%	29.0%	27.1%	28.7%	29.0%
Pretax Income	$63.8	$83.6	$96.8	$94.5	$83.4	$72.6	$83.3	$111.7	$338.7	$355.0	$484.7
Taxes	18.7	24.5	28.6	19.8	25.0	20.2	24.2	32.4	91.9	101.8	140.5
Net Income	$45.1	$59.0	$68.2	$74.7	$58.4	$52.4	$59.1	$79.3	$247.1	$253.2	$344.1
EPS	**$0.26**	**$0.34**	**$0.38**	**$0.41**	**$0.33**	**$0.30**	**$0.33**	**$0.44**	**$1.40**	**$1.40**	**$1.90**
Avg. Shares (mil.)	172.0	174.1	177.8	177.9	179.2	177.3	178.0	179.0	175.4	178.4	181.0
As a % of Revenue											
Total Revenue	100.0	100.0	100.0	100.0	100.0	100.0	100.0	100.0	100.0	100.0	100.0
Cost of Sales	45.7	46.0	45.0	45.9	44.7	48.7	48.4	48.1	45.7	47.6	47.4
Cost of Service	50.9	50.9	51.3	53.9	53.8	54.2	54.0	54.0	51.8	54.0	54.1
Cost of Revenue	46.3	46.5	45.7	46.7	45.8	49.3	49.0	48.7	46.3	48.3	48.2
SG&A	27.5	26.5	27.7	29.1	28.9	28.8	28.4	27.4	27.8	28.3	27.7
R&D	12.5	11.1	10.6	10.6	12.2	12.0	11.6	11.2	11.1	11.7	11.6
Operating Income	13.6	15.9	16.0	13.5	12.9	9.8	10.9	12.7	14.8	11.7	12.6
Pretax Income	14.2	15.2	16.8	14.5	14.0	10.8	11.4	13.2	15.2	12.5	13.0
Net Income	10.1	10.7	11.8	11.4	9.8	7.8	8.1	9.4	11.1	8.9	9.3
Year-Over-Year Growth (%)											
Sales	44	44	49	45	33	21	25	30	46	27	31
Service	37	39	40	37	33	28	32	32	38	31	30
Total Revenue	44	44	48	44	33	22	26	30	45	28	31
Cost of Revenue	40	39	40	42	31	30	35	35	40	33	30
SG&A	38	43	51	58	39	33	30	22	48	30	28
R&D	38	37	19	29	29	33	38	37	30	34	29
Operating Income	82	71	104	39	26	(25)	(14)	22	70	1	40
Pretax Income	87	58	108	45	31	(13)	(14)	18	71	5	37
Net Income	71	59	116	61	29	(11)	(13)	6	74	2	36
Sequential Quarterly Growth (%)											
Sales	(2)	24	5	14	(11)	14	8	18			
Service	10	9	6	8	7	5	9	7			
Total Revenue	(1)	23	5	13	(9)	13	8	16			
Cost of Revenue	(3)	23	3	16	(11)	22	8	16			
SG&A	3	18	10	19	(9)	12	7	12			
R&D	5	8	1	13	5	11	5	12			
Operating Income	(5)	44	6	(4)	(13)	(14)	20	36			
Pretax Income	(2)	31	16	(2)	(12)	(13)	15	34			
Net Income	(3)	31	15	10	(22)	(10)	13	34			

NM = Not Meaningful   *E = Morgan Stanley Research Estimates*   *A = Actual*

Sun Microsystems

($ Millions Except EPS)

	1995A				1996E				Full Year		
	Sep	Dec	Mar	Jun	SepA	DecA	Mar	Jun	1995A	1996E	1997E
Revenue	**$1,273.4**	**$1,475.3**	**$1,505.0**	**$1,648.1**	**$1,485.3**	**$1,751.4**	**$1,860.0**	**$2,040.0**	**$5,901.9**	**$7,136.7**	**$8,350.0**
Cost of Revenue	$761.4	$862.1	$855.1	$920.4	$829.0	$984.7	$1,050.0	$1,152.0	$3,399.0	$4,015.7	$4,780.0
SG&A	329.0	364.3	368.1	411.3	398.6	421.3	445.0	483.0	1,472.8	1,747.9	1,997.0
R&D	129.2	131.9	131.3	137.3	144.7	167.5	171.0	180.0	529.8	663.2	765.0
Operating Income	$53.8	$117.0	$150.5	$179.1	$112.9	$178.0	$194.0	$225.0	$500.3	$709.9	$808.0
Net Interest Expense	(2.7)	(3.1)	(7.6)	(9.5)	(11.6)	(7.4)	(7.0)	(8.0)	(22.9)	(34.0)	(36.0)
Effective Tax Rate	32.0%	32.0%	32.0%	32.0%	32.0%	32.0%	32.0%	32.0%	32.0%	32.0%	32.0%
Pretax Income	$56.5	$120.0	$158.1	$188.6	$124.6	$185.4	$201.0	$233.0	$523.2	$743.9	$844.0
Taxes	18.1	38.4	50.6	60.4	39.9	59.3	64.3	74.6	167.5	238.1	270.1
Net Income	$38.4	$81.6	$107.5	$128.2	$84.7	$126.0	$136.7	$158.4	$355.8	$505.9	$573.9
Earnings Per Share	**$0.20**	**$0.42**	**$0.54**	**$0.63**	**$0.42**	**$0.65**	**$0.72**	**$0.84**	**$1.81**	**$2.63**	**$3.10**
Avg. Shares (mil.)	191.3	195.5	197.4	203.1	199.3	194.3	191.0	188.0	197.0	193.0	185.0
As a % of Revenue											
Revenue	100.0	100.0	100.0	100.0	100.0	100.0	100.0	100.0	100.0	100.0	100.0
Cost of Revenue	59.8	58.4	56.8	55.8	55.8	56.2	56.5	56.5	57.6	56.3	57.2
SG&A	25.8	24.7	24.5	25.0	26.8	24.1	23.9	23.7	25.0	24.5	23.9
R&D	10.1	8.9	8.7	8.3	9.7	9.6	9.2	8.8	9.0	9.3	9.2
Operating Income	4.2	7.9	10.0	10.9	7.6	10.2	10.4	11.0	8.5	9.9	9.7
Pretax Income	4.4	8.1	10.5	11.4	8.4	10.6	10.8	11.4	8.9	10.4	10.1
Net Income	3.0	5.5	7.1	7.8	5.7	7.2	7.3	7.8	6.0	7.1	6.9
Year-Over-Year Growth (%)											
Revenue	33	30	26	17	17	19	24	24	26	21	17
Cost of Revenue	34	31	25	9	9	14	23	25	23	18	19
SG&A	22	24	22	21	21	16	21	17	22	19	14
R&D	20	18	6	23	12	27	30	31	80	42	15
Operating Income	246	78	78	61	110	52	29	26	80	42	14
Pretax Income	250	81	82	66	120	54	27	24	85	42	13
Net Income	131	86	87	65	120	54	27	24	82	42	13
Sequential Quarterly Growth (%)											
Revenue	(9)	16	2	10	(10)	18	6	10			
Cost of Revenue	(10)	13	(1)	8	(10)	19	7	10			
SG&A	(3)	11	1	12	(3)	6	6	9			
R&D	16	2	(0)	5	5	16	2	5			
Operating Income	(52)	117	29	19	(37)	58	9	16			
Pretax Income	(50)	112	32	19	(34)	49	8	16			
Net Income	(51)	112	32	19	(34)	49	8	16			

E = Morgan Stanley Research Estimates.   *A = Actual*

Telecommunications and Related Services

AT&T — Income Statement

($ Millions Except Per Share Data)

	1994				1995						
	1qtr 94	**2qtr 94**	**3qtr 94**	**4qtr 94**	**1qtr 95A**	**2qtr 95A**	**3qtr 95A**	**4qtr 95A**	**1993**	**1994 A**	**1995 A**
Revenues											
Telecom Services	10,449	10,527	10,698	10,689	10,736	11,03	11,33	11,25	39,863	42,363	44,351
Products & Systems	4,074	4,933	5,068	7,086	4,537	5,223	5,144	7,508	17,798	21,16	22,412
Rentals & other serv.	1,38	1,51	1,498	1,827	1,443	1,607	1,522	1,61	6,991	6,216	6,189
Cellular	502	545	577	613	652	724	758	792		2,237	2,926
Financial services and leasing	691	723	808	895	894	923	950	964	2,504	3,11	3,731
Total Revenues	17,097	18,238	18,649	21,11	18,262	19,51	19,704	22,13	67,156	75,094	79,609
Less: Direct Costs	10,14	10,848	10,902	12,487	10,71	11,36	11,43	12,938	40,569	44,384	46,463
	6,952	7,390	7,747	8,623	7,545	8,144	8,266	9,193	26,587	30,710	33,146
Operating Expenses											
SG&A	4,355	4,691	5,000	5,591	4,769	5,022	5,053	5,972	16,782	19,637	20,816
Research & Development	762	708	808	832	847	831	847	776	3,069	3,11	3,301
Contingency/Other	0	0	0	0	0	0	0	0	498	0	0
Total Operating Expenses	5,11	5,399	5,808	6,423	5,616	5,853	5,900	6,748	20,349	22,747	24,11
Operating Income	1,835	1,99	1,939	2,200	1,929	2,291	2,366	2,445	6,238	7,963	9,029
Other Income	11	11	-17	83	147	11	128	11	532	301	508
Non-Operating Expenses					5%	15%	22%	11			
Minority Interest	0	0	0	0	21	28	0	0	0	0	49
Amort LIN							0	0			0
Interest Expense	195	209	176	168	130	172	197	209	566	748	708
Total Non-Operating Expenses	195	209	176	168	15	200	197	209	566	748	757
Pre-Tax Income	1,757	1,900	1,746	2,11	1,925	2,206	2,297	2,354	6,204	7,516	8,780
One Time Charges	0	0	0	0	0	0	0	0	-7,768	0	0
Provision For Income Taxes	$683	$652	$696	$777	$727	$851	$864	$850	$2,230	$2,808	$3,292
Net After-Tax Income	$1,074	$1,248	$1,050	$1,338	$1,197	$1,354	$1,433	$1,504	($3,794)	$4,708	$5,488
EPS Reported	**$0.69**	**$0.80**	**$0.67**	**$0.85**	**$0.76**	**$0.85**	**$0.90**	**$0.94**	**($2.80)**	**$3.01**	**$3.45**
EPS Normalized					10.0%	6.6%	13.8%	10.3%			10.2%
	$0.69	$0.80	$0.79	$0.85	$0.76	$0.85	$0.90	$0.94	$2.94	$3.13	$3.45

A = Actual

19 – 26

Comcast — Consolidated CATV Systems

($ Millions)

	1994 1Q	2Q	3Q	4Q	1995E 1Q	2Q	3Q	4QE	1994	1995E	1996E
Homes Passed	4,248,000	4,270,000	4,292,000	4,314,000	5,507,000	5,528,000	5,549,000	5,570,000	4,314,000	5,570,000	6,927,000
% Change	1.7	1.8	1.7	2.4%	29.6%	29.5%	29.3%	29.1%	2.4%	29.1%	24.4%
Basic Subscribers	2,677,000	2,680,000	2,707,000	2,766,000	3,346,000	3,351,000	3,360,000	3,401,000	2,766,000	3,401,000	4,303,000
% Change	2.8%	3.6%	3.6%	4.5%	25.0%	25.0%	24.1%	23.0%	4.5%	23.0%	26.5%
Basic Penetration	63.0%	62.8%	63.1%	64.1%	60.8%	60.6%	60.6%	61.1	64.1%	61.1	62.1%
Premium Subscriptions	1,932,000	1,992,000	2,052,000	2,134,000	2,815,000	2,869,000	2,886,000	2,900,000	2,134,000	2,900,000	3,669,000
% Change	5.1	9.0%	11.2	14.0%	45.7%	44.0%	40.6%	35.9%	14.0%	35.9%	26.5%
Premium Penetration	72.2%	74.3%	75.8%	77.2%	84.1%	85.6%	85.9%	85.3%	77.2%	85.3%	85.3%
Total Revenue	260.9	266.4	266.6	271.4	347.1	362.5	368.5	372.6	1,065.3	1,450.6	1,701.
% Change	-4.2%	-4.7%	-2.5%	0.5%	33.1%	38.9%	38.3%	39.7%	-2.7%	36.2%	17.3%
Monthly Revenue per Subscriber	$32.66	$33.15	$32.99	$33.06	$34.79	$36.08	$36.60	$36.74	$32.97	$36.06	$37.80
% Change	-6.7%	-7.7%	-5.9%	-3.4%	6.5%	10.5%	10.4%	11.3	-5.5%	9.4%	4.8%
Monthly Revenue per Home Passed	$20.56	$20.85	$20.76	$21.03	$21.07	$21.90	$22.18	$22.34	$20.80	$21.87	$23.29
% Change	-5.6%	-6.3%	-4.2%	-	2.5%	6.5%	6.4%	7.6%	-4.7%	5.2%	6.5%
Operating Costs	134.0	136.	137.7	140.	182.0	179.9	186.5	189.3	547.8	737.7	873.3
% of Revenues	51.4%	51.1	51.7%	51.6%	52.4%	49.6%	50.6%	50.8%	51.4%	50.9%	51.3%
Operating Cash Flow	126.9	130.3	128.9	131.	165.	182.6	182.0	183.3	517.5	712.9	828.3
Operating Margin	48.6%	48.9%	48.3%	48.4%	47.6%	50.4%	49.4%	49.2%	48.6%	49.1%	48.7%
Management Fees and Other Income	0.0	0.0	0.0	0.0	0.0	0.0	0.0	0.0	0.0	0.0	0.0
Total Operating Cash Flow	126.9	130.3	128.9	131.	165.	182.6	182.0	183.3	517.5	712.9	828.3
Cash Interest Expense	58.8	59.9	61.	62.2	84.3	89.0	94.5	96.4	242.0	364.2	390.1
Cash Interest Coverage	2.2	2.2	2.1	2.1	2.0	2.1	1.9	1.9	2.1	2.0	2.1
Noncash Interest Expense	3.8	3.4	3.0	2.6	3.2	3.7	4.3	4.8	12.9	16.0	16.
Total Interest Expense	62.7	63.4	64.1	64.8	87.5	92.7	98.8	101.	254.9	380.2	406.2
Total Interest Expense Coverage	2.0	2.1	2.0	2.0	1.9	2.0	1.8	1.8	2.0	1.9	2.0
Capital Expenditures and Other	34.7	52.3	56.4	20.6	43.9	68.8	69.4	74.7	163.9	256.8	336.3
Discretionary Cash Flow	29.6	14.6	8.4	46.0	33.8	21.	13.8	7.3	98.7	75.9	85.8

Effective 9/30/96 results are pro forma for the EW Scripps cable television systems.
E = Morgan Stanley Research Estimates.

Cox Communications — Consolidated CATV Systems

($ Millions)

	Pro Forma 1994				Pro Forma 1995E				Pro Forma		
	1Q	2Q	3Q	4Q	1Q	2Q	3Q	4QE	1994	1995E	1996E
Homes Passed	4,928,893	4,952,119	4,975,345	5,005,000	4,963,756	4,983,752	4,982,490	5,001,000	5,005,000	5,001,000	4,992,000
% Change	2.2%	2.2%	2.1%	2.0%	0.7%	0.6%	0.1%	-0.1%	2.0%	-0.1%	-0.2%
Basic Subscribers	3,027,630	3,049,775	3,071,919	3,127,000	3,196,184	3,202,098	3,216,469	3,236,000	3,127,000	3,236,000	3,310,000
% Change	3.1%	3.0%	3.8%	4.5%	5.6%	5.0%	4.7%	3.5%	4.5%	3.5%	2.3%
Basic Penetration	61.4%	61.6%	61.7%	62.5%	64.4%	64.3%	64.6%	64.7%	62.5%	64.7%	66.3%
Premium Subscriptions	1,924,603	1,941,637	1,958,671	1,985,000	1,852,365	1,835,261	1,835,363	1,814,000	1,985,000	1,814,000	1,756,000
% Change	-2.5%	-0.3%	1.7	4.0%	-3.8%	-5.5%	-6.3%	-8.6%	4.0%	-8.6%	-3.2%
Premium Penetration	63.6%	63.7%	63.8%	63.5%	58.0%	57.3%	57.1%	56.1%	63.5%	56.1%	53.1%
Total Revenue	303.3	306.4	302.7	316.3	309.4	324.3	328.1	343.3	1,228.8	1,305.1	1,409.3
% Change	6.6%	3.8%	2.3%	4.6%	2.0%	5.8%	8.4%	8.5%	4.5%	6.2%	8.0%
Monthly Revenue per Subscriber	$33.59	$33.62	$32.96	$34.02	$32.62	$33.79	$34.08	$35.47	$33.55	$34.00	$35.75
% Change	3.4%	0.7%	-	0.4%	-2.9%	0.5%	3.4%	4.3%	0.9%	1.3%	5.2%
Monthly Revenue per Home Passed	$20.56	$20.68	$20.33	$21.13	$20.69	$21.74	$21.95	$22.92	$20.67	$21.82	$23.43
% Change	4.1%	1.6%	0.1%	2.4%	0.6%	5.1	8.0%	8.5%	2.3%	5.6%	7.3%
Operating Costs	181.1	182.5	192.4	196.1	188.9	198.3	200.0	208.4	752.0	795.6	840.9
% of Revenues	59.7%	59.5%	63.6%	62.0%	61.1%	61.1%	61.0%	60.7%	61.2%	61.0%	59.7%
Operating Cash Flow	122.3	124.0	110.2	120.3	120.4	126.1	128.1	134.9	476.8	509.5	568.4
Operating Margin	40.3%	40.5%	36.4%	38.0%	38.9%	38.9%	39.0%	39.3%	38.8%	39.0%	40.3%
Management Fees and Other Income	0.0	0.0	0.0	0.0	0.0	0.0	0.0	0.0	0.0	0.0	0.0
Total Operating Cash Flow	122.3	124.0	110.2	120.3	120.4	126.1	128.1	134.9	476.8	509.5	568.4
Cash Interest Expense	5.9	5.9	19.4	14.9	36.4	39.9	37.9	36.0	46.1	150.1	184.6
Cash Interest Coverage	20.7	21.0	5.7	8.1	3.3	3.2	3.4	3.8	10.3	3.4	3.1
Noncash Interest Expense	0.0	0.0	0.0	0.0	0.0	0.0	0.0	0.0	0.0	0.0	0.0
Total Interest Expense	5.9	5.9	19.4	14.9	36.4	39.9	37.9	36.0	46.1	150.1	184.6
Total Interest Expense Coverage	20.7	21.0	5.7	8.1	3.3	3.2	3.4	3.8	10.3	3.4	3.1
Capital Expenditures and Other	59.6	67.3	83.2	88.1	57.8	85.0	106.1	91.8	298.2	340.7	385.7
Discretionary Cash Flow	56.8	50.8	7.7	17.2	26.3	1.2	(15.9)	7.1	132.5	18.7	(1.8)

Pro forma for the Times Mirror cable television acquisition   *E = Morgan Stanley Research Estimates*

MCI Communications

($ Millions Except Per Share Data)

Consolidated	1QA	2QA	3QA	4QA	1QE	2QE	3QE	4QE	1994A	1995A	1996E
			1995			1996E					
Total Revenues	3,561	3,706	3,862	4,136	4,417	4,607	4,806	4,924	13,337	15,248	18,754
											9.46%
Operating Expenses	2,812	2,944	3,068	3,278	3,515	3,659	3,815	3,904	10,636	12,086	14,895
EBITDA	749	762	794	858	901	948	991	1,020	2,701	3,162	3,859
	21.03%	*20.56%*	*20.56%*	*20.74%*	*20.40%*	*20.58%*	*20.61%*	*20.71%*	*20.25%*	*20.74%*	*20.58%*
Depreciation	319	325	328	336	349	364	379	394	1,113	1,308	1,486
SHL Amort.					0	0	0	0			0
Nationwide Amort.				0	0	0	0	0			0
Operating Income	430	437	466	522	552	584	612	626	1,588	1,854	2,373
Interest Expense	-38	-36	-35	-40	-47	-52	-59	-65	-153	-149	-223
Interest Income	46	49	36	16	8	5	2	2	47	147	17
Other	-12	-9	-2	-9	-12	-16	-20	-22	-54	-32	-70
Equity (losses)/Gains in Affiliates	-29	-18	-21	-24	-28	-32	-38	-42		-92	-140
Pretax Income	397	423	444	465	473	489	497	499	1,428	1,728	1,957
Tax Provision	153.0	162.9	169.2	180.0	184.4	190.6	193.8	194.5	541.0	665.0	763
Tax Rate	38.5%	38.5%	38.1%	38.7%	39.0%	39.0%	39.0%	39.0%	37.9%	38.5%	39.0%
Div on Pfd	0	0	0	0					0	0	0
Net Income	244	260	275	285	288	298	303	304	887	1064	1194
EPS	**0.36**	**0.38**	**0.40**	**0.41**	**0.42**	**0.43**	**0.44**	**0.44**	**1.47**	**1.55**	**1.72**
Avg Shares	685	685	688	694	695	695	695	695	640	688	695
Adjustments	0.00	0.00	0.00	0.00					0.00	0.00	0.00
Normalized EPS	**0.36**	**0.38**	**0.40**	**0.41**	**0.42**	**0.43**	**0.44**	**0.44**	**1.47**	**1.55**	**1.72**
Costs as Pct of Long Distance Revenue											11.13%
Telecommunications Expense	51.1%	51.8%	51.8%	50.1%	50.0%	50.0%	49.9%	49.9%	51.9%	51.2%	49.9%
Sales, Oper and Gen	27.9%	27.6%	27.6%	27.4%	27.6%	27.4%	27.4%	27.3%	27.9%	27.6%	27.4%
Depreciation	9.0%	8.8%	8.5%	8.3%	8.3%	8.3%	8.3%	8.5%	8.3%	8.6%	8.4%
Total	87.9%	88.2%	87.9%	85.8%	85.4%	85.1%	85.0%	85.0%	88.1%	87.4%	85.1%
Net LD SG&A						26.8%	26.8%	26.6%			26.8%
Operating Income	**12.1%**	**11.8%**	**12.1%**	**14.2%**	**14.6%**	**14.9%**	**15.0%**	**15.0%**	**11.9%**	**12.6%**	**14.9%**

A = Actual   E = Morgan Stanley Research Estimates.

Sprint — Consolidated Statement of Income 1994–1996E

($ Millions Except Per Share Data

	1995E				1996E				YE		
	1QA	2QA	3QA	4QE	1QE	2QE	3QE	4QE	1994	1995E	1996E
Operating Revenues											
Long-Distance	1752.5	1771.8	1826.9	1885	1936.5	1957.8	2009.6	2064.1	6805.1	7236.2	7968.0165
Local Telco	1140.9	1167.8	1179.9	1216	1209.4	1239.0	1248.3	1286.5	4412.8	4704.6	4983.3
Cellular	203.3	232.8	246	0	0.0	0.0	0.0	0.0	701.8	682.1	0.0
Complementary	277.3	298	295.1	290	292.8	312.9	309.9	304.5	1108.7	1160.4	1220.1
Intercompany	-102.5	-104.8	-105.6	-108	-115.8	-118.4	-119.3	-122.0	-366.6	-420.9	-475.6
Total Revenues	3271.5	3365.6	3442.3	3283	3322.9	3391.4	3448.5	3533.1	12661.8	13362.4	13695.735
Operating Expenses											
Long-Distance	1597	1601	1642	1695	1735	1754	1793	1843	6200	6535	7125.1
Local Telco	869	896	888	925	922	950	933	971	3,391	3,579	3775.2
Cellular Service	173	193	203	0	0	0	0	0	617	568	0.0
Complementary	258	275	271	268	264	281	277	273	1,034	1,073	1094.5
Intercompany	-103	-105	-106	-108	-	-	-	-122	-367	-421	-475.6
Total Expenses	2795	2860	2899	2780	2804	2866	2883	2966	10875	11334	1151
Expenses as Pct of Total Expense											
Long Distance	57.1%	56.0%	56.6%	61.0%	61.9%	61.2%	62.2%	62.1%	57.0%	57.7%	61.9%
Local Telco	31.1	31.3%	30.6%	33.3%	32.9%	33.1%	32.4%	32.7%	31.2%	31.6%	32.8%
Cellular	6.2%	6.7%	7.0%	0.0%	0.0%	0.0%	0.0%	0.0%	5.7%	5.0%	0.0%
Complementary	9.2%	9.6%	9.4%	9.6%	9.4%	9.8%	9.6%	9.2%	9.5%	9.5%	9.5%
Operating Income											
Long Distance	155	17	185	190	201	204	217	221	605	701	843
Local Telco	272	272	292	291	288	289	316	315	1022	1126	1208
Cellular	30	40	43	0	0	0	0	0	85	11	0
Complementary	19	23	24	22	29	32	33	31	75	87	126
Intercompany and Other	0	0	0	0	0	0	0	0	0	0	0
Total	476	506	544	503	518	525	566	567	1787	2029	2177
Operating Margin					2109	2116	2157	2158		3620	3863
Long Distance	8.9%	9.6%	10.1	10.1	10.4%	10.4%	10.8%	10.7%	8.9%	9.7%	10.6%
Local Telco	23.8%	23.3%	24.7%	23.9%	23.8%	23.4%	25.3%	24.5%	23.2%	23.9%	24.2%
Cellular	14.9%	17.3%	17.6%	0.0%	0.0%	0.0%	0.0%	0.0%	12.1	16.7%	0.0%
Total	14.6%	15.0%	15.8%	15.3%	15.6%	15.5%	16.4%	16.1	14.1	15.2%	15.9%
Other Exp, Net *	20.5	14.5	18.	25	28	35	45	75	-1	78	183
Interest Charges	99.2	100	98	65	64	64	64	64	398	362	256
Minority Interest	0	0	0	0					0	0	0
Other/Interest Income **	0	0	0	0	-34	-57.5	-60	-50	0	0	-201.5
Income Bef Taxes	**356**	**391**	**428**	**413**	**460**	**484**	**517**	**478**	**1390**	**1588**	**1939**
Tax Provision	132.1	145.3	158.9	153.6	171.7	180.4	192.8	178.4	498.4	589.9	723.3
Tax Rate	37.1%	37.2%	37.2%	37.2%	37.3%	37.3%	37.3%	37.3%	35.9%	37.1%	37.3%
Net Income	224	246	269	260	289	303	324	300	891	998	1216
Preferred Stock	0	1	1	1	14	7			0	0	0
Net Income	**224**	**245**	**268**	**259**	**275**	**296**	**324**	**300**	**891**	**998**	**1216**
Net Margin	6.9%	7.3%	7.8%	7.9%	8.7%	8.9%	9.4%	8.5%	7.0%	7.5%	8.9%
EPS***	**0.64**	**0.70**	**0.76**	**0.74**	**0.78**	**0.69**	**0.74**	**0.69**	**2.55**	**2.85**	**2.94**
EPS After Non recurr	**0.64**	**0.70**	**0.76**	**0.74**	**0.78**	**0.69**	**0.74**	**0.69**	**2.49**	**2.85**	**2.94**
Avg Shares Outs (MM)	349.5	350.2	350.5	350.5	351	430	437	437	349	350	414

* 1996 Other Expense includes $160M for STV
** 1996 Other Income is based on $3B Received in 2/96 and $500M in 4/96 from FT/DT
***4Q95E EPS including Cellular = $.075 for Fourth Quarter

A = Actual   E = Morgan Stanley Research Estimates

Tele-Communications — TCI Group — Consolidated CATV Systems

($ Millions Except Per Data)

	1994				1995E				1994	1995E	1996E
	1Q	2Q	3Q	4Q	1Q	2Q	3Q	4QE	1994	1995E	1996E
Homes Passed	18,148,000	18,263,000	18,733,000	19,137,000	19,556,000	19,681,000	19,775,000	20,063,000	19,137,000	20,063,000	22,868,000
% Change	1.9%	2.1%	4.3%	6.1%	7.8%	7.8%	5.6%	4.8%	6.1%	4.8%	14.0%
Basic Subscribers	10,881,000	10,923,000	11,349,000	11,695,000	12,035,000	12,093,000	12,168,000	12,467,000	11,695,000	12,467,000	14,526,000
% Change	5.0%	4.3%	7.2%	9.3%	10.6%	10.7%	7.2%	6.6%	9.3%	6.6%	16.5%
Basic Penetration	60.0%	59.8%	60.6%	61.1%	61.5%	61.4%	61.5%	62.1%	61.1%	62.1%	63.5%
Premium Subscriptions	11,002,000	11,327,000	11,947,000	12,417,000	12,623,000	12,781,000	13,020,000	13,234,000	12,417,000	13,234,000	14,411,000
% Change	12.1%	13.3%	17.4%	20.0%	14.7%	12.8%	9.0%	6.6%	20.0%	6.6%	8.9%
Premium Penetration	101.1%	103.7%	105.3%	106.2%	104.9%	105.7%	107.0%	106.2%	106.2%	106.2%	99.2%
Total Revenue	1,019.7	1,039.7	1,019.5	1,104.0	1,169.0	1,262.0	1,310.0	1,333.7	4,182.9	5,074.7	6,096.5
% Change	0.2%	-0.2%	-2.4%	6.2%	14.6%	21.4%	28.5%	20.8%	0.9%	21.3%	20.1%
Monthly Revenue per Subscriber	$31.50	$31.79	$30.31	$31.94	$33.19	$34.87	$35.86	$36.17	$31.38	$35.04	$37.19
% Change	-4.3%	-4.7%	-8.3%	-1.9%	5.4%	9.7%	18.3%	13.2%	-4.8%	11.7%	6.1%
Monthly Revenue per Home Passed	$18.79	$19.04	$18.25	$19.43	$20.27	$21.44	$22.05	$22.36	$18.88	$21.54	$23.42
% Change	-1.6%	-2.2%	-6.0%	0.9%	7.9%	12.6%	20.8%	15.0%	-2.2%	14.1%	8.7%
Operating Costs	555.3	571.3	576.7	634.9	672.0	744.0	784.0	788.7	2,338.2	2,988.7	3,560.0
% of Revenues	54.5%	54.9%	56.6%	57.5%	57.5%	59.0%	59.8%	59.1%	55.9%	58.9%	58.4%
Operating Cash Flow	464.4	468.4	442.8	469.1	497.0	518.0	526.0	545.0	1,844.7	2,086.0	2,536.6
Operating Margin	45.5%	45.1%	43.4%	42.5%	42.5%	41.0%	40.2%	40.9%	44.1%	41.1%	41.6%
Management Fees and Other Income	0.0	0.0	0.0	0.0	0.0	0.0	0.0	0.0	0.0	0.0	0.0
Total Operating Cash Flow	464.4	468.4	442.8	469.1	497.0	518.0	526.0	545.0	1,844.7	2,086.0	2,536.6
Cash Interest Expense	178.0	182.0	203.0	220.0	232.0	232.0	258.0	249.2	783.0	984.2	1,130.4
Cash Interest Coverage	2.6	2.6	2.2	2.1	2.1	2.2	2.0	2.2	2.4	2.1	2.2
Noncash Interest Expense	0.0	0.0	0.0	0.0	0.0	0.0	0.0	0.0	0.0	0.0	0.0
Total Interest Expense	178.0	182.0	203.0	220.0	232.0	232.0	258.0	249.2	783.0	984.2	1,130.4
Total Interest Expense Coverage	2.6	2.6	2.2	2.1	2.1	2.2	2.0	2.2	2.4	2.1	2.2
Capital Expenditures and Other	243.0	356.0	335.0	244.3	225.0	298.0	250.0	239.6	1,178.3	1,012.6	1,193.9
Discretionary Cash Flow	43.4	(69.6)	(95.2)	4.8	40.0	(12.0)	18.0	56.2	(116.5)	89.2	212.2

Pro forma for the Viacom Cable, Columbia Cable, and Chronicle Cable acquisitions

E = Morgan Stanley Research Estimates.

WorldComm — Consolidated Income Statement

($Millions Except EPS)	Normalized 1994A 1qtr 94	2qtr 94	3qtr 94	4qtr 94	1995E 1qtr 95	2qtr 95	3qtr 95	4qtr 95E	YE 1995E	1996E	1997E
Total Revenues	533.9	545.3	568.6	573.0	865.0	894.7	933.6	961.0	3,654.3	4,229.9	4,692.9
Less: Direct Costs	328.0	349.0	365.5	390.9	479.8	492.5	508.3	510.9	1,991.5	2,284.6	2,543.4
%	61.44%	64.00%	64.29%	68.21%	55.47%	55.05%	54.45%	53.16%	54.50%	54.01%	54.20%
Gross Margin	205.9	196.3	203.0	182.2	385.2	402.2	425.2	450.1	1,662.8	1,945.4	2,149.5
	38.56%	36.00%	35.71%	31.79%	44.53%	44.95%	45.55%	46.84%	45.50%	45.99%	45.80%
Operating Expenses											
SG&A	91.4	99.2	100.4	97.3	177.8	183.5	190.8	197.0	749.1	768.8	876.6
	17.12%	18.19%	17.65%	16.99%	20.56%	20.51%	20.43%	20.50%	20.50%	18.18%	18.68%
Synergies					17.5	21.2	23.2	24	85.9		
Total Operating Expenses	91.4	99.2	100.4	97.3	160.3	162.3	167.6	173.0	663.2	768.8	876.6
					18.54%	18.14%	17.95%	18.00%	18.15%	18.18%	18.68%
EBITDA	114.5	97.1	102.7	84.8	224.9	239.9	257.7	277.1	999.6	1,176.5	1,272.8
	21.44%	17.81%	18.06%	14.80%	26.00%	26.82%	27.60%	28.84%	27.36%	27.81%	27.12%
Non-Operating Expenses											
Merger and Restructuring	0	0	11	130.5					0		
Depreciation					44.3	47	49.5	54	194.8	241.2	277.1
Amortization	38.1	40.4	42.6	42.7	30.25	30.25	30.25	30.25	121	123.3	123.3
Minority Interest/Other Expenses	-3.3	0.0	-1.2	-1.0	-0.2	-3.1	-3.7	-2.5	-9.5	0.0	0.0
Interest Expense	10.1	11.4	12.8	13.0	62.3	64.6	62.526	62	251.426	241.9	241.9
Total Non-Operating Expenses	44.9	51.8	165.2	185.2	136.7	138.8	138.6	143.8	557.7	606.4	642.3
Pretax Income	69.5	45.3	-62.5	-100.4	88.2	101.2	119.1	133.4	441.9	570.1	630.5
Provision For Income Taxes	29.0	25.9	49.3	-30.3	34.4	39.5	46.5	52.0	172.3	222.3	245.9
Net After-Tax Income	40.6	19.5	-111.8	-70.1	53.8	61.7	72.7	81.4	269.6	347.8	384.6
Preferred Dividends	6.9	7.0	6.9	6.9	6.9	6.9	3.8	3.8	21.5	21.5	21.5
Income Attributable to Common Shareholders	33.6	12.5	-118.7	-77.0	46.9	54.8	68.9	77.6	248.1	326.3	363.2
EPS - Common Stock	$0.21	$0.08	($0.75)	($0.48)	$0.28	$0.33	$0.37	$0.41	$1.40	$1.74	$1.93
EPS - Fully Diluted					$0.28	$0.32	$0.37	$0.41	$1.37	$1.74	$1.92
Avg. Shares	163.7	163.7	158.3	159.1	166.8	166.8	187.9	187.9	177.3	188.0	188.0
Fully Diluted					198.0	198.0	203.0	203.0	200.5	203.0	203.0

E = Morgan Stanley Research Estimates.

Telecommunications Equipment

ADTRAN — Earnings Model 1994-1997E

($ Millions Except EPS)

	1995A				1996E				Full Year			
	Mar	Jun	Sep	Dec	Mar	Jun	Sep	Dec	1994A	1995	1996E	1997E
Revenue	**$38.1**	**$45.5**	**$48.0**	**$49.9**	**$51.0**	**$58.0**	**$62.0**	**$69.0**	**$123.4**	**$181.5**	**$240.0**	**$300.0**
Cost of Revenue	$19.4	$23.7	$24.6	$25.3	$26.4	$29.9	$31.9	$35.2	$63.2	$93.0	$123.4	$155.4
SG&A	5.4	6.6	7.1	8.2	7.4	8.4	8.8	9.7	17.3	27.3	34.3	41.4
R&D	4.2	4.7	5.1	5.1	5.6	6.3	6.4	7.1	13.8	19.1	25.4	33.3
Operating Income	$9.1	$10.4	$11.2	$11.3	$11.6	$13.5	$14.8	$17.0	$29.1	$42.1	$56.9	$69.9
Other Income	0.3	0.3	0.7	0.9	0.9	0.9	0.9	0.9	(0.0)	2.2	3.4	3.6
Effective Tax Rate	35.4%	34.3%	34.8%	30.0%	33.5%	33.5%	33.5%	33.5%	36.1%	33.5%	33.5%	33.5%
Pretax Income	$9.4	$10.7	$11.9	$12.2	$12.4	$14.3	$15.7	$17.9	$29.1	$44.3	$60.3	$73.5
Taxes (1)	3.3	3.7	4.2	3.7	4.2	4.8	5.2	6.0	10.5	14.8	20.2	24.6
Net Income	$6.1	$7.0	$7.8	$8.6	$8.3	$9.5	$10.4	$11.9	$18.6	$29.5	$40.1	$48.9
Earnings Per Share	**$0.16**	**$0.18**	**0.20**	**$0.22**	**$0.21**	**$0.24**	**$0.26**	**$0.29**	**$0.52**	**$0.75**	**$0.99**	**$1.20**
Avg. Shares	39.0	39.0	39.5	39.6	39.9	40.0	40.2	40.4	36.1	39.2	40.5	40.8
As a % of Revenue												
Total Revenue	100.0	100.0	100.0	100.0	100.0	100.0	100.0	100.0	100.0	100.0	100.0	100.0
Gross Margin	49.0	47.8	48.8	49.3	48.3	48.4	48.5	49.0	48.8	48.8	48.6	48.2
SG&A	14.2	14.5	14.7	16.4	14.6	14.4	14.2	14.0	14.0	15.0	14.3	13.8
R&D	10.9	10.3	10.7	10.3	11.0	10.8	10.4	10.3	11.2	10.5	10.6	11.1
Operating Income	23.9	22.9	23.4	22.7	22.7	23.2	23.9	24.7	23.6	23.2	23.7	23.3
Pretax Income	24.7	23.6	24.8	24.5	24.4	24.7	25.3	25.9	23.6	24.4	25.1	24.5
Net Income	15.9	15.5	16.2	17.2	16.2	16.4	16.8	17.2	15.1	16.2	16.7	16.3
Year-Over-Year Growth (%)												
Total Revenue	58	49	49	37	34	28	29	38	70	47	32	25
Cost of Revenue	54	50	48	39	36	26	30	39	72	47	33	26
SG&A	45	54	55	73	38	27	25	18	45	58	26	21
R&D	39	36	40	38	35	33	26	38	38	38	33	31
Operating Income	91	50	51	14	27	29	32	51	112	44	35	23
Pretax Income	104	57	60	20	32	33	31	46	119	52	36	22
Net Income	109	64	64	29	36	35	34	39	120	58	36	22
Sequential Quarterly Growth (%)												
Total Revenue	4	19	6	4	2	14	7	11				
Cost of Revenue	7	22	3	3	4	14	7	10				
SG&A	15	22	7	16	(9)	12	5	10				
R&D	12	13	9	0	9	12	3	10				
Operating Income	(9)	15	8	1	2	16	10	15				
Pretax Income	(8)	14	11	3	2	15	10	14				
Net Income	(8)	16	10	10	(4)	15	10	14				

A= Actual   E = Morgan Stanley Research Estimates
Note (1): Prior to July 1, 1994, company was an S corporation. Tax information is presented as if the company had been subject to corporate income taxes before this date.

Cascade Communications — Earnings Model 1995–1997E

($ Millions Except EPS)

	1995A Mar	Jun	Sep	Dec	1996E Mar	Jun	Sep	Dec	1995	1996E	1997E
Revenue	$23.5	$29.1	$36.0	$46.2	$50.0	$53.0	$56.0	$60.0	$134.8	$219.0	$350.0
Cost of Revenue	$8.6	$10.6	$13.0	$16.4	$17.9	$19.3	$20.8	$22.2	$48.6	$80.2	$128.1
Sales & Marketing	4.0	4.8	5.6	6.2	7.3	7.6	8.0	8.5	20.6	31.4	52.5
General & Administrative	1.2	1.6	2.0	2.2	2.6	2.7	2.8	3.0	7.0	11.0	17.5
R&D	3.5	4.3	5.4	7.5	8.0	8.3	8.7	9.3	20.7	34.3	54.3
Operating Income	$6.2	$7.9	$10.1	$13.9	$14.4	$15.1	$15.7	$17.0	$38.1	$62.1	$97.7
Other Income	0.6	0.7	1.0	0.9	1.0	1.0	1.0	1.0	3.2	4.0	5.0
Pretax Income	$6.9	$8.6	$11.0	$14.8	$15.4	$16.1	$16.7	$18.0	$41.3	$66.1	$102.7
Taxes	2.6	3.3	4.2	5.7	5.9	6.2	6.4	6.9	15.9	25.5	39.5
Net Income	$4.2	$5.3	$6.8	$9.1	$9.4	$9.9	$10.3	$11.1	$25.4	$40.7	$63.1
Earnings Per Share	$0.14	$0.17	$0.22	$0.30	$0.31	$0.32	$0.33	$0.35	$0.84	$1.30	$2.00
EPS Fully Taxed at 38.5%	NM	NM	NM	NM	NM	NM	NM	NM	NM	NM	NM
Avg. Shares	30.2	30.2	30.4	30.8	30.9	31.1	31.2	31.4	30.4	31.2	31.6
Margin Analysis											
Total Revenue	100.0	100.0	100.0	100.0	100.0	100.0	100.0	100.0	100.0	100.0	100.0
Gross Margin	63.5	63.6	64.0	64.5	64.3	63.5	62.9	63.0	64.0	63.4	63.4
Sales & Marketing	17.1	16.4	15.5	13.4	14.5	14.4	14.3	14.2	15.3	14.3	15.0
General & Administrative	5.0	5.5	5.5	4.7	5.1	5.0	5.0	5.0	5.2	5.0	5.0
R&D	14.8	14.6	15.0	16.2	16.0	15.7	15.5	15.5	15.3	15.7	15.5
Operating Income	26.6	27.0	28.0	30.1	28.7	28.4	28.1	28.3	28.2	28.4	27.9
Pretax Income	29.2	29.4	30.6	32.1	30.7	30.3	29.9	30.0	30.6	30.2	29.3
Net Income	18.0	18.1	18.8	19.8	18.9	18.6	18.4	18.4	18.8	18.6	18.0
Tax Rate	38.5%	38.5%	38.5%	38.5%	38.5%	38.5%	38.5%	38.5%	38.5%	38.5%	38.5%
Year-Over-Year Growth (%)											
Total Revenue	273	243	140	128	113	82	55	30	169	62	60
Cost of Revenue	219	215	129	122	108	82	60	35	154	65	60
Sales & Marketing	235	167	84	37	80	60	43	37	95	53	67
General & Administrative	306	244	159	85	116	65	42	37	157	58	59
R&D	191	166	153	207	130	96	60	24	180	66	58
Operating Income	580	517	195	195	130	91	56	22	269	63	57
Pretax Income	631	571	199	186	123	87	52	21	272	60	55
Net Income	372	332	136	114	124	87	52	21	174	60	55
Sequential Quarterly Growth (%)											
Total Revenue	16	24	24	28	8	6	6	7			
Cost of Revenue	16	23	22	27	9	8	7	7			
Sales & Marketing	(11)	19	17	11	17	5	5	6			
General & Administrative	(0)	37	23	11	16	4	6	7			
R&D	42	22	27	39	7	4	4	7			
Operating Income	33	26	28	38	3	5	5	8			
Pretax Income	32	25	29	35	3	5	4	7			
Net Income	(1)	25	29	35	3	5	4	7			

A = Actual E = Morgan Stanley Research Estimates

DSC Communications — Earnings Model 1993–1996E

($ Millions Except EPS)

	1995A				1996E				Full Year			
	Mar	Jun	Sep	Dec	Mar	Jun	Sep	Dec	1993A	1994A	1995A	1996E
Revenue	**$318.0**	**$360.0**	**$370.1**	**$373.9**	**$350.0**	**$410.0**	**$435.0**	**$505.0**	**$730.8**	**$1,003.1**	**$1,422.0**	**$1,700.0**
Cost of Revenue	$159.3	$182.3	$195.7	$198.8	$190.4	$221.4	$230.6	$266.1	$412.8	$512.7	$736.1	$908.5
SG&A	46.1	50.7	52.6	57.8	56.0	56.6	59.2	68.2	112.7	141.9	207.2	239.9
Other Expense	2.2	2.3	2.3	2.8	2.8	2.8	2.8	2.8	8.5	7.2	9.6	11.2
R&D	46.9	47.9	47.6	47.3	45.5	51.3	53.1	60.6	86.6	127.3	189.7	210.4
Operating Income	$63.5	$76.8	$71.9	$67.2	$55.3	$78.0	$89.4	$107.3	$110.2	$214.0	$279.4	$330.0
Other Income	1.0	3.1	1.7	4.6	1.8	1.8	1.8	1.8	(2.9)	9.2	10.5	7.2
Effective Tax Rate	35.0%	35.0%	33.0%	31.2%	38.0%	38.0%	38.0%	38.0%	25.4%	27.1%	33.5%	38.0%
Pretax Income	$64.5	$79.9	$73.7	$71.9	$57.1	$79.8	$91.2	$109.1	$107.3	$223.2	$289.9	$337.2
Taxes	22.6	28.0	24.3	22.4	21.7	30.3	34.7	41.5	27.2	60.6	97.3	128.1
Net Income	$41.9	$51.9	$49.4	$49.4	$35.4	$49.5	$56.6	$67.6	$80.1	$162.6	$192.7	$209.1
Earnings Per Share	**$0.36**	**$0.44**	**$0.42**	**$0.42**	**$0.30**	**$0.42**	**$0.47**	**$0.57**	**$0.75**	**$1.39**	**$1.63**	**$1.75**
Avg. Shares	117.7	118.2	118.7	118.4	118.8	119.1	119.4	119.7	106.7	116.7	118.1	119.3
As a % of Revenue												
Total Revenue	100.0	100.0	100.0	100.0	100.0	100.0	100.0	100.0	100.0	100.0	100.0	100.0
Cost of Revenue	50.1	50.6	52.9	53.2	54.4	54.0	53.0	52.7	56.5	51.1	51.8	53.4
SG&A	14.5	14.1	14.2	15.5	16.0	13.8	13.6	13.5	15.4	14.1	14.6	14.1
Other Expense	0.7	0.6	0.6	0.8	0.8	0.7	0.6	0.6	1.2	0.7	0.7	0.7
R&D	14.8	13.3	12.9	12.6	13.0	12.5	12.2	12.0	11.9	12.7	13.3	12.4
Operating Income	20.0	21.3	19.4	18.0	15.8	19.0	20.6	21.2	15.1	21.3	19.6	19.4
Pretax Income	20.3	22.2	19.9	19.2	16.3	19.5	21.0	21.6	14.7	22.2	20.4	19.8
Net Income	13.2	14.4	13.3	13.2	10.1	12.1	13.0	13.4	11.0	16.2	13.5	12.3
Year-Over-Year Growth (%)												
Total Revenue	58	57	42	20	10	14	18	35	36	37	42	20
Cost of Revenue	53	56	46	26	20	21	18	34	24	24	44	23
SG&A	51	50	48	38	21	12	13	18	30	26	46	16
Other Expense	(13)	(4)	144	111	30	22	21	(0)	66	(15)	34	17
R&D	90	66	42	18	(3)	7	11	28	27	47	49	11
Operating Income	62	61	28	(5)	(13)	2	24	60	160	94	31	18
Pretax Income	57	59	26	(2)	(11)	(0)	24	52	535	108	30	16
Net Income	42	43	14	(8)	(16)	(5)	15	37	591	103	18	9
Sequential Quarterly Growth (%)												
Total Revenue	2	13	3	1	(6)	17	6	16				
Cost of Revenue	1	14	7	2	(4)	16	4	15				
SG&A	10	10	4	10	(3)	1	5	15				
Other Expense	62	7	1	21	(0)	0	0	0				
R&D	17	2	(1)	(1)	(4)	13	4	14				
Operating Income	(10)	21	(6)	(7)	(18)	41	15	20				
Pretax Income	(12)	24	(8)	(2)	(21)	40	14	20				
Net Income	(22)	24	(5)	0	(28)	40	14	20				

A = Actual   *E = Morgan Stanley Research Estimates*

StrataCom — Earnings Model 1993–1995

($ Millions Except EPS)

	1994A				1995A				Full Year		
	Mar	Jun	Sep	Dec	Mar	Jun	Sep	Dec	1993A	1994A	1995A
Revenue:											
Product	$19.2	$24.9	$36.8	$55.8	$65.7	$72.9	$80.8	$83.8	$61.9	$136.8	$303.2
Service and other	3.9	4.1	4.2	5.3	5.9	7.1	7.3	8.2	12.5	17.5	28.5
Total Revenue	**$23.1**	**$29.0**	**$41.0**	**$61.1**	**$71.6**	**$80.0**	**$88.1**	**$92.0**	**$74.4**	**$154.2**	**$331.7**
Cost of Revenue:											
Product	6.8	8.9	13.4	20.3	23.5	25.9	28.1	28.5	23.1	49.4	106.0
Service and other	2.6	2.8	2.9	3.9	4.0	4.8	5.2	6.2	8.7	12.2	20.2
Total Cost of Revenue	**$9.4**	**$11.6**	**$16.3**	**$24.3**	**$27.5**	**$30.7**	**$33.3**	**$34.7**	**$31.9**	**$61.6**	**$126.2**
Selling, General & Admin.	6.0	7.5	9.8	12.0	15.6	16.6	18.8	19.3	19.5	35.3	70.3
R&D	4.5	5.3	7.2	12.3	12.3	14.2	15.3	16.4	15.2	29.3	58.2
Operating Income	$3.2	$4.5	$7.7	$12.6	$16.2	$18.5	$20.7	$21.6	$7.8	$28.0	$77.0
Other Income	0.3	0.3	0.3	1.0	1.2	1.4	1.0	1.4	1.1	1.8	5.1
Effective Tax Rate	30.0%	30.0%	34.0%	36.0%	36.0%	36.0%	36.0%	36.0%	15.0%	33.8%	36.1%
Pretax Income	$3.5	$4.8	$8.0	$13.6	$17.4	$19.9	$21.7	$23.0	$8.9	$29.9	$82.1
Taxes	1.1	1.4	2.7	4.9	6.3	7.2	7.8	8.3	1.3	10.1	29.6
Net Income	$2.5	$3.3	$5.3	$8.7	$11.1	$12.8	$13.9	$14.7	$7.5	$19.8	$52.5
Earnings Per Share	**$0.07**	**$0.10**	**$0.15**	**$0.23**	**$0.28**	**$0.32**	**$0.35**	**$0.36**	**$0.23**	**$0.55**	**$1.31**
EPS Fully Taxed at 38%	$0.07	$0.09	$0.14	$0.22	$0.27	$0.31	$0.34	$0.35	$0.17	$0.51	$1.27
Avg. Shares (adj. for split)	33.1	33.8	34.6	38.0	39.4	39.7	40.0	40.4	32.8	36.1	39.9
Margin Analysis											
Total Revenue	100.0	100.0	100.0	100.0	100.0	100.0	100.0	100.0	100.0	100.0	100.0
Gross Margin	59.2	59.9	60.3	60.3	61.6	61.6	62.2	62.3	57.1	60.1	62.0
Selling, General & Admin.	25.8	26.0	23.9	19.6	21.9	20.7	21.3	20.9	26.2	22.9	21.2
R&D	19.4	18.4	17.6	20.1	17.2	17.7	17.4	17.9	20.5	19.0	17.6
Operating Income	14.0	15.5	18.8	20.6	22.6	23.2	23.5	23.5	10.5	18.2	23.2
Pretax Income	15.2	16.4	19.5	22.3	24.3	24.9	24.6	25.0	11.9	19.4	24.7
Net Income	10.7	11.5	12.8	14.2	15.6	15.9	15.8	15.9	10.1	12.8	15.8
Year-Over-Year Growth (%)											
Total Revenue	36	61	116	201	210	176	115	51	34	107	115
Cost of Revenue	29	48	101	181	191	164	105	43	29	93	105
Selling, General & Admin.	31	60	98	128	162	120	91	61	28	81	99
R&D	28	48	84	194	174	166	112	34	38	93	99
Operating Income	99	144	278	454	401	311	168	72	72	260	175
Pretax Income	75	124	255	449	395	318	172	69	77	237	175
Net Income	45	85	176	313	352	283	164	69	67	163	165
Sequential Quarterly Growth (%)											
Total Revenue											
Cost of Revenue	14	26	41	49	17	12	10	4			
Selling, General & Admin.	9	23	40	49	13	12	9	4			
R&D	14	27	30	22	31	6	13	3			
Operating Income	7	19	35	70	0	15	8	7			
Pretax Income	42	40	71	63	29	15	12	5			
Net Income	42	35	68	70	28	14	9	6			
	17	35	58	65	28	14	9	6			

A = Actual

Application Software

Adobe Systems — Income Statement Comparisons F1995–F1997E

($ Millions Except EPS)

	F1995				F1996E				F1995(a)	F1996E	F1997E
	2/95	5/95	8/95	11/95(a)	2/96E	5/96E	8/96E	11/96E	F1995(a)	F1996E	F1997E
Revenue	$189	$189	$183	$201	$201	$208	$209	$231	$762	$849	$968
Excluding FreeHand and PhotoStyler	189	189	183	201	--	--	--	--	762	849	968
Licensing	46	45	45	47	49	50	52	53	183	204	231
Application products	143	144	138	154	152	158	157	178	579	645	738
Adobe	123	122	11	132	136	139	138	157	489	570	653
Frame	20	22	26	22	16	19	19	21	90	75	85
Other											
Cost of Goods	34	32	27	37	36	36	35	39	130	147	165
Gross Profit	155	157	156	164	165	172	173	192	632	702	804
Operating Expense	103	109	111	125	120	124	123	132	448	497	570
Amort. of Capitalized Software	3	3	3	3	1	1	1	1	11	2	2
R&D	31	33	35	40	38	38	36	40	138	152	175
Marketing	57	59	60	68	67	70	71	75	244	283	325
G&A	14	14	13	14	14	15	15	16	55	60	68
Operating Income	52	48	45	40	45	48	51	60	184	204	234
Interest Income, net	6	8	7	8	8	8	8	8	29	32	36
Pretax Income	57	56	52	48	53	56	59	68	214	236	270
Taxes	21	21	18	18	19	21	21	25	78	86	98
Net Income (Operating)	36	35	34	30	34	36	37	43	136	150	171
Unusual Item	--	--	--	(42)	--	--	--	--	(42)	0	0
Net Income	36	35	34	(12)	34	36	37	43	93	150	171
Earnings Per Share	$0.50	$0.47	$0.44	($0.16)	$0.44	$0.46	$0.48	$0.56	$1.26	$1.95	$2.19
Operating	--	--	--	0.40	--	--	--	--	$1.80	--	--
Shares Outstanding ('000)	72,888	75,321	76,325	76,488	76,988	77,100	77,200	77,300	75,255	77,147	78,147
Shares used for operating EPS				72,477					74,253		
Growth Rate											
Revenue (yr-yr)	23%	13%	10%	7%	6%	10%	14%	15%	13%	11%	14%
Excluding FreeHand and PhotoStyler	36	25	20	12	--	--	--	--	22	11	14
Revenue (seq.)	1	0	(3)	10	0	4	0	11			
Expenses (yr-yr)	9	(1)	3	9	16	13	11	6	5	11	15
Expenses (seq.)	(9)	5	2	13	(4)	3	(1)	7	--	--	--
EPS (oper.)	68	71	54	(3)	(11)	(1)	9	40	43	8	13
Margin Analysis											
Gross Margin	82.1%	82.9%	85.0%	81.8%	82.0%	82.5%	83.0%	83.0%	82.9%	82.6%	83.0%
Operating Margin	27.3	25.4	24.6	19.7	22.5	23.2	24.3	26.0	24.2	24.1	24.1
Pretax Margin	30.3	29.5	28.6	23.9	26.5	27.0	28.1	29.5	28.0	27.8	27.8
Net Margin	19.1	18.6	18.5	15.2	16.8	17.2	17.9	18.7	17.8	17.7	17.7
Expenses as Pct. of Revenue											
Operating Expense	54.8%	57.5%	60.4%	62.1%	59.5%	59.3%	58.7%	57.0%	58.7%	58.6%	58.9%
Amort. of Capitalized Software	1.4	1.6	1.5	1.3	0.3	0.3	0.3	0.3	1.4	0.3	0.2
R&D	16.2	17.3	19.0	19.7	18.9	18.2	17.2	17.3	18.1	17.9	18.1
Marketing	29.9	31.3	32.7	34.0	33.3	33.6	34.0	32.5	32.0	33.3	33.6
G&A	7.3	7.4	7.2	7.2	7.0	7.2	7.2	6.9	7.3	7.1	7.0
Tax Rate	36.9%	37.0%	35.3%	36.5%	36.5%	36.5%	36.5%	36.5%	36.4%	36.5%	36.5%

Pro forma Restatement includes Adobe, Aldus, Frame and Mastersoft results.
(a) Includes charges from Frame acquisition and restructuring ($31.5MM pre-tax), write off of Ceneca in process R&D ($15MM pre-tax), and write off of goodwill from Silicon Beach ($3.2MM pre-tax).
E = Morgan Stanley Research Estimates   *Fiscal year ends in November.*

FTP Software — Financial Summary F1993–F1995

($ Thousands Except EPS)

	3/94	6/94	9/94	12/94	3/95	6/95	9/95	12/95	F1993	F1994	F1995
Net Sales	19,075	20,879	24,013	29,278	31,314	34,083	37,116	33,863	58,726	93,245	136,376
Cost of Sales	2,717	3,163	3,618	3,593	4,311	4,168	4,693	4,671	7,928	13,091	17,843
Gross Profit	16,358	17,716	20,395	25,685	27,003	29,915	32,423	29,192	50,798	80,154	118,533
Sales & Marketing	3,434	4,119	4,216	4,899	7,083	8,420	11,220	13,883	9,510	16,668	40,606
Product Development	3,476	3,493	8,128	5,418	5,560	4,934	11,533	8,742	9,389	20,515	30,769
G&A	1,903	1,855	2,344	3,260	2,844	3,088	3,562	4,716	5,649	9,362	14,210
Total Operating Expenses	8,813	9,467	14,688	13,577	15,487	16,442	26,315	27,341	24,548	46,545	85,585
Operating Income	7,545	8,249	5,707	12,108	11,516	13,473	6,108	1,851	26,250	33,609	32,948
Investment Income, net	605	714	836	977	1,043	1,253	1,416	2,442	685	3,132	6,154
Pretax Income	8,150	8,963	6,543	13,085	12,559	14,726	7,524	4,293	26,935	36,741	39,102
Taxes	3,212	3,421	2,421	4,712	4,709	5,412	2,765	1,582	10,611	13,766	14,468
Net Income	4,938	5,542	4,122	8,373	7,850	9,314	4,759	2,711	16,324	22,975	24,634
EPS	$0.17	$0.20	$0.14	$0.28	$0.27	$0.33	$0.17	$0.10	$0.65	$0.79	$0.87
Shares Outstanding	28,846	28,231	28,594	29,904	28,721	28,344	28,059	27,982	25,114	29,082	28,262
Growth Rate											
Revenues (yr-yr)	--	47%	58%	65%	64%	63%	55%	16%	--	59%	46%
Revenues (seq.)	8%	9%	15%	22%	7%	9%	9%	-9%	--	--	--
Expenses (yr-yr)	--	69%	133%	75%	76%	74%	79%	101%	--	90%	84%
Expenses (seq.)	14%	7%	55%	-8%	14%	6%	60%	4%	--	--	--
EPS (yr-yr)	--	21%	-10%	33%	60%	67%	18%	-65%	--	22%	10%
Margin Analysis											
Gross Margin	85.8%	84.9%	84.9%	87.7%	86.2%	87.8%	87.4%	86.2%	86.5%	86.0%	86.9%
Operating Margin	39.6%	39.5%	23.8%	41.4%	36.8%	39.5%	16.5%	5.5%	44.7%	36.0%	24.2%
Pretax Margin	42.7%	42.9%	27.2%	44.7%	40.1%	43.2%	20.3%	12.7%	45.9%	39.4%	28.7%
Net Margin	25.9%	26.5%	17.2%	28.6%	25.1%	27.3%	12.8%	8.0%	27.8%	24.6%	18.1%
Expenses as Pct. of Revenue											
S&M	18.0%	19.7%	17.6%	16.7%	22.6%	24.7%	30.2%	41.0%	16.2%	17.9%	29.8%
Product Development	18.2%	16.7%	33.8%	18.5%	17.8%	14.5%	31.1%	25.8%	16.0%	22.0%	22.6%
G&A	10.0%	8.9%	9.8%	11.1%	9.1%	9.1%	9.6%	13.9%	9.6%	10.0%	10.4%
Total Operating Expenses	46.2%	45.3%	61.2%	46.4%	49.5%	48.2%	70.9%	80.7%	41.8%	49.9%	62.8%
Tax Rate	39.4%	38.2%	37.0%	36.0%	37.5%	36.8%	36.7%	36.9%	39.4%	37.5%	37.0%

Fiscal Year ends in December.

Firefox Communications — Financial Summary F1993–F1995

($ Thousands Except EPS)

	F1994				F1995				
	3/94	6/94	9/94	12/94	3/95	6/95	9/95	F1993	F1994
Net Sales	2,301	3,613	3,244	4,378	4,722	5,308	5,684	5,172	13,536
Cost of Sales	436	601	583	799	854	920	872	792	2,419
Gross Profit	1,865	3,012	2,661	3,579	3,868	4,388	4,812	4,380	11,117
Research and Development	347	370	362	349	558	595	634	948	1,428
Sales and Marketing	1,050	1,362	1,973	2,012	2148	2,392	2,612	2,579	6,397
General and Administrative	391	542	539	621	651	663	811	1,094	2,093
Total Operating Expenses	1,788	2,274	2,874	2,982	3,357	3,650	4,057	4,621	9,918
Operating Income	77	738	(213)	597	511	738	755	(241)	1,199
Interest Expense, Net	18	29	40	55	46	(134)	248	91	142
Pretax Income	59	709	(253)	542	465	872	1,003	(332)	1,057
Provision for Income Tax	27	294	(105)	225	186	311	322	(123)	441
Net Income	32	415	(148)	317	279	561	681	(209)	616
Income Attributable to Common Stock	--	366	(197)	--	--	542	--	(225)	419
EPS (before Preference Shares)	$0.01	$0.08	($0.03)	$0.06	$0.05	$0.08	$0.10	($0.05)	$0.08
EPS (with Preference Shares)		$0.07	($0.04)			$0.08			
Shares Outstanding	5,486	5,486	4,569	5,486	5,486	6,656	6,980	4,569	5,486
Growth Rate									
Revenues (yr-yr)	--	224%	165%	138%	105%	47%	75%	--	162%
Revenues (seq.)	25%	57%	-10%	35%	8%	12%	7%	--	--
Expenses (yr-yr)	--	120%	156%	74%	88%	61%	41%	--	115%
Expenses (seq.)	4%	27%	26%	4%	13%	9%	11%	--	--
EPS (yr-yr) (before Preference Shares)	--	NM	NM	NM	400%	11%	NM	--	NM
Margin Analysis									
Gross Margin	81.1%	83.4%	82.0%	81.7%	81.9%	82.7%	84.7%	84.7%	82.1%
Operating Margin	3.3%	20.4%	-6.6%	13.6%	10.8%	13.9%	13.3%	-4.7%	8.9%
Pretax Margin	2.6%	19.6%	-7.8%	12.4%	9.8%	16.4%	17.6%	-6.4%	7.8%
Net Margin	1.4%	11.5%	-4.6%	7.2%	5.9%	10.6%	12.0%	-4.0%	4.6%
Expenses as Pct. of Revenue									
R&D	15.1%	10.2%	11.2%	8.0%	11.8%	11.2%	11.2%	18.3%	10.5%
S&M	45.6%	37.7%	60.8%	46.0%	45.5%	45.1%	46.0%	49.9%	47.3%
G&A	17.0%	15.0%	16.6%	14.2%	13.8%	12.5%	14.3%	21.2%	15.5%
Total Operating Expenses	77.7%	62.9%	88.6%	68.1%	71.1%	68.8%	71.4%	89.3%	73.3%
Tax Rate	45.8%	41.5%	41.5%	41.5%	40.0%	35.7%	32.1%	37.0%	41.7%

Fiscal Year ends in December.

Intuit — Income Statement Comparisons F1994–F1996E

($ Thousands Except EPS)

	F1995E				F1996E				Annual Data		
	10/94	1/95(a)	4/95	7/95(d)	10/95	1/96E	4/96E	7/96E	F1994(b,c)	F1995	F1996E
Revenue	$68,184	$162,773	$98,912	$65,860	$96,773	$213,000	$139,000	$86,277	223,448	$395,729	$535,050
Cost of Goods	17,848	40,393	25,747	21,615	27,167	49,378	33,360	22,432	58,870	105,603	132,337
Gross Profit	50,336	122,380	73,165	44,245	69,606	163,622	105,640	63,845	164,578	290,126	402,713
Operating Expense	48,916	80,271	63,802	57,750	89,294	105,400	83,000	73,200	125,790	250,739	350,894
R&D	10,679	13,524	14,050	15,115	19,912	21,000	20,500	20,200	24,589	53,368	81,612
Customer Service & Tech. Support	13,678	24,520	19,438	15,723	25,040	33,000	23,000	20,000	39,182	73,359	101,040
Marketing	17,758	36,547	25,734	19,556	34,800	44,000	32,000	25,000	49,502	99,595	135,800
G&A	6,801	5,680	4,580	7,356	9,542	7,400	7,500	8,000	12,517	24,417	32,442
Operating Income	1,420	42,109	9,363	(13,505)	(19,688)	58,222	22,640	(9,355)	38,788	39,387	51,819
Interest Income, net	626	548	743	1,896	2,066	1,800	2,200	2,050	2,655	3,813	8,116
Pretax Income	2,046	42,657	10,106	(11,609)	(17,622)	60,022	24,840	(7,305)	41,443	43,200	59,935
Taxes	777	16,210	3,840	(4,411)	(6,696)	22,808	9,439	(2,776)	16,035	16,416	22,776
Net Income (Oper.)	1,269	26,447	6,266	(7,198)	(10,926)	37,214	15,401	(4,529)	25,408	26,784	37,159
Amort. of Purchased Intangibles (b) & Unusual Item	54,864	12,137	10,018	(4,872)	10,081	10,000	10,000	10,000	198,809	72,147	40,081
Net Income (Reported)	(53,595)	14,310	(3,752)	(2,326)	(21,007)	27,214	5,401	(14,529)	(173,244)	(45,363)	(2,922)
Earnings Per Share	($1.36)	$0.33	($0.09)	($0.06)	($0.48)	$0.58	$0.12	($0.33)	($5.37)	($1.11)	($0.07)
Operating (excld. Amort. Intangibles)	0.03	0.62	0.15	(0.17)	(0.25)	0.80	0.33	(0.10)	0.75	0.63	0.80
Operating (Pro Forma w/ 38% Tax Rate)	0.03	0.62	0.15	(0.17)	(0.25)	0.80	0.33	(0.10)	0.76	0.63	0.80
Pro Forma Shares Out. ('000)	41,036	42,902	43,068	42,236	44,027	46,542	46,742	47,342	33,896	42,824	46,163
Shares used to calculate reported EPS	39,276	42,902	40,882	42,236	44,027	46,542	46,742	44,000	32,274	40,762	44,328
Growth Rate											
Revenues (yr-yr)	44%	80%	82%	112	42%	31%	41%	31%	109%	77%	35%
Revenues (seq.)	119	139	(39)	(33)	47	120	(35)	(38)	--	--	--
Expenses (yr-yr)	11	114	77	99	83	31	30	27	104	99	40
Expenses (seq.)	69	64	(21)	(9)	55	18	(21)	(12)	--	--	--
EPS	--	--	--	--	--	--	--	--	--	--	--
EPS (Operating)	(90)	7	79	80	(903)	30	126	(40)	171	(17)	29
EPS (Pro Forma)	(89)	6	79	89	(903)	30	126	(40)	172	(17)	29
Margin Analysis											
Gross Margin	73.8%	75.2%	74.0%	67.2%	71.9%	76.8%	76.0%	74.0%	73.7%	73.3%	75.3%
Operating Margin	2.1	25.9	9.5	(20.5)	(20.3)	27.3	16.3	(10.8)	17.4	10.0	9.7
Pretax Margin	3.0	26.2	10.2	(17.6)	(18.2)	28.2	17.9	(8.5)	18.5	10.9	11.2
Net Margin	1.9	16.2	6.3	(10.9)	(11.3)	17.5	11.	(5.2)	11.4	6.8	6.9
Expenses as Pct. of Revenue											
Operating Expense	71.7%	49.3%	64.5%	87.7%	92.3%	49.5%	59.7%	84.8%	56.3%	63.4%	65.6%
R&D	15.7	8.3	14.2	23.0	20.6	9.9	14.7	23.4	11.0	13.5	15.3
Customer Service & Tech. Support	20.1	15.1	19.7	23.9	25.9	15.5	16.5	23.2	17.5	18.5	18.9
Marketing	26.0	22.5	26.0	29.7	36.0	20.7	23.0	29.0	22.2	25.2	25.4
G&A	10.0	3.5	4.6	11.2	9.9	3.5	5.4	9.3	5.6	6.2	6.1
Tax Rate	38.0	38.0	38.0	38.0	38.0	38.0	38.0	38.0	38.7	38.0	38.0

(a) Operating results include $1.3MM provision ($0.04 per share after tax) for TurboTax & MacInTax replacement disks that may be requested by customers for units shipped through January 31, 1995. (b) Write-offs for purchased R&D, amortization of intangibles and merger-related expenses in connection with the CQ4:93 merger with ChipSoft and CQ3:94 merger with Parsons Technology which were (c) Note that F1994 results exclude F1Q94 ChipSoft operations, due to timing of mergers if included, results for F1994 would have been lower due to ChipSoft pattern of losing money in the October quarter. (d) Reported EPS includes $25.6MM after-tax payment form Microsoft related to termination of proposed merger, and in-process R&D and other expenses associated with purchase of PersonalNews Inc. Includes ChipSoft results after December 12, 1993, and Parsons Technology results after September 27, 1994.

E = Morgan Stanley Research Estimates   *Fiscal Year ends in July.*

Macromedia —Income Statement Comparisons F1995–F1997E

($ Thousands Except EPS)

	F1996				F1997				Annual Data		
	6/95	9/95	12/95(d)	3/96E	6/96E	9/96E	12/96E	3/97E	F1995(a)	F1996E	F1997E
Revenue (c)	$22,343	$25,777	$29,149	$31,831	$36,351	$39,259	$39,337	$42,653	$53,698	$109,100	$157,600
Cost of Goods	4,226	4,675	5,275	6,048	6,761	7,302	7,317	7,933	9,599	20,224	29,314
Gross Profit	18,11	21,102	23,874	25,783	29,589	31,957	32,021	34,720	44,099	88,876	128,286
Operating Expense	12,886	13,977	14,849	16,183	19,629	20,807	20,849	22,819	33,857	57,895	84,105
Sales & Marketing	7,562	7,992	8,326	9,231	11,269	12,170	12,195	13,436	17,846	33,11	49,069
R&D	4,104	4,615	5,097	5,252	6,180	6,281	6,294	6,825	11,42	19,068	25,579
G&A	1,220	1,370	1,426	1,700	2,181	2,356	2,360	2,559	4,590	5,716	9,456
Operating Income	5,231	7,125	9,025	9,600	9,960	11,14	11,17	11,900	10,242	30,981	44,182
Other Income/(Expenses)	296	906	1,418	1,200	1,000	1,000	1,000	1,000	376	3,820	4,000
Pretax Income	5,527	8,031	10,443	10,800	10,960	12,149	12,172	12,900	10,618	34,801	48,182
Taxes	1,105	2,214	3,066	3,240	3,288	3,645	3,652	3,870	1,055	9,625	14,454
Net Income (Oper.)	4,422	5,817	7,377	7,560	7,672	8,505	8,520	9,030	9,563	25,176	33,727
Unusual Item	--	(400)	(225)	--	--	--	--	--	(3,025)	(625)	--
Net Income	4,422	5,417	7,152	7,560	7,672	8,505	8,520	9,030	9,563	24,551	33,727
Earnings Per Share	$0.13	$0.15	$0.18	$0.20	$0.20	$0.22	$0.22	$0.24	$0.19	$0.65	$0.88
Operating	0.13	0.16	0.19	0.20	0.20	0.22	0.22	0.24	0.28	0.67	0.88
Shares Outstanding	35,078	37,316	39,653	38,200	38,280	38,000	38,200	38,400	34,414	37,562	38,220
Growth Rate											
Revenues (yr-yr) (b)	116	119	144%	62%	63%	52%	35%	34%	43%	103%	44%
Revenues (seq.)	14	15	13	9	14	8	0	8	--	--	--
Expenses (yr-yr)	75	85	90	46	52	49	40	41	22	71	45
Expenses (seq.)	16	8	6	9	21	6	0	9	--	--	--
EPS (Operating)(yr-yr)	307	154	243	41	59	54	20	19	187	137	32
Margin Analysis											
Gross Margin	81.1	81.9%	81.9%	81.0%	81.4%	81.4%	81.4%	81.4%	82.1%	81.5%	81.4%
Operating Margin	23.4	27.6	31.0	30.2	27.4	28.4	28.4	27.9	19.	28.4	28.0
Pretax Margin	24.7	31.2	35.8	33.9	30.2	30.9	30.9	30.2	19.8	31.9	30.6
Net Margin	19.8	21.0	25.3	23.8	21.	21.7	21.7	21.2	17.8	23.1	21.4
Expenses as Pct. of Revenue											
Operating Expense	58%	54%	51%	51%	54%	53%	53%	54%	63%	53%	53%
Sales & Marketing	34	31	29	29	31	31	31	32	33	30	31
R&D	18	18	17	17	17	16	16	16	21	17	16
G&A	5	5	5	5	6	6	6	6	9	5	6
Tax Rate	20%	28%	29%	30%	30%	30%	30%	30%	10%	28%	30%

(a) Represents $3MM in merger-related expenses.
(b) Quarterly results not restated for altsys acquisition prior to F1994.
(c) FreeHand contribution represents royalty revenue (6/93-12/94), and MS full product revenue estimates (3/95-present)
(d) Includes $225,000 pre-tax charges related to the acquisition of OSC, Inc.

E = Morgan Stanley Research Estimates   *Fiscal year ends in March.*

Microsoft — Income Statement Comparisons F1994–F1996E

($ Millions Except EPS)

	F1995				F1996E				Annual Data		
	9/94	12/94	3/95	6/95(b)	9/95	12/95 (c)	3/96E	6/96E	F1995(b)	F1996E (c)	F1997E
Revenue	$1,247	$1,482	$1,587	$1,621	$2,016	$2,195	$2,100	$2,000	$5,937	$8,311	$9,973
U.S.	773	876	915	956	1,290	1,317	1,239	1,200	3,520	5,046	5,485
International (a)	474	606	672	665	726	878	861	800	2,417	3,265	4,488
Cost of Goods	186	222	235	234	322	330	294	260	877	1,206	1,197
Gross Profit	1,061	1,260	1,352	1,387	1,694	1,865	1,806	1,740	5,060	7,105	8,776
Operating Expense	624	740	803	855	986	1,079	1,090	1,095	3,022	4,250	5,152
R&D	178	199	219	264	302	313	330	350	860	1,295	1,580
Marketing	395	479	516	505	621	690	680	660	1,895	2,651	3,208
G&A	51	62	68	86	63	76	80	85	267	304	365
Operating Income	437	520	549	532	708	786	716	645	2,038	2,855	3,624
Other Income, net	34	37	43	61	62	76	80	85	175	303	340
Stock Option Expense	0	0	0	0	0	0	0	0	0	0	0
Pretax Income	471	557	592	593	770	862	796	730	2,213	3,158	3,964
Taxes	155	184	196	196	271	310	279	256	731	1,11	1,387
Net Income (Operating)	316	373	396	397	499	552	517	475	1,483	2,043	2,577
Non recurring charge	--	--	--	46	--	(23)	--	--	--	(23)	--
Net Income (Reported)	316	373	396	368	499	575	517	475	1,453	2,066	2,577
Earnings Per Share	$0.51	$0.60	$0.63	$0.58	$0.78	$0.90	$0.81	$0.73	$2.32	$3.22	$3.93
Operating				0.63		0.87			2.36	--	--
Shares Outstanding	622	625	626	635	640	638	642	646	627	630	655
Growth Rate											
Revenues (yr-yr)	27%	31%	28%	25%	62%	48%	32%	23%	28%	40%	20%
Revenues (seq.)	(4)	19	7	2	24	9	(4)	(5)	--	--	--
Expenses (yr-yr)	30	40	44	44	58	46	36	28	40	41	21
Expenses (seq.)	5	19	9	6	15	9	1	0	--	--	--
EPS	29	26	14	13	53	45	27	17	20	36	22
Margin Analysis											
Gross Margin	85.1%	85.0%	85.2%	85.6%	84.0%	85.0%	86.0%	87.0%	85.2%	85.5%	88.0%
Operating Margin	35.0	35.1	34.6	32.8	35.1	35.8	34.1	32.3	34.3	34.4	36.3
Pretax Margin	37.8	37.6	37.3	36.6	38.2	39.3	37.9	36.5	37.3	38.0	39.7
Net Margin	25.3	25.2	25.0	24.5	24.8	25.1	24.6	23.7	25.0	24.6	25.8
Expenses as Pct. of Revenue											
Operating Expense	50.0%	49.9%	50.6%	52.7%	48.9%	49.2%	51.9%	54.8%	50.9%	51.1	51.7%
R&D	14.3	13.4	13.8	16.3	15.0	14.3	15.7	17.5	14.5	15.6	15.8
Marketing	31.7	32.3	32.5	31.2	30.8	31.4	32.4	33.0	31.9	31.9	32.2
G&A	4.1	4.2	4.3	5.3	3.1	3.5	3.8	4.3	4.5	3.7	3.7
Tax Rate	32.9%	33.0%	33.1%	33.0%	35.2%	36.0%	35.0%	35.0%	33.0%	35.3%	35.0%

(a) Does not include OEM revenues.
(b) Represents one-time $46MM merger termination fee paid to Intuit.
(c) $30MM pre-tax gain from sale of certain assets ($0.03 in EPS).
E = Morgan Stanley Research Estimates   Fiscal Year ends in June.

NetManage — Financial Summary F1993–F1995

($ Thousands Except EPS)

	F1994				F1995				F1993	F1994	F1995
	3/94	6/94	9/94	12/94	3/95	6/95	9/95	12/95	F1993	F1994	F1995
Net Sales	9,113	12,056	16,626	23,811	25,812	30,173	32,692	31,226	20,797	61,606	125,446
Cost of Sales	904	1,290	1,663	2,078	2,461	3,289	3,131	3,290	1,896	5,935	13,065
Gross Profit	8,209	10,766	14,963	21,733	23,351	26,884	29,561	27,936	18,901	55,671	112,381
Research and Development	1,252	1,569	2,455	3,950	4,296	4,900	5,201	7,295	3,457	9,226	23,861
Sales & Marketing	2,247	3,053	3,947	6,533	8,815	11,040	11,489	11,898	6,122	15,780	46,117
General & Adminstrative	631	840	1,074	1,649	1,678	1,736	2,355	2,641	1,645	4,194	9,808
Write Off of In-Process R&D	--	--	2,000	--	--	--	--	--	--	2,000	--
Amortization of Goodwill	--	--	78	235	330	339	331	299	--	313	1,298
Acquisition Costs	--	--	--	--	--	--	--	--	--	--	1,701
Loss from Equity Investment	--	--	--	--	--	--	--	--	--	--	306
Total Operating Expenses	4,130	5,462	9,554	12,367	15,119	18,015	19,376	22,133	11,224	31,513	83,091
Operating Income	4,079	5,304	5,409	9,366	8,232	8,869	10,185	5,803	7,677	24,158	29,290
Interest Income, net	368	606	744	807	963	1,176	1,254	1,027	275	2,525	4,494
Pretax Income	4,447	5,910	6,153	10,173	9,195	10,045	11,439	6,830	7,952	26,683	33,784
Taxes	1,779	2,307	2,338	3,865	3,510	3,228	4,004	1,684	3,177	10,289	11,487
Net Income	2,668	3,603	3,815	6,308	5,685	6,817	7,435	5,146	4,775	16,394	22,297
EPS	$0.07	$0.09	$0.09	$0.15	$0.14	$0.16	$0.18	$0.12	$0.17	$0.41	$0.52
Shares Outstanding	38,416	40,664	40,570	41,360	41,992	41,789	42,384	43,330	28,632	40,266	42,831
Growth Rate											
Revenues (yr-yr)	239%	237%	137%	217%	183%	150%	97%	31%	--	196%	104%
Revenues (seq.)	21%	32%	38%	43%	8%	17	8%	-4%	--	--	--
Expenses (yr-yr)	149%	132%	165%	243%	266%	230%	103%	79%	--	181	164%
Expenses (seq.)	15	32%	75%	29%	22%	19%	8%	14%	--	--	--
EPS (yr-yr)	274%	357%	51	163%	95%	84%	91%	-22%	--	144%	28%
Margin Analysis											
Gross Margin	90.1%	89.3%	90.0%	91.3%	90.5%	89.1%	90.4%	89.5%	90.9%	90.4%	89.6%
Operating Margin	44.8%	44.0%	32.5%	39.3%	31.9%	29.4%	31.2%	18.6%	36.9%	39.2%	23.3%
Pretax Margin	48.8%	49.0%	37.0%	42.7%	35.6%	33.3%	35.0%	21.9%	38.2%	43.3%	26.9%
Net Margin	29.3%	29.9%	22.9%	26.5%	22.0%	22.6%	22.7%	16.5%	23.0%	26.6%	17.8%
Expenses as Pct. of Revenue											
R&D	13.7%	13.0%	14.8%	16.6%	16.6%	16.2%	15.9%	23.4%	16.6%	15.0%	19.0%
S&M	24.7%	25.3%	23.7%	27.4%	34.2%	36.6%	35.1%	38.1%	29.4%	25.6%	36.8%
G&A	6.9%	7.0%	6.5%	6.9%	6.5%	5.8%	7.2%	8.5%	7.9%	6.8%	7.8%
Total Operating Expenses	45.3%	45.3%	57.5%	51.9%	58.6%	59.7%	59.3%	70.9%	54.0%	51.2%	66.2%
Tax Rate	40.0%	39.0%	38.0%	38.0%	38.2%	32.1%	35.0%	24.7%	40.0%	38.6%	34.0%

Restated for the acquisition of AGE Logic.
Fiscal Year ends in December.

Netscape Communications — Income Statement 1994–1996E   Restated for 2-for-1 stock split effective February 7, 1996

($ Thousands Except EPS)

	1995				1996E				Annual Data		
	3/95(a)*	6/95(b)*	9/95(c)*	12/95(d,e)	3/96E	6/96E	9/96E	12/96E	Inception** thru 12/94	1995(a-e)	1996E
Net Revenue	$4,738	$11,888	$20,803	$40,616	$43,053	$46,928	$51,855	$58,596	$1,403	$80,656	$200,432
Products	4,496	11,084	19,607	35,437	38,748	42,235	46,670	52,737	1,087	73,236	180,389
Services	242	804	1,195	5,179	4,305	4,693	5,186	5,860	316	7,420	20,043
Cost of Goods	450	1,286	2,838	6,268	6,678	7,278	8,043	9,088	329	11,073	31,087
Products	273	949	2,458	4,742	5,386	5,871	6,487	7,330	162	8,653	25,074
Services	177	337	380	1,526	1,292	1,408	1,556	1,758	167	2,420	6,013
Gross Profit	4,288	10,602	17,964	34,348	36,375	39,649	43,812	49,508	1,074	69,583	169,345
Operating Expenses	5,643	12,147	17,298	31,452	33,366	35,900	39,151	43,361	10,678	71,927	151,778
R&D	1,965	4,017	5,918	10,703	12,485	13,374	14,519	16,407	3,674	24,311	56,786
Sales & Marketing	2,758	6,368	9,441	17,710	17,436	18,771	20,483	22,267	4,469	38,903	78,957
G&A	920	1,762	1,940	3,039	3,444	3,754	4,148	4,688	2,535	8,713	16,035
Unusual Items	500	0	0	2,033	0	0	0	0	2,487	2,533	0
Deferred Compensation	862	413	614	614	614	614	614	614	--	2,503	2,456
Net Operating Expenses - Reported	7,005	12,560	17,912	34,099	33,980	36,514	39,765	43,975	13,165	76,963	154,234
Operating Income - Normalized	(1,355)	(1,545)	666	2,896	3,009	3,750	4,662	6,147	(9,604)	(2,344)	17,567
Operating Income - Reported	(2,717)	(1,958)	52	249	2,395	3,136	4,048	5,533	(12,091)	(7,380)	15,111
Operating Income (Excl. Unusual Items)				2,282						(4,847)	
Interest & Other	18	349	1,318	2,609	2,300	2,343	2,395	2,434	212	4,437	9,472
Pretax Income - Normalized	(1,337)	(1,196)	1,984	5,505	5,309	6,092	7,057	8,580	(9,392)	2,093	27,039
Income Taxes	0	0	0	498	1,911	2,193	2,541	3,089	0	498	9,734
Net Income - Normalized	(1,337)	(1,196)	1,984	5,007	3,398	3,899	4,517	5,491	(9,392)	1,595	17,305
Net Income - Reported	(2,699)	(1,609)	1,370	2,360	2,784	3,285	3,903	4,877	(11,879)	(3,441)	14,849
Net Income (Excl. Unusual Items)				4,393						(908)	
Earnings Per Share - Normalized	($0.02)	($0.02)	$0.03	$0.06	$0.04	$0.05	$0.05	$0.06	($0.14)	$0.02	$0.20
Earnings Per Share - Reported	(0.04)	(0.02)	0.02	0.03	0.03	0.04	0.04	0.06	(0.18)	(0.05)	0.17
Earnings Per Share (Excl. Unusual Items)				0.05						(0.01)	
Shares Outstanding	66,002	66,002	75,602	84,928	85,728	86,528	87,328	88,128	67,490	73,784	87,078
Growth Rate											
Net Revenues (yr-yr)	--	--	--	--	809%	295%	149%	44%	--	5649%	149%
Net Revenues (seq)	--	151%	75%	95%	6	9	11	13	--	--	--
Expenses - Normalized (yr-yr)	--	--	--	--	491	196	126	38	--	574	111
Expenses - Normalized (seq)	--	115	42	82	6	8	9	11	--	--	--
Net Income - Normalized (yr-yr)	--	--	--	--	NS	NS	NS	NS	--	NS	10
Net Income - Normalized (seq)	--	NS	NS	221	(37)	18	19	25	--	--	--
EPS - Normalized (yr-yr)	--	--	--	--	NS	NS	NS	NS	--	NS	7
EPS - Normalized (seq)	--	NS	NS	185	(37)	17	18	24	--	--	--
Margin Analysis											
Product Revenue as % of Total Revenue	94.9%	93.2%	94.3%	87.2%	90.0%	90.0%	90.0%	90.0%	77.5%	90.8%	90.0%
Service Revenue as % of Total Revenue	5.1	6.8	5.7	12.8	10.0	10.0	10.0	10.0	22.5	9.2	10.0
Gross Margin	90.5	89.2	86.4	84.6	84.5	84.5	84.5	84.5	76.6	86.3	84.5
Gross Margin - Products	93.9	91.4	87.5	86.6	86.1	86.1	86.1	86.1	85.1	88.2	86.1
Gross Margin - Services	26.8	58.1	68.2	70.5	70.0	70.0	70.0	70.0	47.2	67.4	70.0
Operating Margin - Normalized	NS	NS	3.2	7.1	7.0	8.0	9.0	10.5	NS	NS	8.8
Pretax Margin - Normalized	NS	NS	9.5	13.6	12.3	13.0	13.6	14.6	NS	NS	13.5
Net Margin - Normalized	NS	NS	9.5	12.3	7.9	8.3	8.7	9.4	NS	NS	8.6
Expenses as Pct. of Revenue											
Operating Expense - Normalized	119.1%	102.2%	83.2%	77.4%	77.5%	76.5%	75.5%	74.0%	761.1%	89.2%	75.7%
R&D	41.5	33.8	28.4	26.4	29.0	28.5	28.0	28.0	261.9	30.1	28.3
Marketing & Selling	58.2	53.6	45.4	43.6	40.5	40.0	39.5	38.0	318.5	48.2	39.4
G&A	19.4	14.8	9.3	7.5	8.0	8.0	8.0	8.0	180.7	10.8	8.0
Tax Rate	NS	NS	NS	9.0%	36.0%	36.0%	36.0%	36.0%	NS	NS	36.0%
No. Employees	150	244	350	630	693	762	839	922	100	630	922
No. Employee Growth (yr-yr)	NS	NS	NS	NS	362%	212%	140%	46%	NS	530%	46%
No. Employee Growth (seq)	NS	63%	43%	80%	10%	10%	10%	10%	--	--	--
L12M Rev. ($'000)/End. Employee	NS	NS	NS	$124	$168	$199	$218	$217	NS	$128	$217
L12M Opex-Reported ($'000)/End. Employee	NS	NS	NS	$106	$136	$155	$167	$165	NS	$114	$165

(a) *Deferred compensation for CQ1:95 includes: $16,000 of R&D; $25,000 of S&M; and $821,000 of G&A. Unusual item includes charge of $500K related to proprietary rights agreement.*
(b) *Deferred compensation for CQ2:95 includes: $117,000 of R&D; $105,000 of S&M; and $191,000 of G&A.*
(c) *Deferred compensation for CQ3:95 includes: $233,000 of R&D; $225,000 of S&M; and $141,000 of G&A.*
(d) *Includes charge of an estimated $2MM related to acquisition of Collabra Software.*
(e) *Includes charge of $2MM related to acquisition of Collabra Software.*

* *CQ1-CQ3:95 not yet restated for Collabra acquisition..*
** *Inception was April, 4, 1994.*   *E = Morgan Stanley Research Estimates*   *Fiscal Year ends in December.*

Spyglass — Financial Summary F1993–F1996

($ Thousands Except EPS)

	F1994				F1995				F1996	F1993	F1994	F1995
	12/93	3/94	6/94	9/94	12/94	3/95	6/95	9/95	12/95			
Net Sales	271	606	686	2,066	2,018	2,184	2,816	3,332	3,845	1,375	3,629	10,350
Cost of Sales	49	80	99	377	368	278	236	273	272	223	605	1,155
Gross Profit	222	526	587	1,689	1,650	1,906	2,580	3,059	3,573	1,152	3,024	9,195
S&M	107	222	208	433	571	533	887	1,085	1,147	605	970	3,076
R&D	93	124	121	171	297	421	589	700	958	370	509	2,007
G&A	164	191	174	265	333	451	535	629	723	565	794	1,948
Gain on Sale of Data Visualization Product Line								(863)				(863)
Total Operating Expenses	364	537	503	869	1,201	1,405	2,011	1,551	2,828	1,540	2,273	6,168
Operating Income	(142)	(11)	84	820	449	501	569	1,508	745	(388)	751	3,027
Other Income	12	38	24	31	42	39	40	443	459	68	105	564
Income before Income Taxes and Change in Acct'g	(130)	27	108	851	491	540	609	1,951	1,204	(320)	856	3,591
Provision for Income Taxes	(52)	10	42	325	196	217	244	758	482		325	1,415
Income before Cumulative Effect	(78)	17	66	526	295	323	365	1,193	722	(320)	531	2,176
Cumulative Effect of Change in Accounting	800										800	
Net Income	722	17	66	526	295	323	365	1,193	722	(320)	1,331	2,176
Accretion of Preferred Stock Dividends	(64)	(65)	(64)	(64)	(64)	(65)	(62)	0	0	(257)	(257)	(191)
Net Income Available to Common Stockholders	658	(48)	2	462	231	258	303	1,193	722	(577)	1,074	1,985
EPS												
Net Income Before Cumulative Effect	($0.01)	$0.00	$0.01	$0.07	$0.04	$0.04	$0.05	$0.10	$0.06	($0.13)	$0.15	$0.25
Net Income	$0.11	$0.00	$0.02	$0.15	$0.08	$0.09	$0.09	$0.10	$0.06	($0.25)	$0.39	$0.23
Net Income Available to Common Stockholders	$0.10	($0.01)	$0.00	$0.06	$0.03	$0.03	$0.04	$0.10	$0.06	($0.23)	$0.31	$0.23
Shares Outstanding	6,800	6,822	6,826	7,242	7,484	7,572	7,942	11,902	12,142	2,514	6,898	8,636
Growth Rate												
Revenues (yr-yr)	--	--	--	--	645%	260%	310%	61%	91%	--	164%	185%
Revenues (seq.)	--	124%	13%	201%	-2%	8%	29%	18%	15%	--	--	--
Expenses (yr-yr)	--	--	--	--	230%	162%	300%	78%	135%	--	48%	171%
Expenses (seq.)	--	48%	-6%	73%	38%	17%	43%	-23%	82%	--	--	--
EPS (yr-yr)	--	--	--	--	-68%	NM	NM	57%	93%	--	-135%	74%
Margin Analysis												
Gross Margin	81.9%	86.8%	85.6%	81.8%	81.8%	87.3%	91.6%	91.8%	92.9%	83.8%	83.3%	88.8%
Operating Margin	-52.4%	-1.8%	12.2%	39.7%	22.2%	22.9%	20.2%	45.3%	19.4%	-28.2%	20.7%	29.2%
Pretax Margin	-48.0%	4.5%	15.7%	41.2%	24.3%	24.7%	21.6%	58.6%	31.3%	-23.3%	23.6%	34.7%
Net Margin	242.8%	-7.9%	0.3%	22.4%	11.4%	11.8%	10.8%	35.8%	18.8%	-42.0%	29.6%	19.2%
Expenses as Pct. of Revenue												
S&M	39.5%	36.6%	30.3%	21.0%	28.3%	24.4%	31.5%	32.6%	29.8%	44.0%	26.7%	29.7%
R&D	34.3%	20.5%	17.6%	8.3%	14.7%	19.3%	20.9%	21.0%	24.9%	26.9%	14.0%	19.4%
G&A	60.5%	31.5%	25.4%	12.8%	16.5%	20.7%	19.0%	18.9%	18.8%	41.1%	21.9%	18.8%
Total Operating Expenses	134.3%	88.6%	73.3%	42.1%	59.5%	64.3%	71.4%	46.5%	73.6%	112.0%	62.6%	59.6%
Tax Rate	40.0%	37.0%	38.9%	38.2%	39.9%	40.2%	40.1%	38.9%	40.0%	0.0%	38.0%	39.4%

Fiscal Year ends in September.

Enterprise and Networking Software

Informix — Sales and Earnings Summary Fiscal 1994–1996E

($ Millions, Except EPS)

	1994A					1995A					Annual Data		
	3/94	6/94	9/94	12/94	CY94	3/95	6/95	9/95	12/95	CY95	CY93	CY94	CY95
Americas	39.7	44.6	56.2	75.0	215.5	58.0	62.9	80.4	92.1	293.4	154.3	215.5	293.4
Europe	39.6	43.3	42.9	50.3	176.0	50.0	65.3	63.1	81.5	259.8	144.1	176.0	259.8
Intercontinental	16.8	17.7	17.8	24.8	77.2	39.8	35.5	37.0	43.5	155.8	54.5	77.2	155.8
DB Tools	26.1	28.5	27.0	35.2	116.8	33.9	38.0	38.8	42.8	153.5		116.8	153.5
DB Servers	48.7	54.5	61.2	82.6	247.0	76.4	85.2	96.8	123.9	382.4		247.0	382.4
Total Licenses	74.8	83.0	88.2	117.8	363.8	110.4	123.2	135.6	166.8	535.9	284.3	363.8	535.9
Services	21.3	22.7	28.6	32.3	104.9	37.4	40.4	45.0	50.3	173.1	68.6	104.9	173.1
Total Revenue	**96.1**	**105.7**	**116.8**	**150.1**	**468.7**	**147.8**	**163.6**	**180.5**	**217.1**	**709.0**	**352.9**	**468.7**	**709.0**
Cost of Revenue	5.0	5.5	6.3	7.9	24.7	7.9	8.2	9.0	12.9	37.8	20.1	24.7	37.8
Cost of Service	9.7	10.9	12.5	12.9	46.0	17.9	21.3	22.9	27.0	89.0	32.9	46.0	89.0
Sales/Mkt	39.9	46.3	48.6	65.7	200.5	64.5	69.6	76.7	83.8	294.6	137.7	200.5	294.6
Research	12.9	15.1	15.9	16.5	60.4	17.5	19.0	21.2	21.6	79.3	43.6	60.4	79.3
Gen/Admin Exp.	9.5	7.2	8.1	9.7	34.5	11.1	12.0	11.9	14.0	49.0	33.2	34.5	49.0
Total Op Costs	77.1	84.9	91.4	112.7	366.1	118.9	130.0	141.6	159.2	549.7	267.5	366.1	549.7
Op Profit	19.0	20.8	25.4	37.3	102.6	28.9	33.6	38.9	57.8	159.3	85.4	102.6	159.3
Other income	1.0	0.8	-0.5	1.1	2.4	0.1	-0.9	2.2	2.4	3.9	1.2	2.4	3.9
Interest expense	-0.1	-0.9	1.0	-1.2	-1.2	1.5	1.6	-0.3	-0.5	2.3	1.4	-1.2	2.3
Special Items	-	-	-	-	-	-	-	-	-	-	-	-	-
Pretax Profit	19.6	20.7	25.9	37.2	103.4	30.6	35.4	40.4	59.7	166.1	87.7	103.4	166.1
Taxes	7.0	7.5	9.3	13.4	37.2	11.5	13.3	15.2	20.9	60.8	31.6	37.2	60.8
Net Income	12.5	13.3	16.6	23.8	66.2	19.1	22.1	25.3	38.8	105.3	56.1	66.2	105.3
Avg Shares(mil.)	135.0	133.5	133.9	135.6	134.5	137.0	138.2	140.0	140.7	139.0	135.6	134.5	139.0
EPS Operating	**0.10**	**0.10**	**0.12**	**0.18**	**0.49**	**0.14**	**0.16**	**0.18**	**0.28**	**0.76**	**0.36**	**0.49**	**0.76**
% Change	12%	10%	126%	30%	35%	47%	61%	50%	58%	55%	-15%	35%	55%
EPS- reported	0.10	0.10	0.12	0.18	0.49	0.14	0.16	0.18	0.28	0.76	0.36	0.49	0.76
% Change	12%	10%	126%	30%	35%	47%	61%	50%	58%	55%	-25%	35%	55%
Growth Y/Y %													
Americas	25.2	22.3	38.6	64.6	39.7	46.1	40.8	43.2	22.7	36.1	26.9	39.7	36.1
Europe	22.0	23.8	12.4	30.5	22.2	26.2	50.7	47.1	62.2	47.6	30.3	22.2	47.6
Asia/Pacific	30.6	37.9	56.4	43.0	41.7	136.3	100.0	107.9	75.3	101.8	83.8	41.7	101.8
DB Tools	-	-	-	-	-	30.0	33.4	43.4	21.8	31.5	-	-	31.5
DB Servers	-	-	-	-	-	57.0	56.3	58.2	50.1	54.8	-	-	54.8
Licenses	20.3	23.1	21.9	42.9	27.9	47.6	48.4	53.7	41.6	47.3	19.8	27.9	47.3
Services	42.7	34.2	61.7	69.8	53.0	75.5	78.1	57.1	55.7	64.9	48.5	53.0	64.9
Total Revenue	**24.7**	**25.3**	**29.7**	**48.0**	**32.8**	**53.8**	**54.8**	**54.5**	**44.6**	**51.3**	**24.4**	**32.8**	**51.3**
Cost of Revenue	-6.7	27.7	23.4	48.0	22.9	57.5	49.3	42.5	62.3	53.4	-6.5	22.9	53.4
Sales/Mkt	38.0	37.8	31.1	72.4	45.6	61.6	50.4	57.8	27.5	46.9	37.1	45.6	46.9
Research	30.8	34.7	42.3	45.3	38.5	35.9	25.8	33.3	30.5	31.2	51.4	38.5	31.2
Gen/Admin Exp.	25.3	-10.1	-5.3	7.5	4.0	16.1	66.8	46.7	44.5	41.8	-2.8	4.0	41.8
Total Op Costs	**30.1**	**29.8**	**30.2**	**55.1**	**36.9**	**54.2**	**53.2**	**54.9**	**41.3**	**50.1**	**26.4**	**36.9**	**50.1**
Op Profit	6.6	9.9	27.9	29.9	20.1	52.3	61.5	53.0	54.9	55.3	18.6	20.1	55.3
% of Revenues													
License margin	93.3	93.4	92.9	93.3	93.2	92.9	93.4	93.4	92.3	92.9		93.2	92.9
Service margin	54.4	52.1	56.3	60.2	56.2	52.2	47.4	49.2	46.3	48.6	5.7	56.2	48.6
Sales/Mkt	41.6	43.8	41.6	43.8	42.8	43.7	42.6	42.5	38.6	41.6	39.0	42.8	41.6
Research	13.4	14.3	13.6	11.0	12.9	11.9	11.6	11.7	9.9	11.2	12.4	12.9	11.2
Gen/Admin Exp.	9.9	6.8	7.0	6.4	7.4	7.5	7.3	6.6	6.4	6.9	9.4	7.4	6.9
Total Op Costs	**80.2**	**80.3**	**78.3**	**75.1**	**78.1**	**80.4**	**79.5**	**78.5**	**73.4**	**77.5**	**75.8**	**78.1**	**77.5**
Op Margin	19.8	19.7	21.7	24.9	21.9	19.6	20.5	21.5	26.6	22.5	24.2	21.9	22.5
Pretax Profit	20.4	19.6	22.2	24.8	22.1	20.7	21.6	22.4	27.5	23.4	24.8	22.1	23.4
Net Income	**13.0**	**12.5**	**14.2**	**15.9**	**14.1**	**12.9**	**13.5**	**14.0**	**17.9**	**14.9**	**15.9**	**14.1**	**14.9**
Eff Tax Rate	36.0	36.0	36.0	36.0	36.0	37.5	37.5	37.5	35.0	36.6	36.0	36.0	36.6
Ratios/BS													
Book Value/shr	1.61	1.62	1.76	2.03	-	2.19	2.39	2.57	3.01		-	-	-
Cash/shr	1.07	1.14	1.20	1.41	-	1.28	1.39	1.51	1.79		-	-	-
Sales/Shr	**2.75**	**2.95**	**3.14**	**3.46**	-	**3.80**	**4.18**	**4.58**	**5.04**		-	-	-
Total Cash	144	152	161	192	-	176	193	211	252		-	-	-
Total Debt	0	0	0	0	-	0	0	0	0		-	-	-
Total Equity	218	216	236	276	-	300	330	360	423		-	-	-
Total Assets	**327**	**338**	**376**	**444**	-	**476**	**532**	**594**	**674**		-	-	-
Receivables	101	102	111	132	-	122	143	172	183		-	-	-
Rec Days Outst	**95**	**87**	**85**	**79**	-	**74**	**79**	**86**	**76**		-	-	-
LTM Sales	372	393	420	469	-	520	578	642	709		-	-	-
LTM EPS	0.37	0.38	0.45	0.49	-	0.53	0.60	0.66	0.76		-	-	-

Fiscal year ends in March.   *LTM = Last 12 Months*

Novell — Sales and Earnings Summary Fiscal 1995–1997E

($ Millions, Except EPS)

	1996E				1997E				Annual Data		
	1/96E	4/96E	7/96E	10/96E	1/97E	4/97E	7/97E	10/97E	FY95E	FY96E	FY97E
Domestic	277	271	302	312	291	316	326	359	1136	1162	1292
International	200	197	218	226	229	219	267	260	904	841	975
Netware 4.0	162	168	210	220	225	230	280	290	430	760	1025
Netware 3.0	125	120	120	115	100	90	90	80	636	480	360
NetWare Other	5	5	5	5	5	5	5	5	21	20	20
NetWare Systems Group	292	293	335	340	330	325	375	375	1087	1260	1405
Unix systems Group	20	15	15	15	10	12	12	12	101	65	46
Information Access/Mgt	75	85	90	100	95	110	115	136	248	350	456
Applications (WordPerfect)	45	30	33	35	35	36	38	42	467	143	151
License Revenue	432	423	473	490	470	483	540	565	1903	1818	2058
Education, Service & Other	45	45	47	48	50	52	53	54	153	185	209
Net Sales	**477**	**468**	**520**	**538**	**520**	**535**	**593**	**619**	**2056**	**2003**	**2267**
Cost of Sales	119	109	113	116	113	125	130	135	493	457	503
Sales & Marketing	152	135	139	142	148	155	166	168	595	568	637
Product Develop.	93	89	89	92	94	95	96	97	366	363	382
G & A	38	32	32	33	34	35	37	38	150	135	144
Total Op Expenses	283	256	260	267	276	285	299	303	1111	1066	1163
Total Expenses	402	365	373	383	389	410	429	438	1604	1523	1666
Operating Income	75	103	147	155	136	128	169	182	452	480	615
Investment Income	14.0	12.0	10.0	8.0	6.0	6.0	6.0	7.0	58.8	44.0	25.0
Interest Expense	1	1	1	1	1	1	1	1	2	4	4
Merger expenses	0	0	0	0	0	0	0	0	0	0	0
Pretax Income	90	116	158	164	143	135	176	190	513	528	644
Taxes	30	39	53	55	49	46	60	65	172	177	219
Net income from ops	60	77	105	109	94	89	116	126	341	351	425
Extraordinary items	-	-	-	-	-	-	-	-	0	0	0
Taxes on extr. items	-	-	-	-	-	-	-	-	0	0	0
Net Income	60	77	105	109	94	89	116	126	341	351	425
Avg Shrs. (mil.)	367	358	349	340	340	342	342	344	375	354	342
EPS-Operating	**0.16**	**0.22**	**0.30**	**0.32**	**0.28**	**0.26**	**0.34**	**0.37**	**0.91**	**1.00**	**1.25**
% Change	-27%	-15%	11%	100%	75%	18%	13%	16%	8%	10%	25%
EPS-Reported	0.16	0.22	0.30	0.32	0.28	0.26	0.34	0.37	0.91	1.00	1.25
Growth Y/Y %											
Domestic Revenue	2	-3	2	9	5	16	8	15	0	2	11
Intl Revenue	-10	-16	-10	9	14	12	22	15	5	-7	16
NETWARE 4	**125**	**115**	**62**	**47**	**39**	**37**	**33**	**32**	**330**	**77**	**35**
NETWARE 3	**-31**	**-25**	**-25**	**-15**	**-20**	**-25**	**-25**	**-30**	**-18**	**-25**	**-25**
TOTAL NETWARE	**13**	**20**	**14**	**17**	**13**	**11**	**12**	**10**	**19**	**16**	**12**
Unix systems Group	-9	-44	-44	-40	-50	-20	-20	-20	-43	-36	-29
Information Access/Mgt	82	48	29	25	27	29	28	36	15	41	30
Applications (WordPerfect)	-69	-81	-69	-36	-22	20	15	20	-21	-69	6
License Revenue	-7	-13	-5	9	9	14	14	15	0	-4	13
Education, Service & Other	67	10	18	7	11	16	13	13	50	21	13
TOTAL REVENUE	**-3**	**-12**	**-3**	**9**	**9**	**14**	**14**	**15**	**3**	**-3**	**13**
Op Expenses	7	-8	-7	-9	-2	11	15	13	4	-4	9
Op Profit	-26	-20	3	76	58	16	11	16	72	3	22
% of Revenue											
Cost of Sales	24.9	23.3	21.7	21.6	21.7	23.4	21.9	21.8	24.0	22.8	22.2
Gross Margin	75.1	76.7	78.3	78.4	78.3	76.6	78.1	78.2	76.0	77.2	77.8
Sales & Marketing	31.9	28.8	26.7	26.4	28.5	29.0	28.0	27.2	29.0	28.4	28.1
Product Development	19.5	19.0	17.1	17.1	18.1	17.8	16.2	15.7	17.8	18.1	16.9
G & A	7.9	6.8	6.2	6.1	6.5	6.5	6.2	6.1	7.3	6.7	6.4
Op Margin	**15.8**	**22.0**	**28.3**	**28.8**	**26.1**	**23.9**	**28.5**	**29.5**	**22.0**	**24.0**	**27.1**
Net Income	12.6	16.5	20.2	20.3	18.1	16.6	19.6	20.3	16.6	17.5	18.7
Eff Tax Rate	33.5	33.5	33.5	33.5	34.0	34.0	34.0	34.0	33.5	33.5	34.0
Ratios/BS											
Book Value/shr	-	-	-	-	-	-	-	-	-	-	-
Cash/shr	-	-	-	-	-	-	-	-	-	-	-
Sales/Shr	-	-	-	-	-	-	-	-	-	-	-
Total Cash	-	-	-	-	-	-	-	-	-	-	-
Total Debt	-	-	-	-	-	-	-	-	-	-	-
Total Equity	-	-	-	-	-	-	-	-	-	-	-
Total Assets	-	-	-	-	-	-	-	-	-	-	-
Rec Days Outst	-	-	-	-	-	-	-	-	-	-	-
LTM Sales	2039	1978	1960	2003	2046	2113	2186	2267	-	-	-
LTM EPS-reported	0.85	0.81	0.84	1.00	1.12	1.16	1.20	1.25	-	-	-

E = Morgan Stanley Research Estimates   Fiscal year ends in March.   LTM = Last 12 Months

Oracle Systems — Sales and Earnings Summary Fiscal 1995–1997E

($ Millions, Except EPS)

	8/95	11/95	2/96E	5/96E	8/96E	11/96E	2/97E	5/97E	FY95	FY96E	FY97E
			1996E				**1997E**				
Total Revenue	**772**	**967**	**1010**	**1420**	**1051**	**1313**	**1374**	**1933**	**2967**	**4169**	**5670**
Oracle Americas	375	446	470	710	518	615	649	980	1416	2001	2762
Oracle Eur./ME/Afr.	280	375	385	510	365	488	501	663	1165	1551	2016
Oracle Asia/Pacific	116	145	155	200	168	210	225	290	385	615	892
Services	405	464	475	565	532	634	650	773	1293	1909	2589
Support	198	225	233	274	252	311	324	381	585	931	1268
Consult'g & Train'g	208	239	242	290	281	323	326	392	710	979	1321
Total Licenses	382	503	535	855	518	679	723	1160	1672	2275	3081
Other licenses	16	20	20	20	21	22	23	24	66	76	90
Product Licenses	366	483	515	835	497	657	700	1136	1606	2199	2990
By Platform											
Unix	247	343	363	617	343	466	494	858	1175	1570	2161
Desktop	61	90	100	148	90	133	142	208	271	400	572
Proprietary	42	46	52	69	64	58	65	70	160	210	257
By Prod. Segment											
Servers	235	344	370	625	341	468	503	845	1111	1574	2157
Dev Tools	67	84	85	95	87	109	111	124	341	331	430
Applic.Group	48	55	60	115	70	80	87	167	154	278	403
Apps-related svs.	74	75	80	110	110	110	115	160	210	339	495
Sales/Mkt Exp.	279	357	360	526	379	489	493	726	1103	1522	2087
Cost of Services	232	255	277	345	322	352	382	476	779	1109	1533
Research	84	93	93	110	110	116	125	138	261	381	489
Corp G&A	52	57	58	62	65	69	79	81	174	229	294
Total Expenses	**647**	**763**	**788**	**1043**	**876**	**1026**	**1079**	**1421**	**2318**	**3240**	**4403**
Operating Profit	125	204	222	377	174	287	295	512	649	929	1267
Net Interest	7.3	2.8	2.3	2.3	2.3	2.3	2.4	2.4	9	15	9
Special charges	-51	-	-	-	-	-	-	-	0	-51	0
Pretax Profit	81.5	207.2	224.3	379.3	176.8	288.9	296.9	514.2	658	892	1277
Taxes	27.7	70.5	76.3	129.0	60.1	98.2	100.9	174.8	217	303	434
Tax rate	34%	34%	34%	34%	34%	34%	34%	34%	33%	34%	34%
Net Income	53.8	136.7	148.0	250.3	116.7	190.7	196.0	339.4	441	589	843
Avg. Shares(mil.)	447	447	445	445	445	445	445	445	443	446	445
EPS-Operating	**0.20**	**0.31**	**0.33**	**0.56**	**0.26**	**0.43**	**0.44**	**0.76**	**1.00**	**1.40**	**1.89**
EPS Growth	45%	46%	38%	37%	30%	39%	33%	36%	57%	40%	35%
EPS Reported	0.12	0.31	0.33	0.56	0.26	0.43	0.44	0.76	1.00	1.40	1.89
Growth Y/Y %											
Oracle Americas	44	43	39	41	38	38	38	38	50	41	38
Oracle Eur./ME/Afr.	23	38	35	34	30	30	30	30	40	33	30
Oracle Asia/Pacific	69	67	58	52	45	45	45	45	71	60	45
Servers	29	44	42	46	45	36	36	35	64	42	37
Dev Tools	-11	9	5	-12	30	30	30	30	5	-3	30
Applic.Group	109	104	82	62	45	45	45	45	64	81	45
Unix	20	36	33	39	39	36	36	39	49	34	38
Desktop	36	64	54	40	47	47	42	40	48	47	43
Proprietary	45	28	41	20	53	26	24	1	23	31	23
Product Licenses	**31**	**41**	**37**	**37**	**36**	**36**	**36**	**36**	**46**	**37**	**36**
Service Sales	**55**	**51**	**43**	**44**	**31**	**37**	**37**	**37**	**54**	**48**	**36**
Total Revenue	**39**	**44**	**40**	**40**	**36**	**36**	**36**	**36**	**48**	**41**	**36**
Total Expenses	**38**	**43**	**39**	**39**	**36**	**35**	**37**	**36**	**47**	**40**	**36**
% of Sales											
Op Margin	16	21	22	27	17	22	21	26	22	22	22
Ratios/BS											
Book Value/shr	2.92	3.27	-	-	-	-	-	-	-	-	-
Cash/shr	1.29	1.24	-	-	-	-	-	-	-	-	-
Sales/Shr	**7.13**	**7.78**	-	-	-	-	-	-	-	-	-
Total Cash	577	554	-	-	-	-	-	-	-	-	-
Total Debt	92	91	-	-	-	-	-	-	-	-	-
TotalEquity	1306	1462	-	-	-	-	-	-	-	-	-
Total Assets	2349	2530	-	-	-	-	-	-	-	-	-
Rec Days Outst	**71**	**71**	-	-	-	-	-	-	-	-	-
Receivables	611	767	-	-	-	-	-	-	-	-	-
LTM Sales	3182	3479	3767	4169	4448	4793	5157	5670	-	-	-
LTM EPS	1.06	1.16	1.25	1.40	1.46	1.58	1.69	1.89	-	-	-

E = Morgan Stanley Research Estimates   Fiscal year ends in March.   LTM = Last 12 Months

Internet/Online Services Consulting and Development

FIND/SVP — Financial Summary F1993–F1995

($ Thousands Except EPS)

	3/94	6/94	9/94	12/94	3/95	6/95	9/95	F1993	F1994
		F1994			F1995				
Revenues	5,932	6,201	6,134	6,090	6,819	7,039	7,398	20,257	24,357
Direct Costs	3,035	3,491	3,295	3,031	3,824	3,752	3,974	10,788	12,852
Gross Margin	2,897	2,710	2,839	3,059	2,995	3,287	3,424	9,469	11,505
Operating Expenses									
Selling, General, and Administrative Expenses	2,672	2,436	2,509	2,744	2,813	2,979	3,108	8,743	10,361
Total Operating Expenses	2,672	2,436	2,509	2,744	2,813	2,979	3,108	8,743	10,361
Operating Income	225	274	330	315	182	308	316	726	1,144
Interest Income	15	13	17	14	15	14	13	60	59
Gain on Sale of Net Assets				80			10		80
Interest Expense	(6)	(6)	(13)	(27)	(47)	(72)	(61)	(25)	(52)
Pretax Income	234	281	334	382	150	250	278	761	1,231
Provision for Income Taxes	105	129	152	172	65	111	120	192	558
Income Before Cumulative Effect of Change in Accounting	129	152	182	210	85	139	158	569	673
Cumulative Effect of Change in Accounting								157	
Net Income	129	152	182	210	85	139	158	726	673
EPS	$0.02	$0.02	$0.03	$0.03	$0.01	$0.02	$0.02	$0.11	$0.10
Shares Outstanding	6,450	7,600	6,067	7,000	8,500	6,950	7,900	6,600	6,730
Growth Rate									
Revenues (yr-yr)	25%	23%	22%	12%	15%	14%	21%	--	257%
Revenues (seq.)	9%	5%	-1%	-1%	12%	3%	5%	--	--
Expenses (yr-yr)	31%	8%	16%	20%	5%	22%	24%	--	268%
Expenses (seq.)	17%	-9%	3%	9%	3%	6%	4%	--	--
EPS (yr-yr)	-50%	100%	50%	-50%	-50%	0%	-33%		-9%
Margin Analysis									
Gross Margin	48.8%	43.7%	46.3%	50.2%	43.9%	46.7%	46.3%	46.7%	47.2%
Operating Margin	3.8%	4.4%	5.4%	5.2%	2.7%	4.4%	4.3%	3.6%	4.7%
Pretax Margin	3.9%	4.5%	5.4%	6.3%	2.2%	3.6%	3.8%	3.8%	5.1%
Net Margin	2.2%	2.5%	3.0%	3.4%	1.2%	2.0%	2.1%	3.6%	2.8%
Expenses as Pct. of Revenue									
S, G & A	45.0%	39.3%	40.9%	45.1%	41.3%	42.3%	42.0%	43.2%	42.5%
Operating Expenses	45.0%	39.3%	40.9%	45.1%	41.3%	42.3%	42.0%	43.2%	42.5%
Tax Rate	44.9%	45.9%	45.5%	45.0%	43.3%	44.4%	43.2%	25.2%	45.3%

Fiscal Year ends in December.

Organization/Aggregation

America Online — Income Statement Comparisons F1995–F1997E

($ Thousands Except EPS)

	F1995(b,d)				F1996E(d)				Annual Data		
	9/94(a)	12/94	3/95(c)	6/95(e)	9/95(f)	12/95	3/96E	6/96E	F1995(a,b,d)	F1996E(d,f)	F1997E(d)
Revenue	$56,936	$76,395	$109,104	$151,855	$197,865	$249,094	$295,965	$351,215	$394,290	$1,094,139	$1,968,798
Service Revenue	50,056	66,966	99,814	138,916	185,086	224,525	265,965	313,215	355,752	988,791	1,694,893
Marketing	--	--	--	--	--	--	--	--	0	--	--
Other Revenue	6,880	9,429	9,290	12,939	12,779	24,569	30,000	38,000	38,538	105,348	273,905
Cost of Goods	32,917	42,847	66,526	87,434	119,077	145,928	177,579	207,217	229,724	649,801	1,161,591
Gross Profit	24,019	33,548	42,578	64,421	78,788	103,166	118,386	143,998	164,566	444,338	807,207
Operating Expense	19,396	26,021	34,244	52,211	66,249	85,328	96,842	113,350	131,872	361,769	605,077
Marketing	11,553	16,069	20,234	29,208	36,729	51,913	57,182	67,341	77,064	213,166	389,825
G&A	6,086	7,028	11,193	17,659	20,480	23,986	28,709	33,014	41,966	106,189	154,235
Product Development	1,757	2,924	2,817	5,344	9,040	9,429	10,951	12,995	12,842	42,415	61,016
Operating Income	4,623	7,527	8,334	12,210	12,539	17,838	21,544	30,648	32,694	82,569	202,130
Other Income, net	689	750	814	770	780	1,425	1,100	800	3,023	4,105	2,800
Pretax Income	5,312	8,277	9,148	12,980	13,319	19,263	22,644	31,448	35,717	86,674	204,930
Taxes	2,121	4,222	3,634	5,192	5,568	6,924	8,605	11,950	15,169	33,047	77,874
Net Income (Operating)	3,191	4,055	5,514	7,788	7,751	12,339	14,039	19,498	20,548	53,627	127,057
Extraordinary Item	(1,710)	(42,785)	(8,101)	(1,599)	(18,013)	(1,749)	(1,032)	(1,032)	(54,195)	(21,825)	(4,128)
Net Income (Reported)	1,481	(38,730)	(2,587)	6,189	(10,262)	10,590	13,008	18,466	(33,647)	31,802	122,929
Earnings Per Share (Diluted)	$0.02	($0.60)	($0.04)	$0.07	($0.10)	$0.10	$0.12	$0.16	($0.50)	$0.28	$1.00
Operating	0.04	0.06	0.08	0.08	0.08	0.12	0.13	0.17	0.27	0.50	1.04
Reported				0.07					(0.55)		
Excluding loss from 2Market		0.10							0.29		
Shares Outstanding (Diluted)	76,428	64,776	67,244	94,328	99,788	105,559	108,000	112,000	67,972	106,337	122,337
Growth Rate											
Revenue (yr-yr)	198%	211	244%	276%	248%	226%	171	131	241%	177	80%
Service Revenue (yr-yr)	250	230	246	270	270	235	166	125	252	178	71
Revenue (seq.)	41	34	43	39	30	26	19	19	--	--	--
Service Revenue (seq.)	33	34	49	39	33	21	18	18	--	--	--
Expenses (yr-yr)	163	178	213	262	242	228	183	117	213	174	67
Expenses (seq.)	35	34	32	52	27	29	13	17	--	--	--
Net Income (Operating) (yr-yr)	953	5,693	333	761	143	204	155	150	706	161	137
EPS (Oper.)	750	9,491	374	567	86	87	59	11	619	85	108
Margins											
Gross Margin	42.2%	43.9%	39.0%	42.4%	39.8%	41.4%	40.0%	41.0%	41.7%	40.6%	41.0%
Operating Margin	8.1	9.9	7.6	8.0	6.3	7.2	7.3	8.7	8.3	7.5	10.3
Pretax Margin	9.3	10.8	8.4	8.5	6.7	7.7	7.7	9.0	9.1	7.9	10.4
Net Margin	5.6	5.3	5.1	5.1	3.9	5.0	4.7	5.6	5.2	4.9	6.5
Expense Percentages											
Cost of Goods Sold/Service Revenue	65.8%	64.0%	66.6%	62.9%	64.3%	65.0%	66.8%	66.2%	64.6%	65.7%	68.5%
Opex/Total Revenue	34.1	34.1	31.4	34.4	33.5	34.3	32.7	32.3	33.4	33.1	30.7
Marketing/Service Revenue	23.1	24.0	20.3	21.0	19.8	23.1	21.5	21.5	21.7	21.6	23.0
G&A/Total Revenue	10.7	9.2	10.3	11.6	10.4	9.6	9.7	9.4	10.6	9.7	7.8
Product Development/Total Revenue	3.1	3.8	2.6	3.5	4.6	3.8	3.7	3.7	3.3	3.9	3.1
Tax Rate	39.9	51.0	39.7	40.0	41.8	35.9	38.0	38.0	42.5	38.1	38.0

(a) Includes $1.7mm in costs related to the merger with Redgate Communications. (b) Restated for the merger with Redgate Communications. Note F1991 and F1992 reflect Redgate operations for the twelve month periods ending Dec. 1990 and Dec. 1991, respectively. (c) Includes estimated pre-tax charges of $20mm related to write offs from ANS acquisition and follow-on to BookLink and NaviSoft acquisitions. (d) Represents $45mm charge associated with ANS acquisition, amortized over 10 years using straight-line method, beginning in F3Q95. (e) Extraordinary item includes $1.1mm pre-tax amortization of goodwill charge and $497K pre-tax charge for merger expenses. (f) Extraordinary item includes $16.9mm pre-tax charge related to write-off of R&D in precess at Ubique and amortization of previously acquired assets.

E = Morgan Stanley Research Estimates   Fiscal Year ends in June.

H&R Block/CompuServe — Financial Summary F1994–F1995

($ Thousands Except EPS)

	F1995				F1996		F1994	F1995
	7/94	10/94	1/95	4/95	7/95	10/95	F1994	F1995
Revenues								
Service Revenues	135,719	163,404	252,528	682,164	199,347	216,464	1,118,566	1,233,815
Franchise Royalties	1,187	3,442	8,931	78,876	1,395	3,582	96,766	92,436
Investment Income	5,151	4,554	4,104	9,894	4,307	2,866	15,256	23,703
Other Income	3,343	1,457	2,451	3,113	13,065	1,001	8,089	10,364
Total Revenues	145,400	172,857	268,014	774,047	218,114	223,913	1,238,677	1,360,318
Expenses								
Employee Compensation and Benefits	44,994	49,908	94,643	252,959	54,904	61,523	404,367	442,504
Occupancy and Equipment	60,910	64,072	74,777	95,769	81,511	89,727	242,391	295,528
Marketing and Advertising	6,443	13,880	17,649	46,933	3,577	16,572	60,783	84,905
Supplies, Freight and Postage	6,680	10,878	20,490	33,494	15,211	17,931	60,182	71,542
Other	31,170	36,148	47,353	47,664	54,428	51,630	162,698	162,335
Purchased Research & Development				83,508			25,072	83,508
Total Expenses	150,197	174,886	254,912	560,327	209,631	237,383	955,493	1,140,322
Pretax Income	(4,797)	(2,029)	13,102	213,720	8,483	(13,470)	283,184	219,996
Income Tax Expense	(1,837)	(777)	5,018	110,333	3,257	(5,172)	119,189	112,737
Net Income from Continuing Operations	(2,960)	(1,252)	8,084	103,387	5,226	(8,298)	163,995	107,259
Net Earnings from Discontinued Operations							9,268	
Net Gain on Sale of Discontinued Operations							27,265	
Net Income	(2,960)	(1,252)	8,084	103,387	5,226	(8,298)	200,528	107,259
EPS from Continuing Operations	($0.03)	($0.01)	$0.08	$0.97	$0.05	($0.08)	$1.54	$1.01
EPS	($0.03)	($0.01)	$0.08	$0.97	$0.05	($0.08)	$1.88	$1.01
Shares Outstanding	105,126	105,000	105,658	105,658	107,103	103,950	106,577	106,197
Growth Rate								
Revenues (yr-yr)	41%	32%	17%	0%	50%	30%	--	10%
Revenues (seq.)	-81%	19%	55%	189%	-72%	3%	--	--
Expenses (yr-yr)	28%	26%	6%	22%	40%	36%	--	19%
Expenses (seq.)	-67%	16%	46%	120%	-63%	13%	--	--
EPS (yr-yr) (from continuing operations)	NM	NM	NM	-47%	NM	NM	--	-34%
EPS (yr-yr)	NM	0%	-33%	-47%	NM	NM	--	-46%
Margin Analysis								
Pretax Margin	-3.3%	-1.2%	4.9%	27.6%	3.9%	-6.0%	22.9%	16.2%
Net Margin (from Continuing Operations)	-2.0%	-0.7%	3.0%	13.4%	2.4%	-3.7%	13.2%	7.9%
Net Margin	-2.0%	-0.7%	3.0%	13.4%	2.4%	-3.7%	16.2%	7.9%
Expenses as Pct. of Revenue								
Total Operating Expenses	103.3%	101.2%	95.1%	72.4%	96.1%	106.0%	77.1%	83.8%
Tax Rate	38.3%	38.3%	38.3%	51.6%	38.4%	38.4%	42.1%	51.2%

Fiscal Year ends in April.

Publishing (Traditional)

Dun & Bradstreet — Sales and Earnings Summary 1994–1995

($ Millions Except EPS)

	1994				1995				Annual Data	
	3/94	6/94	9/94	12/94	3/95	6/95	9/95	12/95	1994	1995A
Marketing Information Services	440.3	483.8	513.5	605.3	527.4	587.4	598.0	675.3	2,042.9	2,388.1
% Change	0.2%	2.6%	9.9%	23.5%	19.8%	21.4%	16.5%	11.6	9.3%	16.9%
Risk Management & Business Marketing, Info. Svs.	385.6	392.0	391.3	436.8	409.2	426.1	428.0	470.8	1,605.7	1,734.1
% Change	2.8%	2.3%	0.9%	4.4%	6.1%	8.7%	9.4%	7.8%	2.7%	8.0%
Software Services	94.8	99.1	94.0	118.0	105.8	108.2	106.0	137.4	405.9	457.4
% Change	-15.0%	-17.3%	-13.4%	-13.0%	11.6	9.2%	12.8%	16.4%	-14.7%	12.7%
Directory Information Services	78.8	103.2	101.8	156.3	77.6	89.9	104.0	152.2	440.1	423.7
% Change	0.5%	2.2%	2.3%	-9.0%	-1.5%	-12.9%	2.2%	-2.6%	-2.4%	-3.7%
Other Business Services	99.7	106.6	102.8	92.0	99.6	95.8	97.4	119.	401.1	411.9
% Change	49.0%	23.8%	8.3%	-	-0.1%	-	-5.2%	29.4%	14.1	2.7%
Total Revenue	**1,099.2**	**1,184.7**	**1,203.4**	**1,408.4**	**1,219.6**	**1,307.4**	**1,333.4**	**1,554.8**	**4,895.7**	**5,415.2**
% Change	2.6%	2.0%	3.9%	6.7%	11.0	10.4%	10.8%	10.4%	3.9%	10.6%
Operating Profit by Segment										
Marketing Information Services	--	--	--	--	--	--	--	--	277.1	337.2
Risk Management & Business Marketing, Info. Svs.	--	--	--	--	--	--	--	--	445.2	405.1
Software Services	--	--	--	--	--	--	--	--	(0.8)	30.3
Directory Information Services	--	--	--	--	--	--	--	--	214.2	204.0
Other Business Services	--	--	--	--	--	--	--	--	88.3	63.8
Corporate Expenses	--	--	--	--	--	--	--	--	(98.5)	(70.5)
Total Operating Income	--	--	--	--	--	--	--	--	925.5	969.9
Operating Costs, Selling & Administrative Expenses	939.4	970.6	953.0	1,107.2	1,046.8	1,087.4	1,072.7	1,238.4	3,970.2	4,445.3
Restructuring Expense/(Income), net	--	--	--	--	--	--	--	--	--	--
Total Operating Income	159.8	214.1	250.4	301.2	172.8	220.0	260.7	316.4	925.5	969.9
% Margin	14.5%	18.1	20.8%	21.4%	14.2%	16.8%	19.6%	20.3%	18.9%	17.9%
Interest Expense (Income), net	(4.0)	3.9	4.3	3.7	6.5	5.3	8.0	1.	7.8	20.9
Other expense (income)	12.0	8.3	13.3	4.9	15.7	12.6	15.5	13.4	38.5	57.2
Pretax Income	151.8	201.9	232.8	292.7	150.6	202.1	237.2	301.9	879.2	891.8
Income Taxes	43.1	57.3	66.1	83.2	41.7	56.0	65.7	83.6	249.7	247.0
Tax Rate (%)	28.4%	28.4%	28.4%	28.4%	27.7%	27.7%	27.7%	27.7%	28.4%	27.7%
Net Income	108.7	144.6	166.7	209.5	108.9	146.1	171.5	218.3	629.5	644.8
Earnings per Share	**0.64**	**0.85**	**0.98**	**1.23**	**0.64**	**0.86**	**1.01**	**1.29**	**3.70**	**3.80**
Average Shares Outstanding (mil)	170.2	170.1	170.0	169.7	169.7	169.6	169.6	169.4	169.9	169.5
Profit Margins (%)										
Marketing Information Services	--	--	--	--	--	--	--	--	13.6%	14.1
Risk Management & Business Marketing, Info. Svs.	--	--	--	--	--	--	--	--	27.7%	23.4%
Software Services	--	--	--	--	--	--	--	--	-0.2%	6.6%
Directory Information Services	--	--	--	--	--	--	--	--	48.7%	48.1%
Other Business Services	--	--	--	--	--	--	--	--	22.0%	15.5%
Corporate Expenses	--	--	--	--	--	--	--	--	-2.0%	-1.3%
Total Operating Income	--	--	--	--	--	--	--	--	18.9%	17.9%

A = Actual
Note: 4Q 1995 excludes $448 million ($1.91 per share) restructuring charge.

Gannett — Sales and Earnings Summary 1994–1996E

($ Millions Except EPS))

	1994				1995E				Annual Data		
	3/94	6/94	9/94	12/94	3/95A	6/95A	9/95A	12/95E	1994	1995E	1996E
Newspapers											
Advertising	492.2	540.2	521.9	598.3	516.7	567.1	508.8	604.3	2152.7	2197.0	2356.9
Circulation	212.1	212.9	210.7	213.7	212.0	214.0	209.4	213.7	849.5	849.1	866.1
Total Newspapers	704.4	753.1	732.7	812.0	728.7	781.2	718.3	818.0	3002.1	3046.1	3223.0
Broadcasting	84.0	107.5	95.2	119.9	97.0	120.9	104.8	122.9	406.6	445.6	481.2
Outdoor Advertising	46.9	63.2	65.9	65.1	50.6	68.6	67.4	67.7	241.1	254.3	272.1
Other	41.3	43.1	38.6	51.6	37.5	43.3	41.8	55.7	174.7	178.3	191.7
Multimedia	--	--	--	--	--	--	--	--	--	--	667.1
Total Revenue	**876.6**	**966.9**	**932.4**	**1048.6**	**913.8**	**1013.9**	**932.3**	**1064.3**	**3824.5**	**3924.3**	**4835.0**
Cost of Sales	516.4	516.1	524.0	550.3	534.2	542.4	546.2	575.0	2106.8	2197.8	2313.2
SG&A	165.9	168.5	167.4	194.3	171.8	174.8	167.0	184.6	696.1	698.1	719.1
Depreciation and Amortization	51.8	51.7	53.7	51.6	50.7	50.3	49.7	51.8	208.8	202.4	207.0
Multimedia	--	--	--	--	--	--	--	--	--	--	475.5
Elimination of Redundant Costs	--	--	--	--	--	--	--	--	--	--	-20.0
Acquisition Amortization	--	--	--	--	--	--	--	--	--	--	44.8
Total Operating Costs	734.2	736.2	745.2	796.2	756.7	767.5	762.8	811.4	3011.7	3098.4	3739.6
Operating Income	142.5	230.7	187.3	252.4	157.2	246.4	169.4	252.9	812.8	825.9	1095.4
Operating Margin (%)	16.3	23.9	20.1	24.1	17.2	24.3	18.2	23.8	21.3	21.0	22.7
Operating Profit by Segment											
Newspaper Publishing	142.7	200.1	167.7	223.5	150.7	205.3	136.3	214.1	733.9	706.5	819.5
Broadcasting	21.2	39.5	27.2	41.0	26.2	47.4	38.5	46.1	128.9	158.2	167.2
Outdoor Advertising	-4.7	8.2	7.0	6.6	-2.8	11.1	9.7	9.5	17.1	27.5	32.6
Multimedia-after amortization	--	--	--	--	--	--	--	--	--	--	146.7
Corporate	-16.6	-17.1	-14.7	-18.7	-17.0	-17.4	-15.2	-16.7	-67.1	-66.3	-70.7
Total	142.5	230.7	187.3	252.4	157.2	246.4	169.4	252.9	812.8	825.9	1095.4
Operating Profit Margin (%)											
Newspaper Publishing	19.1	25.1	21.7	25.9	19.7	24.9	17.9	24.5	23.1	21.9	24.0
Broadcasting	25.2	36.7	28.6	34.2	27.1	39.2	36.8	37.5	31.7	35.5	34.8
Outdoor Advertising	-10.1	13.0	10.6	10.2	-5.6	16.2	14.4	14.0	7.1	10.8	12.0
Total Operating Profit Margin	16.3	23.9	20.1	24.1	17.2	24.3	18.2	23.8	21.3	21.0	22.7
Other Income(expense)	-10.1	-9.3	-10.5	-0.7	-12.3	-12.1	-8.0	-8.0	-30.7	-40.4	-40.0
Interest on Multimedia Debt ($530 mm)	--	--	--	--	--	--	--	--	--	--	-37.1
Interest for Acquisition Financing	--	--	--	--	--	--	--	--	--	--	-107.5
Pretax Income	132.3	221.4	176.7	251.7	144.9	234.3	161.4	244.9	782.1	785.6	910.8
Income Taxes	53.6	89.6	71.2	102.3	58.7	94.9	65.3	99.2	316.7	318.1	387.0
Tax Rate (%)	40.5	40.5	40.3	40.6	40.5	40.5	40.5	40.5	40.5	40.5	42.5
Net Income	78.7	131.8	105.5	149.4	86.2	139.4	96.1	145.7	465.4	467.5	522.1
Earnings per Share	**0.54**	**0.90**	**0.74**	**1.07**	**0.62**	**1.00**	**0.69**	**1.04**	**3.23**	**3.34**	**3.73**
Average Shares Outstanding (mil)	147.0	147.2	143.5	139.3	140.0	140.0	140.2	140.2	144.3	140.1	140.0
Newspapers - Yr/Yr % Change											
Advertising	5.8	5.2	9.8	8.5	5.0	5.0	-2.5	1.0	7.4	2.1	5.0
Circulation	1.0	1.3	1.5	1.3	-0.1	0.5	-0.6	0.0	1.3	0.0	2.0
Total Newspapers	4.3	4.1	7.3	6.5	3.5	3.7	-2.0	0.7	5.6	1.5	5.8
Broadcasting	1.4	-1.4	3.2	6.0	15.4	12.5	10.1	2.5	2.4	9.6	8.0
Outdoor Advertising	-1.9	-1.3	9.8	10.5	7.8	8.5	2.2	4.0	4.5	5.4	7.0
Other	6.2	4.1	-6.2	6.6	-9.1	0.4	8.2	8.0	2.8	2.1	7.5
Total Revenue	3.8	3.1	6.4	6.7	4.2	4.9	0.0	1.5	5.0	2.6	23.2
Expenses as % Revenue											
Cost of Sales as % of Revenue	58.9	53.4	56.2	52.5	58.5	53.5	58.6	54.0	55.1	56.0	47.8
SG&A	18.9	17.4	18.0	18.5	18.8	17.2	17.9	17.3	18.2	17.8	17.2
Depreciation and Amortization	5.9	5.3	5.8	4.9	5.5	5.0	5.3	4.9	5.5	5.2	4.3
Total Operating Costs	83.7	76.1	79.9	75.9	82.8	75.7	81.8	76.2	78.7	79.0	77.3

E = Morgan Stanley Research Estimates   *A = Actual*
Note: Multimedia Inc. assumed acquired at year-end 1995.

Knight-Ridder — Sales and Earnings Summary 1994–1996E

($ Millions Except EPS)

	1994				1995				Annual Data		
	3/94	6/94	9/94	12/94	3/95	6/95	9/95	12/95	1994	1995A	1996E
Newspapers - Advertising											
Retail	174.0	194.8	182.2	241.4	181.8	200.1	172.6	253.3	792.5	807.8	848.1
General	47.1	45.5	40.3	51.6	47.4	47.0	37.7	50.5	184.5	182.5	191.7
Classified	145.4	155.7	155.5	149.8	167.1	175.4	167.4	172.8	606.4	682.7	723.7
Total	366.5	396.0	378.1	442.8	396.3	422.4	377.8	476.5	1583.4	1673.0	1763.5
Circulation	120.7	121.6	120.5	121.8	122.6	123.0	117.5	132.1	484.6	495.3	510.2
Other	14.6	16.6	16.0	19.8	18.3	20.2	20.7	22.7	66.9	81.9	94.2
Lesher Communications	--	--	--	--	--	--	--	--	--	--	108.0
Total Newspapers	501.8	534.1	514.5	584.4	537.1	565.7	516.0	631.4	2134.9	2250.2	2475.8
Business Information Services	129.0	127.4	128.1	129.5	137.5	121.7	122.0	120.4	514.0	501.7	414.7
Total Revenue	**630.8**	**661.6**	**642.6**	**713.9**	**674.6**	**687.5**	**638.0**	**751.8**	**2648.9**	**2751.9**	**2890.5**
Labor and Employee Benefits	268.4	268.0	269.6	283.5	279.6	274.5	269.5	304.4	1089.4	1128.0	1085.0
Newsprint, Ink & Supplements	79.4	79.9	81.8	94.8	94.8	108.0	111.	132.8	335.9	446.8	527.3
Other Operating Costs	181.	181.	178.5	202.3	191.6	183.2	200.8	209.6	743.0	785.1	739.6
Depreciation and Amortization	37.1	37.2	37.4	37.5	37.6	37.1	37.3	39.5	149.3	151.6	151.6
Lesher Communications	--	--	--	--	--	--	--	--	--	--	92.0
Total Operating Costs	566.0	566.3	567.3	618.0	603.6	602.7	618.9	686.3	2317.6	2511.6	2595.5
Operating Income	64.8	95.3	75.3	95.9	71.0	84.7	19.	65.5	331.3	240.3	295.0
Operating Margin (%)	10.3%	14.4%	11.7	13.4%	10.5%	12.3%	3.0%	8.7%	12.5%	8.7%	10.2
Segment Profits											
Newspapers	68.1	102.0	79.3	101.5	77.7	94.7	29.3	79.4	350.9	281.1	341.6
Business Information Services	7.5	5.0	6.4	4.1	6.7	3.1	3.6	-1.4	23.1	12.0	14.5
Corporate Expenses	-10.8	-	-10.4	-9.7	-13.4	-	-13.9	-12.5	-42.7	-52.9	-
Total	64.8	95.3	75.3	95.9	71.0	84.7	19.	65.5	331.3	240.3	295.0
Profit Margin by Segment (%)											
Newspapers	13.6	19.	15.4	17.4	14.5	16.7	5.7	12.6	16.4	12.5	13.8
Business Information Services	5.8	3.9	5.0	3.2	4.9	2.5	3.0	-	4.5	2.4	3.5
Corporate Expenses	-1.7	-1.8	-1.6	-1.4	-2.0	-1.9	-2.2	-1.7	-1.6	-1.9	-2.1
Total	10.3	14.4	11.	13.4	10.5	12.3	3.0	8.7	12.5	8.7	10.2
Other Income/(Expense)	-	-10.0	-12.2	-5.8	-9.4	-5.0	-7.0	-14.0	-41.2	-35.3	-25.0
Pretax Income	51.7	85.3	63.1	90.1	61.6	79.7	12.	51.5	290.1	205.0	270.0
Pretax Margin (%)	8.2%	12.9%	9.8%	12.6%	9.1%	11.6	1.9%	6.9%	11.0	7.4%	9.3
Income Taxes	21.3	35.1	25.8	36.9	26.0	33.1	5.5	20.5	119.2	85.1	114.8
Tax Rate (%)	41.2%	41.2%	41.0%	41.0%	42.1%	41.5%	45.5%	39.8%	41.1	41.5%	42.5
Net Income	30.4	50.1	37.2	53.2	35.7	46.6	6.6	31.0	170.9	119.9	155.3
Earnings per Share	**0.55**	**0.92**	**0.69**	**0.99**	**0.69**	**0.93**	**0.13**	**0.63**	**3.15**	**2.39**	**3.29**
Average Shares Outstanding (mil)	55.2	54.5	53.8	53.5	51.9	50.1	49.4	49.0	54.3	50.1	47.3
Revenue - % Change											
Newspapers - Advertising											
Retail	2.5	1.9	3.9	5.0	4.5	2.7	-5.3	3.0	3.4	1.9	5.0
General	9.8	1.9	10.2	15.6	0.6	3.3	-6.5	0.0	9.3	-	5.0
Classified	7.5	9.8	11.	14.8	14.9	12.7	7.7	13.0	10.9	12.6	6.0
Total	5.4	4.9	7.6	9.3	8.1	6.7	-0.1	7.6	6.9	5.7	5.4
Circulation	3.2	2.3	2.3	0.8	1.6	1.2	-2.4	2.0	2.1	2.2	3.0
Other	12.3	15.5	16.4	26.1	25.2	22.2	29.2	25.0	17.9	22.3	15.0
Lesher Communications	--	--	--	--	--	--	--	--	--	--	--
Total Newspapers	5.0	4.6	6.6	7.9	7.0	5.9	0.3	8.0	6.1	5.4	10.0
Business Information Services	21.6	14.8	16.0	16.6	6.6	-4.5	-4.7	-5.3	17.2	-2.4	-17.3
Total Revenue	8.0	6.4	8.3	9.4	6.9	3.9	-0.7	5.3	8.1	3.9	5.0

E = Morgan Stanley Research Estimates   A = Actual
Note: 4Q 1995 includes $0.20 per share for severance charges.

McGraw-Hill — Sales and Earnings Summary 1994–1996E

($ Millions Except EPS)

	1994				1995				Annual Data		
	3/94	6/94	9/94	12/94	3/95	6/95	9/95	12/95	1994	1995A	1996E
Segment Revenue											
Info. and Media Services	149.3	159.9	149.1	214.6	154.3	168.3	163.8	224.7	672.8	711.1	754.4
Broadcasting	24.4	30.6	27.2	32.5	26.5	30.9	26.9	34.0	114.7	118.3	126.6
C.J. Tower	15.3	15.9	16.5	18.0	17.1	19.9	23.0	23.5	65.7	83.5	95.7
Total Info. & Publications	189.0	206.4	192.8	265.1	197.9	219.1	213.7	282.2	853.2	912.9	976.8
Educational & Prof. Publishing	119.3	126.6	213.2	164.8	121.3	131.6	216.7	178.5	624.0	648.1	684.6
El-Hi	57.0	132.2	270.0	79.0	50.0	170.0	280.0	87.5	538.2	587.5	548.5
Total Educational & Publications	176.3	258.8	483.2	243.8	171.3	301.6	496.7	266.0	1162.2	1235.6	1233.1
Financial Services	194.4	183.1	179.6	188.4	199.4	192.1	194.0	201.4	745.5	786.8	845.8
Total Revenue	**559.8**	**648.3**	**855.5**	**697.3**	**568.5**	**712.8**	**904.4**	**749.6**	**2760.9**	**2935.3**	**3055.6**
Segment Operating Profit											
Info. and Media Services	8.5	20.9	6.7	30.4	11.4	20.1	12.9	32.9	66.5	77.3	89.0
Broadcasting	4.5	10.5	7.8	11.0	6.4	10.7	7.0	11.5	33.8	35.6	38.9
C.J. Tower	1.5	1.9	2.0	2.7	1.6	1.7	2.0	3.2	8.1	8.5	10.1
Total Info. & Publications	14.5	33.3	16.4	44.1	19.4	32.5	21.9	47.6	108.3	121.4	137.9
Educational & Prof. Publishing	-0.9	2.9	37.7	23.6	-3.0	3.2	47.8	27.3	63.3	75.3	84.1
El-Hi	-24.0	18.0	79.0	-10.5	-26.4	28.0	86.5	-9.5	62.5	78.6	66.0
Total Educational & Publications	-24.9	20.9	116.7	13.1	-29.4	31.2	134.3	17.8	125.8	153.9	150.1
Financial Services	58.8	53.3	49.4	55.8	59.3	56.0	57.4	62.4	217.2	235.0	257.0
Total Profit	48.3	107.5	182.5	113.0	49.4	119.7	213.5	127.8	451.3	510.3	545.0
Total Operating Profit	48.3	107.5	182.5	113.0	49.4	119.7	213.5	127.8	451.3	510.3	545.0
General Corporate Expense	-11.5	-13.1	-15.0	-14.6	-12.9	-13.5	-17.2	-18.7	-54.1	-62.3	-65.0
Operating Profit	36.8	94.4	167.6	98.4	36.5	106.2	196.3	109.1	397.2	448.0	480.0
Interest Expense	-11.3	-12.7	-14.2	-13.5	-12.8	-16.3	-16.3	-13.4	-51.7	-58.8	-51.5
Pretax Earnings	25.5	81.7	153.3	84.9	23.7	89.9	180.0	95.7	345.4	389.3	428.5
Income Taxes	10.5	33.7	63.2	35.0	9.8	37.0	74.1	39.4	142.3	160.4	176.5
Tax Rate (%)	41.2%	41.2%	41.2%	41.2%	41.2%	41.2%	41.2%	41.2%	41.2%	41.2%	41.2%
Net Income	15.0	48.0	90.2	49.9	14.0	52.8	105.8	56.3	203.1	228.9	252.0
Earnings per Share	**0.30**	**0.97**	**1.82**	**1.01**	**0.28**	**1.06**	**2.12**	**1.12**	**4.10**	**4.59**	**5.10**
Average Shares Outstanding (mil)	49.4	49.4	49.5	49.6	49.7	49.8	50.0	50.1	49.5	49.9	49.4
Revenue - % Change											
Info. and Media Services	1.1	0.9	-1.9	1.6	3.3	5.3	9.9	4.7	0.5	5.7	6.1
Broadcasting	10.0	10.5	17.2	15.0	8.6	1.1	-1.1	4.6	13.2	3.2	7.0
C.J. Tower	7.3	6.5	10.3	11.7	11.8	24.8	39.4	30.6	9.0	27.0	14.7
Total Info. & Publications	2.6	2.6	1.4	3.7	4.7	6.2	10.9	6.5	2.7	7.0	7.0
Educational & Prof. Publishing	8.5	6.8	11.7	4.8	1.7	3.9	1.6	8.3	8.2	3.9	5.6
El-Hi	--	--	--	-12.9	-12.3	28.6	3.7	10.8	--	9.2	-6.6
Total Educational & Publications	60.4	118.2	153.1	-1.7	-2.8	16.5	2.8	9.1	74.1	6.3	-0.2
Financial Services	12.5	7.0	3.3	5.2	2.5	4.9	8.0	6.9	7.0	5.5	7.5
Total Revenue	19.9	32.1	54.2	2.2	1.6	9.9	5.7	7.5	25.8	6.3	4.1
Operating Profit - % Margin											
Info. and Media Services	5.7	13.1	4.5	14.2	7.4	11.9	7.9	14.6	9.9	10.9	11.8
Broadcasting	18.4	34.5	28.6	33.8	24.2	34.6	26.0	33.8	29.5	30.1	30.7
C.J. Tower	9.8	11.7	12.1	15.0	9.4	8.5	8.7	13.6	12.3	10.2	10.5
Total Info. & Publications	7.7	16.1	8.5	16.7	9.8	14.8	10.2	16.8	12.7	13.3	14.1
Educational & Prof. Publishing	-0.8	2.3	17.7	14.3	-2.4	2.4	22.0	15.3	10.1	11.6	12.3
El-Hi	-42.1	13.6	29.3	-13.3	-52.8	16.5	30.9	-10.9	11.6	13.4	12.0
Total Educational & Publications	-14.1	8.1	24.1	5.4	-17.1	10.4	27.0	6.7	10.8	12.5	12.2
Financial Services	30.2	29.1	27.5	29.6	29.7	29.1	29.6	31.0	29.1	29.9	30.4
Total Profit	8.6	16.6	21.3	16.2	8.7	16.8	23.6	17.0	16.3	17.4	17.8

E = Morgan Stanley Research Estimates   *A = Actual*

Note: 4Q 1995 excludes $26.8 million ($0.31 per share) charge and $23.8 million ($0.28 per share) gain.

McClatchy Newspapers — Sales and Earnings Summary 1994–1996E

($ Millions Except EPS)

	1994				1995				Annual Data		
	3/94	6/94	9/94	12/94	3/95	6/95	9/95	12/95	1994	1995A	1996E
Advertising	83.8	93.0	91.3	99.9	87.1	96.8	94.3	100.7	368.1	378.9	397.8
Circulation	21.2	21.2	21.2	21.4	21.7	21.7	21.7	22.1	85.0	87.2	89.8
Other	3.9	4.4	4.5	5.4	5.0	6.1	5.6	6.5	18.3	23.3	29.1
News & Observer	--	--	--	--	--	--	20.3	31.2	--	51.5	130.0
Total Revenue	**108.9**	**118.6**	**117.1**	**126.8**	**113.8**	**124.6**	**142.0**	**160.5**	**471.4**	**540.9**	**646.7**
Compensation	50.2	50.9	51.3	49.9	51.8	50.3	51.0	50.3	202.4	203.3	207.4
Newsprint and Supplements	14.7	15.9	17.1	19.8	19.1	22.9	24.9	27.3	67.5	94.2	110.7
Other Operating Expenses	22.9	21.8	21.9	24.9	23.4	22.5	23.8	23.9	91.5	93.5	95.4
Depreciation and Amortization	9.5	9.5	9.5	9.7	9.2	9.3	9.6	9.2	38.1	37.3	38.4
News & Observer	--	--	--	--	--	--	19.4	28.1	--	47.5	119.0
Total Operating Expenses	97.3	98.1	99.8	104.3	103.4	104.9	128.6	138.8	399.6	475.8	570.8
Operating Income	11.6	20.5	17.3	22.4	10.4	19.7	13.3	21.7	71.9	65.1	75.9
Interest Expense	0.0	0.0	0.0	0.0	0.0	0.0	2.9	4.1	0.0	7.0	16.0
Interest Income	0.4	0.6	1.0	1.3	1.6	1.6	0.7	0.1	3.2	3.9	0.0
Partnership Losses	1.5	1.5	1.0	1.5	0.7	0.4	-0.3	-0.2	5.5	0.6	-3.5
Other-net	0.0	0.0	0.0	0.0	0.0	0.3	0.0	0.0	-0.1	0.3	0.4
Pretax Income	10.4	19.6	17.3	22.2	11.2	21.2	11.4	17.8	69.6	61.7	63.7
Income Taxes	4.5	8.6	6.6	9.1	4.6	8.7	5.8	7.6	28.9	26.7	29.0
Tax Rate (%)	43.5%	43.9%	38.5%	40.8%	40.9%	41.0%	50.5%	42.7%	41.5%	43.2%	45.5%
Net Income	5.9	11.0	10.6	13.2	6.6	12.5	5.6	10.2	40.7	35.1	34.7
Earnings per Share	**0.20**	**0.37**	**0.35**	**0.44**	**0.22**	**0.42**	**0.19**	**0.34**	**1.38**	**1.17**	**1.16**
Average Shares Outstanding (mil)	28.9	29.5	29.9	30.0	30.0	30.0	30.0	30.1	29.6	30.0	30.0
Revenue - Yr/Yr % Change											
Advertising	3.5	5.0	5.6	6.3	3.9	4.1	3.3	0.7	5.2	2.9	5.0
Circulation	1.2	1.4	1.5	1.8	2.4	2.4	2.4	3.2	1.5	2.6	3.0
Other	16.2	12.3	15.7	33.3	27.9	38.4	23.4	19.6	19.6	26.9	25.0
Total Revenue	3.5	4.6	5.2	6.4	4.5	5.1	21.2	26.6	5.0	14.7	19.6
Expenses - Yr/Yr % Change											
Compensation	1.0	1.2	2.7	0.3	3.1	-1.2	-0.7	0.7	1.3	0.5	2.0
Newsprint and Supplements	3.7	3.0	14.1	23.5	29.6	44.2	45.9	37.6	11.3	39.5	17.5
Other Operating Expenses	3.2	-1.0	3.5	10.0	2.1	2.8	8.5	-3.9	4.0	2.2	2.0
Depreciation and Amortization	9.8	8.8	7.9	2.6	-3.0	-2.3	1.2	-4.7	7.2	-2.2	3.0
Total Operating Expenses	2.7	1.7	5.2	6.6	6.3	6.9	28.9	33.1	4.0	19.1	20.0
Operating Income	10.1	21.1	5.5	5.8	-10.7	-3.9	-22.9	-3.5	10.4	-9.5	16.6

E = Morgan Stanley Research Estimates.   A = Actual

Note: 3Q and 4Q 1994 exclude $5.1 million($0.18 per share) and $0.9 million($0.03 per share), respectively, for favorable tax adjustment.

3Q 1995 excludes a $2.3 million pre-tax charge ($0.04 per share). 4Q 1995 excludes a $0.4 million charge ($0.01 per share).

New York Times — Sales and Earnings Summary 1994–1996E

($ Millions Except EPS)

	1994				1995E				Annual Data		
	3/94	6/94	9/94	12/94	3/95A	6/95A	9/95A	12/95E	1994	1995E	1996E
Newspapers (NY Times & regionals)	358.9	390.0	353.2	412.3	396.1	420.3	382.1	459.4	1,514.5	1,657.9	1,772.3
Affiliated (Boston Globe)	110.0	118.1	117.5	127.0	117.0	126.4	125.0	135.9	472.6	504.3	529.5
Magazines	96.5	108.9	39.4	35.3	40.9	42.9	43.4	40.0	280.1	167.3	177.3
Broadcasting	24.1	18.5	17.0	30.8	17.2	20.8	22.2	24.6	90.4	84.8	97.7
Total Revenue	**589.5**	**635.5**	**527.2**	**605.4**	**571.2**	**610.4**	**572.7**	**659.9**	**2,357.6**	**2,414.1**	**2,576.7**
Raw Materials (excl. Boston Globe)	66.4	68.5	53.0	66.6	65.6	70.1	71.0	93.2	254.4	299.9	344.9
Boston Globe Raw Materials	12.0	12.0	13.0	13.0	14.4	15.6	19.5	19.5	50.0	69.0	79.4
Operating Costs (excl. Boston Globe)	200.7	206.0	180.8	190.9	180.7	184.5	185.0	196.6	778.3	746.8	776.7
Affiliated (excl. raw materials)	38.0	39.0	39.0	39.0	40.6	40.4	41.0	40.2	155.0	162.2	168.7
Amortization (Affiliated acquisitions)	6.3	6.3	6.3	6.3	6.3	6.3	6.3	6.3	25.0	25.0	25.0
Total Costs and Expenses	323.4	331.7	292.0	315.7	307.6	316.9	322.8	355.7	1,262.8	1,302.9	1,394.6
Gross Profit	266.1	303.8	235.2	289.7	263.6	293.5	249.9	304.1	1,094.8	1,111.2	1,182.1
Selling, General, & Administrative	175.5	182.9	154.9	183.3	157.1	161.4	161.7	185.1	696.6	665.4	688.6
Affiliated Expenses	47.5	47.5	47.0	45.0	49.0	50.5	48.0	45.5	187.0	193.0	199.7
Operating Profit	43.2	73.4	33.3	61.4	57.5	81.6	40.2	73.6	211.2	252.9	293.8
Operating Profit by Segment											
Newspapers	38.8	52.5	18.8	36.1	44.1	56.5	21.2	45.9	146.1	167.8	194.9
Affiliated (incl. amortization)	6.3	13.3	12.3	23.8	6.8	14.0	12.5	25.1	55.6	58.4	66.2
Newspapers - total	45.1	65.8	31.1	59.8	50.8	70.5	33.7	71.1	201.7	226.1	261.1
Magazines	0.2	10.0	5.5	3.5	10.2	10.9	7.5	5.0	19.2	33.6	39.0
Broadcasting	4.1	4.7	2.9	7.7	2.7	6.2	4.4	6.1	19.4	19.5	24.4
Corporate Expenses	(6.2)	(7.1)	(6.2)	(9.6)	(6.2)	(6.1)	(5.3)	(8.7)	(29.1)	(26.3)	(30.8)
Operating Profit Margins (%)											
Newspapers	10.8	13.5	5.3	8.7	11.1	13.4	5.6	10.0	9.6	10.1	11.0
Affiliated	5.7	11.3	10.5	18.7	5.8	11.1	10.0	18.5	11.8	11.6	12.5
Newspapers - total	9.6	12.9	6.6	11.1	9.9	12.9	6.7	11.9	10.2	10.5	11.3
Magazines	0.2	9.2	14.0	9.9	24.9	25.4	17.2	12.5	6.9	20.1	22.0
Broadcasting	16.9	25.5	17.1	25.0	16.0	30.0	19.8	25.0	21.5	23.0	25.0
Total Interest Expense & Other	8.7	8.0	6.2	8.4	7.3	6.7	5.6	7.0	31.3	26.7	30.0
Pretax Income	34.5	65.4	27.1	53.0	50.2	74.9	34.7	66.6	180.0	226.3	263.8
Income Taxes	16.7	31.4	12.6	13.8	24.5	34.2	12.0	30.0	74.6	100.7	118.7
Tax Rate (%)	48.5	48.0	46.5	26.1	48.8	45.7	34.7	45.0	41.4	44.5	45.0
Net Income Before Equity Interest	17.8	34.0	14.5	39.2	25.7	40.7	22.6	36.6	105.4	125.6	145.1
Equity - forest products	(0.0)	0.3	1.5	1.5	1.7	2.6	4.3	6.5	3.3	15.0	17.5
Net Income	17.7	34.3	16.0	40.7	27.4	43.3	26.9	43.1	108.7	140.6	162.6
Earnings per Share	**0.17**	**0.32**	**0.15**	**0.41**	**0.28**	**0.45**	**0.28**	**0.45**	**1.06**	**1.45**	**1.70**
Average Shares Outstanding (mil)	106.9	106.3	104.3	98.8	97.8	96.8	96.3	96.0	104.1	96.7	95.5

E = Morgan Stanley Research Estimates　　　*A = Actual*

Times Mirror — Sales and Earnings Summary 1994–1996E

($ Millions Except EPS)

	1994				1995				Annual Data		
	3/94	6/94	9/94	12/94	3/9	6/95	9/95	12/95	1994	1995A	1996E
L.A. Times											
Revenue	239.1	250.0	243.0	297.0	240.3	257.5	245.0	288.0	1,029.1	1,030.8	1,066.9
Operating Costs	221.0	232.0	226.5	264.0	218.8	235.0	225.0	250.8	943.5	929.6	952.8
Operating Profit	18.1	18.0	16.5	33.0	21.5	22.5	20.0	37.2	85.6	101.2	114.0
Operating Margin (%)	7.6	7.2	6.8	11.1	8.9	8.7	8.2	12.9	8.3	9.8	10.7
East Coast Newspapers											
Revenue	232.0	267.3	250.2	284.3	235.9	269.1	241.3	280.5	1,033.8	1,026.9	962.8
Operating Costs	214.0	232.5	233.7	244.5	222.0	238.5	226.2	237.7	924.8	924.4	827.5
Operating Profit	18.1	34.9	16.5	39.8	13.9	30.6	15.1	42.8	109.3	102.4	135.3
Operating Margin (%)	7.8	13.0	6.6	14.0	5.9	11.4	6.3	15.3	10.6	10.0	14.0
Total Newspapers											
Advertising	353.2	394.1	372.2	444.6	357.0	401.7	364.6	434.8	1,564.1	1,558.2	1,557.7
Circulation & Other	117.9	123.2	128.7	136.7	119.2	124.9	121.7	133.7	506.5	499.4	471.9
Total Newspaper Revenue	471.1	517.3	493.2	581.3	476.2	526.6	486.3	568.5	2,070.6	2,057.6	2,029.7
Operating Costs	435.0	464.5	460.2	508.5	440.8	473.5	451.2	488.5	1,868.3	1,854.0	1,780.4
Operating Profit	36.2	52.9	33.0	72.8	35.3	53.1	35.1	80.0	194.9	203.6	249.3
Operating Margin (%)	7.7	10.2	6.7	12.5	7.4	10.1	7.2	14.1	9.4	9.9	12.3
L.A. Times - % change											
Revenue	1.9	2.9	4.7	7.0	0.5	3.0	3.0	(3.0)	4.3	0.2	3.5
Operating Costs	(0.9)	0.0	(0.4)	5.2	(1.0)	4.0	(0.7)	(5.0)	1.1	(1.5)	2.5
Operating Profit	57.4	63.6	266.7	24.5	18.8	25.0	21.2	12.7	60.0	18.2	12.7
East Coast Newspapers - % change											
Revenue	2.2	4.3	5.0	4.6	4.0	1.0	1.0	(1.3)	4.0	(0.7)	3.5
Operating Costs	(0.3)	2.5	2.0	1.9	5.0	5.0	(3.2)	(2.8)	1.6	(0.0)	2.5
Operating Profit	43.4	18.1	78.7	24.7	(23.2)	(12.3)	(8.3)	7.6	31.3	(6.3)	32.1
Total Newspapers - % change											
Total Revenue	2.1	3.6	4.9	5.8	1.1	1.8	(1.4)	(2.2)	4.5	(0.6)	(1.4)
Total Costs	(0.6)	1.2	0.8	3.6	1.3	7.0	(2.0)	(3.9)	1.3	(0.8)	(4.0)
Operating Profits	50.7	30.5	140.6	24.6	(2.4)	0.4	6.5	9.9	42.7	4.5	22.5
Professional Information											
Revenue	198.1	222.7	288.5	296.0	223.3	250.1	296.3	321.3	1,005.3	1,091.0	1,156.5
Costs	182.8	192.6	220.1	235.9	214.6	227.1	248.6	264.8	831.4	955.0	1,000.4
Operating Profits	15.3	30.1	68.4	60.2	8.7	23.0	47.7	56.6	174.0	136.0	156.1
Operating Margin (%)	7.7	13.5	23.7	20.3	3.9	9.2	16.1	17.6	17.3	12.5	13.5
Consumer Media											
Revenue	64.6	67.8	77.2	80.3	74.7	66.9	82.4	77.3	289.9	301.3	326.9
Costs	68.0	69.1	73.8	83.9	79.7	74.0	76.9	78.3	294.7	308.9	316.6
Operating Profits	(3.4)	(1.3)	3.4	(3.6)	(4.9)	(7.1)	5.5	(1.0)	(4.9)	(7.5)	10.4
Operating Margin (%)	3.0	-1.9	4.3	-4.5	-6.6	-10.6	6.7	-1.3	-1.7	-2.5	3.2
Total Professional and Consumer	262.7	290.5	365.7	376.3	298.1	317.0	378.7	398.6	1,295.2	1,392.3	1,483.4
Total Costs	250.8	261.7	293.9	319.7	294.3	301.1	325.5	343.0	1,126.1	1,263.9	1,317.0
Total Operating Profit	11.9	28.8	71.8	56.6	3.8	15.9	53.2	55.6	169.0	128.4	166.4
Operating Margin (%)	4.5	9.9	19.6	15.0	1.3	5.0	14.0	13.9	13.1	9.2	11.2
Other Segments											
Revenue											
Corporate & Other	0.0	0.0	(0.2)	0.0	0.0	0.0	0.0	0.0	(0.2)	0.0	0.0
Eliminations	(0.1)	(0.1)	(0.0)	(0.2)	0.0	(1.2)	(0.2)	(0.4)	(0.5)	(1.8)	(1.2)
Cable (discontinued as of 2Q '94)	123.0	–	–	–	–	–	–	–	123.0	–	–
Total Revenue	**856.7**	**807.6**	**858.7**	**957.4**	**774.0**	**842.4**	**864.8**	**966.7**	**3,488.2**	**3,448.2**	**3,511.9**
Corporate & Other	(15.2)	(16.3)	(16.2)	(21.8)	(15.0)	(21.9)	(16.6)	(23.2)	(69.5)	(76.6)	(65.0)
Operating Profit	32.9	65.3	88.5	107.6	24.1	47.1	71.7	112.4	294.4	255.4	350.7
Profit Margin (%)	3.8	8.1	10.3	11.2	3.1	5.6	8.3	11.6	8.4	7.4	10.0
Interest Income, net	4.0	4.0	4.0	4.0	5.2	3.4	(0.5)	(2.8)	16.0	5.2	(5.0)
Pretax Income	36.9	69.3	92.5	111.6	29.3	50.6	71.2	109.6	310.4	260.6	345.7
Income Taxes	18.5	34.6	46.3	55.8	14.2	24.5	34.1	51.8	155.2	124.7	164.2
Tax Rate (%)	50.0	50.0	50.0	50.0	48.5	48.5	47.9	47.3	50.0	47.8	47.5
Preferred Dividend	13.9	13.9	13.9	13.9	4.7	13.8	13.4	12.1	55.7	44.0	33.8
Net Income	4.5	20.7	32.3	41.9	10.4	12.2	23.7	45.7	99.6	91.9	147.7
Earnings per Share	**0.04**	**0.18**	**0.29**	**0.37**	**0.08**	**0.11**	**0.21**	**0.42**	**0.89**	**0.84**	**1.39**
Average Shares Outstanding (mil)	112.0	112.0	112.0	111.9	123.4	113.2	111.8	108.2	111.9	113.8	106.0

E = Morgan Stanley Research Estimates *A = Actual*
Note: All above periods assume cable disposition and a $1.3 billion cash infusion. All one-time gains and charges are not included.

Tribune — Sales and Earnings Summary 1994–1996E

($ Millions Except EPS)

	1994				1995				Annual Data		
	3/94	6/94	9/94	12/94	3/95	6/95	9/95	12/95	1994	1995A	1996E
Newspapers											
Advertising											
Retail	104.3	112.6	106.8	137.4	110.0	119.2	109.1	134.4	461.1	472.6	486.8
General	35.4	33.5	28.6	37.8	34.1	33.3	26.1	36.8	135.3	130.3	135.5
Classified	95.2	98.7	97.4	93.8	109.1	108.9	103.7	103.3	385.1	425.0	450.5
Total Advertising	234.9	244.7	232.8	269.0	253.1	261.4	238.9	274.5	981.5	1,027.9	1,072.8
Circulation	62.8	61.1	58.6	60.3	62.3	60.6	59.5	67.3	242.8	249.7	254.7
Other	17.2	15.4	19.8	18.7	20.6	21.3	23.1	15.0	71.1	79.9	91.9
Total Newspapers	314.9	321.2	311.3	348.1	336.0	343.3	321.5	356.7	1,295.4	1,357.5	1,419.4
Education	18.9	27.0	23.5	28.9	20.4	27.5	28.5	22.6	98.3	99.1	135.4
Broadcasting and Entertainment											
Television	118.4	168.0	134.5	177.6	134.1	171.2	150.1	174.2	598.5	629.5	679.9
Radio	10.4	16.2	19.5	22.8	24.9	20.5	20.1	22.9	68.8	88.4	94.6
Entertainment	18.1	38.9	26.0	12.4	17.5	29.2	46.8	15.5	95.5	109.0	119.9
Cable/Development	–	–	–	1.3	–	–	–	1.9	1.3	1.9	10.0
Broadcasting and Entertainment	146.9	223.1	180.0	214.2	176.4	220.9	217.0	214.4	762.9	828.8	904.4
Intercompany (primarily newsprint)	0.0	0.0	(1.3)	–	–	–	–	–	(1.3)	–	–
Total Revenue	**480.7**	**571.3**	**513.5**	**591.1**	**532.8**	**591.7**	**567.0**	**593.8**	**2,155.2**	**2,285.4**	**2,459.1**
Operating Profit											
Newspaper Publishing	69.2	76.3	60.4	81.8	70.8	75.0	52.2	72.2	287.7	270.1	283.1
Broadcasting and Entertainment	20.4	50.2	23.7	38.1	28.7	53.0	35.1	43.8	132.4	160.6	185.4
Education	1.3	2.6	(5.3)	4.2	(0.4)	3.9	3.2	(2.1)	2.8	4.6	26.4
Newsprint Operations (QUNO)	(9.1)	(0.6)	3.9	(0.6)	4.1	8.3	11.2	–	(6.4)	23.6	–
Corporate Expense	(6.3)	(6.4)	(6.8)	(6.6)	(7.1)	(7.4)	(7.3)	(8.3)	(26.2)	(30.1)	(27.5)
Operating Income	75.5	122.1	75.9	116.8	96.1	132.8	94.4	105.5	390.3	428.9	467.4
Operating Margin (%)	15.7%	21.4%	14.8%	19.8%	18.0%	22.4%	16.6%	17.8%	18.1%	18.8%	19.0%
Interest Expense/(Income), net	1.2	(0.0)	(0.5)	0.1	(0.1)	0.5	0.6	3.4	0.9	4.4	30.0
Pretax Income	74.3	122.2	76.3	116.7	96.2	132.4	93.8	102.1	389.4	424.4	437.4
Pretax Margin (%)	15.4%	21.4%	14.9%	19.7%	18.1%	22.4%	16.5%	17.2%	18.1%	18.6%	17.8%
Income Taxes	34.2	50.7	28.5	47.5	37.5	50.2	33.4	41.3	160.8	162.5	179.3
Tax Rate (%)	46.0%	41.5%	37.3%	40.7%	39.0%	38.0%	35.6%	40.5%	41.3%	38.3%	41.0%
QUNO (Discontinued)	–	–	–	–	–	–	–	7.3	–	7.3	–
Net Income	40.1	71.5	47.8	69.2	58.7	82.1	60.4	68.1	228.6	269.3	258.1
Net Margin (%)	8.3%	12.5%	9.3%	11.7%	11.0%	13.9%	10.7%	11.5%	10.6%	11.8%	10.5%
Earnings per Share	**0.49**	**0.93**	**0.60**	**0.89**	**0.76**	**1.09**	**0.79**	**0.91**	**2.91**	**3.54**	**3.55**
% Change	36.1%	16.1%	24.9%	11.3%	55.4%	17.5%	31.2%	2.8%	19.2%	21.8%	0.1%
Average Shares Outstanding (mil)	67.1	67.0	67.4	66.9	66.0	65.0	64.9	63.4	67.2	64.8	60.5
Revenue - % Change											
Newspapers - Advertising											
Retail	4.4	6.3	7.0	6.1	5.4	5.8	2.2	-2.2	6.0	2.5	3.0
General	17.3	6.6	15.6	10.3	-3.7	-0.3	-9.0	-2.6	12.2	-3.7	4.0
Classified	12.5	14.4	13.3	17.3	14.5	10.4	6.5	10.1	14.3	10.4	6.0
Total Advertising	9.4	9.5	10.6	10.4	7.7	6.8	2.6	2.0	10.0	4.7	4.4
Circulation	0.4	-0.1	-3.1	-2.7	-0.8	-0.8	1.5	11.6	-1.4	2.8	2.0
Other	-1.1	-8.8	20.3	-0.8	19.8	39.0	16.4	-20.2	2.2	12.4	15.0
Total Newspapers	6.9	6.5	8.3	7.2	6.7	6.9	3.3	2.5	7.2	4.8	4.6
Education	–	–	378.1	77.2	8.0	1.8	21.1	-21.6	–	0.7	12.0
Broadcasting and Entertainment											
Television	5.4	10.8	2.5	25.5	13.2	1.9	11.6	-1.9	11.5	5.2	8.0
Radio	3.6	-4.0	19.9	45.8	139.6	26.6	3.5	0.6	17.2	28.5	7.0
Entertainment	-2.4	-19.7	-45.7	-25.8	-3.5	-24.9	79.9	24.4	-27.5	14.1	10.0
Broadcasting and Entertainment	4.2	2.9	-7.9	23.1	20.1	-1.0	20.6	0.1	4.9	8.6	9.1
Total Revenue	10.6	10.4	5.5	15.0	10.8	3.6	10.4	0.5	10.4	6.0	7.6

E = Morgan Stanley Research Estimates　　　　*A = Actual*
Note: First quarter 1995 EPS excludes a 13 cent gain.
　　　3Q and 4Q 1994 not restated for sale of small newspaper, Times Advocate in California.

HNC Software — Income Statement Comparisons

($ Millions Except EPS)

	F1996E				F1997E				Annual Data		
	Mar-96	Jun-96	Sep-96	Dec-96	Mar-97	Jun-97	Sep-97	Dec-97	FY95	FY96	FY97
Revenues	6.9	8.4	9.6	10.2	9.7	11.7	13.7	15.0	25.2	35.0	50.1
Total Expenses	6.2	7.4	8.1	8.5	8.3	9.7	11.2	12.0	22.1	30.1	41.2
License & Installation	1.2	1.4	1.7	2.0	1.8	2.1	2.6	3.0	3.0	6.3	9.5
Contracts & Other	1.7	2.2	2.2	2.0	2.1	2.5	2.6	2.8	6.9	8.1	10.0
R & D	1.2	1.5	1.7	1.8	1.6	2.1	2.4	2.5	4.8	6.3	8.6
Marketing & Selling	1.3	1.4	1.6	1.7	1.8	1.9	2.2	2.3	4.9	5.9	8.2
G & A	0.8	0.8	1.0	1.0	1.0	1.1	1.4	1.4	2.6	3.6	4.9
Operating Income	0.7	1.1	1.4	1.7	1.4	2.0	2.5	3.0	3.1	4.9	8.8
Net Interest	0.3	0.3	0.4	0.4	0.4	0.4	0.5	0.5	0.8	1.3	1.8
Pre-Tax Income	1.0	1.4	1.8	2.1	1.8	2.4	3.0	3.5	3.8	6.2	10.7
Taxes	0.4	0.5	0.6	0.8	0.6	0.9	1.1	1.3	(0.7)	2.3	3.9
Net Income	0.6	0.9	1.1	1.3	1.1	1.5	1.9	2.3	4.6	3.9	6.8
EPS	$0.07	$0.10	$0.13	$0.15	$0.12	$0.17	$0.21	$0.25	$0.64	$0.45	$0.75
Shares	8.7	8.7	8.7	8.7	9.1	9.1	9.1	9.1	7.1	8.7	9.1
Growth Rate											
Revenues (yr-yr)	35.3%	42.0%	38.2%	42.0%	40.9%	39.1%	43.4%	47.1%	53.0%	38.9%	43.0%
Revenues (seq.)	-4.2%	22.2%	13.6%	6.8%	-4.9%	20.6%	17.1%	9.5%			
Expenses (yr-yr)	34.4%	40.6%	34.6%	33.7%	34.8%	32.0%	37.6%	41.6%	46.8%	36.2%	36.8%
Expenses (seq.)	-2.9%	19.4%	10.8%	4.1%	-2.1%	16.9%	15.5%	7.1%			
EPS	20.9%	28.6%	-63.8%	60.4%	72.1%	68.2%	64.9%	64.1%	104.8%	-29.9%	67.2%
Margin Analysis											
Pretax Margin	14.2%	16.5%	18.4%	20.3%	18.0%	20.8%	22.0%	23.6%	15.3%	17.6%	21.4%
Net Margin	9.0%	10.5%	11.7%	13.0%	11.5%	13.2%	14.0%	15.0%	18.1%	11.2%	13.6%
Expenses as Pct. of Revenues											
Total Expenses	89.4%	87.4%	85.2%	83.1%	85.6%	82.9%	81.8%	80.0%	87.8%	86.1%	82.3%
License & Installation	17.4%	16.6%	17.3%	19.6%	18.6%	17.9%	19.0%	20.0%	11.9%	17.9%	19.0%
Contracts & Other	24.7%	26.2%	23.0%	19.6%	21.6%	21.4%	19.0%	18.7%	27.3%	23.1%	20.0%
R & D	17.2%	18.3%	18.2%	17.9%	16.5%	17.9%	17.5%	16.7%	19.0%	17.9%	17.2%
Marketing & Selling	19.2%	16.5%	16.5%	16.2%	18.6%	16.2%	16.1%	15.3%	19.5%	17.0%	16.4%
G & A	10.9%	9.8%	10.3%	9.8%	10.3%	9.4%	10.2%	9.3%	10.1%	10.2%	9.8%
Tax Rate	36.3%	36.3%	36.3%	36.3%	36.3%	36.3%	36.3%	36.3%	NM	36.6%	36.5%

E = Morgan Stanley Research Estimates   *A = Actual*

19 – 60

VeriFone — Income Statement Comparisons F1995-1997E

($ Millions Except EPS)

	F1996E				F1997E				Annual Data		
	Mar-96	Jun-96	Sep-96	Dec-96	Mar-97	Jun-97	Sep-97	Dec-97	FY95	FY96E	FY97E
Revenues	95.2	113.8	124.5	127.6	117.1	140.0	153.1	156.9	387.0	461.1	567.2
% ch.	22.7%	22.7%	22.7%	22.7%	23.0%	23.0%	23.0%	23.0%	22.5%	22.7%	23.0%
Total Expenses	86.2	98.5	108.5	111.8	106.5	122.1	134.2	137.7	341.2	404.9	500.4
Cost of Revenues	49.8	59.4	64.9	66.5	62.1	74.2	81.2	83.2	202.4	240.5	300.6
R&D	11.2	12.6	14.5	16.7	14.6	16.5	17.2	19.3	45.0	55.0	67.6
S,G & A	25.9	27.2	29.7	29.3	30.6	32.2	36.6	36.0	97.9	112.1	135.4
Interest	(0.7)	(0.7)	(0.7)	(0.7)	(0.8)	(0.8)	(0.8)	(0.8)	(4.0)	(2.7)	(3.2)
Pretax Income	9.0	15.3	16.0	15.8	10.6	17.9	19.0	19.3	45.8	56.2	66.8
Taxes	2.6	4.4	4.7	4.6	3.1	5.2	5.5	5.6	13.3	16.3	19.4
Net Income	6.4	10.9	11.4	11.2	7.6	12.7	13.5	13.7	33.2	39.9	47.4
EPS	0.26	0.44	0.46	0.45	0.30	0.51	0.54	0.55	1.32	1.60	1.90
Shares	25.0	25.0	25.0	25.0	25.0	25.0	25.0	25.0	24.5	25.0	25.0
Growth Rate											
Revenues (yr-yr)	22.7%	22.7%	22.7%	22.7%	23.0%	23.0%	23.0%	23.0%	22.5%	22.7%	23.0%
Revenues (seq)	NM	19.5%	9.4%	2.5%	NM	19.5%	9.4%	2.5%			
Expenses (yr-yr)	22.4%	22.5%	22.6%	24.2%	23.5%	24.0%	23.7%	23.2%	23.4%	23.0%	23.6%
Expenses (seq)	NM	14.2%	10.1%	3.1%	NM	14.7%	9.9%	2.6%			
EPS	14.7%	13.9%	13.6%	22.4%	18.2%	16.8%	18.3%	21.9%	16.1%	16.0%	18.9%
Margin Analysis											
Pretax Margin	9.4%	13.5%	12.9%	12.4%	9.1%	12.8%	12.4%	12.3%	11.8%	12.2%	11.8%
Net Margin	6.7%	9.6%	9.2%	8.8%	6.4%	9.1%	8.8%	8.7%	8.6%	8.6%	8.4%
Expense as Pct. of Revenue											
Total Expenses	90.6%	86.5%	87.1%	87.6%	90.9%	87.2%	87.6%	87.7%	88.2%	87.8%	88.2%
Cost of Revenues	52.3%	52.2%	52.1%	52.1%	53.0%	53.0%	53.0%	53.0%	52.3%	52.2%	53.0%
R&D	11.8%	11.1%	11.6%	13.1%	12.5%	11.8%	11.2%	12.3%	11.6%	11.9%	11.9%
S,G & A	27.2%	23.9%	23.9%	23.0%	26.1%	23.0%	23.9%	22.9%	25.3%	24.3%	23.9%
Interest	NM	NM	NM	NM	NM	NM	NM	NM	NM	NM	NM
Tax rate	29.0%	29.0%	29.0%	29.0%	29.0%	29.0%	29.0%	29.0%	29.0%	29.0%	29.0%

E = Morgan Stanley Research Estimates   *NM = Not Meaningful*

The Authors

Mary Meeker

Mary joined Morgan Stanley in 1991 as the firm's PC Software/Hardware & New Media analyst. Earlier, she served as a technology research analyst at Cowen and at Salomon Brothers. Mary received an MBA in finance from Cornell University in Ithaca, New York, and a BA from DePauw University, in Greencastle, Indiana.

Mary's work has been recognized in various Wall Street Analyst Polls including those conducted by Greenwich Associates, *Institutional Investor*, *The Wall Street Journal*, *Forbes*, and *The Red Herring*.

Mary's research coverage includes PC software companies such as Adobe, Corel, Intuit, Macromedia, Microsoft, and Symantec. In PC hardware, she follows companies that include Apple, Compaq Computer, and Dell Computer. Her new media coverage includes America Online, Avid Technology, Broderbund Software, Electronic Arts, Maxis, Netscape, and The 3DO Company.

Chris DePuy

Chris DePuy is a research associate at Morgan Stanley covering the data networking and telecommunications equipment industries, with a special focus on Internet technology. He holds a Masters degree in engineering from Cornell University and a Bachelors degree from Union College in Schenectady, New York; he is also a registered New York State Professional Engineer. Before joining Morgan Stanley in 1995, Chris worked as a consulting engineer and as a corporate network administrator at Hill Environmental. At Morgan Stanley he has been involved in coverage of Ascend Communications, Cascade Communications, Cisco, Bay Networks, and 3Com.